PRINCE RUPERT OF THE RHINE

By the same author

1660 The Year of Restoration

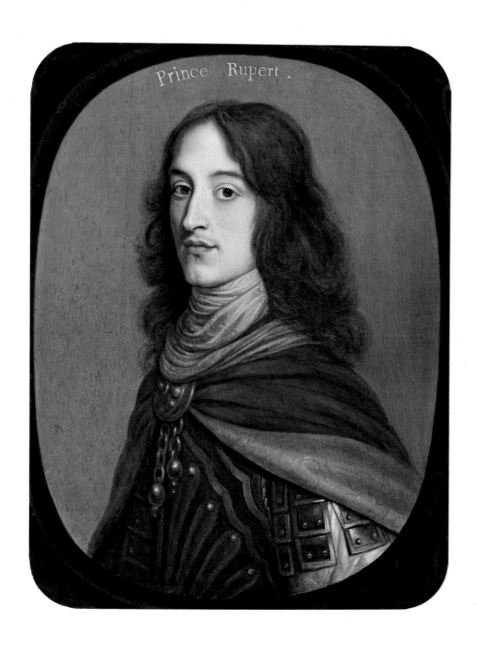

Prince Rupert, attributed to Honthorst

PRINCE RUPERT
OF THE RHINE

PATRICK MORRAH

CONSTABLE

LONDON

First published in Great Britain 1976
by Constable and Company Ltd
10 Orange Street London WC2H 7EG
Copyright © 1976 by Patrick Morrah
All rights reserved

ISBN 0 09 460910 1

Set in Monotype Baskerville 11 pt
Printed in Great Britain by The Anchor Press Ltd
and bound by Wm Brendon & Son Ltd
both of Tiptree, Essex

TO MONICA

CONTENTS

CONTENTS

ILLUSTRATIONS

ILLUSTRATIONS

PREFACE

THERE has been no fully documented biography of Prince Rupert since that of Eva Scott in 1899. (Miss Scott later wrote a revised version, but this was never published.) During the present century many sources have been brought to light or rediscovered, and these include the all-important *Rupert Diary*. This must be my excuse for embarking on a new life of Rupert.

During the summer of 1972, when I was three-quarters of the way through this book, a suitcase full of papers on which I was working, together with a substantial portion of my own manuscript, was stolen from my club. This set me back many months, and some of the loss was irretrievable. Christian charity forbids me to wish the thief every plague, murrain, misery and torment, in this world and the next, that the mind of the devil can conceive. I can only regret that this is so.

Former biographies include the massive three-volume work of Eliot Warburton, with its mass of reproductions of original documents. I have leant heavily on Warburton, as every writer on Rupert must. But Warburton was an inaccurate transcriber, and wherever possible I have checked his work with the original sources.

As regards quotations, my system has been to use my texts as exactly as possible. Thus I have given the seventeenth-century spelling where this is ascertainable; I have, however, expanded certain conventional abbreviations, and I have at times altered the punctuation in the interests of intelligibility. In reference notes I have not given the folio numbers in the case of manuscript sources. Some manuscripts have none, and some are renumbered in various places. I decided to omit them all for the sake of uniformity. It will, I think, be easy enough for anybody who is interested to verify my references.

In the matter of spelling of names consistency is impossible. My general system has been to give them as one would expect to find them spelt at the present day. I have made an exception in the case of Rupert's dog Boye at the urgent request of Brigadier Peter Young, who regards the spelling 'Boy' with aversion. My preference for Stewart over Stuart may be set down as a personal idiosyncrasy, though it has a sound historical basis.

In the seventeenth century the difference between the new style of dating, generally used on the continent of Europe, and the old style used in England was ten days; the first of the month at home, for instance, was the eleventh in France and Germany. In this very confusing matter my method has been to use the old style for events in England and the new for those abroad, hoping I have made no mistakes.

In compiling this work I have received invaluable help from a great number of people. Brigadier Peter Young, whose knowledge of the English Civil Wars is unrivalled, was himself contemplating a life of Rupert but found he had too many other commitments. He kindly put his researches and his notes at my disposal, and in addition read my whole book in manuscript, advising me at all points. My debt to him is great.

Mr Charles Frewer's help has been immense. For many years he has, for his own purposes, been collecting material on Rupert, particularly on the later years of the Prince's career, and he most generously allowed me the use of it all. In addition, having a wide knowledge of the iconography, he kindly acted as art editor.

Dame Veronica Wedgwood, with her unvarying generosity to writers less well endowed in knowledge and capacity than herself, was indefatigable in drawing my attention to sources, and also lent me a number of documents, of some of which I was later robbed. Dr Maurice Ashley read my manuscript and gave me much useful advice. Mr Bernard Thorold, himself engaged on a life of Rupert's brother Maurice, put his researches at my disposal. The Reverend J. R. Powell read my naval chapters with an expert eye, putting me right on a number of points. Dr Margaret Toynbee gave me the benefit of her great knowledge of the Stewarts. Mr Lawrence Josset, the only contemporary English artist working in mezzotint, kindly explained the process to me. The late Donald Nicholas lent me some important manuscript letters before his recent lamented death. Mr Roger Munden assisted me with transcripts, and Mr Geoffrey Strachan, Mrs J. R. Nicol, Mr R. H. C. Steed and Dr Sylvia England with translations.

Mrs Shand, a direct descendant of Prince Rupert, helped me with pictures and information.

I should like to mention all others who have helped me, but space forbids. I can only append a list of some of them, and ask pardon of those omitted: Mr R. C. Anderson, Miss Dorothea St Hill Bourne, Mr Patrick Bushe-Fox, Mr A. C. Cooper, Mr George Edinger, Professor K. H. D. Haley, Mr. P. H. Hulton, Miss Ann Jones, Mrs Philip

Lewtas, Mrs Michael Lind, Mr Gregory Lowe, Mr Robert Mackworth-Young, Miss Teresa Malik, Miss Rachel Marr-Johnson, Sir Oliver Millar, Dr Klaus Mugdan, Mrs H. Nicholls, Mr A. W. H. Pearsall, Miss Mary Pegg, Mrs E. Plant, Mr Colin Ronan, Miss Joan Thompson, Miss Elizabeth Ward; officials of the British Museum, the Public Record Office, the Victoria and Albert Museum, the London Library, the College of Arms, the Hudson's Bay Company, Messrs Glyn, Mills & Co., the Surrey County Council and the Wiltshire County Council.

BOOK ONE

THE KING'S NEPHEW
1619–1642

CHAPTER 1

THE WINTER PRINCE

O F all the sovereigns who have reigned over the people of Britain the most intensely individual was King James I. Everything he did, everything he said, bore the stamp of his personality: autocrat, wit, scholar, controversialist, homosexual, buffoon, he attracted and repelled his contemporaries as he has attracted and repelled historians of later days. On the whole repulsion has predominated, both in his own time and since. For this his personal habits must bear the chief blame. His homosexual propensities are beyond dispute; but it was not his delight in the company of handsome young men that aroused disgust so much as the way he displayed it. He fawned on his chosen minions; he cuddled them in public, and he slobbered over them. Slobbering indeed was one of his unfortunate characteristics. His tongue was too large for his mouth, and when he drank wine, an occupation of which he was very fond, he spilt a lot of it out of the sides of his mouth.

There was much about him that was repellent. He wore the same clothes till they were filthy, and never washed his hands, contenting himself with rubbing the ends of his fingers with the wet end of a napkin. Passionately fond of hunting, he had a habit of plunging his legs into a stag's warm bowels after a kill had been made; this was supposed to be for medicinal reasons, but it was suspected that he derived a perverse pleasure from this unsavoury activity. He was coarse of speech, awkward in gait and unsteady on his feet, and totally lacking in regal dignity.

These defects have tended to obscure the many fine qualities the King possessed. His scholarship was genuine; as an intellectual sovereign he has no equal in the catalogue of British kings and queens, with the possible exception of Alfred, and few among the royalty of other nations. He was a prolific author, his books embracing such diverse subjects as kingship, poetry, theology, demonology and the new custom of tobacco smoking. In his youth he had been something of a poet, like his ancestor King James I of Scotland. He was widely read in all branches of literature, and he had a deep understanding of theology, which he delighted to discuss with the most learned divines in his

3

realm. He was far from being the mere pedant of hostile tradition.

His conversation, pungent and often obscene, was marked by genuine wit and his own brand of pawky humour, combined with down-to-earth good sense. It was hard to get the better of him; prelates and politicians, though they often found him exasperating, soon came to realize that here was a king to whom they could not talk down, who really understood the problems of Church and State, and whose shrewdness not infrequently exposed the superficiality of their own thinking.

Above all, King James was a kindly man, whose not ignoble object was to 'win all men's hearts'. He hated the waste of human life in war, and stubbornly strove to keep his kingdoms at peace: an aim in which he succeeded until the very last months of his reign, when he had lost his grip on affairs. In religion, where his chief interest lay, he was tolerant, preferring discussion and debate to persecution. He would if he could have softened, if not abrogated, the harsh laws that were in force against religious minorities. Here the spirit of the age was against him, and he was unable to mitigate the blood-lust of his subjects.

As a monarch he was constantly contrasted, to his disadvantage, with his predecessor Elizabeth I. The forceful personality of that dominating lady had captured the imagination of Englishmen, who came to look back on her reign as a golden age; and the stranger from Scotland, with his crude manners and unkingly demeanour, was bound to suffer in comparison. By no criterion can James be pronounced a successful ruler. His worst defects were his reliance on his unworthy favourites and a hopeless lack of financial prudence. He lavished fantastic sums on the Earl of Somerset and the Duke of Buckingham – and Buckingham, allpowerful in the later years of the reign, did his best to bring the country to ruin and bankruptcy. Honours were dispensed with reckless abandon, often for cash down; and financial incompetence threatened the fabric of the constitution.

Yet the King's rule was not wholly contemptible. When he allowed himself to use his own judgement he governed capably; his shrewd understanding and his homely common sense often saved him from the worst errors. He had served a long and hard apprenticeship as King of his native Scotland, where he survived conspiracies, assassination attempts and kidnapping; in that turbulent land he had worn down his enemies and emerged as a ruler who could stand comparison with any of his Stewart ancestors.

During his reign in Scotland he had been the hero of one episode which seems singularly out of character. In 1585, when he was nineteen, negotiations began for his marriage to Anne, daughter of King Frederick II of Denmark and Norway; but various factors, including the death of King Frederick, delayed the union, and it was not till 1589 that Princess Anne, having been married by proxy in Copenhagen, prepared to set out for her new home. Her ship, however, was driven by a storm on to the coast of Norway; whereupon the impatient bridegroom, knowing only that the expected vessel had failed to arrive, assumed the role of knight-errant and ardent wooer and set out through stormy seas to seek his bride. He found her at Oslo, promptly had a second marriage ceremony performed, and in due course returned in triumph with his Queen to Scotland.

Queen Anne, eight years younger than her husband, was at this time fifteen years old: a tall Scandinavian blonde and a noted beauty. Her family was ancient and she had been brought up with the strictest attention to court etiquette and in the Lutheran tradition. By nature she was gay and kind-hearted; she loved jewels, ceremonial, and light entertainment. Affairs of state meant little to her, and she never attempted to wield any political influence. At first the marriage was reasonably happy, but in view of the widely different temperaments – not to say tastes – of the King and Queen this could not and did not last. There were two main causes of trouble. In the first place Queen Anne could hardly be expected to take a tolerant view of her husband's sexual predilections, and as his attentions to his male favourites became more blatant she grew increasingly embittered. Secondly she was quite unable to share his intellectual interests. She was not devoid of aesthetic taste or artistic discrimination; the masques that were for some years the glory of the court of James I, scenically designed by Inigo Jones to the texts of Ben Jonson, were inspired by the encouragement given by the Queen, who appeared in many of them herself. She was, too, an enthusiastic builder, and was constantly improving and embellishing her houses at Westminster and Greenwich. But such things were little to the King's taste; his mind ran to weighty learning and intellectual speculation, and here his wife could not follow him.

There was never any complete estrangement; but friction developed fairly early, and squabbles increased as time went on, often in public, to the scandal of the sober-minded and the delight of gossip-writers. In later years the royal couple lived mainly apart.

A further source of friction came from the Queen's religious views. Early in her married life she had cast off the Lutheranism of her childhood, and before the move from Edinburgh to London she became a Catholic. Though never openly declared, her conversion was well known and she never tried to hide it. King James had no personal prejudice against the Church of Rome; his ideal was universal toleration. But his position as sovereign of two Protestant kingdoms was delicate Mary Queen of Scots, the mother whom he had never known and whose existence during her long imprisonment in England had always been a latent threat to his own throne, had been to the last an ardent Catholic; when her death came at the hands of the Elizabethan government she claimed that she died for her religion. Any inclination towards his mother's faith could at any time have endangered King James's position in both his realms. And Queen Anne's correspondence with the Pope and her leanings towards Spain, that power that was always a bogey to the English people, sometimes appeared capable of upsetting the balance of the King's foreign policy. Yet he was tolerant in private as well as in public life. He never attempted to coerce his wife.

Whatever his sexual aberrations, King James did his dynastic duty by his Queen. By the time he succeeded to the English throne in 1603 she had borne him three sons and two daughters, and two more daughters were to follow. But infant mortality was high in the sixteenth and seventeenth centuries, and only three of the seven survived the nursery. These included the first two to be born. Henry Frederick, the eldest of the family, born in 1594 and created Prince of Wales in 1610, grew up into a young man of exceptional brilliance. In contrast with his father he was strong, handsome, brave and vigorous: a fine horse-man and a splendid athlete from his early years. His life was one of con-stant activity; when he was not playing tennis or golf, games at which he excelled, he was exercising himself in arms, shooting with the bow and tossing the pike. Yet though in essence an outdoor boy he was intellectu-ally active too. He was not a scholar like King James, but he had a keen intelligence and an appreciation of poetry; he was one of Ben Jonson's patrons and took a deep interest in that learned dramatist's use of classical sources. But it was in affairs of state that he soon began to exert an influence out of all proportion to his years. His precocity was such that when he was twelve the French Ambassador reported that his pleasures did not savour in the least of a child, that he associated with older people as if he despised those of his own age, and that he was already feared by Lord Salisbury and other leading figures of the English Government. He soon showed that he had a will of his own, and from the time that he entered his teens he interested himself in the political questions of the day, particularly naval and military affairs. He urged a strongly Protestant policy, and when, at the instigation of his Catholic mother, a Spanish marriage was proposed for him, he declared that two religions could not lie in one bed. He formed his own court, which was so much frequented that it came to be looked on as a rival to that of the King. The Prince had little filial veneration for King James, and, in denouncing the imprisonment of Sir Walter Raleigh, declared that no man but his father would keep such a bird in a cage.

Prince Henry was the darling of the English people, who saw in him a future king after their own hearts: a sturdy, fearless warrior who would stamp on popery and lead them to victory over proud Spaniards and two-faced Frenchmen. The subtle and tortuous King James they neither liked nor understood. His open, straightforward, brave-hearted son was their ideal of what a monarch should be.

Almost as popular was the King's daughter Elizabeth, born two years after the Prince, whose devoted admirer she quickly became. As she grew up into a gay, laughing, lovely girl, tall and fair like her mother, her countrymen took her to their hearts as the feminine counterpart of her elder brother. Like him she loved an outdoor life; she enjoyed riding and hunting, and kept a large stable; she was devoted to all animals. She was also well educated and a good linguist, speaking French better than Prince Henry did. What most endeared her to the English was her inexhaustible vitality, of which it is still possible to catch a glimpse from her vivid, uninhibited letters. From childhood her charm and beauty were the theme of poetry; long before Sir Henry Wotton penned his exquisite lines to 'th'eclipse and glory of her kind', bards of lesser calibre but equal enthusiasm vied with each other in singing her praises.

Princess Elizabeth's Protestantism was as pronounced as her brother's. Her formative years were spent at Combe Abbey, near Coventry, under the tutelage of Lord and Lady Harington, whose régime, though it was not one of unrelieved austerity, included long and frequent household prayers whereat, says Miss Carola Oman in her biography of Elizabeth, 'solemn warnings against the Church of Rome and an existence of idle pleasure were repeated with tireless fervour, and as far as the old faith was concerned, the impression made upon the mind of the infant Elizabeth was lifelong'.[1]

The third of King James's progeny who survived infancy presented a sad contrast. Prince Charles, born in 1600, was the second son and fourth child; a second daughter had died at the age of fifteen months shortly before his birth. It looked as though the new prince would follow his sister to the grave; he was sickly and undersized and so weak in his joints that the King toyed with the idea of having his legs encased in iron boots to strengthen them. Mentally too his development was arrested; for a long time he was unable to speak, and when he did it was with a stammer. Contrary to expectations he grew out of the worst of his defects, but he remained shy and withdrawn, a cipher in the shining presence of his elders. His lordly brother regarded him with the somewhat patronizing affection of the strong for the weak. According to a story which, however, has no contemporary authority, he promised that if Charles would go into the Church, which seemed all that he was fitted for, he would make him, when he himself reigned as King Henry IX, his Archbishop of Canterbury.

For Princess Elizabeth a marriage was hoped for that would be worthy of her birth, beauty and accomplishments. A succession of suitors came and went during her childhood. First in the field was the Dauphin Louis, son of King Henry IV of France, to whose ambassador King James diplomatically declared that his daughter had already fallen in love with the young prince's portrait; Elizabeth at the time was six years old, and the future King Louis XIII not yet two. Tentative negotiations dragged on for some years, but religious considerations were a barrier and the project eventually died of inanition.

Other candidates passed in review: the most interesting, in view of the future that might have been, was Gustavus Adolphus, son and heir of King Charles IX of Sweden. But Sweden was at this time at war with Denmark, where Queen Anne's brother now reigned as King Christian IV; and the English King was not prepared to send his daughter to a land where she would be her uncle's enemy.

In 1611, when Elizabeth was fifteen, came the most glittering prospect of all. King Philip III of Spain, autocrat of the enormous Spanish Empire, a pious middle-aged gentleman of blameless life and negligible capacity, found himself a widower through the unexpected death of his wife Margaret, and within weeks of this event let it be known that he was in the market for the English princess. King James was interested, for a Spanish alliance would further his ideal of universal peace. Queen Anne was enthusiastic, and would have been only too glad if the stipulation that her daughter should become a Catholic had been agreed to. But the prospect of a change of faith was acceptable to nobody but the Queen. Elizabeth was adamant in her Protestantism, though her scruples would doubtless have been overruled had not more powerful interests supported her. The forceful personality of the Prince of Wales was thrown into the opposite scale, and the Spanish Ambassador reported that the Prince had 'publicly said that whosoever should counsel his father to marry his sister to a Catholic prince, were a traitor'.[2] If King James had ever wavered on this point he did so no longer; he swore that his daughter should never go out of his kingdom a papist.

There was, however, yet another prince, of impeccably Protestant antecedents, in the offing; and immediately after the collapse of the Spanish project the Electress Juliana, from her castle at Heidelberg, set the wheels turning on behalf of her son Frederick V, Elector Palatine of the Rhine. Young Frederick, born on 15 August 1596, was just four days older than the English princess. He was a graceful youth, trained in martial exercises, a good horseman, well-versed in Latin and French, good-looking, virtuous in his morals and ardent in his religion. He had been a reigning prince since the death of his father, the Elector Frederick IV, the previous year; and his strong-willed mother doted on him.

8

Once started, the negotiations proceeded steadily. With the fading of the Spanish prospects King James became convinced of the advantage of a Protestant alliance, and the young Calvinist prince seemed destined to become the most influential Protestant ruler in Germany. Queen Anne was less enthusiastic – not only for reasons of religion. She had been bitterly disappointed when her daughter's chance of being Queen of Spain fell through, and for her now to accept the proposal of the lord of a small German state seemed by contrast a degradation. But the Queen had no power to do more than complain. Her counsels were disregarded.

Dynastically her scorn was misplaced. The Palatinate was indeed, in area, a small state; but its ruler was the senior representative of the great house of Wittelsbach, and could boast a more illustrious ancestry than could the Stewarts. The Count Palatine of the Rhine, or Palsgrave, had originally been an officer of the imperial household, and the office went back to the time of Charles the Great; the 'Palace Count' had been of similar status to those 'Mayors of the Palace' who had in the eighth century displaced the *fainéant* Merovingians and, in the person of Charles, established the Holy Roman Empire as a reincarnation of the European dominion of the Caesars. The Count Palatine of the Rhine, who administered a district owing allegiance to the Emperor but independent of his direct rule, became the leading prince of the Empire, the first of the four lay electors who, with their three ecclesiastical counterparts – the Archbishops of Mainz, Trier and Cologne – formed the college whose duty it was to meet when the imperial throne became vacant and elect a new emperor.

In the thirteenth century the sovereignty of the Rhenish Palatinate became hereditary in the Wittelsbach family, and so it had continued to the time of Frederick V. There had, however, been various subdivisions. The Dukedom of Bavaria had gone to a younger son, and his descendants now reigned over a larger territory than did the senior branch. Later smaller districts, such as Neuburg, Simmern and Sulzbach, were detached from what remained of the Palatinate; in 1559 the senior line died out, and the Simmern line, in the person of the Elector Frederick III, succeeded to the Palatine dignity. In the early seventeenth century the lands subject to the Elector consisted of two separate areas: the Lower Palatinate, extending on both sides of the Rhine from Alsace to Württemberg and including Heidelberg the capital, and the Upper Palatinate, north of the Danube and west of Bohemia.

The greatest era of the Rhenish Wittelsbachs had been the brief period between 1401 and 1410, when the Elector Rupert III had himself worn the imperial crown. Since then their fortunes had declined, and their influence in the always Catholic Empire had inevitably faded with their change of religion. The Bavarian Wittelsbachs remained Catholic, but the Reformation came to the Palatinate in 1545, when the Elector Frederick II introduced the Lutheran doctrine into Heidelberg. It was a mild and tentative revolution; there was no persecution, and a measure of Catholic ceremonial was retained.

Frederick III, however, the first elector of the Simmern line, introduced the harsher Calvinist régime, and the Palatinate entered upon a period of severe repression. The conflict between Lutheranism and Calvinism persisted for another generation, as Louis VI reversed his father's religious policy. But with the accession of the nine-year-old Frederick IV in 1583, and the administration of his uncle John Casimir, the Palatinate was firmly established as a Calvinist state. Yet compared with others of its kind it was tolerant. There was little bloodshed and a substantial Catholic minority as well as a Lutheran one survived undisturbed in the Lower Palatinate. The Catholic Church was never driven underground as it was in England. The Upper Palatinate, which enjoyed a considerable measure of independence, remained obstinately Lutheran.

Frederick IV, Elector Palatine from 1583 to 1610, was a worthy if rather colourless individual. His interests were primarily religious, and in this direction he succeeded in restoring much of the Palatinate's former influence in Germany. A Protestant Elector Palatine could never be the Emperor's right-hand man as his ancestors had been; Frederick's weight had to be thrown into the anti-imperial scale. He set himself up as the leader of the Protestant princes of Germany, and in the last year of the century, with the Margraves of Brandenburg and Baden, the Duke of Württemberg and his cousin the Count Palatine of Neuburg, he established the Protestant Union, a league of mutual defence which was to be henceforth the rallying-point for the anti-Catholic cause.

Frederick IV was a man of limited intellect, but he encouraged the cultural activities of others. One of the two paramount glories of the Rhineland was the University of Heidelberg, the intellectual centre of Germany. Elector Frederick took the greatest interest in its progress and its studies. He founded a new chair of history and one, rather surprisingly, of Arabic, and he saw to it that the finest scholars were attracted to Heidelberg.

The second great glory of the Rhineland, then as now, was its wine, that wine now generally known by the name of hock (probably an abbreviation of the name Hochheim). The cultivation of the Rhenish vineyards can be traced far back in the Middle Ages, and it was the peculiar distinction of the cultivators that it was they who rediscovered the principle, lost since Roman times, that wine kept better in large receptacles. Hence, from the fifteenth century onwards, came the building of gigantic 'tuns', which became a prestige symbol and reached fantastic proportions.

Some of the best vineyards were in the Lower Palatinate, and it was at Heidelberg that the most famous of the Rhineland tuns was set up. The builder was the Administrator John Casimir, who resolved 'to make a mighty cask, such as there was none other on earth'.[3] The result was the Great Tun, housed in a building adjoining Heidelberg Castle and holding 132,000 litres of wine. The original Great Tun was later to be replaced by even larger casks.

Frederick IV encouraged the wine industry as he encouraged learning at the university. His method, however, was less to foster the cultivation of the vineyards than to devote himself to the whole-hearted enjoyment of their products. The thirst of the most dedicated wine-drinker could hardly make much impression on the contents of the Great Tun; but Frederick IV did his best, and a goodly portion of the splendid liquid travelled down the princely throat. The Elector's addiction, which led to gout and to conscience-stricken entries in his diary, helped to carry him off at the age of thirty-six.

In 1594, soon after he had embarked on personal rule, Frederick had made a marriage designed to strengthen the Protestant alliance. His bride was Louisa Juliana, the orphaned daughter of that Prince of Orange, known as William the Silent, who had been the heart and soul of the revolt of the Dutch provinces against Spain. Prince William's career had ended, amid internal strife and disillusionment, with his assassination in 1584. But his name was still one to conjure with, and the House of Orange remained a rallying-point for the Protestant cause in Europe.

Princess Juliana was a true daughter of her father. She was severe and withdrawn, lacking in any sort of personal charm; watchful over her rights, and by no means immune from jealousy and vindictiveness. But she had all the determination of her race, and would fight to the death for her beliefs and for her family. She was wholly devoted to her Calvinist creed, and the support she brought to her husband was not limited to the dynastic advantage. She was a far stronger character than he was, and buoyed him up in those moments of weakness to which his lack of backbone and his heavy drinking made him subject. After his death her energy was directed to the interests of her eldest son, and it was she who was the moving spirit behind the plans for the English marriage.

With King James and the Electress Juliana in agreement, the conclusion of formalities was only a matter of time. The marriage contract was signed in May 1612, and after further preparations and voluminous correspondence the young Elector Palatine landed at Gravesend on 16 October. He was received with rapture by the English populace, delighted to find him a fine-looking youth, graceful and charming, frank and open in bearing, a fitting consort for their beloved princess. No defects of character were as yet apparent.

Masques, banquets and pageants followed. But there was a shadow over the festivities. The Prince of Wales was not his usual brilliant self; he took part in the early revels, but only with an effort. Then, on 29 October, when a banquet was held at the Guildhall in honour of the Palsgrave (the title generally employed in England), he failed to appear. It was announced that he had an attack of fever, and during the next few days it became known that for some time his health had been causing anxiety. He had been as active as ever, playing tennis and bathing in the Thames; but he had suffered from insomnia and taken to making long rambles by the river at night. He had actually risen from a sickbed to welcome his sister's suitor, but the strain was now becoming too great. He took once more to his bed. Infection was feared, and only his physicians were allowed to visit him. On 6 November he died, apparently from typhoid, and it was recorded that his last words were 'Where is my dear sister?' Such was the bond between them that, when barred from the sick-room, she was said to have even attempted to enter it in disguise.[4]

Prince Henry's death at the age of eighteen suggests one of the greatest might-have-beens in the history of England. Had he lived to be King he could scarcely have failed to stamp his personality on the age in which he lived.

The Prince's death meant the postponement of the royal wedding. He was buried in Westminster Abbey on 7 December, but after Christmas it was decided that court mourning could be relaxed. A betrothal ceremony took place in the Banqueting Hall at Whitehall on 27 December, and in the new year the round of masques and river pageants was renewed. England's poets celebrated the occasion, and fourteen plays were presented before Elizabeth and Frederick at Whitehall. Six of them were by William Shakespeare – *Much Ado about Nothing, The Tempest, The Winter's Tale, The Merry Wives of Windsor, Othello* and *Julius Caesar.*[5] According to tradition *The Tempest*, Shakespeare's last play, was specially written for the occasion; but there is no contemporary evidence of this.

Finally, on 14 February 1613, amid a wealth of Jacobean pomp that severely strained the royal treasury, the wedding ceremony was performed by the Archbishop of Canterbury, George Abbot, in the chapel of Whitehall Palace. King James gave the bride away, and a prominent figure was the twelve-year-old Prince Charles, now Duke of York, who made an agreeable impression by the dignity and self-possession with which he fulfilled the duties that would have fallen to the lot of his dead brother.

In April the Elector Palatine and his bride sailed from Margate, and after a leisurely journey made a joyous entry into Heidelberg on 17 July. In their lovely Rhineland capital they were received with the greatest enthusiasm. They were handsome, charming and very much in love; and Elizabeth's gaiety and vitality made an excellent impression. The next few years were happy and carefree. On 2 January 1614 Elizabeth gave birth to a son and heir, given the names of Frederick Henry. Another son, Charles Louis, followed on 22 December 1617, and a daughter, Elizabeth, on 26 December of the next year.

Had the Elector Frederick been content to remain in the by no means negligible station to which his birth entitled him, he might have continued to rule his dominions prosperously if not with distinction. But he allowed himself to get entangled in events whose scope was beyond both his resources and his personal capacity; to become the key figure in the breaking of the storm that was now to engulf the Empire.

To the east of the Upper Palatinate lay the kingdom of Bohemia, a territory that held a somewhat anomalous position in the Holy Roman Empire. It was an independent kingdom, but its ruler, by virtue of the Golden Bull of the Emperor Charles IV (himself King of Bohemia) of 1356, was one of the four lay electors who decided the occupancy of the imperial throne. Moreover the Bohemian monarchy, in theory elective, had become, like the Empire itself, in practice hereditary in the imperial house of Habsburg. It was thus a Catholic dominion, closely dependent on Vienna; but since the religious revolt of John Huss, burned as a heretic in 1415, the country had been the most explosive centre of dissent in central Europe, and now, in the early years of the seventeenth century, Protestants were in the majority.

The Emperor and King of Bohemia at this time was a mild, elderly gentleman named Matthias. He had no son, and about 1615 it was agreed among the Habsburgs that the succession should go to his cousin the Archduke Ferdinand of Styria. The German dominions of the Habsburgs were docile enough, but in the two kingdoms of Bohemia and Hungary there was always danger of revolt. In the hope of securing a peaceful succession, therefore, the Emperor decided to hand over these two crowns to his heir during his own lifetime.

The Emperor duly abdicated, formal elections were held, and in July 1617 the Archduke Ferdinand was crowned King of Bohemia in Prague. Some months later he was also proclaimed King of Hungary. In Bohemia, however, the Protestant party were planning rebellion. Under the lax and absentee rule of Matthias they had been unmolested, but with the presence in their midst of the new, less tolerant King, they feared suppression of their religious liberties which had been guaranteed by Matthias's brother and predecessor, the Emperor Rudolph II. They decided to strike the first blow.

The result was the incident known to history as 'the Defenestration of Prague', which led to the outbreak of the Thirty Years War. King Ferdinand, seeing trouble brewing, had retired discreetly to Vienna. In his absence, on 21 May 1618, a group of Protestants led by Count Matthias Thurn invaded the Hradschin Palace in Prague, where the imperial commissioners were meeting, and seizing two of them, Slavata and Martinitz, threw them out of the window. The victims fell some sixty feet; they were not seriously hurt, however, as they fell somewhat ignominiously on a dungheap. But this deliberate act of provocation was the spark that set Europe ablaze.

The fighting that followed the Defenestration was desultory and inconclusive. Austrian troops entered Bohemia but were forced to retire. Thurn then led an army into Austria, but had to retreat in his turn. But he and his followers had burned their boats. Ferdinand had in effect been rejected as King of Bohemia, and the next logical step was to elect a new monarch. Who more suitable than the young Elector whose domains bordered on Bohemia, who had already taken his place as leader of the Protestant Union in succession to his father, and who was married to the daughter of the King of England?

This was the moment that the Emperor Matthias chose to die. He succumbed to a fit on 10 March 1619, and though there were other candidates the election of Ferdinand, titular King of Bohemia, was unlikely to be circumvented. It duly took place on 28 August, and the party in power in Prague found themselves in direct revolt against the Holy Roman Emperor.

Meanwhile another revolt had taken place in Hungary, where the Estates chose Bethlen Gabor, Prince of Transylvania, for their King. Before the imperial election the Elector Palatine had written to his wife: 'Instead of Ferdinand gaining a crown at Frankfurt, he may well lose two.'[6] Ferdinand had gained his crown at Frankfurt, but the rest of Frederick's prediction looked like coming true.

Events now moved fast. Before the end of August the Bohemians had formally deposed Ferdinand and elected the Elector Palatine their King, a deputation from the Estates had been sent to Heidelberg to invite his acceptance, and intense diplomatic activity had been set in motion to sound out the opinions of interested princes. Frederick consulted his mother, his ministers and his colleagues of the Protestant Union; Elizabeth wrote to the Marquess of Buckingham, now in the full tide of his ascendancy over James I, and to Archbishop Abbot of

Canterbury, who promptly replied in favour of acceptance. The Electoral Chancellor, Prince Christian of Anhalt, took the same view, and so did many of the German rulers. But two experienced members of the older generation had different ideas. The Electress-Dowager Juliana, despite her ambitions for the advancement of her beloved son, urged him to decline a venture which was at the best uncertain and the failure of which would undoubtedly lead to his ruin. The King of England's reaction to the Bohemian offer was also one of dismay. It struck at the root of James's most cherished plans. Civil and religious peace was his ideal; his aim was to hold the precarious balance in a distracted Europe and dissuade the extremists from flying at each other's throats. Moreover he was at this time negotiating for a Spanish marriage for his son Charles, which would increase his influence on the continent. If his son-in-law were to accept the Bohemian throne the balance would be upset and all Europe would be plunged into a religious war. He himself would be urged to throw his weight behind the Protestant cause and contribute troops and money, with the probability that England would be forced into a war against the Habsburg powers.

His subjects thought differently. When the news came through that Frederick had been offered a crown, that their darling princess could now be a queen, a queen moreover who would be in the forefront of the fight for the Protestant cause, the people's enthusiasm broke loose. Bonfires were lit in the London streets, church-bells were set ringing, and the clergy called on their congregations to pray for the King and Queen of Bohemia. The King's Council, moreover, led by Archbishop Abbot, were in favour of acceptance of the crown. All this was distressing for King James. He was not a popular monarch, and if he failed to support his daughter in what was regarded as a Protestant crusade he would be faced with a formidable opposition; even his throne might be in danger. So when the Elector's envoy, Baron Christopher Dohna, arrived in London to ask for the royal advice, the King was compelled to temporize. He refrained from any direct refusal of support, but replied that he was unable to give the Elector the title of King until he was convinced of the validity of the Bohemian election. He forbade his own subjects to pray for Frederick as King of Bohemia, and he made it as clear as he dared that no practical support from him could be expected.

Meanwhile the Elector had made up his mind. The envoys from Bohemia were pressing, and he could not wait for any reply from England. On 28 September he signed a paper agreeing to meet Bohemian deputies on the frontier. If the conditions offered were satisfactory, he would proceed at once to Prague.

How far Frederick was influenced in his decision by his wife is uncertain. The traditional view, that it was she who, from motives of feminine vanity, plagued him into pursuing his enterprise, has been shown to rest on dubious evidence.[7] In fact, while declaring her readiness to support her husband in whatever course God should ordain, she expressly left the political question to Frederick. At the same time her private feelings can hardly be in doubt. Certainly she longed to be a queen. At the time of her marriage her mother had voiced her scorn at the meanness of the match, saying that her daughter would hence-forth be known as 'Goodwife Palsgrave'. Queen Anne had died in March 1619, but probably the taunt still rankled.

Clearly Elizabeth was not tormented by the doubts that afflicted her husband. With her proud Stewart blood she welcomed adventure, and she had a lively contempt for the enemy in the person of the Emperor Ferdinand II. In a letter to Sir Dudley Carleton, English Ambassador at The Hague at the time of the imperial election, she had written, with that engaging outspokenness that makes her so entertaining a correspondent: 'They have chosen heare a blinde Emperour, for he hath but one eye, and that not verie good. I am afrayed he will be lowsie, for he hath not monie to buy himself cloths.'[8]

The die having been cast, preparations for the journey were quickly made. Elizabeth, although in an advanced state of pregnancy, insisted on accompanying her husband. Frederick Henry, now in his sixth year, was to go with his parents, but the two younger children, Charles Louis and Elizabeth, were to stay with their grandmother at Heidelberg.

The long procession of horsemen and carriages set forth from Heidelberg on 7 October, making its way through Ansbach into the Upper Palatinate. At Amberg, the Upper Palatinate's principal town, the Elector was met by an imperial envoy sent by Ferdinand in a last attempt to dissuade him from accepting the crown. Frederick was not to be dissuaded, and the procession went on to Waldsassen on the Bohemian border. There, on 24 October, the Elector accepted the terms offered and was proclaimed King Frederick of Bohemia.

Next day the King and Queen crossed the frontier into their new kingdom, and on 31 October, amid ardent expressions of loyalty, they made their state entrance into Prague. There they were lodged in that same Hradschin Palace where the fateful Defenestration had taken place some eighteen months before.

On 4 November King Frederick was crowned in the Cathedral of St Vitus; three days later came the turn of his Queen. So far all had gone well. The handsome young King had made an excellent impression, and the tall, fair, graceful Queen seemed likely to capture the imagina-tion of the Bohemians as she had that of the English. In her native country she was already 'the Queen of Hearts'; in Bohemia she now became 'the Pearl of Britain'. But to the Emperor and his followers the new sovereign and his consort bore a different aspect. 'A winter king and queen of snow' was the scornful description that spread across Europe from Vienna; they would melt away when the sun shone.

And after the first fine careless rapture flaws were seen in the demeanour of the royal couple. Elizabeth was gay, charming and vivacious; but she was not always tactful. When the women of Prague waited on her on her name-day, the Feast of St Elizabeth, she failed to appreciate the significance of the traditional gift of confectionery and allowed her courtiers to laugh at the triviality of the present. Deeper criticism arose from the religious prejudices of the King and Queen. Prague was an ancient city of great beauty and great traditions: a polyglot centre where faiths and races met. The Protestant party was now in power, but it was Lutheran rather than Calvinist and iconoclasm was foreign to its nature. Frederick was a rigid Calvinist, to whom relics of the Catholic past were monuments of superstition. Elizabeth, Puritan by upbringing thanks to the Haringtons, accommodated herself with enthusiasm to her husband's way of life. Thus they were led into diplomatic error. Frederick had all pictures and statues taken from the Cathedral, and followed up this unpopular action by ordering the removal of the crucifix and attendant religious statues that from time immemorial had guarded the bridge over the Moldau. Elizabeth supported him, and it was said that she had vowed never to cross the bridge of Prague until such relics of popery had gone.

The time was approaching when the King and Queen would need the undivided allegiance of the people of Bohemia, but so long as affairs continued to have a prosperous look no great rift was noticeable, and Bohemian enthusiasm was as evident as ever when on 17 December (7 December according to the old-style English usage) of the year 1619 the Winter Queen gave birth to a winter prince.

This third son and fourth child, born to a queen in her husband's capital city, was given an imperial name, Rupert, after his ancestor Rupert III, the one member of the Palatine family who had worn the crown of the Holy Roman Empire. Great rejoicings followed his birth. A month later the news reached London, and King James, though officially he still denied the royal title to his son-in-law, 'joyfully asked for a large beaker of wine and drank to the health of the new born prince in Bohemia and of the new king and the queen his daughter. He then took his purse and gave it with all that it contained to this gentleman (who had brought the news), saying to him "Run and tell the good news to the prince and throw the doors open if they are not already open." '9 Three months later, when the little prince was christened with elaborate ceremonial in the Cathedral, his chief sponsor, represented by

17

proxy, was Bethlen Gabor, the Transylvanian prince who was now in power in Hungary.

But the snow had melted, and it was time for the Winter King and Queen to face the summer storm. In April the Emperor called on Frederick to resign his crown under pain of being put under the ban of the Empire. Frederick, who earlier in the month had had his eldest son proclaimed Crown Prince of Bohemia, returned a defiant answer. War was now certain, and during the ensuing months the King of Bohemia toured his territories to rally his supporters to arms and appealed for help abroad. He had little success. The princes of the Protestant Union were wary of being involved in hostilities against the powerful imperial forces. King James was far too canny to commit himself, though he allowed a body of volunteers to enlist under Sir Horace Vere, and Charles Prince of Wales, to whom Elizabeth made a personal appeal, contributed £2,000 to help the cause. Louis XIII of France remained neutral. And in Bohemia itself the response was lukewarm.

The Emperor moved in his own good time. He had four strong armies at his disposal, and with one of them, composed of Spanish troops commanded by Ambrogio Spinola, he struck first at the Lower Palatinate. On 28 August these forces crossed the border and advanced towards Heidelberg.

The great war was now well and truly launched on its long and terrible course, and the prime agent was the inoffensive, ineffectual, well-meaning Elector Palatine Frederick. He now did his feeble best to stem the tide. Sending the Crown Prince for safety to Berlin (Elizabeth refused to leave Prague in the hour of danger), he joined his army in the field to defend his hereditary domains. But his troops were ill-trained, ill-clad and ill-armed, and were no match for Spinola's seasoned army.

Autumn rains brought a slight respite; then the Emperor struck again. At the beginning of November a second, Bavarian, army entered Bohemia from the west and marched on Prague in an endeavour to cut off the capital from Frederick's forces. Its commander, Marshal Bucquoy, had been disabled by a wound and the expedition was led by Count Johann von Tilly, who was to prove himself one of the most formidable generals of the Thirty Years War.

King Frederick managed to get back to Prague, and his forces, such as they were, took up a defensive position on the Weissenburg, 'the White Mountain', just outside the city. Imminent conflict seemed unlikely; but shortly after midday on Sunday, 8 November, Tilly attacked. Frederick was dining comfortably in the Hradschin Palace, on the western side of the Moldau; by the time he had risen from table the issue had already been decided.

The Battle of the White Mountain was one of the shortest and most decisive actions on record. It had lasted barely an hour when Frederick's forces, commanded by Christian of Anhalt, streamed into Prague in headlong flight. In the palace all was confusion; the royal coach was hurriedly summoned, and the King and Queen headed a precipitate flight across the river. A fateful episode of this ignominious scene has been described by Miss Oman in words that cannot be bettered:

> Much frenzied packing was done on that dark November afternoon, but Frederick's chamberlain, on a last progress through the deserted royal apartments, discovered something important which had been left behind. He picked it up, and hurrying down to the courtyard, was just in time to catch the last coach drawing away from the palace doors. Not until the bundle 'thrown in' by Christopher Dohna rolled from the 'boot' on to the floor of the carriage and burst into a roar, did his astonished fellow-travellers discover that the infant Prince Rupert was amongst them.[10]

Such was the first recorded adventure of Prince Rupert of the Rhine and of Bohemia. It had a suitably martial flavour; but retreat in the face of the enemy, in this case hardly voluntary, was not characteristic of the career that was to follow.

CHAPTER 2

FIRST VENTURES IN ARMS

AFTER his spectacular departure from the Hradschin Palace on 8 November 1620, the young prince disappears for a time into the shadows of history. His father had given him the resounding title of Duke of Lusatia, but it is as plain Prince Rupert, one of a constantly growing family of young Palatines, that he appears in the occasional references that are to be found to his exiled childhood.

That night was the last the King and Queen of Bohemia were to spend in their transitory kingdom. There was no hope of holding Prague, and Frederick and Elizabeth now reaped the reward of their undiplomatic behaviour. Loyalty to the Winter King and Queen was not strong enough to face adversity. The people of Prague shut the gates against the defeated troops, and the burghers implored their sovereign to make good his escape before further disaster came to the city. Frederick had no choice. Early on the following morning, with Elizabeth and the infant Rupert, he set out towards the north-east. That day Maximilian of Bavaria, head of the junior branch of the Wittelsbachs, took possession of Prague in the name of the Emperor Ferdinand.

At Breslau in Silesia Frederick appealed to the Protestant Union for help in retrieving his fortunes. But no help was forthcoming for a hopelessly beaten prince, and no course was open but continued flight. The next objective was Brandenburg, whose ruler, the Elector George William, had married Frederick's sister Catherine, and with whom the young Prince Frederick Henry had taken shelter. But George William, a Lutheran, had little sympathy for his Calvinist brother-in-law, particularly in the hour of defeat, and had no intention of embroiling himself with the Emperor on his behalf. He was anxious to get rid of his embarrassing guests as quickly as possible, but since Elizabeth, who at one stage of the journey was compelled to ride pillion behind a young English soldier named Ralph Hopton, was pregnant as usual, he allowed them to stay in his castle of Kustrin, some miles north of Frankfurt-on-Oder. There, in the new year, the Queen's fourth son and fifth child was born. The baby was named Maurice after the Prince of Orange, his great-uncle, one of the most illustrious soldiers of his time.

It was an opportune compliment. Maurice of Nassau, Prince of Orange and Stadtholder of the United Provinces, was the son of William the Silent and brother of the Electress Palatine Juliana. And he it was who, when the princes of Germany were falling over each other in their eagerness to be rid of the unfortunate couple who had been so rash as to raise the standard of revolt in the name of the Protestant alliance, offered the exiles an honourable residence at The Hague. There they arrived on 14 April 1621, bringing Rupert with them but leaving the baby Maurice in Berlin with his aunt, the Electress of Brandenburg. Charles Louis and Elizabeth were also in Berlin; after the fall of Prague the whole of the Palatinate was quickly overrun by imperial troops, and though the garrison of Heidelberg held out for some months the Electress Juliana, with the two young children, took refuge with her daughter.

During the years that followed the Winter King led a life of constant and ineffectual activity. His capable mercenary general, Count Ernest von Mansfeld, won a few successes for him in the Lower Palatinate, and the war gradually spread over most of Germany. Frederick moved from camp to camp and did what he could to stir up allies, but he was no longer a serious military factor in the situation and hostilities proceeded with little reference to the man whose action had started them.

He was only intermittently at The Hague, where his Queen now settled down in permanent residence. She was no more reconciled to defeat than he was, and her voluminous correspondence did more for the cause than her husband's fruitless wanderings. 'The grey mare', wrote her brother Charles, 'is the best horse.'[1] Her vitality was undimmed, and the style of her letters grew racier with the years. She addressed her correspondents with colloquial affection. Sir Jacob Astley was 'Honest little Jacob',[2] and a playful letter to the Earl of Carlisle began: 'Thou ugly, filthy, camel's face . . .'[3]

For the rest, she managed to enjoy life at The Hague. Prince Frederick Henry of Orange, brother of Maurice, put his palace at her disposal on her arrival, and later she was given a house by the States of Holland. The States also assigned her an income to add to her pension from England. It was not sufficient for her needs, and the Palatine family were constantly in debt; but no adversity could subdue Queen Elizabeth's natural gaiety. She hunted constantly, and took what part she could in the social life around her. She indulged to the full her love of animals and kept a menagerie of pets which, according to her youngest daughter, she preferred to her children.

These children continued to arrive on the scene with unfailing regularity. In 1622 a daughter was born who in compliment to the host country was named Louise Hollandine; in 1623 came Louis; in 1624

Edward; in 1626 Henrietta Maria; in 1627 Philip; in 1628 Charlotte; in 1630 Sophia, and in 1632 Gustavus Adolphus. Such a brood was enough to tax the attentions of any mother, let alone one with Elizabeth's commitments and responsibilities; and whether or not Sophia's strictures were true she certainly decided that her family would be better brought up at a distance. Once more Prince Maurice came to her aid. He obtained from the university city of Leyden, north of The Hague, the loan of a house called the Prinzenhof, and here the young Palatines passed their childhood.

The Crown Prince had reached The Hague soon after his parents. Frederick Henry was a solemn child who early in life assumed his responsibilities as heir to the Palatine house. On 11 May 1621 he sent a progress report to his grandfather of England:

> Sir, we are com to the Haag from Sewneden to see the King and the Queene, and my little brother Rupert, who is now a little sicke; but my brother Charles who is at Heydelberg is, God be thanked, very well, and my sister Elizabeth, and shee is a little bigger and stronger than he. So I kisse your Majesties hand, and I pray God to blesse you. Your majesties Grandchild, Fred Henry.[4]

At first only Frederick Henry, Rupert and Louise formed the ménage at Leyden, over which the strict Mme de Plesseus presided. To further their education the two boys were entered at the university. But in 1624 Charles Louis joined them from Brandenburg, and four years later Elizabeth and Maurice, while as the younger children emerged from the nursery they too were sent from The Hague. In later life the youngest but one painted a forbidding picture of the Leyden régime:

> At Leyden we had a court quite in the German style. Our hours as well as our curtsies were all laid down by rule. My governess, whose name was Mme. de Ples, had held the same post with my father when he was a child, and from this fact her probable age may be guessed. She was, however, assisted in her duties by two daughters, who looked older than their mother. Their conduct was equally upright towards God and man. I believed that they prayed to God, and never disturbed man, for their appearance was frightful enough to terrify little children. They taught me to love God and fear the Devil, and brought me up strictly according to the good doctrine of Calvin.
>
> I learned the Heidelberg catechism in German, and knew it by heart, without understanding a word of it. I rose at seven in the morning, and was obliged to go every day en deshabillé to Mlle. Marie de Quat, one of the ladies before mentioned, who made me pray and read the Bible. She then set me to learn the 'Quadrains de Pebrac', while she employed the time in brushing her teeth; her grimaces during this performance are more firmly

fixed in my memory than the lessons which she tried to teach. I was then dressed and prepared by half-past eight to endure the regular succession of teacher after teacher. . . .

Everything was so arranged that we knew on each day of the week what we were to eat, as is the case in convents. On Sundays and Wednesdays two divines or two professors were always invited to dine with us. They believed that I should turn out a prodigy of learning because I was so quick, but my only object in applying myself was to give up study when I had acquired all that was necessary, and be no longer forced to endure the weariness of learning. After dinner I rested till two o'clock, when my teachers returned to the charge. At six I supped, and at half-past eight went to bed, having said my prayers and read some chapters in the Bible.[5]

It all sounds reminiscent of the Harington régime which Elizabeth of Bohemia had endured as a child. She and Frederick were both devoted Calvinists, and doubtless they saw no reason to depart materially from a curriculum which they themselves had found eminently satisfying. Nevertheless this highly coloured passage cannot be accepted unreservedly as evidence of the conditions under which Prince Rupert grew up. The lively, gossiping Electress Sophia of Hanover had an acid pen; she wrote her memoirs when she had moved far from the beliefs and loyalties of her childhood; and she was speaking of a time when the elder boys, including Rupert who was eleven years her senior, were no longer at Leyden. The boys were taught by tutors from the university, broader in view and more tolerant than the de Plesseus gorgons; and none of them showed any sign in later years of resenting the discipline under which they had been educated. All, in greater or lesser degree, inherited their mother's vitality, and there are indications that the young Palatines, far from being repressed, were addicted to any amount of the rowdy mischievousness natural to a bouncing brood of un-inhibited youth. Among themselves they acquired nicknames which are some guide to their developing characters. Charles Louis, bitter and sardonic in his comments on others, was 'Timon'; Elizabeth, studious and devoted to the classics, was 'La Grecque'; Rupert was 'Robert le Diable' for his rough manners and fierce temper. Nobody appears to have ventured on a nickname for the grave and respected Frederick Henry.

Rupert is commonly thought of as being German. So he was, if only the direct male line is considered. But all royal families are of mixed blood, and Rupert's was as mixed as any. His grandfathers were German and Scottish, his grandmothers Dutch and Danish. And this again is to take account only of one side of each line. A generation or two back reveals English and French blood, and a little further would show relationship with almost every princely line in Europe. Rupert was a princeling of the Holy Roman Empire; he had been born in Bohemia and grew up in the Netherlands. Eventually he was to give his allegiance to his mother's country. In his early days he was a cosmopolitan and a wanderer, while giving his first loyalty to his father's house and ready always to fight for the restoration of the family's dominions.

He early developed a gift for languages. Before he was three years old his father recorded proudly that he was 'fort savant d'entendre tant de langages'.[6] If we accept the testimony of his earliest biographer,[7] he made modern languages his particular study. Unlike his sister Elizabeth, 'hee was not ambitious', we are told, 'to entertaine the learn'd tounges, as qualifications that require soe much tyme to the improving and preserving them and which a Prince has rarely occasion to use, either in Court or Camp'. By his thirteenth year, continues the writer, he could understand and be understood in all Europe; his High and Low Dutch (Dutch and German) 'weere not more naturally spoken by him, than English, French, Spanish and Italian'. And 'latin hee understood'. Thus early were his eye to the future and the practical bent which was always to distinguish him made evident.

Equally practical, and in accordance with his temperament, was his ardent application to military training. 'While hee thus happily learnt to Speake,' says the author of *The History of Prince Rupert*, 'hee more happily learnt to act. Warr was his great inclination, and in Peace he made it his principall Study. . . . Hee framed his body and his mind continually to that glorious exercise, considering hee should have need of both, desiring to bee Captain and Souldier too. This made him delight in the exercise of the horse, and the use of his Armes, in Learning Fortification, and all other notions which might render him Knowing and prosperous.' Another contemporary biographer paints a similar picture, speaking of the young Prince 'also applying himself to riding, fencing, vaulting, the exercise of the pike and musket, and the study of geometry and fortification; wherein he had the assistance of the best masters; beside the inclination of a military genius, which shewed itself so early, that at eight years of age he handled his arms with the readiness and address of an experienced soldier'.[8]

For the rest, Rupert took part in the normal occupations of a young prince, albeit in exile. He rode and he hunted, and he may at this time have learned to play tennis, a game to which he had a lifelong devotion and in which, like most things to which he turned his hand, he attained a high degree of skill. At this time also he had his first chance of developing his talent for drawing. The painter Honthorst was a friend of the Palatine family, with whom he resided for a time at The Hague. Honthorst took a great interest in the children, visited them at Leyden, and gave tuition to those of them who were inclined that way. His favourite pupil was Louise, the artist of the family: a pupil so attentive to her master's teaching that a number of her pictures have been attributed to him. But Rupert was a close second, a draughtsman of considerable promise.

Such was Rupert in his boyhood: 'Robert le Diable', a swashbuckling and no doubt arrogant lad, strong and active, devoted to arms and outdoor exercises, yet with a quick brain, a keen, inquiring mind and considerable artistic talent. He had his Scottish grandfather's penetrating brain but was wholly without that scholarly monarch's academic interests; nor had he King James's unfortunate personal characteristics. From his mother he inherited his mental and physical vitality, and from her and his Dutch grandmother the strength of his character and his fighting spirit; from the latter also his rather sombre stubbornness. But from the Palatine side of his family, or at least his immediate forbears, nothing is obviously traceable except perhaps his loyalty to the Calvinist creed, to which he always remained faithful though he never allowed it to influence his public conduct. As regards his absorption in things military, Rupert's upbringing played a greater part than heredity. He had been born in time of war; before he was a year old he had been caught up in retreat from battle. Since that day he had grown up in an atmosphere of potential strife, for always the goal before his exiled family was the restoration by force of arms of their hereditary domains if not the kingdom of Bohemia. Rupert with his bellicose temperament looked forward to playing his part in the coming struggle; from his earliest years he was determined to be a soldier.

It was in any case a normal career for a younger son. Rupert came only third in the succession. The important member of the rising generation was the eldest son. The Crown Prince was his father's pride and joy: a prince of boundless promise, an old head on young shoulders, wise and kindly, courtly and level-headed, with a deep sense of the responsibilities that rested on him. As Henry Prince of Wales had been to the Stewarts, so was Frederick Henry to the Palatines.

Then, in 1629, came tragedy. Prince Maurice of Orange had died four years before, and one of his bequests to his nephew Frederick was a share in a Dutch company which was carrying on operations to intercept Spanish galleons bringing treasure from the Indies. The company's fleet had now returned to Amsterdam with its spoils, and King Frederick travelled from The Hague to view the ships and arrange for payment of his share. He took with him his eldest son, now fifteen years old.

All went well on the outward journey. But the money could not be allocated at once, and Frederick, short of cash as usual, decided to travel home on the ordinary packet-boat. In the Haarlem Meer it was rammed by a heavy Dutch vessel and sank. There were few survivors.

25

Some sailors managed to rescue Frederick, but as he was hauled from the water he heard his son's despairing cry: 'Save me, Father!' Then the boy vanished.

The young hopeful of the family was no more; and the heir was now Charles Louis, 'Timon', the cool, smooth, precocious, self-centred boy who was his mother's favourite but nobody else's. It was a poor exchange.

For the Winter King it was the beginning of the end. For years he had been subject to melancholia and increasing nervous irritability. He had not the inner strength that enabled his wife to surmount misfortune. Now he sank into despair. His son's dying cry, it is said, rang in his ears to his own dying day.[9]

Yet, ironically enough, it was in the days which followed that hope arose of the fulfilment of King Frederick's dreams. The Thirty Years War was extending its tentacles beyond the confines of Germany; Spain and France were becoming involved. The alliance between the Habsburg powers, Spain and the Empire, was close, and Spanish troops were already in the Palatinate. Now the government of King Philip IV, headed by Gaspar de Guzman, Count-Duke of Olivarez, saw its way to work for the recovery of the revolted Spanish Netherlands. This brought the France of Cardinal Richelieu into the fray, though not yet to the extent of actual hostilities. Richelieu was not prepared to see any further advance of Spanish power, and this Prince of the Church, chief minister of the Catholic King Louis XIII, did not hesitate to throw the weight of French influence into the balance on the Protestant side. The issue was no longer which religious faction should prevail in Germany. The prize was the domination of Europe; the conflict was between Habsburg and Bourbon. And in the summer of 1630 Richelieu unleashed a hurricane from the north. Its name was Gustavus Adolphus.[10]

Gustavus II of Sweden was one of the great generals of history. In 1630 he was thirty-six years old and had been on the throne for nineteen years. During that time, in addition to consolidating his kingdom under a strong central government, he had built up an army which had no equal in Europe. It was consummately trained and admirably disciplined. Gustavus had studied the military methods of Prince Maurice of Orange, and Dutch instructors had been employed to train his gunners. In both artillery and cavalry the King attached supreme importance to mobility. He introduced light guns, 4–pounders which a single horse could carry, and used them to support his attack when and where they were needed. So with the cavalry. The horseman of the early-seventeenth-century army was armed with musket and pistols, clad in heavy armour and mounted on a beast built rather for stamina than for speed. Cavalry were little more than mounted infantry, trained to advance at a slow trot with frequent halts to dismount and fire volleys in support of the infantry. Gustavus brought in lighter horses and reduced his horsemen's armour to the minimum of helmet and breastplate. He trained them to advance with all possible speed, to fire only when within close range of the enemy, and to use their swords in the final attack.

The paramount principle of mobility informed also Gustavus's actual tactical reforms. Instead of massing his troops in columns he formed them into small squares, infantry and cavalry alternately; each square having room to manoeuvre on its own. His musketeers stood in files, the first wheeling to the rear after firing and the next taking their place for the next volley. Thus, even with the laborious loading process of that era, something like continuous fire was maintained, and the square formation enabled direction to be changed with the minimum of delay.

Gustavus Adolphus was an ardent Protestant, who viewed the Catholic Empire with unwavering hostility. He was also a statesman with a firm grasp of grand strategy, and from a practical standpoint what he feared was the establishment of imperial power over the Baltic ports and consequent threats to the Scandinavian kingdoms. In such circumstances Richelieu had little difficulty in inducing him to accept his destiny as the Protestant champion of Europe against the encroachments of Catholic Austria.

King Gustavus landed at Usedom, on the Baltic coast, on 4 July 1630, giving as his pretext the Emperor's intervention in Poland and the threat to the Protestant religion. Within a month he had taken possession of Pomerania. At the beginning of 1631 he signed his treaty of alliance with France; then he struck southwards across Germany. There were no forces in the north capable of resisting his highly trained army, and his success brought allies to his side. He failed to relieve the Protestant city of Magdeburg, key fortress of the Elbe, which fell to Tilly's forces in May; but the victorious troops, less well disciplined than those of Gustavus, destroyed the city so effectually that its strategic significance was lost. It was no longer capable of serving as a base. Tilly withdrew, and Gustavus continued his advance.

In September these two illustrious commanders met face to face at Breitenfeld, four miles north of Leipzig. The result was a brilliant victory for the Swedish King; Tilly's army was routed, and its general severely wounded.

There was now no stopping Gustavus. He swept westwards through Saxony and Hesse, and by November was on the borders of the Palatinate.

Here King Frederick drifted into the picture. One of Gustavus's declared objects had been the restoration of the Elector Palatine to his hereditary estates, and ostensibly it remained so. Frederick therefore hurried from The Hague to join his declared liberator at Frankfurt-on-Main. The outcome was yet one more disappointment in the futile career of the Winter King. Gustavus received him with the utmost respect, according him the honours of a king; but that was as far as he was prepared to go. The conqueror was now master of the Rhineland and of all northern Germany. The way seemed open to Austria, and he was dreaming of Swedish dominance in Europe and the imperial title for himself. He was not prepared to surrender any part of his authority, and his dazzling prospects were not to be jeopardized for the sake of any pledged word to a discredited prince who would be no asset to his cause. Frederick might return to Heidelberg as Elector Palatine, but only as a puppet, a vassal of the King of Sweden. With what remaining dignity he could muster, Frederick declined the humiliating terms offered. He lingered in the area, but his last hope had gone.

Gustavus continued his victorious progress, sweeping into Bavaria and forcing the passage of the Danube at Donauworth; then, in April 1632, he inflicted a second defeat on Tilly near Ingolstadt. The imperialist general, now over seventy years old, received a mortal wound.

This was the limit of Gustavus's triumphant advance. His worthiest foe was no more, but Albert von Wallenstein, a commander no less eminent than Tilly though less steadfast to the imperial cause, had still to be reckoned with. Wallenstein fought only for his own interests, and his capricious movements had been the bane of Ferdinand for years. Now he decided to come to the aid of the Emperor, uniting his own forces with those of Maximilian of Bavaria, and Gustavus was forced to turn north again to deal with the new threat. On 16 November the final, fatal battle was fought – in a heavy mist – at Lutzen, fifteen miles west of Leipzig. Wallenstein was defeated, but when the mist cleared King Gustavus Adolphus was found dead on the field.

Before the month was out the man who a few weeks before had seemed to have all Germany at his feet was followed to the grave by Frederick of Bohemia, a failure to the last. The plague was raging in the Rhineland, and Frederick, wandering indecisively, made little effort to avoid the stricken area. The attack of which he was a victim is said to have been a slight one, but the Winter King had no will to live. On 29 November he died at Mainz.

The fifteen-year-old Charles Louis was now the titular Elector Palatine, but there was little prospect of a restoration. The only hope of support lay in the Winter Queen's brother Charles, King of England, Scotland and Ireland since the death of his father seven years before. On 12 December 1632 the four eldest boys wrote to their uncle, committing 'ourselves and the protection of our rights into your gratious armes; humbly beseeching your Majestie so to loock upon us, as upon those who have neither friends nor fortune, nor greater honour in this world, then to belong unto your Royall bloud'. The letter was signed 'Charles, Rupert, Maurice, Edward'.[11]

To this pathetic appeal King Charles returned a gracious answer. 'I can truly say that I have lost more than you,' he wrote, 'for you have only changed your father, since I will now occupy the place of the deceased; but I have irreparably lost a brother.'[12] At the same time he promised Elizabeth the continuance of the allowance granted to her husband, and invited her to bring all her children to England. The Queen, however, was not prepared to leave the continent while there might yet be a reaction in Germany in favour of the new Elector Palatine. Moreover she was embarrassingly in debt and the move would cost money.

Meanwhile life in the Netherlands went on much as before. In his last years Frederick had spent most of his remaining funds on building a country home at Rhenen, in the province of Utrecht, and here the family passed some of their most carefree hours. Rupert indulged his growing passion for hunting, and it may have been at Rhenen that a curious adventure befell him, though it is ascribed by its recorder to a later time. He was hunting in the company of Sir Thomas Billingsley, and a fox went to ground, followed by 'a dog which the prince loved'. Rupert tried to pull the hound out but got stuck in the hole; whereupon Billingsley caught hold of the Prince's legs. Finally the other hunters came up, pulled away the tutor, who pulled out Rupert, who pulled out the hound, which pulled out the fox.[13]

The number of Elizabeth's children was now reduced to ten: Frederick Henry was gone, and two others, Louis and Charlotte, had died in infancy – a small proportion of mortality in that age, evidence of the healthiness of the breed. In 1631 the boys were joined at Leyden by their cousin Johann of Zweibrucken-Veldenz, son of Frederick's sister Louisa and of the same age as Rupert. He was accompanied by his tutor, Heinrich Stern, and their letters home presented a cheerful picture of family life which may serve as a corrective to Sophia's forbidding description. The children 'all live very happily and affectionately together,' reported Stern.[14] Johann told of riding expeditions, of vaulting, fencing, pike-swinging, dancing and lute-playing. 'I am very well here,' he wrote, 'and very happy in such good company, with so many different exercises and amusing games.'

During this time Rupert was straining at the leash. For years now he had been training himself in arms, and he longed for active service in the field. After his father's death, says the author of *The History of Prince*

Rupert, 'nothing then was left to comfort him, but the Liberty which hee promised himselfe of speedily goeing to the Army'.

In 1633, when he was in his fourteenth year, he had his way. In the previous year his great-uncle Prince Frederick Henry of Orange, brother and successor of Maurice, had advanced into the Spanish Netherlands and seized Venloo, Roermund and Maestricht on the Meuse. Now he was besieging Rhynberg, and he proposed to Queen Elizabeth that Charles Louis, who would sooner or later have to fight for his inheritance, should join his forces for training in war. The Queen consented, whereupon Rupert pleaded to be allowed to go too. His mother agreed to this also, saying that he could not be too soon a soldier. 'Last Wednesday,' wrote Johann on 2 May, 'my two eldest cousins went to the field with the Prince of Orange.'[15]

This first venture in arms lasted only a few weeks. The Queen, always solicitous of the moral welfare of her children, had apparently heard tales of the depravity of the soldiery – revelations which one would think could hardly have been new to her. At any rate, 'upon a suggestion that the army would corrupt and debauch him',[16] she recalled her second son to The Hague before May was out. Charles Louis presumably, with his two years' seniority, was considered proof against temptation.

Rupert was deeply aggrieved; but his humiliation was of short duration. Prince Frederick Henry, 'who loved him very dearly',[17] made representations to his mother, who thereupon had second thoughts. The young prince was soon back before Rhynberg, which fell to Frederick Henry of Orange in October. The two boys were said by the English envoy Honeywood to have distinguished themselves by their 'ingenuous and manly carriage';[18] the Prince of Orange, Honeywood further reported, 'could not show more tendernesse of them, or joy more in them, if they were his own'.[19]

Back at The Hague at Christmas 1633, Prince Frederick Henry celebrated his victory with a 'solemn running at the ring', a tournament on the old medieval model. Prince Rupert took part and again distinguished himself, though since he was only just fourteen the author of the *History*, writing at a later date, may be suspected of letting his enthusiasm carry him away in his lyrical description of the part played by the young warrior:

> . . . The first Course was runn for honour of the Ladyes; never were horses better managed, or armes more skilfully handled, all being ambitious to signalise themselves in this cause by showing the greatest gallantry and addresse; 'till our young Prince appeared, every one promised to him selfe to bear away the palme; but the gracefull aire, which accompanied all his actions, weere such as drew the eyes and hartes of all the spectatours

towards him, and the hopes of the Contenders from them – for his per-
formances that day, showed hee had not only the advantages of all in
birth and meene, but in bravery and addresse; for hee won the Prize with
as many acclamations as if hee had gained a battail or conquered a
Kingdome.[20]

The ladies moreover, continues the writer, 'contended among themselves which should Crowne him with the greatest and most welcome
gloryes'. And of course there was one 'more eminent than all the rest,
both in Quallity and beauty', who 'would not that her esteeme should
bee drown'd in noises, or goe along in the Crowd of common admirers'.
One would like to know the name of this first recorded feminine admirer
of Rupert, but his biographer tells us only that her loveliness 'transcen-
ded that of the rest of her sex, as much as his worth had the noblest of
his, and that it was not possible that the greatest bravery could bee
showed without the admiration of the greatest beauty'.

The tournament over, Rupert returned to Leyden to continue his
education, but 'his thoughts were so wholly taken up with the love of
arms, that he had no great passion for any other study'.[21] And in 1635
he was allowed once more to serve with Prince Frederick Henry's
forces. This was a more serious campaign. France, now fully committed
to hostilities, had sent 25,000 men, under Marshals de Châtillon and
de Brézé, to fight the Spaniards in Brabant in uneasy alliance with the
Dutch. In the event the fighting was inconclusive, but Rupert had a
more thorough taste of active warfare than had fallen to his lot during
the siege of Rhynberg. He was present at the capture of Tirlemont,
which the French troops ruthlessly sacked; at the siege of Louvain,
which was unsuccessful; at the passage of the river Florival; and at the
first stages of the siege of the strong fortress of Schenkenseyan.

Here he showed that he possessed the true qualities of a soldier. For
he renounced all distinctions of rank, choosing to serve as an ordinary
trooper in Prince Frederick Henry's Guards. Determined to learn the
rudiments of military order and discipline the hard way, he 'delivered
himself up to the common duties and circumstances of a private soldier,
in all sorts of fatigues and hazards'.[22] Fatigues and hazards he took in
his stride, but discipline was harder to master. Through the laudatory
passages of the *History* one can detect signs that the Prince's officers
must have found young Rupert no easy trooper to control: '. . . he
shewed an early bravery to the astonishment of the eldest Souldiers;
he would have done more would they have suffer'd him, but care was
taken of him, who tooke non of him selfe'. Moreover, this private
soldier, fifteen years of age, apparently did not hesitate to question the
strategy of his commander-in-chief:

31

. . . nor could he accommodate his thoughts to the Pollitique reasons of the Prince of Orange, who as it was thought might have made better advantage of the French Army, if it had conduc't to the interest of those to whom hee was generall. An active Prince as ours, was alwaies for Charging the enemy, hee knew noe other cunning or mistery of State, then to Fight well, believed Valour was more the virtue of his age than prudence, and thought it lesse honourable for him to bee a great Politician than a good Souldier. But hee must be guided by his Generalls orders and not his owne; hee knew obedience was better than victory, and that before wee overcome others wee should learne to overcome our selves. This hee had leasure to understand before the end of the Campaigne when affaires moved not soe fast as hee desired.[23]

Thus early do we find evidence of those qualities of Rupert, his impatience, his arrogance, his conviction that he knew better than anybody else, that were to cause him much trouble in the years ahead. But it is clear that he did make some effort to 'overcome himself'. When the campaign broke up for the winter and he returned once more to The Hague, he must have been a wiser, more experienced, altogether a more mature being, than the eager boy who had first set out for the wars two years before.

His next adventure, of a very different nature, was to have a profound influence on the shape of his future career. For it took him to England.

CHAPTER 3

MOTHERLAND

SINCE the death in 1612 of Henry Prince of Wales, the shy, under-sized, stammering boy who was his younger brother had grown, largely through sheer will-power, into a respected figure of regal dignity. Charles's stammer was still with him and he was still small (five feet five or six inches is the usual estimate), but he had achieved a grace of manner that impressed itself on all who met him. King of England, Scotland and Ireland since 1625, he had dispensed with parliaments after the first four years of his reign, and under his personal rule England, free from foreign wars, had blossomed and prospered to a degree that was the envy of her neighbours.

King Charles differed from King James as widely as a son can differ from his father. He was solemn, withdrawn, intensely earnest; the bawdy boisterousness that had characterized the first Stewart King of England was alien to his nature. His private life was one of immaculate purity. He was deeply religious, and the Church of England in which he had been brought up was to him the most sacred institution in the world. While he lacked his father's intellectual interests, King Charles had a deep devotion to, and appreciation of, the visual arts. His own taste was faultless and his sense of beauty and understanding of painting enabled him to build up a royal collection that has seldom been equalled. He patronized Rubens and made Van Dyck and Dobson (whom he dubbed 'the English Tintoret') successively his court painters. At the same time he set himself to beautify his palaces and his capital city. Inigo Jones was his Surveyor-General, and as such could count on the fullest support from his royal patron in all his schemes of archi-tectural improvement. Hence the English court, which in the previous reign had been notorious as the abode of ribaldry and debauchery, became a symbol of gracious living, stately and formal indeed but en-hanced by beauty and good manners. Whatever his faults, Charles I was a highly civilized man.

In matters of administration he was conscientious and took pains to understand the problems that faced his government. At the same time, as Dame Veronica Wedgwood has shown,[1] he revealed, at any rate in the

33

early years of his reign, a lack of application. Even during the period of his personal rule his attendances at meetings of his Privy Council, the central organ of government, were irregular; he could always be distracted by the pleasures of the hunting field or the calls of his art collection. He had a high sense of both his rights and his duties as governor of his country, but did not want to be troubled with matters of detail. Only under the grim pressure of war would he abandon this casual attitude.

Like his father he held the most exalted view of kingship. The monarch ruled by divine right; sovereignty was a gift conferred by God, and whatever its holder might do, however far short of divine perfection his conduct might be, he could not be called to account for it. His duty indeed, as the father of his people, was to rule them with paternal benevolence; to promote their well-being with all the power at his command. But he must be judge in his own cause on how far he succeeded in doing so. It was not for his subjects to question his actions; their obedience must be absolute. He was accountable to God alone.

Charles I was fundamentally a weak man. He had shown strength of character in schooling himself for kingship, in dedicating himself to the assumption of an authority for which he was not originally destined, and for which his personal characteristics ill fitted him. But his air of command was superficial. He was unsure of himself, lacking in decisiveness, feeling always the necessity of leaning on the shoulders of those endowed with more resolution and more forceful personalities than his own. He had worse faults than these. His actions often gave an impression of deviousness, which was again the manifestation of weakness. Faced with opposition he would take refuge in a mass of verbiage which he felt free to interpret in his own way and to his own advantage, and he was apt to persuade himself that, since his opponents were inspired by disreputable motives, any methods he might use in dealing with them were justified. In many of his dealings it is difficult to acquit him of bad faith.

In his relations with his friends also the defects of his character are apparent. He was capable of base ingratitude: the result not so much of callous indifference as of his belief in his divine authority. From those who served him he expected everything, and recognized no obligation to give anything in return. The highest possible service to the King was the duty of every subject. For that service no reward was required; if the King chose to confer any, it was simply out of his princely benevolence.

Before his accession to the throne Prince Charles had fallen under the spell of his father's favourite George Villiers, Duke of Buckingham. Buckingham, a man of mediocre capacity and little political judgement, had the flamboyant self-confidence needed to dominate the emotionally insecure prince, and his ascendancy continued after Charles became King; for the first three years of the reign he was the real ruler of England. In the meantime the King had married Henrietta Maria, youngest daughter of that dashing monarch King Henry IV of France. Henrietta, nine years younger than her husband, was fifteen at the time of her marriage in 1625. She inherited many of her father's characteristics: his gaiety, his determination, his vigour and his courage. She was not beautiful (a defect which Van Dyck convincingly disguised), nor was she particularly intelligent; but she had abundance of charm, wit and vivacity, together with a wilful nature, strong likes and dislikes, and a capacity for enmity.

The marriage was at first unhappy. Henrietta's frivolity offended the grave King, while the Queen resented the influence of Buckingham, who treated her with overbearing insolence. But Buckingham was assassinated in 1628, and then a curious thing happened. After three years of marriage, freed from the discordant influence of the favourite, the young King and Queen fell deeply and enduringly in love. Once again King Charles felt the need to lean on a stronger nature than his own. Henceforth she was his guide and mentor, except in matters of religion.

Queen Henrietta was a devoted Catholic. Her faith, and her dream, were the conversion of her husband's country from the schism which, at the time of her arrival in England, was less than a century old. Charles was equally rigid in his devotion to the Church of England. To him the Anglican establishment was all in all: the one focus of loyalty from which he would not swerve. Here at least he never showed weakness.

Like his brother before him Charles I was devoted to his sister Elizabeth. He had chafed at his father's ambivalent attitude towards the Palatinate question, and in his private capacity had done all he could to show where his sympathies lay. Yet when he became King he found that there was little he could do to help the exiles. Official military aid towards recovery of the lost territories was out of the question. England in any case had no standing army, and the most the King could do was to declare his approval of the raising of volunteer units. Nor was he in a position to supply financial aid on any useful scale. England in the mid-1630s had an air of prosperity, but in the absence of parliament the King was dependent on the ancient dues of the Crown. He had no money to spare.

Nevertheless it was in the King of England that the hopes of the exiled Palatines chiefly lay. Queen Elizabeth, sanguine of temperament, was convinced that her brother needed only to be persuaded of the necessity and of what was required of him. And who could better persuade him than the Prince Elector himself? Charles Louis completed his eighteenth year in the winter of 1635; now he was of age, and formally assumed his father's titles (other than that of King of Bohemia, which was not hereditary). His royal mother decided that the time was ripe for a visit to England.

King Charles's agreement was obtained, and Charles Louis arrived at Dover in November 1635. He was received most graciously. 'The Earl Marshal from the King,' wrote a correspondent, 'and the Lord Goring from the Queen went to *Gravesend* to attend him, who the same Night brought his Highness to the King, who received him in the Queen's withdrawing Chamber, using him extraordinary kindly; the Queen kissed him. He is a very handsome young Prince, modest, very bashful, he speaks *English*.'[2] He was lodged in Whitehall, and one of his first visitors was the Spanish Resident Nicolaldi, who to the surprise of other diplomats gave him his title of Prince Elector Palatine, 'saying, his Master doth so, and commanded him to do the like'.[3]

Whether Charles Louis was really 'very bashful' may be doubted. At eighteen he was an accomplished diplomatist, cool, shrewd, intelligent, with graceful manners and a keen eye for the main chance. He was cold-hearted and selfish, but his aims were not contemptible. From infancy the Palatines had been brought up to keep one prime objective in view, the restoration to the family of their ancestral lands. Now, in England and as heir to the family fortunes through the death of his elder brother, Charles Louis took a good look round him and set himself to cultivate all circles which might be useful in achieving his aim. He did not limit himself to the court. While he got on excellently with his uncle, he seems to have seen what was not yet apparent on the surface, that King Charles's personal rule was far from secure. The opposition which had been in evidence in the King's early parliaments was gathering strength behind the scenes; its leaders were the Puritan landed gentry, men such as John Pym, John Hampden and Oliver St John, Lord Saye and Sele and the Earl of Warwick, and with some of these Charles Louis, a natural ally by reason of his Calvinist upbringing, took care to ingratiate himself.

And now Rupert, the campaign of 1635 over, was at a loose end. His brother was making himself popular in England, and this led to a proposal that the second surviving Palatine son should follow. In this case the initiative is said to have come from King Charles, but doubtless there had been diplomatic prompting from The Hague. There were misgivings in England: '. . . he is not so welcome at Court,' wrote the Venetian Ambassador, 'because they fear that by degrees they will all come and will take root'.[4] And the Winter Queen herself had little confidence that the younger prince, with his unpolished manners, would make as good an impression as his brother had done. To Sir Henry Vane she wrote:

> I fear that *mon envoyé* will not make altogether so many compliments as my lord of Carlisle doth; yet I hope for blood sake he will be welcome, though I believe he will not much trouble the ladies with courting them, nor be thought a very *beau garçon*, which you slander his brother with, for I fear it is but a slander what you say of him, and to shew you have not forgot to be a courtier. . . . Give your good counsel to Rupert, for he is still a little giddy, though not so much as he has been. I pray tell him when he does ill, for he is good-natured enough, but doth not always think what he should do.[5]

Contrary, however, to these anxious prognostications, Rupert made himself immediately popular in England, so much so that he was soon eclipsing his brother in public esteem. He arrived in February 1636, and was received, as Charles Louis had been, with every mark of affection by the King and Queen. He was enchanted with all he saw, and his spontaneous, ingenuous delight pleased his hosts more than the suave appreciation shown by the elder brother.

The young Prince, now just sixteen years old, made his English trip a glorious holiday. The two brothers, though they were often together on ceremonial occasions, otherwise saw little of each other. Charles Louis pursued his devious intrigues, while Rupert threw himself into the pleasures of the most cultivated court in Europe. He hunted with the King at Oatlands; he viewed with delight the magnificent royal collection of pictures, and admired the splendid new Banqueting Hall in Whitehall, designed by Inigo Jones and with a ceiling painted by Rubens; his portrait was painted by Van Dyck; he enjoyed the masques and pageants, on land and on the river, that were the joy of Queen Henrietta Maria; and he basked in the admiration of the ladies of the court.

He made friends with surprising ease. Within weeks of his arrival in England the rough-tempered boy, who appeared to his mother and others a crude swashbuckler fit only for camp life, found himself in a courtly and cultured circle of high literary distinction. At its centre was Endymion Porter, a courtier whose qualities were as exceptional as his name. He was partly of Spanish blood, an experienced diplomat, a minor poet and a connoisseur of the arts, a man of wit and learning; and at his house in the Strand he and his charming wife Olivia entertained the leading literary figures of the day. Among his friends were Robert Herrick, Sir William Davenant, Sir John Suckling, Edmund Waller and Thomas Carew. Rupert became a frequent visitor to the house, and in this rarefied atmosphere, utterly different from anything he had known before, he achieved a popularity which in itself showed that there was more in his character than his mother had perceived. The Porters were delighted with him, while of the others the poet Davenant in particular became a fervent admirer.

Rupert had other friends than these. Sir Thomas Roe, explorer and diplomat, Elizabeth of Bohemia's 'Honest Fatte Thom', who was now in temporary retirement in England, kept a fatherly eye on him and sent progress reports to The Hague. Commenting on both brothers to Queen Elizabeth on 20 July 1636, he wrote:

It is not the first time your Majesty confessed to me . . . your affection to the Prince Elector, but now I must approve and admire your judgment, for there was never any fairer subject of love. . . . Yet this doth not detract from Prince Rupert, whom I have observed of a rare condition, full of spirit and action, full of observation and judgment. Certainly he will *reussir un grand homme*, for whatsoever he wills, he wills vehemently; so that to what he bends, he will be in it excellent. I am glad he stays here while he cannot be employed in a school of honour, for his Majesty takes great pleasure in his unrestfulness, for he is never idle, and in his sports serious, in his conversation retired, but sharp and witty when occasion provokes him.[6]

It seems to have been now too that Prince Rupert became intimately acquainted with that fascinating character William, Lord Craven, though he must almost certainly have known him earlier. Craven was the son of Sir William Craven, a self-made man who had come to London from his native Yorkshire early in the reign of Elizabeth I and had amassed a large fortune by commerce, becoming Warden of the Merchant Taylors' Company in 1593 and Lord Mayor of London in 1610. Eight years later Sir William died, and Craven the younger, inheriting his father's wealth, embarked on a military career. He served under both Maurice and Frederick Henry of Orange in the Low Countries, and in 1632, at the age of twenty-six, accompanied Frederick of Bohemia in his final effort to win back the lands of the Palatinate, earning the commendation of Gustavus Adolphus for his gallantry. It was at this time that he fell under the spell of the Winter Queen. He lived to be over ninety, and to the end of his life he dedicated himself and his resources to the service of the Queen and her family with single-minded devotion.

Craven was a born knight-errant, who asked nothing more of life than the chance to do battle in the cause of his lady. In stature he was small, and he abounded in eccentricities of manner which excited the affectionate amusement of the irreverent young Palatines at The Hague. Given a barony by King Charles in 1627, he lived on and off at The

Hague, where he could keep an adoring eye on his Queen, ready at all times to do her bidding. But he was in England at the time of the princes' visit, and set himself with characteristic enthusiasm to further Charles Louis's schemes for raising support. At the same time he watched over the fortunes of the younger brother, and helped him with money and advice.

But much as he relished the company of these kind and influential friends, Rupert's deepest devotion was reserved for the King and Queen. He was young and impressionable, and the grave dignity and stately courtesy of King Charles, the vivacity of Queen Henrietta, and the splendid ceremonial of the court over which they presided, made a profound impression on him. Here and now, it seems safe to conjecture, he saw in his uncle and aunt a fitting object for the loyalty that was the mainspring of his nature; he would be happy to serve them in whatever contingencies might arise in the future. The Queen made much of him, and hence arose a new source of anxiety for his mother over the water. Henrietta Maria was the most ardent of Catholics, and her dearest wish was to bring all her friends into the fold of the Catholic Church. In Rupert she discerned a possible convert, and she encouraged his aesthetic interest in ritual and ceremonial in the hope of inducing a change of faith.

She was not alone in her efforts. Olivia Porter was a Catholic, and her husband, if not one himself, was at least highly sympathetic to that Church. And in the summer of 1636 there was a new addition to the Porter circle when Monsignor George Conn arrived in England as papal agent to the Queen. Among those who served the Catholic Church in England during the days of persecution this cultured Scottish priest takes a high place. He was a scholar and a lover of the arts, and with his tact and moderation he established the happiest relations with the tolerant King, which enabled him to work quietly for the welfare of his co-religionists without raising the antagonism which at that time was aroused so easily by any attempt to better their lot. With Rupert he was soon on terms of friendship, discussing pictures with him, explaining the doctrines of his Church, and even making tentative plans for a future visit of the Prince to him when he returned to Rome.[7]

One would much like to know how far Rupert moved towards conversion; but the evidence is scanty. Certainly he was attracted, and this seems to have been the only time in his life when he may have wavered in his allegiance to the Calvinist creed. He never paraded it; in an age when it was customary to proclaim one's religious beliefs loudly and firmly he was consistently reticent about his. It may be that in reality religion meant little to him, and that his steadfastness was a matter of loyalty rather than conviction; or it may be simply that he considered, in contrast with the conventions of his time, that his religion was a private matter that concerned nobody but himself.

His leaning towards Rome in 1636 has been dismissed by most historians as a youthful aberration, induced by delight in ceremonial and the dazzling personality of the Queen. But it is possible that it went deeper. The Queen certainly thought that his conversion was imminent, and Rupert himself, when he finally returned to The Hague, convinced his mother that a few days more in England would have made him a Catholic. On hearing this Henrietta commented to Conn that, had she realized this, she would have found some means to keep him in England.[8]

It was Charles Louis who first raised the alarm of his brother's possible conversion, writing to his mother that Rupert was 'always with the Queen and her ladies and her papists'.[9] In a later letter he wrote:

> . . . My brother Rupert is still in great friendship with Porter; yet I cannot but commend his carriage towards me, though when I ask him what he means to do, I find him very shy to tell me his opinon. I bid him take heed he do not meddle with points of religion amongst them, for fear some priest or other, that is too hard for him, may form an ill opinion in him. Besides M. Con doth frequent that house very often, for Mrs. Porter is a professed Roman Catholick. Which way to get my brother away, I do not know, except myself go over. . . .[10]

Queen Elizabeth, visualizing her son already in the arms of the Scarlet Woman, tried in vain to get him to come home. She appealed to Sir Thomas Roe to induce the young man to return so that he could take the field with the Prince of Orange, as 'he spends his time but idly in England'.[11] Sir Thomas was sympathetic, but tactfully advised the Queen to recall her son gently. 'His spirit is too active to be wasted in the soft entanglings of pleasure,' he wrote. 'He will prove a sword for all his friends if his edge be set right. There is nothing ill in his stay here, yet he may gather a diminution from company unfit for him.'[12]

Rupert had a will of his own, and he was enjoying himself much too much to allow himself to be sent home. And the King and Queen loved having him with them. Queen Elizabeth wrote once more to Roe: 'You may easily guess why I send for him, his brother can tell you else. I pray you help him away, and hinder those that would stay him.'[13] But it was of no avail. Queen Henrietta said she would not let her nephew go, and Elizabeth resigned herself to the situation.

So Rupert was reprieved. But his mother's appeals were perhaps not without their effect, for in this summer of 1636 his uncle and aunt and his English friends began to cast their eyes around to see what could be done to find him employment and provide for his future. One suggestion put forward was marriage. The Palatine family were always short of money, and an alliance with a wealthy heiress would benefit them all. There was one available in France – the daughter of the Duc de Rohan, a distinguished Huguenot soldier who had fought under Henry IV. Negotiations were set on foot, and in September Charles Louis wrote to his mother that overtures were going ahead. 'I think it is no absurd proposition,' he added, 'for she is great both in means, and birth, and of the religion.'[14]

Queen Elizabeth was in favour of the match; and so, it would appear, was Marguerite de Rohan. Rupert, however, showed no enthusiasm. He was quite happy as he was; passing his time, according to the Venetian Ambassador, 'by amusing himself in the society of the ladies . . . without any preoccupations besides what his own youthful inclinations at present supply him'.[15] It is unlikely that he had ever seen his suggested bride or knew very much about her; however, it is perhaps significant that her attractions as set forth in diplomatic correspondence were her wealth, her high birth, her influential connections and her Protestantism. Mention of beauty was conspicuous by its absence, though at one stage the Earl of Leicester, the English Envoy in Paris, half-heartedly described her as 'handsomer than is necessary'.[16] The project was pursued in England and in France, but with little urgency. Negotiations dragged on for a number of years, and then came to nothing.

Yet Rupert was not devoting himself exclusively to dalliance, for another scheme was maturing which had a far greater appeal for him. This was nothing less than the establishment of a principality for him in Madagascar. This island contained a few Arab settlements, and the interior was reputed to be inhabited by mysterious tribes of fearsome savagery. The Portuguese had reported its discovery in 1500 and had named it the island of St Lawrence. Since then a few Portuguese missionaries had landed and made courageous attempts to spread the gospel among the coastal tribes, but with little success.

The idea of an English colonization of Madagascar seems to have taken root early in 1636. An expedition was to be fitted out with Rupert as leader, and he was to be Governor of the island when the objective had been attained. Even in those days of colonizing ardour the plan was widely regarded as fantastic and impracticable, but Rupert at least took it seriously. He was fired with ambition, and devoted himself, with that intensity of application which was one of his characteristics, to the study of shipbuilding. In March, with his brother and the King, he paid a visit to Woolwich, where under the supervision of Phineas Pett, the master-shipwright, a great new warship, the *Sovereign of the Seas*, was being built. The fleet had been neglected in King James's time; his son was now repairing the damage, and for this purpose had extended the levying of 'ship money' to the inland counties, an act which was shortly to have fateful consequences. The *Sovereign of the Seas*, with its three gun-decks and 105 guns, was to be the pride of his ship-money fleet, one of the largest and most beautiful vessels afloat. The keel had been laid in the previous December, and out of the waste timber two small pinnaces were built at the King's command. When he and the Palatine princes went to Woolwich on 28 March 1636, Pett recorded that they 'stood in the windows of my lodgings to see the two pinnaces launched, which was performed to their great content, and named the Greyhound and Roebuck'.[17] Prince Rupert, who had grown up in a maritime country but whose active adventures to date had all been on land, had found a new enthusiasm.

Not so his mother. Elizabeth was horrified, particularly so as, in the mood of the moment, a second suggestion was being put forward that Charles Louis should lead an expedition to the West Indies. If her two eldest sons should both go gallivanting off to the ends of the earth, what would become of the Palatinate? She would 'have none of her Sons to be Knights-Errant'.[18]

Nevertheless the plans went ahead. The East India Company, to whom the King appealed for advice, would have nothing to do with the venture, but an order in council was passed for the fitting out of twelve men-of-war and twenty-four merchantmen, with Rupert as Admiral and Captain Bond as his lieutenant. Endymion Porter, one of the movers of the scheme, was commissioned by the King to inquire into the prospects, and according to Warburton he wrote a pamphlet describing the prospective wealth of Madagascar in glowing colours.[19]

Another literary supporter was Sir William Davenant, who was inspired by the occasion to produce a poem of 446 lines (few of them of much merit) dedicated to Prince Rupert. It describes a dream in which the poet was

> steer'd unto an Isle,
> Between the Southern *Tropick* and the *Line*;
> Which (noble Prince) my prophecie calls thine: . . .[20]

Rupert soon appears at the head of his fleet, then lands and prepares for battle, but meets only minor resistance. And so the gallant Prince opens his reign and a new golden age:

> Here in a calme began thy regall sway;
> Which with such cheerfull hearts, all did obey,
> As if no Law, were juster than thy word:
> Thy scepter still were safe, without a Sword.

And here *Chronologers* pronounce their stile;
The first true Monarch of the *Golden Isle*:
An *Isle*, so seated for predominance,
Where Navall strength, its power can so advance,
That it may tribute take, of what the East
Shall ever send in traffique to the West.[21]

Had Rupert ever got to Madagascar he might perhaps have found his dominion somewhat different from that portrayed in Davenant's poetic imagery. But Davenant was a leader of literary society, and his poem caught the imagination of contemporaries and helped to swell support for Rupert's enterprise.

Pending the fitting out of the ships – and officialdom worked no more rapidly then than at other periods of history – there was for the moment nothing more to be done. Meanwhile the round of ceremonies and entertainments continued. In August the court went on its summer progress, and Charles Louis and Rupert were of the company. And it was now that Prince Rupert first saw Oxford. This was the highlight of the princes' stay in England. William Laud, Archbishop of Canterbury, was Chancellor of the University, and under his supervision the city and the colleges bustled about to ensure that the royal visit should be a success. The bellman was sent round to 'require all persons to remove their blocks and dirt from before their doors, and to pitch all places that were faulty, and that presently they go about it, heavy penalties were denounced against all who disobeyed these orders, and the scavenger was directed to set himself to work to rid the streets of dirt, filth, rubbish, and all manner of uncleanness'.[22] Instructions were issued to the undergraduates which have a perennial ring. They were 'to appear nowhere abroad without their caps, and in apparel of such colour and fashion as the statute prescribed, and particularly they were not to wear long hair, nor any boots, nor double stockings rolled down or hanging loose about their legs, as the manner of some slovens is, nor to wear their gowns hanging loosely, with their capes below their shoulders'.[23]

It was a crowded two days, in which the Palatine princes played a prominent part, being the highest-ranking visitors after the King and Queen and travelling with them in the royal coach. They arrived at Oxford on 29 August, and were met a mile outside the city by the Chancellor, heads of houses and dons in their scarlet gowns, and representatives of the town. After a speech by William Strode, the Public Orator, 'the Chancellor, in the name of the University presented to the King a Bible in folio, with a velvet cover, richly embroidred with the King's Arms in the midst, and also a costly pair of Gloves. To the Queen another pair of Gloves, to the Prince Elector Hooker's Books of

Ecclesiastical Politie with Gloves, and to his Brother Rupert Caesar's Commentaries in English, illustrated by the learned explanations and discourses of Sir Clem. Edmonds'.[24] Laud had evidently given careful consideration to the gifts; Caesar's *Commentaries* in English were eminently suitable for a youth of martial attainments whose favourite study was not Latin.

The royal party proceeded to Christ Church, with halts for more speeches on the way, and that evening they saw in Christ Church Hall a play by Strode himself called *Passions Calmed, or the Settling of the Floating Island*. Laud, who wrote a lengthy account of the Oxford visit, said cautiously that the play 'was very well penned, but yet did not take the court so well'.[25] Lord Carnarvon, who was in the royal party, was blunter in his criticism. It was, he said, 'the worst that ever he saw but one that he saw at Cambridge'.[26]

Next morning the King and his nephews attended matins in Christ Church Cathedral, after which the two princes were conducted to the House of Convocation to be made Masters of Arts. So Rupert, donning a scarlet gown and being invested by Sir Nathaniel Brent, Warden of Merton College, became a graduate of the University of Oxford. In compliment to Laud he and Charles Louis were entered as members of St John's, which was the Archbishop's college.

There were of course more speeches, including one in Latin from Laud; and then, after a tour of the colleges, the princes returned to Christ Church to attend the King. The Queen having availed herself of the feminine privilege of being 'not ready', the rest of the royal party visited the recently expanded Bodleian Library. Dinner at St John's College followed and before the day ended there were two more plays – *Love's Hospital* by George Wilde and *The Royal Slave* by William Cartwright – which seem to have found more favour than Strode's luckless effort.

Between the plays there was a banquet at which the King and Queen and Charles Louis sat together at the high table, and Rupert at a lower one with lords and ladies of the court. Finally there was a private supper at Christ Church, after which the visitors, whose stamina must have been severely tested, retired to rest. At eight o'clock next morning, the university dignitaries saw them off along the Woodstock road.

In such diversions, which Rupert evidently enjoyed in spite of the speeches and the sermons, the year 1636 drew to its close. But Madagascar had not been forgotten, and in the early months of 1637 there was more talk of the venture. The Winter Queen was as adamant as ever in her opposition. 'As for Rupert's romance of Magadascar,' she wrote to Roe in April, 'it sounds like one of Don Quixote's conquests, where he promised his trusty squire to make him king of an island.'[17]

Roe still advised her to bide her time. He too was convinced that the Madagascar scheme was absurd, but saw that the best course was to allow events to shape themselves.

There was much coming and going between London and The Hague. Elizabeth sent her trusted counsellor Johann von Rusdorf to England to drum some sense into her errant son. Rupert listened to his admonitions, said nothing, and remained undeterred. Meanwhile King Charles had sent his own envoy to The Hague to sound his sister on her future plans for Rupert. This envoy was Colonel George Goring, younger son of Lord Goring and commander of one of the English regiments of foot in the Dutch service. He reported that he found the Queen was disposed to recall her son, as 'she had a belief that he would lose his time in England'.[28] He added that the Elector had mentioned to his mother the sending of some land forces into France, 'which he judges a fit command for him'.[29]

Events in fact were moving towards new continental adventures, and it was this that finally put paid to the Madagascar project. Charles Louis's assiduous undercover work had not been in vain, and plans for the recovery of the Palatinate lands were maturing. The Emperor Ferdinand II had died in February; his son, Ferdinand III, was as yet an unknown quantity, and Richelieu was planning active moves against the Empire. King Charles promised his nephew a fleet and encouraged the raising of volunteers. Money began pouring in, and a subscription list was headed by the King and Lord Craven with £10,000 each. The King also promised Charles Louis £12,000 a year for the support of any army he might be able to raise. Richelieu asked for a force of 6,000 Englishmen to support the French action, and Charles Louis requested that the command should be given to Rupert. This proposal, however, came to nothing.

Rupert turned to the support of his brother's fortunes with all the enthusiasm of his nature. 'The dream of Madagascar, I think, is vanished,' wrote Roe in patent relief to Elizabeth on 8 May, 'and the squire must conquer his own island. A blunt merchant called to deliver his opinion, said it was a gallant design, but such as wherein he would be loth to venture his younger son.'[30] The Queen for her part was anxious that the young soldier should return to the service of the Prince of Orange, in company with her next son Maurice.

Now that action was in prospect, Rupert was wholly in accord with his mother's and his brother's designs. Arrangements were quickly made for bringing the English visit to an end, and on 26 June the Palatine brothers embarked in the *St George* at Greenwich, escorted by the English royal fleet and accompanied to the coast by the Earl of Arundel and to Holland by the Earls of Northampton and Warwick, Lord

Craven and Lord Grandison. Yet Rupert, eager as he was to fight for the family fortunes in the field, left at least part of his heart in the country he had come to love so well. A correspondent wrote to Lord Wentworth: 'Both the Brothers went away unwillingly, but Prince *Rupert* expressed it most; for, being a Hunting that Morning with the King, he wished that he might break his Neck, that so he might leave his Bones in *England*.'[31]

CHAPTER 4

IMPERIAL CAPTIVE

AFTER paying their respects to the Winter Queen at The Hague the brothers once more separated. Charles Louis went into Westphalia to arrange for the support in his projected campaign of the Swedish forces under Marshal Johan Banér. Rupert, impatient for action and at a loose end until his brother's return, hastened once more to join the Prince of Orange, who was now besieging Breda.

There is insufficient evidence to determine the nature of the relations existing at this time between Charles Louis and Rupert; but it seems likely that, even if no personal rift had as yet occurred, it was at least in the making. They had gone their own ways in England. The Elector, in his long and frequent letters to his mother, seldom mentioned his brother; when he did, it was in the somewhat exasperated tones of an elder compelled to divert his attention from his own vital concerns to watch over the conduct of an errant junior. Rupert's feelings are more difficult to fathom, since he did not put them on paper. It may be surmised, however, that he resented the assumption of superiority on the part of one so different in temperament and outlook from himself.

At Breda he found himself in the more congenial company of his younger brother Maurice, next in age to himself. These two had been apart during their early childhood, the newly born Maurice having been left in Berlin when Rupert was taken by his mother to Holland. In the adolescent years at The Hague and Leyden there is nothing to show that their friendship amounted to any more than that between others of the family. Now, however, when Rupert was in his eighteenth year and Maurice in his seventeenth, the fortune of war brought them together, and a comradeship began which was to remain the closest in both their lives.

Rupert arrived at the siege with Northampton and Grandison, who had accompanied him and Charles Louis from England. Maurice was already before Breda, and in the besieging army were a number of English officers whose names were to become familiar a few years later. At this time four English regiments of foot and several troops of horse were in the pay of the States of Holland, and among the future

47

Cavaliers were Sir Jacob Astley, George Goring, Henry Wilmot, Charles Gerard and Charles Lucas. The Parliamentarian Philip Skippon, and George Monk, who was to fight for each side in turn in the Civil War, were others whose fame lay in the future.

At the siege Rupert soon found opportunities to display his soldierly qualities and to show how well grounded he was in military training. 'Nothing could soe well please our young Prince,' says the *History of Prince Rupert*, 'in the pationate desire hee had still to acquire greater glory, hee let noe day passe in that seige, without doeing some exploite at which the whole army was surprized, and his example inspired them with soe much courage and tooke soe much from the enimy, that in a short tyme, they became masters of the place.' The author of the *History* was apt to let his enthusiasm run away with him, and it may be doubted whether the fall of Breda was brought about by the inspiring example of a seventeen-year-old volunteer soldier. But the soberer and more factual account in the *Life of Prince Rupert* shows that he made a practical contribution to victory. On one occasion

> . . . General Morgan had the opening of the trenches; and Sir Jacob Astley commanded under him. Prince Rupert and Prince Maurice put themselves upon the *perdu*; and crept up so close to the enemy's works, that they could hear the soldiers discourse on the other side, and made a discovery of their design to issue out, waiting till they were just upon the point of a sally. Whereupon the Princes instantly retired, and gave the besiegers so seasonable notice of it, that they were presently ready for them, and beat them in again with loss.[1]

In this exploit it is possible that Prince Frederick Henry's army was indebted not only to Rupert's alertness and enterprise but to his skill as a linguist. We are not told in what language the defenders were conversing; the Breda garrison was Spanish, but the Spanish army included troops of various nationalities. From his earliest years Rupert had found it easy to master foreign tongues, and at a period shortly after this he was said to be fluent in six.

In the next action in which the young prince was engaged he showed, as well as courage, a sublime contempt for orders from above when they conflicted with his own wishes. The Prince of Orange sent in an attack against a 'hornwork', or fortified outpost, which he considered so dangerous that he expressly forbade Rupert to expose himself in it. 'But he slipped himself, nevertheless, as a volunteer into the party, and came off untouched, leaving a great many of his companions behind him.'[2] Monk, Goring and Wilmot took part in this operation. Monk led a 'stand of pikes'; Wilmot and Goring were both wounded, the latter being lamed for life. A comic incident was also recorded. 'A Bergundian officer was stript and lay among the dead upon the hornwork, a good while after started up, Messieurs, est de poynt de Quartière? They cald him Jack ffalstaff upon and he carry'd the name.'[3]

Breda fell on 10 October 1637, and its reduction ended the year's campaign. Young Maurice was sent, with Prince Edward the next Palatine brother, to complete his studies in France, while Rupert returned to The Hague to join Charles Louis. Whatever his private relations with his eldest brother, he was eager to join him in striking a blow for the family inheritance. The Elector had been able to raise a force of some 4,000: 2,500 horse and dragoons and 1,500 foot. Banér had co-operated to the extent of sending a body of troops under James King, a Scottish mercenary serving with the Swedish forces. Rupert was given the command of a regiment of horse; it was the first time he had the actual command of a unit. Lord Craven, who had presumably accompanied Charles Louis on his mission to the Swedes, and who had made a personal contribution of £30,000 to the enterprise, led a regiment of Guards. Other officers named were Ferentz and Loe, who had the title of 'field-marshal',[4] and the Swedish colonel Count Königsmark.

By October 1638 Charles Louis was ready to take the field, though what he hoped to achieve with so small a force is something of a mystery. The Emperor Ferdinand III had underlined his father's policy by confirming the grant of the Upper Palatinate, with the Electorate, to Maximilian of Bavaria, while indicating to Lord Arundel, the English envoy, that he would give up the Lower Palatinate only on condition of its being purchased at a heavy rate. It was a long march to Heidelberg, and the young Elector can hardly have been so deficient in military flair as to have imagined that he could force his way through the imperial armies to his ancestral territory. What does seem surprising is that the Prince of Orange, a soldier of great experience and capacity, should have encouraged the venture.

Charles Louis, with Craven's money, had purchased the Westphalian town of Meppen from its Swedish overlord, but no sooner had this place been named as the rendezvous for the forces than it was overrun by imperial troops. Undeterred, the Elector proceeded to advance by way of Brentheim, about thirty miles further south, and then south-eastwards towards Minden. He himself was in command of the expedition, but he seems to have exercised little control. His military capacity was slight, and in the climax to the brief campaign events took their disastrous course uninfluenced by him.

Rupert, on the other hand, was in his element, and a reconnaissance gave him an early opportunity to distinguish himself. The advancing army passed near an unidentified imperialist garrison which in the *Life of Prince Rupert* is called 'Rhennius' (possibly Rheine), and Craven and Richard Crane accompanied Rupert to 'take a view of the town'. The *Life* relates that, finding three troops of the garrison drawn up before the town, Rupert sent out three troops to beat them in. Then the Prince, going in on the forlorn hope, made his first cavalry charge, 'which was so exemplary to all about him, that notwithstanding their odds of number, they beat them into their garrison, and followed them so close that they wanted very little of entering the town with the enemy'. During this charge a soldier with a 'screwed gun' (an early form of rifle) took aim at Rupert at a range of ten yards but misfired. Finally Rupert and his company, 'having seen and alarmed the place, returned to the Elector's troops'.[5]

There is little in this short account of Rupert's 'first charge' to indicate how far it foreshadowed that form of attack which was to become his own peculiar contribution to military tactics. Despite the new ideas introduced by Gustavus Adolphus, the cavalry charge at this time was generally little more than a trot with frequent halts for firing volleys. Yet Rupert 'beat them into their garrison, and followed them so close that they wanted very little of entering the town with the enemy'. It may have been a more or less spontaneous departure along new lines, induced by his dashing and headlong leadership. In any case its success must surely have set him thinking on the possibilities of cavalry as a weapon of its own, irrespective of fire-power.

The Elector's army continued its march and laid siege to Lemgo in Münster, some twenty miles south of Minden, where the Swedes had a garrison. But hardly had the Elector sat down before Lemgo than news arrived that the Austrian Count Hatzfeldt was approaching towards the river Weser, with a force greatly outnumbering his own, to cut him off. Charles Louis had no chance of defeating such a body, and on 16 October he abandoned the siege and began the retreat towards Minden. There were two possible routes – by way of Rintelen to the west or of Vlotho to the east. Here General King took over. He was probably the most experienced officer present, but his advice was fatal; he urged the adoption of the Vlotho route, though this meant 'falling into the very mouth of Hatsfield'.[6] Next morning the Elector's troops had not advanced more than half a mile when they found the Count waiting for them with eight regiments of cuirassiers, a regiment of Irish dragoons and 1,800 foot. The Irish were commanded by Colonel Walter Devereux, a soldier of fortune who four years before had gained notoriety by killing Wallenstein with his own hands after that turbulent warrior had fallen foul of Ferdinand II.

King rode ahead to reconnoitre from the top of a hill, and gave it as his judgement that it was a good place in which to draw up, but not before he had sent away his own baggage, 'which received a very ill construction'.[7] The Swedish cavalry commander Königsmark now came up and expressed his dislike of the position taken up. Rupert, with a reasonableness not always in evidence, 'told him that he would take his directions, and follow him wherever he pleased (he commanding then as eldest Colonel)'.[8] Königsmark thereupon 'drew down all the horse into an enclosed piece of ground, and very courteously gave the Prince Elector's horse the van',[9] though it was his own turn to occupy that post of honour. He said that he would 'do the part of a trusty second',[10] but proved a better promiser than performer. King meanwhile had ridden off to bring up the foot and cannon.

At this point the imperialists launched their assault. The first attack fell on Charles Louis and Ferentz in the van. Both were beaten back, and now came Rupert's turn. He beat the enemy from their ground and forced them back, though without any assistance from Königsmark. Here the *History of Prince Rupert* takes up the tale:

> . . . I may say our Prince in a great degree sustained the Courage of his Party. He did more then can bee said, and as in the former course of his life he had surpassed others this day hee surpassed himselfe; the ardour of his Courage engaged him, not considering how hee was seconded, and the first tyme he recollected himselfe to give orders to his men, hee found hee was single in the adverse partie, but not knowne.

The reason why he was not known was that he was wearing a white ribbon in his helmet, so as to be recognized by his troops, and it so happened that the enemy were wearing a like mark of distinction.

And now Lord Craven came to his aid, forcing his way through the imperialist troops with two troops of the Elector's Guards. The enemy, however, with the advantage of numbers, sent in another regiment, that of Lieutenant-Colonel Lippe, while Major-General Westerholder with 800 horse fell upon the rear. Rupert and Craven were completely surrounded, but Rupert was still unrecognized.

> . . . And whilst a thousand thoughts weer revolving in his mind, the way to make his escape, Hee perceived a Cornet of his Brothers Army verry vigorously charged and incompassed with a body of the Enemy; the reasons of his owne safety, could not longer retaine his Courage, nor keepe him concealed, when soe noble an action was presenting of makeing himselfe knowne. Hee stayed not longer therefore to consider, but fell uppon them with soe much fury, and shooke soe much terror in the enemy, that imediately he freed the Cornet. This was done with too great hazard of his Life, for all their rage and fury was turned against him. There it was a souldier more bould than the rest, laid hould on his bridle, which the Prince cleared by cutting of at one blow the fingers of his hand that held

it, and after that not without doeing great execution on the Enemy, hee forced his way through them, and joyned himselfe againe to his party, to their unspeakable encouragement. . . .[11]

But Rupert's personal gallantry could neither turn defeat into victory nor effect his escape. Weight of numbers prevailed, and the whole of the Elector's force was routed. Rupert made one last attempt to clear a hedge and so get out of the enclosure, but his tired horse refused. Craven and Ferentz forced their way to his side, and only when Craven had been twice wounded did the three of them give up the struggle. Rupert surrendered to Colonel Lippe, who, 'having a curiosity to see his face, struck up his helmet and looking earnestly at him, demanded of him what he was, who answered that he was a Colonel; "Sacramet!" (says Lip) "it is a young one".'[12]

The other principal officers got away. Königsmark had taken his regiment off without striking a blow. Charles Louis and King had ridden off the field, and narrowly escaped drowning in the Weser. 'The Elector lost his whole Army that day,' says the *History*, 'and had hee not taken a resolution to save himselfe, by swimming over a River, hee had lost his life, or liberty'. Königsmark's conduct had been contemptible. King, who had so prudently sent his baggage away before the fighting started, was suspected of treachery. On Charles Louis it is not easy to pass judgement. He certainly left Rupert to his fate, but only when his own troops were hopelessly beaten; it does not appear that there was anything he could have done at this stage to rescue his brother. He had taken the first shock of the imperialist attack, and he seems to have fought bravely enough at the outset.

Rupert, who was at first taken for the Elector himself, was delivered into the custody of Devereux, 'with whom the Prince imediately treated about his escape, and gave him five pieces in earnest of a further reward'.[13] Devereux would doubtless have accommodated his captive, 'but Hatsfield appeared at that moment and prevented him'. The three distinguished prisoners were escorted to Warendorf, where they were detained for some weeks while Craven recovered from his wounds. Thence they were taken to Dillenburg and then to Bamberg on their way to Austria. At a place called in the *Life* 'Sansuffle' 'a woman would have assisted him [Rupert] in his escape: but there was no opportunity'.[14]

At Bamberg he was separated from his fellow-captives, who soon afterwards were allowed to ransom themselves. Rupert was too important a prisoner to get away so easily. Craven, who paid £20,000 for his own liberty, offered double that sum for leave to share the Prince's captivity, but this was not permitted. Finally, in February 1639,

Rupert found himself lodged in the fine castle of Linz on the Danube.

Exaggerated reports of his fate reached the outside world. On 14 November 1638 Edward Nicholas, one of the clerks of the council at Whitehall, wrote to Sir John Pennington: 'We have received sad news of the defeat of the Prince Palatine's army at their first entrance into action. The Palsgrave hardly escaped by swimming over a river; his brother (Prince Robert) is taken prisoner, and since dead of his many wounds, having fought very bravely, and (as the Gazette says) like a lion. . . .'[15]

Queen Elizabeth, uncertain of the outcome, reacted in a manner that lacked something of maternal solicitude. She was still obsessed with the bogy of her son's possible conversion to Rome, and writing to 'Honest Thom' Roe of her relief that her favourite Charles Louis was safe, and had 'lost no honnour', she added: '. . . and if I were sure where Rupert is, I should not be so troubled; if he be prisoner, I confess it would be no small greef to me, for I wish [him] rather dead than in his ennemies hands.'[16] And a fortnight later, when the truth was known, she reiterated this sentiment: 'I confess the overthrow of the troupes doth not much trouble me, they are not so manie, but Ruperts taking is all. I confess in my passion I did rather wish him killed, I pray God I have not more cause to wish it before he is gotten out.'[17]

Rupert, however, was neither dead nor converted to Rome; he was in fact enjoying a reasonably comfortable existence at Linz. In the seventeenth century the lot of a prisoner of war of noble birth was seldom hard; it was a matter of honour to treat such a one with every courtesy and with due regard for his comfort. And Rupert with his brave spirit and proud bearing won the respect of his captors. Hatzfeldt had already taken a liking to him, and the Governor of Linz, Count von Kuffstein, though at first, being responsible for his prisoner's custody, he kept him under strict guard, soon became a friend.

Yet the mere fact of captivity, with its restriction of movement and enforced inactivity, was in itself irksome to one of Rupert's ardent and restless temperament. But though he never ceased to devise plans for regaining his liberty he quickly found occupation. It was now that his artistic and scientific interests developed. The author of the *Life of Prince Rupert* tells us that he 'diverted himself sometimes with drawing and limning',[18] and that he perfected an instrument for drawing in perspective which many years later he was to present to the Royal Society. For outdoor exercise he could at first only walk in Kuffstein's garden. But later he was allowed to ride (presumably in the castle grounds) and to play tennis.

Another marked trait of Rupert's was a characteristically Stewart love of animals. One of his companions in his captivity was 'a rare bitch called Puddle which my Lord Arundell gave him, which doggs were so renowned that the Great Turk gave it in a particular instruction to his embassador to endeavour the obliging of one of them'.[19] This passage might be read as recording that 'Puddle' was the name of this particular bitch, but it probably means simply that she was a poodle. If 'bitch' is correct, she was presumably the mother of the more famous 'Boye' (the more usual contemporary spelling) who was Rupert's constant companion in his Civil War campaigns. But it is at least as likely that the chronicler got the sex wrong and that this was Boye himself. For reference to another and more unusual pet shows a bewildering confusion of gender: 'A Hare likewise was bred up to that extraordinary tameness, that he lay upon the Prince's bed. . . . As soon as the dore was unbolted the hare would leap down off the Prince's bed, and go open it with her mouth and at night retire to her bed again.'[20] We are not told how cordial were the relations between the poodle and the hare, but the fact that apparently both throve together is a tribute to the Prince's perseverance and his way with animals.

Rupert had human companions too. Count von Kuffstein was the father of a large family, his eldest child being a sixteen-year-old daughter, Susanne Marie, 'one of the brightest beauties of her age . . . a young Lady noe lesse excelling in the beauty of her mind, then of her body, in whom the high birth, vertue, courage, bravery of meene and misfortunes of our Prince made farr more sensible impressions then they did in her father, and render'd him a Person to her altogether Illustrious'.[21] She loved him, it would appear, for the dangers he had passed; but whether he loved her that she did pity them we cannot be sure. The author of the *History of Prince Rupert* was romantically inclined. 'Neither had the Prince an indifferency for this Lady, for hee never named her after in his life, without demonstrations of the highest admiration and expresing a devotion to serve her.' It may have been so. Rupert, for all his dedication to the sterner side of life, was not insensible to feminine charms. But there is no evidence that the affair went very far, or that it had any lasting effect. In later life Susanne had three successive husbands. Rupert was not one of them. Whatever the nature of Susanne von Kuffstein's friendship, it was beneficial to Rupert. Her father evidently doted on her, and it was largely through her influence that the prisoner's conditions were eased.

The Winter Queen's fears for her son's religion were justified to the extent that serious efforts were made to convert him. The Emperor was anxious to recruit him for the Catholic cause, and it was doubtless on his instructions that Kuffstein, himself a convert from Lutheranism, made overtures to his captive. They were wholly unsuccessful. Rupert, who had listened with interest and sympathy when Queen Henrietta and Monsignor Conn had expounded the mysteries of their faith, would have no truck with any persuasions from those who had power over his person. It was a matter of honour to him not to yield to duress. Kuffstein asked him to go with him to visit his Jesuit advisers; Rupert refused unless he was also allowed to go elsewhere. Kuffstein then suggested that he should receive the Jesuits at the castle; Rupert would not agree unless he could have other visitors too.

So the months dragged on into years, and Rupert remained a prisoner. Outside Germany there was ceaseless diplomatic activity. His mother, once her fears of his apostasy had been calmed, exerted all her efforts on his behalf. 'Honest Thom' was bombarded with letters, and he himself journeyed to the Imperial Diet at Ratisbon in the hope of negotiating terms for Rupert's release. Elizabeth solicited the help of her brother, and King Charles wrote personally to the Emperor; while Charles Louis made a half-hearted attempt to get one of his followers, Thomas Essex, admitted to Rupert's presence. But none of these moves bore fruit.

In the summer of 1639 Charles Louis was himself a prisoner. He had hopes of the alliance of Duke Bernhard of Saxe-Weimar, and rashly attempted to visit him in Alsace, travelling incognito by way of Paris. Cardinal Richelieu, however, had plans of his own for the Saxe-Weimar army, and the Elector's diplomatic ineptitude gave him an excuse to arrest him. Moreover the three younger Palatine brothers – Maurice, Edward and Philip – were all in France at the time; and all three were likewise placed under restraint.

With five sons in one or another form of detention Queen Elizabeth had enough on her mind to distract any mother. Her buoyant spirit, however, was not downcast; she continued writing vigorous letters, and made feverish efforts on behalf of all her wayward progeny. After a time Charles Louis was allowed to take up residence with Lord Leicester, where he lived in the height of luxury, and Maurice to return home to The Hague. Edward and Philip were kept as hostages, and it was not till April 1640 that they were released. Charles Louis was under restricted movement until the following July.

There remained Rupert, and on his behalf diplomatic manoeuvres continued. There was at one time a hope that, by the good offices of Charles I, he might be exchanged for Prince Casimir of Poland, who had been taken prisoner by the French. 'I have written into England,' wrote Elizabeth to Roe, 'that the French may be well satisfied to offer the change and not to release Prince Casimir without Rupert as they did promise my Brother, which my Brother has given my Lord of Leicester commission to doe.'[22] But King Charles had little diplomatic influence in those quarters, and Richelieu had his own game to play.

According to the *Life of Prince Rupert* the exchange was vetoed by Roe, who was then at Ratisbon, on the ground that 'none but the Archduke Leopold (who was the Emperor's brother) could be a fit exchange for his Majesty's nephew'.[23] Such a suggestion would have been singularly unhelpful, since the Archduke was nobody's prisoner; but it is inconceivable that Roe could have been so stupid as to raise such an objection on a point of etiquette. The author of the *Life* (and of the *Diary*, which records the same incident) must surely have got it wrong.

His mistake may have been caused by the part that this Archduke Leopold did in fact play in the events that led up to Rupert's release. Towards the end of 1639 definite terms were offered to the captive. The first was that he should submit to the Church of Rome. But 'hee made them know, hee looked not uppon the offer as a favour, but an affront; that hee had not learnt to sacrifice his Religion to his interest, and yet hee would breath out his last in Prison, before hee would goe out through the gates of Apostacy'.[24]

Faced with this uncompromising opposition, the Emperor now asked simply that Rupert should formally ask pardon for the crime of rebellion against the Holy Roman Empire. This request, as anyone who knew Rupert could have predicted, met with an equally firm refusal; 'the Prince disdain'ed to aske for it, for doeing his duty, and to make himselfe criminall by an unjust acknowledgment when his action merited only honour and approbation'.[25]

The Emperor now advanced to his third and most important proposition. Ferdinand III, a capable ruler and a good soldier, a man of culture and a generous enemy, had shared the general admiration for Rupert's conduct in adversity. The real reason for his insistence on keeping him a prisoner in Austria was that he hoped to gain his allegiance and his services as a military commander. So he offered him his freedom on condition that he should take a command in the imperial forces against France and Sweden, which powers were now united in a league against the Empire. There was nothing inherently unreasonable in the offer. The Thirty Years War was the happy hunting-ground of mercenaries, and professional soldiers served on one side or the other as their interests dictated. Anybody less scrupulous than Rupert might have jumped at the chance, particularly as Richelieu's recent arrest of his brother supplied a good excuse for fighting against France. But Sweden was the stumbling-block. Gustavus Adolphus had been his father's noblest ally, and Swedish forces had fought by his own side in the recent campaign, even though not very creditably. So once again he refused, saying he would never fight against the champions of his father's cause.

Deadlock was complete, and in his exasperation the Emperor listened to the representations of Maximilian of Bavaria, who, always fearful of a Palatine restoration in his newly gained territories, urged that Rupert, if allowed too much latitude, would engage in intrigues against the Empire. For a time the Prince's movements were more strictly controlled; Kuffstein was ordered to cease his civilities, and a guard of musketeers was sent to Linz to watch over the dangerous prisoner.

This phase was brief; and it was here that Leopold von Habsburg came on the scene. The young Archduke, who was five years older than Rupert, had recently been appointed to the command of his brother's forces: a bad appointment, for he was an indifferent military commander. He was, however, a young man of attractive character, popular throughout Austria and a particular favourite of his imperial brother; he was gentle and warm-hearted, and his piety had won him the nickname 'the Angel'.

The Swedish army was advancing towards Ratisbon, and early in 1640 the Archduke was sent westwards to meet it. On the way he passed through Linz and expressed a particular desire to meet Prince Rupert. These two, Leopold the Angel and Rupert the Devil, the fervent Catholic and the austere Calvinist, were immediately attracted to one another, and a warm and lasting friendship sprang up between them. Leopold showed his regard in practical form; he wrote at once to Vienna on the prisoner's behalf and 'moved the Emperour for his freedome'.[26] Ferdinand for his part responded warmly. He had acted reluctantly in curtailing Rupert's privileges, and he was far more inclined to follow his brother's counsel than that of Maximilian. He was not indeed yet ready to free his prisoner, but the recent restrictions were at once cancelled and the former indulgences actually increased. Rupert was now allowed to leave the castle, on parole, for days at a time, and the Austrian nobles responded by inviting him to their houses and giving hunting parties in his honour.

So the months passed pleasantly enough. 'The onely thing the Emperor now requires is his friendship and that hee will never serve against him and honour, Justise, gratitude and generosity obleiged him to bow heere, hee houlding it ill becoming him to imploy his sword against the person who had put it into his hand, and to make use of the favour he had received to the prejudice of the giver.'[27] Yet still there was procrastination, and it was not till late in the following year that the final act was performed. The prisoner's fate had become a subject of fierce dissension in the imperial family. The Emperor was warmly sympathetic towards Rupert, and so was the Empress Maria Theresa, Philip III of Spain's daughter, perhaps with affectionate memories of the English King to whom she had so nearly been betrothed. But the Duke of Bavaria vehemently opposed any suggestion of release, and his

57

Duchess, Ferdinand's sister, 'came and fell on her knees to the Emperor to hinder it'.[28]

In the end the Archduke Leopold and the Empress carried the day. Prince Rupert, after nearly three years of captivity, was offered his freedom on the sole condition of never more drawing his sword against the Emperor. Rupert was still a little reluctant to consent to conditions; but this time he wavered, and to salve his conscience wrote to his English uncle to ask his advice. King Charles gave more than advice; he issued an order. He was himself in increasing trouble with his subjects, and he wanted Rupert's help in the armed conflict that was looming in England. So he 'commanded the Prince to grant soe reasonable a condition'.[29]

Satisfied now that he could in honour submit, Rupert relaxed his proud attitude. He was particularly grateful to Sir Thomas Roe, who was still at Ratisbon and had never ceased in his efforts to secure his release; and his letters show him in an unusually chastened frame of mind. 'I could not let pass this occasion,' he wrote to Roe on 21 August 1641, 'without giving you very great thanks for your pains, and the affection you show in my business. I leave all the conditions to your disposing, for I know you are my friend, and so I am assured you will do nothing against my honour.'[30]

Roe, finding his young protégé in this mood, evidently took the opportunity of giving him some fatherly advice, for at the end of September came a still less characteristic letter:

> . . . I must give you a greate dele of thankes for the reale frendshippe you shewed me in remembering me of my faults, which I confesse, and strive, and shalle the more hereafter, to mend. . . . But assure yourselfe that it has been only from an evill costum, which I hope, in short time, to mend. Desiring you to continue this your frendshippe in letting me know my faults, that I mai have to mend them, I rest yor Lordshippe's most affectionat frend.
>
> Rupert

When in the autumn of 1641 Rupert was at last freed, he had been nearly three years a prisoner. The manner in which he was set at liberty is recounted in the *Life of Prince Rupert*:

> . . . His Imperial Majesty having appointed an extraordinary hunting in the Lower Austrian country, the Prince was at the chase, and meeting with the Emperor, as by chance (though it was looked upon to be so designed by the Emperor), the Prince presented himself to his Imperial Majesty, and having kissed his hand (which signifies enlargement), he was thereupon finally released. At this hunting it was his Highness' good hap

to kill the first boar with a spear, an exploit that is highly accounted of in the empire. . . .[32]

It now remained only for the released Prince to pay a visit of courtesy to the imperial court. It was arranged that Roe should go with him, and on 14 October Rupert wrote once more to his mentor, thanking him warmly for his support and promising to follow his advice in all points.

News of Rupert's release was received with rapture at The Hague. 'I cannot express my thankfulness sufficiently,' wrote Queen Elizabeth to Roe. 'Dr Spina [Palatine Envoy at Vienna], I think, is in love with you, for he writes so fully how you have wrestled with so much labour to overcome all difficulties. I send you a letter for Rupert, where I command him to follow your advice in all he shall do there, and to return hither as soon as honestly he can. . . . I must confess the Emperor has shewed a great generosity in this. . . .'[33] (So grateful was Elizabeth that for once she alluded to the Emperor by his imperial title. As a rule she always called him 'the King of Hungary', since he had been elected Emperor without the Elector Palatine's vote.) Charles Louis, who was again in England, also congratulated Roe, telling him how pleased King Charles was.

In Vienna Rupert made himself as popular as he had done elsewhere. At first he was worried about the state of his finances. But friends in the Netherlands, of whom Craven was almost certainly one, sent him a timely gift of money, together with handsome garments and a magnificent coach, so he was able to make a dashing appearance in the imperial capital. The Emperor, who had met his guest for the first time at the hunt near Linz, was delighted with him. He received him in private audience, hunted and played tennis with him, and introduced him to the society of Vienna. Ferdinand still had hopes of winning him to his own allegiance; but here Rupert could not be moved. All he wanted now was to get home, and as soon as courtesy permitted he prepared for his journey to The Hague. His plan to travel by way of Innsbruck was abandoned at the Emperor's suggestion; Ferdinand gave him the friendly advice that it would be unwise to venture within the power of the Duke of Bavaria. So he made instead for Prague, visiting his birth-place for the first time since, more than twenty years before, he had escaped anticipating his imperial captivity by being thrown into the boot of a coach.

From Prague he proceeded to Dresden, furnished with an introduction from the Emperor to the Elector John George of Saxony. The Elector invited him to a banquet, but the austere young Prince astonished his host by his temperate habits. 'Being in his passage at the Elector of Saxe's, and desiring to be excused from drinking up at the rate of the company:

what shall we do for him then (says the Elector) if he cannot drink, and so invited him to the entertainment of a hunting.'[34]

Rupert went on by water to Cologne, travelling by day and night and reaching Prague five days before Christmas. Boswell, the English Ambassador, wrote to Roe:

> Prince Rupert arrived here in perfect health, but lean and weary, having come that day from Swoll, and from Hamburg since Friday noon. Myself, at eight o'clock in the evening, coming out of the Court gate, had the good luck to receive him first out of his waggon, no other creature in the Court expecting his coming so soon. Thereby himself carried the news of his being come to the Queen, newly set at supper. You may imagine what joy there was.[35]

There was general rejoicing, and most of the credit went to Roe. The Winter Queen wrote again to him in gratitude, and so did her eldest daughter Elizabeth, 'La Grecque', delighted to see once again the brother to whom she was so closely attached and with whom, alone of the family, she could discuss the scientific studies in which she was now making formidable progress.

Nevertheless there was a problem to be faced. Now Rupert was home, how was he to be employed? He could not return to Prince Frederick Henry's army because of his pledge to the Emperor. There was no money to spare at The Hague, and the Queen now had three other sons on her hands; Edward and Philip were back from France, and Maurice home after a short campaign with the Swedes in the Upper Palatinate.

It was a problem soon solved. Affairs in England were moving to the grand climax, and Rupert in spite of his mother's misgivings, for she still feared the influence of Henrietta Maria, once more turned his eyes towards the land where he had found such happiness.

BOOK TWO

THE KING'S GENERAL
1642–1646

CHAPTER 1

RAISING AN ARMY

B Y the early months of 1642 affairs in England were moving rapidly towards the supreme crisis. The façade of prosperity which hid the defects of King Charles's personal rule had been cracking for a number of years. The ship-money episode of 1634–7 showed up the rift that divided the nation. Disturbed by the ravages in coastal areas caused by raids from Barbary corsairs and Dunkirk privateers, and by the building up of French and Dutch naval strength, Charles I determined on the construction of a powerful fleet. To provide funds he extended the exaction of ship money (in lieu of the provision of ships), traditionally the responsibility of the maritime counties alone, to the inland shires. Hostile reaction was immediate, and John Hampden, a wealthy and respected Buckinghamshire landowner, won the name of a patriot by refusing to contribute to his country's defences. In the test-case that followed, a majority of judges in the Court of Exchequer decided against Hampden, but from then onwards the collection of ship money became increasingly difficult, while the Puritan party opposed to the King's authoritarian rule took heart from the publicity accorded to Hampden's anti-monarchical stand.

More serious was the disastrous effect of the King's policy in Scotland. King James had understood perfectly the stubborn nature of his own countrymen, particularly in the matter of their devotion to the Presbyterian creed, and had been careful not to try to coerce them too far. Charles had neither the judgement nor the tact of his father; the Church of England was all in all to him, and with the earnest encouragement of Archbishop Laud he decreed that the full ceremonial of Anglican worship should be imposed on the northern kingdom. The result was a riot in Edinburgh, an assault on its bishop who was stripped of his vestments, the signing of the National Covenant denouncing 'the re-establishing of the Popish religion and tyranny', and the abolition of episcopacy by the General Assembly of the Kirk of Scotland.

This outright defiance of the royal authority led King Charles, ill equipped and short of money as he was, into two fatal campaigns against his Scottish subjects. The first was a bloodless affair, patched up by a compromise peace which settled nothing. It had two results: the Puritan opposition was again strengthened and encouraged by the King's patent weakness, and the King in his troubles sent for his strongest and most capable adviser, Thomas Lord Wentworth, at this time Lord Deputy of Ireland.

Wentworth, now created Earl of Strafford, set to work immediately, in conjunction with Laud, to restore the King's authority. But it was too late. The Scots had hardly pretended to observe the terms of peace, and the Puritan gentry were busy organizing themselves under the leadership of John Pym into an effective opposition. King Charles felt himself bound to undertake a second northern campaign, and to finance it Strafford advised the immediate summoning of Parliament.

Parliament met on 13 April 1640, and was dissolved less than a month later. In that time its temper was clearly shown: no funds were voted, and Pym presented a catalogue of grievances which he demanded should be remedied before any financial support was forthcoming.

Having dissolved the Short Parliament, King Charles embarked on his second campaign against the Scots. It was brief and calamitous. The King reached York at the head of a weak and as yet ill-disciplined army, and at the same time the Scots crossed the border and occupied Newcastle. A few skirmishes, notably that at Newburn, settled the issue, and Charles was forced to sign a humiliating armistice by which the Scots were to be paid £850 a day for the upkeep of their army and to continue to occupy Northumberland and Durham as security.

The King was now helpless, and there was nothing for it but to appeal once more to the national legislature. That most fateful assembly in the story of England known to history as the Long Parliament assembled on 3 November 1640, and took up with renewed zest the work of its predecessor. Strafford, as the power behind the throne, was the prime target of attack. In the early years of the reign he had sided with the critics of royal policy, and his erstwhile colleagues now flung themselves upon him like a pack of hungry wolves. The envenomed hatred with which Pym and his followers hounded Strafford to his death is not pleasant to contemplate. They impeached him for high treason, and when this ridiculous charge failed they brought in a bill of attainder. It passed both Houses, though only by a small majority in the Lords, and then every pressure was brought to bear upon Charles to grant it the royal assent. Public emotion was deliberately stirred up, and the King found himself practically besieged in Whitehall by a mob howling not only for Strafford's blood but for that of the Queen, against whom as a papist all the passions of religious hatred had been systematically fostered. Faced with the cruellest dilemma of his life, the King surren-

dered. The bill of attainder was signed, and on 12 May 1641 Strafford
was beheaded on Tower Hill. It was a betrayal that to the end of his
days weighed heavily on King Charles's conscience.

From then on things went from bad to worse. The King was beaten,
and he made only half-hearted attempts to stay the pace of revolution.
But there were two points on which he would not give way: he would
not agree to the abolition of episcopacy, and he would not relinquish
control of the militia. There the battle continued to rage; but King
Charles was at a hopeless disadvantage, and he gradually came to
despair of a peaceful solution. On 10 January 1642, after his abortive
attempt to arrest a peer and five members of the House of Commons,
including Pym and Hampden, he left Whitehall with his wife and
children, never to return until the last moments of his life.

The royal family went first to Hampton Court, and thence to
Windsor. In February they moved to Dover. The King's eldest daughter
Mary, now ten years old, had been married in the previous May to the
fifteen-year-old Prince William, son and heir of Frederick Henry of
Orange. The ceremony had taken place at Whitehall, and among those
present was Charles Louis, who 'se trouva a la noce, mais non pas au
disner ny souper'.[1] After a symbolical consummation (the bridal pair
had been put to bed together for an hour under supervision), Mary
remained in England, but she was now to join her husband in Holland,
accompanied by her mother. This was the ostensible purpose of
Henrietta Maria's journey; actually she had a more urgent design,
which was to pawn the crown jewels on the continent and raise men
and money for the royal cause.

It was at Dover that Prince Rupert met once again his beloved uncle
and aunt. Queen Elizabeth had been opposed to his visiting England,
for the usual reason: 'I know that the Queen will use all means possible
to gain him, to the prejudice of the Prince Elector and his religion',[2]
she wrote to Roe. But Rupert was now more than ever determined to
be his own master, and he clearly saw the opening for his services in his
uncle's country. Charles Louis, busy in England ingratiating himself
with both sides, tentatively suggested a command for his brother in
Ireland, where the native Irish had risen against the English Government. But the suggestion was received coldly by the parliamentary
leaders, and was dropped. So when Rupert sailed for England it was
simply with the avowed purpose of thanking King Charles for the part
he had played in securing his release from captivity.

Prince Rupert reached Dover in the *Expedition*, an English ship, on
17 February 1642, and there, kissing the hand of the man whom henceforth he was to regard as his sovereign lord, he 'offer'd his Majesty his
service there if there should be any occasion, which his Majesty re'cd

with gracious acknowledgements'.[3] It was four and a half years since the King and the Prince had met. In that brief period both had undergone searing experiences. King Charles, who had told Rupert's elder brother in 1637 that he was 'the happiest King in Christendom',[4] was now a worn and worried man, a fugitive in his own kingdom, overwhelmed by events that had got beyond his control. Rupert, the eager, impressionable boy who had wanted to leave his bones in England, was a seasoned soldier, hardened by three campaigns and by three years as a prisoner of war. His appearance is well known, for of few men of his time do so many portraits survive. That by Honthorst in the Landesgalerie, Hanover, painted about this time, shows a handsome, refined face, with a somewhat disdainful look and all the pride of race that was his, and dark flowing locks of shoulder-length. His physique was magnificent; at a later date he was described as taller than King Charles II, whose height is estimated at six feet two inches. He was an athlete, a splendid horseman and utterly tireless. His majestic appearance was enhanced by the elegance of his attire. A contemporary described him as 'always very sparkish in his dress'.[5] At twenty-two his character was largely formed. Intensely earnest in everything he undertook, he was haughty, overbearing, impatient of opposition. His three years of imprisonment had probably accentuated his fierce temper, the natural harshness of his personality; while at the same time they had provided him with opportunities for peaceful study and for development of his artistic and scientific interests, so that he emerged a complete and many-sided man, not an intellectual where book-learning was concerned, but with deep knowledge of those subjects which held his attention, particularly the art of war. And for all his hardness and intractability when crossed, in his sunnier moods he had a charm that captivated a wide cross-section of his contemporaries. It had been felt by Count von Kuffstein, the Archduke Leopold, and the Emperor Ferdinand III; and others were to be as strongly affected by it in the years to come. He was wholly sincere, transparently honest, and his most abiding characteristic was loyalty. That loyalty he now laid at the feet of King Charles of England.

The arrival of such a man, with his ardour, his integrity and his proved capacity, was heart-warming to his uncle in this great crisis of his reign, when he was uncertain whom among his advisers he could trust. The Prince for his part appreciated the situation and was not diffident in offering advice.

Hee knew they having without reason departed from their Allegiance, by reason they would never bee reduc'd to it, His Councell therfore to the King was, to put himselfe with all the speed hee could into a Posture of defence; when the sword was in his hand, the rebells would better understand his reasons, and hee might use it as little as he pleased, but it was not without troble, yt hee determin'd in his judgment to imploy force against a nation which hee loved, and hated only in their infidellity; yet finding noe other meanes to engage them to their obedience, hee advised to take armes and resist force with force.[6]

This advice was all very well, but the King was not in a position to act on it. As yet he had not the resources to enable him to 'put himself into a posture of defence'. Moreover he did not yet feel able to avail himself of Rupert's services. To all appearances he had burned his boats; but, vacillating by nature, he still shrank from the final appeal to arms; still hoped that, against all odds, some accommodation with his rebellious subjects might yet be reached. If some such attempt were made, the presence by his side of so martial a figure as his nephew would be, to say the least, embarrassing. It was therefore decided that Rupert should return to Holland as escort to Queen Henrietta Maria and her daughter. On the continent he would be able to keep in touch with his aunt, and when all hope of peace had gone he could return once more to England to serve his uncle.

So Rupert, who 'did then very ill brook of the sea',[7] embarked in the *Lion* with the English Queen, Princess Mary and their retinue – among whom, it is interesting to note, was the young Duchess of Richmond, daughter of the murdered Duke of Buckingham. They arrived at The Hague on 11 March (NS), and were met by the Prince of Orange and his son, and by Elizabeth of Bohemia and her two youngest daughters, Henrietta and Sophia. The Winter Queen's distrust of her sister-in-law was put aside, and she welcomed her with open arms as a royal companion in distress. 'The Queen of Bohemia is very frequently with the Queen,' wrote Sir William Boswell to Roe, 'and most kind they are to one another.'[8]

For the next five months Rupert remained in Holland, with little to do beyond seconding Queen Henrietta Maria's efforts for the royal cause. By selling and pawning her own and the King's jewels the Queen raised men, arms and money, and by August the first instalment was ready for England. By that time the first shots had been fired. After Rupert's departure King Charles had gone north and taken up residence in York, and in April he was refused admission to the fortress of Hull, where the Governor, Sir John Hotham, had agreed to hold the castle and magazine for the Parliament. It was an act of open defiance, and King Charles retired discomfited. Among those in his train was the Elector Charles Louis, selected apparently as one with a foot in both camps who might be relied upon to use his influence with Hotham. But the Elector, cool and calculating as always, had decided that the time had come to dissociate himself from all connection with the royal cause. He slipped away from York, and after communicating his intentions to the Parliament crossed quietly over to Holland.

By this time both sides were preparing for open war. The two Houses of Parliament passed a militia bill, legally invalid since it lacked the royal assent. They then issued an ordinance, assuming control of the trained bands that made up the militia. Charles for his part issued commissions of array to his supporters in all counties, requiring them to raise forces, hold musters, and report to the King on the military state of their areas. In July he chose his principal commanders. The Earl of Lindsey, Lord High Chamberlain of England, 'a person of great honour and courage and generally beloved',[9] was declared General of the Army. Sir Jacob Astley, a splendid veteran, sixty-three years old, who had fought with Prince Rupert in the Low Countries, was made Sergeant-Major-General of the foot. Command of the horse was reserved for Rupert, for whom the King now sent. The Prince's appointment was confided to Queen Henrietta, who 'assur'd him of being Generall of the Horse'.[10]

Rupert accordingly set out once more for England in August 1642. His intention was to sail in the *Lion*, the same ship which had brought him and the Queen to Holland earlier in the year. Here there was a hitch, thus described in the *Rupert Log-book*:

His H was to take Passage in the Lyon, the same that carry'd over the Q: one ffox Commander. The P being aboard, there came a letter to ffox to dissuade him from carrying over the Prince. It was writt by a person from whom that Illustrious ffamily had deserv'd better things. The Ffootman that brought it being casually enquired of about that letter, he innocently discover his message.

The *Rupert Diary* is more explicit on the origin of this letter:

He was to come over in the Lyon: one Capt ffox commander. He took him into his ship. and whilst they were there the Queen Bohemia (Honywood) sent a letter to ffox, which the ffootman that brought betray'd, and it was to dissuade the Capt from carrying him over.

It would seem then, from this rather puzzling passage, that it was the Winter Queen who tried to prevent her son from crossing to England. The reference to 'Honywood' may mean either that the letter was actually written by Sir Robert Honeywood, who was steward of her household, or, perhaps more probably, that the compiler of the *Diary* derived his information from him. The Queen's action, if the evidence is to be accepted, was underhand as well as disloyal; and one can but suspect the influence of Charles Louis. The Elector had now chosen his allegiance, and on his return to Holland had sent a message to Parliament 'wherein he professed sorrow for these distractions, and protested that, whilest he was in the Court of *England*, he had by all means endeavoured to bring the King into a good opinion of his Parliament; acknowledging that his owne interest, and that of the Protestant Religion *in Germany*, did more depend upon the happinesse of the English Parliament, than upon anything else under God'.[11] The last thing the calculating Elector would wish would be to have a brother fighting against the cause which he had espoused.

Be that as it may, Rupert evidently used his powers of persuasion on the now reluctant Captain Fox; at any rate he embarked in the *Lion*. But misfortune befell him once more. A storm blew up in the North Sea, and the *Lion* was forced back into the Texel shoals in the extreme north of the Netherlands; whereupon 'Fox would needs have the Prince go ashore, promising that so soon as ever the wind served he would meet him again at Goree: whereupon the Prince landed and went to the Hague, and Fox went afterwards to Goree, where he set his Highness's trunks and people ashore, but his Highness heard no more of him after'.[12]

These intrigues and betrayals must have considerably ruffled Prince Rupert's none too even temper, but he turned for help to his ever constant friend the Stadtholder, Prince Frederick Henry of Orange, who promptly provided him with a Dutch ship of forty-six guns, commanded by Captain Colster, together with a smaller vessel, a 'galliot', to carry the arms and supplies.

With Rupert when he embarked for the second time were a number of professional soldiers with experience of continental warfare, mostly under Prince Frederick Henry. Among them were Daniel O'Neill, a tough Irishman who had had an adventurous career and had fallen foul of King Charles by allying himself with the enemies of Strafford, and two officers, the engineer Bernard de Gomme, and the 'fireworker' Bartholomew La Roche, whose selection indicates the importance attached by Rupert to the technical aspects of warfare. De Gomme in particular was to become one of his closest advisers on military engineering. But perhaps the most important of the Prince's companions was his favourite brother Maurice, from now on his most loyal and most enthusiastic supporter.

This time the wind was fair, and 'the seas contributed to the designes of the Prince, yet his mind went faster than his vessell, and the Zeale hee had speedily to serve the King, made him thinke dilligence was lazy' [13] He was uncertain where to find the King, and proposed landing either at Scarborough or Tynemouth. But on reaching the English coast he and his followers had their first clash with the Parliamentary forces. Off Flamborough Head they were challenged by a ship called the *London*, which demanded the right of search. 'The Prince was there in a mariner's cap,' says the author of the *Life of Prince Rupert*, 'who said he would not be searched.' There followed a chase to northward, and Rupert and his followers got away to Tynemouth, which stood for the King, and got ashore in boats. From there they got safely into Scarborough.[14]

At Scarborough it was learned that the King had set up his military headquarters in Nottingham, and without delay the Prince, with Maurice, O'Neill and others, took horse and set off southwards. Here Rupert's impetuous haste brought him more trouble, for he met with an accident, on the exact nature of which accounts conflict. There was a hard frost (unseasonable even in an English August), and according to the *Life of Prince Rupert* 'the Prince's horse stumbling came quite over with him, and pitching him upon his shoulder put it out of joint'.[15] The *Rupert Diary*, on the other hand, says that he 'brake his thigh'. Whatever the nature of the accident, it fortunately happened within half a mile of a bone-setter's house; equally fortunately the bone-setter was a Royalist supporter. He 'set it in the highway, and in conscience took but one half of what the Prince offered him for his pains'.[16] Within three hours Rupert was once more on his way, and he reached Nottingham that night. The account in the *Life* is presumably the correct one; a fractured thigh could hardly have been disposed of so easily.

Rupert arrived at Nottingham to find that the King was now in Coventry. Even his enthusiasm was unequal to a further forty-eight-mile ride, and he retired to bed for some much needed sleep. But his rest was disturbed by an incident that provided perhaps his first glimpse of the nature of staff work in the royal army. The Military Governor of Nottingham at this time was Colonel George Lord Digby, son and heir of the Earl of Bristol; and at this moment the King sent to him for two petards from the Nottingham arsenal. Digby, an amateur soldier, however, had no idea what a petard was, and in this worrying situation had recourse to the soldier-prince who had just so opportunely arrived. Rupert accordingly was aroused from his well-earned sleep to go down to the arsenal to look for petards. There was not one to be found in the place. There was, however, a professional officer at hand, Captain William Legge, Master of the Royal Armoury, more knowledgeable and more resourceful than Lord Digby. The searchers 'found two great Apothecarye Morters, which Col. Leg made into a kind of a Pettard';[17] and this was sent off to the King.

The main interest of this curious story lies in the fact that thus, on the same night, Prince Rupert was brought into contact with two men who were to play important parts in his future: one to plague him with his intrigues for many a long day, the other to prove one of his staunchest and most devoted friends, and to be major of the regiment of horse that the Prince now began to raise.

Next day, which would appear to have been 21 August, Rupert set off again to join the King, who was in fact on his way back to Nottingham. They met at Leicester, where Rupert formally took over command of the cavalry, consisting of some 800 untrained horse, though there was a fair cadre of professional officers. Uncle and nephew then proceeded back together, and on 22 August King Charles set up his standard at Nottingham Castle. The civil war between King and Parliament was now officially in being, though there had already been some serious fighting.

The armies engaged in the conflict that now engulfed the country were of an amateur nature.[18] England had a martial tradition but no 'regular army'. The Ango-Saxon *fyrd*, the feudal levies of Norman and Plantagenet times, the baronial forces that fought out the civil wars of the fifteenth century, had been raised, here as elsewhere, on an *ad hoc* basis, and had been adequate to the occasions for which they served. But the great mercenary armies, trained in varying degree, which had arisen on the continent since the middle of the sixteenth century, had no British counterpart. England, strong at sea and secure behind the barrier of the Channel, had felt no need to build up strong land forces. The development of a powerful central monarchy had accentuated this tendency. It had been the policy of the Tudors to destroy the private armies of the great nobles, weakened as these already were by the struggles that had gone before, and with their own growing strength the Tudor sovereigns had been able to reduce their security forces to the minimum. In the seventeenth century the King had only a token force consisting of the Gentlemen Pensioners of the Yeomen of the Guard, with the regular garrisons of the royal castles and forts; also the Honourable Artillery Company, a volunteer body dating from 1507. In the country at large there were trained bands, the territorials of the day: infantry units raised for local defence, with troops of horse and magazines of arms and ammunition under the command of the lords-lieutenant of shires. These trained bands were not bound to serve beyond the limits of their own counties.

So when King Charles rashly embarked on hostilities against the Scots in 1638 he found himself compelled to improvise an army out of almost nothing. This he did largely by calling on the English soldiers who for generations had been serving as volunteers in the continental wars. Many came back to fight for their King when he called on them, a mass of armed individuals rather than complete units, but Charles managed to form them into a respectable force. Above all, he was able to count on the services of officers with extensive military experience. Many of these had been in the Dutch army; many more were Catholic exiles who had served in the Spanish and Austrian forces.

It is estimated that some 6,000 horse and 24,000 foot were raised for the campaigns against the Scots between 1638 and 1640 – a larger force than might reasonably have been expected. They were inadequately organized, and their discipline at first left much to be desired. It is unlikely that they would have distinguished themselves against the hardy Scots but in the event the Scots wars produced no battles worthy of the name.

Something very much more drastic in the way of raising military forces was required in the struggle that was now beginning, and throughout the summer of 1642 both sides were busy preparing for the coming war. Loyalties were divided in all areas and in all ranks of society, but roughly speaking the King had control of the north and west of England, Parliament of the south and east. Thus the Parliamentarians had the resources of the more populous and industrially developed part of the country at their disposal. Most important of all, they held London, the capital, with all its wealth, its manpower and its armoury in the Tower. They also held the ports of Bristol, Plymouth and Hull with their arsenals; the officers of the fleet had with few exceptions declared for Parliament, and this meant that arms and stores from abroad could not reach the King without running the Parliamentary blockade. From the beginning of the Civil War the strategic advantage lay with the Parliament.

It was the Parliament also which first began to levy troops. The Militia Ordinance, which asserted its right to raise forces without the authority of the King, was passed by the House of Commons on 5 March. From the beginning of June, in all those counties over which the Parliament could exercise authority, officers were commissioned to raise troops of horse and regiments of foot and dragoons (mounted infantry), and the lords-lieutenant were made responsible for recruiting.

In the capital the Roundheads, as they were now coming to be called, could count on the great asset of the London trained bands, a force of some 6,000 men of far better quality than most of their counterparts elsewhere in the country: 'unique in that they alone could on occasion be induced to operate away from home'.[19] They were well drilled, well paid and well armed; and the money and resources of the City of London made their quick expansion possible.

On 13 July Robert Devereux, Earl of Essex, was given his commission as Captain-General of the Parliamentary forces. This son of Elizabeth I's rebellious favourite was a worthy, brave, conscientious, lethargic, unimaginative man who had drifted without much conviction into the ranks of the opposition in the early days of the Long Parliament. Previously he had served on the continent in defence of the Palatinate, though without seeing much fighting, and then in Charles I's first campaign against the Scots. In war he was a chivalrous foe and a considerate commander, but his defects as a general in the field were glaring. As Brigadier Peter Young has emphasized, he had an incurable habit of allowing the enemy to get between his army and his base,[20] and he was incapable of listening to advice or learning from experience. S. R. Gardiner summed him up in a devastating sentence: 'Since the days of Nicias no general at the same time so devoted, so incompetent, and so self-satisfied, had been placed at the head of an army.'[21]

The Royalist army had at least the advantage of an established commander whose authority and whose right to the position no man could question. King Charles was, and remained, Captain-General of his own forces. He had little military experience, and was hesitant in taking decisions, but he took his duties seriously, was painstaking in attention to detail, and unlike Essex showed himself able to learn both from his own experience and from the example of others. He worked with the assistance of a council of war composed of generals and administrators and was sedulous in attendance at its meetings.

The King issued his commissions of array in June, and shortly afterwards the Royalist army began to take shape. Commissions were given to individual officers, who raised volunteers by beat of drum and organized them into troops and companies. If the Roundheads held the great advantage of possessing the ports, the capital, the arsenals, and the funds to raise and pay their troops, this was to some extent counterbalanced by the greater number of influential noblemen, with their resources of men and horses, and in many cases with military experience, who sided with the King. Charles was chronically short of money to pay his troops, and without the self-sacrificing fervour of his wealthier subjects, such as the Earls of Newcastle and Worcester, who expended vast sums in paying as well as arming and clothing the men they recruited, he would have been quite incapable of raising the forces required. As it was, though the Roundheads had the advantage of numbers, the Royalist forces, as was soon to be made clear, at the opening of the war made up the more efficient fighting force.

The normal establishment of an infantry regiment in the Royalist army was some 1,200 men, commanded by a colonel and divided into ten companies. But units were seldom up to strength. They consisted of pikemen and musketeers, interspersed within the companies; in battle the pikemen were generally placed in the centre, and the musketeers on the wings. The pike, up to eighteen feet in length, could be used as a weapon of defence to resist a charge, placed at an angle from the ground and held with hand and foot, leaving the pikeman free to use his sword with his other hand. The musket, a matchlock with a maximum range of about 400 yards, was a cumbersome weapon. Its rate of fire has been estimated at one round every three minutes.

It was in the cavalry, Prince Rupert's special sphere, that the Royalists, or Cavaliers, most notably excelled the Roundheads. The nobility and gentry, with their tenant yeomen farmers, and their out-door servants, who flocked in large numbers to the King's standard, were horsemen from boyhood and brought their own mounts when they joined the army. For the business of war they lacked both training and organization, but they formed a potential force of high promise that needed only time and the touch of an experienced military hand.

Five hundred men made up a regiment of horse, but this again was the full complement which was seldom realized. 'In practice,' says Brigadier Young, 'a normal regiment had six troops of about 70 officers and men, a total of 420.'[22] There were three field officers – colonel, lieutenant-colonel and major – to a regiment, and each troop was commanded by a major or captain. Troopers wore 'back and breast' plate armour and a 'pot' helmet, and were armed with sword and pistol. The dragoons came under the cavalry commander but were dressed like the infantry. They rode light horses, Welsh cobs and big New Forest ponies, and carried sword and carbine.

In artillery the Roundheads were superior, once again owing to their command of the seaports and the arsenals. But a royal train of artillery of twenty guns had been organized, and further supplies were hoped for from the Queen, now busy in Holland, if she could elude the Parliamentary blockade. When King Charles moved his headquarters to Nottingham the train was left at York under the highly capable Lieutenant-General Sir John Heydon, who rapidly produced a respect-able artillery force out of most unpromising material.

The types of gun in use during the Civil War were as follows:

	Calibre of cannon (inches)	Weight of cannon (lbs)	Weight of shot (lbs)
Cannon	7	7,000	47
Demi-cannon	6	6,000	27–30
Culverin	5	4,000	15–16
Demi-culverin	$4\frac{1}{2}$	3,600	9–10
Saker	$3\frac{1}{2}$	2,500	5–6
Minion	3	1,500	4
Falcon	$2\frac{3}{4}$	700	$2\frac{1}{2}$
Falconet	2	210	$1\frac{1}{4}$
Robinet	$1\frac{1}{4}$	120	$\frac{3}{4}$

Out of these, demi-cannons, culverins, demi-culverins, falcons, falconets and robinets were represented in the King's train of artillery at the opening of the war.

For the time being Prince Rupert was responsible only for the cavalry. He was indeed in a peculiarly privileged position. He had been made a Knight of the Garter at Nottingham, and as the King's nephew he held a more exalted position (as distinct from his military appointment) than any other man in the royal army. Moreover he was authorized to by-pass the Council of War if he thought fit, and to receive his orders only from the King himself: an unwise concession on the part of King Charles in view of the proud Lord Lindsey's position as General of the Army. As General of the Horse, however, Rupert had one immediate and overriding duty; to transform his force of motley irregulars into a trained body capable of fighting and winning a battle which might be forced upon the Cavaliers almost any day now. It was like trying to turn a number of fox- and stag-hunts into troops of horse.

Rupert therefore repaired once more to Leicester, where the horse were quartered under Henry Wilmot, who as Commissary-General of the Horse was now his second-in-command; and there he devoted all his superabundant energy to the task in hand. It was formidable enough. According to Clarendon the horse 'were not at that time in number above eight hundred, few better armed than with swords'.[23] The troopers were able and willing, and were well mounted; but neither military tactics nor military discipline came within their experience.

Details of the training imposed by Rupert are lacking. One can judge only by results; and the results were impressive. Recruits came in rapidly, and within a matter of weeks the small and unorganized force became a cavalry body of some 4,000 men who quickly showed that they understood what was expected of them and could prove their worth in battle. Discipline is a slow growth, and Rupert's horsemen were never easy to control. When incidents in which allegedly they got out of hand are considered, it should be borne in mind how short a time he had to weld them into an integrated force.

Rupert's conception of the role of cavalry in battle was a development from that of Gustavus Adolphus. Gustavus, with the paramount principle of mobility in mind, had reformed the entire system of European warfare, both in theory and in practice, with the constant aim of offensive action in place of the elaborate siege operations that had dominated military thought of the sixteenth century. His essential contributions to tactics, in the words of his latest and fullest British biographer, were 'his restoration, both to cavalry and infantry, of the capacity for the offensive: his intensification of the firepower of all arms

75

as a necessary preliminary for such action; his insistence upon mobility; and his success in solving the problem of the satisfactory combination of the different arms of the service'.[24] His principal innovation in the use of cavalry has already been described. They were no longer mere mounted infantry, advancing in mass at a slow pace with frequent halts to fire volleys from their pistols. Gustavus took away their heavy armour, reduced their ranks to three, and laid stress on the sword as the main cavalry weapon. 'In attack, the first rank only was permitted to fire its pistols (and even then only one pistol of the pair); and firing was forbidden until they could see the whites of the enemy's eyes. The second and third ranks kept their pistols charged, against an emergency; but their real weapon was the sabre: the pistolling was little more than a gesture towards current military convention. After the first rank had fired, the attack was pressed home at the gallop.'[25]

Rupert now took this a stage further. He saw that Gustavus Adolphus had not gone far enough. Under the Swedish system the horse were interspersed with bodies of foot who advanced with them firing volleys. Thus the cavalry were restricted to the pace of the infantry until the last volley was fired, by when there was little time to break into a gallop and the advantage of speed and mobility was largely lost. About 200 yards are necessary to set up speed for a real charge.

Rupert took the cavalry charge to its logical conclusion. He usually, though not always, did away with the supporting infantry contingents; his cavalry acted on their own. There was to be no firing at all before the enemy ranks were broken; the cavalry were to advance at the gallop, sword in hand, and rout the enemy by the sheer impetus of the charge. In this Prince Rupert was to prove a real innovator; his cavalry tactics broke new ground in seventeenth-century warfare.

On 5 September Rupert moved his headquarters from Leicester to Queniborough, six miles to the north-east; and from there he rode tirelessly about the country raising men and money. His methods were sometimes high-handed, founded on his experience of continental warfare in which living off the country was tolerated to an extent of which England had no experience. One of his first actions brought a prompt repudiation from King Charles of a kind that was a rare occurrence in the relations between the two. On 6 September the Prince wrote as follows to the Mayor of Leicester, a city of more than doubtful loyalty:

Mr Mayor,

His Majesty, being confident of your fidelity to do him all possible service, willed me this day to send for you to my quarters, and there to deliver to you his pleasure. But I, perceiving you are dissuaded from coming (by whom or on what pretences I know not), have here sent you his Majesty's demand. His Majesty being now somewhat necessitated by the vast expenses he hath been this long time enforced to, for the safeguard of his Royal person against the rebellious insurrection of the *true* malignant party, who are now too well known, and their irreligious intentions too plainly discovered by all his loving and obedient servants, doth earnestly require and desire you and his good subjects of the City of Leicester, forthwith to furnish him with two thousand pounds sterling, which he with much care will take order to see repaid in convenient time, and that his Majesty's gracious promise, I hope, will seem much better security than 'The Public Faith', which is the usual assurance that the party which call themselves the Parliament do give. And you must trust them on it, if you assist not his Majesty hereby to defend you against them. You must *do no less than your former* expressions have spoken you, which induces me not to doubt of receiving the demanded sum to-morrow by ten of the clock in the forenoon, that I may be

Your friend,
RUPERT

P.S.   If any disaffected persons with you shall refuse themselves, or persuade you to neglect the command, I shall to-morrow appear before your town, in such a posture, with horse, foot, and cannon, as shall make you know it is more safe to obey than to resist his Majesty's command.[26]

Faced with this peremptory demand from a commander so near at hand, the Mayor hastily sent off £500 on account. But at the same time a protest was made to the King, who lost no time in writing to the Mayor and aldermen of Leicester:

Trusty and well-beloved,
    We greet you well. We have seen a warrant, under our nephew Rupert's hand, requiring from you and other inhabitants of Leicester, the loan of £2,000, which, as we do utterly disavow and dislike, as being written without our privity or consent, so we do hereby absolutely free and discharge you from yielding any obedience to the same, and by our own letter to our said nephew, we have written to him to revoke the same, as being an act very displeasing to us. We indeed gave him direction to disarm such persons there as appeared to be disaffected to our person and government, or the peace of this our kingdom, and should have taken it well from any of our subjects that should voluntarily assist us with the loan of arms and money; but it is so far from our heart or intention, by menaces to compel any to it, as we abhor the thoughts of it, and of this truth our actions shall bear testimony.

Given at our Court at Nottingham,
9th September, 1642.[27]

Rupert plainly had still much to learn about England, and fierce

77

actions such as this aroused the misgivings of Cavaliers. In the main, however, his advent and his dynamic activity galvanized the royal cause into new life and raised the morale of the army. 'Of so great virtue is the personall courage and example of one great Commander,' wrote a contemporary. 'And indeed (to do him right) he put spirit into the King's army, that all men seem'd resolved. . . .'[28] And the *History of Prince Rupert*, which ends with the opening of the war, gave him this valediction: 'There was noe more consternation in the Kings Troops now every one growes assured, the most timorous were ashamed to show feare, under such a Generall, whose valour was increased by the great esteeme was had of him, & hee prepares to support his new dignity, by acting new miracles.'

CHAPTER 2

EDGEHILL

THE Parliamentary army, some 15,000 strong, was concentrated at Northampton. Strategically this position was ideal, for Northampton lies almost directly between Nottingham and London, and the King was thus debarred from marching on the capital, which was his obvious objective; only by its capture could victory eventually be won. A frontal attack was out of the question, and his only hope was to out-manoeuvre and outflank the army opposed to him.

On 9 September Lord Essex left London to take up his command. The King was still concentrating his forces, and if Essex had attacked promptly on his arrival at Northampton he might well have demolished the royal army almost before it was in being; but he was not the man to administer a quick, decisive blow. On 13 September King Charles left Nottingham, marching westwards towards Shrewsbury.

Rupert, still recruiting his cavalry with furious energy, had already seen action of a kind when with 500 men he attacked Caldecote House in Warwickshire, owned by Colonel Purefoy who was then serving the Parliament. An interesting account of this incident, which appears to have taken place on 11 September, comes from a hostile source, the fiercely Puritan chronicler John Vicars, whose story throws light on Prince Rupert's methods of warfare. According to Vicars, Rupert approached the building, a very strong and well-built house of stone, 'upon a Sunday morning a little before prayer time (a fit day and time of the day for such prophane theeves and robbers to act their wicked designes of thefts and rapines)', and demanded surrender. Inside the house were 'only the Mistresse of the House, one or two Daughters; one Mr. *George Abbot* her Son in law, a very resolute and stout young Gentleman, three Serving-men, and three Maid-Servants'; and the tiny garrison put up a stout resistance. Abbot and the serving men kept up a continuous fire, the ladies charged the muskets, and two of Rupert's officers were killed. Rupert then fired the barns, stables and outhouses, but it was not until ammunition was running short that Mrs Purefoy opened the doors, fell on her knees, and craved quarter for herself and her family. The Prince was astonished when he found how small the garrison was, and when he 'understood for certain of the paucity of their number, and considered their brave valour and resolution, he admired and wondred at it, raised the Gentlewoman from her knees, saluted her kindly (the greatest act of humanity, if not the onely, that ever I yet could heare he expressed to any honest English) and granted her request fully and freely'. He then sought out George Abbot, telling him that 'he was worthie to be a chief Commander in an Armie, and proferred him such a place in his Army if he would go with him, but he modestly refused it. However, here the said Prince fairly performed his promise, and would not suffer a penny worth of his goods in the house to be taken from them and so departed'.[1] Vicars may well have exaggerated the extent of the resistance put up, but his grudging admiration for Rupert's chivalrous conduct, coming as it does from one who regarded the Prince as the devil incarnate, speaks for itself.

A less favourable assessment of Rupert's activities at this time comes from another contemporary, Thomas May. 'Many Townes and Villages he plundered,' wrote May, 'that is to say *robb'd* (for at that time, first, was the word *plunder* used in *England*, being born in *Germany*, when that stately Country was so miserably wasted and pillaged by forraigne Armies;) and committed other outrages upon those who stood affected to the Parliament, executing some, and hanging-up servants at their Masters doores, for not discovering of their Masters.'[2] However, May, secretary to the Parliament, was an avowed propagandist, wrote at his masters' direction, and gives no instances of the behaviour he specifies.

Immediately after the Caldecote House episode Rupert and the King met, apparently on the Leicestershire side of the county border; for an episode is recorded in the *Rupert Diary* which indicates the difficulties the royal commanders faced in dealing with the local affiliations of the trained bands. The Leicestershire men had been told either to march with the King into Warwickshire or to leave their arms for others; but when they came to the border they refused to do either. 'Whereupon the King desir'd Prince Rupert to take their Armes from them. So the Prince, Pr Maurice, and the Sheriff with a troop of Dragoons askd if they would march. They sayd nay. Whereupon the Prince clap'd his Pistol to the head of the man that spoke and then they all layd down and after their Example Nottinghamshire and Darbishire did the like.'

Rupert behaved in a typically high-handed fashion. But though the militiamen were within their rights in refusing to march beyond the county boundaries, they were less so in declining to lay down their arms at the command of their King and Captain-General. The incident, however, is mainly of interest as showing that thus early was Rupert taking the lead in matters which officially did not concern him; the trained bands had nothing to do with command of the horse. The King, in fact, had already come to lean on the shoulders of the Prince; and indeed it may well have been Prince Rupert's influence that prompted the King's strategy in moving from Nottingham to Shrewsbury.

This strategy was sound. In making for the Welsh marches the King was going through country that was fundamentally loyal, and he was able to gain a substantial number of recruits on the way. What was perhaps more important was that he had the enemy guessing. Essex did not know what the King was up to; he might be preparing to outflank him by marching down the Severn valley. So on the sound military principle of not losing contact with the enemy he abandoned his strategic position at Northampton, six days after the King had left Nottingham, and marched westwards also, keeping a line some thirty to forty miles south of the royal army, in the direction of Worcester.

The King marched by way of Derby and Stafford. Prince Rupert joined him in Staffordshire with the horse, and in the county town he brought off a feat of marksmanship that survived in the local folklore. Dr Robert Plot, writing some forty years later, recorded that,

> . . . standing in Captain *Richard Sneyd's* garden at the high-house there, at about 60 yards distance, he made a shot at the *weather-cock* upon the Steeple of the Collegiat Church of St. *Mary* with a screw'd Horsmans pistol, and single bullet, which pierced its *taile*, the *hole* plainly appearing to all that were below: which the King then present judging as a Casualty only, the Prince presently proved the contrary by a second shoot to the same effect: the two *holes* through the *weather-cocks* taile (as an ample testimony of the thing) remaining there to this day.[3]

This was a remarkable performance with a 'horseman's pistol' of 1642.

Bridgnorth was the next stop, and here news was received that Essex's troops were approaching Worcester, where Sir John Byron had recently arrived with some money and some of the college plate from Oxford, which he had briefly occupied for the King. The King therefore sent Prince Rupert to join Byron and assist his withdrawal from the threatened city.

Rupert rode to Worcester with his brother Prince Maurice, Wilmot, Sir Lewis Dyve, Digby, Sir Charles Lucas and Lord Crawford. The force consisted of seven troops of horse and a regiment of dragoons, and at Worcester they were joined by a troop of a hundred gentlemen raised by the Earl of Northampton. The total strength was somewhere between 500 and 1,000 men. The allotted task was fulfilled, and on 23 September Byron set out to join the King, his march covered by Rupert's troops. There was, however, no question of holding Worcester. The medieval walls were decayed, and there was no reserve of ammunition. Rupert was in favour of immediate withdrawal, but when news came that some of Essex's horse were drawn up at Powick Bridge, south-west of the city on the river Teme, it was decided to move out in that direction for a reconnaissance. According to the *Rupert Log-book* the decision was taken at a council of war: 'The P. being wholly tho' one chief Officer was very much against it.' What this means is not clear; it seems more likely that it was another officer (perhaps Wilmot) who was in opposition than that Rupert allowed himself to be overruled. At any rate the force drew up in a field between the town and the bridge, and Wilmot went forward to reconnoitre. He reported no enemy in sight, whereupon Rupert and his Cavaliers, who had had no rest since leaving Bridgnorth, took off their armour and lay down on the grass in the warm afternoon sunshine.

Wilmot's reconnaissance, however, had been singularly inefficient. Powick Bridge led into a narrow lane terminating in a field just below that in which Rupert's troops were resting. Over the bridge and up this lane came a body of Parliamentary horse under Colonel Sandys and Captain Nathaniel Fiennes, rather greater in strength than the Cavaliers. Suddenly the resting troopers became aware that this force was begin-ning to deploy in the field immediately below them. This sort of situa-tion called forth all Rupert's gifts of dash, initiative, leadership and quick-wittedness. There was no time to put on the discarded breast-plates. He leaped on to his horse, shouted an order to his men, and charged. Maurice and the rest of the officers were little behind him, and the Royalist force, unorganized and in disarray, galloped sword in hand against the enemy.

It was Rupert's first cavalry charge in England. It was unpremedi-tated, wildly impetuous, and wholly successful. The Cavaliers dashed in among the Roundheads before they could organize their line, and drove them back into the lane. Though Sandys and a few of his men made a gallant stand there, the remainder were driven headlong back over the bridge, many plunging through the river.

Casualties were small: about fifty Roundheads were killed, many of them being drowned when they were driven into the river. Sandys was captured, and died later of his wounds. On the Cavalier side Prince Maurice, Wilmot, Dyve and Lucas were wounded, but none of them seriously. Rupert was unscathed.

The Cavaliers did not pursue the enemy beyond the bridge. They returned to Worcester with more than fifty prisoners, and retired the same night to Tenby. The fight at Powick Bridge was of minor military significance, but its moral effect was tremendous. The young victor's reputation soared sky-high. 'In a moment the untried, unknown Prince Rupert was the hero of all the bold young men who served the King, and the terror of the Parliament.'[4]

Elizabeth of Bohemia, by Honthorst, 1635

Frederick V, Elector Palatine, by Honthorst

On the following day Rupert himself sent, by Richard Crane who was knighted for this day's work, a brief, soldierly despatch to the King announcing the result of the action. To Essex went a letter of a different nature which serves as a reminder that the General of the Horse was still only twenty-two years old:

My Lord,
    I hear you are General of an army, sent by the agreement of both Houses of Parliament (under the pretence of subduing some malignant persons) unto these parts, but we greatly fear you aim at some higher power, namely, your own sovereignty. If your intents are such, give but the least notice thereof, and I shall be ready, on his [Majesty's] behalf, to give you an encounter in a pitched field, at Dunsmore Heath, 10th October next. Or, if you think it too much labour and expense to draw your forces thither, I shall as willingly, on my own part, expect private satisfaction as willingly at your hands for the same, and that performed by a single duel; which proffer, if you please to accept, you shall not find me backward in performing what I have said or promised. I know my cause to be so just that I need not fear; for what I do is agreeable both to the laws of God and man, in the defence of true religion, a King's prerogative, an Uncle's right, a Kingdom's safety.
    Now have I said all, and what more you expect of me to be said, shall be delivered in a larger field than a small sheet of paper; and that by my sword and not my pen. In the interim I am your friend, till I meet you next,

RUPERT

How far this letter was expected to be taken seriously, or whether it was devised for propaganda purposes, it is difficult to decide. But Essex declined the invitation to settle the Civil War by a duel.

One place where Prince Rupert's growing fame as a Royalist commander was decidedly unwelcome was The Hague. The Elector Charles Louis believed his uncle's cause to be already lost, and he had no love for lost causes. So far as he concerned himself with England, his aim was to ingratiate himself with the Parliament, and nothing could be more awkward for the realization of his schemes than to have a brother (let alone two) dealing out death and desolation to the Parliamentary forces. His mother's feelings were more mixed. Her sympathies were with her brother, but she was in a difficult position. Her pension from England came from the tonnage and poundage revenues, and these had been seized by the Parliament, which now cut off the allowances paid to her and her family. She was as usual in serious financial difficulties, and King Charles had no money to spare for her.

The faithful family friend Sir Thomas Roe, who had retired a sick man to England and accepted the authority of Parliament though he never renounced his allegiance to his King, was appealed to over Rupert, and wrote in perplexity to Charles Louis: 'I wish that you and the Queen would write to him, yet the case is very tender; I know not what to advise, for all things are in extremes and must be guided with much wisdom.'[6] To this letter the Elector replied in a tone of ill-mannered exasperation, saying that neither he nor his mother could 'bridle my brother's youth and fieryness at so great a distance, and in the employment he has'.[7]

Charles Louis's letter is dated 6 October. Some days later there was presented to Parliament a paper, dated 5 October, under the title 'The Declaration and Petition of the Prince Palsgrave of the Rhyne, and the Queene his Mother, disclaiming and discountenancing Prince Robert, in all his uncivill Actions which he useth in this Kingdom, desiring both Houses of Parliament not to stoppe their annual Pensions due to them for this Cause, which they cannot help'.[8] This document may or may not be authentic. No signatures are appended, and it is possibly a piece of skilful anti-Royalist propaganda. It does, however, bear the imprint of Charles Louis's personality and of his undoubted influence over his mother at this time. In the following February it was reproduced in London as a pamphlet with the title *The Best Newes That ever was Printed. Prince Ruperts resolution to bee gone to his Mother who hath sent for him.* In this the declaration is followed by a passage, redolent of wishful thinking, to the effect that Prince Rupert had declared to the King that

> . . . he had information by letters from Holland that his Royall mother was much discontented and troubled in minde for his residence here in England, and was very desirous that he should take leave of his Royall Unkle the King of England, and to goe to Holland to her, whereby shee might import her mind unto him, he being willing to fulfill his mothers desires, and sorry for his first coming over, declared his resolution to his Majesty that he was now resolved to leave England, desiring his Majesty not to be displeased thereat; and that according to the utmost of his power, hee would endeavour to send over such able Commanders, as should finish what he had begun.

Meanwhile, on Rupert's withdrawal from Worcester, Essex occupied the city, where his troops expressed their religious fervour by sacking the Cathedral. Rupert returned to the King at Shrewsbury, and after consultation the next step was planned. Again it was strategically sound. By marching westwards to Shrewsbury the King had lured Essex from his strong position at Northampton. Now, while Essex busied himself with fortifying Worcester, Charles determined to retrace his steps and strike south-eastwards; if he could get to London before his opponent the war might well be won.

The royal army had grown substantially, and though recruits were still coming in the King wisely decided to wait no longer. On 12 October he marched; Essex was outmanoeuvred, and allowed the royal army to slip past him. It was a week before he left Worcester in pursuit, marching due east in the hope of intercepting the enemy. Once again the Cavaliers had the initiative. They would probably have to fight a battle on their way, but they would be between the Roundhead army and its base at London.

By the evening of Saturday, 22 October, the King was at Edgecote, south-east of Warwick and half-way between there and Banbury, which was held for the Parliament. Essex, who had made good time since his belated start, was on his track and had reached Kineton, some ten miles south of Warwick.

It was Rupert who discovered how close the Roundheads were. He meant to quarter at Lord Spencer's house at Wormleighton, five miles from Edgecote, and on that Saturday evening he sent his quartermaster with some troopers into the village. Essex had had the very same idea, and in Wormleighton the two bodies clashed. In this small skirmish the Royalists were victorious: '. . . the P's Quarter Master took eleven Prisoners, and brought them in, by which meanes we had Intelligence where the Enemy was'.[9]

The question now was whether the royal army should continue on its way, racing Essex to London, or turn and do battle with his army. Rupert was for falling on the enemy immediately with his cavalry, without waiting for the rest of the King's forces, trusting to the element of surprise to throw the Roundheads into confusion. But at a council of war it was deemed best to notify the King immediately and await his command. Rupert's advice now was that the army should move back westwards and take up a position on the brow of Edgehill, there to await the Roundhead advance. King Charles agreed, and the following brief letter was sent to Rupert at Wormleighton:

Nephew,
    I have given order as you have desyred; so I doubt not but all the foot and canon will bee at Eggehill betymes this morning, where you will also find

Your loving oncle and
Faithful frend, CHARLES R.

4 o'clock this Sunday morning [10]

Edgehill, a ridge three miles long, rises 300 feet from the plain, facing north-west. The scene is little changed today, except that the slope behind the Royalist position is mantled by trees, and was thus described by the late Lieutenant-Colonel A. H. Burne:

> The slope is steep, reaching a gradient of 1 in 4. Though now fringed with a belt of trees, it was open ground at the time of the battle except for one small clump. The plain between the hill and Kineton was fairly open in the centre, though there was some scrub and furze, and a single hedge ran between what are now Thistle and Battle Farms. This hedge still exists, a track running alongside it. On the Cavalier right wing there were five or six hedges between the two armies, but the other wing was very enclosed on the Kineton side with a number of small fields and orchards.[11]

Here the King drew up his army in the early morning of 23 October. Essex, who had apparently been intending to relieve the Parliamentary garrison at Banbury, advanced at dawn and took up a position on the low ground to the north, facing the Royalist forces on the brow.

The two armies were fairly evenly matched, for both had in the field upwards of 14,000 men, including between 2,000 and 3,000 horse. Essex probably had heavier metal if not more guns in his artillery, but this advantage was offset by the fact that at least seven of his guns, escorted by Colonel John Hampden's brigade of foot, had failed to keep up with the main body.

The Royalist army is thought to have consisted of 2,800 horse, 1,000 dragoons, 10,000 foot and twenty guns. The infantry regiments were organized in brigades, or *tertias* as they were called. So far the cavalry do not seem to have had any brigade organization, possibly because Rupert was waiting to select his brigade commanders until he had seen how his senior officers acquitted themselves under fire.

The battle was preceded by an unseemly wrangle which illustrated the unwisdom of the King's decision to make Rupert independent of Lindsey's authority as General of the Army. Lindsey wanted the infantry drawn up in the simple line formation of the Dutch school of warfare. This was not acceptable to Rupert, whose youthful arrogance seems to have been particularly in evidence at this time. He had already fallen foul of the King's Secretary of State, Lord Falkland, by objecting to receiving from him his uncle's commands, and had received a dignified snub from that highly respected nobleman. Now he interfered with Lindsey's dispositions; as a disciple of Gustavus Adolphus he demanded that the infantry should form up in the 'Swedish Brigade' system of squares. This was more complicated than the Dutch formation, and difficult for inexperienced troops, particularly at a moment's notice. Nevertheless Rupert prevailed. He was supported by Patrick Ruthven, Earl of Forth, an experienced Scottish soldier who had recently joined the King, while Sir Jacob Astley, who as Sergeant-Major-General in

THE BATTLE OF EDGEHILL

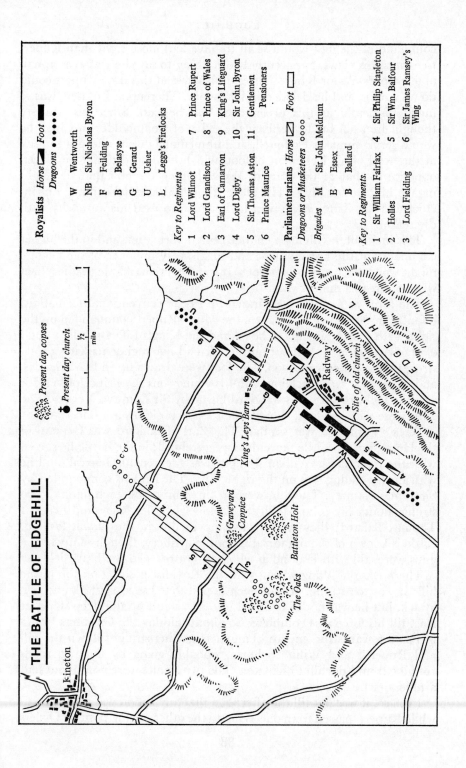

Royalists *Horse* ▨ *Foot* ●●●●●●
  Dragoons ●●●●●●

W   Wentworth
NB Sir Nicholas Byron
F   Feilding
B   Belaysse
G   Gerard
U   Usher
L   Legge's Firelocks

Key to Regiments

1   Lord Wilmot
2   Lord Grandison
3   Earl of Carnarvon
4   Lord Digby
5   Sir Thomas Aston
6   Prince Maurice
7   Prince Rupert
8   Prince of Wales
9   King's Lifeguard
10 Sir John Byron
11 Gentlemen
    Pensioners

Parliamentarians *Horse* ▨ *Foot* ☐
  Dragoons or Musketeers ○○○○

Brigades
M   Sir John Meldrum
E   Essex
B   Ballard

Key to Regiments.

1   Sir William Fairfax
2   Holles
3   Lord Fielding
4   Sir Philip Stapleton
5   Sir Wm. Balfour
6   Sir James Ramsey's
    Wing

⁂ Present day copses
✛ Present day church

0   ½   1
      mile

Kineton

King's Leys Barn

Graveyard
Coppice

Battleton Holt

The Oaks

Radway

Site of old church

EDGE HILL

command of the foot would seem to have had more right than Rupert to express his views, apparently had nothing to say; he was ever a man of few words. As for King Charles, in his eyes at this time Rupert could do no wrong, and he decided in his favour. Thereupon Lindsey 'was so much displeas'd at this preference, that he said, Since his Majesty thought him not fitt to perform the office of Commander in Chief, he would serve him as a Collonell, and immediately went and put himself at the head of his Regiment of foot, which he desir'd might be placed opposite to that of the Earl of Essex, hoping thereby that he might ingage him personally'.[12] His place (though the actual commander-in-chief was the King) was given to Forth, who used his authority with discretion.

This incident, involving a change both in formation and in the higher command, at the last moment and in the very presence of the enemy, might well have proved disastrous. It is indeed remarkable that its effect was not greater than it was.

The army as a whole was drawn up in the conventional formation: infantry in the centre, cavalry on the wings. Rupert commanded on the right, with four regiments of horse and the King's Life Guards: a total of about 1,700 men. Wilmot on the left had five regiments with a total strength of a little over 1,000. The foot were drawn up in five brigades, and in the rear was the King with his young sons the Prince of Wales[13] and the Duke of York, his standard borne by Sir Edmund Verney. The guns were with the foot, though their exact positions are uncertain.

Essex's formation was similar. The Earl of Bedford was General of the Horse, but was little more than a figurehead; in the battle he stayed with the reserve. Sir William Balfour was Lieutenant-General, and he with Lord Feilding was on the right wing. The left was commanded by Sir James Ramsey. The foot were in three brigades, each about 4,000 strong, under Sir John Meldrum, Colonel Charles Essex and Colonel Thomas Ballard; they were drawn up in line in the Dutch fashion. Little is known of the organization of the artillery, though many of the guns were still with Hampden who had not reached the battlefield.

There was one thing wrong with the Royalist position on top of the hill: it was too strong. It had been hoped that Essex would launch an attack, but he was not to be lured into an assault up the steep slope, at least till his force was complete. So about midday the Cavaliers began to move towards the enemy, the foot marching straight down the hill and Rupert's and Wilmot's horse probably going by the two roads running from Edgehill to Kineton. The two armies were now about half a mile apart.

Even so, it was not till the afternoon that any action was seen. Meanwhile Rupert 'passed from one Wing to the other, giving positive Orders to the Horse, to march as close as was possible, keeping their Ranks with Sword in Hand, to receive the Enemy's Shot, without firing either Carbin or Pistol, till we broke in amongst the Enemy, and then to make use of our Fire-Arms as need should require'.[14] The battle started about three o'clock when the Roundhead guns opened fire. A desultory artillery duel followed, while the Royalist dragoons were sent out to beat off some Roundhead dragoons and musketeers who had advanced under cover of the hedge. Then Prince Rupert advanced with his cavalry.

Just before he did so a horseman rode forward from the enemy ranks towards the Prince, tearing off his orange scarf as he did so. Lieutenant John van der Gerish had come to announce that his troop commander, Sir Faithfull Fortescue, 'resolv'd to yield: and that the signal should be the shooting off his Pistol to the ground'.[15] But the time was too short to enable Rupert to notify his subordinate commanders.

Now the time had come for Prince Rupert to put his theory of the cavalry charge into operation in a regular battle. His men advanced in an orderly manner, then broke into a gallop and burst into the ranks of Sir James Ramsey's horse. The movement was as triumphant as had been the more impromptu charge at Powick Bridge. The impetus was irresistible. The Roundhead cavalry broke and bolted, while the supporting musketeers were cut to pieces. Ramsey himself was carried along with the retreating stream for some two miles till he escaped by leaping a ditch. During the charge Fortescue and his men changed sides as promised, but some of them were killed by Sir William Killigrew's troop, part of the King's Life Guards, who did not know of the arrangement.

The bulk of Rupert's horsemen swept on to Kineton, where they fell to looting Essex's baggage train. The Prince has been much criticized for letting them get out of hand so that their services were lost. But it is easier to start a cavalry charge than to halt it; Rupert had trained his men to attack, but he had not had the time to teach them the very difficult art of keeping their ranks after a break-through.

Rupert himself was in no doubt what should be done, and he managed to stop three troops. There is abundant evidence that he did not himself pursue the enemy too far. There is in the London Library a copy of the second edition of Heath's contemporary chronicle, published in 1676, annotated in a seventeenth-century hand by somebody who seems to have been an eye-witness of some of the events described. In his account of Edgehill Heath writes: 'Prince *Rupert* following the chase to Keynton-Town, fell there on the Waggons *Essex* had left behind him, and returned not to the Field, (which also had been totally the Kings) until Colonel *Hambdons* Regiment, and some other Forces which were coming to joyn with Essex, forced him with their Canon out of the Lanes wherein he continued his pursuit.'[16] But in the margin the annotator has written: ' 'Tis a great mistake, for R: did not pursue at all but returnd to the King himselfe.'

Wilmot on the left had charged simultaneously, and also successfully. Lord Feilding's regiment was swept from the field, and Sir William Fairfax's regiment of foot was also routed. Wilmot, with a smaller body of men than Rupert, may have controlled them better, for they did not follow through with the same recklessness. But this may be accounted for by the fact that his break-through was not so complete, and that the ground on the left wing was more difficult for cavalry.

Meanwhile the infantry in the centre were also on the move. As Rupert and Wilmot went forward, Sir Jacob Astley knelt and uttered the famous prayer that has echoed down the ages: 'O Lord! thou knowest, how busy I must be this day: if I forget thee, do not thou forget me.'[17] Then, rising to his feet, he gave the order 'March on Boys!' and led the infantry forward.

The gruelling struggle that followed, and Lord Lindsey's gallant part in it, were vividly described by Clarendon: 'The foot of both sides stood their ground with great courage; and though many of the King's soldiers were unarmed and had only cudgels, they kept their ranks, and took up the arms which their slaughtered neighbours left to them; and the execution was great on both sides, but much greater on the earl of Essex's party.'[18] The Earl of Lindsey, fighting gallantly, had his leg partly shot off; whereupon his son Lord Willoughby, at the head of the King's Regiment of Guards, ran to his father's assistance. Both were taken prisoner, and Lindsey died later of his wounds.

It was indeed Sir William Balfour, the Scottish Lieutenant-General of the Parliamentary horse, in charge of the reserve, who changed the fortune of the day and saved the Roundheads from outright defeat. Rupert's cavalry were scattered, Wilmot's were still engaged on the Royalist left; judging his moment, Balfour, with the two regiments at his command, led two charges against the Royalist infantry. In the first he broke through Colonel Richard Feilding's brigade in the centre, and reached the Royalist guns. Having failed to spike them for lack of nails, he then withdrew and prepared for his second charge.

The King had all this time been behind the foot, but when Balfour made his first charge he rode forward, with the Duke of Richmond and the Earl of Dorset, to put heart into his infantry. At the same time he sent the two young princes, Charles and James, under the personal charge of the great physician William Harvey, with Sir William Howard, Sir John Hinton, Edward Hyde and others, to the rear. There they narrowly escaped capture. It seems that when Balfour drew back some of his men rode on, just as Rupert's had done; for when the princes were seemingly in a position of safety up the hill 'they saw a body of horse advancing directly towards them from the left hand of the King's foot'.[19] These were soon seen to be enemy troopers. The boys were thrilled to be in action, and the eleven-year-old Prince Charles, crying that he 'feared them not, and drawing a pistoll out of one of [his] holsters, and spanning itt, resolved to charge them'.[20] He was dissuaded by Sir John Hinton, 'most humbly, but at last somewhat rudely', and the princes were taken off to a barn for safety.

The King succeeded in rallying his men, who stood their ground nobly. But now came Balfour's second charge. Essex's foot also advanced, and this time his troops actually reached the King's standard. Sir Edmund Verney defended it with his life, but when he was struck down it was seized by an ensign and carried back in triumph to the Roundhead lines.

Darkness was coming on, and the final stages of the battle saw confused fighting all along the line. But there was one more dramatic incident. Sir Charles Lucas, from the Royalist left, led a counter-charge of 200 men against Essex's rear, and Captain John Smith of Lord Grandison's regiment, catching sight of the captured royal standard, dashed into the Roundhead ranks, killed one soldier and wounded another, and crying 'They shall have me with it, if they carry it away'[21] recaptured the banner.

There was no further Roundhead advance. Hampden had at last arrived, but too late to affect the issue. The Cavaliers, while unable to launch another attack, had not lost the ground they had made. In the old Anglo-Saxon phrase, they 'had possession of the place of carnage'. Both armies were exhausted; they spent a cold and miserable night in the field, and all next day remained facing each other. Then Essex withdrew to Warwick, and the King to Edgecote.

Neither side could claim a tactical victory. But the Royalists had achieved their object, which was to prevent the enemy barring their way to London. Yet in the event they did not follow up their advantage. Could they have done so, and so put an end to the war? The question has been argued ever since. Banbury was taken on 27 October, and Rupert was for pushing on, proposing the formation of a flying column of 3,000 horse and foot to seize the capital in a sudden assault. But some of the King's councillors, it would appear, were nervous of what Rupert would do. They felt that this prince from abroad failed to understand their feelings as Englishmen; they had no wish to see their own capital sacked. But in truth the King's shattered army was in no condition for an assault. The carnage had been heavy on both sides; estimates of the total killed at Edgehill vary between 1,000 and 6,000. The lower total is probably nearer the mark, but out of less than 30,000 engaged this is considerable, when one considers that the number of seriously wounded was proportionately high.

As for Rupert's idea of a shock force, this might or might not have worked. The attack would have to have been quick and furious, and it would have come up against the London trained bands, a by no means contemptible force of some 8,000 men. Brigadier Peter Young, whose survey of the situation is the latest and most authoritative, is inclined to think that Rupert's plan may have been over-optimistic.[22]

The conclusion of the campaign of 1642 was anti-climax. The Royalists occupied Oxford, henceforth to be their capital city. Essex's army limped back to London, and though the King advanced to Reading on 4 November there was now no question of capturing London. Negotiations for peace were proposed, and a 'cessation of arms was agreed'. But before matters progressed any further Essex, with his cavalry and the trained bands under Sergeant-Major-General Philip Skippon, marched out of the city towards the King, and Charles took the view that the 'cessation' was no longer in force. He ordered Rupert to seize Brentford, held for the Parliament by Lord Brooke's and Denzil Holles's regiments; and this the Prince did on 12 November, attacking at dawn and annihilating the garrison. His troops got out of hand, and there was a certain amount of looting which was a godsend to the Parliamentary pamphleteers. No civilian life, however, seems to have been lost.

Essex thereupon drew up his forces on Turnham Green. His strength was greater than the King's, and Charles dared not risk a battle. The royal army withdrew to Hounslow, and the campaign was over.

There can be no question that the Cavaliers had lost it. The Parliament maintained control of London, and all hope of a quick end to the struggle had gone. A long-drawn-out war of attrition lay ahead.

CHAPTER 3

FRIENDS AND ENEMIES

A FTER the retirement from Brentford King Charles, with Prince Rupert and his other principal officers, took up winter quarters in Oxford. The university city, which was to be capital of Royalist England for the next three years and more, had been occupied by Sir John Byron with his regiment of horse for about a fortnight in August and September 1642. After his departure for Worcester it had fallen to the Roundheads under Lord Saye and Sele, but their stay was hardly longer. The university was strongly Royalist, and though the town, in traditional enmity, inclined towards the other side, Saye decided that Oxford was an unsuitable site for a Parliamentary garrison. Early in October the Roundheads evacuated the city, which was occupied by the Royalists a week after Edgehill. Work was immediately begun on fortifying the town, and the army was quartered in the city and in the surrounding fortresses and garrison towns that formed the outer defences, the most important being Reading, Abingdon, Banbury, Wallingford, Faringdon, Boarstall House north-east of Oxford, and Donnington Castle near Newbury.

As the court and army settled down, university life was inevitably disrupted. Buildings were taken over to be used as magazines, college plate was requisitioned (payment being promised 'after the rate of 5s the ounce for white and 5s6d for guilt plate as soone as god shall enable us'),[1] and from 1643 onwards regiments of auxiliaries were recruited for the defence of the city. A governor was appointed in the person of Sir Jacob Astley. The King and his court took up residence in Christ Church, while Rupert and his brother Maurice, who had long since recovered from the slight wound he had received at Powick Bridge, were quartered at the house of the town clerk.

During this lull in the fighting Rupert's life was one of ceaseless activity. He was constantly riding over the countryside, recruiting, inspecting, raising money from reluctant supporters, reconnoitring the ground, reporting on garrisons, encouraging and threatening the fainthearted. A few entries from the journal of his marches during November and December 1642 may give some idea of his activity:

93

[November] 21. Munday, to Abingdon: where the Troope quarterd.

22. Tuesday, back to the King at Reding.

29. Tuesday, back with the King to Oxford, to winter quarters.

December 5, Munday, to Tame, in Oxfordshire.

6. Tuesday, faced Ailesburye.

7. Back to Oxford.

22. Thursday, marcht all night to Deddington.[2]

In the new year the pace increased. Towards the end of January we read:

21. Satterday, to Kirtleton.

22. Sunday, to Bracklye, in Northamptonshire.

24. Tuesday, to Daventrye.

26. Thursday, to Southam, in Warwickshire.

28. Satterday, to Butlers Marston by Edgehill.

29. Sunday, to Shipton on Stoure.

30. Munday, laye all night in the feild at Halling, by Sudelye Castle.

Februarye 1. Wednesday, to Northlech in Glocestershire.[3]

These exercises in perpetual motion soon made Prince Rupert a legend to friend and foe. He was even credited with occult powers, and Robert the Devil took on a new diabolism. He was here, there, everywhere: even, according to some reports, among the Roundhead forces. A pamphlet with the title *Prince Roberts Disguises*, published in London in November 1642, gives an awestruck account of his ingenuity. On one occasion, according to this, when reconnoitring near the Roundhead lines he met a man taking a load of apples and pears to sell to Essex's troops. He bought the man's whole stock, and then changed clothes with him, saying he wanted to sell the fruit himself for a joke. Then he went off through the Roundhead positions, 'selling his apples at any rate, viewing their strength, and in what kind they lay, and retourned backe againe, took his Horse, gave the fellow another piece, with this charge, to goe to the Army and aske the Commanders how they liked the fruite Prince *Robert* in his owne Person did but this morning sell them'.

In a similar adventure after Edgehill the Prince was said to have taken shelter from the rain in an alehouse, where 'he met with a fellow that was rideing to *Warwick*, but stayed there by chance to drinke, to sell Cabbage Nets, to boyle Cabbage in'. He bought the nets, paying the man double the price asked, and 'borrowed his Coate and told him he would ride upon his Horse some foure miles off, to put a tricke upon some friends of his, and returne at Evening, leaving his own Nag, and his Coate behind, also he left a Crowne in the Hostisses hand for them to drinke while his returne'. In Warwick Rupert sold the nets, heard

94

all the news he could garner of the enemy's movements, and on his return to the alehouse 'sent them word by him that he bought the Nets of that he had been with them, and withall he wished him to tell them that it should not be long ere he would to requite their kindnesse send them Cabbage'.

In a third episode he was recorded as travelling from Brentford to London by river and viewing the defences disguised as a woman. The sight of an unknown woman six feet three inches tall taking a good look at the fortifications might be expected to have excited comment, but of this we are not told.

Whether anything resembling these exploits really took place is dubious. The stories were 'related to an Inne-Keeper at *Colebrooke*, who was toule it in a merry humour by one of the Cavaliers': hardly the most reliable form of historical evidence. The Scarlet Pimpernel tone of the adventures does not ring altogether true, presenting as it does the romantic picture that grew up of Rupert as the archetype of the gay and dashing cavalier. Rupert was indeed dashing, but he was hardly gay. His normal mood was one of grim determination, and his dash was the expression of tactical policy. He was intensely earnest in all he did, and it is difficult to visualize him in the joyous leg-pulling role depicted by the pamphleteer. A more likely hero of these tales would have been Wilmot or Goring.

The most curious thing about the stories is that they should have been retailed in a pamphlet printed in Roundhead London and presumably designed as anti-Royalist propaganda. For anything better calculated to pour ridicule on Roundhead security, or to raise the morale of the Cavaliers and enhance the popularity of their commander, would be hard to conceive.

Rupert's popularity among his troops was indeed immense at this time. His dynamic leadership, his willingness to bear all the burdens of the army, his care for his men's welfare, had made him the darling of the rank and file. His military competence, shown in the success of his cavalry charges and his constant harassing raids on the enemy forces, together with his devotion to duty and his long hours in the saddle, won the confidence of his officers. 'I must confess I have neither desire nor affection to wait upon any other general,'[4] wrote Sir Arthur Aston, an experienced soldier who had fought as far afield as Muscovy in the service of Gustavus Adolphus, in August 1643. ' 'Tis not advance of title I covet but your commission,' wrote Thomas Sandford.[5] And Sir Lewis Dyve, writing a little later, implored the Prince's 'gratious acceptation of the fervent desire I have to sacrifice my life at your feet'.[6]

As in the case of many other leaders, junior officers imitated his mannerisms and his dress. On one occasion, according to Sir Edward Southcote, he inadvertently initiated a fashion which even today has not wholly disappeared. Southcote, writing early in the eighteenth century to his son Philip, told how his own father, Sir John, volunteered to fight for the Royalist cause, 'very ambitious to get into Prince Rupert's favour, being he was the greatest hero as well as the greatest beau, who all the leading men strove to imitate, as well in his dress as in his bravery'. And the Prince 'one day on a very cold morning . . . tied a very fine laced handkerchief about his neck, which he took out of his coat pocket; and this appeared so becoming that all his mimics got laced pocket handkerchiefs and made the same use of them, which was the origin of wearing laced cravats, and continued till of late years'.[7]

In the eyes of the men who fought under him Rupert could do no wrong. In those of his Roundhead enemies he could do no right. By the end of 1642 a pamphlet war was in full swing, and vituperation poured from the London presses. Rupert was accused of every imaginable military crime – of looting and rapine, of massacring women and children, of torturing and murdering prisoners of war. Vague and unspecific as most of the charges were, they constituted a more formidable attack than the retailing of romantic stories of wanderings through the enemy lines in disguise; and that Rupert was not unaffected by them was shown when he himself entered the lists with a pamphlet with the title *Prince Rupert his Declaration*, issued by the Oxford University printer.

How far the wording of the *Declaration* was Rupert's own work there is no means of knowing; probably it was drafted for him by a secretary or a member of his staff, possibly by Sir John Birkenhead, editor of the Royalist newspaper *Mercurius Aulicus*. Rupert himself was capable of writing good straightforward English, though his style is seldom sparkling. But by this date he cannot have been much practised in the literary use of his mother's tongue, and the *Declaration*, inspired as it may have been by the Prince, must have been put together by an Englishman. It is a competent statement, the dignified tone of which contrasts favourably with the virulent scurrilities of his opponents.

'It will seem strange (no doubt),' began the pamphlet, 'to see me in print, my known disposition being so contrary to this scribbling age; and sure I had not put my self upon a Declaration if in common prudence I could have done otherwise.' Then, after alluding to the 'malicious lying Pamphlets' that 'are printed against mee almost every morning', Rupert proceeded to answer Lord Wharton, who had fought in the Parliamentary army at Edgehill and subsequently in a speech at Guildhall had assailed the Prince's conduct of the battle. He briefly and effectively answered Wharton's denigration of the courage and discipline of the Cavalier troopers; then in a vigorous counter-attack he dealt with the charges brought against him of countenancing atrocities:

> Now for barbarousness and inhumanity to women and children, wherewith his Lordship and those impudent unpunished papers cried daily in the streets do continually slander us, I must here professe, that I take that man to be no Souldier or Gentleman, that will strike (much lesse kill) a woman or a child, if it be in his power to doe the contrary: And I openly dare the most valiant and quick-sighted of that lying Faction, to name the time, the person, or the house, where any child or woman lost so much as a hair from their head by me, or any of our souldiers. In a battel, where two Armies fight, many one hath unfortunately killed his dearest friend, very often those whom willingly he would otherwise have spared; and whether any woman or child were killed in this fight is more than I can justly say: I am sorry if there were. I speak not how wilfully barbarous their souldiers were to the Countesse *Rivers*,[8] to the Lady *Lucas* in *Essex*,[8] and likewise to the like persons of quality in *Kent*, and other places: Whom have we ever punished for speaking against us, as they most Jewishly whipped to death a Citizen of *London*, for saying no more than what was included in His Majesties Proclamation. But since they name plundering, whose monies? Nay whose Armes have we taken away; unlesse theirs, who actually had, or at least declared they would use them against His Majesties Army? And for that little cloth borrowed for our souldiers (wherewith their Pamphlets make such a noise) His Majesty by Gods help will see it better paid for, then any thing they have taken up on *publick Faith*. What house have we ransacked, as they did the Earle of Northamptons?[9] mangling and cutting in pieces rich chaires, beds, stools and hangings; drinking as much and as long as they were able, then letting the rest run out upon the floore, when as the very Earle of *Essex* his house at *Chartley* suffered not the least damage by us. What Churches have we defaced, as they did at *Canterbury, Oxford, Worcester*, and many other places? whose pockets have we pickt ever to the value of three pence, under pretence of searching for letters, as they lately did in *Gloucestershire*, and particularly the last week at Windsor and Vxbridge?

Against the charge that the Royalists were an army of 'Popish Cavaliers', Rupert pointed to his services to the Protestant cause in Europe. And his pamphlet ended with an eloquent peroration:

> . . . I think there is none that take me for a Coward; for sure I feare not the face of any man alive, yet I should repute it the greatest victory in the world to see His Majesty enter *London*, in peace, without shedding one drop of bloud: where, I dare say (God and His Majesty are witnesses I lye not) no Citizen should be plundered of one penny or farthing, whereby that ancient and famous City would manifestly perceive how desperately it hath been abused by most strange, false and bottomlesse untruths, for

which some body (without repentance) must be ashamed at the day of Judgement, if they escape a condigne legall punishment in this world: I therefore conclude with this open profession (and I am confident our whole Army will say *Amen* unto it) he that hath any designe against the Protestant Religion, the Lawes of England, or hopes to enrich himself by pillaging the City of London, let him be accursed: And so, whether peace or warre, the Lord prosper the work of their hands who stand for GOD and King CHARLES.

RUPERT.

Needless to say, the *Declaration* did not go unanswered. Two Roundhead pamphlets quickly appeared in London. The first, the anonymous *Answer to Prince Rupert's Declaration*, was vague and inept, and Rupert took no notice of it. The second, *The Parliaments Vindication, in Answer to Prince Ruperts Declaration*, by 'S. W. Esquire', contained a little more meat. It renewed the charges of pillage and plunder, and asked 'who were they that compelled divers of our most eminent Captaines to ride starke naked on horse backe, while they followed them with reproachfull and contumelous speeches, calling them Parliament rogues, and Parliament dogges, was it not Prince Rupert souldiers, and the Cavaliers, and who were they that drove our men like beasts before their army?' There followed a specific allegation: '. . . they tooke a religious Gentleman, and having fastened a cord to his feet dragg'd him about the town of Thistleworth,[10] and being weary of their cruelty cryed at last why do we trouble our selves any longer with this Parliament dogg, and so shot him at last with his Pistoll'.

Rupert's accusations with regard to Lady Rivers and Lady Lucas were countered with charges of looting the houses of Lord Saye and Lord Stamford and of turning the porch of Kingston Church into a stable. Charges against the Cavaliers of robbing travellers on the highways followed: '. . . and being not satisfied with that money which they bear about them, they have stripped men and women starck naked even to their shirts and smocks, and so left them to the mercy of a darke and cold night, to find the way home or else to perish in the fields'.

Rupert permitted himself one more riposte. In *Prince Rupert his Reply to a Pamphlet, Entituled, The Parliaments Vindication*, he poured scorn on 'S.W.', pointing to the latter's refusal to disclose his name and to the lack of concrete evidence to support his denunciation: '. . . he affirmes it from the testimony of men in the Moone, for surely upon this earth they have no residence'. He disclaimed all knowledge of the murder of the 'religious gentleman' at 'Thistleworth', but to the charge concerning the treatment of prisoners he replied:

. . . if the souldiers did as the law of armes allowes them, strip some of their

Captaines, was I ingaged either to prohibite them the making the best of their prisoners? or obliged to recloth those Captaines that were devested of their apparell? For driving their men like beasts before our army, belike the said Gentleman imagines wee are bound in courtesie to go a foot, and give their men (our prisoners) our horses.

Papers printed for propaganda purposes in time of war are the worst form of historical evidence. Roundhead pamphlets were issued with the main object of blackening the reputation of the Cavaliers in general and Prince Rupert in particular; truth entered into consideration only in so far as, if the accusations were too wild, they would not be believed. From now on throughout the war the Royalists were to be charged with all manner of atrocities; but, as in the pamphlet quoted above, most of the specific allegations against Rupert concerned the conduct of his troops without the suggestion that war crimes had been committed at his order. His detractors, in fact, were unable to convict him, even in their own eyes, of any offence beyond imposing inadequate discipline.

Most modern historians acquit Rupert of barbarous conduct in war. The charge of allowing his men to get out of hand at times certainly has some substance, but so has the defence that in the earlier stages of the war he was commanding a motley force of amateurs who could only gradually be brought under strict military discipline. As was seen in his reply to *The Parliaments Vindication*, he sanctioned rough treatment of prisoners when it was in his view in accordance with the 'law of arms'. He was not averse from reprisals, and at a later stage of the conflict he executed a number of prisoners in retaliation for the massacre by the Roundheads of the King's Irish soldiers. Repugnant to modern thought as is the cold-blooded killing of prisoners, this action did not go beyond the accepted custom of war in the seventeenth century. Moreover it effectively checked the growing tendency to barbarity that was making itself felt. Taken as a whole, the English Civil War was humanely conducted in comparison with the murderous struggle that was going on at the same time in Germany. Rupert had served his apprenticeship in that toughest of schools of war, but his standard of behaviour can stand comparison with that of any English commander on either side. His conception of military honour was of the highest, and many instances of his soldierly chivalry and of his courtesy to his foes could be cited. His behaviour to Mrs Purefoy and her gallant garrison at Caldecote House in 1642, vouched for by a fanatical enemy, was typical of his attitude.

Charges of plundering are less easily dismissed. There were loud and frequent complaints of the seizure and looting of property by Prince Rupert's Cavaliers, and he himself became 'Prince Robber' to the Parliamentary pamphleteers. Undoubtedly he was apt to behave in a high-handed manner, as in the case of the Mayor of Leicester. Here again his continental training must be considered. Living off the country was an established custom in the Thirty Years War, and the royal army had to be paid and fed. The Parliamentarians, chiefly through their control of the City of London, were at a financial advantage throughout the war, and if the King had not resorted to methods unfamiliar to England he could not have kept his forces in the field. It was Rupert's job to see that his men, whose pay was usually in arrear, did not go hungry, and that supplies were maintained; and he did it by the most effective means that lay to hand. Yet there is abundant evidence that he did not countenance indiscriminate plunder. Where this occurred it was rigorously punished.

It was not only the slanders of the Roundhead pamphleteers that Rupert had to combat. From the first days of the establishment of the Royalist headquarters at Oxford he had enemies, and influential ones, at the court there; some also among his senior officers in the army. That he was so often at loggerheads with those who served the same cause as he did was to a great degree his own fault. He was violent and intolerant, and he could not brook opposition. He saw things in black and white; those who differed from him were in his eyes guilty of wilful obstruction. He was sadly deficient in tact, and showed little respect for his elders. Even Sir Philip Warwick, a warm admirer, wrote that 'a little sharpness of temper of body, and uncommunicableness in society or council, (by seeming with a pish to neglect all another said, and he approved not) made him less grateful, than his friends wished; and this humor soured him towards the Councillors of Civill affairs, who were necessarily to intermix with him in Martiall councills'.[11]

King Charles himself gave his nephew his warm support, so far as his vacillating nature allowed. Nor were the King's secretaries of state hostile. Sir Edward Nicholas, the senior of the two, was the most honest, trustworthy and unselfish of the royal councillors; he served the King consistently and efficiently without indulging in intrigues or taking sides among factions. His relations with Rupert were always cordial if not noticeably demonstrative. The other secretary was the more distinguished Lucius Cary, Viscount Falkland, a man of culture, intellect and lofty character. Falkland had rebuked Rupert on the eve of Edgehill when the Prince objected to taking the King's orders from him. 'It was his office to signify what the King bad him,' he said on that occasion; 'which he should always do; and that he [the Prince] in neglecting it neglected the King'.[12] But this not unjust reproof was evidence simply of Falkland's exalted view of his high office and of the dignity of the King; it does not appear that there was any further friction between the two men.

The same cannot be said of the Chancellor of the Exchequer, Sir John Culpeper. Culpeper, who had fought at Edgehill, was a brave soldier and a capable administrator, but a man of blunt manners and hot temper. In this he was not unlike Rupert himself; he resented the younger man's attitude, and a personal dislike grew up between them for which, perhaps, each was equally responsible.

Then there was the lawyer Sir Edward Hyde, who at this time held no official post but was in the confidence of the King, drafting many of the royal proclamations and declarations. In later life, as the Earl of Clarendon, Hyde was to write the story of his times on a majestic scale and in orotund prose of rare quality. It is to this great work, the *History of the Rebellion and Civil Wars in England*, that we owe much of our knowledge of the squabbles that went on in Oxford and of the characters of the men who figured in them. But one must beware of trusting Clarendon's judgements too far. He was an honest man, loyal to his King and whole-hearted in his devotion to the royal cause. But his narrative is the record of a man of intense prejudices intent on self-justification, while his position at this time was one of less importance than the *History* suggests. He recognized the Prince's qualities as a soldier, but represents him as little more than a swashbuckling troublemaker, invariably in the wrong in every dispute that arose.

It is at first sight surprising that Hyde should have been so prejudiced against Rupert. They were alike men of integrity, whose single-hearted aim was the winning of the war; alike in their loyalty to the King and in their hatred of muddle and inefficiency. The truth seems to be that Edward Hyde was one of those civil administrators imbued with an innate detestation of their military counterparts. To him all professional commanders were obstinate blockheads, necessary in the field but a menace and a nuisance in council. His comments on Prince Maurice, who was a soldier pure and simple, were even more virulent than those on Rupert. Sir Charles Lucas was another soldier who displeased Clarendon, and even Jacob Astley seems to be somewhat disparaged in his description.

A more insidious enemy was George Lord Digby, son and heir of the Earl of Bristol but also himself a peer. Digby, at this time about thirty years of age, also held no official post but was much in favour with the King. He was a young man of great charm, handsome in a rather soft way, elegant, witty and cultivated. Yet his whole career, before as well as during the Civil War, proved his untrustworthiness. He had acted both for and against Strafford, and similarly in the affair of the five members he had been in surreptitious consultation with the intended victims while actually urging on King Charles the desirability of decisive action. Digby was a born intriguer; if there was a string to be pulled, he would pull it. He was volatile, sanguine, filled with dreams of self-aggrandisement. He fancied himself both as soldier and as politician: imagining himself at one moment as leading the Royalist forces to victory, at another as the statesman who would bring the two sides together in a lasting peace. By his graceful manners, his eloquence and his mastery of the arts of the courtier he had insinuated himself into the innermost counsels of the always impressionable King, where his capacity for stirring up trouble for others was virtually unlimited.

Rupert had first come into contact with Digby in the somewhat ludicrous episode of the petard at Nottingham. Probably the sense of having made himself ridiculous on that occasion continued to rankle in Digby's mind; at any rate he intrigued tirelessly against Rupert and worked constantly to undermine his influence. Yet such were the vagaries of his mercurial nature that there were moments when he swerved towards ardent support of the Prince, for whom it seems that in spite of himself he had a grudging admiration. Had Rupert been more of a courtier he might have made of him a useful, though certainly not a reliable, ally. As it was, he treated him with contempt. He had no opinion of him as a soldier and despised him as a man; and he made little attempt to hide his opinion.

In a rather different category were the two playboys of the royal army, Goring and Wilmot. Colonel George Goring, the Alcibiades of the English Civil War, was a brilliant soldier who had fought with distinction on the continent, receiving a wound at Breda in 1637 which lamed him for life. In Holland he had been on friendly terms with the Palatine family and is believed to have carried on a flirtation with Princess Louise, though how far it went is uncertain. Returning to England, he devoted himself to a life of roistering debauchery. Drinking and wenching were his favourite occupations, but with civil strife in the offing he took care to ingratiate himself with both sides. He became Governor of Portsmouth, took part in the Army Plot of 1641, and then betrayed it to Parliament. The Parliamentarians thereupon confirmed him in his post at Portsmouth, but when hostilities broke out he declared for the King. Yet when, in September 1642, Portsmouth was blockaded, he surrendered it with scarcely a blow and sailed for Holland. Probably he could have done nothing else, but in view of his record his action was regarded with suspicion. He was now back in England, as General of the Horse to the Earl of Newcastle.

Goring was as unreliable and untrustworthy as Digby, but his treacheries were more open. Digby was as plausible as he was devious, exercising an unfortunate influence on Royalist policy; Goring cared only for himself and made hardly a pretence of any more virtuous motive. Yet when sober he was as good a commander as the Royalist forces could boast, and his jovial dissipations made him popular with his troops. Though scarcely industrious, he was quick in action and decisive in an emergency.

Henry Wilmot, Commissary-General of the Horse, had also served with Rupert on the continent. Son and heir of the first Viscount Wilmot, who had had a long military career, mostly in Ireland, he was both a less dangerous opponent and a less valuable ally than Goring. They were alike in many ways. Wilmot like Goring put pleasure always above duty, though his tastes ran more to the bottle than to the bed. He was fat, good-natured and easy-going, and so long as his amusements were not interfered with he served the Royalist cause well. Wilmot was a capable but a lazy soldier; at Edgehill he had led his cavalry with great success on the left wing, but when towards the end of that day he was urged by Falkland to undertake a second charge his reaction was characteristic. 'My lord,' he is recorded as saying, 'we have got the day, and let us live to enjoy the fruit thereof.'[13] There was to come a time when his loyalty to King Charles I would be suspected, though probably unjustly; but he was more firmly attached to the Prince of Wales, one of whose closest friends he became. He was to have his finest hour in the dark days of 1651, as the resourceful and debonair companion of the young King Charles II in his wanderings through republican England after defeat in the Battle of Worcester.

Though Rupert was at first on good terms at least with Goring, he was out of sympathy with both him and Wilmot, and they with him. He was undoubtedly right in his assessment, but here again his tendency to see everything in black and white did him disservice. Both men had valuable military qualities which were not in over-abundant supply in the King's army; and Rupert might have made better use of their services than he did.

Rupert had friends, at court and in the army, as well as enemies. One of them was James Stewart, Duke of Richmond and Lennox, closely related to the King and one of the highest noblemen in the country. Richmond, seven years older than Rupert, was a young man of spotless honour respected by all parties. He early attached himself to the Prince's interests, and his friendship was unswerving. He had married, in 1637, a lively young widow who was the daughter of the famous Duke of Buckingham. Mary Duchess of Richmond was now on the continent in attendance on Queen Henrietta Maria. Her relations with Prince Rupert will be discussed later. It is enough to say here that when she came back to England she became as close a friend of the Prince as was her husband, and the intimacy between the three of them provided a copious source of scandal for the enemy pamphleteers.

In the army Rupert from the first gathered round him a knot of trusted soldiers on whom he could rely and who formed in a sense his personal staff. Such were Sir Charles Lucas, a gallant young officer who had been wounded at Powick Bridge; Henry Lunsford, an excellent tactician; Sir John and Sir Thomas Byron, both professional soldiers; and Charles Gerard, rash and hot-tempered but a loyal follower, who had distinguished himself at Edgehill. Others were Sir Lewis Dyve, Lord Grandison, Sir Arthur Aston and Sir William Neale. Most valued of all was William Legge, whom Rupert had encountered first at Nottingham. 'Honest Will' Legge was a blunt, down-to-earth soldier as free from guile as he was from personal ambition. He was Rupert's most faithful servant, as staunch in his loyalty as was Richmond. As time went on the trust and intimacy between the Prince and Legge grew steadily, as is revealed in their correspondence. Legge wrote to Rupert with uninhibited candour, always with his best interests at heart. Rupert wrote to his beloved Will with an informality which he seldom showed in letters to anybody else.

Dearer to Rupert than any of these was his younger brother Maurice. This prince has been dismissed by a number of historians as an ill-mannered boor, distinguished only by a measure of military capacity. This is largely on the authority of Clarendon, who wrote of him in a more than usually vitriolic passage: 'The prince had never sacrificed to the Graces, nor conversed amongst men of quality, but had most used the company of ordinary and inferior men, with whom he loved to be very familiar. He was not qualified with parts of nature, and less with any acquired; and towards men of the best condition, with whom he might very well have justified a familiarity, he maintained at least the full state of his birth, and understood very little more of the war than to fight very stoutly when there was occasion.'[14] Evidence to support this assessment is conspicuously lacking. Like Rupert, Maurice did not suffer fools gladly. Doubtless he was sometimes brusque, and one suspects that Sir Edward Hyde had felt the lash of the young man's tongue or at least met with a suspicious *hauteur*, typical of the young soldier confronted by a wily political lawyer. Doubtless also, as a soldier, Maurice preferred the company of his men in the field to that of the soft-spoken courtiers at Oxford. This is hardly to be held against him. For the rest, Maurice, like his brother, to whom he bore a strong resemblance both physically and mentally, was honest and straightforward and wholly devoted to the cause he served. He resembled Rupert also in that his pre-eminent quality was loyalty, and the prime object of that loyalty was the brother whom he had chosen to follow in arms.

Yet none of these devoted followers was Prince Rupert's closest companion. The being who most fully shared his life, scarcely ever leaving his side, was the faithful and beloved Boye, whom he had brought with him from the continent. Boye was a big white poodle, as is shown both in caricatures of the time and in the portrait, almost certainly painted by Princess Louise, which is now in the possession of the Nicholas family. He was big and strong, and could run with his master's horse; and the Countess of Sussex recorded that when Rupert was hunting in Buckinghamshire 'he kailde fife buckes, shote them and his doge boy poullede them down'[15] – no mean feat for any poodle. The bucks were probably red deer.

To the Parliamentary pamphleteers Boye was a 'devil dog', credited with supernatural powers. 'He is Weapon-proof himselfe,' wrote one who called himself 'T.B.',[16] purporting to be a Roundhead spy at Oxford, 'and probably hath made his Master so too. My selfe, and the rest whom you have employed to be of the conspiracy against him, have alwaies fail'd of our attempts, as if something more than Witchcraft watcht over him. . . . He can goe invisibly himselfe, and make others doe so too.'[17] The familiarity between dog and man is thus castigated: '. . . he salutes and kisseth the Prince, as close as any Christian woman would, and the Prince salutes and kisseth him backe againe as favorily, as he would (I will not say any Aldermans wife, but) any Court-Lady, and is as little offended with his Breathing. Then they lye perpetually, in one bed, sometimes the Prince upon the Dogg, and sometimes the Dogg upon the Prince; and what this may in time produce, none but the close Committee can tell.' And T.B. reached this conclusion: 'Is not this a Dogg that is no Dogg, but a Witch, a Sorceresse, an Enemy to Parliament, (that is, to Church and State) a meer Malignant Cavalier-Dogg, that hath something of Divell in or about him?'

It is unlikely that 'T.B.' was a genuine Roundhead spy. His pamphlet has all the appearance of being a Royalist satire on Puritan propaganda. But there are other publications which indicate that, at least for propaganda purposes, the Roundheads were ready to attribute to Boye the diabolical powers that they discerned in his master. Belief in witchcraft was widespread, and it was probably genuinely believed that Boye was Rupert's familiar.

Among the Royalist soldiers, naturally, the amiable poodle was immensely popular. 'Sergeant-Major-General Boy' became virtually the army's mascot, and roistering Cavaliers drank healths to him, even, as another horrified pamphleteer recorded, 'upon their knees, yay drinking Healths to Prince Rupert's dog'.[18] He was a great favourite with the King, who 'himself never dines nor supps, but continually He feeds him. And with what think you? even with Rumps and Sidesmen of Capons, and such Christianlike Morcells. And if this be not to prophane, I know not what is.'[19] Whatever the privations of war, Boye did not do too badly.

Such were some of the characters, human and otherwise, friendly and hostile, by whom Prince Rupert was surrounded in the early days after Edgehill. Rupert's most influential enemy, however, was not yet in the country. Strange to say, she was to be that Queen who had been his adored friend and patroness in the happy days before the Civil War.

CHAPTER 4

CAVALIER ASCENDANCY

WITH the renewal of active hostilities in the early months of 1643, a coherent strategic pattern becomes discernible on the Royalist side. The broad position at this time was that Parliament held the south and east of England, with the coastline from Flamborough Head to Plymouth, the Channel ports and, above all, London and the lower Thames valley. The King's forces held the northern counties with the northern and eastern areas of Yorkshire, parts of Lancashire and Nottinghamshire, the whole of Wales except for the south-western tip, and Cornwall in the west. The plan was for a concentric movement on London. The admirable and reliable Sir Ralph Hopton, commanding in Cornwall, would advance south of the Thames, with the eventual object of cutting off the Roundheads' water trade below London. Simultaneously the Earl of Newcastle would bring the northern army southward through the Midlands. The King meanwhile would consolidate his position at Oxford and hold off Essex's forces until the pincer movement made a concerted triple advance on the capital possible.

It cannot be said with certainty that it was in Rupert's brain that the plan originated. There was nothing very profound in the conception; it was in great degree dictated by the strategic situation. Rupert, however, was the most highly professional of the royal counsellors, the man on whose military advice King Charles was coming increasingly to rely, and the probability is that, whether or not the Prince devised the project in the first place, it was he who worked out the details of how it was to be implemented.

Hopton, whose nominal commander, with the title of Lieutenant-General of the Six Western Counties, was the Marquess of Hertford, was early in the field. His difficulty was the usual one of persuading the trained bands to serve outside their own county, but he raised an army of volunteers and on 19 January won the Battle of Braddock Down. Then, with Cornwall firmly in his hands, he advanced into Devon.

In the north Newcastle had a harder task, for opposed to him were substantial Roundhead forces under Lord Fairfax, controlling much of the West Riding. Fairfax was a mediocre commander, but he had with him his brilliant son Sir Thomas, a resolute and dashing soldier. Newcastle, who before the war had been governor to the Prince of Wales, was a grandee with many admirable qualities but little military experience. His forces were numerically superior to those of his opponents, but he himself was no match in the field for Thomas Fairfax. With him, however, was Goring; and also with him, as a sort of chief of staff, was James King, that experienced Scottish professional soldier who had played so equivocal a part in Rupert's fate at Lemgo. Indecisive fighting, rather to the advantage of the Cavaliers, had taken place before the end of 1642; and on 30 March Goring defeated the younger Fairfax on Seacroft Moor.

Rupert for his part took the field in January, and his first exploit in 1643 was the storming of Cirencester, a town of great importance to the Royalists, for on its possession depended the line of communication to the south-west. Rupert therefore planned an attack in conjunction with Lord Hertford, who was to advance from South Wales. The Prince left Oxford on 6 January and marched all day and night through stormy weather. 'This night,' records the journal of his marches, 'we sawe the strange fire falling from heaven, like a bolt; which with severall cracks, brake into balls, and went out, about steeple height from the ground.'[1] On the following day he was in front of the town; but Hertford failed to arrive and this first attempt failed. Rupert withdrew to Bibury.

On 21 January he again marched from Oxford, with a force some 4,000 strong, and this time made a feint to the north, 'to which purpose he marched by with his Army as if he intended to attempt *Sudley Castle*, which had not long before been taken by *Massey*, but suddenly turning again, fell upon them [the Cirencester garrison] unexpectedly with his whole Force'.[2]

The attack took place on 2 February. In an hour and a half the town was stormed. The attack began with an assault by a 'forlorn hope' led by Wilmot. Colonel Lewis Kirke followed up with the main body of foot, and at the same time Rupert brought up the cavalry to seize the turnpike at the west end of the town. There was fierce resistance, but the Cavaliers were soon inside, the market-place was captured and the streets were cleared, though for some time Roundhead troops continued firing from windows.

The losses were very unequal. Eleven to twelve hundred Parliamentarians were taken prisoner, and perhaps as many as 300 killed. The Cavaliers admitted to a loss of only about fifteen or twenty men. Their trophies included five cannon and seventeen standards and colours.

How much Cirencester suffered for its resistance cannot easily be estimated. It was the custom to sack a town that stood a storm. Some houses were burned, and horses, sheep, oxen, cattle, wool and cloth went to mount, feed and clothe the King's army. The usual accusations of barbarity were made. According to a Parliamentarian account, the Cavaliers 'fell to plundering that night, all the next day, and on Saturday, wherein they shewed all the barbarous insolence of a prevailing enemy'.[3]

The prisoners were put into a church and strictly guarded. Many of them were stripped, we are told by the same Roundhead writer, 'of their utmost garments', while 'their friends were not suffered to bring them a cup of water into the church that night, but what they thrust in at the backside, having broken the windowes'.[4] They were afterwards marched to Oxford, bound two and two with ropes or match, and many were compelled to take up arms for the King – a dubious policy, for they lost no time in attempting to desert.

The fall of Cirencester struck terror into the neighouring garrisons. Sudely and Berkeley Castles were abandoned; so were Tewkesbury, Devizes and Malmesbury. Rupert left his brother Maurice and his regiment of horse, with Colonel Kirke and 1,000 foot and dragoons, to secure Cirencester, and garrisoned Malmesbury with 400 foot under Lieutenant-Colonel Herbert Lunsford and Captain Curson's troops from his own regiment. On the Monday following the storm the gentlemen of Gloucestershire assembled at Cirencester, at the Prince's invitation, and agreed to contribute £4,000 a month and £3,000 immediately to raise a regiment to guard the county.

The capture of Cirencester and Malmesbury left the King's army in control of most of Gloucestershire. In the lower Severn valley the Parliamentarians still held Gloucester and Bristol, but their frontiers had been thrown back. Oxford was the more secure for Prince Rupert's victory.

The Prince himself returned to Oxford, where he appears to have been lodged in Christ Church. A deputation from the Parliament, consisting of the Earls of Northumberland, Salisbury, Pembroke and Holland, was now in the city, and negotiations for peace were in progress. Prince Rupert's victory, however, made the King less anxious to listen to Parliamentary proposals, and the talks came to nothing.

Bristol was the next objective, and on 7 March Rupert moved to Chipping Sodbury, advancing the next day to Durdham Down above the city. Here, however, there was a setback. Two Bristol merchants, Butcher and Yeoman by name, had planned to admit the Royalists to the city, but on Durdham Down news was received that the plot had been discovered and the conspirators executed. Without help from within, Rupert's forces were not strong enough to take Bristol. On 10 March he was back in Oxford.

Meanwhile Queen Henrietta Maria, bringing much needed arms and military stores, had arrived back in England. Never in her life did she put up a more gallant show than now. On the day that Cirencester fell she sailed from Scheveningen in the *Princess Royal*, attended by eleven transports packed with men and ammunition. The convoy was assailed by a furious storm, and for nine days the *Princess Royal* seemed in hourly danger of sinking. The Queen's ladies were in terror, but Henrietta never lost her high spirits. 'Comfort yourselves,' she proudly assured them. 'Queens of England are never drowned.'[5] The ships were forced back to Scheveningen, but within a fortnight Queen Henrietta was at sea again. This time she had better weather and on 22 February, escorted by the great Dutch Admiral van Tromp, she landed with her precious cargo at Bridlington.

Early next morning came a further adventure. Four Parliament vessels under Captain William Batten had arrived in the bay and began firing at the transports that lay waiting to unload. The Queen's lodging was close to the shore, and she awoke to find herself under fire. Undaunted as ever, she announced cheerfully that she would lead the defence in person, but as the bombardment continued she was induced to leave the building and take refuge in a ditch. On the way she suddenly turned back; she had left behind her pet dog Mitte. With Mitte safely in her arms, the Queen joined her ladies in the ditch, but the cannonballs continued to fly until van Tromp threatened to break his neutrality by opening fire unless the bombardment ceased. With the fall of the tide Batten retired, and a few days later the 'Generalissima', as she now styled herself, proceeded to York to join Lord Newcastle, who had sent an escort of 1,000 Cavaliers to meet her at Bridlington.

At York the Queen had her first meeting with James Graham, Earl of Montrose, who had come south to give warning that the Argyll government of Scotland was likely to send an army to the support of the Roundheads. Montrose had earlier inclined towards the Presbyterian opposition, but he had been disillusioned by the excesses of the Covenanters and from 1641 onwards he was unswerving in his allegiance to King Charles. He was to prove the staunchest and most brilliant upholder of the royal authority in the northern kingdom. Henrietta was captivated by him; the King, however, out of contact with Montrose's powerful personality, preferred the counsels of the Duke of Hamilton, and the Earl's warnings were disregarded.

At Oxford the pressing need was to open up a line of communication by which the Queen could bring her arms and ammunition to headquarters. The Earl of Newcastle was in control of most of Yorkshire, but between York and Oxford the country was dominated by the Roundheads. It was therefore decided that Prince Rupert, with a force of

12,000 horse and dragoons and 600–700 foot, should march north towards Lichfield; 'which if he could reduce, and settle there a garrison for the King, lay most convenient for that northern communication, and would with it dissolve other little adjacent holds of the enemy, which contributed much to the interruption'.[6]

Rupert set out in the last week of March, followed by a stream of sometimes contradictory letters from the King. Among the volunteers in his train was, rather surprisingly, Lord Digby, who 'understood Prince Rupert is going northward, and requests permission to accompany him'.[7] Digby was a romantic, and his gesture may merely have reflected his desire to shine as a knight in arms; but it is equally possible that he was anxious to make contact as soon as possible with the impressionable Queen.

On the last day of the month the Prince reached Stratford-on-Avon, and on Easter Monday, 3 April, he was before Birmingham, a town 'of as great fame for hearty, wilfull, affected disloyalty to the King, as any place in England'.[8] The town was captured without difficulty, though the handful of defenders, drawn from the garrison of Lichfield, put up a brave resistance. Some houses were set on fire, however, and the usual cry of atrocities was raised. A Roundhead pamphlet, *Prince Rupert's Burning love to England*, made the most of the opportunity:

> . . . They beastly assaulted many women's Chastity, and impudently made their brag of it afterwards, how many they had ravished; glorying in their shame, especially the *French* among them, were outragiously lascivious and letcherous. . . .
>
> Nor did their rage here cease, but when on next day they were to march forth of the Towne, they used all possible diligence in every street to kindle fire in the Towne with Gunpowder, Match, Wispes of Straw, and Besomes burning coales of fire, etc. flung into Straw, Hay, Kid piles, Coffers, Thatch, and any other places, where it was likely to catch hold; many of which attempts were successlesse and found after their departure, yea, it is confidently related, that they shot fire out of their Pistols, wrapping lighted Match with powder or some other ingredients with formes of slugs, or bullets in brown Paper, which themselves confessed was the Lord *Digbies* device, the English Firebrand. . . .[9]

The reverse side of the coin is shown in a private letter sent from Walsall 'by a Worthy Gentleman to his friend in Oxford' two days after the fall of the town. Relating how the defenders sallied forth calling their assailants 'Cursed doggs, devilish Cavaliers, Popish Traytors', this unnamed worthy proceeds:

> . . . This could not but incense the soldiers, and the Prince to make his passage into the Towne, was forced to give orders for firing a house or

two; but they retiring and flying, upon his entrance into the Towne he immediately gave order for quenching of the fire which was done accordingly, and no more hurt was done on Monday. But yesterday his Highnesse being to march from thence, and fearing what those great provocations might worke with the souldiers, he gave expresse command that no souldier should attempt to fire the towne. And after his departure thence some souldiers, (as yet unknown) having fired the Towne in diverse places, he immediately sent to the inhabitants of the towne, to let them know that it was not done by his command, and therefore wished them to quench it, but the wind being high and the fire encreased, it could not be so soone extinguished as was to be desired![10]

There the matter must rest. As usual in these cases, it is impossible to be sure of the truth in the face of conflicting partisan statements: with the qualification that the letter from Walsall, being a private communication sent almost immediately after the occurrence, seems worthy of the greater credence.

From Birmingham Rupert advanced northwards to capture Lichfield. This was a tougher proposition, for though the town was open the cathedral close was strongly fortified, and defended by a well-trained garrison under a competent commander, Colonel Rowsewell; '. . . the wall,' says Clarendon, 'about which there was a broad and deep moat, was so thick and strong that no battery the prince could raise would make any impression'.[11] Rupert entered the town on 8 April, but his force, consisting mainly of cavalry, was ill-equipped for a siege, and the garrison resisted stoutly.

Here the Prince's interest in, and knowledge of, the science of military engineering came to his aid. Mining as an act of war was unknown in England, but familiar to continental soldiers, and being now in mining country Rupert sent Colonel Hastings out to recruit skilled men. Hastings raised a unit of fifty miners from Cannock Chase and Rupert set them to work to tunnel under the wall of the close. At the same time, to strengthen his meagre force of foot, he 'persuaded many officers and volunteers of the horse to alight and bear their parts in the duty, with which they cheerfully and gallantly complied; and in less than ten days he had drawn the moat dry, and prepared two bridges for the graff'.[12] During this time there were fierce sallies from the garrison, and both Legge and Digby, together once more as at Nottingham, were wounded. Legge was also taken prisoner.

Legge's captivity was brief, but another prisoner met a grim fate. The story comes from a Roundhead source: 'So he [Rupert] sent for all the ladders within eighteen miles, intending to scale. But in the scaling, our men killed eight of his men and took one, which they hanged three yards from the wall, like a sign, and bid Prince Rupert shoot him down. Then Prince Rupert swore, "God d—— him, he would not give one man quarter".'[13]

Rupert had received sufficient provocation to justify him in carrying out his threat; but just at this moment a letter from the King arrived enjoining his nephew to 'have a care of spilling innocent blood . . . and hereof fail not, as you desire the good of us, who desire nothing more than the good, happiness, and peaceable government of our kingdom, and not the effusion of the blood of our subjects, mercy being the brightest attribute of a king.'[14] Rupert's anger cooled, and the next day he sent a trumpeter to ask the garrison if they would yield on quarter. The answer was defiance.

By 20 April all was ready for the assault, and the mine – which on the testimony of Rupert himself (or at least of his personal staff) was 'the first that was sprung in England'[15] – blew a twenty-foot breach in the wall. The Cavaliers poured through and some furious fighting took place. In this assault the defenders held their own, but next day they agreed to surrender on honourable terms, and the garrison marched out with colours flying, trumpets sounding and matches lighted. Rupert personally congratulated Colonel Rowsewell on his gallant resistance.

Lichfield, however, was the nearest Prince Rupert got to the northern army on this expedition. For a serious threat had developed nearer base. Throughout the winter Lord Essex had remained inactive in his winter quarters at Windsor. Now he moved, and the King suddenly found that Reading, one of the key fortresses surrounding Oxford, faced a serious threat. Reading had a strong garrison of 3,000 men, with twenty guns, under Sir Arthur Aston, a capable and experienced soldier; but Essex was approaching with the full strength of his army, estimated at 15,000 foot and 3,000 horse.

On 15 April King Charles wrote to Rupert, then preparing for his assault on the close at Lichfield: 'Nepheu I thought necessary to advertise you that the Rebells have ataqued Reading, not to recall you (though I could be content you were here) but to desyer you to hasten Northward. I wryte not this to make you raise your seige but that you lose no more time in it then you must needs. I suppose that this direction needs no wais retard my Wyfes coming for though she should not bee so soon reddie I believe you have wherewithall to doe bothe. . . .'[16]

King Charles was clearly in two minds, and this characteristic letter was hardly calculated to ease Rupert's dilemma. On the following day, however, the Prince's duty was made clear in a further missive:

Nephew Upon further debate this day I have resolved to desyre you to come to mee with what dilligence you may and with as much force as you can leavinge so much behinde you with Colonel Hastings as to defend that Country. This I confesse is somewhat differing from what I wrote to you yesterday leaving the particular reason of the change to Sect Nicholas' letter. Never the less wee heere suppose that what you will leave behinde you will be able to doe what I writ concerning the Earle of Newcastle to whom I have sent another dispache about the same business with but a little variation. So I rest Your loving Oncle & faithfull frend.

Charles R.

Oxford 16 Ap. 1643

I hope you will have done your worke about Lechfeald before this can come to you.[17]

Rupert had no choice. The junction with the Queen and her badly needed supplies must be postponed. As soon as Lichfield had fallen he retraced his steps southward, and on 25 April joined the King at Wallingford.

On the following day King Charles attempted to force his way with nine regiments of foot across Caversham Bridge, on the outskirts of Reading, now beseiged by Essex's army. But the two Roundhead infantry regiments of Lord Robartes and Colonel Henry Barclay, safely ensconced in a strong position called Harrison's Barn, were sufficient to hold an army at bay. The Cavaliers battered their position with ordnance, including a 24-pounder, but when about midday their infantry attacked they met with a hot reception.

The main body of the Roundheads lay between the barn and Caversham Bridge and was not even engaged. Had the Reading garrison made a vigorous sortie the King's efforts might have been crowned with success; but it was in fact too late. Aston, the Governor, had been put out of action by the fall of a brick on his head, and Colonel Richard Feilding had taken over command. Feilding, who had no means of knowing that help was at hand, had already hung out a flag of truce; and he felt that he could not in honour break off the negotiations. Prince Rupert's part in this affair is related as follows in the laconic sentences of the *Rupert Log-book*:

. . . the P. spoke to ffielding over the River by Reading to know if he wanted anything; he sayd they wanted Powder, but that they were in treaty, and were offer'd terms to march out of the town. (The Garrison being 3 or 4,000 strong). His H. told him that there was no treating to be admitted, the king being there in Person; and that for Powder he might be furnished when he pleas'd passing over a *Quantity* in a Boat for the Present. But notwithstanding all this he insisted upon it, and a councell of Warre was call'd and the town delivered up to the great and generall dissatisfaction of the Souldiery.

So Reading fell. Feilding was forthwith court-martialled and sentenced to death. But here Rupert intervened. As a soldier he understood

Prince Rupert as a boy, by Ravesteyn

Prince Rupert in 1642, by Honthorst

Feilding's dilemma, and his natural generosity in military matters would not allow him to acquiesce in the execution of an officer whose error had been one of judgement only. Through the agency of the young Prince Charles he interceded with the King, and Feilding was reprieved. His regiment was given to Sir Jacob Astley, but he continued to serve as a volunteer: proof that his conduct had not been inspired by treachery.

Back with the King's main army, Rupert resumed his restless activities. Essex now posed a real threat to Oxford, and the Prince worked unceasingly to frustrate him, harassing the Parliamentary army in a succession of guerilla raids. The *Journal of Prince Rupert's Marches* gives an idea of his movements during May and June:

Maye 1. Munday, the camp beyond Culham bridge by Abingdon, begun.
   4. Thursday, the Prince to Abingdon.
   7. Sunday, marcht all night to Newberrye.
   8. Munday, pursued the Enemyes 4 miles: and back to Abingdon.
  18. Thursday, 2 Regiments of horse sent after the Enemye, towards Farindon: the Prince marcht out 4 miles: and returned that night to Abingdon.
  19. Fryday, to Oxford . . . . .
June 2. Fryday, marcht all night to Pangbourne.
   3. Satterday, back to Abingdon: and that night to Oxford.
   8. Thursday, towards Stoken churche, to view the Erle of Essex: returned by night to Abingdon.[18]

A sympathetic letter to Rupert, dated 11 May, from the always friendly Secretary Nicholas, while naming no names, gives an illuminating picture. 'The King is much troubled,' wrote Nicholas, 'to see your Highness discontented, and I could wish that some busy-bodies would not meddle as they do with other men's offices, and that the King would leave every officer respectively to look to his own proper charge, and that his Majesty would content himself to overlook all men to see that each did their duties in their proper places, which would give abundant satisfaction, and quiet those that are jealous to see some men meddle, who have nothing to do with affairs.'[19]

Meanwhile the Royalist fortunes looked brighter in the west of England. Lord Hertford and Prince Maurice had linked up in Somerset with the Cornish force under Hopton, whose personal influence had achieved the not inconsiderable feat of persuading his sturdily independent Cornishmen to serve beyond the borders of their county. And now when the combined force of some 7,000 men was advancing to try conclusions with Sir William Waller, at this time the most competent of the Parliament's higher commanders – his western victories had won him the title of 'William the Conqueror' – Rupert struck a blow in the centre with one of his most brilliant exploits.

A type of minor operation common in the Civil War was the beating up of the enemy's quarters, which brought results at small cost. Spies could easily locate the villages where enemy troops were quartered, guides with local knowledge were not hard to find, and the security of the soldiery lying snug in houses and barns often left much to be desired. The slow rate of fire of seventeenth-century muskets meant that the attacking horsemen could be in the midst of their sleeping victims before the sentries could loose off more than a few shots. The episode which led to the action at Chalgrove Field was an example of this kind of operation.

Essex had moved forward to Thame, twelve miles east of Oxford, on 10 June, and his troops lay loosely quartered in the villages round about. On 17 June he sent a detachment of 2,500 horse and foot north-west-ward to take Islip; but finding the Cavaliers ready for them the Parliamentarians abandoned their design. That same afternoon Rupert marched out of Oxford at the head of a mixed force some 1,800 strong – about 1,000 horse, 350 dragoons under Sergeant-Major-General Lord Wentworth, and between 400 and 500 foot under Colonel Henry Lunsford.

Colonel John Urry, a Scots soldier of fortune who was to make a habit of changing sides, had deserted Essex a few days previously, bringing with him first-hand knowledge of the layout of his quarters and, more important, the news that a convoy with £21,000 for the pay of the Parliamentarian army was expected. The Prince intended therefore to march through Essex's quarters causing as much havoc as possible, and, if he could, to intercept the convoy, though it was like looking for a needle in a haystack to discover wagons at night in the wooded skirts of the Chilterns.

Sending Will Legge on ahead with an advanced guard, Rupert crossed the river Thames at Chislehampton, bypassed Tetsworth where the Parliamentarians had a strong guard, and by three o'clock on the morning of 18 June had reached the hamlet of Postcomb, where Colonel Herbert Morley's troop of Sussex horse was quartered. While the Royalist dragoons were dismounting, some of the Roundhead troopers had time to get on horseback and escape, only those in the nearer houses being surprised. Nine prisoners were taken, and one of Morley's cornets, besides arms and horses.

This little affair took half an hour. Rupert then pushed on under the ledge of hills not far from Stokenchurch and before 5 a.m. reached Chinnor, four miles south of Thame and the very farthest enemy quarter towards London.

While Legge's advanced guard entered the village, the rest of the force surrounded it. This time the surprise was complete. The men quartered there, some 200 dragoons of Sir Samuel Luke's regiment, newly raised in Bedfordshire, had been in the saddle all the previous day on the Islip expedition. A few officers valiantly defended the house where they lay, but most were easily disposed of. The Royalists estimated that about fifty of the Bedfordshire men were killed; as 120 were taken, few can have escaped. Unfortunately the conductors of Essex's convoy heard the alarm, and the Cavaliers just missed them when they drove their carts into a wood.

The fight at Chinnor had taken about an hour and a half, and it was high time for Rupert to make good his retreat. But it seems that he was trailing his coat, for he withdrew in a leisurely manner, giving the enemy a chance to confront him. And so it turned out. Between seven and eight o'clock news was brought that a body of the enemy had been discovered in a village to the left. Soon afterwards the Roundheads began to skirmish with Rupert's men, consisting of his own and Lord Percy's regiments of horse, the former commanded by Lieutenant-Colonel Daniel O'Neill and the latter by Percy himself. At nine o'clock Prince Rupert halted in Chalgrove cornfield, two miles south-east of Chislehampton, and, as Percy and O'Neill closed up, bodies of enemy horse and dragoons were seen coming down the hill from the direction of Easington and Thame.[20]

Rupert now took care to secure his retreat over Chislehampton Bridge; he sent Colonels Lunsford and Washington with all the foot and dragoons to occupy both ends of the bridge, and Lieutenant-Colonel John Russell of Wentworth's dragoons to line the hedges along the lanes leading there, hoping that the enemy might be drawn into an ambush.

The two forces were now parted only by a hedge. The Parliamentarians brought their dragoons up near the middle of it, and their forlorn hope to one end. Their main body, eight troops, faced Rupert's Life Guards and his regiment. Among them, though Rupert did not know it, was the illustrious Parliamentarian Colonel John Hampden. He had been staying near at hand, and hearing the alarm had risen from his bed and joined, as a volunteer, the first band of Roundhead troops he met.

At this juncture several officers advised Rupert to continue his retreat, but the Prince judged otherwise. The rebels, he said, being so near, might bring the Cavaliers' rear into confusion. 'Yea,' he added, 'this insolency is not to be endured.'[21] Then, says the anonymous Cavalier officer who tells the story: 'His Highness facing all about, set spurs to his Horse and first of all (in the very face of the Dragoons) leapt the headge that parted us from the rebels. The Captain and rest of his Troop of Lifeguards (every man as they could) jumped over after him; and as about 15 were gotten over, the Prince presently drew them up into a Front till the rest could recover up to him. At this the rebels' Dragooners that lined the headge fled: having hurt and slain some of ours with their first volley.'[22]

Meanwhile O'Neill had taken Rupert's regiment round the left end of the hedge and had begun the encounter with the main enemy body. These, when they saw the Cavaliers face about, had pulled up quickly and made a stand. 'To say the truth,' wrote the Cavalier officer, 'they stood our first charge of pistols and swords better than the rebels have ever yet done since their first beating at Worcester: especially those of their right wing for their left gave it over sooner: for that the Prince with his Lifeguards . . . charging them home upon the flank . . . put them in rout at the first encounter.'[23] Percy with some troops of his regiment also fell upon the Roundhead left, while Major Thomas Daniel attacked their right with the Prince of Wales's regiment, and the Roundheads were totally routed.

Hampden rode off the field with a wound in his shoulder. It was found that a bone was broken, and after a week of pain he died.

John Hampden was the darling of the Parliamentarians. It does not appear that he had any great natural talents, but 'his power and influence', wrote Clarendon, 'was greater to do good or hurt than any man's in the kingdom, or than any man of his rank hath had in any time: for his reputation of honesty was universal, and his affections seemed so publicly guided that no corruption or private ends could bias them'.[24]

Prince Rupert stood his ground in Chalgrove Field for about half an hour; then, when it was clear that no further action was to be expected from the Roundheads, he retired in leisurely fashion over Chislehampton Bridge, sending the turncoat Urry to report his success and receive the knighthood with which King Charles was wont to reward the bearers of good tidings. At about two o'clock the Prince reached Oxford with well over a hundred prisoners and the trophies of this classical raid, his troopers proudly displaying Colonel Morley's cornet, Sir Samuel Luke's guidons and two of the orange colours of Sir Philip Stapleton's regiment of horse.

The *Rupert Diary* succinctly summed up the effect of Chalgrove Field on the Roundheads: 'Upon the Death of Hamden their Army lessen'd, their Counsells stop'd; Essex retyr'd to Lond: and then the Parliament began their new modell.' This example of hindsight is an indication that the *Diary* was put together many years later, and it oversimplifies the outcome: the formation of the New Model Army was as yet in the future, and Chalgrove was not its occasion. Nevertheless Rupert's victory did have the moral results implied, turning the tables and counteracting the effects of the loss of Reading. The Royalists had regained the initiative, and the Parliamentary commanders, dispirited by the death of Hampden, fell into hesitations and divided counsels; the pressure on Oxford relaxed.

There was good news too from the north, where on 30 June Lord Newcastle defeated the Fairfaxes on Adwalton Moor. This victory left the Royalists in almost complete control of Yorkshire, and on 3 July the Queen set out to join her husband with 3,000 foot, 1,000 horse and six cannon. And once more Rupert advanced northward to meet her.

Essex tried to intercept him, but he was no match for the dynamic energy of the Prince. At Buckingham his men attacked while Rupert was shaving. 'He had hardly finished, and went out and beat them.'[25] On the remainder of his march the Prince was barely molested, and on 11 July he met Queen Henrietta at Stratford-on-Avon. Two days later, on the site of the Battle of Edgehill, they were joined by the King, and on the following day the three of them rode together into Oxford.

The arrival of the Queen meant that the city took on more the character of a court than of a garrison. Intrigue was rife, and Digby, sparing no pains to make himself agreeable to his royal mistress, was in his element; soon the nucleus of a 'Queen's party', critical of the higher military command, was discernible. To Rupert there was another source of interest, for among the ladies of the Queen's train was the Duchess of Richmond. The Prince had met her when he escorted Queen Henrietta Maria to Holland on the eve of the Civil War. At an earlier date she had been suggested as a child-bride for his eldest brother Frederick Henry, but this proposal came to nothing. She was now twenty years old, and Rupert was captivated by her charm. Roundhead scandal was soon busy with reports of their intimacy, but one obvious fact that could not be glossed over was that the friendship of the Prince and the virtuous and honourable Duke of Richmond waxed rather than waned.

Rupert in any case allowed himself little time for dalliance. More important to him was the fact that the men, arms and ammunition brought by the Queen made a useful addition to the royal army. And in the meantime the western forces had done splendid service. On 5 July Hopton, with the assistance of Prince Maurice, had defeated Waller at Lansdown, on the outskirts of Bath: a victory which was by no means decisive and which was marred, first, by the death in action of the Cornish leader Sir Bevil Grenville, and, second, by the incapacitation next day of Hopton himself, severely injured by the explosion of a powder-wagon. But better was to come. Both armies moved eastward

into Wiltshire, and as they faced each other north of Devizes Prince
Maurice paid a flying visit to Oxford to ask for reinforcements. Wilmot
and Sir John Byron joined him with a substantial body of horse, and on
13 July, the day the King and Queen were reunited at Edgehill,
Maurice and Wilmot won one of the most complete victories of the
whole war, totally routing Waller's army on Roundway Down and
driving the remnants back towards the west.

In these propitious circumstances the time was ripe for another
attempt on Bristol and completion of the reduction of the west. The
task was entrusted to the General of the Horse rather than to Lord
Forth, who as Lieutenant-General of the Army acted mainly as Chief
of Staff to the King, and on 18 July Prince Rupert set out from
Oxford.

The strength of his force is not precisely known, but it comprised two
wings of horse under Sir Arthur Aston and Colonel Charles Gerard,
nine troops of dragoons, and three tertias (brigades) of foot under
Colonel-General Lord Grandison, Colonel Henry Wentworth and
Colonel John Belasyse, besides a substantial train of artillery commanded by Bartholomew de la Roche and Captain Samuel Fawcett.
His fourteen regiments of foot are said to have been 'all very weak'[26]
and no doubt they were, compared with their war establishment, but
even so they probably mustered about 5,500 men.

The first objective was Gloucester, but on 20 July, as Rupert was
approaching the city, he received intelligence that Waller, with some
500 to 600 survivors of his defeated army, had got there the night before.
The Prince decided to get in between Sir William and Bristol, and so
cut him off, but Waller, 'not loving to be cooped up in a siege',[27] slipped
away to Evesham. From there he made for London to pursue his vendetta against the Parliamentary Commander-in-Chief, with whom he
was habitually at loggerheads. 'Waller is gone as fast as he can to
London,' wrote Lord Percy, Royalist General of the Ordnance, to
Rupert from Oxford on 22 July, 'to complaine of my Lord of Essex for
betraying of him which he will have soe much reason for as the Houses
certainly will resent it highly this will cause much distraction in these
affaires and I hope we shall take the advantage of it'.[28]

With Waller out of the way, Rupert now decided to leave Gloucester
alone and make an immediate attack on Bristol, the second city in the
kingdom. Turning southwards, he reached Westbury College on 23
July, Maurice having met him on the way, and spent the afternoon
reconnoitring. Accompanied by Aston and others, he rode with his
Life Guards and Colonel Washington's dragoons over Durdham
Down and along the banks of the Avon to Clifton Church, which was
within musket-shot of Brandon Hill Fort. Seeing the group of officers

in the churchyard, the defenders fired two or three cannon-shot at them, but without result.

A council of war was held and a plan drawn up for simultaneous attacks by Rupert on the north side of the town and Maurice on the south from the Somerset side – Lord Hertford, Maurice's nominal commander, 'saying to the Pr: go to the Councill of War, for I understand nothing'.[29]

The Bristol forts commanded the high ground overlooking the city. This meant that the line was a long one, about four miles, and required a substantial garrison to man it. The forts were all palisaded, but their ditches, though about eight or nine feet deep, were somewhat narrow. In de Gomme's opinion the 'curtain' or line of earthworks connecting the forts, 'was of mean strength, and not comparable to those of Oxford'.[30] The rocky nature of the ground precluded sapping and mining, and so the council of war decided to storm them.

Waller had drawn out 1,200 men from the city when he went to the fatal field of Roundway Down, and so the Governor, Colonel Nathaniel Fiennes, eldest son of Lord Saye and Sele, had a garrison of only 300 horse and 1,500 foot, exclusive of townsmen: he had, however, about a hundred guns of various sizes. Fiennes, though he had fought at Powick Bridge and Edgehill, was not a soldier of great experience, and what he had had was not very happy.

At 11 a.m. on Monday, 24 July, Prince Rupert, having drawn up his army on the edge of Durdham Down, sent his trumpeter to summon the city in his own name and Hertford's. On Fiennes's refusal to surrender, the Cavaliers now set to work in earnest, occupying houses and hedges near the enemy works and siting batteries to play upon Windmill Hill Fort, Prior's Hill Fort and Brandon Hill Fort; the second of these was less than 300 yards from its target. Meanwhile the infantry on both sides exchanged musket-fire, and in some places the Royalists pushed forward within pistol-shot of the works, but by nightfall little practical advantage had been achieved.

On Tuesday a further council of war was held, and orders were issued for a co-ordinated attack at dawn on the following morning, 26 July. Directions were given 'to entertain the enemy with alarms all night: and when they heard the losing [presumably 'loosing'] of signal shot off, with the two demi-cannons from my Lord Grandison's post, they should fall on generally'.[31]

Despite the care Rupert had taken to co-ordinate the attacks of the two armies, the Cornish troops crossed the starting-line ahead of their time. Before three o'clock in the morning the Cavaliers on the northern front could see and hear their volleys, 'which giving as the alarm, the Prince sent to have the signal shot'.[bb] Then the assault was launched.

At the outset it did not go well. The western army was everywhere repulsed with loss, and Rupert's men at first fared no better. Grandison and Colonel John Owen were both wounded, and after an hour and a half's fight no progress had been made. The officers of Wentworth's tertia had held a conference about midnight and had resolved to fall upon the line between Brandon Hill and Windmill Hill Forts: a good decision as there was dead ground at the foot of both the hills. Two officers were shot and four or five soldiers killed, but the survivors, gallantly led by Wentworth and Sir Edward Fitton, dashed up to the works. Once up to the line, 'they were almost in covert under St Michael's-hill, and so under the hill, that the Windmill fort could not see them; yea, the spur and barn on their right hand sheltered the forwardest of them from Brandon Fort also. Being gotten to the line, Lieutenant Wright, Lieutenant Baxter, with others, throwing hand-grenades over among the enemies, made them stagger and recoil a little: so that ours more courageously coming on to storm over the line, the enemies quitted it, and ran towards the town'.[33]

Meanwhile Lieutenant-Colonel Edward Littleton, of Richard Bolle's regiment, who was acting as Wentworth's brigade major, abandoned his duties as a staff officer and rode along the inside of the line with a fire-pike, quite clearing the place of its defenders, who ran off in a panic shouting 'Wildfire!' Fiennes's troop of horse counter-attacked with a charge, but the fire of dragoons and musketeers and the resolute conduct of some officers, who ran at the horsemen with fire-pikes, saved the day.

This good news was soon brought by Will Legge to Prince Rupert, who was with Belasyse's tertia. These troops now fell on once more, with Rupert, 'whose very name,' wrote one who fought under him, 'was half a conquest',[34] himself leading some of them into the enemy's works. 'Thence his Highness returning to fetch up his own troop, his horse's eye was shot out under him; after which, without even so much as mending his pace, he marched off on foot leisurely till another horse was brought him.'[35]

Belasyse's men were now sent to support Wentworth's tertia at 'Washington's Breach', as the place where they had broken in came to be known after Colonel Henry Washington, the dragoons commander. The line was broken by about 4 a.m., but the worst was not over though the Cavaliers' good luck did not desert them yet. A fort just inside the line called Essex-work, which covered the suburbs and the quay, fell more by luck than good judgement. Some Royalists who had newly got in were charged by some enemy horse before they could get into order, and ran into a lane to take cover, not knowing that the Parliamentarians had the strong Essex-work fort there. The men in the fort, thinking they were being attacked in force, turned and ran.

Wentworth and Washington soon came up to consolidate this new gain.

By this time Aston's cavalry were inside the line supporting the foot. Wentworth pushed on and, getting near the quay, sent word to the Prince that it was in his power to fire the ships and so endanger the houses nearby. Rupert, however, 'setting all his mind to preserve the city, gave no allowance to it'.[36]

The bitterest struggle now ensued. For two hours Belasyse, supported by Aston, waged a hard fight for the Frome Gate, the Roundheads making sorties with horse and foot, covered by musketry from windows. Lieutenant-Colonel Henry Lunsford, who had already been wounded in the arm, was now shot through the heart. Belasyse himself was wounded, and the tired soldiers began to flag. But reinforcements were at hand, in the shape of Herbert Lunsford of the Lord General's regiment with men of Lord Grandison's tertia who beat the enemy through the Frome Gate and into the town. Many brave officers and soldiers were lost in this conflict, but the Roundheads also were 'paid soundly; and this made them think of nothing but parley',[37] knowing that Rupert could now bring his guns up to the very gates, firing the ships and houses at his leisure.

All this time Rupert 'rode up and down from place to place, where most need was of his presence, here directing and encouraging some, and there leading up others; generally it is confessed by the commanders that had not the Prince been there, the assault, through mere despair, had been in danger to be given over in many places'.[38] He now set up his command post at Washington's Breach; as the enemy still held the forts on Brandon Hill and Windmill Hill, this was not the safest of places. The garrisons, however, fired but little; seeing themselves cut off from the city, they felt that by shooting they would only make their conditions worse when surrender came.

This was not long delayed. Deciding to reinforce success, Rupert sent to Maurice for 1,000 Cornish foot, but by the time they arrived Fiennes had sent out a drum to desire a parley. The Prince consented on condition that the Governor should send out hostages of good quality, and that the parley should last but two hours.

The terms of surrender were arranged that evening. Fiennes's officers were allowed to march out with their horses and swords, but the foot had to lay down their arms and the horse to leave their firearms. All cannon, ammunition and colours fell into the victors' hands.

When next day the Parliamentarians marched out there was some disorder, for they began to depart two hours before the time appointed; 'some were plundered out of the town; seeing our officers, who should have restrained their soldiers, were not yet come'.[39] According to de Gomme, such plundering as was done was the work of stragglers and sharks, that follow armies merely for spoil and booty';[40] but there were also among the offenders some soldiers who had suffered similar ill-usage at the surrender of Reading and now thirsted for revenge. Whatever was done had no countenance from Rupert, who descended on the plunderers in a fury. The Prince, *'who uses, not only in point of honour but of religion too, to make good his word,* was so passionately offended at the disorder, that some of them felt how sharp his sword was'.[41] Fiennes himself, in his later defence of his conduct before Parliament, paid generous tribute to both Rupert and Maurice:

> I must do this right to the Princes, contrary to what I find in a printed pamphlet, that they were so far from sitting on their horses, triumphing and rejoicing at these disorders, that they did ride among the plunderers with their swords, hacking and slashing them, and that Prince Rupert did excuse it to me in a very fair way, and with expressions as if he were much troubled at it.[42]

Thus England's second city, with all its wealth and shipping, fell to the Cavaliers. The moral effect was very great. Berkeley Castle was abandoned shortly afterwards, and the Earl of Carnarvon, marching through Dorset with 450 horse and dragoons, quickly took Dorchester and Weymouth and relieved Corfe Castle.

The capture of Bristol was immediately followed by a dispute characteristic of Rupert's deteriorating relations with the court. Lord Hertford's part in the assault had been negligible, and Prince Maurice as his lieutenant-general had tended to act as though his superior were not there and to assume an independent command. Hertford, though he had no illusions as to his own military talent, resented such behaviour, and complained that the two princes had conducted their operations without reference to him as General of the Western Army. To show his authority, as soon as Bristol had fallen, he in his turn ignored Rupert and announced the appointment of Sir Ralph Hopton as Governor of the city. But Rupert had already written to the King asking for his own appointment as Governor; and Charles, unaware of any difference of opinion, had readily granted the petition of Bristol's conqueror. Rupert's enemies at court vehemently espoused the candidature of Hopton, who had continued to exercise his military administration during his recovery from the severe injuries received in the explosion after Lansdown.

The situation was saved by King Charles, who for once acted both decisively and with perfect diplomacy. First he wrote to Hopton to the effect that, 'haveing heard that the Marquess of Hertford haveing intended to make you Governor of our recovered Cittye of Bristoll, and wee haveing thought fitt to confer the same upon our Nephew Prince

Rupert, Wee have thought it necessarie to assure you, that in this wee have bin so far from intending you thereby any disrespect, as we never heard, nor imagined that you should have bin named to that command'. He added that 'wee too much esteeme our Nephew P. Rupert, to make him a means of putting any disrespect upon any Gentleman especially upon one wee so much esteeme as you, then to give you any distast'.[43] Next he rode over himself to Bristol and took personal charge of affairs. Having congratulated his nephew on his military success, he confirmed him in the governorship according to his promise, and at the same time indicated to him the way out of the *impasse*, so that the Prince 'immediately sent a commission to Sir Ralph Hopton, (who was now so well recovered that he walked into the air) to be his lieutenant-governor, signifying likewise to him, by a confidant who passed between them, that though he was now engaged for some time (which should not be long), to keep the superior title himself, he would not at all meddle in the government, but that he should be as absolute in it as if the original commission had been granted to him'.[44] Finally, the King promoted Maurice to the rank of general and took Hertford back with him to Oxford under the tactful pretext that he needed his experienced counsel at headquarters.

So honour was satisfied all round. Rupert had the highest regard for Hopton, and provided his own request was not slighted had no objection to handing over the effective command to him. Hopton for his part, according to his own account, 'abhoring verie much that His Majesties affaires should be disturbed by any concernment of his, disposed all his endeavours to the composing the business between the two great Lords, and for himselfe wholy submitted to his Majestie's pleasure'.[45] Rupert had certainly behaved tactlessly in ignoring Hertford's legitimate authority, although Clarendon's characteristic comment may be taken with a grain of salt: 'Many were very much troubled to see prince Rupert, whose activity and courage in the field they thought very instrumental, incline to get the possession of the second city of the kingdom into his hands, or to engage himself so much in the civil government as such a command soberly executed must necessarily comprehend, and this, as it were, in contempt of one of the prime noblemen of the kingdom.'[46] As for the King's intervention it makes one feel that the royal cause would have been much strengthened if he had more often acted with such authority and such confidence in his own capacity.

With Bristol in Royalist hands, the only major Parliamentary stronghold to hinder an advance on London from the west was Gloucester, garrisoned by a powerful force under Colonel Edward Massey. King Charles therefore turned north to besiege this town. With him went

Rupert, who, however, would seem from the first to have had mis-givings about the King's strategy. It may be that he would have pre-ferred to march eastwards at once, leaving Massey entrenched behind him; but if Gloucester were to fall quickly no harm would be done. Such was not to be. Charles summoned the city on 9 August, promising generous treatment to the inhabitants; the reply, preserving the usual fiction of allegiance to 'King and Parliament' even in direct confronta-tion with the King himself, was firm defiance:

> We, the Inhabitants, Magistrates, Officers, and Souldiers within this Garrison of *Gloucester*, unto his Majestie's Gracious Message returne this humble Answer, That we do keepe this City, according to our Oath and Allegiance, to and for the use of his Majestie and his Royall Posterity; and do accordingly conceive ourselves wholly bound to obey the Com-ands of His Majestie signified by both Houses of Parliament; and are resolved, by God's helpe, to keepe this City accordingly.[47]

Massey, nevertheless, did appear for a time to waver, throwing out hints of surrender; but nothing came of these and he was probably playing for time. It soon became apparent that the siege was likely to be a long one. In these circumstances Rupert became more and more doubtful of the wisdom of the royal strategy, and was reluctant to exercise command.

Late in August Montrose arrived in the camp before Gloucester, bringing news that the Scottish Covenanters were arriving to join forces with the Roundheads. The King, as before, attached little importance to this intelligence. At the time of the first Scots War Montrose had been in opposition, and Charles seems always to have been reluctant to recognize the value of his services. But consultations in Oxford were decided on, and on 26 August Montrose rode with the King and Rupert to the Royalist capital. Lord Forth remained in command of the troops before Gloucester.

It was while uncle and nephew were on their two-day visit to Oxford that an incident took place which was of the highest significance. Three rebel earls – Bedford, Holland and Clare – had come from Westminster to offer their submissions to the King. All had been prominent in the Parliamentary cause, and King Charles was hesitant in his attitude to them. Some of his councillors, however, were opposed to any accommodation with such renegades, and the Queen took the lead in cold-shouldering them. Rupert took the opposite view. To him the overriding consideration was the advisability of encouraging deser-tions from the enemy ranks, some of which might be of more value than those of the three earls. So he used his influence to intercede for the penitents. The Prince had his way, and the three earls entered the service of the King. But here for the first time was a definite indication of a rift between Rupert and his aunt.

The King and his nephew returned to Gloucester. But now the Parliament had moved. Under the influence of John Pym, still the brains and inspiration of the rebel cause, it was decided that Gloucester must be relieved. At the end of August Essex left London with 8,000 foot and 4,000 horse. Moving north of Oxford, he swept through the Cotswolds, brushing aside a small Cavalier force at Stow-on-the-Wold on the way. On 8 September he marched unopposed into Gloucester; the garrison were down to their last barrel of gunpowder.

Tactically this march of Essex's was one of his finest military feats. The strategic concept may not have been his, but its effect was characteristically to cut him off from his base.

The King had withdrawn his troops when news came of the approach of the relieving force. This strategy may or may not have been Rupert's; it would accord with his known lack of enthusiasm for the siege of Gloucester. In any case it was sound. There was now once again a chance to march on London with the main Parliamentary army isolated in the rear. The plan was to take up a position across the road by which Essex must return, beat off his army in the battle which must ensue, and then continue the march to the capital.

In the event it was a near thing. Essex showed unwonted energy. While the King, evidently expecting the enemy to march by the Warwick road, took up positions at Pershore and Evesham to the north of Gloucester, the Parliamentary commander moved rapidly south and on 15 September surprised Cirencester, quickly disposing of the Cavaliers quartered there and seizing some forty cartloads of valuable supplies. Then he marched hard to the south, making for the road running from Hungerford through Newbury to London.

The Cavaliers had for the moment been outmanoeuvred. Their intelligence seems to have been faulty, and Essex had gained valuable time. Moreover, King Charles was in one of his vacillating moods. As soon as Prince Rupert knew what had happened he mustered his cavalry on Broadway Down, ready for pursuit to the south, but 'the K and Counsell depending upon country Intelligence would not order it'.[48] A curious scene followed. Rupert, impatiently awaiting orders to move, went off with a page and two gentlemen, about six o'clock in the evening of 16 September to seek the King, and 'seeing a light at a house came in, and saw the K and the Lord Percy at Pickett, and the Generall was present'.[49]

To the mind of posterity this picture of the King and Lord Percy playing a quiet game of picquet in the middle of war in a Cotswold farmhouse, with Lord Forth, the Lord General, looking on, is not without its charm. To Rupert it had none. The need for action was urgent, and he brusquely demanded permission to march at once. After a short debate the King issued the necessary orders, and Rupert, detailing Lieutenant-Colonel George Lisle to follow with 1,000 musketeers, 'marched that night and next day, and came to ffarendon to refresh'.[50]

At Faringdon news was received that Essex was passing over Aldbourne Chase, intending to enter Newbury that night; once there, nothing could stop him getting to London. But if Rupert could head him off and force him back into Hungerford he could still be intercepted. Instantly the Prince attacked. A fierce cavalry charge threw Essex's rearguard into confusion, and by the time the Royalist horse were beaten off all hope of getting into Newbury had vanished. Essex led his troops across the Kennet at Hungerford, putting the barrier of the river between him and his pursuers, and the delay enabled the King, whom Rupert's vehemence had galvanized into action, to lead his infantry into Newbury on the following day, 19 September.

The expected confrontation took place, therefore, to the south-west of the town of Newbury. Before dawn on 20 September the Parliamentarians advanced and took possession of Bigg's Hill and Round Hill, overlooking the Royalist lines, and Essex deployed his men along the lanes and hedges at the foot of the two hills.

The strength of the two armies was approximately equal, each having some 14,000 men: the Cavaliers were stronger in cavalry, the Roundheads in infantry. King Charles commanded his own army, with Lord Forth at his side. Prince Rupert led the horse and Sir Jacob Astley the foot. The guns – some twenty pieces, sixteen of them brass – were under the command of Lord Percy as General of the Ordnance.

On the other side the Parliamentary horse were divided into two wings, commanded by Sir Philip Stapleton and Colonel John Middleton. The artillery, believed to have been of about the same strength as the King's, were under Sir John Merrick, while the foot – which included 5,000 men of the London trained bands – were in two divisions, one commanded directly by Essex and the other by that skilled and hardened veteran Sergeant-Major-General Philip Skippon.

The Cavaliers, deployed in line to the south of Newbury, effectively barred the road to London, and in the circumstances Rupert was in favour of defensive tactics. The Roundheads, he argued, must attack, cut off as they were from the capital; all the Royalists had to do was to stand firm and keep them from their base, and from supplies. But Rupert was overruled, and it was the Royalist army which launched the attack.

The battle that followed lasted all day. The Royalist cavalry attacked on both wings; Sir John Byron on the right, nearest Newbury, and

Rupert on the left. Byron, receiving orders at 5 a.m. to attack Round Hill, 'full of enclosures and extremely difficult for horse service',[51] made ground but was forced back by the Roundhead infantry and artillery. It was in this action that Lord Falkland fell. The gentle, intellectual Secretary of State was weary of bloodshed and bowed down with the unsought cares of state, and it would seem that he deliberately threw his life away. Choosing to serve as a volunteer, 'he was very cheerful, and put himself into the first rank of the Lord Byron's regiment, which was then advancing upon the enemy'.[52] And when the attack took place he charged recklessly forward, riding through a gap in a hedge while Byron was arranging to have the gap enlarged. Falkland and his horse were immediately killed. 'Thus fell that incomparable young man, in the four and thirtieth year of his age, having so much despatched the business of life that the oldest rarely attain to that immense knowledge, and the youngest enter not into the world with more innocence',[53] to be the subject of an imperishable passage of English prose from the pen of his friend Edward Hyde.

Byron charged again, but the Roundhead infantry stood firm. Meanwhile on the left, in ground more suitable for cavalry, Rupert deployed his horse on Wash Common and set himself to clear Stapleton's troops from Enborne Heath. He charged three times, and resistance was fierce, but at last Stapleton was driven back. According to Bulstrode Whitelock, a personal encounter took place between the two commanders. Stapleton, 'desiring to cope singly with the Prince, rode up, all alone, to the troop of horse, at the head of which Rupert was standing with Digby and some other officers. Sir Philip looked carefully from one to the other until his eyes rested upon Rupert, whom he knew; then he deliberately fired in the Prince's face. The shot took no effect and Sir Philip, turning his horse, rode quietly back to his own men.'[54]

Casualties were heavy, and the Royalists suffered another grievous loss with the death of the gallant Earl of Carnarvon. Rupert had no further success. Skippon rallied his infantry and the weakened Royalist force could not dislodge them.

In the centre there was confused fighting and stalemate. Lord Robartes drove the Royalists back, but further attacks forced Essex to send in his reserves. Now came the crisis of the battle. Skippon, with only one regiment left in reserve, stabilized the Parliamentary centre, and here again the London trained bands held their ground while Sir John Merrick brought up the big guns. An artillery engagement followed, and a further cavalry charge by Rupert; but no further advance could be made.

Fighting continued till seven o'clock in the evening, with much loss of life but little change in the control of ground. But the Cavaliers had run short of ammunition, and that night the King held a council of war. Rupert was in favour of holding on at all costs, but Percy declared that only ten barrels of powder were left, and the King allowed himself to be persuaded by this argument. Orders were given for a withdrawal towards Oxford, and next morning the Roundheads, finding the road clear, proceeded on their way to London.

Rupert did not rest. Next morning he took his cavalry in pursuit of Essex and harassed his rearguard in the neighbourhood of Aldermaston. But these tactics could not affect the issue.

Thus the Cavaliers lost another chance of victory. What became known as the First Battle of Newbury was a confused affair, more significant in its results than in its conduct. In some ways it was Edgehill in reverse, for where the former battle had left the road to London clear for the Royalists (a result of which they failed to take advantage), Newbury left it clear for the Parliamentarians.

In the extensive fighting that had taken place throughout the year 1643 the King's forces had more than held their own. In the field they had again and again proved themselves superior to their opponents; the Parliament could not as yet boast a commander remotely comparable with Rupert, but they had failed to achieve the knock-out blow which alone could bring them victory. The economic odds were always increasing against the Royalists. Time was not their ally, and if it was to be a win on points the victors would be the Roundheads.

CHAPTER 5

DEFEAT IN THE NORTH

At the end of 1643 Prince Rupert was at the height of his military reputation. In so far as Newbury was a strategic setback, it did not reflect upon him. Everything he had undertaken in the military field had been successful in greater or lesser degree; he was the idol of his troops and the terror of the Roundheads. But at Oxford the clouds were gathering. Rupert's brusque manners, and his inability to suffer fools gladly, were increasing the hostility of the courtiers who were temperamentally opposed to him in the first place, and it began to be apparent that a small knot of intriguers were at work, doing their best to undermine his influence with the King.

At their head was Digby, a far more formidable figure than he had been hitherto. For First Newbury had had, so far as Rupert was concerned, one most unfortunate consequence. With the death of Lord Falkland one of the secretaryships of state became vacant, and on 28 September, largely through the influence of the Queen, the post was given to Digby. From then on the new Secretary's enmity to Rupert grew. It appears to have had little logical foundation. As a colonel of horse Digby had served by his own choice under the Prince in the summer campaign, and had fought gallantly at Lichfield; he had never questioned the capacity of the younger man (Digby was thirty, Rupert twenty-three) as a leader in the field. The antagonism was doubtless partly personal: Rupert had little regard for Digby either as soldier or as administrator, and never troubled to hide his opinion. But Digby was an opportunist. Signs of a rift between the Prince and the Queen had appeared in the affair of the three rebel lords, and Digby, who was always working towards further extension of his influence through his intimacy with Henrietta, saw the advantage of abetting her in her growing animosity towards Prince Rupert.

The Queen was now to become Rupert's most influential enemy. Again there was no adequate reason why she should be so. She was as dedicated as anybody in the kingdom to the ousting of the rebellion against her husband's authority, and she could hardly fail to see that Rupert was the most powerful instrument to that end that the royal

131

cause possessed. But the Generalissima wanted things her own way. She had always exercised a dominant influence over her hesitant, easily swayed husband; she now saw that influence challenged by the strong-willed, martial nephew to whom she had become so devoted six years before. Then he was her adoring slave; now he emerged as a rival. The episode of the rebel lords showed her which way the wind was blowing.

Some hints of the enmity Rupert was arousing, both from his royal mistress and from others, are given in a letter to him from Lord Percy, another of the Queen's intimates. On 23 July 1643, when Rupert was preparing to attack Bristol, Percy wrote to him: 'The Queene's health doth begin to mend which is a great blessing to us all, the King hath desired her to imploy herselfe to make you Wilmott and Culpeper friends and the like to all the rest of us, she thinks it fitt to be done for the present as the Ks affaires stand and soe do I too.'[1] Here Queen Henrietta appears as a peacemaker, but in Percy's next letter, sent a week later, a note of petulance appears; 'Your best frends doe wish that when the power is put absolutely into your hands you will comply soe farre with the King's affaires as to doe that which may content many, and displease fewest; your success in armes I hope will not make you forgett your civility to Ladyes this I say to you from a discourse the Queene made to me this night wherein she told me she had not received one letter from you since you went though you had writt many, which is a fault you must repaire.'[2] And on July 30 Percy wrote: '. . . for that I writt of the Queene I hope you will give her noe more the advantage to lay that fault to your charge'.[3] In a postscript to this last letter Lord Percy wrote: 'I had an expresse command to present the Duchesse of Richmonds service to you.'[4] Among those in the Queen's confidence who did their best to counter the designs of Rupert's enemies the Duke and Duchess of Richmond were pre-eminent. There was another who may be bracketed with them. Highest in Henrietta Maria's counsel stood the commander of her bodyguard, Henry, Lord Jermyn, a fat, supple courtier whose intimacy with his mistress was such that after Charles I's death there were rumours that she had married him. Jermyn has had a bad press from historians. Doubtless he was selfish, self-indulgent and unprincipled. In the worst days of Royalist hardship he contrived personally to be well fed and well clothed. But to Rupert he was the best of friends.

Faced with intrigues at court, and with disaffection among a section of his officers (Wilmot in particular was drifting further and further into opposition to his authority), Rupert became progressively more irritable and intractable, thereby increasing the enmities of his critics and stirring up more trouble for himself. During the winter of 1643–4 he resumed his restless activities, covering wide areas of ground, harassing Parliamentary bodies of troops where he could, but fighting no major engagements. He was seldom in Oxford, and he was afflicted always with anxiety lest in his absence the unstable King should yield to counsels of the Queen or Digby which would conflict with his own plans for victory. His agent at Oxford was Arthur Trevor, a voluminous correspondent who acted in a similar capacity for the Marquess of Ormonde, the King's Deputy in Ireland. 'The army is much divided,' wrote Trevor to Ormonde in November 1643, 'and the Prince at true distance with many of the officers of horse.'[5]

Whatever the machinations of the Queen and Digby, and whatever suspicions Prince Rupert might entertain, King Charles did not waver in his trust of his nephew, on whom in the new year he conferred a fresh honour. Apart from his Knighthood of the Garter Rupert had as yet received no English title. Now, however, the King decided to call a Parliament, to sit in Oxford as a counterweight to the 'pretended' Parliament at Westminster and to raise money for the 1644 campaign. He intended that Rupert should sit in the Lords, and on 24 January 1644 the Prince was created Duke of Cumberland and Earl of Holderness. Apart from his parliamentary seat the advancement made little difference to his position; nor did it make much impact on the world at large. To the end of his life he continued to be known as Prince Rupert; the title of Duke of Cumberland occurs only on official documents.

In January 1644 came a momentous event – the invasion of England by a Scottish army, of the likelihood of which the Earl of Montrose had twice warned King Charles. In September 1643, after Newbury, members of both Houses of the Westminster Parliament, in the presence of commissioners from Scotland, signed the Solemn League and Covenant by which they nominally committed themselves to the Presbyterian creed as adopted by the northern kingdom. In return the Scots agreed to support the English Parliamentarians in arms, and on 19 January some 20,000 troops under Alexander Leslie, Earl of Leven, began to cross the Tweed. Leven had led the northern forces in the Scots wars of 1639–41, and after the restoration of peace had sworn that he would not bear arms against the King again. He salved his conscience now by the usual fiction: he was not fighting against his sovereign but coming to his rescue, with the altruistic aim of delivering him from his evil advisers.

The menace of this new accession to Roundhead strength could hardly be exaggerated. It meant above all that hope had gone of Lord Newcastle's forces marching south to join the intended pincer movement on London. Newcastle, whose headquarters were in York, would have to concentrate all his resources on holding his position in the north of England; and even that might prove to be beyond his powers.

There was, however, a counterpoise to the Scottish invasion in the shape of reinforcements from across the Irish Sea.

Since the outbreak of civil war in England, Ireland had been in a more than usually turbulent condition. Lord Ormonde held Dublin for the King, but Parliamentary forces operated in the north and the south, while the Catholic Irish, fearful of Puritan domination, had formed their own state under the name of the Catholic Confederacy. The Confederacy's fight was against the Parliament, not the King; but inevitably it assumed the form of a revolt against all English rule, and Ormonde was forced to use all his military strength to maintain his position. In the autumn of 1643, however, he succeeded in coming to terms with the Confederacy, and the 'Cessation', as it was called, enabled him to release some of his troops for service in England. About twelve regiments of foot and one of horse crossed St George's Channel, most of them being sent to Chester where John Lord Byron (he had received a peerage after Newbury) was in command.

In these circumstances Prince Rupert was given, for the first time, an independent command. Byron, brave and loyal but a ruthless soldier, had not given satisfaction. When the first units from Ireland arrived he set himself to clear Cheshire of its Roundhead garrisons, but met with little success. At Barthomley, south-east of Crewe, he attacked the village church in which some Roundhead troops were holding out. When they refused to surrender, he stormed the building and put all those inside to the sword, soldiers and civilians alike, a justifiable action according to the laws of war, but perhaps hardly politic. Then, in freezing weather, he laid siege to Nantwich. Disaster followed. Sir Thomas Fairfax, who had recently captured Gainsborough in Lincolnshire, marched across country to the relief of Nantwich. He attacked on 25 January, and his troops, maddened by news of the massacre at Barthomley, hurled themselves on the Cavaliers with irresistible fury. Byron was completely defeated; most of the infantry surrendered, and the remainder, with the cavalry, retreated to Chester.

When the news reached Oxford it was decided that an abler hand than Byron's was needed in the north-west. Even before the Nantwich defeat the King had resolved to send Rupert to the area, and on 5 February the Prince was appointed President of Wales and Captain-General of the counties of Cheshire, Lancashire, Worcestershire and Shropshire, with power to appoint commissioners for the levy of taxes and troops. He set out for his new command next day, and on 19 February established his headquarters at Shrewsbury.

Here he set to work with his wonted energy; touring the garrisons, recruiting officers and men, retraining Byron's demoralized troops, and taking over the reinforcements as they arrived from Ireland. He was hampered as usual by lack of money, arms and ammunition, and his demands for supplies frequently met with obstruction at Oxford from Percy, John Ashburnham the army paymaster, and others. Jermyn, however, exerted himself with some success to see that Rupert was supplied, using his influence with the King and Queen and with the newly called Oxford Parliament; and Trevor, writing incessantly, kept him informed of all developments, while also fighting the battle of supplies.

With Ormonde in Ireland Rupert's relations were cordial. James Butler, twelfth Earl and first Marquess of Ormonde, was as remarkable a figure as was to be found in that age. Now thirty-three years of age, he was the head of one of the greatest houses in Ireland. He was a man of lofty spirit, uncompromising uprightness of character, invincible courage and haughty temper. In his early days he had clashed with Thomas Wentworth, the future Earl of Strafford, when that forceful administrator was engaged in restoring order in Ireland. Faced with an order from Wentworth that no swords should be worn in Parliament, Ormonde marched in ostentatiously wearing his, and when an official tried to take it off him answered that 'if he had his sword it should be in his guts'.[6] Wentworth, admiring the young man's mettle, wisely backed down, and Ormonde, also recognizing a kindred spirit, thereafter became his staunchest supporter. Throughout a long lifetime James Butler combined the fiercest independence with unswerving loyalty to the English crown.

Rupert's new appointment had not come without a characteristic attempt by Digby to make trouble between him and Ormonde. The Secretary of State affected to consider that the command in the northwest should have gone to the latter. On 20 February he wrote to the Marquess: 'I have written unto your excellence formerlye the reasons of prince Rupert's commission for those parts, whereof you had the command; but lett mee withall assure you, that I knew not of it till it was done, I beinge not then soe happye as to have any part in his highnesses counsells.'[7] Ormonde brushed aside the innuendo, replying coolly that he regarded the appointment of Rupert as very fitting. Rupert for his part received every co-operation from the Irish Lord-Lieutenant, who sent him all the men and arms he could spare.

While consolidating his command, Rupert had his share of skirmishing, of which the journal of his marches gives brief details. On 4 March he 'marcht all night towards Draiton', and on the following day, Shrove Tuesday, 'he beate Hilton and Fairfax from thence, and quartered there that night': on Ash Wednesday, 'after dinner, home to Shrewsburye'.[8] The *Rupert Diary* fills in the details to a slight extent: 'Drayton in Shropshire, Col. ffairfax with 700, and the P. had 100 horse.

The Enemy draws into a Close, and made it fast . . . and the P came to the gate with his own troop, till his Regiment came up and then beat them all to pieces.' 'Col. ffairfax' was probably Sir William Fairfax, cousin of Sir Thomas.

It was in these days that Prince Rupert performed his harshest act of reprisal against the Roundheads. Particular anger had been stored up against the troops from Ireland, who in Parliamentary parlance were 'Irish papists', though they were nothing of the sort. To Rupert it was a matter of no moment what was their nationality or religion; atrocities in breach of the rules of war quenched all feelings of mercy in his breast. This was what happened:

> About this time the Enemy at Nantwich, and other garrisons thereabouts had taken 13 of the P's men and had hanged 'em. After this the P. took 14 of the Enemy, and hangd 13, and sent the 14th to tell his Masters. And withall that if they hangd any more of his men he would hang two for one, which stopt that efflux of blood ever after. Essex sent to ask the P if he had any order to hang his men. The P return'd he did it as a souldier, and not by any Particular direction as it seems the Perliament forces in those garrisons had from the Parliament for hanging up the Ps men.[9]

Rupert's main task, however, was not skirmishing with minor bodies of the enemy, let alone punishing them for their misdeeds by executing prisoners. Affairs in the north were critical, and Rupert's object was to take his western army into Yorkshire to relieve the pressure on Lord Newcastle. Newcastle's strength was insufficient to hold off the Scots for long, and unless help came York, the greatest Royalist stronghold in the north, must fall in a matter of months. To Newcastle's solicitations were added those of the Earl of Derby, whose dauntless wife was valiantly defending Lathom House in Lancashire. She was related to Rupert, for she had been born Charlotte de la Tremoille, daughter of the Duc de Thouars and granddaughter of William the Silent, Prince of Orange; she was thus a cousin of the Elector Palatine Frederick V and a niece of Rupert's still living grandmother, the strong-minded Dowager Electress Louisa Juliana. Her kinship certainly weighed with Rupert, and when Lord Derby wrote from Chester of her critical situation he felt bound in honour to go to her aid as soon as he was in a position to do so.

The immediate and urgent need, however, was the relief of Newark-upon-Trent, a Royalist stronghold of the most vital importance. Newark, strongly fortified, lay on the Fosse Way, the Roman road that runs from Leicester to Lincoln, at the centre of communications between Newcastle's army in the north and the King's capital and headquarters. In Royalist hands it could keep open a route between York and

Oxford; if it should fall to the Roundheads communications between the northern and central Cavalier armies would be cut.

In February 1644 Sir John Meldrum, the Parliamentary commander in Nottinghamshire, advanced on Newark with a force of about 7,000 men – 2,000 horse, 5,000 foot, eleven guns and two mortars. On 29 February he laid siege to the town. The Governor of Newark was Sir Richard Byron, younger brother of Lord Byron and one of six brothers who fought for the King in the Civil War. He had a garrison less than 2,000 strong, including 300 horse. He could hope for no help from Newcastle, who was fully occupied with the Scots. Relief could come only from Rupert's forces in the west, and on 7 March the King wrote to his nephew, urging him 'to use all possible speedy meanes to succour a place of soe [great?] consequence unto Us; than which you cannot doe us a greater pleasure in this State of Our Affairs'.[10]

Five days later came a more definite order. Rupert, who was then at Chester, 'received *March* the Twelfth a Command from his Majesty to draw what Forces he could together, and march to the relief of Newark'.[11] Writing to him on the same day, the King concluded his letter: '. . . as for Newark, I believe before this, you will have understood my full directions, which I hope will not be the lesse powerfull, being the more civill: for an earnest desyre to you is as much as a perremptory command to others, from Your loving Oncle, & most faithfull frend, Charles R'.[12]

Rupert lost no time. On 13 March he moved back towards his headquarters at Shrewsbury, 'speeding away Major *Legg* [General of the Ordnance] before to chuse out so many commanded Musqueteers of the *English* (of late come out of *Ireland*) as might be spared out of that Garrison'.[13] Rupert reached Shrewsbury on the 14th, and next day, Friday, was at Bridgenorth, where he was met by the troops that Legge had raised – 1,120 men under Colonel Tillier – who came by boat down the Severn. Rupert had his own troop and regiment of horse, 'with 20 of Major General *Urrey's*; with these Forces he drew along 3 Field-pieces'.[14]

Rupert now marched north-eastwards in the direction of Newark, recruiting his meagre forces by drawing every available man from the Royalist garrisons along the way. On Saturday he reached Wolverhampton, and on Sunday, 17 March, was at Lichfield. At this point Essex, apprised of the Prince's sudden activity, sent out a force of cavalry to observe his movements; Ashburnham gave Rupert notice of this in a pithy communication: 'Sir, Since this inclosed was sealed, there is intelligence come that the strength that followeth your Highness is nine hundred dragoons, and one regiment of horse; which I hope will all be damned.'[15]

Nothing further is heard of this force, which had little chance of catching up with Rupert. He for his part pressed on: on Monday to Ashby-de-la-Zouch, on Tuesday to Rempstone on the Nottingham-shire border. On Wednesday, 20 March, he halted at Bingham, ten miles south-west of Newark. At Ashby-de-la-Zouch he had been joined by Lord Loughborough and by Major-General George Porter, son of his old mentor Endymion Porter who was now a member of the Oxford Parliament. The Prince's strength had risen to some 3,300 horse and a little over 3,000 foot.

Rupert's movements were well known to the Parliamentary com-manders; yet still Meldrum was taken by surprise. He could not believe that the Prince, with what at the outset was a totally inadequate force, could so increase his strength and at the same time march so fast as to constitute a threat to the besieging army. 'Hitherto had the Marches been so speedy, as Fame itself was prevented.'[16] There were indeed doubts whether the objective could be Newark. As late as 19 March the Northamptonshire Committee reported to Sir Samuel Luke, Parliamentary Governor of Newport Pagnell, that Rupert 'may come to Leicester or Newark'.[17] Deceived by the speed of Rupert's march, Meldrum failed to make adequate dispositions for defence until it was too late.

The town of Newark lies on the south-east bank of the Trent, which at this point branches into two, to form an island, two and a quarter miles long and a mile and a half wide, to the north-west of the town. The medieval castle, the Royalist garrison's strong-point, stood between the Fosse Way and the Trent, commanding the bridge which carried the Great North Road across the river and overlooking the whole of the island. North of the town, on the east bank of the river, lay a fortified position known as the Spittal, the site of a medieval hospital. To the east, some 1,500 yards from the church, is Beacon Hill, the highest point in the area.

Until 20 March Meldrum had done nothing to deter Rupert's advance beyond sending out a body of horse under Sir Edward Eartop to prevent his junction with Loughborough, which it failed to do. Then, convinced at last that a serious attack was imminent, he held a council of war at which it was decided to concentrate the army at the Spittal while sending a detachment of horse over Muskham Bridge at the north of the island to fetch provisions. It would appear from a passage in the *Rupert Diary* that the Prince had anticipated this latter move, and that Porter was caught napping: 'The Enemy had sent their horse to a little River where G:Porter lay. And the P directed that he should not let them go there without following them. But he let 'em march away, and gave no notice, to the great displeasure of the P.

The Enemy had no knowledge of the Ps coming notwithstanding.'

Meldrum's movements took place on the night of the 20th, and the news that his force were marching northwards reached Prince Rupert at Bingham in the small hours of the morning. Thinking that they were retiring, he acted immediately so as not to lose control. The *Diary* has a curious sidelight: 'The P dream'd the Enemy was beaten this night, and told Legg of it.' One would not expect the severely practical prince to be influenced by dreams, but in this case perhaps the confidence in victory thus induced inspired him with more even than usual of his dynamic energy. Leaving the infantry, gunners and the main body of horse to follow as best they might, he set forth at a gallop with the van of his cavalry at 2 a.m., and rode hard through the night, skirting the town of Newark to the south-east and making for Beacon Hill. On the hill were posted some of Meldrum's horse, but their orders were not to fight and they fell back as the Cavaliers approached. By daybreak on 21 March Rupert was on the crest of Beacon Hill, from where he could see the Roundhead army drawn up near the Spittal, 'and four Bodies of Horse posted to receive him, at the very descent of the Hill'.[18]

Rupert attacked without waiting for his main body to come up. His meagre forces were drawn up in two lines: he was himself on the right with his own troop of Life Guards, seconded by Loughborough's troop and with Gerard's in reserve. At 9 a.m. he launched one of his now famous cavalry charges, leading his troopers down the hill, breaking into a gallop on the lower slopes, and falling with a furious onslaught on the Roundhead horse below. As the Cavaliers advanced they shouted their field-words 'King and Queen', to which the Parliamentarians replied with the cry 'Religion'.

As usual, the shock effect of the charge was tremendous, but Colonel Rossiter and Colonel Francis Thornhagh put up a vigorous defence. According to Mrs Hutchinson, wife of the Roundhead Governor of Nottingham, Thornhagh launched a counter-attack, 'where, they say, he charged the prince himself, and made his way and passed very gallantly through the whole army, with a great deal of honour, and two desperate wounds, one in the arm, the other in the belly'.[19] Rupert was certainly in the thick of the fray, and indeed came as near as ever he did to falling in action. The fight, says his biographer, 'was maintained very fiercely on both sides; the Prince himself having advanced so far into the Enemies Ranks, that being observed and known, was dangerously assaulted by three sturdy Souldiers, whereof he slew one with his own Sword, a second was Pistolled by one of his Gentlemen, the third being ready to lay hand on the Princes Coller, had it almost chopt off by Sir *William Neal*. Being thus dis-ingaged with a shot only in his Gauntlet, he furiously charged through them, routing and pursuing them to their own works at the Spittle'.[20] Rossiter at least appears to have retired in good order.

There was now a lull while the main Cavalier body came up. Meanwhile Meldrum's defeated horse fell back across a bridge of boats on to the island. Once reinforced, and with his army once more complete, Rupert was master of the situation. He sent Colonel Tillier with part of the 'Irish' foot and some horse to the north-east to attack the bridge of boats. Here he was bombarded by the Roundhead guns and had to fall back out of range. At the same time Meldrum's line of communication over Muskham Bridge was cut off, for 'three Companies of Colonel *King's*, and three *Nottingham* Companies (unknown to Sir *John*) quitted the Fort where they lay, passed over *Muscombe*-Bridge, brake up the Bridge, and so secured themselves'.[21] Rupert got 500 horse into the western part of the island, and the Parliamentary forces were invested on all sides – 'the late Blockers found themselves now beseiged'.[22] Finally Sir Richard Byron, with part of his garrison, sallied forth from the castle into the island. Rupert, it appears, had early established communication with Byron. According to Warburton he got a message through to him during the night in cryptic terms: 'Let the old drum on the north side be beaten early on the morrow morning'[23] – the 'old drum' being Meldrum. The story, however, rests on no sure foundations; and it was well on in the day when Byron made his sally.

Meldrum's position was now hopeless. He had victuals for only two days, and the party he had sent out over Muskham Bridge the day before had no hope of getting back. Nor could Meldrum himself retreat over that bridge. Any counter-attack was doomed to failure, and if he tried to hold his ground he could quicky be starved out. The only course was to surrender, and at nightfall he sent a trumpet to the Prince for a parley. The terms were generous. Officers and men were to march away with arms, colours and drums; the Prince was to send a convoy 'to protect them from any injury Two Miles from His utmost Quarters towards Lincoln'.[24]

Once again it appears that some of Rupert's soldiers got out of hand, and that there was trouble over observing the terms of surrender. According to Mrs Hutchinson 'the prince broke all these conditions, and pillaged them to their shirts, and sent many captains quite naked away'.[25] She was a highly prejudiced witness, and her testimony may be discounted. Rushworth's account, however, can be taken as substantially accurate:

Accordingly *Meldrum* and his Forces marched out, but complained, that contrary to the Articles they were spoiled of their Colours, Swords, Pikes, *etc.*, which the Kings Party excused, by alledging, that they attempted to carry away more than was Conditioned; and that some of theirs had been so used before at *Lincoln*, and expecially that the same was against the Prince's Mind, who slashed several of his soldiers for the same, and sent back some Colours they had taken.[26]

The relief of Newark was one of Prince Rupert's most brilliant exploits. The battle was comparatively bloodless; some 200 Roundheads fell, it has been estimated, and less than 100 Cavaliers.[27] But the victory over superior forces was complete. Rupert had achieved surprise by the sheer speed of his movements and the sureness of his control over hurriedly raised forces; his tactics were faultless, and his cavalry leadership as effective as ever.

Rejoicing at Oxford knew no bounds. King Charles hastened to congratulate his nephew, saying that the victory '(as all your other victories) gives me as much contentment in that I owe you the thanks as for the importance of it, which in this particular, believe me is no lesse than the saving of all the North'.[28] Yet the writing was on the wall. For all their military successes the Royalists were growing no stronger. They had failed to strike a decisive blow; failed, above all, to take London. Money was increasingly scarce, and it was becoming more and more difficult to pay the troops, who were forced to live off the country with the inevitable consequence of marauding and growing unpopularity. The great nobles who had done so much to support the cause out of their own pockets were feeling the draught; they could not indefinitely face the constant drain on their resources.

The strength of the Parliamentarians, on the other hand, was growing. Politically they were in no better shape than they had ever been. Pym had died in the previous December, and as yet no clear successor had emerged to give unity to the direction of policy. With the coming of the Scots a Committee of Both Kingdoms had been established at Westminster to organize the general conduct of the war. Its principal members on the English side were Oliver St John, the Solicitor-General, and Sir Henry Vane the younger. Of the Scottish commissioners the most forceful and the most influential was John Lord Maitland, 'a bulky red-headed young man of great learning and prodigious memory, a cold heart, a shrewd head, and a wrathful, spluttering eloquence'.[29] The Committee had wide powers, and gave orders to the generals in the field; but its path was not unobstructed. It enjoyed no unity of direction; it could not rely on the support of the Commons; and it was distrusted by the military commanders.

Nevertheless, in spite of the uncertain guidance of the Committee of Both Kingdoms, in spite also of the mutual jealousies of the army commanders and the declining authority of Essex, the Roundhead forces were becoming better organized. Instead of the haphazard raising of troops that characterized the early stages of the conflict, formations had been established in groups of counties; of these the army of the Eastern Association, raised in that part of England most firmly in the grasp of the Westminster Parliament, was the most formidable. In the north Lord Fairfax had a substantial army, and his son Sir Thomas was emerging as the most dashing and inspiring leader on the Roundhead side, the only one at this stage of the war who could stand comparison with Prince Rupert. Further north still the Scots under Lord Leven posed a gigantic threat to Newcastle's position at York. They had not yet been involved in serious hostilities, but their potential was enormous.

Moreover the morale and efficiency of the troops were improving. In 1642 and 1643 the Parliamentarians, man for man, had been palpably inferior to their opponents. Early in the war an uncouth but astute back-bencher named Oliver Cromwell, who had commanded a troop of horse at Edgehill, put his finger on the basis of the trouble in a conversation with John Hampden, who was his cousin. Long afterwards he recorded the gist of what he had said:

> 'Your troopes,' said I, 'are most of them old decayed serving-men, and tap-sters, and such kind of fellows; and,' said I, 'their troopers are gentlemen's sons, younger sons and persons of quality: do you think that the spirits of such base and mean fellows will be ever able to encounter gentlemen, that have honour and courage and resolution in them?' Truly I presented to him in this manner conscientiously; and truly I did tell him: 'You must set men of a spirit: and take it not ill what I say, – I know you will not, – of a spirit that is likely to go on as far as gentlemen will go: – or else I am sure you will be beaten still.'[30]

Since that day Oliver Cromwell had risen in the world. He was a member of the Committee of Both Kingdoms, and a power in the land. But his chief activities were military. Not a professional soldier before the war, he studied his craft with all the intensity of his nature. He was now a senior officer in the army of the Eastern Association, and virtually second in command to its general, the Earl of Manchester. There he put into practice the principles he had expounded to Hampden. For the dash and spirit of loyalty that animated the Cavaliers he substituted the driving force of religion. A stern Puritan, he inspired his men with the fervour that possessed him. The Royalist forces were represented as papists and sinners, enemies of the true Protestant religion, whom it was a spiritual duty to destroy. Other commanders followed his lead, and the conflict from the Roundhead viewpoint assumed more and more the character of a holy war.

Cromwell too proved himself, in the purely military sphere, a first-rate trainer of troops, particularly cavalry. He imposed rigid, indeed severe, discipline, and showed that he possessed the pre-eminent quality of procuring the loyalty of his men. With his keen eye and brain he was able to learn from his enemies. He observed the success of Rupert's cavalry charges, and saw where lay their one weak point: the difficulty of halting the impetus of horses in full gallop when once the objective was gained. This he set himself to remedy by stern discipline and incessant training.

For the Cavaliers there were more immediate dangers at hand. With Newark relieved it was time to concentrate once more on the main objective – the relief of the pressure exercised on Lord Newcastle by the northern Parliamentarian armies. Newcastle himself was importunate, and on 25 March he wrote to Rupert from Durham with the quaintly phrased stateliness characteristic of his correspondence:

May it please your Highness,

In the first place I congratulate your huge and great victories, which indeed is fit for none but your Highness. For all the affairs in the North I refer your Highness to this bearer, Sir John Mayne, who can tell your Highness every particular; only this I must assure your Highness that the Scots are as big again in foot as I am, and their horse, I doubt, much better than ours are, so that if your Highness do not please to come hither, and that nay very soon too, the great game of your uncle's will be endangered, if not lost; and with your Highness being near, certainly won: so I doubt not but your Highness will come, and that very soon.

Your Highness's most passionate creature,

W. NEWCASTLE[31]

Rupert can have had no doubt of the urgency of the situation. But he was not yet ready to resume his northward march. After a few days at Newark he turned back to his headquarters at Shrewsbury, where the immediate tasks of recruiting, organizing and training his forces went on. All the time he had to contend with the intrigues and divided counsels in Oxford. As usual, Digby was working to undermine the Prince's influence with King Charles; also as usual, Richmond and Jermyn were doing their best to smooth matters over and to see that Rupert's interests were not neglected. His most powerful enemy, however, was soon to be out of the way. The reunion of the King and Queen in the previous year had not been fruitless, and the now pregnant Henrietta Maria, in delicate health, decided that Oxford was no place for her. The west country, she felt, would be a more peaceful place for her confinement. On 17 April the King escorted her to Abingdon, and there they parted; as it turned out, for ever. The Queen proceeded to

Exeter, where on 16 June she gave birth to her ninth and youngest child, the Princess Henrietta Anne.

Oxford was indeed anything but safe. From the south it was threatened by Waller, who on 29 March defeated Forth and Hopton at Cheriton, six miles east of Winchester; thereby regaining for the Parliament a considerable part of Hampshire and Wiltshire. To the east lay Essex, inactive as yet but with a considerable army at his disposal. To the north-east was Lord Manchester with the formidable army of the Eastern Association, which could be used in support either of an attack on Oxford or of the northern advance on York. The western half of the country was still in Royalist hands, but Prince Maurice, with his army of 6,000 men, had been tied up since the middle of March in a prolonged siege of Lyme, one of the few Parliamentary strongholds left in the south-west.

On 25 April Rupert, now nearly ready to march, paid a visit to Oxford, at the urgent demand of the King, to attend a council of war. Among those present were Forth (about this time created Earl of Brentford), Wilmot, Hopton, Sir Jacob Astley, Digby and Culpeper. Rupert gave his advice. It was to strengthen the garrisons of Oxford, Wallingford, Abingdon, Reading (which had been reoccupied as a result of First Newbury) and Banbury, and to reinforce them with all the foot available; to keep a good body of horse about Oxford, free to manoeuvre where required; and to send the rest to reinforce Prince Maurice in the west. These measures would, in Prince Rupert's view, be sufficient to hold off the threat from Essex and Waller while he himself went north to the aid of Newcastle.

His advice was adopted, and on 5 May the Prince returned to Shrewsbury. Hardly was his back turned when the plan was changed. The decision now taken was to abandon Reading, demolish its fortifications, and withdraw its garrison of 2,500 men to reinforce the Oxford garrison. Essex and Waller were now both on the move; the former had marched out from London and was advancing towards Reading over the Chilterns, while Waller moved towards the same objective through Farnham, Bagshot and Basing. On 19 May Roundhead forces entered the abandoned town.

The Oxford garrison was thus strengthened. Nevertheless the threat to the city was acute, and became more so when a week later Abingdon was also abandoned. Had the Parliamentary armies' movements been efficiently co-ordinated, or had the Committee of Both Kingdoms been able to exert its authority, not only would Oxford have fallen, but a defeat would almost certainly have been inflicted on the central Royalist army which it could hardly have survived. As it was, distrust and jealousy among the Roundhead generals frustrated the strategy devised in London. The intention had been that not only Essex and Waller, but Manchester too, should advance on Oxford. But Essex and Waller detested each other; Essex was jealous of Manchester's growing power; and Manchester for his part was more concerned with the conflict in the eastern counties than with the larger issues of the war. In the event Manchester made no move to join the other two commanders, who themselves reduced co-operation with each other to the minimum.

Yet divisions on the Parliamentary side were only half the story. It was in fact the King who saved the situation. As happened from time to time in his vacillating career, at the moment of crisis he took his own decision and acted on it. If Oxford were besieged he could hardly hope to hold out for more than a few weeks. But if he slipped out of the city with sufficient troops before his line of withdrawal was cut he might draw the Roundhead armies after him in pursuit and then either elude them or take his chance in the open field.

This was the decision taken. On the night of 3 June King Charles, with a force estimated at 3,000 foot, 4,000 horse and some light artillery,[32] marched out of Oxford between the two hostile armies and, turning westwards, made for the Cotswolds. He took with him the Prince of Wales, the Duke of Richmond, Digby, Wilmot, Percy, Culpeper and Astley; leaving behind him his second son the Duke of York, the majority of his council, and Sir Arthur Aston, Governor of the city.

Events turned out as the King had calculated. As soon as they found their quarry had eluded them, the Roundhead generals set off in pursuit; Essex to the north, Waller to the south. But the King had a good start. He marched through the Cotswolds, turning north at Burford and arriving at Worcester on 6 June. Essex and Waller, following, met and conferred at Chipping Norton. It was the parting of the ways. There was no chance of agreement between them, and Essex, in defiance of his orders, declared his intention of taking no further part in the campaign but of marching south-west to the relief of Lyme.

Waller went on to Evesham. Meanwhile the King, who had marched on northwards towards Bewdley, doubled back on his tracks and was again at Worcester on 15 June. He then returned through the Cotswolds in the direction of Oxford, Waller failing to cut him off. There was further manoeuvring, which brought the King and the Parliamentary commander to the neighbourhood of Banbury, close to Edgehill where the first great battle of the war had been fought.

The two armies met on 29 June at Cropredy Bridge, three and a half miles north of Banbury; and there the King won a meritorious victory. Waller was trapped between the two halves of the royal army and was eventually forced to retire across the bridge with considerable losses.

Cropredy Bridge, with the manoeuvres that led up to it, was not a decisive victory, but it saved Oxford from capture and the central Royalist army from destruction. The King's surprise march had outwitted and divided his opponents, and from first to last he had handled his troops with consummate skill while facing enemy commanders of far greater experience.

Meanwhile Prince Rupert was advancing on York. There Newcastle's position was precarious. The siege started on 22 April 1644, when the northern army under Lord Fairfax and the Scots under the Earl of Leven sat down before the city. Early in the following month they were joined by the Earl of Manchester, who on 6 May stormed Lincoln and then advanced to York with his army of the Eastern Association. And with him was Oliver Cromwell. The total strength of the three besieging armies amounted to more than 20,000 men,[33] and they formed a ring around the city – Manchester on the north side, Leven on the west, Fairfax on the east. Newcastle, with a few horse and 4,000 to 5,000 foot as his garrison, had retired within the walls.

Rupert left Shrewsbury for the north on 16 May; his army, according to one who took part in the march, consisted 'of 2000 horse and 6000 ffoote, or about (as is supposed) drawne out of the Countyes of Hertford, Woster, Stafford, Salop, Chester'.[34] Instead of taking the direct road north-eastwards towards York he struck due north, with the intention of capturing a western port, to serve as a link with Ireland, and of storming the Parliamentary strongholds in Lancashire which would otherwise be a menace to his rear when he moved eastwards.

His exact movements can be traced in the *Journal of Prince Rupert's Marches*. On the first day he reached Petton, near Wem; on Saturday, 18 May, he was at Whitchurch, eighteen miles north of Shrewsbury; moving eastwards, he arrived at Market Drayton on the 20th, and Betley, east of Newcastle-under-Lyme, on the 21st. Turning north again through Staffordshire and Cheshire, he was at Sandbach on the 22nd and at Knutsford on the 23rd. On the way he gathered reinforcements, drawing out from Chester all the men who could be spared and leaving Will Legge to command the depleted garrison. At Knutsford he beat a Roundhead force in a minor skirmish, and from there he advanced to Stockport.

Here his forces 'beat their way over ye Passe of Stopford',[35] and the welcome result was the raising of the siege of Lathom House. Here the gallant Countess of Derby, Rupert's cousin, had held out for eighteen weeks with a tiny garrison, refusing all demands for her surrender. 'Go back to your commander,' she had replied to the last summons, sent by Colonel Rigby, 'and tell that insolent rebel, he shall have neither persons, goods, nor house. When our strength is spent, we shall find a fire more merciful than Rigby's, and then, if the Providence of God prevent it not, my goods and house shall burn in his sight; myself, my children, and my soldiers, rather than fall into his hands, will seal our religion and our loyalty in the same flame.'[36] Lord Derby had joined Rupert, and was with the relieving forces when his spirited lady's long ordeal ended.

This was on 25 May. The besiegers of Lathom House withdrew to Bolton: a fact unknown to Rupert, who sent his Quartermaster-General, that Colonel Tillier who had distinguished himself at Newark, forward with the vanguard to secure quarters in the town. Bolton was known as 'the Geneva of England' on account of its strong Puritan sympathies, and Tillier found himself opposed by a strong enemy force. He managed to entrench himself in the outskirts, and here Rupert joined him with the main body on 28 May.

The storming of Bolton followed. Rupert and Derby led a cavalry charge, and the defenders were forced back within their lines. But their foot, 5,000 of them behind strong entrenchments, put up a formidable resistance. Then the Roundheads perpetrated an act of derisive defiance which sealed their fate. 'During the time of the Attaque they took a prisoner (an Irishman) and hung him up as an Irish papist.'[37] This was the sort of action that stung Rupert to fury. He threw himself from his horse, put himself at the head of his infantry, and led them in an attack that proved irresistible. The town was stormed, and the Roundhead troops suffered severely for their action. A report made to Sir Samuel Luke at Newport Pagnell says that Rupert, with a strength now of 14,000 men, 'went against Bolton where he was thrice repulsed, and on the 4th assault took it, and in it 1,500 prisoners, and put them all to the sword'.[38] There is no corroboration of the charge of killing prisoners in cold blood, but undoubtedly the town was sacked. The *Rupert Diary* admits that 'a great slaughter was made of the Enemy'; but it also states that '700 got into the Church, and the P gave them quarter'.

From Bolton Rupert proceeded to Bury, where on 30 May 'Lord Goring's Horse came to us'.[39] Then, after a brief rest, he retraced his steps to Wigan, a loyal town which gave him an enthusiastic welcome; and on 11 June after a brief siege he captured Liverpool, where he showed his care for his men by writing to the Bishop of Chester requesting that 'a general collection may be forthwith made in all churches within your diocese'[40] for the relief of the wounded. Liverpool gave him the western port he needed; his line of communication with Ireland was secure, and he was ready to advance to the relief of York.

There was little time to lose. Newcastle could not hold out much longer; six days was one estimate. Rupert was being bombarded by instructions, many of them contradictory, from the royal headquarters, now moving through the West Midlands. And it was while he was at Liverpool that he received from his master the most fateful letter of the Civil War. It was dated 14 June from Ticknill, near Ashby-de-la-Zouch. King Charles had not yet decided on his strategy in the face of the threat from Waller's army, and it was evidently in a mood of uncertainty and despondency that he wrote to Rupert:

Nepueu/first I must congratulat with you, for your good successes, asseuring you that the things themselfes ar no more welcome to me, than that you are the means: I know the importance of the supplying you with powder for which I have taken all possible wais, having sent both to Ireland & Bristow, as from Oxford this bearer is well satisfied, that it is impossible to have at present, but if he tell you that I may spare them hence, I leave you to judge, having but 36 left; but what I can gett from Bristow (of wch there is not much certaintie, it being threatned to be beseiged) you shall have

But now I must give you the trew stat of my Affaires, wch if their condition be such as enforses me to give you more peremptorie comands then I would willingly doe, you must not take it ill. If Yorke be lost, I shall esteeme my Crowne litle lesse, unlesse supported by your suddaine Marche to me, & a Miraculous Conquest in the South, before the effects of the Northern power can be found heere; but if Yorke be relived, & you beate the Rebelles Armies of both Kingdomes, which ar before it, then but otherwise not, I may possiblie make a shift, (upon the defensive) to spinn out tyme, untill you come to assist mee: Wherefor I comand and conjure you, by the dewty & affection which I know you beare me, that (all new enterpryses laid aside) you immediatly March (according to your first intention) with all your force to the relife of Yorke; but if that be eather lost, or have fried themselfes from the beseigers, or that for want of pouder you cannot undertake that worke; that you immediatly March, with your whole strength, to Woster, to assist me & my Army, without which, or your having relived Yorke by beating the Scots, all the successes you can afterwards have, most infallibly, will be uselesse unto mee: You may belive that nothing but an extreame necessity could make me wryte thus unto you, wherefor, in this Case, I can no wayes dout of your punctuall complyance with

Your loving Oncle & most
faithfull frend

I comanded this bearer   Charles R.[41]
to speake to you
concerning Vavisor

This letter, clearly from a desperate and hard-pressed man, was hardly a model of lucidity. But to Rupert its main import was clear. He was commanded to march at once to York, and not only to relieve the city but also to defeat the armies of Fairfax, Manchester and Leven in the field. His creed was loyalty and obedience and he would obey, whatever his own judgement of the situation might be. It is said that Culpeper, on hearing that the letter had been sent, exclaimed to the King: 'Why, then, before God you are undone, for upon this peremptory order he will fight, whatever comes on't.'[42]

Rupert, in deciding where his duty lay, had no doubt that the King's letter must be his justification. In after years he never produced it in his own defence, though it was said that he 'carried this letter about him to his dying day'.[43]

Some blamed Digby for the letter, among them Sir Philip Warwick who wrote that 'the Lord Digby had this year given a fatall direction unto that excellent Prince Rupert to have fought the Scotch army'.[44] What Digby's advice was there is no means of telling, but it is impossible to believe that he drafted the letter. Every line of it, with its tortuous phrasing and worried tone, bespeaks the King himself.

The burden of the King's letter was not the only one the Prince had to bear at this time. The intrigues of the hostile courtiers, clustering around King Charles as he moved through the Midlands, were such that Rupert's patience, never of the strongest, was strained to breaking-point. If we are to believe Arthur Trevor, he even threatened to throw in his hand and leave the kingdom to its fate. Writing to Ormonde from Chester on 29 June, Trevor had this to say about what had been going on:

> Prince Rupert, by letter from court, understands that the king growes dayly more and more iealous of him and his army; and that it is the common discourse (at the openest places where men can discover themselves) of the Lord Digbye, lord Percy, sir John Culpeper, and Willmot, that it is indifferent whither the parliament or prince Rupert doth prevayle; which did so highlye jesuite prince Rupert, that he was once resolved to send the king his comission and gett to France.
>
> This fury interupted the march ten dayes; but at length tyme and a frend, the best coolers of the blood, spent the humour of travayle in him, though not that of revenge; to which purpose hee hath sent his letter to the king for the removeall of them from his councell; and if this be not done, hee will leave this warr and sit downe.[45]

Whatever Trevor may have meant by the verb 'to jesuite' it is plain that Rupert was in a white heat of fury. He was engaged in a mission that might well seal the fate of the kingdom, and to have to look over his shoulder to guard against the petty spite of those who should have given him their support was almost more than he could bear. It must have taken all the tact of the 'frend', who one may surmise was Richmond, or possibly Jermyn, to keep him to his allotted task.

But the mood of black rage passed, or at least was overcome. Rupert was the King's servant; he would never desert his master so long as he could still be of service. As to the ten-day delay in Lancashire, Trevor in attributing this to the dispute with the courtiers was probably right in a sense; Rupert needed supplies of arms and ammunition from head-quarters, and Percy, as General of the Ordnance, was dilatory in providing them. But there is no evidence that Rupert purposely wasted time, and it would be most unlike him to do so. He was up against great odds, and it would be suicidal to move before he was in a position to carry out his design.

Once he resumed his march he certainly lost no time. On Friday, 22 June, he moved north from Lathom House, which he had made his temporary headquarters, to Preston: on the following day north-east to, Ribchester, and on Sunday the 24th, following the line of the Ribble to Clitheroe on the Lancashire–Yorkshire border. Next day he was at Gisburn in Yorkshire, and on 26 June at Skipton Castle, where he stayed three days 'to fixe our armes, and send into Yorke'.[46]

The next step was to occupy Denton, near Otley, a house belonging to none other than Lord Fairfax. Twenty-three years earlier, two mem-bers of that prolific family, William and John Fairfax, had fought and died in defence of the Palatinate, and a portrait of one of them hung in the gallery at Denton. Rupert saw it, and his reaction was thus recorded by a younger member of the family, Brian Fairfax: 'At the sight of this picture the generous Prince Rupert, who lay at Denton, in his march to York, Anno 1644, commanded the house should not be injured for his sake. Such force hath gratitude in noble minds,/ Such honour ever Virtue's shadow finds.'[47] This was on 29 June, and on the 30th Rupert advanced to Knaresborough, only fourteen miles from the city of York which now lay due east of him. With the reinforcements brought by Goring, and those he had been able to recruit on his march, he now had some 15,000 men under his command.

The road from Knaresborough led to the south side of York, and as soon as the Roundhead generals had intelligence of Rupert's latest advance they swung their forces westwards to meet him, crossing the Ouse by a bridge of boats at Poppleton, north-west of the city, massing their armies on the open ground of Marston Moor to block the Knaresborough road, and leaving the northern gate of York unguarded.

There followed one of those swift and imaginative manoeuvres that showed Prince Rupert's true qualities as a commander. Putting out a cavalry screen to deceive the enemy, he suddenly wheeled his main force northwards, crossed the Ure at Boroughbridge and then the Swale at Thornton Bridge, swung south-east again, sent a party ahead

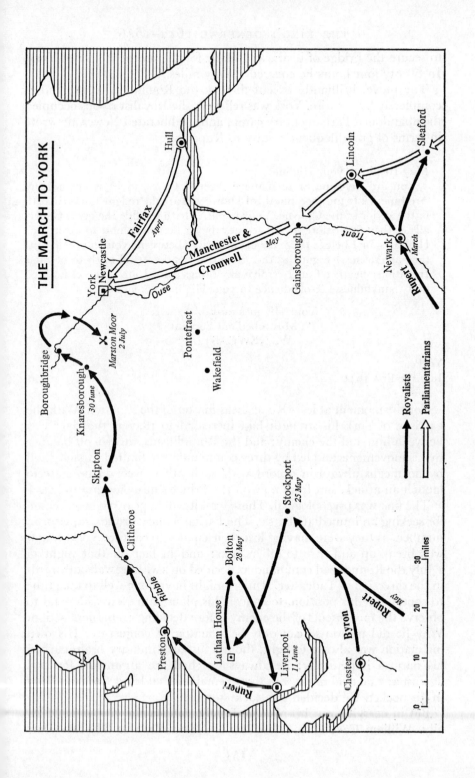

THE MARCH TO YORK

Royalists ■►
Parliamentarians ▷

Hull
Fairfax April
Newcastle
York
Ouse
Marston Moor 2 July
Boroughbridge
Knaresborough 30 June
Skipton
Clitheroe
Ribble
Preston
Rupert
Latham House
Liverpool 11 June
Bolton 28 May
Stockport 25 May
Chester
Byron
Rupert May
Manchester & Cromwell May
Gainsborough
Trent
Pontefract
Wakefield
Lincoln
Sleaford
Newark Rupert March

0   10   20   30 miles

to secure the bridge of boats, and made for the northern gate of York. In twenty-four hours he covered twenty miles.

The move, brilliantly executed, took the Roundhead commanders completely by surprise. York was relieved, the Royalist troops occupied the abandoned Parliamentary camp, and the liberated Newcastle wrote in terms of grandiloquent ecstasy to Rupert:

> May Itt please your Highnes
> You are welcome Sr so manaye severall wayes, as itt is beyond my Arethmetick to number, but this I knowe you are the redemer of the North & the savior of the Crowne. Your name Sr hath terefide the great Generalls & they flye before itt. Itt seemes theyer designe is nott to meet your Highness for I beleve theye have gott a river betweene you and them butt they are so nowlye gone as ther is [no] sertentie att all of them or their Intentions, neyther Can I resolve any things since I am made of nothing butt thankfulnesse & obedience to your Highnes comandes

Your Highnes most obligde &
Most obedient Servant
W. NEWCASTLE[48]

Yorke
July the first 1644

For the moment at least Rupert was master of the situation. With the garrison of York his strength had increased to 18,000; the river was between him and the enemy; and the Roundheads, thrown off balance by his movements and led by three commanders of limited capacity and by no means always in accord with each other, were in no state to launch an attack. But from now on the Prince's mistakes multiplied.

The first was psychological. There was, it will appear, no good reason for seeking an immediate battle. The Parliamentary armies, superior in numbers as they were, having lost their chance to capture York, might well break up and turn to other tasks; and in fact on that night of 1 July the Roundhead commanders decided on a withdrawal southwards in the direction of Tadcaster. Rupert might have done well to take time to consolidate his position, to concert his plans with Newcastle, and to observe the movements of the enemy before deciding on his next action. Why he did not do so can only be a matter of conjecture. His own inclination was always to fight, though his keen military brain curbed his natural impetuosity; he always weighed the arguments for and against any tactical move. But there remained that letter from the King in his pocket. He decided to attack at once.

But in carrying out his plan he fatally mistook the character of his ally. William Cavendish, Marquess of Newcastle, was fifty-two years old; a grandee and a magnifico, stately and courtly in address; of little military capacity though a sound administrator; a man of kindly nature but proud and sensitive, quick to take offence at any apparent slight to his authority.

This was just the mistake Rupert made. To Newcastle he was a valuable ally who had come to his rescue at a critical moment; his letter of 1 July had been an expression of gratitude, couched in his usual style of hyperbolic courtesy. Rupert, however, took the words 'obedience to your Highnes comandes' literally. He himself was the commander, and Newcastle had put himself under his orders. He proceeded to act accordingly.

It appears, though it is not quite certain, that Rupert did not enter York on 1 July. Instead he sent Goring, who was General of the Horse in Newcastle's northern army, to convey his wishes that the Marquess should lead his forces out of the city at four o'clock on the following morning to join Rupert on the march to Marston Moor. Even for Rupert, who was not renowned for tact, such conduct would seem to be singularly graceless, not to say inept. Yet there may have been reasons for it. Brigadier Peter Young has pointed out that 'in the seventeenth century there were strange mysteries of protocol to confuse the issue',[49] and suggested that the Prince felt that if he were to wait personally on Newcastle it might be taken as tacit admission of the latter's seniority. Rupert was of higher rank than the Marquess; he was a duke in the peerage of England as well as a royal prince; he was determined to assert his authority. Yet Newcastle was nearly thirty years older, a magnate in the northern counties, and commander of an independent army. He was certainly affronted.

From this time onward Newcastle made at least a show of complying with Rupert's wishes, but in a dilatory way and with the air of a sulky child who has been slighted. And Newcastle's chief military adviser was Lord Eythin, the Scottish general who as James King had played so equivocal a part when Rupert was taken prisoner at Lemgo. There was little love lost between Eythin and the Prince. According to Sir Hugh Cholmley, who wrote his account of Marston Moor some years later, Newcastle gave order that Rupert's instructions should be followed, and 'accordingly all the fort were at 2 a clock that night drawn in a body expecting to march out of the city, when there came an order from General King, that they should not march till they had their pay whereupon they all quitt their colours and disperse'.[50] Cholmley adds that many of the men were engaged in plundering the enemy's abandoned trenches, and that Eythin denied having sent any such message, 'but that it being pay day the soldiers would not out of the city without it and raised this of themselves'.

Whatever the truth of the matter, and whatever the part played by Eythin, it is clear that there was something approaching a mutiny among the men of the York garrison. Their ordeal in the beleaguered city had lasted more than two months, and it is hardly surprising that they got out of hand. Once again Rupert was at fault; it was expecting rather a lot of them to order that they should at once march out to battle, and he seems hardly to have bothered to find out the state of their morale.

So it was that Prince Rupert, ready himself at four o'clock in the morning, was kept waiting for five hours for Newcastle. Meanwhile the chance of a surprise attack slipped away. The Parliamentary withdrawal had already started, and the foot were on their way to Tadcaster, but some Roundhead patrols clashed with Rupert's cavalry, whereupon the infantry were hastily recalled. In the words of the *Rupert Diary*, 'the P would have attaq'd the Enemy himselfe in their Retreat, if he had not expected the Earles[51] assistance; but at last instead of 10000 men he had not above 2500, and those all drunk'.

The meeting took place at 9 a.m.[52] Rupert controlled his temper, and allowed himself only the comment: 'My Lord, I wish you had come sooner with your forces, but I hope we shall yet have a glorious day.'[53] Rupert then suggested an immediate attack, which would perhaps have been better launched earlier, without waiting for the drunken 2,500; but Newcastle demurred, saying 'he had 4,000 good foot as were in the world',[54] and it would be better to wait for them. Rupert, apparently less high-handed now he was in the presence of the Marquess, allowed himself to be dissuaded.

It was four o'clock in the afternoon before Eythin turned up, bringing with him the Whitecoats, hardened Yorkshire veterans who were the best infantry in the north of England. They were under good discipline now, and the effects of the previous night's debauch had worn off, as was to be shown before nightfall. But by the time they arrived the Roundheads had reassembled their armies.

So the day wore away, with both forces consolidating their positions; the Cavaliers now facing south, the Roundheads north. There was some minor skirmishing, and at one point the Royalists took a prisoner who was asked by Rupert: 'Is Cromwell there?'[55] Thus far had the reputation of the obscure captain of the Edgehill fight advanced in the eyes of his opponents.

The ground on which the biggest battle of the Civil War was now to be fought consisted of open moorland between the villages of Tockwith to the west and Long Marston to the east, some two miles apart. Just in front of the Royalist position ran a deep ditch fringed by hedges. The Roundheads on the south side were on slightly higher ground than that

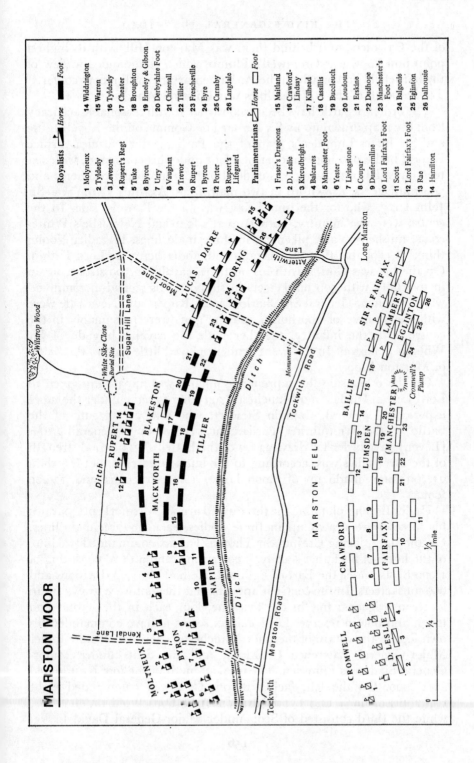

of the Cavaliers, and behind them was Marston Hill, with its highest point now known as Cromwell's Plump, which commanded a view of the battlefield and on which the Parliamentary generals met to confer.[56] To the north of the Royalist lines was Wilstrop Wood.

The orders of battle have been reconstructed with reasonable accuracy from the map drawn up by Sir Bernard de Gomme on the Royalist side and Sir James Lumsden's plan of the Parliamentary armies. Prince Rupert had 6,000 horse and 11,000 foot under his command, with six-teen guns. His right wing was under Lord Byron, with 2,600 horse and 500 musketeers, drawn up in two main lines. Assisting Byron was Sir John Urry, who for the time being was on the Royalist side. In the centre were the infantry, both Rupert's foot and Newcastle's White-coats, musketeers and pikemen, in three main lines. Brigadier Young thinks it probable that the overall commander here was Lord Eythin. On the left was Goring with his northern cavalry, 2,100 strong, again in two lines with 500 musketeers in support. His second-in-command was Lieutenant-General Sir Charles Lucas. Rupert and Newcastle were with the reserve of 700 horse, and the guns were presumably in the centre with the infantry, together with the cavalry brigade of Sir William Blakiston. In the event artillery played little part in the Battle of Marston Moor.

On the other side the supreme command was apparently given to Lord Leven, Fairfax and Manchester agreeing to serve under the more experienced general. Captain Stewart, who sent an account of the battle to the Westminster Parliament, records that 'Generall *Lesley* [Leven] gave order for drawing up of the Battell'.[57] The total strength of the three allies was, according to the latest researches, not less than 21,200 men, made up of 8,000 horse, 1,000 dragoons and 12,200 foot.[58]

Under Leven's planning the three allied armies were not kept separate; his forces were drawn up in three bodies, each in three main lines. On the right, facing Goring, Sir Thomas Fairfax commanded two lines of the horse of his father's army, 3,000 strong, and a third consisting of 1,000 Scots under the Earl of Eglinton. He had also 500 dragoons and 600 musketeers. In the centre it appears that the foot were drawn up in fourteen brigades: five in the first line, four each in the second and third, and one in reserve. Lord Fairfax seems to have commanded his own foot in the centre of the line: Manchester's on the left were under Major-General Lawrence Crawford, and the Scots under Major-General Sir James Lumsden. The total strength of the foot is estimated at 11,000. On the left, facing Byron, Cromwell commanded eight regiments of horse and two of dragoons; he himself led the first line, while the third consisted of Scots under Major-General David Leslie.

Cromwell's strength was about the same as Thomas Fairfax's on the other wing.

Leven decided to attack. He cannot have known of the dissensions in the opposite camp, but his forces were superior and he probably reasoned that, in view of the previous withdrawal of his own infantry and their hasty reassembly, and the lateness of the hour, Rupert would conclude that no action was likely; he would thus achieve surprise. And so it turned out. Eythin was far from co-operative, and Rupert, whatever his private views on the subject, for once sacrificed the initiative.

There are three main versions of what happened. According to Cholmley's, which is probably the most reliable, Eythin disagreed with Rupert's marshalling of the army as being too near the enemy, and in a place of disadvantage. He then advised against an attack, saying: 'Sir, your forwardness lost us the day in Germany, where yourself was taken prisoner.' Rupert allowed himself to be persuaded, 'and therefore gave order to have provisios for his army brought from York, and did not imagine the enemy durst make any attempt; so that when the alarum was given, he was set upon the earth at meat a pretty distance from his troops, and many of the horsemen were dismounted and laid on the ground with their horses in their hands.'[59] A 'particular relation' concerning Marston Moor, 'found in a paper of notes by Clarendon on the affairs of the north', is included in his *History of the Rebellion*. It gives the following account:

> When Lt.-generall Kinge came up, prince Rupert showed the marq. and the earle [*sic*] a paper which he sayd was the draught of the battell as he meant to fight it, and asked them what they thought off it. Kinge answered, 'By God, sir, it is very fyne in the paper, but there is no such thinge in the ffeilds.' The prince replyed, not, etc. The marq. asked the prince what he would do? His highness answer'd, 'We will charge them tomorrow morning.' My lord asked him whether he were sure the enemy would not fall on them sooner? He answered 'No'; and the marquisse therefor going to his coach hard by, and calling for a pype of tobacco, before he could take it the enemy charged.[60]

The Duchess of Newcastle, who wrote a life of her husband designed above all to laud and justify his actions, says nothing of any argument between Rupert and Eythin but records that the Marquess asked Rupert what he wanted him to do, and that Rupert replied that he would begin no action till early in the morning; whereupon Newcastle went to rest in his coach. 'Not long had my Lord been there, but he heard a great noise and thunder of shooting, which gave him notice of the armies being engaged.'[61]

However much these accounts may differ in detail, the essentials are not in dispute. Clearly it was Rupert's decision to postpone action till the following morning. If anybody saw the danger of an attack at that hour of the evening (it was seven o'clock or later) it was Newcastle: Rupert discounted it, and so allowed himself to be taken by surprise when, at the moment when he and his troops were eating their supper in the ditch and behind it, the whole Roundhead line swept down the slope upon them. As it did so a storm of rain and thunder broke over the field, extinguishing many of the Royalist musketeers' matches and leaving them only the butt-ends of their weapons to meet the advancing pikemen. The Parliamentary foot, 'going in a running march',[62] were soon over the ditch.

On the Roundhead left Cromwell's first charge, aided by Crawford's infantry, also carried the ditch. As they did so, Byron, not waiting to be attacked, counter-charged and met them head-on. In doing so he showed characteristic impetuosity; 'by the improper charge of the Ld Byron', says the *Rupert Diary*, 'much harm was done'. It appears to have been Rupert's plan to delay his counter-attack till his men could charge, with the support of musket-fire, when Cromwell's horse had the hedge and ditch behind them. Byron not only met the enemy at a disadvantage but masked the fire of the Royalist infantry. Cromwell's 'Ironsides' were perfectly disciplined; their controlled charge was too much for Byron's men, who broke and fled.

Rupert decided that he must personally repair the situation. Leaving his command post, he rode off to his right wing to rally his men. Cholmley relates what happened:

Upon the alarum the Prince mounted to horse and galloping up to the right wing, met his own regiment turning their backs to the enemy which was a thing so strange and unusual he said "swounds, do you run, follow me,' so they facing about, he led them to a charge, but fruitlessly, the enemy having before broken the force of that wing, and without any great difficulty, for these troops which formerly had been thought unconquerable, now upon a panic fear, or I know not by what fate, took scare and fled, most of them without striking a stroke, or having the enemy come near them, made as fast as they could to York. . . .[63]

Cholmley probably exaggerated the rout. There was some hard fighting, during which Cromwell was wounded, though not seriously. Whether or not he left the field to have his wound dressed is uncertain; however, he was soon rallying his men for any further counter-attack Rupert might put in with his remaining cavalry.

It was on this wing that the Roundheads' initial success was most complete. In the centre Lord Fairfax's and Manchester's foot, supported by the Scots, were pressing forward. They broke through the first line, capturing three guns in the process; but when they came up against Newcastle's Whitecoats they met with fierce resistance. Newcastle himself came forward, put himself at the head of a troop of gentlemen volunteers, and led them in a charge. Fairfax's infantry were held up, and for the moment forced back.

On the eastern wing Sir Thomas Fairfax attempted, like Cromwell, to drive the Royalist cavalry off the field; but he was far less successful. The ground was more difficult on this right wing, broken up by ditches and clumps of furze. Fairfax himself charged gallantly with 400 men, breaking through part of Goring's line and riding in pursuit towards York. But the bulk of the Royalist horse had the best of it, and when Fairfax returned to the field he found himself among the victorious Cavaliers and in imminent danger of capture. 'I was gotten in among the Enemy,' says his own account of the battle, 'which stood up and down the Field in several bodies of Horse. So, taking the Signal [a white handkerchief, or a piece of paper] out of my hat, I passed through, for one of their own Commanders; and so got to my Lord of Manchester's Horse in the other Wing; only with a cut in my cheek which was given me in the first charge, and a shot [which] my horse received.'[64]

The Royalist charge, led by Goring and Sir Charles Lucas, had routed the rest of Fairfax's cavalry. Some of Goring's horse got out of hand and fell to looting the enemy's baggage; but most of the force remained intact. In this part of the battle the Cavaliers had triumphed.

Goring's success was exploited and had its effect on the centre. Here the Royalist foot were with difficulty holding out when Lucas swung the second line of Goring's cavalry to the right against their assailants. The sequence of events is not easy to determine, but either at this moment or slightly earlier Sir William Blakiston's cavalry brigade, in reserve in the centre, launched an attack on Lord Fairfax's infantry opposite. The result was wild confusion among the right and centre of the Roundhead infantry. Many of Fairfax's men turned and fled, and the panic spread to the Scots on their right.

This temporary Royalist success in the centre had a quite remarkable effect on the Parliamentary high command. The sight of the panic-stricken soldiers, bolting to the rear past Cromwell's Plump, convinced Leven's staff that 'the battle was irretrievably lost, seeing they were fleeing upon all hands, therefor they humbly entreated his excellence to retire, and wait his better fortune'.[65] And Leven took their advice without further investigation, riding from the battlefield and not drawing rein till he reached Leeds. Lord Fairfax acted equally promptly, making for his house at Cawood. Of the three allied army commanders only Manchester remained in the field.

Yet the battle was very far from being lost. Cromwell on the left was still fighting it out with Rupert, who returned no more to his command post. The details are impossible to disentangle. Cholmley's account makes it appear that Rupert attacked immediately Byron's men began to break, and that he was defeated in a single action. But it is probable that there was more than one counter-charge, and that fierce fighting continued for most of the time that the Royalists were pulling the battle round at the other end of the field. As Brigadier Young remarks, in an action such as this 'the winning side was the one with the last reserve'.[66] This advantage was with the Parliamentarians. It was David Leslie's Scots cavalry, charging in from the flank, who delivered the *coup de grâce*. Rupert's horse were routed, and he himself, cut off from his own Life Guards, is said to have hidden himself in a beanfield as the defeated troops swept by. He escaped capture, but took no further effective part in the battle.

The last phase was at hand as darkness came on. Having dealt with Rupert, Cromwell's horse, keeping admirable formation, wheeled to the right. Sir Thomas Fairfax joined them with such of his own cavalry as he had managed to keep with him, and the whole of the Roundhead left wing swung round to take the Cavalier centre in the flank. The scene here was now one of the wildest confusion, but those Royalist foot who still maintained discipline fell back as the attack developed, and the Whitecoats took up a defensive position in White Syke Close in front of Wilstrop Wood.

Cromwell now executed the brilliant manoeuvre that finally turned the tables. Supported by Leslie, he led his cavalry right round behind the Royalist line and confronted Goring on the eastern wing. It was an extraordinary situation. The whole front had swung round on a south-north axis; the Cavaliers were being forced back to the south-east, in the direction in which they had originally hoped to advance; and Goring, turning about, stood in what had been Fairfax's station to face an attack from the very spot from which he had first charged. And at this crucial point in the battle the higher command on both sides had virtually ceased to exist. Leven and Lord Fairfax were far away; Rupert was cut off from his army. Manchester was content to follow his forceful subordinate, and Newcastle and Eythin, if they were still in the field, exercised little influence.

How long this last phase took is uncertain; but the battle ended in moonlight. Cromwell had gained the initiative. Goring's cavalry were now in considerable disorder, and proved no match for Cromwell's Ironsides. These were supported by the Scots infantry, who had stood firm under Baillie and Lumsden and now rallied to the attack. Lucas had been taken prisoner, and Goring's horse were now totally routed. Goring himself escaped from the battlefield and fled into Lancashire.

The end was at hand. With the advance of Manchester's army the resistance of the Royalist infantry crumbled – with one gallant exception. Newcastle's Whitecoats in White Syke Close, after all their comrades had fallen or surrendered, refused quarter and resisted almost to the last man. The three principal generals of the Royalist forces made their way to York, which obviously could not now be held for long. Rupert arrived there late at night. Separated from his troops and surrounded by the enemy, he had 'killed 4 or 5 with his owne hands, and at last hee brake strongly through them'.[67]

Marston Moor, where nearly 40,000 men were engaged, was probably the biggest battle ever fought on English soil. It was an action of inextricable confusion, out of which it is difficult to weave a coherent narrative. Many gallant deeds were performed, but tactical direction at the highest level was almost totally lacking. Only Cromwell seems to have had throughout a clear idea of what he was doing and intended to do, and he was undoubtedly the chief agent of victory.

Casualties on the Royalist side were heavy. It has been estimated that the dead numbered more than 4,000, with 1,500 taken prisoner. The Parliamentarians suffered much less: possibly as few as 300 killed, though many were wounded.

It is hard to account for Rupert's failure. Till now his military career in England had been one of almost unbroken success. In the most exacting circumstances he had proved himself masterful, self-confident, resourceful; decisive alike in planning and execution. His admirers had come to look on him as invincible. Yet at Marston Moor he made mistake after mistake. He mishandled Newcastle; then insisted on joining battle when, after his brilliant march to the relief of York, there was no need to do so. Having made that decision, he failed to fall on the enemy when they were in disarray and in semi-retreat. Then, when his forces were in action, he abandoned the direction of his armies and involved himself with the affairs of one portion of the front. His was the supreme command, but he can hardly be said to have exercised it. The truth would seem to be that for once he was uncertain of himself; that he was acting against his own better judgement, and that this induced hesitation and confusion of mind. Left to himself, he would perhaps not have chosen to fight the Roundheads on Marston Moor. But there was that letter from the King. He had no means of knowing of Charles's victory at Cropredy Bridge, and he may have truly thought that the kingdom was lost if he did not fight and defeat the armies arrayed against him. He had failed. But his spirit was unbroken. The *Rupert Diary* tells us of the conversation that took place between the Prince, Newcastle and Eythin when they met in York on that night of disaster; and the contrast in their reactions to defeat is revealing:

. . . Sayes Geall King what will you do? Sayes the P I will rally my men.
Sayes Geall King now you what Ld Newcastle will do?

Sayes Ld Newcastle I will go into holland (looking upon all as lost).

The P would have him endeavour to recruit his fforces. No (sayes he)
I will not endure the laughter of the Court, and King sayd hee would go
with him; and so they did and left the Governour of York with what force
he had, to defend himself. . . .

So Prince Rupert retraced his steps to Shropshire to recruit new
forces for the King; York and the north were irretrievably lost, but
there might still be hope in the west. He left many gallant men behind
him, who would fight no more; and doubtless he grieved for them. One
individual casualty must be mentioned, for it was assuredly not the
least of the Prince's sorrows. Boye, his beloved poodle, had been tied
up at the opening of hostilities. But he slipped his collar and followed
his master into battle. He was found among the dead on the field of
Marston Moor.

EXTINCTION OF HOPE

REJOICING in London, when the news of Marston Moor reached the Parliament, knew no bounds. Pamphlets sang the praises of the northern generals (who in truth had not covered themselves with much glory) as the prospect of final victory loomed in sight. The extreme Puritan element exulted particularly in the death of Boye, and in Rupert's obvious grief. A poem was soon in circulation with the title 'A Dogs Elegy, or Ruperts Tears', of which a few lines will indicate the tone:

> Lament poor *Cavaliers*, ay, howl and yelp
> For the great losse of your *Malignant Whelp*,
> Hee's dead! Hee's dead! No more alas can he
> Protect your *Dammes*, or get Victorie.
> How sad that *Son* of *Blood* did look to hear
> One tell the death of this shagg'd *Cavalier*,
> Hee rav'd, he tore his Perriwig, and swore,
> Against the Roundheads that hee'd ne'er fight more:
> Close couch'd, as in a field of *Beanes* he lay,
> Cursing and banning all that live-long day;
> Thousands of Devills Ramme me into Hell,
> Or may I live and die an Infidell,
> The Day's quite lost, wee are all confounded,
> And made a prey to every paltry *Roundhead*; . . .

There was corresponding dejection among the Royalists, aggravated by the fact that false rumour, spread by the premature flight of so many of the Roundhead troops, gave high hopes destined quickly to be dashed. The King had moved westward again after Cropredy Bridge, and he was at Evesham when, on 5 July, 'His Majesty had a brief express from *Newark*, implying that Prince *Rupert* had on *Tuesday* before utterly defeated the *Scots, Fairfax* and *Manchester's* Armys before York'.[1] Then came reality.

Rupert's critics at court of course made the most of his defeat, especially when it was learned that he had left York to its fate. Clarendon records bitterly that

. . . the like was never done or heard or read of before; that two great Generals, whereof one had still a good army left, and the other had the absolute commission over the northern counties and very many considerable places in them still remaining under his obedience, should both agree in nothing else but in leaving that good city and the whole country as a prey to the enemy – who had not yet the courage to believe that they had the victory.[2]

Clarendon, however, was no soldier. Rupert's judgement was based on sound military principles as understood in his day. York after Marston Moor was indefensible (it surrendered to the Fairfaxes on 16 July) and if Rupert had attempted to hold it with his now shattered force he would have faced not only inevitable defeat but also the risk of being cut off from all contact with the King's forces to the south. The only hope lay in moving once more towards the west and reassembling and consolidating the remains of his army.

The King himself continued to give his nephew his complete support. He refrained from all recrimination, deep though his disappointment must have been, and his letters were as cordial as ever. 'As concerning your generositye & particular Fidelity & Frendship to me,' he wrote a few weeks after Marston Moor, 'I have an emplicit faith in you: this at all tymes shall be made good by your loving Oncle & faithfull frend Charles R.'[3]

In truth the position did not yet seem hopeless. There were still substantial forces in being in the west, with the prospects of further recruitment there and in Wales. The King's own military prestige had never been greater, while the higher Parliamentary command was disorganized and disunited. And a counter-offensive was shortly to be mounted in Scotland which, ephemeral though it was to prove, for the brilliance of its design and execution had no parallel in the Civil War.

Prince Rupert's movements after Marston Moor can be followed in the journal of his marches, though the details there given cannot easily be reconciled with the succinct statement in the *Rupert Diary* that he 'march'd away into Shropshire . . . taking with him all the Northern Horse which the E of Newcastle left with his; and brought them into his quarters in Wales'. The *Diary* doubtless telescoped events, for the *Journal* makes it clear that the Prince's route back to his headquarters was anything but direct and that he did not re-enter Shropshire before the end of July.

On the day after the battle he moved to Thirsk, where 'Sir Robert Clavering came to us with 1,300'.[4] On 4 July he moved on to Richmond, 'staying for the scattered troopes';[5] this would appear to have been the most northerly point in England that he ever touched. Here he met Montrose, who had crossed the border to help him but arrived too late.

All the Scottish general could now do was to supply some troops to reinforce Rupert's depleted forces: then he went north again to organize his gallant, desperate rising on behalf of his King in his own country.

From Richmond Rupert proceeded on 7 July to Bolton Castle; then to Ingleton, to Hornby in Lancashire, to Garstang, to Preston, and north to Kirkby Lonsdale in Westmorland, where he arrived on the 18th. He then turned south again to Garstang and Preston, and on Monday, 22 July, 'to Latham hall. Erle of Darbye gone'.[6] Thence to Liverpool, and on the 25th to Chester. At this point there is a gap of nearly a month in the *Journal*, but he was still at Chester on 5 August. Towards the end of that month he was recruiting in Wales.

Meanwhile King Charles in the south, having defeated Waller and relieved the pressure on Oxford, now turned to deal with Essex. The Parliamentary commander, after relieving Lyme, had decided to invade Cornwall; and as he moved westwards the King, joining forces with Sir Richard Grenville and Prince Maurice which gave him an army estimated at 16,000 men, arrived on 26 July at Exeter.

In the campaign that followed, King Charles was very much in command of his troops. His success at Cropredy Bridge had given him the confidence he so badly needed, and he acted with authority and vigour. Essex reached Bodmin on 28 July, and at the same time Charles advanced to Launceston, twenty miles away. Grenville, who had been blockading Plymouth, simultaneously advanced from the south-west, and Essex, with his army of 10,000 men, found himself in the gravest danger. He moved south to Lostwithiel, and on 6 August the King called on him to surrender and come over to him, promising him 'eminent Marks of my Confidence and Value'.[7] Essex refused, and King Charles was poised for an attack when movement was delayed by a sensational incident.

Wilmot, Lieutenant-General of the Horse and now Viscount Wilmot of Athlone by the death of his father, had been falling increasingly under suspicion as a subversive influence; according to Clarendon 'during the whole march he discoursed in all places that the King must send to the Earl of Essex to invite him to a conjunction with him, that so the Parliament might be obliged to consent to a peace'.[8] Suddenly, on 8 August, the blow fell. The King's army was encamped at Boconnoc, three miles east of Lostwithiel, and there, in the presence of his troops, Wilmot was arrested, deprived of his command, and charged with high treason. He was sent under guard to Launceston, and thence to Exeter.

The causes of this dramatic reversal of favour, conducted with the maximum of publicity, are not easy to unravel. Wilmot was always a

Royalist, and was to live to become one of the most intimate friends of the next King of England. He does appear to have been in communication with Essex, but further light was not destined to be thrown on the charge of treason. The King, grateful no doubt for Wilmot's good service at Marlborough, Cirencester, Roundway Down and elsewhere, offered him the chance of leaving the country as an alternative to standing trial. A few weeks later Wilmot departed to France.

Rupert was only indirectly involved. When preparing for Wilmot's fall the King had sent to his nephew for Goring, whose reputation stood high after his conduct at Marston Moor; and Goring was now given the vacant post. Wilmot with his easy-going ways was popular with the troops, and while Rupert, who was far away at Chester, probably had nothing to do with Wilmot's arrest (though he certainly cannot have been displeased at it), the King evidently thought it politic to associate his nephew's name with what had been done. 'Immediately after [Wilmot's dismissal] His Majesty attended by the Principal Officers of His Army rode to every division of the Horse, and there declared, that at the Request of his Nephew Prince *Rupert*, and upon his Resignation, he had made Mr. *Goring* General of the Horse, and therefore commanded them to obey him.'[9] At the same time Percy, the far from competent General of the Ordnance, a close supporter of Wilmot, resigned and was replaced by Hopton. From the military point of view both changes were for the better.

The Wilmot crisis turned out to be a nine days' wonder and the Royalists closed in on the enemy. Grenville entered Bodmin and blocked Essex's way to the north, while Goring and Sir Jacob Astley occupied St Blazey and St Austell, south-west of Lostwithiel. Essex was hemmed in on all sides, with but a tenuous link with the sea at Fowey. The Committee of Both Kingdoms had promised support, and the Earl of Warwick was on his way with the Roundhead fleet; but contrary winds held him up, and Essex's position was becoming desperate. It became more so when on 21 August Prince Maurice and the Earl of Brentford (Lord Forth's new title) stormed Beacon Hill, east of Lostwithiel.

The end came with the close of the month. At 3 a.m. on 31 August Sir William Balfour, Parliament's most brilliant cavalry leader, broke out of the trap in a skilful surprise manoeuvre, but the foot under Philip Skippon were demoralized, and on 1 September Skippon surrendered; a total of thirty-six cannon, 10,000 small arms, and several wagon-loads of powder and match, badly needed by the Royalists, were given up. Essex had not waited for the end. He escaped by sea in a fishing-boat and was rowed out to one of Lord Warwick's ships.

Almost simultaneously with the King's victory in the south-west, there began, in Scotland, the war's most brilliant military episode. Montrose had been lingering in the north, hoping for help in creating a diversion in his own country in support of his King. But after his meeting with Rupert at Richmond he was forced to realize that no assistance could be expected from that quarter. Undismayed, he decided to launch his venture on his own.

In July a force of Irish, sent by the Earl of Antrim, had landed in the Macdonald country in the Western Highlands, thus providing the only rallying-point for a Royalist rising in Scotland. The Marquess of Argyll, leader of the Covenanters, sent a force from Edinburgh to engage the invaders, and as he did so Montrose laid his plans. King Charles, though he still did not fully trust his most loyal supporter in the northern kingdom, had in February named him Lieutenant-General in Scotland, and in May had created him a marquess. Armed with the King's commission, Montrose on 18 August slipped over the border with only two companions, disguised as their groom, and a few days later presented himself in the Irish camp.

He was promptly accepted as leader, and in the days that followed, with the magnetic qualities of leadership he possessed, he persuaded the clansmen, Stewarts and Robertsons as well as Macdonalds, to rally to the royal cause. Quickly he found himself in command of 2,000 men – ill-armed, ill-clad, but hardy Highland warriors with intimate knowledge of the hills – and at their head raised the King's standard at Blair Castle. He then marched rapidly into the Tay Valley, reinforced on his way by his own clan, the Grahams, who like others who joined him had been called out to fight the Irish invaders, and made for Perth where a force of Covenanters, 700 horse and 6,000 foot, awaited him under Lord Elcho.

Montrose, outnumbered by at least two to one, confronted Elcho on 1 September at Tippermuir, three miles outside Perth. Elcho attacked with his cavalry, but the Highlanders, from slightly higher ground, hurled themselves on them with wild yells and brandishing their primitive weapons, and the Lowland horsemen broke in terror. Fired to enthusiasm by Montrose's leadership, the Irish then attacked and overran Elcho's infantry. By sunset the rout was complete and Montrose entered Perth in triumph.

It was the first of a series of dazzling victories. From Perth he turned north-eastwards, gathering forces as he went, and on 13 September took Aberdeen. Argyll was now in pursuit with substantial forces, but Montrose drew back into the hills and turned south again through the Spey valley. It was now that he displayed his genius for guerilla warfare. His ragged force of Highland clansmen, increasing all the time as the fame of his leadership spread, had neither training nor (in the military sense) discipline. But Montrose could control them, and by his speed of movement he left Argyll helpless, leading him some 200 miles through the Highlands, harassing him with lightning raids while the Covenanters' army, in a state of growing demoralization, never caught sight of their elusive foe's main body. At Fyvie Castle he allowed them to catch up with him, and then, after inflicting severe damage on them, vanished once more into the hills. Argyll could pursue no further. He returned to Edinburgh and then, having laid down his command, made for his own lands in the Campbell country to the west.

There Montrose fell on him. Winter was approaching, and the mountain passes were, according to normal military canons, impassable. But Montrose led his wild clansmen through the November snows, and in mid-December descended on Argyll's stronghold at Inverary. Argyll was taken completely by surprise, and like Essex after his Cornish defeat made his escape by sea. By the end of the year Montrose was master of the Highlands.

Only gradually did the news of these successes infiltrate into the royal circle, and their effect on the military situation in England was small. If Montrose hoped by his operations to relieve the pressure exerted by the Scots army south of the border, he was not immediately successful. Leven remained obstinately in the north of England. On 19 October he stormed Newcastle-upon-Tyne, which he had been besieging since Marston Moor; but this was the Scots' only activity. Argyll was left to fight Montrose with no assistance from the south.

Meanwhile King Charles, after his triumph in the south-west, left Grenville to blockade Plymouth, still in Roundhead hands, and moved eastwards with the aim of relieving the garrisons of Banbury Castle, Basing House and Donnington Castle, all under severe pressure from the Parliamentary forces. These forces were in poor shape, and the commanders were bickering as usual; but could they but unite they could put some 17,000 men into the field while the King had not more than 10,000. Essex had landed at Southampton and was endeavouring to restore his shattered army. Waller was in the Farnham area on the borders of Hampshire and Surrey, while Manchester, still with Cromwell as his right-hand man, was advancing towards Reading.

Moving from Devon into Dorset, the King halted at Sherborne, and on 20 September he sent for Rupert, who had now established his headquarters in Bristol. A consultation took place, and Rupert clearly saw that for King Charles to court battle without reinforcements would be rash, to say the least; the Roundheads might be disorganized, but they were potentially very much stronger than the King's forces. Better to wait till the levies which Rupert was busily recruiting in Wales and the west could be brought to join him. So 'there it was resolved we should draw all our forces together, and make our Rendezvous at Marlborough, and the Kg then promised the P . . . that he would not engage the Enemy till the P came to him'.[10]

The King therefore moved on while Rupert returned to Bristol. General Charles Gerard had done good recruiting work in Wales, and the Prince busied himself in assembling the forces raised and preparing to join the King. Charles, however, with the self-confidence born of his recent victories, ignored the promise he had made to his nephew. Instead of turning north to meet Rupert at Marlborough, he continued to advance due east to relieve Basing and Donnington. On 15 October he entered Salisbury.

The Roundheads succeeded in combining to meet the threat. Essex had fallen sick (or claimed to have), but the remnants of his army were led north by Skippon and Balfour; Waller, after being driven from Andover in a skirmish with Goring, fell back to Basingstoke, and there was joined on 19 October by Manchester. Skippon arrived there on the following day, and the three armies, though with no clear overall command, were concentrated in force. It was the situation which Rupert had foreseen, and against which he had attempted to guard by making his uncle promise to wait for him.

The King pressed on, reaching Whitchurch on this same 20 October, and Kingsclere on the following day. A battle was now inevitable. 'This speedy Advance at that time,' wrote Sir Edward Walker, 'was by some esteemed the first and only Error that had been committed since His Majesty left *Oxford*, for now we were engaged and could not in Honour retreat; neither could we give any Relief to *Basing*, the Rebels then lying about it'.[11]

Too late, King Charles realized the danger. He turned north on the 22nd to Newbury, where he took up a strong position north of the town. But the Parliamentary armies were on his heels. With a strength of 17,500 horse and foot, they advanced on Newbury, while the King reduced his own strength to 9,000 by sending a brigade of horse to the relief of Donnington. On 27 October the Parliamentary armies attacked. They were fully informed of the Cavaliers' strength and dispositions by Sir John Urry, who had chosen this moment to make one of his periodical changes of side.

The Second Battle of Newbury was chiefly remarkable for the out-flanking movement by which Waller, marching thirteen miles by night round the north of the Royalist position, took the King and Prince Maurice in the rear. The fighting, which went on for most of the day, ended in favour of the Roundheads, but that night the King skilfully slipped away northward between the attacking armies, making for Bath and a junction with Prince Rupert, while most of his army escaped to Wallingford and Oxford.

Rupert was horrified. His uncle had ignored his advice, broken the promise he had made him, and thrown away the advantage his previous successes had given him. The Prince had apparently no notion what the King was up to until after the battle. 'Oct 28 the P marched to Marsfield; & meets one Coll Tuke Heleby; who told him the Kg would speak with him in Bath; and that he had been beaten; which was an astonishment to the P; it being contrary to his promise.'[12]

The Prince's advice was now to march back to Oxford, and this was done. His Welsh levies under Gerard were now with him, and the possibility was discussed of a counter-attack on the Parliamentary armies at Newbury. Meanwhile the King was in a chastened mood, and anxious to show that his confidence in his nephew was undimmed. Earlier in the year the question of giving Rupert supreme command of the royal armies had been mooted; now it was put into practice.

It had become obvious that the Earl of Brentford was no longer equal to his duties. He had been a good, brave and loyal officer, but he was old and tired, and had taken to the bottle. He had been wounded at Newbury, and was now persuaded to retire. His command was given to Prince Rupert, who on 6 November 1644, in a ceremony on Bullingdon Green, was declared General of all the King's forces in England, as well as Master of the Horse. Yet Rupert considered it politic that he should not be officially commander-in-chief. 'For when the King declared his nephew prince Rupert to be general, in the place of the earle of Brayneford, his highness desired that there might be no general in England but the Prince of Wales, and that he might receive his commission from him; which his majesty took well; and so that commission of generalissimo was likewise given to the Prince, when in truth it was resolved that he should act no part in either, but remain quiet in Bristol, till the fate of all armies could be better discerned.'[13] The nominal generalissimo was at this time fourteen years of age, and an ardent admirer of his cousin.

At last Prince Rupert was supreme commander of the royal armies under the King, with the principal voice in laying down strategy. But it was late in the day.

Three days afterwards the King and Rupert advanced on the Parliamentary armies in the neighbourhood of Newbury. The objective was the relief of Donnington Castle and the recovery of the ordnance left there; all of which was accomplished without difficulty. The Roundhead higher command was already disintegrating, and little resistance was offered; but the Royalists did not feel equal to launching a full-scale attack – 'it was not then thought fit to fight, tho' the P was for it'.[14]

Some minor skirmishing took place at Donnington which was later dignified by the name of the Third Battle of Newbury.

So the year 1644 drew to its close with little more in the way of serious fighting. The intrigues at Oxford were renewed. The mercurial Digby had for a brief space swung over to Rupert's side, but now he was working as hard against him as ever, in temporary alliance with Goring, who since his appointment as Lieutenant-General of the Horse in place of Wilmot had nourished hopes of being appointed to an independent command. Neither Goring nor Digby trusted the other, but they were ready to combine against Rupert and Digby encouraged Goring's ambition.

Faced once more with the machinations of his enemies, Rupert fell into one of his blackest moods. He had expected, in addition to his other promotions, the post of Colonel of the Life Guards; it would hardly have added to his authority, and it is unlikely that he would have objected very strongly to its being given to another, had not Digby been involved. As it was, he actually contemplated throwing in his hand and leaving the kingdom, as is recounted in the *Rupert Diary*:

> ... ffrom thence they came to Malmsbury & there by the advice of the Earle of Bristol [Digby] they would not let the P have the Command of the Guard; but says it was a Comand apart and it was given to the Ld Bernard Steward Bro: to the D of Richmond, to the great displeasure of the P. but by the persuasion of ffriends he submitted, tho' he was resolved to have layd down his command upon it.

This is an indication that Rupert was feeling the strain of more than two and a half years of war and almost incessant activity. It is not the only one. Thomas Carte prints a letter from Arthur Trevor which contains an unexpected passage: 'Prince Rupert is soe much given to his ease and pleasures, that every man is dishartened that sees it. This citty of Bristoll is but a great house of baudry, and will ruine the king; and by all I see, prince Rupert is resolved to lye by it.'[15]

Trevor was always a good friend to Rupert, and would not be inclined to spread false rumours to his detriment. He was garrulous, however, and prone to exaggeration. But there are difficulties in the way of accepting the genuineness of this letter. It is dated '13*th of Octo.* 1644' from Bristol, and its contents in general indicate that it was written before Second Newbury. Yet it states that 'the prince of Wales is made generalissimo, and prince Rupert capt. generall of all the king's armyes'[16] and these appointments were not made till 6 November. It adds, moreover, that 'the ould general Forth hath layd downe his commission, and since that tyme, with a fall from his horse, hath broke his shoulder'.[17] Brentford (Forth) was wounded at Newbury, and there is no mention of his having been injured before. The discrepancies seem irreconcilable.

Certainly the picture is not convincing. Rupert had a savage temper, and was quite capable of throwing in his hand, or at least threatening to do so, in a moment of stress if he felt himself slighted; but it is hard to imagine him, so long as he held the King's commission, giving up the struggle and wallowing in idle dissipation or drunken self-pity. His loyalty and his determination were stronger than that.

If Rupert did in any way lose his grip, he was soon himself again. During the winter of 1644-5 there was intense political activity both in Oxford and in London, and Rupert with his newly acquired authority took an active part. Towards the close of 1644 new negotiations for peace were inaugurated, and the Prince met the Parliamentary commissioners when they arrived in Oxford. There was little hope of an accommodation; both sides were mainly concerned to spin out time. The King would not budge an inch in the matter of a religious compromise; nor would he have any truck with the long list of his supporters who were to expect no pardon – a list headed by the names of Rupert and Maurice. This amused the King's two nephews. *'At the reading of the excepted persons names,'* wrote Bulstrode Whitelock, who was himself one of the commissioners, *'which the Earl of Denbigh read with great courage and temper: P. Rupert and P. Maurice being present when their names were read as excepted persons, they fell into a laughter, at which the King seemed displeased, and bid them be quiet.'*[18]

These preliminaries led in the new year to the long-drawn-out and futile negotiations known as the Treaty of Uxbridge.[19] Here the King's chief delegate was the Duke of Richmond. Rupert was in close touch with his friend as always, and took a keen interest in the discussions. He had begun to despair of an outright military solution, and to consider that the King's best hope might lie in negotiation. But there was never a chance. There were some things on which King Charles would never yield, and for their part the Parliamentary leaders were concerned to propose terms which they were sure would not be accepted.

They were intent on other matters, and from their point of view the Treaty of Uxbridge served to gain time for the momentous changes now projected at Westminster. The Committee of Both Kingdoms were disillusioned with the military situation. Their commanders in the field were at loggerheads. Essex was a broken reed, and now dissension had broken out between Manchester and his Lieutenant-General of the Horse, Cromwell. Two parties had emerged among the Roundheads. On the one hand there were the Presbyterians, who wanted a strict form of religious government in alliance with the Scots. Against them were those now coming to be known as 'Independents', sectaries of various descriptions who stood for the toleration of all creeds provided they were opposed to traditional Anglicanism (and of course to

Catholicism). Cromwell, whose political influence was constantly increasing, was emerging as the leader of the Independents, and he had the support of St John and Vane on the Committee of Both Kingdoms. Against them stood Manchester and the Presbyterians. But there was a corresponding military cleavage too. The Independents, and Cromwell above all, advocated prosecuting the war with all possible zeal. Manchester and his followers were inclined towards an accommodation with the King; the prospect of defeat in the field seemed to them hardly more perilous than that of victory if it should lead to dictation by the sectaries.

The quarrel came to a head in December, with Manchester and Cromwell denouncing each other in the Lords and Commons. Then the Parliamentary leaders moved. Factions in the army could be quelled only by removing their leaders, and a motion was introduced in Parliament that for the duration of hostilities no member of the Lords or Commons should hold any military or naval command. The Self-Denying Ordinance passed the House of Commons on 19 December. In the Lords the struggle was protracted, but the Committee of Both Kingdoms pressed the case with skill and subtlety, and in April 1645 the opposition succumbed.

The ostensible object of the Ordinance was to repair the disorganization of the army. This it achieved. But there was a deeper design – to ensure the triumph of Oliver Cromwell and the Independents. This was shown when, by a series of extensions of his commission, Cromwell himself was allowed, despite the Ordinance, to retain his command without giving up his seat in the House of Commons.

The Self-Denying Ordinance was a measure of far-reaching importance. Whose brain-child it was is uncertain. Cromwell had supported it from the outset; but Dame Veronica Wedgwood considers that the Ordinance 'had that about it which suggests the Parliamentary skill, the deceptive smooth approach of Harry Vane'.[20]

Its military result was the formation of a new, unified, formidable professional army. Under the Ordinance Essex, Manchester and Waller all laid down their commands, and out of their combined forces the New Model Army was formed. It was to consist of eleven regiments of horse, twelve of foot, and one of dragoons: a total of 22,000 men. County committees were ordered to recruit the necessary reinforcements, and provision for regular pay was made through the resources of Parliament and the City of London.

The command was given to Sir Thomas Fairfax. It was the wisest possible choice. Fairfax had proved himself an inspiring leader, popular with his troops and always ready to set a personal example of dash and courage; his military merits were recognized by friend and foe alike.

Moreover, though he inclined to the Presbyterian interest, he was no leader of a faction. He was content to be a soldier, and took no part in political intrigue. As his major-general in command of the foot he had the experienced and capable Philip Skippon. There was as yet no commander of the horse but the name of Oliver Cromwell, unrivalled as a trainer of cavalry and a tried commander in the field, was obviously kept in the organizers' minds. The New Model Army began to form at Windsor at the beginning of April 1645.

Throughout the winter Rupert was as active as ever, preparing for the spring offensive; but he had little enough to show for his pains. On 11 January he attacked Abingdon, abandoned in the previous summer, and penetrated into the town; but a counter-attack by General Richard Browne, the Governor, drove the Cavaliers back with considerable casualties. One result of this action was the loss of Sir Henry Gage, the Governor of Oxford, who died of wounds. In his place Rupert secured the appointment of his loyal friend Will Legge.

In Scotland Montrose continued his brilliantly successful campaign. Argyll had taken the field once more, and on 2 February Montrose won a resounding victory over his forces at Inverlochy; and now Leven was forced to detach some troops from his forces in the north of England as reinforcements for Argyll.

Elsewhere things looked black for the Royalists. Prince Maurice had succeeded to the command in Wales and the Marches, though without the extensive authority that Rupert had wielded. He found the difficulties too much for him, and on 29 January he wrote from Worcester to Rupert appealing for greater powers: 'I shall not need to mention any other particular than that which concerns the enlargement of my commission, and there I desire no farther latitude than the same from you which you had from the King. . . .'[21] A month later he failed to avert the fall of Shrewsbury, his brother's previous headquarters, which surrendered after a surprise attack by Parliamentary forces.

In the west a new phenomenon had appeared. War-weariness, was not confined to the armies. Many months of military exactions, foraging, billeting of troops and general living off the country had aroused the hatred of the people, and now the yeomen and peasants of Worcestershire, Herefordshire and Dorset were rising against their oppressors. Known as the 'clubmen', and armed with whatever bucolic weapons they could raise, they plagued the armies of both sides indiscriminately. But it was the Cavaliers who principally suffered.

At least part of the trouble in the west was caused by Goring, who in December 1644 had been appointed Lieutenant-General of Hampshire, Sussex, Surrey and Kent, and set up his winter quarters at Salisbury. Goring's oppressions and exactions caused widespread discontent. He was for the moment in favour with King Charles, from whom he extracted, probably by the agency of Digby, the privilege of taking his orders directly from the King. Rupert was furious at his authority being thus curtailed, and he evidently expressed his feelings to Goring, who on 22 January replied with a bland insolence all his own: 'Your Highness is pleased to think yourself disobliged by me, for desiring my orders under the King's hand. As I remember, sir, the reason I gave his Majesty for it, was the having more authority by that to guide the Council of this army to his obedience; and one reason I kept to myself, which was, I found all my requests denied by your hand, and therefore desired my orders from another.' He subscribed himself 'Your Highness's most dutiful and obedient Servant, George Goring'.[22]

The Treaty of Uxbridge had reached total deadlock, and in February the conference broke up. The Roundheads, scenting victory, prepared in growing confidence for what seemed likely to be the final offensive. The Independents, with their rejection of all compromise, were in the ascendant. In January the aged Archbishop Laud, who had been a prisoner of the Parliament throughout the war, was executed on Tower Hill; and this act of vindictiveness was followed by the hanging at Tyburn of a humbler victim, the Jesuit Father Henry Morse, who was chiefly noted for his work among the London sick in time of plague.

With the threat of renewed and more ruthless Parliamentary action it was decided at Oxford that it would be advisable for the King and the Prince of Wales to separate; for both to fall into the hands of the enemy would be irreparable disaster. The young Prince was therefore sent to Bristol, where on 5 March he set up his headquarters as nominal General of the West.

Rupert too moved westwards, setting up a new headquarters at Ludlow and increasing his forces by recruitment in Wales. His plan of campaign was for the King to link up with him and his brother Maurice at Hereford and for the combined armies to march north, relieve Chester and Pontefract, and drive back the Scottish army. Events were to determine otherwise.

Rupert's hopes and misgivings are shown in his letters to Will Legge. On March 11 he wrote: 'Hasten the ammunition . . . On Thursday we meet at Wellington; on Friday [cipher Rupert] and Maurice will join, if possible, near Ellesmere. If this succeed there will be some hopes left. . . . I am going about a nobler business; therefore pray God for me, and remember me to all my friends.'[23] On the 24th a further letter contained a clear reference to the machinations of Goring in his western command:

Dear Will,

Our army now is marching towards Herefordshire, to refresh after the Dutch fashion. You can easily imagine what it is that pressed us to go thither; it is not for fear of the enemy, for they are but weak, and keep their holds. Hasten the King with ordnance, horse, and foot, and doubt nothing. We are few, but shrewd fellows as ever you saw; nothing troubles us but that Prince Charles is in worse, and pray God that he were here. I expect nothing but ill from the West; let them hear that Rupert says so. . . .[24]

Rupert reached Hereford on 17 March. On the last day of the month he wrote to Legge saying he was making for Bristol. Another letter, dated 13 April, told Legge that the next of the Palatines, Prince Edward, was anxious to join Rupert and Maurice.

Had Edward come, there would have been four Palatine brothers in England. For Charles Louis was in London, set up in lodgings in White-hall by the Parliament, to whom as the probable victors he had now wholly committed himself. It was common report that he aimed at nothing less than the crown of England, as the Parliament's nominee should his uncle be defeated and deposed.

For the moment Rupert met with success. On 19 April, with Maurice, he relieved Reeston Castle, south of Chester, and a few days later suppressed a rising by Herefordshire clubmen, treating the countrymen with leniency. He was then joined by Astley, and routed Colonel Massey, Governor of Gloucester, at Ledbury.

But now the New Model Army was on the march. With remarkable speed Sir Thomas Fairfax had welded his new command into an efficient fighting machine, and at the end of April he took the field. His orders from the Committee of Both Kingdoms were first to relieve Taunton, besieged by Goring, and on 30 April he marched westward with 11,000 men. In the meantime Cromwell, with an independent force, was threatening the King's central army. On 23 April he defeated the Earl of Northampton at Islip, and next day induced the Governor of Bletchingdon House, Colonel Francis Windebank, to surrender. Windebank was condemned to death at a court-martial, and was executed at Oxford on May in spite of an attempt by Rupert to get him reprieved. Cromwell then moved westward into Berkshire and attempted to capture Faringdon Castle, but was beaten off on 29 April.

In May events moved fast. At the beginning of the month King Charles summoned his two nephews to meet him at Oxford, and at the same time Goring was ordered up from the west with his troops. The King had decided once more to leave Oxford with his army; with Rupert and Maurice he moved again into the Cotswolds, and on 8 May a general rendezvous was held at Stow-on-the-Wold. Sir Marmaduke Langdale had brought in the northern cavalry, and Lord Astley (Sir Jacob had recently been ennobled) his force of infantry. The King's total strength was some 5,000 foot and 6,000 horse.

Here, at a council of war, the strategy to be adopted was argued out. Rupert was still in favour of the northward march. Montrose was at the height of his triumphs; Leven was weakened by having to send reinforcements into Scotland, and his men, casting their eyes towards the troubles in their own country, had little interest in the southern struggles; their discipline was poor. Moreover Langdale's northern horse, had recently inflicted a defeat on Lord Fairfax at Pontefract, suggesting that a decisive campaign might free the north of England from Lord Fairfax and the Scots, avenge Marston Moor, open up communications with Montrose, and enable the royal army then to turn south again and engage Sir Thomas Fairfax's New Model Army without the danger of an enemy in the rear.

On the other side Digby and Goring were eager to try conclusions with the New Model Army as soon as possible. It would be hard to argue that they were wrong, though their motives were suspect. Goring was mainly concerned to safeguard his independent position in the west, while Digby was in one of his moods of optimism and his views were unencumbered with military knowledge. But the solution adopted was the worst possible one. The King, vacillating as he was so apt to do, agreed to a compromise. He and Rupert would march north, while Goring with his 3,000 horse would return into Somerset and head off the younger Fairfax now on his way to Taunton. Rupert acquiesced in this division of the forces: partly, it was suspected, for the sake of getting rid of Goring, who was becoming increasingly unreliable and more and more addicted to periods of drunken inactivity.

Meanwhile Fairfax had been diverted. He had got only as far as Blandford in Dorset when orders reached him from the Committee of Both Kingdoms to change his objective to Oxford. He detached a small force to continue to Taunton (which was relieved on 11 May), and retraced his steps.

King Charles and Rupert were on their way northward. At Evesham, where Rupert installed Will Legge's brother Robert as Governor, they were joined by a further force under Sir Henry Bard; while Sir Charles Gerard, after a successful action in South Wales, was able to send more reinforcements. On 9 May Montrose had won another splendid victory at Auldearn, which put paid to any question of Leven's moving south as the Committee of Both Kingdoms were urging him to do. The King and Rupert pushed on to Market Drayton, where they were joined by Lord Byron, and then eastwards to Stone and Tutbury on the borders of Staffordshire and Derbyshire.

It was at Tutbury that they heard of the new threat to Oxford. This was on 22 May, and on the same day Fairfax was joined by Cromwell and Browne and sat down before the Royalist capital.

No great alarm was felt. The risk had been calculated, and it was to be expected that the Roundheads would move when they found their main enemy had gone north. 'Oxford,' writes Clarendon, 'was known to be in so good a condition that the loss of it could not be in any degree apprehended, and nothing could more reasonably have been wished than that Fayrefax should be thoroughly engaged before it.'[25] Nevertheless, the threat could not be ignored. Rupert sent an urgent message to Goring enjoining him to bring his cavalry to a rendezvous at Market Harborough; and to draw Fairfax off from Oxford it was decided 'to fall upon some place possessed by the Parliament'.[26]

The place selected was Leicester, and thither the King's army marched. On 28 May a further reinforcement of 1,200 horse arrived under Sir Richard Willis, the Governor of Newark, and on the following day Leicester was invested. There was no sign of Goring, who in fact had retired to Bath and was taking little interest in the campaign.

Leicester was not strongly fortified, and was occupied by only a weak garrison; but when Rupert summoned the town on 30 May he found himself defied. Thereupon, at midnight, he stormed the town, attacking on three sides and breaching the walls within an hour. Having refused to surrender, the town was sacked, the shops and houses being ruthlessly pillaged. There were wild reports in the Roundhead pamphlets – the dread spectre of Magdeburg was once more raised – and however much they may have been exaggerated there was undoubtedly great loss of life. Clarendon admits that 'the conquerors pursued their advantage with the usual license of rapine and plunder, and miserably sacked the whole town, without any distinction of persons or places, churches and hospitals as well as other houses [being] made a prey to the enraged and greedy soldier to the exceeding regret of the King; who well knew that, how disaffected soever that town was generally, there were yet many who had faithful hearts to him, and who he heartily wished might be distinguished from the rest: but those seasons admit no difference of persons'.[27] Rupert at least did what he could to prevent a massacre. The Roundhead Sir Samuel Luke wrote within a few days of the storm: 'I hear that at the taking of Leicester at their first coming in they put men, women and children to the sword. In the end, Prince Rupert coming in, his mercy put an end to their cruelties, so far as it concerned the English. The Scots were all put to the sword, being 200 in number.'[28]

The storming of Leicester had the desired effect. Fairfax, on orders from Westminster, abandoned the siege of Oxford and moved north to meet the royal army. On 5 June he marched north-east towards Newport Pagnell, which he reached three days later. On the 10th he was joined by Cromwell, who was now officially appointed his lieuten-

Portrait of King James I,
carved by Prince Rupert

Portrait of Queen
Christina of Sweden,
drawn by Prince Rupert

Prince Rupert's dog, 'Boye'

ant-general in the New Model Army. The Committee of Both Kingdoms gave him a free hand, and he prepared to attack.

Before Fairfax's movements were known a further Royalist council of war had taken a decision to which once more Rupert was opposed. He was confident that Fairfax would break up the siege of Oxford, and was in favour of continuing the northward march, drawing the Roundheads after him so that he could turn and fight them on ground of his own choosing. The council, however, overruled him in favour of a plan to relieve Oxford. It was a fatal decision. When Langdale's northern horse learned that they were not to move in the direction of their own homes they broke into mutiny and rode off to Newark. The Cavaliers, their strength still further depleted by having to leave a garrison in Leicester, made a futile march south to Daventry while Fairfax and the New Model Army were moving northward to their left.

From Newport Pagnell Fairfax marched west to Stony Stratford and on 12 June the Royalists learned at Daventry that he was only five miles to the east of them. That night they withdrew to Market Harborough, where Goring had been ordered to meet them. But there was no Goring, and nor had Gerard joined them as expected. Rupert again urged the resumption of the northward march; it was not too late. But Digby, now supported by John Ashburnham, again had the last word; the King, not for the first time, allowed military expertise to yield to civilian enthusiasm. 'That Night,' wrote Sir Edward Walker, 'an Allarum was given, that Fairfax with his Army was quartered within six Miles of us. This altered our design, and a Council being presently called, resolutions were taken to fight; and rather to march back and seek him out, than to be sought or pursued, contrary (as 'tis said) to Prince *Rupert's* Opinion; it being our unhappiness, that the Faction of the Court, whereof the most powerful were the Lord *Digby* and Mr. *Ashburnham*, and that of the Army ever opposed and were jealous of others.'[29]

On 13 June Fairfax reached Guilsborough, four miles south of the village of Naseby. And that night his vanguard entered Naseby and surprised and captured some Royalist soldiers who had been on patrol and were now refreshing themselves in the village inn.

The news reached Market Harborough in the middle of the night. There was now no question of avoiding a battle, and immediate preparations were made to march out of the town and meet the enemy in the neighbourhood of Naseby.

The odds were formidable. The Royalist forces had been depleted in one way or another during the recent manoeuvres, though the mutiny of the northern horse was over and Langdale had them under control. Details of the total strength are given by Clarendon as follows:

. . . The main body of the foot was led by the Lord Ashley, (whom the King had lately made a baron) consisting of about two thousand and five hundred foot; the right wing of horse, being about two thousand, was led by prince Rupert; the left wing of horse, consisting of all the northern horse, with those from Newark, which did not amount to above sixteen hundred, was commanded by sir Marmaduke Langdale. In the reserve were the King's life-guard, commanded by the earl of Lindsay, and prince Rupert's regiment of foot, both which did make little above fifteen hundred; with the King's horse-guards, commanded by the lord Bernard Stuart, (newly made earl of Litchfield,) which made that day about five hundred horse.[30]

This makes a total of a little over 8,000 men. Clarendon, however, may have over-estimated the figures, and the most usual estimate is 7,500. Against these the Roundheads numbered not less than 12,000 – some 6,000 horse and rather more than 6,000 foot – and the total may have reached 14,000. The odds, in fact, were not far off two to one.[31]

The Royalists drew out of Market Harborough early on the morning of 14 June, and took up a defensive position on the ridge running from East Farndon to Oxendon, extending for about a mile and a half, two miles south of Harborough. Four miles to the south ran the Naseby ridge, immediately north of the village, and here Fairfax brought his army during the night. The King and Rupert had their troops in position by eight o'clock, and Rupert then sent his scoutmaster, Francis Ruce, out to reconnoitre the enemy's dispositions. Ruce seems to have been singularly inept, for although Fairfax was already taking up his position he came back saying he had been two or three miles forward but had seen no sign of the enemy.

This was not good enough for Rupert, and he promptly went forward for a personal reconnaissance. He soon came in sight of the enemy, but to his surprise they were moving not forward but back. What had happened was that Fairfax, accompanied by Cromwell with a detachment of his cavalry, had also been doing a reconnaissance and had moved forward from the Naseby ridge. There was boggy ground in front, and Cromwell suggested that Rupert would never put in a cavalry attack at such a point. As the object was to bring him into battle, it would be better to draw back to the top of the ridge and let the Cavaliers move forward over the bad ground and then attack uphill. Fairfax agreed, and the two generals led their horsemen back to the top of the hill. It was this movement that Rupert saw. He jumped to the conclusion that the Roundheads were, for some reason, withdrawing, and hoped to catch them on the wrong foot with an immediate attack. He sent a message back to the King, asking for the army to come up as soon as possible, and selected a position on Dust Hill, overlooking the open space called Broad Moor. According to Sprigge, the army 'made so much haste, that they left many of their ordnance behinde them'.[32] Fairfax meanwhile drew up his army not on the top of Naseby ridge but just below, so that most of it was hidden from the Royalists.

The Cavaliers' dispositions were as described by Clarendon – Rupert with his cavalry, and with his brother Maurice, on the right in front of what is now called Prince Rupert's Farm; Astley with the foot in the centre; Langdale's horse on the left straddling the road from Naseby to Sibbentoft. King Charles was in personal command, but he had promptly acceded to his captain-general's request for him to bring up the army, and it seems probable that the battle plan was Rupert's. In that case the Prince must be held responsible for the surprising decision that he himself should command the right-wing horse, instead of leaving this to Maurice and taking his natural position at the King's side with the reserve. As at Marston Moor, he seems to have been over-anxious to take an active part in the fighting rather than to exercise his proper function of command.

Fairfax meanwhile had drawn up his army in similar formation below the brow of the Naseby ridge. Cromwell commanded the cavalry on the right, facing Langdale; Commissory-General Henry Ireton was in command on the left, facing Rupert. In the centre the foot were in three lines under Skippon. A 'forlorn hope' of 300 musketeers was placed in front on the left. Eight guns were interspersed between the infantry regiment – more than the Royalists could boast, for they had been able to bring up only six light sakers. Artillery, however, played little part in the Battle of Naseby.

There was one unusual feature in the Roundheads' plan of battle. Running from the left of their line to the Royalist right was a wooded sector called Sulby Hedges, and behind these hedges were placed 1,000 dragoons under Colonel Okey. It was a dangerous position, for these men were forward of the line of battle and at right-angles to it, and a flanking movement might cut them off; but if, as expected, the Royalists launched a cavalry charge straight ahead towards Ireton's horse they could be enfiladed from the hedges. This manoeuvre is said to have been on a last-minute order by Cromwell in his capacity of cavalry commander, perhaps decided on when he saw who was leading the Royalist right wing.

Such was the position when the two armies faced each other about ten o'clock in the morning. Although the main body of Fairfax's army was invisible below the ridge, Rupert must by now have realized his mistake in thinking there had been a withdrawal. Nevertheless he adhered to his plan of attacking first, and the King ordered a general advance. As the Royalist army moved forward, the Parliamentarians marched up to the top of the ridge; concealment was no longer important.

The Royalists advanced in good order. On the right the tactics followed a familiar pattern. Rupert and Maurice led the horse forward at a brisk pace, keeping close to Sulby Hedges so that the field of fire of Okey's dragoons was limited; in fact such ragged volleys as were brought to bear caused little trouble. As they reached the valley they broke into a gallop, the cavalry charge that now was Rupert's trademark. At the same time Ireton, an inexperienced but a valiant commander, advanced down the hill to meet them. There was a clash, a mêlée, and Ireton broke through. His success was only momentary; 'he himself with great resolution fell in amongst the Musquetiers, where his horse being shot under him, and himself run through the thigh with a Pike, and into the face with an Halbert, was taken prisoner by the enemy'.[33] His capture put an end to the action. Rupert swept through the opposition, gathering momentum and pursuing the broken cavalry to the baggage-train which was about level with Naseby Church.

Rupert's less than 2,000 men had routed the 2,700 under Ireton; yet again the famed cavalry charge had proved irresistible. The baggage-train defenders refused quarter and put up a firm resistance, and Rupert decided to waste no time on them. Now came the task of pulling the troopers together and taking them back to wherever they might be needed in the main battle. This, as always, took time. Rupert's men were well organized; they were no longer the semi-trained enthusiasts of Edgehill. But a body of charging horsemen cannot be brought back into parade-ground formation in a moment. It was an hour before they were ready to return, and in this time many things had happened on the rest of the front.

In the centre the fighting was furious. Astley had some 4,000 men; Skippon probably nearly double that number. Yet the Cavaliers had the best of it. It was close-quarter fighting. 'The Foot on either side hardly saw each other,' wrote Sir Edward Walker, 'until they were within Carabine Shot, and so only made one Volley; ours falling in with Sword and butt end of the Musquet did notable Execution; so much as I saw their Colours fall, and their Foot in great disorder.'[34] Skippon himself was severely wounded, though he refused to leave the field. The Roundheads were being beaten back all along the line until Fairfax threw in his reserves, leading them forward himself to redress the balance. The New Model Army commander-in-chief was in his element. His helmet was struck off in the battle, and Whitelocke paints a vivid picture of him 'riding in the Field bare-headed up and down from one part of his army to another, to see how they stood, and what advantage might be gained, and coming up to his own Life Guard commanded by Colonel *Charles*

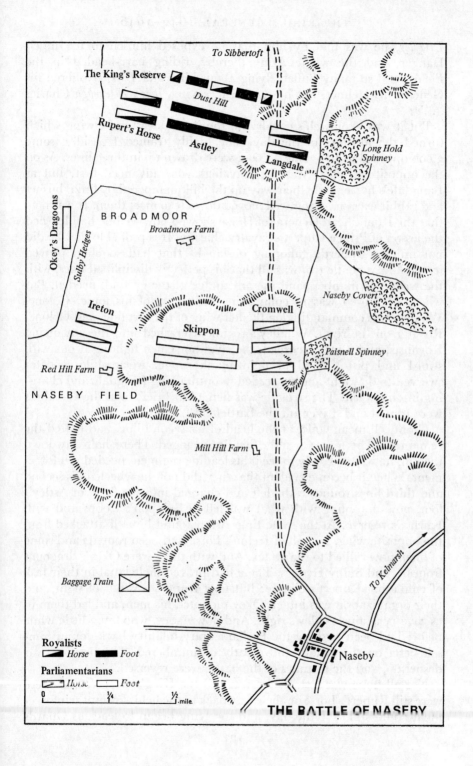

To Sibbertoft

The King's Reserve

Dust Hill

Rupert's Horse

Astley

Langdale

Long Hold Spinney

Okey's Dragoons

BROADMOOR

Broadmoor Farm

Sulby Hedges

Naseby Covert

Ireton

Cromwell

Skippon

Red Hill Farm

Paisnell Spinney

NASEBY FIELD

Mill Hill Farm

Baggage Train

To Kelmarsh

Naseby

Royalists
Horse   Foot

Parliamentarians
Horse   Foot

0   ¼   ½
                  1 mile.

THE BATTLE OF NASEBY

D'Oyley, he was told by him that he exposed himself to too much Danger, and the whole Army thereby, riding bare-headed in the Fields, and so many Bullets flying about him, and *D'Oyley* offered his General his Helmet, but he refused it, saying, *it is well enough* Charles . . .'35

But it was Cromwell's cavalry on the Roundhead right wing which turned the fortunes of the day. The highly trained Ironsides, some 3,000 opposed to Langdale's 1,600, were drawn up in three lines. As on the opposite wing, it was the Cavaliers who advanced first. But as Langdale's horse made their way up the hill, hampered by furze-bushes and rabbit warrens, Cromwell moved down it to meet them. It was now that the Roundhead General of Horse showed how well he had learned the lesson of Prince Rupert's cavalry charges. It is probable that he did not imitate Rupert's galloping onslaught that had so often proved irresistible; a gentle trot was all that his perfectly disciplined lines, with the weight of numbers and the advantage of the ground, needed. But where he scored was in committing only part of his force. Colonel Whalley was commanding on the left wing of the first line, and Colonel Rossiter on the right. Whalley's regiment crashed into the advancing Royalists, and a mêlée ensued, the rival horsemen fighting it out with sword and pistol, fired at point-blank range. Meanwhile Rossiter swerved to the right and succeeded in outflanking Langdale and charging in on his left. The struggle was fierce but brief; soon the Cavaliers were routed and driven off the battlefield.

Cromwell meanwhile, at the head of his second line, had halted the remainder of his force when the first line engaged. There, half-way down the hill, he waited coolly to see if his leading regiment needed reinforcement. When it became evident that they did not, he wheeled his second and third lines round to the left and charged into the flank of Astley's foot, now grappling with what was left of Skippon's troops and with Fairfax's reserve. At the same time Astley found himself attacked from the opposite wing. Not all of Ireton's horse had been routed; and some of them now rallied to the attack. And with them were Okey's dragoons from beyond Sulby Hedges. These had proved ineffectual in their task of enfilading Rupert's charge; but now Rupert was out of sight, and their organization was intact. Okey mounted his men, and led them in as cavalry against Astley's right. And now Astley, who but a little while before had been pushing the Parliamentary infantry back, found himself beset on three sides and greatly outnumbered. The position was desperate, and the fortunes of the battle were reversed.

Not all hope was lost. There was still the King's reserve, and there were still Rupert's horse on their way back to the field. Prompt reinforcement could still save the day, and the King began to lead his Guards forward towards the left flank. Then came the curious incident that proved fatal to his cause. It is thus related by Walker:

> At this instant the King's Horse-guards and the King at the Head of them were ready to charge those who followed ours, when a Person of Quality, 'tis said the Earl of *Cornwath*, took the King's Horse by the Bridle, turned him about, swearing at Him and saying, Will you go upon your Death? and at the same time the Word being given, March to the right Hand, (which was both from assisting ours or assailing them, and (as most concluded) was a civil Command for every one to shift for himself) we turned about and ran on the Spur almost a quarter of a Mile, and then the Word being given to make a Stand, we did so; though the Body could never be rallyed.[36]

Robert Dalzell, Earl of Carnwath, was a Scottish peer of no military distinction. Clarendon in his account of this episode definitely ascribes the action to the earl and calls him 'a man never suspected for infidelity, nor one from whom the King would have received counsel in such a case'.[37] Infidelity seems hardly to enter into the matter; Carnwath may be presumed to have been genuinely concerned for the King's safety. But it is plain that he panicked, that it was no business of his to interfere, and that his action was deserving of a court-martial. It is equally plain that King Charles, taken off his guard, lost control of the situation and allowed chaos to ensue. His fatal hesitancy may have come over him at the critical moment.

If only Rupert had been there it may be taken as certain that he would have averted the disaster. Where exactly he was at this precise moment is unknown. Walker says that 'by this time Prince *Rupert* was come with a good body of Horse from the right Wing'[38] but evidently he had not reached the spot where the King and Carnwath were. The reserve troops were in confusion and had lost their impetus, and he was too late to rally them.

There was little more. Fairfax marshalled his forces and prepared for a final assault. It was never delivered. The battle, which had lasted a bare three hours, was irretrievably lost, and the King led the scattered remnants of his army from the field. Cromwell's horse pursued them almost to Leicester, celebrating their victory by slaughtering 'above 100 Women and Souldiers Wives, and some of them of Quality',[39] whom they overtook on the way. All the Cavaliers' baggage fell into the hands of the enemy, including the King's cabinet containing his personal correspondence, of which the Parliamentarians were able to make good use in propaganda.

Casualties were not heavy. A recent estimate puts the total of Royalist dead at under 1,000, and of the Roundheads at not more than

150.[40] Naseby was not a battle on the scale of Marston Moor, but it was more decisive in its results.

It was a near-run thing, as Wellington said of a later and greater battle. Up to almost the end it might have gone the other way; and the Cavaliers with greatly inferior forces put up a magnificent fight against the highly professional New Model Army. Strategically the cardinal error had been to send Goring and his 3,000 horse back to the west; tactically the mistake was for Rupert to command on the right instead of staying with the King. Whether or not this was Rupert's fault must remain uncertain. It is possible that King Charles, confident of his military capacity, preferred to exercise full command himself and ordered his nephew to attack where he did. We shall never know.

At least a mile from the correct site stands an obelisk recording the outcome of the battle in the following stately phrases:

TO COMMEMORATE
THAT GREAT AND DECISIVE BATTLE
FOUGHT IN THIS FIELD
ON THE XIV DAY JUNE MDCXLV
BETWEEN THE ROYALIST ARMY
COMMANDED BY HIS MAJESTY
KING CHARLES THE FIRST
AND THE PARLIAMENTARY FORCES
HEADED BY THE GENERALS FAIRFAX AND CROMWELL
WHICH TERMINATED FATALLY
FOR THE ROYAL CAUSE
LED TO THE SUBVERSION OF THE THRONE
THE ALTAR AND THE CONSTITUTION
AND FOR YEARS PLUNGED THIS NATION
INTO THE HORRORS OF ANARCHY AND CIVIL WAR
LEAVING A USEFUL LESSON TO BRITISH KINGS
NEVER TO EXCEED THE BOUNDS
OF THEIR JUST PREROGATIVE
AND TO BRITISH SUBJECTS
NEVER TO SWERVE FROM THE ALLEGIANCE
DUE TO THEIR LEGITIMATE MONARCH
THIS PILLAR WAS ERECTED
BY JOHN AND MARY FITZGERALD
LORD AND LADY OF THE MANOR OF NASEBY
AD MDCCCXXIII

It is a fair epitaph. After Naseby there was never any chance of a Royalist victory in the English Civil War. And nobody saw this more clearly than Prince Rupert.

CHAPTER 7

BRISTOL AND AFTER

HAVING retreated to Leicester 'in disorder enough',[1] the King with his beaten army went on to Ashby-de-la-Zouch, where he arrived early on the morning of 15 June. It might have been expected that Fairfax, after the decisive victory of Naseby, would pursue these disorganized remnants without delay and prevent them linking up with those of the other Cavalier forces still in being. Instead he followed them only as far as Leicester, which fell to him on the 18th. Doubtless he took the view that King Charles was now a beaten man, that the final Parliamentary triumph could not be long staved off, and that therefore he need not hurry in following up his victory. Better to consolidate his position, wipe up pockets of resistance, and advance in good order and at a leisurely pace with the growing strength of the New Model Army.

His decision gave the King time to continue his retreat without precipitate haste. Charles with his two nephews, with Digby, and with his cavalry, moved by way of Lichfield, Wolverhampton and Bewdley to Hereford, which he reached on the day after the fall of Leicester. Here King and princes parted. This may well have been partly, and certainly ostensibly, for strategic reasons; but Rupert's distrust of Digby had flared up into open hate. Digby, plausible as ever, was putting it about that the disaster of Naseby was the fault of Rupert; and as Rupert had fought against his will, whereas the King on Digby's advice had insisted on seeking battle, the Prince was furiously resentful. On 18 June he wrote from Bewdley to Will Legge at Oxford:

... Pray let me know what is said among you concerning our last defeat. Doubtless the fault of it will be put upon [cipher Rupert]. Since this business, I find Digby hath omitted nothing which might prejudice [Rupert], and this day hath drawn a letter for the King to Prince Charles, in which he crosses all things that befel here in Rupert's behalf, I have shewed this to the King, and in earnest; and if, thereupon, he should go on and send it, I shall be forced to quite generalship, and march ... towards Prince Charles, where Rupert hath received more kindness than here. ...[2]

Whether or not the King sent the letter drafted by Digby to Prince Charles is not known; presumably not, for Rupert's patience was almost exhausted and he would almost certainly have carried out his threat to 'quit generalship'. This he did not do; he did, however, 'march towards Prince Charles'. He could stand Digby's company no longer, and the fickle King for his part may well have considered the atmosphere so electric that it would be best to separate the two. Accordingly, on 26 June, Prince Rupert rode to Cardiff and then, crossing the Severn, proceeded to Barnstaple, where the young Prince of Wales, in not altogether nominal command of his father's western army, had withdrawn from Bristol where the plague was already raging. Meanwhile Prince Maurice returned to Worcester, and at the beginning of July the King moved by easy stages to Raglan Castle in Monmouthshire, seat of the Catholic Marquess of Worcester.

Meanwhile Digby, nervous at the turn events had taken, and conscious that he had perhaps gone too far, was attempting to win Will Legge over to his side; a move anybody less sanguine would have ruled out as impossible. In a long letter from Hereford, undated but clearly written at the end of June, he wooed the Governor of Oxford with an effusion of flattery and cajolery, while at the same time, in a characteristic *volte-face*, paying tribute to Rupert and exonerating him from the charge of insisting on battle against the advice of others:

> . . . As for the particular aspersion upon him which you mention of fighting against advice, he is very much wrongd in it whether you meane in the generall or the particular of that day for in the generall when contrary to the advice of soe many it was once resolved yt wee should march the waye wee did, it was then the unanimous opinion of all that if Fairfaxe should follow us neere wee ought to turne upon him & fight with him before he could ioyne with the Scots & for the particular time place & circumstances of our fighting that day His Highness cannot be said to have gone against my ld Asteley or any mans advice for I am confident noe man was askt upon the occasion. I am sure no Councell called. I shall only say this freely to you yt I think a principall occasion of our misfortune was the want of you with us for had you been there I am persuaded yt when once we were come up too neare them as yt they could not goe away from us you would at least have asked some questions, whether having store of provisions with us, wee should rather have tryed to bring them to our Post then to have assaulted them instantly in theirs. . . . Well let us looke forwards; Give your Pr good advice, as to caution and value of counsell & God will yet make him an instrument of much happiness to the King & Kingdom & yt being I will adore him as much as you love him though he should hate as much Your faithfullest frein & servant

George Digbye[3]

No letter could be more typical of Digby. Equally typical of its writer was the reply. Blunt Will Legge told Digby firmly that he had been informed on Digby's authority – by his servant, one Felton – that Rupert had fought in opposition to Astley's advice, and 'with people much distracted for the great loss, these words went far to the Prince's prejudice'. Legge continued:

> ... I am extremely afflicted to understand from you that Prince Rupert and yourself should be upon so unkindly terms. . . . But, my Lord, I often found this a hard matter to hold between you; and truly, my Lord, your last letter to me gives me some cause to think your Lordship not altogether free from what he often accused you of as the reason of his jealousies; which was, that you did both say and do things to his prejudice contrary to your professions, not in an open and direct line, but obscurely and obliquely; and this way, under your Lordship's pardon, I find your letter, in my understanding, very full of. For, where your Lordship would excuse him of the particular and general aspersions, yet you come with such objections against the conduct of that business, as would, to men ignorant of the Prince, make him incapable of common sense in his profession. . . .[4]

Legge brushed aside Digby's flattering suggestion that if he himself had been at Naseby the result might have been different, and after further refutation of Digby's contentions he ended his letter with the forthright pronouncement: 'And assure yourself you are not free from great blame towards Prince Rupert, and no man will give you this free language at a cheaper rate than myself, though many discourse of it.'[5]

After a few days with the Prince of Wales at Barnstaple Rupert took up his post at Bristol, the King's main stronghold, and did what he could to strengthen the city's defences. To add to his troubles, the clubmen were being obstreperous. Goring in the west had tried to recruit some of them into the Cavalier forces, but they were unreliable auxiliaries and with arms in their hands they became more dangerous than ever. Rupert made similar attempts to enlist their support, but in vain; their guerilla forays were a constant anxiety.

Rupert was active scouring the country in his wonted manner and striving to put heart into his sadly stricken troops. But he had lost all hope of ultimate victory. On 21 July he crossed the Severn for a brief conference with the King at Crick, near Chepstow. What passed between them is unknown, but three days later Rupert received from the King, now at Newport, a letter which, in Charles's most circumlocutory style, informed his nephew that he had 'taken a resolution which is differing from what I was most inclined to when I saw you last', and that 'the particulars being of some length and greatest secrecy, I have commanded Digby to write, I not having time myself to do it'.[6] This resolution, as rumour soon reported at Bristol, was to leave the western forces and make a secret journey to join Montrose. To Rupert such a project seemed disastrous. On 28 July he wrote to the Duke of Richmond:

My Lord,

It is now in everybody's mouth, that the King is going for Scotland. I must confess it to be a strange resolution; considering not only in what condition he will leave all behind him, but what probability there is for him to get thither. If I were desired to deliver my opinion, which your Lordship may declare to the King. His Majesty hath now no way left to preserve his posterity, kingdom, and nobility, but by a treaty. I believe it a more prudent way to retain something, than to lose all. If the King resolve to abandon Ireland, which now he may with honour, since they desire unreasonably; and it is apparent they will cheat the King, having not five thousand men in their power. When this has been told him, and that many of his officers and soldiers go from him to them, if he have no more consideration of such as stay, I must extremely lament their condition, being exposed to all ruin and slavery. One comfort will be left: we shall all fall together. When this is, remember I have done my duty.

Your faithful Friend,
RUPERT.[7]

Bristol, July 28, 1645.

For three years Prince Rupert had been his uncle's most ardent supporter in the prosecution of the war, standing out uncompromisingly against any suggestion of accommodation with rebels. Now he had joined the peace party. The change of outlook needs examination. Undoubtedly Rupert was war-weary. The strain of those three years of incessant conflict had been tremendous, and even his iron constitution and dynamic energy could not be expected to hold out for ever. From the beginning he had borne the brunt of the struggle, and to him more than to any other general had fallen the task of transforming a disjointed mass of volunteer enthusiasts into a cohesive army, while at the same time exercising constant activity in the field. And all through the crowded months he had had to contend with the intrigues of his domestic enemies within the Royalist fold. In his two last and greatest battles he had fought against his better judgement, and the result had been defeat all the more bitter for the succession of victories he had previously enjoyed. It was enough to shake the stoutest resolution.

Yet it would be contrary to everything we know about Rupert to suppose that personal considerations of any kind were uppermost in his change of heart. He looked at the situation with the eye of a soldier. The King's cause was lost. Almost the whole of England was under the control of the Roundheads. The Royalists still held Wales and part of the West, the country around Oxford, and a portion of Nottinghamshire centred in Newark. All the rest, except for a few scattered outposts, was in rebel hands. Montrose was still pursuing his triumphant course in Scotland, but he was far away, separated from the King by vast tracts of enemy-occupied territory.

In military terms the preponderance was enormous. The New Model Army was becoming daily more formidable, a trained professional force, well paid and admirably commanded. There were two other Parliamentary armies in the field: those of the Western Association and the Associated Northern Counties. The Scots, moreover, were still to be reckoned with. With the Royalist defeats Leven had ceased to look over his shoulder at his native land. He advanced southwards through the Midlands, and was now threatening Worcester.

The Royalist forces were totally inadequate to fight such odds. Naseby had left King Charles with about 4,000 horse, and during the weeks that followed he scraped together some 3,000 foot of varying quality. These had been reinforced in South Wales by about 3,000 men under Gerard. There was also the western army, 7,000 strong, under Goring, who had failed to appear at Naseby and instead laid siege to Taunton, where the Roundhead Robert Blake, destined to win his greatest fame at sea, put up a gallant defence. But at the end of June Fairfax moved. With the main weight of the New Model Army he marched south at astonishing speed, leading his troops through Wiltshire to Dorset and advancing on Taunton from the south. Goring raised the siege, and Fairfax, joined by Massey with the Western Association army, attacked him with 14,000 men near Langport in Somerset. The Battle of Langport, on 10 July, was the last large-scale battle of the First Civil War. Goring was defeated, and the King's forces in the west were hopelessly enfeebled.

Such was the military situation in July 1645. And just at this time there were published in London the details of the King's private correspondence captured by the Roundheads after Naseby. It consisted largely of letters from the Queen, who was now in Paris, together with copies of the King's letters to her. These revealed the royal negotiations to procure both men and money from various foreign powers, France and Denmark in particular; and also the King's intention to land an Irish army in England. Strategically he was justified, but the mention of foreign troops alienated many of his supporters; even more so the invitation to Irish papists, regarded in the climate of the time as little better than savages.

When all this is considered, it can hardly be a matter of surprise that in Rupert's eyes the only sane policy was to sue for peace. The war was lost, but the Crown might yet be saved. What he did not appreciate was King Charles's exalted sense of his mission in life and his devotion to his Church which forbade him to compromise with his religious ideals.

Richmond showed Prince Rupert's letter to the King, and Charles's reply, sent from Cardiff on 4 August 1665, made clear his attitude:

> . . . if I had any other quarrell, but the Defence of my religion crowne & friends you had full reason for your advice for I must confesse that speaking ether as a mere soldier or statesman I must say ther is no probabilitie but of my ruine; yet as a Christian I must tell you that Godd will not suffer Rebelles & traitors to prosper or this cause to be overthrown & whatsoever personall punishments it shall please him to inflict upon mee must not make me repyne, much lesse give over this quarrell, and there is little question that a composition with them at this time is nothing else but a submission which, by the Grace of Godd, I am resolved against whatsoever it cost mee.

He bade his nephew 'noewise to hearken after treaties', and after explaining his religious outlook in detail he concluded: 'Lastly bee confident that I would not have put you nore myself to the trouble of this long letter had I not a great estimation of you & full confidence in your friendship'.[8]

Rupert accepted this reasoned exposition of the King's attitude, coupled as it was with renewed assurances of his uncle's continuing trust and friendship. His task now was to ensure that Bristol should be able to hold out for the King. It was no easy assignment. Fairfax after his defeat of Goring was mopping up the west at leisure; on 23 July he had captured Bridgwater, and on 14 August he stormed Sherborne Castle, the last Royalist stronghold in Dorset. In Bristol itself Rupert had a line four miles long to defend with a garrison of 1,500 men, a force which would be insufficient even with modern weapons. There was still plague in the city, and morale was dangerously low. Rupert had himself captured Bristol two years before, and knew how difficult it was to defend. Nevertheless he appeared confident, and on 12 August sent to the King 'a very cheerful letter' in which 'he undertook to defend it full four months'.[9]

In the meantime King Charles pressed northwards. Nothing more was heard for the time being of any secret journey on his own, but on 5 August, feeling secure with Bristol in Rupert's hands, he moved from Cardiff with a small force hoping ultimately to establish a link with Montrose; on the way he sent an order to the Prince of Wales to escape to France if he was in danger of capture. Marching through the Welsh mountains and eluding the enemy forces, he reached Doncaster on 18 August. Here, finding himself in danger of being surrounded, he was forced to retreat and moved south-east to Huntingdon. His march through enemy country was a remarkable feat at this stage of the war, but it achieved nothing and on 28 August he entered Oxford, still his capital city but itself increasingly insecure. He left two days later, and at the beginning of September was back in the west. On the 4th he relieved Hereford, which had been besieged by the Scots, and from there he returned to Raglan Castle.

After the fall of Sherborne Castle Sir Thomas Fairfax, with Cromwell at his side, marched north to Bristol, and on 21 August 1645 sat down before the city. His army, about 12,000 strong, was encamped on both sides of the Avon; a Parliamentary naval squadron closed the mouth of the river and made relief by sea impossible. Rupert, surrounded and blockaded by sea and land, was cut off from all communication with other Royalists. The King wrote from Hereford signifying his intention of marching to his relief, but the letter never arrived.

For a fortnight there was skirmishing on the outskirts of the city, in which Rupert lost Sir Richard Crane, who had commanded his Life Guard throughout the war, and Astley's younger son Bernard. The Prince harried the besieging army ceaselessly, but heavy rain hampered his horsemen, and Fairfax, with the weight of numbers on his side, was not seriously perturbed. On 4 September he summoned Rupert to surrender the city, and with his demand he coupled a personal appeal to the humanity of the Prince and to his regard for the English people's services to the Palatine family. After propounding the usual Roundhead claim that the Parliament stood for the true rights of the Crown, and that the King was 'misled by evill Counsellours', Fairfax referred to Rupert's 'royal birth, and relation to the Crown of England, your honour, courage, the vertues of your person'. He said that, if the Prince should decide to surrender rather than allow the shedding of blood and the sacking of so noble a city, 'it would be an occasion glorious in it self, and joyful to us, for restoring of you to the endeared affection to the Parliament, and people of *England*, the truest friend to your Family it hath in this world'.[10]

It was an eloquent appeal, and Rupert had a deep respect for Fairfax. But he was bound in honour, and whatever his private view of his chances of success in defending Bristol he was not prepared to surrender until all hope had gone. He refused the summons, but asked for permission to communicate with the King. Fairfax, not unnaturally, refused to grant this, and Rupert then played for time by putting forward proposals for terms, including completely free movement for all the garrison, which went far beyond anything Fairfax was likely to grant. A few more days were expended in argument, but Fairfax was not deceived. On 9 September he laid his plans for storming the city.

Rupert for his part had made what preparations he could. Supplies had been concentrated, and the city's inhabitants ordered to lay in victuals for six months ahead. The Prince had consulted his colonels of posts, and at a council of war the judgement was passed 'that notwithstanding, the Works and Line were very defective, the Circuit large, our numbers few; yet if we could repell one General Storm, the Enemy would be discouraged from attempting the second time, and the season of the Year might advantage us, and incommode them'.[11] Three courses of action were discussed. First Rupert offered to try to break through Fairfax's army with his horse, leaving the rest of his force to defend the fort and castle. This suggestion was rejected as being 'neither safe nor honourable'.[12] The second course was to withdraw to the castle and the great fort, or citadel, and hold them as long as possible. This also was turned down; the stronghold could not accommodate all the horse and foot, and those who were left outside, as well as the Cavaliers' loyal supporters in the town, would be at the mercy of the enemy. So the third course was adopted, and 'we were all resolved to fall upon the best general defence that could be made of the whole, wherein we might all share alike'.[13]

Fairfax attacked at 2 a.m. on 10 September. The assault was opened 'by setting on fire a great heap of straw and Faggots on the top of an hill, and the shooting off four great guns against *Pryers-fort*, from the place where the *General* was to recide all the time of the storm, which being accordingly given, immediately the storm began round the City, and was terrible to the beholders'.[14] Rupert's guns answered, and there was fierce resistance; but after an hour's hard fighting the Roundheads broke the Royalist line at two points and entered the town.

The Prior's Hill Fort defenders to the north of the city held out with the greatest gallantry. But numbers told, and at 5 a.m. the fort fell and its remaining defenders died; 'our men,' records the Roundhead chronicler, 'were so little prepared for to shew mercy, by the opposition that they met with all in the storm, and the refusal of quarter when it was offered, that they put to the sword the Commander (one Major *Price* a Welchman) and almost all the Officers, Souldiers, and others in the Fort'.[15]

By daybreak Rupert adjudged the situation hopeless. Fairfax had a stronger force, particularly in artillery, than he himself had had when he had captured Bristol in 1643. The Roundhead troops were pouring into the town, and the Prince was forced to withdraw towards the castle; but in doing so he was cut off from those who still held out in the perimeter forts, and who faced the fate of the Prior's Hill garrison. Moreover the well in the great fort was in an unfinished state (one wonders why) and men who withdrew there would soon run short of

water. There was no news of any relieving force on the way, and further
resistance could only end in disaster.

Once more Rupert consulted his officers, and at his council of war it
was agreed, though not unanimously, that it would be better to capitu-
late and save part of the garrison than doom the whole to annihilation.
At eight o'clock in the morning Rupert sued for terms.

The terms were generous. Rupert and his men were to march out
'with Colours, Pikes, and Drums, Bag and Baggage',[16] horses and swords
were retained, but firearms only in the case of 'the Prince's lifeguard'
(presumably a company of foot). The sick and wounded were to remain
unmolested in the city, and allowed to return to the King when recovered. Convoy was to be provided for the troops 'to any such Garison
of the King's as the Prince shall name, not exceeding fifty miles from
Bristol',[17] and the citizens were to be protected from plunder and violence.
There was a hitch in carrying out these terms. 'The next day upon some
Insolencies of the Soldiers, his Highness sent to Sir *Thomas Fairfax*, that
the Articles were violated, and that if there was not a present redress,
he would stand upon his own defence, and rather die than suffer those
injuries; and thereupon for his Highness satisfaction we had liberty to
march with our Arms unto our Quarters.'[18]

The defeated Cavaliers then marched out of Bristol. Proceedings
were conducted with grace and dignity. Fairfax was the soul of courtesy,
and personally escorted his vanquished foe for two miles over the downs.
Rupert too played his part to perfection. 'The Prince,' it was recorded
in a newsletter, 'was clad in scarlet, very richly laid in silver lace,
mounted upon a very gallant black Barbary horse; the General and the
Prince rode together, the General giving the Prince the right hand all
the way.'[19] And Rupert, according to a Parliamentary newspaper, remarked to a Roundhead officer that 'he never received such satisfaction
in such unhappiness, and that if ever in his power he will recompense
it'.[20]

The Royalist 'robber prince', who for the past three years had been
looked upon by the Roundheads as next of kin to the devil himself,
made a singularly gracious impression on some who now met him in the
flesh for the first time. Colonel John Butler, who escorted him as far as
Woodstock, wrote from there to Sir William Waller:

I had the honour to wayte upon his Highnesse Prince Rupert with a
convoy from Bristow to this place; and seriously I am glad I had the
happinesse to see him, for I am confident we are much mistaken in our
intelligence concerninge him. I finde him a man much inclyn'd to a happy
peace, and will certainly imploy his interest with his Majestie for the
accomplishinge of it. Therefore I make it my request to you, that you will
use some meanes that no pamphlet be printed that may derogate from his

worth for his delivery of Bristow. On my word he could not have held it, unless it had bin better man'd.[21]

Far otherwise was the reception of the news of the Bristol surrender at the King's court; had Butler but known it, he or Waller could not have been more wildly astray than to rely at this moment on Rupert's 'interest with his Majestie', particularly in the matter of accomplishing a happy peace. King Charles heard what had happened when he arrived back at Raglan Castle. His reaction verged on the hysterical. He promptly returned to Hereford, and from there, without waiting for any explanation from his nephew, sent off what was probably the bitterest letter Prince Rupert ever received.

Hereford, 14 Sept. 1645.

Nephew,

Though the loss of Bristoll be a great blow to me, yet your surrendering it as you did is of so much affliction to me, that it makes me forget not only the consideration of that place, but is likewise the greatest trial of my constancy that hath yet befallen me; for what is to be done? After one that is so near to me as you are, both in blood and friendship, submits himself to so mean an action (I give it the easiest term) such I have so much to say that I will say no more of it: only, lest rashness of judgement be laid to my charge, I must remember one of your letters of the 12 Aug., whereby you assured me, (that if no mutiny happened,) you would keep Bristoll for four months. Did you keep it four days? Was there any thing like a Mutiny? More questions might be asked, but now, I confess, to little purpose. My conclusion is, to desire you to seek your subsistence (until it shall please God to determine of my condition) somewhere beyond seas, to which end I send you herewith a pass; and I pray God to make you sensible of your present condition, and give you means to redeem what you have lost; for I shall have no greater joy in a victory, than a just occasion without blushing to assure of my being

Your loving oncle and most
faithful friend.[22]

With the letter and the pass the King sent a revocation of all Rupert's commands and commissions. At the same time Will Legge, for no other reason than that he was the Prince's friend and supporter, was deprived of the governorship of Oxford and placed under arrest.

The violence of King Charles's reaction to the surrender of Bristol was out of keeping with all that had gone before. True, the blow was a heavy one. The great port of Bristol, the only substantial seaport remaining to the Royalists, was an asset of vital importance; without it even the King could see that his cause was doomed. Yet in all the misfortunes and disappointments in previous years the one constant had been Charles's trust and support of his nephew. After every setback Rupert had been reassured of his uncle's confidence; even the disaster of Marston Moor had not shaken the King's trust. Yet now, unheard and without any attempt at inquiry, the Captain-General of the King's armies found himself dismissed, disgraced, and bidden to go at once into exile.

Modern historians have united in acquitting Rupert in the matter of the surrender. Militarily he was justified; the city at the time of Fairfax's attack was indefensible, and prolonged resistance would have led only to the slaughter of soldiers and civilians. The Prince had no means of knowing that the King was planning a relief expedition, which in any case would almost certainly have been ineffectual. Yet the fact remains that only a month previously Rupert had assured his uncle that he could defend the city for four months; and this he had signally failed to do.

This failure to fulfil his promise weighed heavily with the King. Also he could not forget that earlier in the year his nephew had advocated the ending of the war by treaty. These circumstances combined to prompt suspicion, eagerly fed into the royal ear by Digby, that the Prince had sold the pass, had not tried to hold Bristol, but had hastened to hand the port over to the enemy as a means of bringing about the end of hostilities. The courtesies that had passed between Rupert and Fairfax inclined the King's mind in the same direction.

A brief passage in the *Rupert Diary* supplies the vital clue to King Charles's actions: 'Then the P had a letter from the King to discharge him of the Generallship, and Leg of the Government of Oxford. Bristol [Digby] having made a suggestion that he held correspondence with the P. Elector, tho' he never wrote one letter to him.'

For Charles Louis was still in London and by an unfortunate coincidence had just at this time been granted a pension of £8,000 a year by the House of Commons. It was being freely bruited about that he was aiming at the English throne; if Charles should be deprived of his crown, and his children barred from the succession, the Elector Palatine would, after his mother the Queen of Bohemia, be the next heir. That Rupert, who detested his brother's outlook and had held no communication with him since the start of the Civil War, should have been a party to Charles Louis's aims and even conspired with him to betray his master for the sake of a share in the spoils, was an idea so preposterous that up to this time King Charles would have brushed it aside with contempt. But now the King was in despair; he was always susceptible to his nearest adviser's voice, and in his agony of mind he allowed himself to listen to Digby's insinuations.

Prince Rupert, having parted from Fairfax and his escort, arrived at Oxford on Monday, 15 September. And it was here, two days later, that he learnt of his fate. 'Wednesday, by letter from the King,' says the journal of his marches, 'the Lords discharged the Prince of his Generallship: cashiered his Regiments of Horse and Foote, his troope [Life Guards] and firelocks. That daye was Colonel Legg discharged of his Government of Oxford, and confin'd to his house.'[23] It was Sir Edward Nicholas, the Secretary of State, who had always been a good friend to Rupert, to whom the painful task of carrying out the King's orders was entrusted. With a copy of the letter to Rupert, Nicholas was sent a warrant for the arrest of Legge, and also 'a warrant to be directed to what person shall bee thought fittest for the apprehendinge my Nephew Rupert, in case of such extreamitye as shall bee hereafter specifyed, and not otherwise'. Elaborating this point, the King went on: 'The warrant for my Nephews commitment is onlye that you may have the power to doe it, if in stead of submittinge to, and obeying my commands in goeinge beyond sea, you shall finde that hee practise the raysinge of mutinye or any other disturbance.'[24]

That King Charles should think his nephew capable of raising a mutiny rather than submit to his commands shows how far his mind had been poisoned against Rupert. The Prince accepted his dismissal with dignity. 'I went to Col. Legge's house,' reported Nicholas to the King, 'where Prince Rupert dined, and desiring to speak privately with him in the withdrawing room, I presented to him first his discharge, and after that your letter, to which he humbly submitted, telling me that he was very innocent of anything that might deserve so heavy a punishment.' At the same time Nicholas took the opportunity to put in a word of sympathy for the victims of the King's wrath and the condition in which they found themselves. His letter went on:

> . . . And now I may not omit to acquaint your Majesty that I hear Prince Rupert hath not 50 *l.* in all the world, but is reduced to so great extremity as he hath not wherewith to feed himself or servants. I hear that Col. Legg is in no more plentiful condition, which I hold it my duty to mention, as not unfit for your consideration. Your Majesty will herewith receive a letter from Prince Rupert, who I believe will stay here till he hears again from you, for that he cannot, without leave from the rebels, go to embark himself, and without your Majesty's license I hear he will not demand a pass from the rebels. . . .[25]

Rupert, however humbly he might submit to the King's commands, was not the man to sit down meekly under the indignities he had received. He might be willing to go into exile, but not before he had presented his case to the King in person and vindicated his honour and his military reputation. The rather incoherent letter which he sent to his uncle by the hand of Nicholas at least made clear his intentions:

> . . . How I have behaved myself from the beginning until this misfortune of your commands engaged me in Bristol; from inferior persons I shall not desire greater justification or applause than I have received from your Majesty, therefore I pass [over] all former times without mention, to come to this, of which I only say if your Majesty had vouchsafed me so much patience as to hear me inform you, before you had made a final judgment (I will presume to present thus much), that you would not have censured me, as it seems you do, and that I should have given you as just satisfaction as in any former occasions, though not so happy. But since there is so great appearance that I must suffer, that it is already decreed, what otherwise I should have desired to have given your Majesty an account [of], now I am obliged to seek for my own clearing that what you will have me bear may be with as much honour to me as belongs to integrity. If your Majesty will admit me to that opportunity, I desire to wait on you to that end as soon as I can, when I know I have leave for it, which I humbly desire to have. If I must be so unfortunate [as] not to be allowed it, since the first duty that I owe, which is to your Majesty, is not suffered me to perform, wherein else I should rest, in the next place I owe myself that justice as to publish to the world what I think will clear my carriage in all this business now in question from any foul deed or negligence, and vindicate me from the desent of any prevailing malice though I suffer [by] it. . . . Wherever I am or how unhappy so ever, and by your will made so, yet I shall ever retain that duty to your Majesty which I have ever [entertained], as your Majesty's most obedient nephew and faithful humble servant, Rupert.[26]

Rupert was determined to see the King. Digby, enjoying his triumph and knowing how easily it could be blown away by a confrontation between uncle and nephew, was equally determined that he should not do so. The King must be kept away from Oxford, and from any place where the Prince could easily come to him. For the moment Digby prevailed. Under his influence the King prepared to move north once more, still with the ultimate aim of linking up with Montrose, who it was now hoped would be in a position to invade England.

Rupert therefore proceeded to his next step, of which he had given warning to his uncle – the public vindication of his own actions at Bristol. The *Declaration of His Highness Prince Rupert with a Narrative of the State and Condition of the City and Garrison of Bristol, when His Highness Prince Rupert came thither: of the actions there during the siege, of the treaties, and rendition thereof*,[27] printed at Oxford, told the whole story of the siege in lucid military language. Supported with documents, with the proceedings of the council of war, and with details of the defences signed by the engineer officers de Gomme and Mansfield, it demonstrated in unequivocal terms the reasons for Rupert's decisions and showed that his actions, whether right or wrong, were dictated by military considerations alone. If the surrender had been longer delayed, the peroration declared, 'the city had thereby been exposed to the spoil and fury of the enemy, so many gallant men who had so long and faithfully served his Majesty, whose safeties his Highness conceived himself in honour obliged to preserve as dearly as his own, had been left to the slaughter and rage of a prevailing enemy'.[28]

The King marched north through the mountains of North Wales, and on 23 September attempted to relieve Chester, where Lord Byron was still holding out. On the following day his forces were badly cut up at Rowton Heath, although the garrison still maintained their hold; thereafter it was decided that the northward expedition must be abandoned. A safe haven then had to be found for the King; Worcester was first considered, but the Governor there was Prince Maurice, who, recently recovered from a serious illness, was known to be indignant at the treatment of his brother. Digby was opposed to such a location for this reason, and likewise he was equally opposed to any return to Oxford. Eventually it was decided to break through enemy territory to Newark. Through Bridgnorth and Lichfield the hazardous journey was accomplished, and on 4 October the King and his followers safely reached the Royalist enclave. Nearly a hundred miles of Roundhead occupied territory lay between Newark and Oxford, and Digby calculated that he had effectively prevented a meeting between uncle and nephew.

Rupert thought otherwise. As soon as he heard that the King was at Newark, the scene of one of his own greatest triumphs, he resolved to make his way through the enemy country and, with or without permission, confront his uncle face to face.

He set out on 8 October at the head of about eighty of his followers who volunteered to accompany him. He tried to induce Richmond to be of their number, but the Duke would not leave Oxford; probably he was unwilling to give countenance to a venture that might be construed as an act of defiance to the King. At Banbury Rupert was joined by his brother Maurice with another party of volunteers, bringing the total to 120. On 20 September King Charles had sent his younger nephew a letter in which he expressly dissociated him from Rupert's misdeeds; but Maurice's first loyalty, even though he held the King's commission, was then and always to his brother.

Thus Rupert, deprived of all his commands, yet once more found himself leading a band of men in arms, albeit a small one, in the sort of daring adventure in which he revelled. When the news of his design reached London, the Parliament sent orders for his interception, and

1,500 horse were posted at various places where he might be expected to march; but Rupert, moving through Northamptonshire with his usual speed and certainty, was too swift for them. At Burghley House, the Duke of Buckingham's seat on the river Welland, there was a Roundhead garrison; 'and as he marched by it the Garrison came out and one that was Governor there had been formerly in his High: troop. The P. drew his troop into 2 Divisions in a broad highway there and the Governor came with the Grosse of his Body, & knowing the P came up with his Pistoll & mist ffire, and then cry'd for quarter but the P shot him dead. And then in a short time the rest fled.'[29]

On went the princes, and only towards the end of the march did they meet any serious resistance. At Belvoir Bridge, some twelve miles south of Newark, they were stopped by Colonel Rossiter with 300 horse. 'The P stood first toward the Horse, as if he would charge them and then upon a sodain turned and fought 'em and beat them twice; by which the other forces of the Enemy being allarm'd, they came up to the P. Sayes the P to his People, we have beaten 'em twice; we must beat them once more, and then over the passe and away which accordingly they did; and then the P sent away his Papers & Baggage to Belvoir Castle.'[30]

Rossiter once more prepared to attack, and this time Rupert took evasive action. He had been to Belvoir before, on his carefree visit to King Charles's court ten years before; and he remembered a cross-country route he had learned when 'hunting & shooting of conyes'. Down this path he led his volunteers towards the castle, pursued by Rossiter's cavalry. 'The Enemy sent 40 horse after the P, and the rest follow'd the grosse of the troop. When they came near they cry'd P.R. will you have quarter. The P commanded his people to come close together, and to turn when he turn'd. The Army came down the hill in disorder, and the P beat them, and Ld Molineux killing a man upon a good mare, the P now mounted himself, and he fast and swiftly went to bevoir: But some of the Baggage the other way was lost, and about 14 men.'[31]

King Charles once again turned north. His fortunes were at the lowest ebb, for Montrose's glorious campaign in Scotland was at an end. After two more splendid victories at Alford and Kilsyth, in July and August, the Marquess was defeated on 13 September at Philiphaugh, near Selkirk, by David Leslie, who had arrived from England. The nature of his warfare made victory dependent on sustained success in the field. So long as he was winning, he was sure of the loyalty of the brave, undisciplined Highlanders who formed his guerilla army. When he failed they melted away, became once more a rabble, and squabbled among themselves. Montrose retreated into the Highlands, and was no longer a factor in the English Civil War.

The extent of the disaster was not yet known at Newark. Indeed it was rumoured that after Philiphaugh Montrose had rallied and was again approaching the border; if a junction could be effected there might still be hope. This was one reason for advancing northward; but Digby, who was now all-powerful with the King, had a more personal reason. He had learned that Prince Rupert was on his way to Newark and he therefore prevailed on his master to march out of that town towards Rotherham, with the object of advancing further if the news should be satisfactory. But at Welbeck reports came through of Montrose's retreat and the King decided to turn back.

He did so without Digby. Even in these unpropitious circumstances the strange decision was made to send the northern horse into Scotland, still with the avowed object of linking up with Montrose. Digby was given the command, with the title of Lieutenant-General of the Forces North of the Trent, and with the experienced Sir Marmaduke Langdale as second-in-command. This expedition got as far as Dumfries, but there the forces disintegrated, and Digby and Langdale escaped to the Isle of Man.

King Charles returned to Newark on 14 October, and there he learned that Rupert and Maurice were at Belvoir Castle. He was no better disposed towards his elder nephew than he had been since the fall of Bristol. Digby's malice had done its work, helped as it was by a series of poison-pen letters sent from Oxford by Digby's agent Edward Walsingham. These letters, partly in cipher, were designed to show that Rupert was not only a defeatist but a traitor, and hinted that he was aiming at the Crown. 'As even now I came through the garden of Christchurch,' said the writer in a letter sent on 16 September, 'a gentleman met me, and took me into the inner garden, and told me he would show me our [318, cipher for ruler?]. Fancy, when I came there, I found Prince Rupert and Legge with the Lord 116 walking gravely betwixt them on the further side. I seemed to take no notice of the gentlemen's meeting, but came away resenting to see the gentry and nobility stand there bare at a distance as if his Majesty had been present.'[32] In another, speaking of Rupert's wish for a treaty, Walsingham wrote: 'Assure yourself, my Lord, that though this be Prince Rupert's aim here pretended, 'tis but the medium to his real one, yet it is so plausible that you would bless yourself for to see how it is cherished by all that are either malcontent, timorous, or suspected.' And he went on: 'Surely there is no way left for his Majesty to recover, prosper, and give life to his discouraged party but by expressing his high dislike and distrust to Prince Rupert, which is most certainly sold away whatever fair glosses may be put upon it.'[33]

The letters were contemptible, but, shown to Charles by Digby, they had helped to feed the distrust which had been nurtured in the King's mind since his nephew's first tentative proposal for a peace. Now he was prepared to believe that the Prince was coming with an armed force to overpower him and compel him to make peace. He wrote at once to Rupert at Belvoir, 'commanding him to stay there until further Order, and intimating His Displeasure at his not giving Obedience to His former Command'.[34]

Rupert's reply was open defiance. The next day, 16 October, he rode into Newark with his brother by his side, and his offence was aggravated by the enthusiastic reception given him by his supporters in the town. The Governor of Newark was Sir Richard Willis, later to become notorious as the alleged betrayer of the Royalist secret organization the 'Sealed Knot'; while one of the senior officers in the town was the Prince's faithful follower Charles Gerard, recently raised to the peerage as Lord Gerard of Brandon. These two rode two miles out of the town to meet the recalcitrant Prince with an escort of a hundred horse, 'and as it were in defiance bring him into the Town to the Governor's House; which was more of Duty than the Governor ever paid to His Majesty coming three times thither'.[35] It is scarcely to be wondered at if the unfortunate King thought himself faced with the ultimate degradation, a rebellion against his rule within his own family and his own household.

An uncomfortable scene followed. Rupert and Maurice strode into the presence of the King, and Rupert, without any ceremony, curtly announced that he had come to render an account of the loss of Bristol and to clear himself. The King behaved with his usual dignity. He said little (and what he did say has not been recorded) to his unmannerly nephew, but left the room and went to his supper. The two princes followed, and Charles submitted to the humiliation of eating his supper with his nephews standing over him and demanding redress. He coped with the situation as best he could by asking Prince Maurice a few questions while completely ignoring the elder brother.

Graceless as his conduct had been, Prince Rupert got his way. Much as the King must have resented the way his nephew had forced himself into his presence, he was evidently impressed with his sincerity. At least Rupert was not in rebellion; all he wanted was to vindicate his reputation in the eyes of his sovereign lord. And next day King Charles granted the Prince's request for a court-martial to inquire into the whole question of the surrender of Bristol. Members of the court were the Earl of Lindsey, the Earl of Cork, Lord Astley, Lord Belasyse, Lord Gerard, Sir Richard Willis, and John Ashburnham. On 21 October the King declared their judgements. He had himself deposed that:

... we did not believe our said nephew to be guilty of any the least want of courage or fidelity to us, in the doing thereof; but, withal, we believed that he might have kept the castle and fort a longer time; we having absolutely resolved speedily to have drawn together all the forces we possibly could, and to have hazarded our own person for his relief. . . . To which our said right dear nephew answered, that whatever he did therein, was by the advice of the Council of war of that garrison; and that he could not, in his judgement, possibly expect such relief.

And at the second sitting of the court:

> . . . upon a serious consideration of the whole matter, we were then pleased to declare, that we were fully satisfied that our said right dear nephew, Prince Rupert, is not guilty of any the least want of courage or fidelity to us, or our service, in that action: and we then gave leave to the Lords and others, above specified, to declare their opinions on that point. Who, upon our leave, and a full consideration of the narrative formerly delivered, did unanimously concur with us; declaring, likewise, that our said right dear nephew is not guilty of any the least want of courage or fidelity to us, or our service, in that action.[36]

It was not a complete vindication. As Clarendon commented, the Prince 'was absolved and cleared from any disloyalty or treason in the rendering of Bristol, but not of indiscretion'.[37] But his honour was redeemed, and if the matter had been allowed to rest there complete reconciliation between uncle and nephew could have been immediately effected. Rupert, however, was in one of his most prickly moods; he had not been restored to any of his commands, and he was still smarting under a sense of injustice. The King for his part could not forget his nephew's defiance of his authority, or the part played by the Governor of Newark. Charles had decided to quit the town and make his way once more to Oxford, and was reluctant to leave Willis there in Rupert's company. He therefore sent for him privately and ordered him to change places with Lord Belasyse, commander of his Horse Guard. Willis was furious. The transfer could be regarded as promotion rather than degradation, but he saw it only (and certainly rightly) as a punishment for taking Rupert's part. And Rupert himself took a similar view.

So it was that there was a second unseemly scene in the King's presence, followed by an episode in which Rupert's conduct is adjudged by Warburton 'the greatest error, if not crime, that the history of his life contains'.[38]

On Sunday, 26 October, when the King had returned from church and was preparing for dinner, Willis, with the two princes, Gerard and about twenty officers of the garrison, burst into his presence. Willis 'addresseth himself to Him and tells Him, that what His Majesty said to him in private was now publick and the talk of the town, which was to his Dishonour'.[39] Rupert then intervened with the comment that Willis was being removed because he was his friend, and Gerard added that this was a plot by Digby, whom he would prove a traitor. The King tried to draw Willis away for another private talk, but Willis refused to go with him and demanded public satisfaction.

This was too much to be borne, and the King ordered them all out of the room. They departed 'both confounded and ashamed'.[40] Rupert, however, 'shewed no reverence, but went out proudly with his hands at his sides'.[41]

Willis and the princes returned to the Governor's house, and on the way 'their Coach overthrew and they all fell in the Dirt'.[42] Doubtless this did not improve their tempers. The King immediately proclaimed Belasyse Governor, and before nightfall received a petition from the protesters 'desiring Sir *Richard Willis* might receive a tryal by a Court of War, and if they adjudged him faulty, then to be dismissed his Charge; or else Passes for themselves and so many Horse as well would go with them; and withal hoping His Majesty would not esteem this action of theirs to be a Mutiny'.[43] On this last item the King commented drily that 'He would not Christen – though it looked very like one'.[44] As for the request, he would not make a council of war the judge of his actions; but anybody who wanted a pass to leave the kingdom should have one the next morning.

Accordingly the officers presented themselves next morning to receive their passes and take their leave. Gerard 'expressed some sence of Folly in this Action',[45] but in this he was alone. Rupert and his friends left that afternoon for Belvoir Castle. According to one account their departure was preceded by a further scene, with Rupert this time really on the brink of armed rebellion. According to Joshua Moore, Rupert 'remained much dissatisfied, and together with all those officers and soldiers which were in his train, consisting of 200 horse, drew them up . . . into the market place'. The King thereupon ordered Belasyse to draw up his Guards. Moore continues:

> Being told the Prince was at the head of his, the King took horse and marched with swords and pistols ready to the Market-place to have charged the Prince in case of resistance. But first he called upon him and said: 'Nephew, why are you thus in arms?' who answered, 'to defend ourselves against our enemies.' The King replied: 'I command you to march out immediately to Belvoir Castle and to stay there till the passes be sent to you to go beyond the seas.' The Prince then with great duty and obedience went out to Balverton Gate and marched to that Castle ten miles distant.[46]

That this circumstantial story has some substance can hardly be doubted. Moore was Belasyse's secretary and biographer, and was in a position to know what happened. But at the same time he may well have been prejudiced in favour of Belasyse and ready to represent the conduct of his master's rival Willis and his friends in a bad light. How near Rupert was to mutiny cannot be stated with certainty; however hot his temper, it is difficult to imagine him proceeding to such an extreme. The episode is not mentioned by Walker or Clarendon, neither of them noticeably sympathetic to Rupert. And a Parliamentary journal, describing the departure, says that the princes marched out from Newark, 'the King looking out of a window, and weeping to see them as they went'.[47] It seems likely that Moore at least exaggerated.

Rupert and Maurice had their passes from the King; but it was impossible for them to leave England without permission from the Parliament. Rupert therefore sent Lieutenant-Colonel Henry Osborne to London to ask for passes for himself, his brother and the rest. There was protracted correspondence, but the final answer was that they could have the passes on giving a promise never again to bear arms against the Parliament. This promise they refused to give. Taking to arms once more, they fought their way to Worcester, and thence to Woodstock.

Here they were within distance of the King, who had returned to Oxford where he released Will Legge from house-arrest. Legge immediately set himself to restore friendship between the King and Rupert, imploring the Prince to make a suitable submission. 'The first discourse I had with him [the King] was concerning you,' he wrote on 21 November, 'where he gave me a relation of the unhappy breach between you, which I would to God had never been. . . . I have not hitherto lost a day without moving his Majesty to recall you, and truly this very day he protested to me he would count it a great happiness to have you with him, so he received that satisfaction he is bound in honour to have, and what that is, you will receive from the Duke of Richmond.'[48]

A letter which may have carried even more weight with the Prince bore no date or signature:

May it please Yr Highnesse

This nyght I was with the King, whoe expresses greate kindnesse to you, but beleevs Yr partinge with him was soe much the contrary as Yr Highnesse cannot think it but a finill. How truly Sir his Majestye conceaving it soe in my oppinion tis fitt you should make sume hansume applycation, for this reason, because my Lord Duke and others here are much Yr servants, And all that are soe wish yre return to Courte, though it be but to part frendlye but I think it necessary you prepar the waye first by letters to the King. Sir I have no designs in this but Yr service. and if you understand me rightlye that will prevayle soe much as you will consyder what I saye, before you resolve the contrarye . . . tis Yr Uncle you shall submit to

And a Kinge not in a condition he meryt What others may saye I know
not but really Sir may I speak my opinyon as a person that values you
above all the world besydes. I am confident you know how faithfully my
harte is to your Highness And how much I am

Your Highnesses most obedient humble
Servant

Oxford this Thursday night 3 o'Clock.[49]

The reference to 'my Lord Duke' makes it at least possible, if not
probable, that this correspondent was the Duchess of Richmond.

Then on 25 November came a second letter from Legge, couched in
particularly affectionate terms:

> My dearest Pr:
> Your Brothers man would not doe me the favour to call on me for this
> Letter although I tould him I had it redye. I am of oppinion you should
> write to your unkle, seeinge your stay hath been so Longe in his quarters,
> (in Civillity you ought to doe it) and if you offered your service to him yet
> and submitted yourselfe to his disposeinge and advice, many of your
> frinds think it could not be a dishonour but rather the contrary, seeinge he
> is a Kinge, your unkle, and in effect a parent to you; if it were possible for
> me to come where you are I would not faile to com to you, or if you can
> com neere I shall doe the same! God of heaven bless you. Dearest Prince,
> your faithfullest poorest servant
> Will: L.[50]

Faced with these appeals from those who were dearest to him,
Rupert swallowed his pride and capitulated. He wrote to the King
humbly acknowledging the error of his conduct at Newark and asking
what he should do. After some further correspondence King Charles
'sent him, by Col. Leg, a Paper, that was to confesse, etc.'.[51] Rupert
replied by sending a blank paper with his name subscribed; 'the K.
with tears in his Eyes took this so well, that all was at peace'.[52]

Complete submission brought complete reconciliation. On 9 December the Prince returned to Oxford, 'and the K embraced him; and (as
hath been sayd) repented much the Ill Usage of his Nephew'.[53] But
uncle and nephew were soon to part for the last time.

The war was virtually over; the King now recognized that he was
beaten. On Rupert's return he revealed to him his latest design: to leave
Oxford secretly and throw himself on the mercy of the Scottish army,
now in the neighbourhood of Newark. The Prince opposed the plan,
and even obtained a signed statement that the step was being taken
against his advice. But when the King, as so often, proved obdurate, he
asked to be allowed to accompany him – 'But the K sayd he would be

discovered by his talnesse'.[54] On 27 April 1646 King Charles left Oxford.

There was little more. On 1 May Fairfax laid siege to Oxford, and there was no hope of defending the city for long. There was some skirmishing, and Rupert, Maurice and Gerard did their share, Rupert being slightly wounded: '. . . a Lt of the Enemyes shot the P in the shoulder and skin'd his hand, so that his pistoll fell out of his hand and it shot his enemyes horse'.[55] Remarkably enough, this was the Prince's only wound in a war in which he had hazarded his person as had few others in high command. The skirmish was nothing more than a delaying action. The King's council made the inevitable decision to treat, and on 20 June Oxford surrendered.

Fairfax's terms were characteristically generous. As regards Rupert and Maurice, they were given leave to quit the country with their servants while being allowed to stay six months longer provided they did not approach within twenty miles of London. This provision led to further trouble. The princes wanted to go within the forbidden distance, and Fairfax gave them special permission. Their object was the ostensibly unlikely one of meeting with their elder brother Charles Louis. The carnage of the Thirty Years War was ending at last; negotiations were in train for a peace, and it was hoped that the Elector Palatine would be restored to at least a part of the family inheritance. Rupert and Maurice had a stake in the Palatinate too, and a family conference was deemed necessary.

The three brothers met at Guildford on 1 July. Nothing is known of the details of their discussions; the reunion could hardly have been a cordial one. But it aroused the wrath of the rulers in Parliament, though in fact Guildford is more than twenty miles from London. They held that Fairfax had no right to grant the princes a dispensation from the terms agreed on, and in retaliation ordered the princes to leave England within ten days. The brothers were probably not reluctant. They made their way to Dover, and on 5 July Prince Rupert took ship for Calais. Maurice left three days later, accompanying the great Dutch sailor Admiral van Tromp to Holland.

The end of the First Civil War was not the end of Rupert's career as a soldier; he was to do a little fighting on the continent during the next few years. But the actions he fought there were unimportant, and it is on his Civil War record that his military capacity must be judged. He was certainly in the forefront of the generals engaged, and equally certainly stood first among the Royalists. Only Hopton's record can stand comparison with his; Goring, though a great man in a fight, was too little able to discipline himself or his army and showed little talent for independent command.

On the Parliamentary side Sir Thomas Fairfax was a commander of much the same pattern as Rupert: bold, indefatigable, able to inspire his men by personal example of intrepidity and skill at arms. Cromwell, who rose from captain to lieutenant-general during the war, enjoyed independent command only in three relatively unimportant actions and five minor sieges; his great military triumphs lay in the future. How far he was responsible as Fairfax's right-hand man for that general's successes it is not easy to determine. Certainly he was a brilliant cavalry leader and a magnificent trainer of troops; but much of his reputation rests on his own words. He was accustomed to hold forth in later years on how he had won the Civil War with God as his second-in-command. Fairfax on the other hand was a silent and a modest man, who had little to say on his victories, though he did write an account of his campaign in the north.

Of the other Roundhead generals Waller, who won his nickname of 'William the Conqueror' by a series of easy victories in the opening months of the war, was a skilful if cautious tactician; but his one great victory at Cheriton was offset by the disaster at Roundway Down and his repulse at Cropredy Bridge. Essex was at best an officer of very ordinary ability. Certainly Rupert, in spite of ultimate failure, can challenge comparison with any of them.

It is generally accepted that during the first campaigns of the war, those of 1642 and 1643, the Cavaliers displayed a grasp of strategy which was quite lacking on the Parliamentarian side. In 1642 Rupert saw the need to reach London with all possible speed. It is clear that in 1643 the Royalists intended to make a triple advance on the capital with their northern, Oxford and western armies. Probably this plan was conceived by Rupert rather than by King Charles or his professional adviser, Lord Forth. Likewise the strategy for 1644 to hold the Parliamentarians round Oxford while attempting to clear the north was the Prince's.

So much for the higher direction of the war. There is considerable evidence of the Prince's ability to conduct a campaign. The stroke which cut off Essex at First Newbury was his and his alone; his relief of York was perhaps the neatest operation of the whole war, and that of Newark was a masterpiece of aggressive action.

Descending to the tactical level, we find at first glance a rather unsatisfactory picture. The Prince was present at five of the major battles of the war, and in only one – Newark – was the Royalist army completely successful. At Marston Moor the Cavaliers were badly routed, and the responsibility was primarily Rupert's. In the other three battles the

King himself commanded. At First Newbury the cavalry fought well under most adverse circumstances, while both at Edgehill and at Naseby the wing which Rupert commanded was successful, in the latter case against odds of two to one. The fact remains, however, that in the one really great battle where he exercised supreme command he met with irretrievable disaster.

In the storming of towns as well as in the numerous other combats, actions and skirmishes where he commanded, particularly when he was taking the offensive, Rupert's record was one of almost unvarying success. The abortive attempt on Abingdon in January 1645 and the unsuccessful defence of Bristol were his only failures.

In the matter of his most renowned tactic, the cavalry charge, he was a true innovator. It was virtually irresistible, and almost invariably he swept away all opposition. Where he failed was in rallying and re-forming his troops of horse when the charge was done; but only long training of men and horses could achieve this. Cromwell managed it; but Cromwell had more time and more resources. Rupert was the pioneer; Cromwell learned from his enemy's mistakes and built on the foundations he laid.

His most hostile critics have always granted that Prince Rupert possessed in no ordinary degree the qualities required of a successful cavalry officer: outstanding personal courage, the gift of taking in a situation at a glance, and that of quick decision. His skill and delight in the technical side of his profession, though well enough known to military historians, have not always been noticed by writers of the eminence of S. R. Gardiner or Sir Charles Oman, both of whom seem to have thought Rupert a mere *sabreur*. If that was indeed their view they seriously underrated the Prince, who was not only a tactician but a strategist, while such of his letters as have come to light reveal a con-siderable talent for administration.

The conclusion must be that, young as he was, he was the only man on the Royalist side who had the knowledge, the ability and the stature required to fight a successful campaign against the formidable odds that at length prevailed.

Tichnell 14. June 1644

Nephew

first I must congratulat with you, for your good suc=
cesses, assuring you that the things themsellfs ar no more welcome
to me, then that you ar the means of. I know the importance of
the supplying you with powder, for w[hi]ch I haue taken all possible
ways, hauing sent both to Ireland & Bristoll, as from Oxford
this week no lesse then 600 is already sent to you, and 600 more is
a prouiding, but if... you that I may spare them, pro=
uided, I shall have 800 powder, hauing but 36 left, but w[ha]t I
can get from Bristoll, w[hi]ch there is not much certainty upon
being threatened to be siedged you shall heare.

But now I must giue you the true state of my affaires, w[hi]ch if
their condition be suche as enforces me to giue you more peremptory commands
then I would willingly doe, you must not take it ill. If Yorke
be lost, I shall esteeme my Crowne litle lesse, unlesse supported by
your suddaine Marche to me, & a Miraculous conquest in the
South, before the effects of the Northern powers can be found
here, but if Yorke be relieued, & you beate the Rebells Armies
of

both which are... but are before it, then, (but other=
ways not) I may possibly make a shift,
(upon the defensiue) to spinne out tyme, untill you come to assist mee:
Wherfor I command & conjure you, by the dutty & affection w[hi]ch I know
you beare me, that (all new enterpryses laide asyde) you immediatly marche,
(according to your first intention) with all your force to the relife of Yorke:
but if that be either lost, or freed... from the siege, or you haue
that for want of Powder, you cannot undertake that worke; that
you immediatly march... with your whole strength, directly to Wost[er],
to assist me & my Army, w[i]thout w[hi]ch, or your hauing relieued
Yorke, by beating the Scots, all the successe you can afterwards haue
most infallibly, will be uselesse unto mee: You may belieue that noth=
ing but an extreame necessity could make me thus write unto
you, wheerfor in this case, I can no wayes doute of your punctuall
complyance with

I commanded this bearer to speake
to you concerning Vernon.

Your louing Oncle & most faithfull
frend
Charles R.

Portrait of Prince Rupert, by Lely

BOOK THREE

THE KING'S ADMIRAL
1646–1660

SOLDIERING IN FRANCE

P RINCE Rupert landed at Calais on 10 July 1646, and two days later
rode to Boulogne. On 14 July he reached Beauvais, and on the 23rd
St Germain-en-Laye, north-west of Paris, where Queen Henrietta Maria
presided over what remained of the English royal court. With her was
the Prince of Wales, who after leaving England with Hyde and others
had just arrived from Jersey to join his mother in exile. 'Thursday, to
St Germains,' runs the last entry in the *Journal of Prince Rupert's Marches*,
'where wee found the Prince our Master. Blessed be God, for his and
our deliverance, from the Parlament.'[1]

Rupert was warmly welcomed by Prince Charles, who was now sixteen years old, and also by the French royal family. Queen Henrietta,
however, at first received her nephew coldly. 'Here his H was ill entertain'd by her Majesty,' records the *Rupert Diary*, 'till the Q: of France
took his part.' This Queen of France was Anne of Austria, Regent since
the death in 1643 of her husband King Louis XIII. Richelieu had
died a few months before his master, and the effective ruler of France
was now the supple Italian Cardinal Mazarin, who had been the earlier
prelate's protégé. The new King, Louis XIV, was not quite eight years
old.

It was not Queen Anne's advocacy alone that altered Henrietta
Maria's attitude to Rupert. A more influential advocate, probably,
was her husband. King Charles was now at Newcastle, virtually a
prisoner of the Scots; but he was still able to write to his wife, and in a
postscript to a letter dated 5 August 1646 he wrote: 'If thou see Pr.
Rupert tell him that I recommend him to thee, for albeit his passions
may sometimes make him mistake, yet I am confident of his honesty
and courage, having at least [last?] behaved himself very well.'[2] And so
the Queen, for the time being at least, was reconciled with her nephew.

Nevertheless it was French court favour that was most valuable to
Rupert at this time. He was still only twenty-six, and war-weary
though he had undoubtedly been in the closing stages of the English
conflict he was now eager for new military employment. There was
also the money question. Little enough is known of Prince Rupert's

financial position at this or any other stage of his life; but certainly he was never a rich man, and in 1646, with the loss of his army command, he must have been hard up. There was no money to spare at St Germain, where many of the courtiers (though not Jermyn) were reduced to penury. It was essential that Rupert should find something to do.

This did not prove difficult. The war that had ravaged Europe for twenty-eight years was drawing to an end, more through the exhaustion of nations and armies than from hope of a satisfactory peace; but a desultory campaign between French and Spanish forces was being waged on the borders of France and Flanders, and Mazarin, at the Queen Regent's instigation, was only too glad to enlist the support of a soldier of Rupert's reputation. Gaston Duc d'Orléans, uncle of the French King, was also an advocate, and Rupert was offered the rank of Maréchal de Camp, roughly equivalent to brigade commander, with 'a Regt of ffoot, a Troop of Horse, and the Comand of all the English in ffrance'.[3]

On this occasion Rupert, always so scrupulous of his honour, appears not to have raised the question of his promise, given five years before, never again to fight against the Emperor. Presumably he salved his conscience with the consideration that only the Spanish army was involved in hostilities with the French in this particular theatre of war. He did, however, refuse to accept without the permission of the English King, and when this had been obtained he reserved to himself 'a liberty of entering at any time into the Service of the Kg of Great Brittagne, if there should be occasion'.[4]

These points settled, Rupert raised his English forces. There was no lack of recruits, for the defeated Cavaliers in exile on the continent were delighted to serve under the Prince once more. Soon he found himself at the head of between 1,500 and 2,000 men. Among those who applied was Goring, but Rupert refused his services and Goring promptly accepted a Spanish commission.

In the meantime Rupert appeared briefly in the unaccustomed role of courtier. Queen Henrietta Maria had set her heart on arranging a marriage between her son Prince Charles and his cousin Anne Marie Louise de Bourbon, Duchesse de Montpensier, known to history as 'la Grande Mademoiselle'. It would have been an advantageous match, for Anne Marie, the daughter of that veteran intriguer Gaston d'Orléans, was the greatest heiress in France, having been left an enormous fortune by her mother. She was three years older than the Prince of Wales: a tall, commanding blonde, intelligent, high-spirited, imperious, and with an exalted idea of her own importance. Prince Charles had been Rupert's devoted admirer since the days of Edgehill, and he now called on his services to assist him in paying court to the royal lady. Rupert the linguist was recruited to act as interpreter between the couple, and accompanied the young man to Fontainebleau. He appears to have done his best, but the courtship was not a success. Neither party was enthusiastic. Prince Charles had already embarked on his career as a philanderer, which he was to pursue with energy to the end of his life; and he was not attracted to his overpowering cousin. His own ignorance of French was more diplomatic than real: a fact which Mademoiselle, though her first impression was that 'he neither spoke, nor in any manner understood the French language',[5] quickly divined. 'What is strange, and hard to believe,' she wrote in her memoirs, 'is, he told Prince Rupert, his cousin, who served as an interpreter, that he understood everything I said, although he knew nothing of French.'[6] The truth was that Charles had little wish for personal contact or prolonged conversation with his intended bride; his taste ran to less impressive and more pliant damsels.

Mademoiselle, for her part, had her eye on bigger game. Ferdinand III had recently become a widower, and the glittering prospect of the Empire was dangled before her. The penniless and exiled English Prince had hardly a chance, even if he had wanted it.

So the matchmaking faded out; Rupert failed to make his mark as Cupid. In the event Mademoiselle was destined to remain unwed for many years, and when she did at last marry, in her forties, the match was generally regarded as a *mésalliance*.

In the summer of 1647 Prince Rupert and his English troops were posted to the Flemish border. The campaign that followed in that much fought-over area, however, bordered on the ridiculous. The Spaniards were besieging Armentières, and Rupert was ordered to join the relieving force. As some 20,000 Spanish troops were engaged, and the French amounted to not more than 7,000, the prospects were not hopeful. The senior French commander was the Comte de Gassion, an officer of gay and dashing gallantry, erratic military judgement, and considerable eccentricity. Associated with him, however, was the Danish Marshal Rantzau, a much-battered veteran who had fought under Condé at Rocroi in 1643 and who had little respect for Gassion; and the curious seventeenth-century device seems to have been employed of allotting the military command to different generals on different days.

When Rupert arrived Gassion greeted him cheerfully and promised him 'un bel Action demain'.[7] The *belle action* that ensued, as described in the *Rupert Log-book*, quickly opened the Prince's eyes to the French marshal's carefree methods of warfare:

. . . the next day after Gassion went to view the Enemye Line on the other side of the River; taking the P along with him: under the protection of certain Hedges they came up near to the River side where Gassion spake to the P: to stay behind till he call'd him, whence the P stayd with two others. then Mr Gassion advanc'd to a little house like a fferay house upon the side of the River. The P. heard the Stroke of the Ore as if a Boat were coming over the River; but darst not give Gassion any notice of it, for fear of Discovering him to the Enemy. The Mareschall stay'd there till the People out of the Boat were Landed: who sent one before to see if the house were clear, and coming on the further side of the House he came upon the Back of Gassion as he was peeping at the Armye another way. But Gassion having a presence of witt, set a good face on't and rebukt the souldier as if he had been one of their own officers. O faiz tu la, va tan a ton quartier, what the devill do yo do here go to your Quarter. So the Souldier stopped at it taking him for one of their own officers. This pause of the Souldier gave the marischall time to run for't to get a Hedge; and the Enemyes flynt lock firing after him. He got in very great disorder over a Ditch, and the P: coming up to him to bring him off (he said) mort dieu ce m'arrive toujour. I have allwayes thus luck. To which the P reply'd Je n'en doubt poynt, si vous faiz come la souvent.[8]

Gassion's conduct, if foolhardy, had at least been resourceful, but hardly prudent for a commander-in-chief. And in this manner he continued. On the following day he marched his troops towards the enemy camp 'on the other side of the River where the passage was clear, with a Pretence to fall upon the Line'.[9] At this point, perhaps at the insistence of Rantzau, he called a council of war, and Rantzau asked Rupert 'what that mad man Gassion intended to do',[10] as the ground ruled out all possibility of an attack by the horse. Rupert then gave his opinion: it was inadvisable to attack with the inferior forces at their disposal. He was supported by the council, and Gassion was overruled. The French drew off, and the Spaniards were allowed to take Armentières.

Having taken it they marched westwards towards their garrison of La Bassée, the French marching parallel with them. On the way Gassion once more indulged his *penchant* for viewing the enemy in person at close quarters. Asking Rupert if he was well mounted, he suggested that they should 'go see the army'.[11] Rupert agreed, and leaving Rantzau behind the two generals went off together, with two or three others, to have a look at the Spanish troops. They were promptly ambushed from behind a hillock, and a troop of Spanish horse tried to cut them off from their own forces. Gassion and the Prince got over a little slough, and two of Rupert's officers who had been left behind came up with some volunteers to help them. One was Robert Holmes, who had fought gallantly under Prince Maurice at Roundway Down and was to be one of Prince Rupert's most trusted servants in the future; the other, named Mortaigne, was Rupert's Gentleman of the Horse and had been with him all through the Civil War. They beat off the Spaniards as they were attempting to cross a rivulet, but both were wounded: Holmes in the leg, Mortaigne in the hand. Mortaigne got back to Rupert, but Holmes, whose 'legg was shot in pieces just under the knee',[12] was left lying on the ground. Thereupon Rupert, 'seeing that nobody would engage to bring him off, went himself with Mortaigne, who being wounded in the hand could give little help, his H: took him up behind with great danger and difficulty, and so brought him off, not any of the ffrench volunteers coming in to his assistance'.[13]

From this time onwards relations between Rupert and Gassion, understandably, deteriorated. And worse was to follow.

The Spaniards now moved south-east to Landrecies, and orders came for the French to relieve this garrison. The attempt failed, and Rupert was left to effect a retreat with three regiments of German horse. This he did, beating off 6,000 of the Spaniards' best men who were sent out against him. Gassion came to tell him that his cannon were stuck fast in the mud, but Rupert asked for reinforcements, which Gassion gave him, and 'undertook to make good the Retreat and bring off the Cannon which Gassion was in doubt whether he should leave behind or no'.[14] The Prince was as good as his word, and drew off the whole force without the loss of a man.

It was presumably during this retreat that the first real clash between Gassion and Rupert took place. Gassion left the Prince at 'a small redoubt they had made with 25 horse'.[15] Rupert here beat off a number of attacks, but the position evidently could not be defended for long, and the Prince prepared to withdraw. Thereupon 'Gassion desir'd him to stay as long as he could there, and the P sent him word it was not his day of command, and came away'.[16]

Friction between the two was apparently reported to the highest quarters, and Gassion received a rebuke, though its terms are obscure. The *Rupert Diary* adds at this point: 'The P was not well us'd by Gassion, which was understood, and he was chequ'd from the Court, enquiring whether he would be a Croat or a Generall.' There were Croats on both sides, light horsemen who harried the flanks of the enemy.[17] Possibly they had become a byword for indiscipline and lack of order.

Rupert at least, in this miserable campaign, had done nothing to diminish his military reputation, and he now brought about the only tangible success of which the French army could boast. La Bassée, to the north-west, was the next objective. Rupert took his horse ahead, leaving the foot to follow, and arrived almost at the same time as a relief force of 300 or 400 men consisting largely of English cavalry of Goring's troops. These were all captured by Rupert, and most of them consented to take service under him. With his augmented horse, and with the foot that now came up, the Prince laid siege to the town, and in three weeks the Spanish garrison capitulated.

Gassion had had no part in the siege, and according to Warburton now 'did manifestly envy the Prince the honour of taking it, not having allowed him so much as passing for the facilitating of the work'.[18] This apparently led him, in the final episode of his relations with Rupert, to the most disreputable piece of behaviour of which he was guilty. It is thus recounted in the *Rupert Log-book*:

> At La Basse Gassion envites the P one day to take the Ayre with him; and his H accompany'd him but his businesse was to carry him to Bysters to talk to his Bayliff about Oates and Hay; and he took 80 horse of the Guards along with him. A Boor taking notice of this sent and fetch'd a Party of about 100 flint locks to try and interrupt them in their Return. As they came back the P: discover'd a Dogg sitting upon his tayle and looking towards the Wood. Whereupon his H gave Sr Wm Reeves (who was then his Page) his Cloak, and riding through the Park up to Gassion who was about 40 yards in the head of them with some officers with him. Have a care Sr (sayes the P) there's a Party in the Wood. The word was no sooner spoken but they had a salvo from the Enemyes Ambush bothe before and behind. So they were forc'd to break through the ffire. Sr Wm Reeves with some others being taken Prisoners, the Governor of Armeniers very civilly return'd him again. When they had broken through Gassion fac'd about towards the Enemy. Sayes Gassion mort dieu Il faut rompre le col assez bougres La; let's break the necks of those Rogues, and taking his foot out of the stirrup the P with some few officers took it that he was alighting, and that the whole party should do the like; and so to fall upon the ambush with Sword and Pistol. The P: and some officers alighting from their horses, Gassion in the mean time march'd away with the Horses; the Enemy following the P: and those Officers on foot; and there his H rec'd a shot in the head. . . .

Rupert escaped from the ambush and returned to Gassion, who remarked politely that he was sorry to see the Prince was wounded. 'Moi aussi' was Rupert's terse retort.

The story of this campaign is told from Rupert's point of view,[19] and I know of no French account to provide a counter-balance. It is possible that in this last incident some genuine misunderstanding may have taken place which could explain away what appears on the surface to have been an act of deliberate treachery. At any rate the result to Rupert, who as a rule seemed to bear a charmed life, was in this case an injury which was to trouble him to the end of his life.

It was the end of the campaign for him, and for this he is unlikely to have been sorry. He returned to La Bassée for treatment, and from there moved to Béthune. By September 1647 he was back at St Germain.

About the same time the Comte de Gassion was killed by a musket-shot in the head while besieging Lans.

King Charles had been handed over by the Scots to the English Parliament, and from Hampton Court, where he was now a prisoner, Rupert received a letter which put the seal on the reconciliation between uncle and nephew. The King assured the Prince that since they had last met all Rupert's actions had more than confirmed the good opinion he had of him; and he added that, 'next my children (I say next) I shall have most care of you, and shall take the first opportunity either to employ you or have your company'. A postscript referred to Rupert's wound, of which the King had not heard 'before I was assured of your recovery; for which nobody, without compliment, is gladder than myself'.[20]

Rupert's wound, though it never completely healed, did not incapacitate him for long, and he was once again eager for action. This time, however, it was of a different nature. There was no more campaigning with the French for him, and he was now at liberty to pursue his private feuds. Digby, after a series of adventures that took him to Ireland and Jersey, arrived in France at the beginning of October. Rupert awaited him at St Germain; and all the injuries he had suffered at this man's hand now urged him to vengeance. The time had passed when he and Digby had, despite all their differences, at least been fellow-soldiers devoted to the cause of their King. Neither was in official employ now, and Rupert felt free to call his enemy to account.

He was not the only one. On his way from Rouen to Paris Digby received a challenge from that other intriguer Lord Wilmot, who accused him of writing letters to his prejudice to the Queen.[21] Digby, puzzled, pointed out that the letters in question had been written long before, and that since then there had been a formal reconciliation between the two of them; but Wilmot stuck to his point and demanded satisfaction. After some negotiations through Daniel O'Neill, who had attached himself to Digby, the two agreed to meet at St Germain, but Digby insisted that he had done no injuries to Wilmot 'but the same that he was forced by the duty of his place to do to the King's own nephew Prince *Rupert*'.[22] To this Wilmot replied that Rupert would not seek satisfaction that way, and then, so Digby told O'Neill, drew him aside and 'desired him to be very careful of himself, for he knew there was foul play intended him by Prince *Rupert*'.[23]

Arrangements for this duel hung fire, and in the meantime Prince Rupert issued his challenge, sending a French friend, M. de la Chapelle, to Digby the morning after his arrival at St Germain with the message that 'he expected him with his sword in his hand at the Cross of *Poissy*, a large league off in the forest with three in his company'.[24] Digby replied that he would willingly meet the Prince immediately, but having no horses of his own and being unable to procure any without arousing suspicion at court he would have to come on foot and would be half an hour late. Thereupon Rupert himself sent horses to meet Digby and his party half-way.

The duel, however, was not destined to take place. Word of the challenge had reached the court, and the Queen took steps to stop it. The instrument she chose was Jermyn, who went to Digby before he set out and gave him the order. Digby, however, was not easily put off. He had received Rupert's challenge and deemed himself in honour bound to accept it; and he replied with the surprising suggestion that Jermyn should join his party as one of his seconds. His proposal deferred the prevention of the duel, but not quite in the manner Digby had suggested. Jermyn had always been Rupert's loyal friend, and Digby's cool request roused him to anger. He expressed himself ready to defy the Queen's order, but in his own way; 'the Lord *Jermin* with some passion,' wrote O'Neill, '(as I conceive he had reason) reply'd, if you will force me to such extremities, I will be of the party, but it shall be against you.'[25]

Digby and Jermyn then went off to the meeting-place by different routes; Digby picked up the horses sent by Rupert, and at Poissy the two antagonists with their seconds (Rupert's now included Jermyn) prepared for the encounter. That was as far as it got. The Queen's Guards appeared on the scene, as Jermyn presumably knew they would; and simultaneously arrived the Prince of Wales, who had been hunting in the forest nearby. The whole party were arrested and taken back to St Germain, where the Queen ordered an immediate inquiry into the whole business to be held by Lord Culpeper, Lord Gerard, Lord Wentworth and Sir Frederick Cornwallis.

The result, surprisingly, was complete reconciliation between Rupert and Digby. Rupert's anger had cooled, and he 'most discreetly and most nobly declar'd, that he was far from making a quarrel with the Lord Digby upon any thing he had done against him as Secretary of State, tho' of never so much prejudice to him: but that this resentment was upon speeches that he was inform'd the Lord Digby had publish'd highly to his dishonour'.[26] The formula gave Digby the chance to withdraw without loss of honour, and Culpeper and his colleagues 'found his Lordship so forward to clear himself of an imputation so prejudicial to him, as that having publish'd the pretended words concerning his Highness, and on the other side his Highness so generous in not demanding or expecting from the Lord *Digby* any thing that might misbecome him, that the business was that night concluded in the presence of the Queen and the Prince of *Wales*'.[27]

The reconciliation had a sequel. The postponed meeting between Digby and Wilmot took place near Paris on 9 October, and in agreeing to it Digby declared that 'the Lord Willmot had given his Lordship such ungentlemanlike provocations, as he would rather have answer'd with an affront than with his sword, but for another thing that had interven'd; which was the only ground upon which he could then fight with him, namely, that the Lord *Willmot* had been author to the Lord *Digby* of so unworthy a scandal upon Prince Rupert, as to tell his Lordship that his Highness would not seek right of him in a way of honour, but that he intended his Lordship foul play'.[28]

In the duel Wilmot was wounded in the hand. So Rupert was avenged upon another of his enemies by the agency of the one who had injured him most of all.

But Rupert had not yet finished with his private enmities. Lord Percy, as General of the Ordnance in the King's army, had not only shown himself incompetent but had subjected the Prince to incessant frustration by his dilatoriness in providing arms and ammunition. How far this was deliberate it is hard to say, but Percy had always been ready to intrigue with Rupert's enemies at court, and Rupert's resentment had been smouldering for years.

Now he seized his opportunity. In April 1648, on the excuse of being injured by something said by Percy, he rode up to him on a hunting expedition and, laying his hand on his bridle, demanded satisfaction. Percy replied haughtily that he would immediately give it and that there was no need to seize his bridle, and the two men dismounted and fought there and then. After the second pass 'Percy was run through the fleshie part of his right side much backwards, and in that passe they closed, and falling both to the ground Percy's hand was hurt.'[29] They were then separated, and Percy's wounds were found not to be serious.

During this period immediately following the end of the English Civil War Rupert, in spite of his spells of unemployment, made no move to visit his mother. Maurice stayed quietly at The Hague, but Rupert kept aloof. Probably he was resentful of the part Queen Elizabeth had played throughout the hostilities, keeping in close touch with her favourite son Charles Louis and thus by inference inclining to the side of the Parliament. This is of necessity guesswork, for no letters survive to reveal the feelings of either. It does not appear that Elizabeth wrote to her second son at all at this time, and she seldom mentioned him in her correspondence with the eldest.

The Winter Queen had in any event enough to exercise her mind in the conduct of two other members of the family – her two youngest sons. Prince Edward, gayest and handsomest of the Palatines, had been living mainly in Paris, employed happily in revelries and gallantries suitable to his age and station, and fighting at least one duel. His proposal in April 1645 to join Rupert in England had come to nothing, but the twenty-year-old Prince was soon involved in a different sort of adventure.

In May the news leaked out that Edward had secretly married a highly-placed lady eight years older than himself. Rupert was one of the first to be informed. Jermyn wrote to him from Paris on 5 May 1645: 'Your Highness is to know *a romance story* that concerns you here, in the person of Prince Edward. He is last week married privately to the Princess Anne, the Duke of Nevers' daughter. . . . She is very rich; six or seven thousand pounds a-year sterling is the least that can fall to her, maybe more: and is a very beautiful young lady.'[30]

Edward had done extremely well for himself. Anne de Gonzagues, besides being the daughter of the Duc de Nevers, Montferrat and Mantua, was sister of the Queen of Poland and was a shining figure in Parisian society, noted for her beauty, charm and wit. It was felt in her circle that she had thrown herself away on an impoverished exile, and the Queen Regent of France was at first furious and ordered Edward to return to Holland; but she soon relented. Edward and Anne cared nothing for the sensation their romance had caused. They were in love, and remained so.

There was nothing in the bride's worldly circumstances to make the Winter Queen disapprove of the marriage. But shattering news was to follow. Anne de Gonzagues was a devoted Catholic, and it was not long before it was learned at The Hague that Edward himself had been received into the Catholic Church. Elizabeth reacted as she had reacted to Queen Henrietta Maria's attempt to convert Rupert to the faith eight years before, and wrote in distraction to Charles Louis, who was equally dismayed. Deep-seated hatred and distrust of Rome were the mainspring of the Queen's anger; but with the Prince Elector political considerations were uppermost. The possession of a papist brother would do him no good with the English Parliament.

Mother and son continued to discuss the matter in correspondence, but there was nothing they could do except console themselves with the conviction that neither the romance nor the conversion would last. They were wrong. The marriage proved happy and successful, Edward remained a faithful Catholic, and the couple became popular and respected ornaments of French society. Charm combined with wealth, moreover, was not without its influence at The Hague. Before many years had passed Prince Edward was again on good terms with his mother.

This episode threw Queen Elizabeth into a frenzy of anxiety for her youngest surviving son. In 1646 Prince Philip was eighteen years old;

a true Palatine, fiery, unruly and impetuous. At this time he was intent on raising some troops to serve with the Republic of Venice, a project that his eldest brother viewed with misgiving. 'I could wish either my brother Rupert or Maurice would undertake the Venetian employment,' wrote Charles Louis, 'my brother Philip being very young to undertake such a task.'[31]

But before he could leave The Hague Prince Philip became the central figure in a highly sensational incident in which the Winter Queen was herself involved. Among the hangers-on in Elizabeth's circle was a certain Jacques de l'Epinay, Sieur de Vaux, an attractive but brash young French exile with a reputation as a lady-killer. The Queen was enchanted with him, and so possibly was her second daughter Louise. Elizabeth, unconventional and careless of her reputation as she was, admitted him to an unqueenly intimacy and allowed him such liberties as walking beside her with his hat on: liberties which deeply offended her friends and at least one of her children. Inevitably the young man became more and more insolent, and Philip in particular became furiously resentful.

The storm broke in June 1646. Wild rumours soon spread, and it was said that the spark which ignited the fire was the Frenchman's boast that he had enjoyed the favours of both Queen Elizabeth and Princess Louise.[32] Certainly something occurred which brought Prince Philip to a determination to avenge in blood the insult to his family. He had already warned de l'Epinay to keep away from his mother's palace, and now, on the night of 20 June, he ran into him close to the house. A brawl ensued, and the two young men and their respective attendants were separated by the watch. Next evening Philip again encountered de l'Epinay as he was returning from a dinner-party. Philip leaped from his coach and threw himself on his adversary; de l'Epinay just had time to draw his sword before the Palatine prince plunged his hunting knife into his throat. De l'Epinay fell dying, and Philip got back into his coach and bolted to the Spanish Netherlands frontier.

The scandal was deeply felt in the Palatine family. The Winter Queen fulminated against her youngest son, but Philip won warm support from other members of his house. Louise's sentiments are not recorded, but her elder sister Elizabeth had strongly disapproved of de l'Epinay and is said to have been temporarily estranged from her mother through her support of her youngest brother. Rupert evidently shared her views. There is no evidence that he bothered himself one way or the other about what Prince Edward had done; doubtless, in accordance with his usual principles, he regarded his brother's choice of both bride and religion as entirely his own affair. But to judge from a letter from Charles Louis to his mother, dated 10 July, Rupert, who arrived in France just at this time, fully supported Philip. 'My brother Rupert sending this bearer to your Majesty about his business,' wrote the Elector, 'I cannot omit to accompany him with my humble request in favour of the suit he hath to you in my brother's behalf,' Charles Louis went on to justify Philip's behaviour in view of 'the affront he received, of the blemish had lain upon him all his life-time if he had not resented it; but much more that of his blood, and of his nearness to you, and to him whose ashes you have ever professed more love and value than to any thing upon earth.'[33]

There, so far as the famliy were concerned, the matter rested. There could be no question of Elizabeth's receiving Philip back into favour, since he could not set foot in Holland. He went over to England where his eldest brother, with the consent of Parliament, helped him to raise 1,000 men for Venice. But he did not stay long in Venetian service. The rest of his short life he spent as a soldier of fortune; fighting now in one army, now in another.

In the years 1646 to 1648 Rupert's character appears in its most sombre and least attractive light: irascible, quarrelsome, vindictive. He was restless and discontented, and the effects of his wound were doubtless troubling him. He needed new employment worthy of his talents and his loyalties. The opportunity was now at hand.

CHAPTER 2

FOR THE KING AGAIN

WHEN the Civil War petered out with the collapse of the Royalist armies, the last senior commander to make a stand for the King was that splendid infantry veteran Lord Astley. Making his way through Worcestershire towards Oxford with 3,000 men, he was defeated near Stow-on-the-Wold by a much superior Roundhead force on 21 March 1646. And in the hour of surrender he addressed his captors in words that have become almost as celebrated as his famous prayer before Edgehill. 'You have now done your work, and may go to play,' he said as he seated himself calmly on a drum; and then he added: 'unless you will fall out amongst your selves.'[1]

Within eighteen months it was clear that Astley's suggestion was coming true. The victors were split into two main factions, with a number of sub-groups that were a nuisance to both. In the background was another factor, the Scots army which had withdrawn within the borders of its own country but had by no means relinquished its interest in English affairs.

In Parliament the Presbyterians were in the majority. Their aim was to impose their own ecclesiastical system, in alliance with the Scots, on the whole of Great Britain, and to use the monarchy for their own purposes. Against them the Independents, increasingly strong in the army, stood for the right of congregations to follow their own individual religious principles and resented the attempt of the Presbyterians to lay down the law for all. Among the Independents, as a powerful minority section, stood the Levellers under John Lilburne, who agitated for the overthrow of the existing constitution and the setting up of a republican and democratic régime. In the army Cromwell was, politically speaking, the acknowledged leader, though Fairfax was still in command. Parliament was anxious to disband the New Model as soon as possible, and offered its members the choice of demobilization or service in Ireland, where there was still armed resistance; but it lacked the power to enforce its demands. Pay was in arrears, and the army leaders were in no mood to throw away the power their possession of armed force gave them. Signs were not wanting that the Commons must soon find themselves overawed by Cromwell and his men.

The prize for which the two main parties contended was the person of the King. The Scots had handed King Charles over to the English Parliament, but the army leaders manoeuvred to get him into their power. As diplomatic manoeuvres continued, the rift between Army and Parliament widened. At the same time the troops were getting out of hand. The conduct of the soldiers and the increasingly obvious threat of a harsh military dictatorship, coupled with the signs of disillusion in the Roundheads' ranks, led to a popular reaction in favour of the King and to the feeling that the time was ripe for his restoration to power. The result was the series of Royalist risings known as the Second Civil War.

At the end of 1647 King Charles made contact with the Scots commissioners in England, and on 26 December made with them a secret agreement, known as the 'Engagement', by which the Scottish army was once more to invade England in return for his undertaking to suppress the Independents and establish Presbyterianism for a minimum period of three years. The Scots did not recross the border till the following July, but in the meantime the spark had been ignited. In March 1648 the Governor of Pembroke, Colonel John Poyer, declared for the King, and Royalists rose in Essex and in Kent. Fairfax marched against the southern insurgents while Cromwell first subdued the Welsh Royalists and then turned north to meet the Scots. But the unrest in the coastal areas helped to bring about the most promising development for the royal cause. In May a substantial portion of the fleet threw off the Roundhead yoke and sailed for Holland to put itself at the disposal of the Prince of Wales.

The Parliamentary fleet at this time was commanded by Vice-Admiral William Batten, the sailor who had fired on Queen Henrietta Maria when she returned to England in 1643. Batten, a professional 'tarpaulin' seaman ill at ease in politics, had taken over from the Lord High Admiral, the veteran Earl of Warwick, when the latter resigned his post under the Self-Denying Ordinance. For the first few months of 1648 he had been superseded by Thomas Rainsborough, a convinced republican, but Rainsborough's unpopularity with the crews led to a near mutiny, and Batten was recalled. How far he was initially concerned in the decision of the disaffected ships to declare for the King is uncertain, but the Parliamentary leaders evidently did not trust him. They recalled Warwick to the supreme command and ordered the Vice-Admiral to repair to him at Portsmouth; whereupon Batten, after an unsuccessful attempt to induce the ships' commanders at Portsmouth to join him, himself sailed for Holland in a frigate. There the Prince of

Wales knighted him and appointed him Rear-Admiral of what now constituted the Royalist fleet. The Prince himself was titular Admiral, but though he intended to sail in command of his fleet he sent at once for his cousin Rupert to be his Vice-Admiral and virtual commander of the Royalist naval force.

Rupert had never yet commanded at sea; but the appointment was in no way unusual. In the seventeenth century, as in the days of Drake, no clear division between land and sea warfare was recognized; nor were the army and navy regarded as distinct and separate services. Officers were transferred from one to the other as circumstances dictated. Moreover Rupert was by no means ignorant of nautical matters. He had grown up in the maritime atmosphere of the Dutch republic; during his first visit to England before the Civil War he had shown deep interest in shipbuilding and the affairs of the navy, hoping as he did at that time to sail at the head of a fleet to Madagascar; and his keen brain had been devoted to mastering the details of all forms of warfare and of military and naval technique. He was an obvious man for the post.

He lost no time in answering the call. His French hosts were anxious to retain his services, and he was offered a variety of appointments; but he had always made it clear where his first loyalty lay, and retained the right to leave France and serve his King whenever he should be required to do so. On 29 June 1648 he left Paris for Calais, thence proceeding to The Hague.

It was his first visit to Holland since 1642, but once again there is no record of any immediate contact with his mother. It is probable, however, that they did meet. Whatever Charles Louis might be doing in London, the Winter Queen was now a full supporter of her brother's cause, as she was soon to prove; and any animosity that Rupert may have felt seems to have been dispelled. Prince Maurice, moreover, was with his mother, and hastened to join Rupert in the fleet.

Happy to be serving his King once more, the Prince was in his sunniest mood. 'Prince Ruperts carriage was such at Callice and throughout the jorney thither,' wrote Lord Hatton to Sir Edward Nicholas, 'that I protest I was overjoyed to see itt both for the publicke and the Princes happiness in his company; and I wish from my hart he were soe well att sea as that his councells might assist the Prince [of Wales]. Certainly, Sir, hee appeares to me to be a strangely changed man in his carriage, and for his temperance and abilities I thinke they were not much questioned.'[2] There was little delay. On 22 July the little fleet set sail from Holland for the Downs, the Channel roadstead off Deal between the North and the South Foreland. The Prince of Wales, as Admiral, flew his flag in the frigate *Satisfaction*.

227

There were, however, the usual dissensions among the Royalists as to the best course to pursue. Some of the more hot-headed exiles who had joined the fleet on Prince Charles's call were in favour of immediately trying conclusions with the Parliamentary navy: a rash challenge which would almost certainly have been disastrous. Batten and Joseph Jordan, who had joined the Royalists with him, were for sailing to Scotland. The Scots army under the Duke of Hamilton had now crossed the border, and the Earl of Lauderdale was conferring on the Duke's behalf with the Prince of Wales in the *Satisfaction*. Rupert, characteristically, urged a more daring tactic which would have taken the fleet in the opposite direction. His plan was to make for the Isle of Wight and rescue the King; then, with his royal master on board, to sail up the Thames and rouse the people in his name.

This plan, might have succeeded. But a different one found favour in the eyes of the seamen, who had to be conciliated in view of their doubtful loyalty. This at least appeared practical. The fleet had to be victualled and the crews paid, and money and supplies were as usual short. The plan was to blockade London and hover about the mouth of the Thames, capturing ships leaving or returning and claiming them as prizes of war.

Faced with these divided counsels the royal fleet achieved little. Rupert's plan was rejected, but two landings were attempted on the east coast. Colchester had been seized for the King, and the Royalists first sailed into Yarmouth Roads with the idea of putting a force ashore to relieve the town. But the number of fighting soldiers aboard the ships was small, and the attempt was easily repulsed. So back they went to the Downs. The three castles of Walmer, Deal and Sandwich had also revolted from the Parliament, and on 14 August a force of 500 men was landed near Deal. This again was a failure; the men were beaten off without difficulty.

So the seamen's plan was adopted. The royal ships lingered for a month in the Downs and at the mouth of the Thames, taking a few prizes. Then towards the end of August came the news of Hamilton's defeat by Cromwell at Preston, which put an end to all hopes of a Royalist victory in the Second Civil War. The Prince of Wales decided to take his fleet back to Holland.

Their return was not without incident. The disaffected seamen of the *Satisfaction*, eager for more prizes, broke into mutiny, demanding to be taken to Lee Road where Warwick's fleet lay; their wrath was centred on Culpeper and Lauderdale, whom they blamed for the decision to withdraw, and they threatened to throw them both overboard. The situation was saved by the coolness and courage of the Prince of Wales, who faced the seamen on deck, explained to them the reasons for his decision (principally the shortage of provisions), and 'gave them so kind words, that at length his ship was after a sort, content to go for Holland'.[3]

No sooner had the mutiny been quelled than Warwick's fleet was sighted coming out of Lee Road, whereat the Prince of Wales 'greatly reioyceing cutt a caper',[4] declaring his resolution to fight the enemy; and the seamen saluted him 'by throwing up their capps, and great acclamations of joy'.[5] But it was not Warwick's tactics to fight at this point. When he saw the Royalist fleet bearing down on him he withdrew before it, seeking the advantage of the wind. His adversaries, taking his withdrawal for retreat, pursued all day, till at nightfall the two fleets anchored at about a league's distance from each other.

At daybreak both prepared for a battle which, wrote the wife of one of Prince Charles's officers, 'would have been the most cruel fight that ever England knew'.[6] Batten, if we are to accept an anecdote related by Pepys many years later, showed what would appear to be signs of terror, and in his fear fell foul of Prince Rupert. 'Mr. Coventry,' wrote the diarist on 4 June 1664, 'discoursing this noon about Sir W. Batten (what a sad fellow he is) told me how the King [Charles II] told him the other day how Sir W. Batten, being in the ship with him and Prince Rupert when they expected to fight with Warwicke, did walk up and down sweating with a napkin under his throat to dry up his sweat. And that Prince Rupert, being a most Jealous man, and particularly of Batten, doth walk up and down, swearing bloodily to the King that Batten had a mind to betray them today, and that the napkin was a signall; "But, by God", says he, "if things go ill, the first thing I will do is to shoot him".'[7]

But the fight was not to be; for 'at that instant there fell so great and sudden a gust of wind, that we had nothing else to save us from the sands that are dangerous in that place, but by casting anchor, which we did within cannon shot one of another, where we lay till next morning'.[8] So for a second night the fleets lay at close quarters, but on the following morning, 'our victuals spent and our mutineers satisfied, we weighed anchor, and set sail for Holland'.[9]

Warwick weighed anchor too, and followed the Royalists. There was one more incident, in which again Batten appears in a dubious light. It is thus related in the *Rupert Log-book*:

... Just as they were setting sayle, a boat gave them advice that they had seen ships which they believd the Portsmouth fleet standing up the River, but this would not be believ'd. At night the P standing upon the Deck in the Constant Reformation, Patison (the Master of the Ship) Cry'd out to his H that he saw a light, and askt what he should do. The P: told him that he believ'd it was the Portsmouth ffleet, and Patison with the rest of the Seamen were of that Opinion. Whereupon the P: advised the stearing toward them; which he did accordingly as they were upon their Course. Batten spake to the King [the Prince of Wales] Sr (sayes he) whither do we steer. Will yor Maty have him steer out of the way for every Collier that he sees. The Swallow and 2 or 3 ships more steer'd with the Portsmouth fleet, and hail'd them, and bade them follow, they answer'd yea yea; being then at anchor, expecting the Tide to carry them into the River. But the King stearing his Course for Holland, the rest follow'd; and this was the Losse of the Portsmouth fleet, which would have furnish'd the Kg with Provisions and might have been had for the Asking.

This not very lucid passage seems to suggest that Rupert thought the Portsmouth fleet was ready to come over to the Prince of Wales, and that the chance was lost through the pusillanimity of Batten. Or the supposition may have been that the Portsmouth ships would mistake the Royalist fleet for Warwick's, and would thus fall into their enemies' hands. In any case it would have been a gamble. The Portsmouth fleet did join Warwick's, and Rupert's manoeuvre might have meant the Royalists being caught between the two. It may be that in this case Batten's judgement was right.

The Royalist fleet now proceeded on its way towards Holland, making for the harbour of Hellevoetsluis, south of The Hague, where it arrived on 4 September. Warwick followed close behind, and there was a race for possession as the Parliamentarians tried to get into the harbour first: a race won by the Prince's ships through the ruse of a Royalist captain who happened to be then on shore.

The Business was who should first get possession of the Harbour. The Constant Reformation was nearest, and Warwick sent a good sailing ffrigatt to get possession before them. So the P's Boat and the Other rac'd for the Harbour. Theirs was nearest and got a shore first. Capt Allen being then on shore, and pretending to be their friend ask'd for the Rope to ty it fast, and as the boat was putting off again, he let slip the rope, and back went the frigatt; so that his Hi got first possession. Where they hauld in all the ships except the Convertine which upon the next Spring Tide they got in too.[10]

So the two fleets remained; the Prince of Wales's ships in the inner harbour, Warwick's in the outer. The Dutch authorities accepted their presence; there was nothing they could do to prevent it. But the crews, though within shouting distance and indulging in frequent brawls in the taverns on shore, were unable to fire on each other because in a neutral port. It was an explosive situation, in which the enforced truce might at any moment be violated. But to avert an international incident the Dutch sent a squadron of ships which anchored between the two fleets, declaring that in case of any violence they would join in against the aggressor.

The first war expedition of the new Royalist fleet had been singularly fruitless. No naval action had been fought, attempted landings on the English coast had been half-hearted and ineffectual, and the only successes had been the capture of a few prizes whose cargo at least served to keep the King's ships and crews in being. Nor had Rupert played a dominant part. His tactics had been unimpressive, he had allowed himself to be overruled on vital strategic decisions, and in the time of greatest crisis it was the young Prince of Wales, not his battle-hardened cousin, who rose to the occasion. Rupert seems at this juncture to have lacked his usual self-confidence. It was his first venture in naval warfare, and he may have felt that he had not yet mastered the new medium.

Once back in Holland, however, he came into his own. The fleet was in a desperate condition, and the Prince set himself to the task of making it a seaworthy and efficient fighting instrument with all his accustomed energy. The first problem was supplies, and Rupert threw himself into the role of purveyor, bargaining for food and commodities, superintending the sale of the prizes, and scrutinizing prices to eke out the slender resources of money available. No detail was too small for him. 'Concerning the pork,' wrote one of his subordinates, 'he tells me he doth not think there can be so great a quantity provided suddenly. He hath not yet provided any shirts or apparel for the men.'[11]

Pay was a virtually insoluble problem. Nominally a seaman of that time received 24 shillings a month: by no means an inadequate wage in seventeenth-century values. But payment was frequently many months in arrear. Only prizes could compensate; and no new prizes could be taken with the fleet shut up in harbour. But Rupert did what he could, and the men appreciated his efforts. When a deputation of sailors waited on the Prince of Wales at The Hague and were told there was no money to hand out, they expressed themselves contented with the promise of shares in the next prizes. Hyde told Rupert that they had 'behaved themselves very civilly'.[12]

Discipline was the most vital problem. The morale of the fleet was low: partly through inaction, partly through lack of pay. Some men were seduced from their allegiance. The fact that the ships' commanders had come over to the Prince of Wales did not mean that all members of their crews felt the same way. Many indeed, pressed men as they were, had little interest in what cause they fought for; they were concerned for pay and plunder. And when they met ashore the better-paid, better-clothed seamen of Warwick's fleet, they were susceptible to their blandishments. But like sailors and soldiers at all times they responded

to strong leadership. And this was what Rupert provided. At one point
Warwick sent one of his principal officers, Captain Moulton, to the
Prince's ship to beg leave to speak to some of his men. Rupert said 'yes
in his hearing; but if he spake any thing amisse he would throw him
over board'.[13] The request was not pursued.

Mutiny was quelled with a firm hand. Clarendon, who relates
Rupert's doings at this time with a grudging admiration, says that he
'with notable vigour and success suppressed two or three mutinies, in
one of which he had been compelled to throw two or three seamen
overboard by the strength of his own arms'.[14] This is probably an exaggeration of what actually occurred. The mutiny was in the *Antelope*,
'upon a Complaynt about Victualls; and his H coming told them such
as did not like the service might be gon, for he could find people to
suite in the Kgs ships without them. So they stood murmuring, without
giving any Answer'.[15] Then towards Michaelmas Prince Rupert had
the ships unrigged 'to prevent any embezzlement or disorders';[16] and
he sent to the *Antelope* for twenty of their best men to help in the work.
But 'they plainly refusing to come, his Highness went on board himself,
with some half-a-score resolute gentlemen, and called positively for
twenty of their best foremast men, and walked upon the deck to see his
commands obeyed; when the seamen, instead of complying, gathered
about his Highness, and one bold fellow among the rest cried out "one
and all," upon which the Prince immediately caught him in his arms
and held him overboard, as if he would have thrown him into the sea.
The suddenness of this action wrought such a terror upon the rest, that
they returned forthwith to their duty.'[17]

Thus some degree of order was maintained in the fleet. Next Rupert
turned his attention to security, planting guns and erecting fortifications on the harbour walls. At this the States of Holland protested, but,
says the *Rupert Log-book*, 'the P return'd answer that if the States would
answer for the Protection of the ffleet, his H would depend upon it; but
other wise having taken charge of the ffleet by his Mateys Commission
he was resolv'd to protect them as well as he could'.

Rupert's exertions were tremendous; but he was not suffered to
devote all his energies to the fleet. A new Cavalier court had been
established at The Hague, and faction was at work again. In the midst
of his naval anxieties the Prince was involved, in the autumn of 1648, in
a new and serious quarrel with Lord Culpeper. A preliminary clash had
taken place before the expedition to England. Culpeper wished to
exclude the Duke of Buckingham from any command in the Second
Civil War 'unless he would be solely under the Earl of Holland and
declare for the Covenant and such popular wayes as he called them'.[18]
Buckingham was the son of King James I's favourite and the brother

of Rupert's devoted friend the Duchess of Richmond; and Rupert resented the slight on him. 'Prince Rupert stucke to itt and wee carried itt against him [Culpeper],'[19] wrote Hatton. But Rupert's judgement was hardly vindicated. Buckingham's rising in Surrey, in which his brother Lord Francis Villiers was killed, was a dismal failure.

Culpeper was not the man to forget such an episode; he and Rupert had always disliked each other. Clarendon in his account of what happened contrives to put the blame on Rupert, representing him as acting under the influence of Sir Edward Herbert, the Attorney-General, against whom Hyde (the future Earl of Clarendon) had a personal vendetta, and who, according to him, 'had the absolute ascendancy over the prince'.[20] Herbert was certainly Rupert's friend, but there is no reason to suppose that his advice and opinions carried more weight with him than those of others. Indeed the idea of anybody having an 'absolute ascendancy' over Prince Rupert is almost laughable.

The quarrel broke out at a meeting of the Prince of Wales's council. A cargo of sugar which had been captured at sea was to be sold, and Rupert proposed that the sale should be entrusted to Sir Robert Walsh, an Irishman who had distinguished himself at Edgehill but whose later history was suspect. Clarendon's account proceeds:

> . . . the lord Culpeper spoke against him [Walsh] with some warmth, that might be thought to reflect a little upon prince Rupert, who had proposed him. Upon which, asking what exceptions there were to Sir Robert Walsh, why he might not be fit for it, Culpeper answered with some quickness that he was a known cheat; which, though notoriously true, the prince seemed to take very ill, and said he was his friend, and a gentleman; and if he should come to hear of what had been said, he knew not how the lord Culpeper could avoid fighting with him. Culpeper whose courage no man doubted, presently replied, that he would fight with his highness; to which the prince answered very quietly that it was well; and the council rose in great complexity.[21]

Hyde tried to induce Culpeper to apologize to Rupert, but Culpeper, in a furious rage, refused to consider any such thing. Meanwhile Rupert told his friend Herbert what had happened. Herbert was, according to Clarendon, 'the unfittest man living to be trusted with such a secret';[22] but there does not appear to have been anything indiscreet or reprehensible about the course he took. He simply went to the Prince of Wales and suggested that he should intervene to compose the quarrel. The Prince authorized him to act as mediator, and Herbert returned to Prince Rupert and 'so far prevailed with his highness, who would have been more choleric if he had had less right on his side, that he was willing to receive a submission, and promised that the other should receive no affront in the mean time'.[23] Culpeper, on the other hand, at first refused all Herbert's efforts to effect a reconciliation; but after some days he changed his mind, and went with Hyde to Prince Rupert's lodging, 'where he behaved himself very well, and the prince received him with all the grace could be expected; so that so ill a business seemed to be as well concluded as the nature of it would admit'.[24]

It was not quite the end of the affair, for Walsh, having heard of what had passed at the council, confronted Culpeper in the street and, after an argument, hit him in the face. Thereupon the Prince of Wales reported the affront to the States of Holland, who banished the offender from The Hague.

Without more certain knowledge of Walsh's character it is impossible to pronounce on the rights and wrongs of this quarrel. Walsh seems to have been, at the least, a man of violent temper, and later suspicions suggest that he was not to be trusted; Rupert, moreover, did not always show himself a good judge of character. But Clarendon, who is the only authority for the episode, was spiteful and prejudiced, particularly against Herbert, who appears, notwithstanding the narrator's asides, in a favourable light. Yet even Clarendon admits that it was Rupert who showed a conciliatory spirit and behaved magnanimously as soon as Culpeper recovered from his temper.

More satisfactory were Prince Rupert's relations with Montrose. The gallant Marquess, a fugitive from Scotland, was now in Brussels, anxious as ever to strike a blow for his King and ready to return to his native country and lead another Royalist movement. From Brussels he wrote to Rupert on 7 September 1648:

Sir: Your Highness may justly think strange, what should embolden me to this freedom; never having done myself the honour to have used the like heretofore, nor being favoured with your commands now to do it. But when your Highness shall be pleased to know, that I was ever a silent admirer of you, and a passionate affecter of your person, and all your ways, you will be pleased to allow me recourse to your goodness and generosity: And the rather, that your Highness sees I am for the present at such distance *with all interests,* as no end but naked respect can now prompt me to it: Which, if your Highness shall do me the honour to take in good part, and *command me to continue,* I shall hope it will not wrong the King your uncle's service, nor what may touch your Highness, both in relation to those and these parts; in either of which I should presume to be able to do you some small services. So, hoping your Highness will pardon this boldness, and take it from the true fountain, I shall only say, that I desire to be ever, Sir, your Highness's most humble, faithfull, affectionate servant,

MONTROSE.[25]

Rupert replied with equal warmth, his letter being dated 20 September from The Hague. 'The noble kindness I see your Lordship still preserves for the King,' he wrote, 'makes me much to covet that we may be happy to serve him together.'[26]

These two kindred spirits had last met on the morrow of Marston Moor. They would gladly have come together again now; but there were obstacles in the way. Montrose spoke for himself alone, with his prestige and his personal authority over his Highland followers. But there was a strong Royalist reaction throughout Scotland, and the ruling Presbyterian party were negotiating with Prince Charles; the Earl of Lauderdale was at this time at The Hague. To Lauderdale and his party Montrose was anathema, and for this reason the Marquess was unable to visit the Royalist court.

Rupert was naturally sympathetic to Montrose; but he was willing to suppress his own inclinations in the interests of the Royalist cause, and the Presbyterians seemed to offer the best hope of a restoration. Indeed he showed remarkable forbearance. For the Scots insisted that, should Prince Charles land in Scotland, neither of the Palatine princes should accompany him. Charles objected to this clause in the agreement, but it was Rupert who resolved the deadlock by proposing a compromise: he would agree not to go on any expedition to Scotland provided his absence was not made a formal condition. This satisfied Lauderdale, who was impressed by the Prince's magnanimity.

Negotiations proceeded at a leisurely pace, and it would be some time yet before Charles could embark on a Scottish expedition. Meanwhile Rupert, who continued to correspond with Montrose, was officially put in command of the fleet. In fact he was in charge already, but the Prince of Wales was titular Admiral. When the Prince proposed to hand over to his cousin, Rupert at first demurred, suggested that it would be more suitable for him to serve under the nominal command of the Duke of York, now just fifteen years old. But Prince Charles would have none of this, and at the end of October Rupert was appointed Admiral with 'all the powers he formerly exercised on land'; his authority being 'unlimited on the coasts of the three kingdoms'.[27]

The reason for the appointment at this time was that the fleet's next task had been decided. As soon as it could get out of Hellevoetsluis harbour it was to sail to the coast of Ireland, to give what support it could to the Marquess of Ormonde, who had returned there and was rallying the Royalists. A commander with a free hand was needed, and Clarendon, who absurdly accuses Rupert of having intrigued for the post, admits that 'there was in truth nobody in view to whom the charge of the fleet could be committed but prince Rupert'.[28]

Shortly after this the main obstacle to the Irish venture was removed.

For two months Warwick's and Rupert's fleet had been watching each other in harbour. Now the Parliament decided that there was nothing to be gained by continuing to blockade the Royalists; and their ships were needed at home. On 21 November Warwick sailed for the Downs.

Preparations were speeded up. Money of course was urgently needed. The Queen of Bohemia pawned her jewels for the support of the fleet, and Lord Craven came forward once more. Craven had remained at The Hague during the English Civil War, attendant on his beloved Queen and grieved at the rift within the family. Now he promised 'what I have in my power'.[29] He had already taken charge of Black, Rupert's favourite horse, and assured Rupert that had he the means Black 'should have a city erected for to lodge him, at least he shall now be as carefully looked unto, until your Highness be pleased to command him again'.[30] The reference to means may imply that even his apparently inexhaustible purse had suffered from his bounty in the cause of the Palatines, but he was now and always a very rich man.

There were still points to be settled. The use of the standard presented some difficulty, as it could be flown only by a Lord High Admiral, an appointment reserved to the King; the Prince of Wales was not empowered to confer the title. But Warwick as the Parliament's Lord High Admiral flew the standard, and it was felt that Rupert, to maintain his authority in the eyes of the seamen, should have the same privilege. It was finally decided that he should be empowered to hoist the standard at his discretion if the situation demanded it.

A more serious question concerned his position in relation to that of Ormonde, who was Lord Lieutenant of Ireland. Attempts to cause ill-feeling between the two were not wanting. Digby was up to his old tricks, and on 27 November he wrote in insidious terms to Ormonde:

> One thing I thinke it necessary to advertise you of, that prince Rupert hath sett his rest to comand this expedition of the fleete, and the councell have complyed with him in it; insoemuch as, if it arrives safe in Ireland, you must expect him there alsoe. I hope his aime is only at the honour of carying the fleete thither through soe much hazard, and then returning to the prince; but if he have any further designe of continuing to comand the fleete, or of remaineing in that kingdom, I feare the consequences of it, knowing what aplications have been made to him formerly, and how unsettled and weake a people you have there, apt to catch at any thing that's new, to interupt the course that they are brought into (I feare) with litle good affection. . . .[31]

Hyde also was concerned that there would be friction, fearing that 'prince Rupert would not live with amity towards the marquis of Ormonde as was necessary for the public service'.[32] And with lesser men the situation might indeed have led to jealousy and recrimination. But Ormonde was above such pettiness. He brushed Digby's insinuations aside, and the question of status was tacitly ignored.

Just when everything seemed to be ready, Will Legge arrived with an urgent message from the King. Legge, in and out of prison, had been ceaselessly working in England for the escape of his royal master from his captivity in the Isle of Wight, and the letter he now brought read as follows:

> Dearest Nephew,
> For want of a cipher, I have chosen this most trusty messenger, Will Legge, to acquaint you with a business which is of great importance for my service; for I have commanded him to desire in my name both your advice and assistance. Of which, knowing your affection to me, I am so confident that I will say no more, but only to desire you to give full credit to this bearer, and to give him a quick despatch, for his sake who is
>
> > Your loving uncle and most
> > faithful friend,
> > CHARLES R.[33]
>
> Newport, Saturday, 28th October, 1648.

The copy of this letter which Warburton reproduced bore the endorsement: 'By Sir William Compton and Sir Edward Lisle, who is yet living in the Isle of Wight, with instructions to provide a ship, and not to acquaint any of the Privy Council with it, nor the Prince of Wales himself, unless he thought fit.'

Such was the trust reposed by the King in his nephew. But it was too late for the Prince to go himself to the rescue of his uncle as he would have liked to do. He was committed to the Irish expedition, and all he could do was to send a ship to the Isle of Wight. But it all came to nothing. The King failed in his last attempt to make his escape.

Legge returned to England, where he was apparently left unmolested. On 15 January 1649 he wrote to Rupert with an ominous prediction: 'My deare P. after my Long imprisonment, I have the Liberty to continue within 20 miles of London, but iff a pass be sent me to depart the kingdom, and then goe, I must, if not sooner; we are heere in a most miserable condition, by the Estate of my Gratious Master, who I feare will eare Long perish in the hands of Murderers!'[34] When and where this letter reached Prince Rupert is uncertain. It is unlikely to have been in Holland. For on 21 January the Prince sailed with the fleet for Ireland.

His destination was Kinsale on the south coast of Munster, seventeen miles from Cork, where Ormonde had landed in the previous September. Rupert as Admiral was in the *Constant Reformation*, a ship of 52 guns;

his Vice-Admiral was his faithful brother Maurice, in the 46-gun *Convertine*, and his Rear-Admiral the veteran Sir John Mennes in the *Swallow* (40 guns). With the three flagships were five smaller vessels – frigates, ketches and a hoy. The *Antelope*, the least seaworthy of the Royalist ships, whose guns had been sold to provide money for equipping the rest of the fleet, was left behind at Hellevoetsluis.

The seventeenth-century warship was seldom of more than a thousand tons. It was a tall, stalwart vessel, with stern towering high above the water-line; the bow was dominated by the forecastle, a square fort rising from the upper deck, carrying guns and capable of defence even if the rest of the ship was in the possession of an enemy. The other guns were ranged in two broadsides along the main deck, with field of fire on either side of the ship. Vessels were classified in six rates: first-rates of 80 guns or more; second-rates of from 52 to 80; third-rates of 44 to 60; fourth-rates of 32 to 50; fifth-rates of 12 to 32; smaller ships were sixth-rates.[35]

With the small Royalist fleet were three Dutch East-Indiamen which had joined the Prince for escort; so that a total of eleven ships sailed down the Channel. On 22 January the Parliament fleet under Vice-Admiral Moulton (the officer who had wanted to address Rupert's men in the *Constant Reformation*) was sighted off Dover, and a battle seemed likely. Rupert, audacious as usual, steered directly towards the rival fleet, and Moulton, apparently deceived by the presence of the Dutch vessels into thinking the force stronger than it was, retired inshore and took shelter under the forts. Rupert sailed on and reached Kinsale on the last day of the month.

On arrival Rupert fortified the harbour and made contact with Ormonde, who was raising what troops he could in the south of Ireland. But there was little enough that the Prince could to to help him. Ormonde wanted him to blockade Dublin harbour and prevent the entry of Parliamentarian reinforcements; but this, Rupert considered, was beyond his power. He had neither the ships nor the men that such an enterprise would require. All he could do was to cruise around off Kinsale in search of prizes. In this he was not unsuccessful. Any ship in alliance with Parliament was lawful game, and Rupert made sufficient captures not only to keep his own fleet in being but even to send some contributions to his needy comrades at The Hague.

In the second week of February the terrible news reached Kinsale for which Rupert, if he had received Legge's letter, must have been not unprepared. Oliver Cromwell, now in virtually undisputed power in England, had abandoned compromise and forced the issue by bringing the King to trial, creating his own tribunal for the purpose. On 30 January Charles I had been beheaded in Whitehall.

Fury, consternation and sorrow filled the hearts of the Royalists in exile. 'Though, when your Highness left this place,' wrote Hyde to Rupert, 'there was no reason to expect any good news from England, yet the horrid wickedness which hath been since acted there, with those dismal circumstances which attended it, was so far beyond the fears and apprehensions of all men, that it is no wonder we were all stuck into amazement with the deadly news of it, that we have not yet recovered our spirits to think or do as we ought.'[36] And Hyde concluded his letter: 'I beseech your Highness, if you send any vessels this way, vouchsafe two or three lines to Charles II, who will be much encouraged by it.'[37]

To Rupert the tragedy was overwhelming. He had had his differences with his uncle, but he had loved and honoured him as he loved and honoured no other man; his whole adult life had been dedicated to his service. At the same time as Hyde's letter came an official commission appointing him Lord High Admiral, as the new King now had power to do. Rupert thereupon issued a declaration in which he gave vent to his grief and anger. 'The bloody and inhumane *murther* of my late dread *Uncle* of ever renowned famous memory,' he wrote, 'hath administred to me fresh occasion (if I had no other motives which might further my indignation against the usurped power in England, to bee assistant both in councell and the best of my personall power, as bound by affinity to my deare Cousen now *Charles the second King of Great Britaine, and all other his late Fathers Dominions*) to take vengeance upon those *Arch-Traytors*, pretending the name of *Parliament*, and keeping a perpetuall *Sessions*, of blood-thirstinesse and murthering *Massacre* at Westminster.'[38] He asserted that he had never desired the supreme naval post, but would have been well satisfied with 'an inferior place where I might have had the freedome, in part to bring such great Traitors and Rebels to condigne punishment'.[39] But he was resolved to use all his power to restore his cousin to the throne from which these murderers had barred him.

The Palatine family were united in grief. The Winter Queen, who had not seen her brother since her wedding nearly forty years before, was as deeply affected as anybody; and Charles Louis, who had been all this time in London, quitted England finally and irrevocably. It has been suggested that this was because he had given up all hope of gaining the English crown himself, but there is no reason to doubt that he was genuinely shocked at what had happened. 'My brother the Prince Elector is here,' wrote Sophia, the youngest sister, in a letter addressed to Rupert, 'and cares no more for those cursed people in England, for he had done his duty to the King, which he might have avoided, as his affairs require him at Cleves.'[40] In this letter Sophia rebuked her brother for not writing, saying that 'we have no news of "Rupert the devil" except what comes out in print'. But her letter never reached its destination, being intercepted in transit by the Parliament's agents.

Prince Edward wrote to his mother: 'I will die without regret, when I have steeped my hands in the blood of those murderers.'[41] He was in no position to do that, but visiting The Hague at this time he relieved his feelings by affronting the Parliament's envoys in the streets: an action which brought him a threat of expulsion from Holland.

Rupert had a new incentive for action, for revenge filled his heart; but he could only continue to cause what harassment he could. He opened up a link with the Scilly Isles, which still held out for King Charles II, and in March sent out four ships, led by Sir John Mennes in the *Swallow*, to cruise in those waters. They were back at Kinsale with five prizes at the beginning of April. Rupert's depredations were now being taken seriously at Westminster, and on 24 March the Council of State decided to send their senior 'General-at-Sea', Edward Popham, to tackle him with such ships as were available. Popham was delayed in the Downs by various causes, but in mid-April he sailed in the *Charles*, with three other ships, and in May he captured two of Rupert's ships which were trying to land soldiers in the Scillies.[42] These two were the *Guinea*, commanded by that Thomas Allin whose ruse had won Rupert's fleet its place in the inner harbour of Hellevoet-sluis, and the *Thomas*, commanded by Captain Jeffries.

On 13 May the other two generals-at-sea, Robert Blake and Richard Deane, arrived at Plymouth, where they were joined by Moulton with his ships. The whole fleet, consisting of ten or more vessels, then sailed for Kinsale, where they arrived on the 21st. Popham then returned to London to report, while Blake and Deane kept watch on Rupert at Kinsale.

This put an end to Rupert's activities. He was secure in Kinsale harbour, which he had strongly fortified. But he was hemmed in by the Parliamentary fleet, which he was not powerful enough to attack. 'Thus both sides resigned themselves to a period of watching and waiting.'[43] All he could do was to recruit seamen in the seaport towns of southern Ireland; but without being able to capture prizes he had difficulty in paying them.

This static situation continued throughout June and July. Then, on 15 August, Oliver Cromwell landed at Dublin with 12,000 men. From there he marched north to the seaport of Drogheda, which after a week's siege he stormed on 10 September; the entire garrison of 3,000, commanded by Sir Arthur Aston, were put to the sword on the personal orders of Cromwell, who forbade his soldiers to give quarter. In addition to the troops, all Catholic priests found in the town were killed on the spot. Cromwell then turned south to Wexford, which fell to him on 11 October. The Drogheda massacre was repeated, leaving in Ireland a legacy of hate which has not yet been obliterated.

Soon after this Cromwell dug himself in for the winter; but the campaign could have only one end. His terror tactics, condemned both at the time and by subsequent historians, from the military point of view had the desired effect. The native Irish were panic-stricken, and Ormonde could no longer hope for any effectual support from them. Nor were the English troops immune from the terror inspired by Cromwell's name. Six days after the fall of Wexford the garrison of Cork went over to the enemy.

Undoubtedly Prince Rupert's failure to blockade Dublin harbour had allowed Cromwell to land unopposed. But with his limited resources he could hardly have put up more than a token resistance; nor could he have kept up an effective blockade throughout the summer months. Ormonde fully accepted Rupert's judgement of his helplessness; in his view the only thing that could have saved the situation was the presence of the King himself, and this he continued to urge.

Rupert, it was clear, could now be of no further service to Ormonde. Nor was his own position at all comfortable. He was trapped between an enemy fleet, superior to his own, and a hostile garrison on shore. If he was to continue to serve his King at sea it could now be only from farther afield. He had foreseen this possibility, and as early as 13 March had written to King John IV of Portugal asking if a naval base could be made available in his country, and had received a favourable reply. Now it was time to take advantage of the offer. But first there was the problem of getting out of Kinsale harbour. Rupert held a council of war at which it was proposed to attack the blockading fleet; but it was decided that the odds were too heavily weighted, and the more cautious plan was adopted of equipping the seven best ships and taking the chance of escaping from harbour on a dark night.

In the event the issue was once more decided for him by the elements. A sudden wind blew Blake's fleet out to sea, and on 20 October Rupert slipped past it with his seven ships, making for the Tagus.

Yet again a Royalist venture had ended in frustration. But Rupert was undaunted; so long as he had life there was hope. His new line of action was to take him half across the world in the service of the cause to which he was dedicated.

CHAPTER 3

CONFRONTATION WITH BLAKE

R UPERT had seven ships with him when he sailed from Kinsale. As
before, he himself was in the *Constant Reformation*, carrying 52 guns;
Prince Maurice as Vice-Admiral was in the *Convertine* (46 guns), and
Sir John Mennes, a veteran of proven loyalty and long experience of
the sea, as Rear-Admiral in the *Swallow* (40 guns). With them were
four frigates, the *Scott* (30 guns), the *Mary* (24), the *Blackmoor Lady* (18)
and the *Black Knight* (14).[1] In the Bay of Biscay the fleet became separated because of bad weather; contact was re-established off Finisterre,
but in sailing southwards from there a further separation occurred.
'Some Leges from shore,' Rupert reported to King Charles who had
moved to Jersey,

> it happened that in the night by a mistake of a fight alle our Fleete except
> Sr Jo: Menes lost me, and the next morning A shippe apering wch we
> chased alle day but in vain, we were put to Leeward of our first rendezvous
> the Isle of Bayone [the Bayona Isles off the north-west coast of Spain],
> whither we imagined our Fleete had sayled. Wee therefore plyed as much
> to windward as wee could two dayes after wee made early in the morning
> 7 shipps to Windward wee gave chase to them & they to us wch proved
> to be our Fleete. Marchall [Captain Marshall, commanding one of the
> frigates] being come in with a prize and my Bro: having taken another
> made up the 7 shipps. Marchalls prize was a Newfoundland man out of
> which we tooke all her fish and fierd the hulk therof.[2]

So started Prince Rupert's privateering exploits in southern and
western waters. His object from the first was the capture of prizes on the
high seas, to provide funds for the Royalist cause as well as to keep his
own fleet in being. Any ship belonging to or in alliance with the rebel
régime in England was fair game. To the Parliamentarians his activities
appeared as piracy, but to Rupert they were patently legitimate. It was
he, the Lord High Admiral of the King of England, who was asserting
the rule of law and the freedom of the seas; his enemies, who had de-
throned and murdered their King, were outlaws who should be granted
no mercy; while those in other countries who gave them active support

were upholding the cause of anarchy. Yet Rupert certainly allowed himself latitude in his interpretation of what constituted alliance with the rebels, and the charges of piracy levelled against him were not confined to England.

Proceeding on their southward way, Prince Rupert's ships captured two more prizes, the *John Adventure* and the *Hopeful Adventure*, English vessels bound from London to San Lúcar, which 'being proude English'[3] put up a valiant fight. Then without further adventure they arrived, towards the end of November 1649, at the mouth of the Tagus.

The King of Portugal had already given his sanction to Rupert's visit, and now before entering the Tagus the Prince sent a message to Lisbon announcing his arrival. John IV, the first sovereign of the House of Braganza, had nine years before put himself at the head of the insurrection which had thrown off the yoke of Spain after sixty years of subservience. He was a capable ruler and a courtly gentleman, whose sympathies lay with the dispossessed royal house of England. Rupert found himself 'receaved and entertayn'd with all possible expressions of love & frendshippe'.[4] 'The King of Portugal gives him all kind of assistance,' wrote Elizabeth of Bohemia happily to the Duchess of Richmond, 'and is extremely kind and civil to him and Maurice'.[5] King John's advisers, however, were less enthusiastic. The *de facto* rulers of England were strong and Charles II was weak. Portuguese support for the House of Stewart would almost certainly bring about a Parliamentary alliance with the ever-menacing power of Spain.

For the moment the King had his way. Rupert and Maurice were invited to Lisbon, and a treaty was signed whereby 'the ministers and officers of the King of Great Brittaine should have power to make adjudification of such prizes as should be taken at sea by his Majestys fleete; and after such adjudification to sell and dispose of the same, in any of the portes of the Kingdome of Portugall'.[6] No inquisition was to be made into the antecedents of the prizes brought in, 'because it doth not belong to his majestie (the King of Portugall) or his ministers to judge of the qualities or titles of merchandizes which confederate nations with that Crowne doe bring to sell in the ports thereof'.[7] In the event of ships belonging to the English King's enemies entering a Portuguese port while the royal ships were there, they were to be detained in harbour for three days after the King's ships put to sea.

More than this could hardly have been hoped for, and Rupert proceeded to sell off some of the proceeds of his sea operations, reporting cheerfully to King Charles that he had 'made a Bargine which I veryly beleeve will yeld £40000 I hope more'.[8] One prize, however, was a source of trouble. While lying off Cascais Roads and awaiting authorization to enter the Tagus, Rupert had seized a large English ship, the

Roebuck, bound for Lisbon from Brazil. The vessel was adapted as a warship and equipped with thirty-six guns; but her cargo was Portuguese, and this led to a prolonged dispute with the Portuguese authorities.

The wrangle continued for several months and was at last settled in Rupert's favour, the *Roebuck* being declared a lawful prize. But relations with the Portuguese Government were deteriorating, and the *Roebuck* affair was not the only symptom. King John was consistently friendly, but his principal minister, the Count of Miro, intent on the continuance of trade with the *de facto* government of England, was anxious to get rid of the embarrassing guest in the Tagus. He therefore put all the obstacles he could in Rupert's way, and the Prince found that the Portuguese merchants with whom he had been negotiating the sale of his prizes' cargoes were reluctant either to continue the purchases or to pay for what they had already received. More prizes were needed, and it was proposed that Prince Maurice should go to sea with a party of ships to look for English ships; but the Portuguese were not prepared to sanction the use of Lisbon as a base for such operations, which could lead to war with the Parliamentary régime. It was held, wrote the Secretary of State to Rupert, 'that considering the present state of this Kingdome and its commerce it would be noe way convenient to make a warre or shew any hostility, nor yet to give any assistance or favour against those English that follow the parliament; and that his Majesty should rather equally entertaine and receive all of the English Nation, for with it hee had renewed the contracts of peace and amitye that was alwayes between the two nations'.[9]

This was on 23 December (NS). A month later, on 27 January 1650, after further correspondence, there came from the same quarter a more forthright request. To avoid further embroilments and disputes, said the minister, it was his government's desire that 'your Serenitye should reembarke all into your shippes, and with all brevity hasten your departure'.[10]

A more direct indication that his serenity had outstayed his welcome could hardly have been given; yet Rupert made no move to go. His ships were now anchored in Oeiras Bay, west of Lisbon, and he exercised his time in reorganizing his fleet, pursuing his sales of cargoes as well as he could, selling off two of his smaller frigates, and converting some of his prizes into warships. In the intervals he and his brother, secure in the personal favour of King John, disported themselves at the Lisbon court, hunting regularly and making themselves popular with the Portuguese clergy, who 'began to fill the pulpits with how shameful a thing it was for a Christian King to treat with rebels'.[11] Rupert also won the goodwill of the people of the country, displaying the geniality and the mastery of the common touch which he was able to produce when he was in the right mood; 'this, with his liberality and complaisance to all sorts of people, they having been accustomed to a Spanish gravity, were surprised by such unusual favours from so great a person'.[12] In this way he counteracted the diplomacy of the hostile minister of the King of Portugal.

The interlude did not last long. It was obvious that, once Rupert's movements were known to the 'Commonwealth', the name by which the English state that had ceased to be even nominally a monarchy was now known, little time would be lost in following him, and that as soon as the worst of winter was over a Parliamentary fleet would make for Portugal. This indeed was the principal fear of the Portuguese ministers.

Rupert's arrival at the Tagus was known in London by the end of November, and on 4 December the Council of State issued its orders. Deane was sick, and the command of the expedition was given to Robert Blake, who had blockaded Rupert at Kinsale. He was ordered to Plymouth while the preparation of the fleet went forward.

Blake, a Somerset man, was, like Rupert, a soldier turned sailor, though unlike Rupert he had done no soldiering till approaching middle age. Now fifty years old, he had fought with distinction for the Parliament in the Civil War, particularly in his own west country where he had tenaciously defended Lyme and Taunton. Before the war he had been a prosperous merchant; he came of a family of shipbuilders, and almost certainly had some experience of the sea. In the years to come he was to prove himself one of the finest naval commanders of the age; resolute, resourceful, cool-headed, he mastered the craft of seamanship and sea warfare as few of his contemporaries, in England at least, were able to do.

At the end of the year Blake was informed that the fleet was ready, and instructed to proceed to Portsmouth and confer with Edward Popham, the third General-at-Sea. On 17 January 1650 he received his detailed instructions. He was 'to pursue, seize, scatter, fight with, or destroy, all the ships of the revolted fleet, and other vessels adhering to them'.[13] If any foreign ships should join the Royalists, he was to fight these too.

It was another six weeks before Blake felt able to leave the Solent. He sailed from Cowes on 1 March with fifteen ships, carrying a total of 454 guns. His flagship was the *St George*; with him were Moulton as Vice-Admiral in the *Leopard* and Richard Badiley as Rear-Admiral in the *Happy Entrance*. Charles Vane, brother of Sir Henry, accompanied the fleet as envoy to the King of Portugal, who, however, had accorded no diplomatic recognition to the Parliamentary régime.

Blake arrived in Cascais Roads on 10/20 March,[14] and promptly wrote to King John asking for his co-operation in exterminating pirates, 'that most nefarious tribe, the enemies of the world'. His letter continued: 'Since the brothers Rupert and Maurice are an important part of them, who have now for several years been carrying on piracy with the ships of the British Commonwealth which were carried off by treacherous revolt, and with some others they have captured, to the great damage of many, but to the greatest of our own countrymen, who [we?] cannot but deem it the work of some special providence that they have been detained in your harbour till the arrival of our fleet.'[15] Blake trusted that the King would allow the Commonwealth ships free use of his port and would oppose no obstacle to hostilities against Rupert's fleet.

It was scarcely likely that the King or his ministers would willingly acquiesce in the opening of hostilities in a Portuguese harbour. But Blake did not wait for an answer to his letter. On 21 March, with his four leading ships, he sailed towards Rupert's fleet in Oeiras Bay. He did not reach his objective. The Portuguese forts in the harbour opened fire, though without doing any damage; and at the same time the wind dropped so that Blake was forced to anchor in an exposed position. An envoy from the King explained that the forts had fired without orders, but also complained of Blake's entry into the harbour uninvited. Blake stood his ground, however, and for the moment was allowed to stay where he was.

Vane meanwhile had been negotiating with the Portuguese court, and on 28 March he reached an agreement with King John. Blake was to be allowed to anchor inside Oeras Bay in the event of heavy weather, but he was to take no aggressive action against Rupert without the written authority of the King. The weather was already bad enough in Blake's eyes to fulfil the conditions, and he promptly took advantage of the permission, anchoring two miles below Rupert, whose ships lay close to Belem Castle.

For some months the two fleets confronted one another. The situation was remarkably similar to that which had prevailed at Hellevoetsluis, with the crews meeting on shore and brawling in the taverns, and Blake's men doing their best to seduce Rupert's from their allegiance. As in the earlier episode, they in many cases succeeded. There was, however, considerably more nautical activity than in the days of Warwick's blockade. King John gave order that no more English warships should enter the Tagus. Vane contended that this was showing partiality in favour of the Royalists, who could be joined by ships of any other nation while Blake was allowed no reinforcements. Point was given to his complaint when on Good Friday, 15 April, two French men-of-war entered the river to support Rupert and anchored by mistake among

Blake's ships. Blake seized them, and demanded of their captain that they should not ally themselves with Rupert; whereupon the French agent at Lisbon made a forceful protest to the King. It was upheld, and Blake was compelled to release the ships, which promptly joined the Royalist fleet.

The next incident was on shore, when Rupert and Maurice were ambushed by a party of Blake's men while hunting; 'which pitiful design being descried, and glad of an escape, some went to their long home, and others by a willing and forced mistake, went aboard our fleet instead of their own'.[16]

Rupert was quick to retaliate, and in his retaliation made use of his scientific ingenuity. In the words of the *Rupert Sea Narrative*,

> that they might know that he had wit as well as courage, he soon after endeavoured a requital; for having fitted a bomb-ball in a double-headed barrel, with a lock in the bowels to give fire to a quick-match, sent it a-board their Vice-Admiral in a town-boat with one of his soldiers clad in a Portugal habit, to put into the stern-boat as a barrel of oil, to keep it for him till he hailed up the side without, 'refreshing for the men'; but, being come to the ship's stern, those ports being unfortunately shut, before he could get to the transom-port, he was known, and taken.[17]

Warburton adds that the man was afterwards recovered by Rupert, but does not give his authority.

Honours were thus even in these cloak-and-dagger activities; both attempts had failed. There followed a war of words. Rupert issued one of his most grandiloquent declarations, addressed to the King of Portugal, in which he denounced the Parliamentarians as 'nothing else, but tumultuous, factious & seditious souldiers, and other disorderly, disobedient and refractory persons comspiring together, and reteining nothing of the ancient form and Government of lawfull Parliaments',[18] and called on the Portuguese not to endure 'such insolency to be com-mitted by these People, who being Rebells to their Prince, & having in Law no right of priviledge in War, are to be deemed and esteemed as Pirates and Sea Rovers'.[19] King John should take action against these rebels, and secure the freedom of the port for the English Royalists.

Vane in his answer showed an equal command of invective. He asserted the claim of the Parliamentary régime to be the true govern-ment of England, and declared the friendship of the Commonwealth for the kingdom of Portugal; 'neither doe wee take itt for any disparage-ment to us our parliament & nation, that wee are so vile in the esteeme of this Vagabond Jerman, a Prince of Fortune, whose highnes is nothing else than haughtinooo, hio Principality meere piracye, the plurality of his person an affectation so singular that no reall prince can chuse but smile at itt, who after he was cudgelled out of England from his trade of plundering did in a short time sett up at sea'.[20]

With both sides soliciting his support, and each accusing the other of piracy, the King of Portugal, whose own sympathies were never in doubt, could only hope that both English fleets would move out and leave him in peace. At the end of May there seemed to be some hope of this, when Blake took his ships back to the entrance to the harbour, out of range of the castle and forts. He was apparently hoping that Rupert would take the opportunity to withdraw from the Tagus, and that he would then, with his stronger fleet, be able to attack him in the open sea.

Rupert, however, was not to be lured into battle; and the deadlock remained. At the same time the Council of State in London decided to reinforce Blake. On 25 May Popham left Plymouth in the *Resolution*, accompanied by seven other ships. With him went new instructions for Blake. He was to surprise or destroy Rupert's ships wherever he found them; to demand from the King of Portugal freedom of those ports in which Royalist ships were sheltering; and, in the event of a refusal, to 'seize, surprise, and detain in the way of justice all such ships, merchants, or others, belonging to the King of Portugal, or any of his subjects'.[21] The English Commonwealth was ready for war with Portugal.

While Popham was on his way, Portugal's Brazil fleet put to sea and was promptly intercepted by Blake. According to the author of the *Rupert Sea Narrative*, this was the fault of the Count of Miro, who assured the King that the fleet would be allowed to pass. As it was, Blake had not yet received his new orders and did not interfere with the Portuguese ships; but there were nine English vessels among them, and these he captured and added to his own fleet.

Popham arrived on 5 June, and from this date the Commonwealth and Portugal were virtually in a state of war. Vane was recalled from the court of Lisbon, and shortly afterwards went home to England to report. Blake and Popham sent a final demand to King John for the surrender of Rupert's ships, which the King was naturally unwilling to grant. Thereupon the Generals-at-Sea prepared to carry out their new instructions, and King John prepared to give active support to Rupert.

For the moment nothing much happened beyond the seizure by Blake of a few Portuguese fishing-craft, interpreted as the first act of war. Blake's fleet was short of water, and Badiley, the Rear-Admiral, was sent off to Cadiz with seven ships to bring back supplies. King John for his part ordered thirteen ships to be got ready under the veteran Admiral João de Sequeira, for the support of Prince Rupert. The King himself, it was said, was anxious to join the fleet, but was dissuaded by his council.

It was not until the end of July that any action was seen, and then it was little enough. Rupert took the initiative. The time had come, he decided, to break through the blockade and take his chance in the open sea. The Parliamentary ships were in Cascais Bay, and his plan was that the Portuguese fleet should get between him and the enemy, and that at nightfall, carrying no lights, his ships should slip past unnoticed. It did not work out that way. On the morning of 26 July, 'after long preparation and much noise',[22] Rupert came out with twenty-six men-of-war and eighteen caravels (small vessels), headed by a French ship of forty guns which had also joined him; but his Portuguese allies hung back, and thus his plan was ruined.

On the approach of the Royalist ships Blake and Popham weighed anchor and stood out to sea with their adversaries to windward. Then, with a shift of the wind to the south, they tacked and got to windward, whereupon Rupert tacked too and the two fleets sailed southward on a parallel course. There was some ineffectual firing, and Rupert's flagship, the *Constant Reformation*, was hit by a ricochet; but nothing conclusive occurred, and Rupert, failing to weather Cape Espichel, returned at the close of the day and anchored at the mouth of the Tagus. The Parliamentary fleet followed, but, 'having a lee shore, and a leeward tide and being in the indraught of the harbour',[23] were afraid to set too close inshore and kept out to sea.

Next morning there was little wind, and the two fleets watched each other throughout the day, though in the evening Blake and Popham 'gave order to the *Assurance* being then come to us, to alarm them in the night thereby to keep Prince Rupert in apprehension that he might not steal away'.[24] On the 28th Badiley's ships reappeared with his supplies from Cadiz, and Rupert, his plan of escape frustrated, returned to the river.

It was deadlock once more. Rupert had been thwarted by the dilatoriness of his allies, but his own seamanship had been undistinguished. King John had watched the action from the cliffs of Cascais, and he must have been sorely disappointed both at the conduct of his own captains and at the failure to relieve his coasts of his guests whose presence was becoming an increasing embarrassment.

Meanwhile the Council of State at Westminster were becoming concerned at the difficulty of supplying so many ships so far from home, and they accordingly instructed the Generals-at-Sea to decide how many could be dispensed with. After some discussion it was decided that Popham should leave for England with eight ships, leaving Blake in sole command in the *George* with eight other vessels – the *Leopard*, *Bonaventure*, *Phoenix*, *Expedition*, *Constant Warwick*, *John*, *Hercules* and *Merchant*. Popham left at the beginning of September. The Brazil prizes had already been sent home.

When Popham had gone, Rupert made another attempt to break out from the Tagus, but he was intercepted by Blake who had with him only two ships besides the *George*. Rupert returned to Lisbon. Once again he and his allies had failed, this time being ignominiously out-manoeuvred by a force a fraction of the size of their own.

The next episode came a week later, when Portugal's homeward-bound Brazil fleet was sighted by Blake. This time, armed with his new instructions, he had no inhibitions about seizing Portuguese vessels, and after a fierce fight destroyed one ship and captured seven others, with 4,000 chests of sugar.

This crippling loss made the Portuguese King more than ever anxious to deprive himself of Rupert's company. He was still personally sympa-thetic, but as long as he harboured the Royalist admiral he could expect to be plundered by the Parliamentarian fleet. Blake, however, after his fight with the Brazil escort, needed to refit and revictual and was forced to sail for Cadiz. There he was welcomed by the Spanish authorities, always ready to support an enemy of Portugal. This left the Tagus open; an outcome which Blake regarded with equanimity. With the ending of resistance in Ireland, and the firm establishment of Cromwell in power in England, there was no chance of Rupert returning to any home port. There was no haven in sight for him, and he would be more vulnerable at sea than under the shelter of the Tagus forts.

All parties were therefore agreed on the advisability of Rupert's departure. King John went personally to his ship to ask him to go, and gave him all aid in refitting and victualling his fleet. That fleet was now reduced to six ships – the *Constant Reformation, Swallow, Black Prince, Second Charles, Henry* and *Mary*. Their total complement has been estimated at less than a thousand men.[25]

With these six ships Prince Rupert left the Tagus on 12 October 1650. He had no clear destination, and could exist only by capturing prizes in those enterprises that to his enemies were plain piracy. 'Now misfortunes being no novelty to us,' wrote the author of the *Rupert Sea Narrative*, 'we plough the sea for a subsistence, and, being destitute of a port, we take the confines of the Mediterranean Sea for our harbour; poverty and despair being companions, and revenge our guide'.[26]

Rupert with his six ships sailed down the west coast of Portugal and through the Straits of Gibraltar, passing south-west of Cadiz where Blake was refitting his fleet; it is not evident that either admiral was conscious of the proximity of the other. Sailing along the coast of Andalusia, the Royalists soon had their first success, for on a dark night they encountered a fleet of English merchantmen bound for Malaga. The merchantmen in the dark mistook Rupert's ships for Blake's, and two of them were captured. Others escaped, but the *Second Charles*, in pursuit of one of them, lost contact with the rest of the fleet. Rupert burned the smaller of his two prizes, after removing her cargo, and then sailed on south to Tetuan, on the North African coast, chosen as the first rendezvous.

There was no sign of the *Second Charles*, and after waiting a day or two in Tetuan Bay Rupert turned north to the coast of Spain, and about the end of October appeared off Estepona. One of the English ships, the *Culpeper*, was at anchor there and Rupert's ships made a somewhat half-hearted attempt to seize her. There was an exchange of shots, and the *Culpeper* was damaged; but the guns of Estepona Castle opened fire on her behalf, and Rupert found it advisable to take his fleet off.

He now made for Malaga, in hopes of a greater prize; for the remainder of the English merchantmen had arrived there. His plan was that the *Henry*, probably posing as the merchantman *Roebuck*, should sail ahead and anchor between the English ships and the mole, so preventing them from getting into the harbour; Rupert would then attack with the rest of his ships by night. The plan miscarried. There was disaffection aboard the *Henry*, and some of the crew stole into the pinnace and rowed ashore, where forts gave the alarm to the Parliamentary vessels. The merchant fleet thereupon entered the harbour, and next morning a Spanish galley came out to investigate. There was an exchange of civilities, but Rupert was clearly not welcome, and he quickly stood off to sea and made his way eastwards.

His next objective was the smaller port of Velez Malaga, a few miles along the coast. Here four English ships had taken refuge, and Rupert demanded their surrender in the name of the King of England. The local Spanish commander, Don Gaspar Ruys de Alarcon, played for time and desired the Prince to take no hostile action until he had sent to Madrid and ascertained the wishes of the King (Philip IV). In the meantime he regarded the English ships as being under the protection of the Spanish crown.

Rupert was in a defiant mood, and according to a Spanish account he 'gave answere, he could not comply with his order if he took not his advantage of the occasion he had lighted on, to find Captaine Morley, one of the foure and cheefest traytors, who had signed the sentence of death of the King of Great Britanie, his uncle; that he had now bin three yeares in pursuit of him, and that the Captain Generall ought to deliver him, not to be guilty of the damages and inconveniences which might follow'.[27] Mr R. C. Anderson has pointed out that nobody named Morley signed the death-warrant of King Charles, but that another account says that Rupert 'demanded the master of a London ship, who had signed the Petition against a Personal Treaty',[28] and that this was probably misinterpreted by the Spaniards. Be that as it may, the

Spanish authorities refused to deliver Morley, and after some bickering Rupert agreed not to fire on the English ships unless they fired first. But he said nothing about any other mode of attack, and he stayed at anchor 'until he had fitted a fireship to send into the road'.[29]

What actually happened is a matter of dispute. According to the Spanish account, the captains of the English ships were assured that the use of fireships would be against the agreement reached, and that they would in that event be defended by the Spaniards; but that 'in the darke of the night some of the Prince's fyre boates drew towards them, and burnt Captaine Morley's ship, and one other, the men that belonged to them having left them'.[30] The *Rupert Sea Narrative* on the other hand says that the English captains 'prevented that design, for, all things being made ready to sheer aboard with them, they suspecting it was to board them, landing their best goods, set fire to their ships, and escaped to land by the light thereof'.[31] Both versions agree that an attack by fireships was planned, whether or not it was carried out, and on this occasion Rupert, evading the spirit of his agreement by juggling with words, seems to have fallen below his customary standard of military honour.

In any case the sole result of the incident was that two English merchantmen had been destroyed; the Royalists had gained no prizes and captured no cargo. Rupert wisely decided that he could do no good by staying, and before dawn had proceeded eastward on his marauding way. Motril, thirty miles further on, was the scene of the next action. There were three English ships there, and Rupert by shot and fireship destroyed them all; then was forced to sail on by fire from the Spanish forts. Once again there was no result but destruction, and Rupert had come perilously near to an act of war against Spain.

Early in November he was joined by the *Second Charles*. She had narrowly escaped an encounter with Blake in the Straits of Gibraltar, and had fled east with a prize to join her admiral. Where the reunion took place is uncertain. The *Rupert Sea Narrative* says that it was 'betwixt Cape de Gatte and Cape Palos',[32] but Gata is at the southern tip of the Gulf of Almeria and Palos nearly twenty miles east of Cartagena, and the distance between the two capes is nearly a hundred miles. As Rupert had only recently left Motril, it was probably not far beyond Cape de Gata; but his fleet at this time seems to have been strung out between the capes in small groups of ships out of touch with one another, a dangerous situation should an enemy appear.

And Blake was on the move again. The time had come, he decided, to strike a crippling blow at Rupert's fleet. He led his fleet eastwards, and at Malaga on 6 November had news of Rupert's movements. He promptly put to sea again, and on 13 November captured the *Henry*, which was sailing alone. Turning towards Cartagena, he then sighted five more Royalist ships. These were the *Second Charles*, the *Black Prince*, the *Mary*, and two prizes, the *Malagonian* and the *William and John*.

These vessels had come together a few days before. With them were Rupert in the *Constant Reformation* and Maurice in the *Swallow*, but the two princes had broken away to chase an English ship, the *Marmaduke* of London, towards the African coast; the rest of the fleet were ordered to rendezvous at Formentera, the southernmost of the Balearic Isles. These ships, says the *Rupert Sea Narrative*, 'contrary to order in hopes of booty, stood in for Cape de Gatte',[33] but it is doubtful if they could in any case have escaped the vigilance of Blake.

The Parliamentary admiral attacked at once, and five frigates closed in on the *Black Prince*. Captain Marshall in the *Second Charles* turned to support her, but was driven off and joined the other three ships, which had made for the shelter of Cartagena harbour. The *Black Prince* was chased eastwards and driven ashore, where her crew set her on fire to prevent her capture.

Blake blockaded the ships at Cartagena, and on 15 November sent in a demand to the Governor that he should be allowed to destroy these 'notorious pirates and destroyers of all trade . . . before they join themselves unto the French, which is likely to be their refuge'.[34] He then entered the harbour and anchored close to the Royalists, undeterred by a few shots fired from the Spanish forts. He was visited by the Governor, who requested him to use no force pending a decision by the King of Spain. Blake reluctantly consented, but next day the matter was decided by the elements. The four ships attempted to escape from the harbour, but a sudden storm drove them ashore and all were completely wrecked.

From this disaster Rupert's fleet could never recover. It was some time before the Prince knew what had happened, and when he did he was as full of fight as ever; but never again would his venture be a serious menace to republican England's shipping.

Blake continued to hunt for Rupert, but in vain. In the meantime he had been recalled by the Council of State, which ordered him to hand over to William Penn, to leave some of his smaller ships and to return to England with the rest. The order had been made before anything was known of the successful pursuit of Rupert's fleet. When the news came through it was countermanded. But Blake had already sailed for home.

Rupert and Maurice meanwhile, having captured the *Marmaduke*, made for the rendezvous at Formentera. When the rest of the fleet failed to appear, Rupert left instructions under a stone, with a white flag over it, for the ships to go on to Cagliari in Sardinia. This message, dated 15 November 1650, was actually found by Blake in his final pursuit, but there is no record of Rupert and Maurice arriving at Cagliari. The next objective was Toulon, but the weather once more intervened. In heavy seas the *Constant Reformation* was separated from the other two ships, and Rupert was driven south-east to the coast of Sicily. The *Swallow* and the *Marmaduke* reached Toulon safely on 5 December.

Maurice at Toulon found himself in a delicate situation. It was not to be expected that the presence of these privateering princes would be regarded by any power from whom they sought shelter as other than a nuisance. In this case the situation was complicated by the fact that France was in the throes of her own civil war, the Fronde. Louis XIV was still a child, and for some years there was armed conflict between, on the one hand, the Queen Mother Anne of Austria with her adviser Cardinal Mazarin, Richelieu's successor, and on the other a number of princes and nobles who for the most part fought for their own particular ends, the prize being possession of the King's person with consequent control of government. Toulon at this time stood for the faction headed by the Prince de Condé, whose career provided so strange a parallel to Prince Rupert's.[35] It therefore behoved Maurice to pay court to Condé's followers, with always in the background the possibility that a change of allegiance might demand a different approach. The admiral in charge of the port was amicable, but advised him to be very careful of the safety both of his own person and of the ships.

Maurice followed the admiral's advice. For some days he refused to leave his ship, giving as his excuse his 'grief for that sad separation from his brother';[36] but the authorities showed themselves friendly, and having to look after the disposal of his prize goods he agreed to go on shore.

On the very day that he was due to do so (probably about the new year) the *Constant Reformation* appeared off Toulon and anchored in the roads. Neither Rupert nor Maurice had any idea whether the other was alive or dead, and the reunion was affecting. They landed together, and were received with great ceremony. Rupert now took over control, and set himself with his customary energy to the task of refitting what was left of his fleet. The prize goods were sold to the Leghorn merchants, and the usual bargaining and haggling took place. The good offices of the Duc de Vendôme, Grand Master of Navigation, enabled Rupert to furnish his ships with stores, and the Prince even acquired two more ships. With his prize money he bought the *Jeremy*, renaming her the *Honest Seaman*; and a Captain Craven joined him with an English vessel from Marseilles, the *Speedwell*, which he now called the *Loyal Subject*. A third change of name was the *Revenge of Whitehall* for the *Marmaduke*.

The Royalist fleet was thus increased from three ships to five, and

Rupert was soon ready to put to sea again. While the refitting was going on, the survivors of Cartagena came straggling in, bringing to Rupert and Maurice the first news of the disaster. They were in a miserable condition. The Spanish authorities had at first hedged when Blake blockaded the Royalist ships, but when those ships were wrecked, and it was clear who was the victor, they came down heavily on the side of the Parliament. The wrecked ships and all the goods that could be salvaged were declared the property of the English Parliament; the Governor of Cartagena refused to provide for the support of the Royalist sailors, saying that 'he has not received any order to make them an allowance, and will not part with a penny';[37] and no passes were given to officers, seamen or soldiers unless they enlisted in the King of Spain's service. Some did so, according to Clarendon: '. . . two or three hundred of them marched over land, and were compelled to list themselves in the Spanish Service at land, where they for the most part perished'.[38] Others, including the captains of the ships, escaped without passes, and eventually arrived at Toulon.

The future Clarendon, who in his account of this episode has his chronology hopelessly muddled, was himself in Madrid at this time. He and Lord Cottington were on a mission to King Philip as ambassadors of Charles II, trying to raise money for the Royalist cause; and the captains of Prince Rupert's ships appealed to them for help. They did what they could, but their protests at the treatment of the seamen were brushed aside. Spain had decided where her interests lay, and Hyde and Cottington could no more help the King of England's subjects than they could help the King himself.

The arrival of the sailors at Toulon at least provided some valuable personnel for the five Royalist men-of-war; Rupert, 'being weak in ships, endeavoured to be strong in men'.[39] But a sordid episode ensued when the captains proceeded to lay the blame on each other for what had happened at Cartagena. Rupert, though he scrupulously would not use the form of a court-martial since he was in a foreign port, was forced to inquire into a series of charges and counter-charges. The most serious was a wrangle concerning the action in which the *Black Prince* was attacked and driven ashore, supported only by the *Royal Charles*. The *William and John*, commanded by Thomas Allin, had also been in a position to give support, and it was now alleged that Allin, 'more careful of his booty than his honour, clapped by a wind, and stood in close-hauled for the harbour'.[40] This was a grave charge, but before a verdict could be pronounced Allin, perhaps to Rupert's relief, disappeared from Toulon; and the matter was allowed to drop. Allin was to have a distinguished naval career in the future as one of Prince Rupert's trusted commanders.

This tiresome business concluded, Rupert prepared for his next adventure. The Mediterranean, he had decided, was no longer a possible sphere of action. Spain was hostile, and Penn was cruising between Sardinia and Majorca with a force which, though smaller than Blake's, was too strong for Rupert's five ships to tackle. Rupert had to seek his fortune further afield, and it is probable that he was already resolved to sail for the West Indies, where a number of islands were still for King Charles. But for the moment he kept his plans to himself. The immediate necessity was to elude Penn.

Rupert, 'with Five Men of War and two Fire-ships',[41] left Toulon on 17 May 1651. He first sailed eastward, then turned south and made for North Africa; there he proceeded westward along the Barbary coast towards the Straits of Gibraltar. He was well on his way before Penn woke up to the fact that he was at sea.

Rupert's immediate object was to get out of the Mediterranean, but there was still the need to capture prizes. Moreover he was filled with rage at the behaviour of the Spanish Government. Just short of the Straits he took a Genoese vessel, the *St Michael the Archangel*, justifying his action by the flimsiest of excuses: '. . . she was made a prize by way of reprisal, in lieu of a caravel of ours, taken by the Genoese in the Straits, and *partly through the clamour of the seamen*, who, in a tumultuous manner petitioned her confiscation, *being bound for a Spanish port*'.[42] Passing through the Straits, the Royalists sailed north-west along the coast of Spain, and off Santa Maria on 18 June took a second prize, this time a genuinely Spanish vessel, the galleon *Nuestra Señora de Lusoldad y entiro Quristo*, homeward-bound from the West Indies, 'which we surprised by putting out the Parliament flag, as their confederate'.[43]

Rupert was delighted with his Spanish prize, which was reported as being worth 100,000 crowns; and he issued a declaration emphasizing his motive of revenge against the Spaniards. 'His reasons were, First, Their giving Protection and free Port to the King's Rebels . . . denying the same to his Majesty's Ships, contrary to the agreement between both Crowns. Secondly, Their forcing the Marriners that were put on shore by *Blake* to serve the Rebels against their wills.'[44]

With his five warships, two prizes and two fireships, and with money and supplies replenished, Rupert now turned south-west to Madeira, where he arrived some time in late June. The Mediterranean venture was over, and he was once again within the dominions of his friend John IV, King of Portugal. He had achieved little, and as a sea commander had made a poor showing in comparison with his great antagonist Blake. But he had kept the King's flag flying, and there was plenty of fight in him yet.

CHAPTER 4

IN WESTERN SEAS

A T Madeira Rupert and Maurice were welcomed by the Portuguese Governor, who visited them on board, and later received them in the fort and took them sightseeing, showing them 'what was worthy seeing on the island'.[1] They sold part of the prize goods and took the rest into their ships, leaving the captured Spanish vessel as being unserviceable. Then, having 'enjoyed these welcome freedoms and correspondences with strangers',[2] they set sail southwards for the Canary Islands.

Now trouble arose. Rupert, it is clear, could by no means count on the loyalty of his crews, or even of his captains. Not all shared his single-minded devotion to his King; many of the sailors had been recruited by force, or joined him in the hope of gain. He was fully aware of the danger, and therefore had kept secret his design of sailing for the West Indies, there to join with the loyal islanders in support of King Charles II. Now, however, the captains had begun to suspect what was in their commander's mind, and the majority were opposed to the dangerous voyage across the Atlantic, with little hope of prizes on the way.

Discontent was accentuated when it was found that no prizes were to be had in the Canaries, and on 7 July 1651[3] Rupert called a council of war to decide on future plans. He proposed to make for the Cape Verde Islands to the south, where they could revictual 'secure from storms or enemies'.[4] These islands were a natural starting-point for the West Indies, and there was immediate opposition. Fearnes, Prince Rupert's flag-captain in the *Constant Reformation*, and one other commander supported the plan; but the rest, led by Chester, Maurice's flag-captain in the *Swallow*, stood out for the Azores, 'concluding that to be the fittest place to victual in: giving out likewise that there we might meet with the English East India fleet'.[5] Rupert did not feel strong enough to oppose the wishes of the majority of his senior commanders, and against his better judgement he consented to sail once more north-westwards.

The little fleet arrived at São Miguel in the Azores at the end of July. It now consisted of five ships: the *Constant Reformation*, the *Swallow*, the

Loyal Subject, the *Revenge of Whitehall*, and the Genoese prize *St Michael the Archangel*. The *Honest Seaman* under Captain Marshall had been separated from the rest during the voyage from the Canaries and made independently for the Azores rendezvous at Terceira.

The Azores were another Portuguese possession, whereas the Canaries were Spanish; and once again the Royalists were warmly welcomed. The Governor of São Miguel invited the princes ashore and showed them 'all the Monasteryes and places of note in the Town',[6] and Rupert was invited to choose whatever diversion or entertainment the island could afford. He stayed only one day, however. Leaving a party of men to see to the victualling, he left for Terceira, and on the way captured another Spanish galleon, the companion of his former prize, with which she had lost contact during the voyage from the West Indies.

At Terceira the *Honest Seaman* was waiting, so Rupert's fleet was now increased to seven ships. Not for long, however: for disaffection now bore fruit. While Rupert was negotiating with some English merchants for supplies, Captain Goulding of the *St Michael the Archangel* sailed with his crew for England to join the Parliamentary navy.

Rupert's troubles were multiplying. His own flagship the *Constant Reformation* was in a far from seaworthy condition, and there was no suitable harbour where repairs could be carried out. Disaster loomed ahead, and the trouble started when Rupert, after more than a month at Terceira, set out to return to São Miguel to continue his victualling. A gale blew up, so that the ships could hardly keep their course; and in this stress the flagship sprang a leak. Fearnes managed to get her into São Miguel Road, and 'as soon as they were at anchor they try'd by stitching of Bownetts to stop the Leak; but to little purpose, for they did not know where it was'.[7] Rupert then got a diver aboard to search for it, but this was in vain too.

In spite of the dangerous condition of his ship Rupert found it necessary to move between the two islands, and once more set sail for Terceira. He was still hoping to bring his captains round to the idea of a West Indies expedition, which was now openly the object of any move southward; and in mid-September,[8] either at Terceira or at São Miguel, he called another council. It was a move of desperation; Rupert once again proposed a southern voyage, but

> finding the ffaction to be now grown Strong and Confident, even to the degree of avowing their Animosityes in their Cups, concerting their Intentions in private meetings and Caballs, and tampering the very Domestiques of his H: the Prince in a just indignation at these Audacious Proceedings order'd severall of their Cabbins to be pull'd down, commanded the Capt of his Guards not to suffer any meetings after the watch was set, nor any Candle to be lighted between Decks, but in such places as

were appoynted for the Ships use: and all too little to obviate so dangerous a distemper.[9]

When the crisis came, however, it was not caused by mutiny. On or about 26 September, when provisioning was not yet completed, the fleet was driven out of Terceira by a violent storm. The ships were forced to run before the gale, and the flagship's leak grew to unmanageable proportions. The storm continued for three days, increasing rather than abating. The *Swallow* and the *Honest Seaman* bore up with the *Constant Reformation*, and kept as close as they could, but the other ships were left far to windward. The flagship's pinnace, which was being towed astern because it was too large to be hoisted in, broke adrift, and when the *Swallow* tried to hoist her own boat in it sank by the ship's side. The *Constant Reformation* was almost beyond help.

The crew worked desperately. A hundred and twenty pieces of raw beef were pushed in and pressed down with stanchions, and for a time it seemed that the men were gaining on the leak. But at six o'clock on the morning of 30 September 'the Admiral started a But-head that brought in so much water as no Pumping could keep her free'.[10] For another four hours the furious work continued, and the ship kept firing her guns to give the other vessels notice to keep near her. But at length it was recognized that all hope had gone. The guns were thrown overboard to lighten the ship, but 'all was labor lost, for the water grew so fast upon them that they could not stand on the hold to Bale'.[11] The *Honest Seaman* ran alongside the ship in the hope of taking some men off, but 'their Resolutions being to live and dy together, there was not any man that endeavoured to escape'.[12]

Prince Maurice in the *Swallow* was in agony for his brother. Rupert waved to him to come up under the stern, 'desiring to commit something to his knowledge before his death'; and Maurice 'commanded his Master to lay him aboard, being resolved either to save his Brother or to perish with him'.[13] But he was met with flat disobedience. The *Swallow*'s officers refused to put him in a position where he was certain to lose his life without any hope of assisting Rupert. Then the two princes tried to speak to each other, 'but the hideous noise of the winds and seas drown'd their voyces'.[14]

Rupert had never been closer to death. He faced it with characteristic resolution and magnanimity. In the words of the *Rupert Sea Narrative*:

P. Maurice seeing himselfe disappoynted one way, made Tryall of another: and perswaded his officers to put out a small boat which he had aboard to endeavour the saving of his Brother. And this they seemed willing to do; but were so long about it that in the meantime the Princes men perceiving their Masters resolution to perish with the Vessel, earnestly besought his

H: to endeavour the saving of himself in a small boat which they had yet left; who generously thank'd them for their care, but refused their offer, and told them that as they had run all ffortunes fformerly with him, so hee was now resolv'd, upon this last Pinch, not to forsake them. His men perceiving that no entreatyes would prevaile pickt out a crew of generous Ladds, hoisted out their Boat, and by force put the Prince in to it, desiring him at parting to remember that they dy'd his true and faithfull servants. Being clear of the Ship, they Row'd up to the nearest Vessell which was the *Honest Seaman*.

This vivid account of how Rupert's life was saved finds corroboration in the *Rupert Log-book*, in which a tabulation of events includes the entry: 'His H. carry'd out of the Admiral by force'. A report was also made by Fearnes, and the author of the *Sea Narrative* drew attention to this in the following words:

We have here deliver'd a true and faithful relation of this dismal Calamity from a Person that was an Eyewitnesse of the whole Action; & tho' this might suffice in a case of this quality, for the satisfaction of a curious Reader we shall yet subjoyn another Relation of the same disaster which was drawn by the hand of Capt fferns who was preserved by the same means as the Prince himselfe, and in manner as above mentioned.

In the margin of the *Narrative* appear the words: 'Here insert the relacion'. The relation is not in the manuscript, but Fearnes's report is among the Firth Transcripts in the Bodleian Library at Oxford, and on the strength of it some historians have suggested that Rupert left of his own free will.[15] Yet in truth the account in 'Capt Fearnes relation of the loss of the Admirall' differs little from that in the *Sea Narrative*. The relevant passage is as follows:

... the officers in generall begg'd of the Prince, yt hee would please to putt himselfe to the mercy of the sea in a little yaule which was uppon the Decke, which rowed with 4 oares, soe wee hoisted out the yaule, and by force made the prince goe in her, & his Highness page Rivers & 7 more of his men, (2 leaped into the yaule after) his highnes the Prince was unwilling to leave us, but wee knew if the Prince could set on bord any of the 2 other shipps which was very doubtfull in soe poore a bote, yt then wee tould his highnes there might be some possibilitie to save some of us, by his Highnes perswasion to them. It pleased God his Highnes got safe on board of the Honest Seaman, which was a miraculous thing. ...

There was general agreement that Rupert had to be forced into the boat, whatever happened afterwards. He then did what little he could to save his comrades. Once on board the *Honest Seaman*, he sent the boat back to save as many men as it could, naming Captain Fearnes, Captain Billingsley and his faithful French supporter Mortaigne in particular. Fearnes accepted the offer and was saved, 'the other two chusing rather to dy among the souldiers, than by leaving them to preserve themselves'.[16] As soon as Fearnes and his companions had been put aboard the *Honest Seaman*, the boat sank.

Rupert's efforts were not yet exhausted. 'This fatall disaster wounded the Prince to the very soule; nor would he yet give over his Endeavours for the saving of his people even to the extreme hazzard of himself.'[17] He ordered the man at the helm in the *Honest Seaman* to edge the ship towards the *Constant Reformation* in the hope of getting some of the men on to his bowsprit; but the flagship was so full of water that she could not stir, and the *Honest Seaman* could not get near enough to take the sailors off. So 'these Brave people having now a certain Death before them, layd aside all other cares to prepare themselves for that'.[18] At nine o'clock that night the *Constant Reformation* went down with the loss of 333 lives.

Next morning, the wind having slackened, Prince Maurice was able to take his brother aboard his own ship. Relations were not very happy there, for Chester, the *Swallow*'s flag-captain, had defied Maurice's order to him to go to Rupert's help at the height of the storm. Nor had his conduct in the later stages been any better. According to Pitts, Rupert's secretary at this time, 'when he saw the ship perishing he made no action at all for their boat to help to save the men, but walked upon the deck, and said, "Gentlemen, it is a great mischance; who can help it!"'[19] It was patent insubordination, but Chester was supported by his officers, and Maurice in the peculiar circumstances was in no position to enforce discipline.

Rupert had for the moment discarded all authority. The loss of his flagship and her crew had struck him to the heart, and he had succumbed to depression; with all his tenacity he seems to have been given to a sort of romantic melancholy when down on his luck. He had another reason for not asserting himself. The attitude of the governors of the various islands was suspect; some of them belonged to the faction of the Count de Miro. The reception of the princes in the Azores had so far been friendly; but the weaker their power the less certain would be their welcome. The loss of the flagship could turn the scale, and it was advisable to give the impression that the *Constant Reformation* was still at sea. So Rupert lay low in his cabin, leaving everything to his brother.

The *Loyal Subject* and the *Revenge of Whitehall* had been driven westwards to the island of Fayal, and Maurice now sailed his two remaining ships thither to meet them. But at Fayal, where he arrived on 19 October, further bad news awaited him; the *Loyal Subject* had dragged her anchors during the storm and been wrecked on the rocks. The Royalist fleet was now reduced to three ships. (No more mention is made of the Spanish prize, which had perhaps perished in the storm.)

The position was precarious. Much treasure had been lost with the *Constant Reformation*, and difficulties of repair and revictualling were acute. And at this juncture an episode occurred which showed how just were the fears of the attitude of the Portuguese governors. Maurice received intelligence of a Spanish galleon which had arrived off Pico, to the east of Fayal, with a starving crew and was negotiating to surrender with her cargo to the Portuguese in return for victuals. Maurice thereupon sent the *Honest Seaman* and *Revenge of Whitehall* 'to make demand of part of her lading for the King of Great Brittagne; that being an open Road; and no ship there to protect her'.[20] Before they arrived the ship had surrendered to the Portuguese, but they remained in the vicinity to make certain of the situation. Satisfied that the surrender had been made before they had come on the scene, their captains then offered them assistance in getting the prize in, and this offer was accepted by the Portuguese.

Maurice had been on doubtful ground in interfering in the first place, but the conduct of his captains thereafter had been impeccable. Evidently, however, they were not trusted; for when, their offer of help having been accepted, they moved farther in towards the shore, they found themselves fired on. The Portuguese, meanwhile, hauled the Spanish ship in and beached her. The *Honest Seaman* returned the fire, but as soon as it ceased an envoy was rowed ashore to ask the reason for the shooting. The Portuguese promptly arrested him, and 'after severall affronts and without reasoning the matter they committed him to the custody of the ffort'.[21] Worse was to follow. The English ships returned to Fayal, but on the way chased a vessel which turned out to be Portuguese. When she ran up her Portuguese flag the pursuit was called off, but the Governor of Fayal made this a pretext for imprisoning all the English officers who were on shore for the business of victualling.

Both sides had been at fault: the English Royalists probably more so than the Portuguese. But the significance of the embroilment was plain. The princes could count on no co-operation from the governors of Fayal and Pico, who were now only too glad of any excuse to show their hostility. In the circumstances Prince Rupert aroused himself from his torpor and decided to conceal his presence no longer. He sent in a peremptory demand for the release of all his men, 'signifying to the Governors how desirous he was to continue the amity and ffair correspondence that had formerly past betwixt the Kg of Portugal and Himself, and that if matters might be honourably composed, he should content himself to passe by all the indignityes that had been lately put upon him; but that otherwise he was resolved to endeavour the recovery of his men by fforse; and that he would immediately send the King of Portugal a Particular of the Affronts that had been put him'.[22]

It was a shock to the governors to discover that Rupert was on board the *Swallow*. The majesty of his presence and the thunder of his threats had an immediate effect. The governors hastened to assure him that it had all been a mistake. The prisoners were all set at liberty, and every assistance was offered in the equipping and victualling of the Royalist fleet.

Rupert was once more in command. The victualling proceeded apace, and on 27 October the English ships returned to Terceira for more provisions. The Prince was now convinced, however, that he must find some more suitable place to careen his vessels. And once again he turned his eyes southward, with the West Indies as the ultimate goal. This time he was determined not to be baulked by opposition within the fleet. After putting in at São Miguel to take in bread and other stores, he sent his secretary Pitts privately to each officer in each ship 'to require their opinion immediately in writing what course they judg'd safest for their Common preservation'.[23] Thus having no time to listen to persuasion and agree on a joint policy, the majority of the officers voted for the West Indies. Chester disagreed, and when he found himself circumvented he asked to be allowed to quit the fleet. Rupert was only too glad to let him go.

On 7 December 1651 Rupert sailed south to the Canaries. His hope was to capture some prizes there, but in this he was disappointed. There were none to be had, and the weather was bad. He therefore decided to make for Cape Blanc on the West African coast, in the kingdom of Arguin (an island now part of Mauritania), where there was 'a very good harbour, and naturally secure, few or none coming there but such as are distressed by Leake or other mishappes in their traffique to the Southward'.[24]

When Rupert reached this harbour on 26 December there was one small Dutch ship there. Fearful of piracy, this vessel fled at his approach, but after a little he succeeded in making contact with her captain and convincing him that he had no hostile designs on her. The meeting was useful; there was a Dutch settlement on an island some twelve leagues away, and the Netherlanders were able to supply the Prince with deal planks and other necessaries for careening his ships. The Royalists set up tents on the shore, hauled in the ships, and set to work to refit the battered vessels.

Contact with the African natives was more difficult. They were a tribe of Mohammedan nomads, typically shy and distrustful, owing nominal allegiance to an island chieftain, the Sant of Sal. There was fish in abundance in the harbour, but Rupert wanted meat for his men, and the only way to get this was to trade with the natives. This proved impossible, and on 1 January 1652 he led an expedition of a hundred men into the interior to make contact, peaceful or otherwise. It was a foggy morning, and eighteen miles from the coast he came on an encampment before the nomads were aware of his approach. They promptly fled, leaving behind their tents and their flocks of sheep and goats, 'which was a seasonable relief to those that in a manner had only Milk for their sustenance'.[25] Rupert, still anxious for trade, pursued the natives; but no friendly communication was possible, and in an attempt to stop their flight one of the Englishmen shot a camel on which a man was escaping with his family. 'But the rider soon remounted another, that sav'd himself and his wife, but for hast left a Male child behind them, which by Providence was guided to his H, as a New Yeares gift'.[26] The terrified little boy clung to the Prince, and when the party, abandoning any further attempt at negotiation, returned to base with their booty, the child went with them.

The natives followed at a distance, and when they were in sight of the ships they sent out two men with a flag of truce, offering now to treat with the English for the return of the boy and the supply of cattle. How they communicated, and in what language, is not recorded. Presumably some among them could speak a European tongue, probably Portuguese or Dutch, and Rupert's linguistic gifts perhaps came in useful once more. At any rate it was arranged that they should return in two days for negotiations. On 3 January they appeared on top of a hill and demanded a hostage before they would send a delegate to treat. Rupert was doubtful of their honesty and refused to detail a man, but one of his soldiers volunteered and the Prince allowed him to go.

The outcome was unfortunate. The nomads' delegate spun out time by endlessly discussing the return of the child, and offering nothing concrete in return; and Rupert, suspecting that some treachery was planned, set a guard on him and forbade any of his men to venture beyond the lines on pain of death; 'which order notwithstanding, one of the Princes men stole behind a cliffe, and went beyond his bounds, which the Moors perceiving, they set upon and slew him, before any man culd come into his Rescue'.[27] Blood having been shed, any hope of accommodation was gone. The nomads bolted, and Rupert, intent on rescuing his hostage, pursued with a body of men. It was no good. They found some blood, but no body, and could only conclude that the man had been murdered and thrown into the sea. Meanwhile the delegate escaped in the confusion and got back to his own people.

So Rupert returned to his ships, and kept with him his little native hostage, who stayed with him until after his return to Europe. He was just a month in the neighbourhood of Cape Blanc. Before he left he arranged for the Dutch ship to sail to France with some of his prize cargo, consisting mostly of ginger and sugar, for the benefit of King Charles. At the same time, in letters to the King and to Sir Edward Herbert, he made it plain that the first charge on the goods must be the settlement of debts he had incurred for goods supplied, on the King's behalf, at Toulon a year before. These debts were not discharged, and the episode was to have repercussions at a later date.

Rupert and Maurice sailed from Cape Blanc on 26 January, this time south-westwards to the Cape Verde Islands. But they had not yet seen the last of Africa. A vain chase of two English vessels brought their fleet to Santiago, the main island of the Cape Verde group and a Portuguese possession. The Governor was friendly and after an exchange of civilities 'gave the Prince notice of some English ships that were trading to Guinny, and fortifying themselves upon the River Gambiere, offering his H both pilots and souldiers to guid him up the River, and to strengthen him for an attempt upon the Fort'.[28]

Rupert with his severely reduced fleet was in need of prizes, and he gladly embraced the Governor's offer. On 21 February, with Portuguese pilots on board his ships and accompanied by a Portuguese caravel full of soldiers, he sailed eastwards for the Gambia River. The help he received, however, did not fulfil expectations. On the first night the caravel disappeared, 'tho' the weather was fair',[29] and the Portuguese pilots proved incompetent, running both the *Swallow* and the *Revenge of Whitehall* (now Prince Maurice's flagship) aground at the mouth of the river on 27 February.

No serious damage was done, and Rupert soon procured more satisfactory pilotage. Going ashore to reconnoitre, he 'found the track of a Christian (for it was the print of a Shooe) whereupon his H appoynted some to run as fast as they could, to get betwixt him and his boat; and so took him'.[30] This man revealed that his ship, the *Krokodil*, belonged to the Baltic duchy of Courland, which owned a fort now being built in the neighbourhood. The Duke of Courland was a distant cousin of the Palatines, and the master of the *Krokodil*, when brought to see Rupert, expressed his friendship and told him where to find the English ships in the river. When, however, the Prince asked for his services as a pilot, he seemed to think he might be departing from his duty to his own overlord; so a little comedy was performed, thus described in the *Rupert Log-book*:

. . . His H demanded of him to Pilote him into the River: His answer was I'll be layd neck and heals ffirst, So you must (sayes the P) and earse too if you don't Do't. Why do so (sayes he) and so he was layd neck and heeles:

why then, sayes he if I must, I must (to show that he was forc'd to't). So upon that he was eas'd and Piloted the P into the River.

Thus acting under compulsion, the Courlander successfully led Rupert into the channel, where on 29 February he captured a small English ship, the *John*. On board this vessel was a Negro interpreter known as 'Captain Jaques',[31] who now attached himself to Rupert and was to prove a faithful and reliable ally in the adventures that followed.

Having manned his new prize, and put Robert Holmes in command, Rupert came to anchor beside the *Krokodil*, where he was invited by the Governor of the Courland fort. This worthy, so far from resenting the requisitioning of the services of his ship's captain, offered all possible help, 'tho' he himself had more need of the Princes assistance than the Prince of His; being himself in danger to be taken'.[32] Doubtless it was a useful alliance on both sides and Rupert, acting on information from the Governor, sailed on up-river and captured a Spanish pink of ten guns. An English ketch, the *Supply*, put up a fight and escaped into the Vintaire, a tributary of the Gambia, where lay the main English ship, the *Friendship*, of 400 tons and with twenty-nine guns. Prince Maurice followed in the *Revenge of Whitehall*, but had to anchor when night fell. Next day, however, he entered the Vintaire, and after an exchange of gunfire the *Friendship* surrendered on promise of quarter and of freedom for the captain.

The ketch had hidden in a creek, but her presence was betrayed by a native and she too was captured, Rupert putting her under the command of the captain of his guards and sending her off to find another small vessel higher up the river. Thereupon the local inhabitants, 'understanding them (the small vessel's crew) to be the Prince's enemyes, and upon what grounds, were glad of the Princes arrival and in a hope of ingratiating themselves cutt off the men of the ketch that the P was going to seek. But his H abhorring to countenance Infidels in the shedding of Christian Blood gave them to understand by the Portuguese that liv'd among them how ill he took it.'[33]

It had been a highly successful action, after months of frustration, and Rupert was able to reorganize his fleet. The *Friendship* was renamed the *Defiance* and made the Vice-Admiral, Maurice shifting his flag from the *Revenge of Whitehall*, to which Captain Marshall moved from the *Honest Seaman*. Holmes commanded the *John*, Captain Clarke took over the *Honest Seaman*, and Captain Craven the Spanish pink. This prize, however, was soon found to be unfit for service and was broken up, the hulk and some guns being left for the Courlanders.

It was mid-March before the fleet, now grown to six ships if the ketch *Supply* is included, was reassembled, and Rupert sailed down the river to return to the Cape Verde Islands, But further adventures were in store.

Emerging from the Gambia, the Prince came to anchor off a town whose name is given as 'Realch', where he waited for some of his ships to catch up. With Captain Jaques, who was apparently a native of the place, on board, he hoped to trade with the natives on shore for refreshments, and at first all was friendliness. But friction soon arose. One of Prince Maurice's seamen, who 'tho' a native of that place had lived long among Christians, and embraced the Christian faith',[34] went ashore to visit his parents and failed to return. It would surely have been better to let him go, but Rupert was furious at the desertion and set out himself in the ketch, with Holmes and a hundred men, to get the man back by force. From the ketch he sent off a small boat to find a secure landing-place in a creek, but 'the surf going High, the Boat was cast away, the men getting shore; the negroes flocking towards them in great numbers'.[35] They were in acute danger of massacre, and Rupert sent Holmes in another boat to their rescue. But this boat too overturned, and Holmes and his men found themselves in as dangerous a position as the others.

The situation was saved by Captain Jaques, who was on shore. Seeing the tumult, he made his way into the crowd of natives, among whom he evidently had much influence, and induced them not only to spare the sailors but to restore their belongings to them, and then took the rescued men up to his own house, 'where he gave them a very kind Entertainment'.[36] But more trouble was in store. Rupert sent another boat to bring off the men, but when it had done so the commander, misunderstanding his orders, told Holmes that Rupert had ordered him to bring Jaques off as well. Holmes and another man therefore went back ashore to fetch Jaques.

At this point Prince Maurice's pinnace captured a native canoe, and one of the Africans in it was unfortunately shot dead in the sight of those on shore. Fury naturally broke out again, and Holmes and his companion were seized and put under guard. It speaks well for the character of their captors that they were not instantly murdered.

Rupert 'was so much mov'd at this way of proceeding that he declared his resolution either to bring them off or to perish'.[37] But he subdued his impetuosity and resolved to try diplomacy before hazarding the lives of his men. He made contact with Jaques, who undertook to discuss the release of the prisoners, the captured canoe and its crew playing the part of hostages. A day was spent in negotiation, and when nothing was achieved Rupert went himself in his pinnace to treat, having given order that all ships should man their pinnaces, which at a signal should make towards him; at a second signal the canoe was to be released.

Rupert anchored near the shore, and with Jaques as interpreter arranged for the natives to free their prisoners as soon as they saw the canoe released. But it had been a trick. Jaques, 'finding that his countrymen intended to keep their prisoners, ran down presently to the seaside, and call'd to them to retake the canoe if possible'.[38] It was too late. The canoe was light and well manned, and quickly made the shore.

The situation was desperate, and it brought out all Prince Rupert's martial qualities. As the natives thronged the shore, sending volleys of arrows towards the boats, the Prince anchored his pinnace close up and opened fire, preparing to leap ashore with his men as soon as the other pinnaces came up. The Africans ran into the sea up to their necks, diving to avoid the shots. Rupert continued to fire, and then was himself wounded, receiving an arrow 'deep into the flesh above the left Papp, which calling instantly for a knife, he presently cut forth himself'.[39]

The encounter could have had but one end. The odds were overwhelming, and Rupert would certainly have died rather than leave Holmes and his companion to their fate. But once again Jaques came to the rescue. In the excitement of the battle he gathered a party of his friends, seized the two prisoners from their guards, and got them aboard Prince Maurice's pinnace: 'An instance of gratitude and fidelity that may serve for an example to those that ought to know better.'[40] There was no need now to continue the fight. When Rupert discovered what had happened he called off the pinnaces, which made their way to the ships. The only casualty was the ketch, 'which being supply'd mostly with new men, the crew mastered the officers, and carry'd her away'.[41]

Rupert sent a message to Jaques assuring him that if he would make his escape from his angry compatriots he would be amply rewarded for his faith and pains. But the gallant Jaques, 'presenting his humble service to the Princes, and wishing them good fortune . . . return'd this answer, that he had done nothing he was affrayd to justify'.[42]

There was nothing to stay for now, and on 29 March Rupert, whose wound was evidently not serious, weighed anchor and sailed once more for the Cape Verde Islands, arriving at Maio, east of Santiago, on 5 April. There were two English ships there, and one, the *Lisbon Merchant* of Plymouth, was quickly captured by Rupert in the *Swallow*. The other, a smaller vessel, got away, and Maurice, after pursuing her westwards in the *Defiance*, anchored in Santiago Road in company with the *Honest Seaman*. The rest of the fleet assembled at Maio.

There was a paucity of fresh water there, and Rupert took his ship to join Maurice, leaving only the *Revenge of Whitehall* and the *John* at Maio. Four days later a Danish ship and two English flyboats (small, swift-sailing vessels) anchored close to the *Revenge*, thinking her to be a harmless merchantman. Rupert turned back to effect the capture of the English vessels, but was forestalled by Marshall in the *Revenge*. The English masters gave intelligence of other ships to be found at Sal, and Rupert now decided to send the new prizes to Santiago, escorted by Holmes in the *John*, and go himself with the *Swallow* and the *Revenge* to seek more victims at Sal.

Only the *Swallow* completed the voyage. The *Revenge of Whitehall* had performed her last service for the Royalists. Rupert had taken more prizes than he could safely man, being forced to dilute his loyal crews with men from the captured ships and with African natives. Some of the Englishmen were doubtless pressed seamen who cared little what master they served, but others were convinced Parliamentarians ready to rise against their captors as soon as opportunity showed itself. Such a one was William Coxon, who had been mate of the *Supply* when the ketch was captured in the Gambia River. He had then been transferred to the *Revenge of Whitehall*, and ever since had been watching for a chance to lead a mutiny. Now that chance had come. Sal was some seventy miles north of Maio, and with the winds against them the two ships, sailing on opposite tacks, were frequently out of touch with one another.

Coxon later wrote a report of the episode for the Council of State, painting a vivid picture of his Royalist captors:

> . . . these plagues and pests of human society, who wished that London were altogether in flames, the Tower of London sunk as far below as it is above the ground, and that Cromwell's heart's blood were out; which curses, we doubt not, will, by the divine hand of justice, fall upon their own heads, when they are full ripe for destruction; for their delights in cursing and swearing and in plundering, sinking, and despoiling all English ships and goods they can possible lay their talons upon, Prince Rupert being not ashamed of openly to declare that, providing he might but ruin and destroy the English interest, especially the estates of the merchants and mariners of London, and the owners and proprietors of all ships belonging to the same, he cared not whether he got a farthing more whilst he lived, than only what would maintain himself, confederates and fleet.[43]

Coxon and his confederate, Hill by name, laid their plans well. There were 115 men on board the *Revenge*, and Coxon and Hill managed to recruit twenty-five whom they could trust not to betray their design. On the night of 22 April the mutineers manned key points in the ship; Captain Marshall was overpowered; officers were attacked with pistols and hatchets; those captured were put in chains in the great cabin; and the *Revenge of Whitehall* sailed for Plymouth under her old name of *Marmaduke*.

Rupert knew nothing of what had happened. Arriving alone at Sal, he stood for Boa Vista to ask if the *Revenge* had touched there. By now he suspected the truth, and giving her up for lost he returned to Maio, rejoining the rest of his fleet at Santiago.

Here a final refitting took place. There was more trouble among the crews, for 'the Master's Mate of one of the Prizes was tryed at Counsel of War for endeavouring to betray his trust; which being clearly prov'd against him, he was executed the same day'.[44] One of the flyboats was found unserviceable, and her hulk given to 'the Religious people of the Charity'.[45] But at last everything was ready, and on 9 May 1652, after all these months of delay, Prince Rupert set out across the Atlantic for the West Indies. With him were five ships – the *Swallow*, the *Defiance*, the *Honest Seaman*, the *Lisbon Merchant* (renamed the *Sarah*) and the *John* – and one flyboat.

He was several months too late. The West Indies at this time included Spanish, French, Dutch and English possessions; there were English settlements in Barbados, St Kitts, St Croix, Nevis, Antigua and Montserrat. All these at the time of the English civil wars were staunchly Royalist, and Rupert's intention had been to link up with the settlers and use the islands as bases for sea warfare on behalf of his King. But he had spent too much time in his quest for prizes. Sir George Ayscue had left Plymouth with a Parliamentary fleet in August 1651, and in October attacked the Royalist colonists in Barbados, the principal English possession. The Governor, Lord Willoughby, put up a stout defence, but the odds were too much for him. During the next few months Ayscue established Parliamentary authority throughout the English West Indies so firmly that he was able to leave for home at just the time that Rupert was preparing for his westward voyage. Rupert knew that Ayscue had reached Barbados, but did not know the extent of his conquest. He stubbornly refused to change his plans and made for Barbados. But on the Atlantic voyage the *Swallow* sprang a serious leak, which was not handled with the maximum of efficiency. Dealing with it drove the fleet off course and past Barbados. Eventually Rupert fetched up at St Lucia, where a small English settlement had been wiped out by the native West Indians. Here the leak was repaired, and all the fleet assembled except the flyboat, which had taken in too much sail and fallen away to leeward.

The next port of call was Martinique, where the French Governor received the Prince with friendly courtesy but gave him the bad news that the Parliamentarians were now the masters of all the English islands. From Martinique he touched in at Guadeloupe, also a French possession, and then proceeded to Montserrat, arriving off the island on Whit Sunday, 5 June. Thence to Nevis, where he attacked the shipping and indulged in a sharp encounter with the guns of the fort, in which he lost his secretary Pitts. According to the *Rupert Sea Narrative* Pitts had a presentiment of death: '. . . it was remarkable that this Gent wrote severall Memorials, in case of his death, the night before; . . . which made people afterwards conclude that he had some presage of his misfortune, for he had been in the whole action before, without doing anything like this.'

Rupert next steered northward up the west coast of St Kitts, where 'the Fleet got into the French Rode called la Bastara [Basseterre] and sayld from thence along the Coast for the Old Rode where the English inhabit'.[46] Here they came under fire from the fort, and Rupert, finding his masts badly exposed and afraid of being becalmed, turned back and anchored at Sandy Point in the French part of the island. He was cordially greeted by the French authorities, and allowed to take in water, 'but proposing other matters of greater consequence, his H. concluded by the Governors refusal of them that this was not a place for Him to trust to, in regard of the strict league between them and the English'.[47] The French colonists were not going to be dragged into any alliance against the Parliamentarians.

Continuing north-westwards, Rupert put in to careen on 24 June at the Virgin Islands, mostly uninhabited but providing good anchorage. While the work was proceeding, some carpenters, new men from the prizes, who had been sent ashore to cut stanchions, seized the pinnace and sailed westwards to the neighbouring island of Puerto Rico. Puerto Rico was garrisoned by a powerful Spanish force, and Rupert, who since Cartagena had not hesitated to commit acts of war against Spanish ships, was afraid of the results of the intelligence the carpenters might take. His provisions were running short, and the Spaniards might take action to prevent his procuring more. So he 'was enforced to Retrench, and to bring every man to four ounces of bread a day; and everything else in proportion; holding himself likewise to the same allowance; by whose example his People were induced to undergo the Hardship with the greater Chearfulness'.[48]

He also took steps to establish a defensive position on shore. The harbour he had chosen was named Dixon's Hole, but came to be called Cavaliers' Harbour and was later to be known as Rupert's Bay. Here the Prince set up tents and mounted eight guns taken from the ships. He also sent the *Sarah* off southwards to Santa Cruz to get water, and there she found the flyboat which had been lost off St Lucia and brought her back. No attack came from Puerto Rico, and the Royalists stayed two months at Cavaliers' Harbour. They then set fire to the *Sarah*, the *John* and another ship which was probably a prize, as unserviceable; this left the *Swallow*, the *Defiance*, the *Honest Seaman* and the flyboat. On 29 August Rupert and Maurice set off on their next adventure.

'And now the storm-blast came, and he was tyrranous and strong.' The greatest disaster of the voyage was at hand: the overwhelming tragedy which affected Rupert perhaps more deeply than any other incident in his life.

His destination is uncertain. Perhaps he meant only to cruise at random in the hope of prizes. But he steered north-north-east between the islands until he reached latitude 21°, 'the wind blowing Trade at E.N.E.'.[49] Then he tacked to weather the islands, 'and stood to the Southwards untill by Computation he was within 12 leagues of the land Anguilla bearing Southward by East: The weather being fair but a great Northern Sea'.[50] On 13 September he was seventy miles north of Sombrero. Then the hurricane struck. It was of tremendous force, and the fleet was quickly scattered; Rupert's flagship, the battered, leaky *Swallow*, was helpless in the dreadful seas. The seamen could not stand on the deck. 'This storm forc'd the P to take in all his sayles except the Mayn-course, with which he toy'd untill 8 of the clock, but the Tempest then increasing tore the sayl from the yard (being of double new Canvass) rolling now in the trough of the Sea, they strove to set the Mizne to keep her up; so that they lay now at the mercy of the winds and the Waves near a Lee-shore, and the weather so thick that they could not see a ships length before them.'[51]

For four days the *Swallow* was hurled hither and thither, miraculously escaping wreck: '. . . it pleased the Divine providence in these deplorable conditions, being 12 at night, and within half a league of a high Rock called Sombrera; that the Admiral drove (as was afterwards concluded) betwixt that and an Island called Anguilla, where never any ships were known to passe before; without seeing or understanding any thing but the calamity and the danger'.[52] The last sail was ripped away, and in the morning the ship narrowly missed a long ledge of rock, escaping through a sudden change of wind.

The officers had little idea where they were. In fact they were back in the Virgin Islands. On 17 September they were off the uninhabited St Ann's Island, where Rupert, 'with a great deal of danger',[53] was able to anchor in twelve fathoms of water. The hurricane was still raging, and there was still the problem of getting into harbour; but 'being in this distresse, a person that was a Prisoner abord the Admiral for endeavouring to debauche some of the seamen, and in that time in Irons, being a very good Pilote, made a proposal to his H that upon condition of his being set at Liberty he would do the best he could to bring the ship into harbour: upon which terms he was set free, and he brought his H safe into a place called Gasper Bay in the Virgin Islands'.[54] Next day the storm subsided, and the *Swallow* was able to make her way back to her former anchorage.

Rupert, the *Swallow* and her crew were safe. But they were alone. The *Honest Seaman*, as later was revealed, had been driven far to the west and wrecked off Hispaniola. The *Defiance* and the flyboat, the former with Prince Maurice on board, had vanished from human ken.

To Rupert the blow was irreparable. Maurice had been dearer to to him than any other human being; the most loyal of brothers, the perfect second-in-command. They had been companions from boyhood. Maurice had hastened to Rupert's side in the dark days after the surrender of Bristol, even defying the King for his sake; and he had stood by him, brave and dependable, in all the perils at sea during the past three years. Now he was dead. Rupert had little hope that he could have survived the storm, but for years he clutched at any straw that might give a clue to his brother's fate. There were reports innumerable. Maurice had been the only survivor from his ship and was a prisoner of the Spaniards. He had been cast ashore in the Virgin Islands. He had been driven southward and captured by Algerian pirates. Two years after the hurricane the Winter Queen wrote to her eldest son: 'As for your brother Maurice, I shall shortlie know, if it be true that he is there at Algiers and so alive, but I ame councelled not to make anie great inquirie because, if he be there and knowes, they may stretch his ransome so high as it will be hard to get it, or alse they may for monie giue him into Cromwells hands, wherefore Rupert must be verie carefull that it be not too much openlie done.'[55]

After the Restoration, presumably at the instigation of Prince Rupert, the various attested statements were collated into a comprehensive report.[56] Most agreed that the *Defiance* had been wrecked off Puerto Rico and Maurice imprisoned there by the Spaniards, many of them specifying a castle called 'the More' as his place of incarceration. But all were hearsay. In June 1663 a certain Fredric de Schamps wrote to Rupert enclosing the following document:

1663, June (16)–26 – Deposition of William Beauchamp, Frenchman, that having been captured by the Spaniards, he was taken prisoner to the town of St. Domingo, where, after his release, he heard some mariners of a ship from Porto Rico talking to those of St. Domingo upon the shore. Seeing a great Flemish ship in the port the Porto Rico men said it was like the English ship which was lost on the coast of Porto Rico. Those of St. Domingo asked if many had been saved, to which the others replied that not a man was saved, as those that escaped the sea were all massacred, and that Prince Maurice was lost

The men of St. Domingo asked if they had massacred him, too, and one of them replied no, but that they had made him drink a cup of chocolate, which was as much to say that they had poisoned him.[57]

Twelve years after the storm Robert Holmes had an encounter with a Spanish ship off the Cape Verde Islands, and Mr Richard Ollard has recently revealed a passage in his account of the incident which may be held to clear up the mystery. The Spanish ship was taking a new governor, Don Francisco Velasco, out to Puerto Rico, and Holmes invited him and others on board to dine with him. His account proceeds:

> Amongst some others that came along with this Gentleman there was a Dominican Friar who spoke good English and lived many years upon the Island of St. John Porto Rico. I asked him whether he was in that Island about that time that prince Rupert was in the West Indies. He told me he was. I asked him whether he did not heare of any prisoners, Englishmen, that were brought thither about that time. He told me that he heard of none, but withall that there were severall of the best officers of that island and other Gentlemen that lived upon the same 30 or 40 yeares on board their shipp, which were able to give me the best account of anything I had a mind to know. I desired him to speak to Don Francisco De Velasco to send for them, which he did grant. . . . Then I got this Father to tell them the storie how wee lost prince Maurice in a Hurricane about that island and some people did say that the prince did save his life But was kept prisoner in a Dungeon at St. John Porto Rico. They assured me there was no such thing as any prisoner there; nor any men saved; but [that] about that very time I spoke of, upon the Southward side of the Island they found a shipp cast away and several pieces of the wreck came ashore; and amongst the rest a Goulden Lyon which some of them saw and a great quantitie of pipestaves markt MP as all prince Maurice his casket[s] were. This confirmed me that he was lost thereabouts.[58]

Back at Cavaliers' Harbour, Rupert spent three days refitting the *Swallow* for sea. Considering the battering she had received, this must be accounted remarkably quick work. However deeply he may have felt the loss of his brother, his spirit was unbroken, and having taken in a good store of fresh water he was ready for action again. Provisions were short, and with his one ship he must try to take more prizes. He set sail on 25 September, making for Guadeloupe. At first his luck was out, but on 5 October he captured a small English ship of ten guns. At Guadeloupe, where he arrived on 10 October, he was given a friendly reception and supplied with all he wanted.

Rupert had hoped to get news of Maurice at Guadeloupe. Of course there was none, but he encountered some Dutch ships whose captains told him that the English Parliamentary régime was now at war with the Netherlands, and also that two English ships were in harbour at Antigua. Thither he sped. He had lost his brother, but he still had his second-best officer, Robert Holmes, who had joined the *Swallow* when the *John* was destroyed and so survived with his admiral. Rupert now

Portrait of Prince Rupert and Dudley, by Vignon

Battle of Texel, 11 August 1673, by van de Velde

sent Holmes ashore with fifty men to attack the fort of Antigua, and while a brisk action took place he captured the ships without resistance, their masters and crews having gone off to loot a wrecked Spanish galleon.

Returning to Guadeloupe, Rupert took on 11 November a 200-ton English ship bound for Barbados and laden with provisions. He now had four prizes. It was all he could manage; more he could not man. He was well supplied, and there was nothing further he could do in the West Indies. He himself was in poor health. The strain of the past months had been too much even for his constitution; he was a sick and tired man. It was time to make for home.

Touching at Dominica and again at the Virgin Islands without important incident, Rupert at length left West Indian waters on 12 December, making for the Azores. On 16 January 1653 he reached Fayal, expecting to be hospitably received by the Portuguese. He was swiftly disillusioned. Portugal was now in amity with Cromwell's government, and the last guest likely to be welcome was the piratical Royalist prince. To his surprise and annoyance he found himself under fire, and when he tried to send a boat ashore the Portuguese waved to it to keep off and would not allow a landing. At São Miguel he met the same treatment.

The only thing to do was to make straight for France, and after a spell of foul weather Rupert directed his course for the coast of Brittany. There were a few minor adventures on the way, but on 4 March he entered the Loire with his four prizes and anchored off St Nazaire. Next day he proceeded up-river to Paimboeuf, where his French pilot ran the *Swallow* aground. At length he was able to set foot on land, proceeding to Nantes, where he promptly fell ill.

Behind him the *Swallow* gradually disintegrated as she lay at anchor.

A COURT IN EXILE

RUPERT'S illness at Nantes was serious but brief. He had been sickening for some time, and the malady, described as a flux (a discharge of blood from the bowels), was doubtless brought on by exhaustion and bad food as much as by anything else. So long as he was at sea, responsible for the lives of his men, he kept himself going by sheer will-power. Once on shore he succumbed.

News of the return of the wanderer was received with excitement at St Germain. He had been away so long, and in the last two years so little had been heard of him, that the name of Rupert had taken on an almost legendary character. When he heard of the Prince's arrival and illness King Charles II wrote to him:

> My dearest Cousin,
>
> I am so surprised with joy in the assurance of your safe arrival in these parts, that I cannot tell you how great it is, nor can I consider any misfortunes or accidents which have happened, now I know your person is in safety. If I could receive the like comfort in a reasonable hope of your brothers, I will not tell you how important it would be to my affairs, when my affection makes me impatient to see you, I know the same desire will incline you, after you have done what can be only done by your presence there, to make what haste to me your health can endure, of which I must conjure you have such a care as it may be in no danger; I have sent Colonel Owen, whom you know to be a very honest man, to do you such service as you shall direct him: . . . I will say no more to you at present, only to assure you I shall be very impatient till I see you, that I may myself tell you with how much kindness I am
>
> My dearest Cousin,
Your most affectionate Cousin,
CHARLES R.
>
> For my dear Cousin Prince Rupert,
>   Paris, March 22, 1653.[1]

Two other letters reached Rupert at the same time. 'For God's sake, sir,' wrote Hyde, 'in the first place look to your health, and then to the safety of what you have there, and then lose no minute of coming away.'[2] And Jermyn, in a friendly letter, assured the Prince that 'the Queen is very entirely your constant friend'.[3]

Equal enthusiasm was shown by the French court. The young King Louis XIV, as soon as he heard that Rupert was fit to travel, invited him to Paris, and 'complimented him in an extraordinary manner, sending the first Gentleman of his Bedchamber to salute him, and congratulate his happy Recovery'.[4] On 29 March (OS), leaving Holmes to look after the prizes, Prince Rupert left for the French capital, where he received a hero's welcome.

His physical strength and iron constitution had ensured him a quick though not complete recovery. But the years of wandering had left their mark on him. For more than four years he had been almost continually at sea, suffering every hardship that wind and weather could inflict, often short of the bare necessities of existence, frequently on the run from more powerful enemies, always bearing the burden of command while battling against overwhelming odds; he had had to bear the loss of many men who had served him with courage and devotion, and of ships he had come to love. Above all, he had lost the faithful brother who had been dearer to him than any other being. No man can emerge from such experiences unscathed. Rupert had always been short-tempered, intolerant, impatient of opposition. Now he became more silent, more morose, though less impetuous. He had aged in those four years. Though still but thirty-three, to those around him he was a veteran, the hard-bitten survivor from a sterner age. Nor was his health ever quite as robust as of yore.

Much had happened during his long absence. Three years before his return King Charles had finally thrown in his lot with the Scottish Presbyterians, and had landed in Scotland and been crowned at Scone, but in so doing had accepted the Covenant and abandoned his noblest subject, Montrose, who had once again been planning to raise the Highlands for his King. Deserted by his master, Montrose was captured by his enemies and met the undeserved death of a traitor as gallantly as any soldier struck down in fair fight.

The betrayal of Montrose was perhaps the most shameful episode of Charles II's life, recalling his father's desertion of Strafford. Subsequently the young King to some extent redeemed himself by his spirited advance with a Scottish army into England, where he was defeated by Cromwell at Worcester on 3 September 1651, and by his gay and resourceful adventures as a fugitive thereafter, when he made his way through England in disguise, displaying dash and gallantry and rejoicing in the courageous loyalty of humble and simple people who risked their lives for their King. With the irrepressible Wilmot at his side he had finally escaped by sea from Shoreham, and since then had been living from hand to mouth in Paris and at St Germain, dependent on the charity of the French court and plagued by dissensions among his own followers and family.

There were changes in the Palatine family too. The indomitable old grandmother, the Dowager Electress Louisa, had died in Brandenburg in 1644, and now there had been two more deaths among the Winter Queen's children. The hot-headed Philip had fallen at Rethel in 1650, fighting in the ranks of the French against the Spaniards. In the following year Princess Henrietta, gentlest and loveliest of the sisters, was married to Sigismund Rakoczy, brother of the Prince of Translyvania. Five months after the wedding, at the age of twenty-five, she died. Another five months, and her husband followed her to the grave.

But the most momentous change concerned Charles Louis. The Thirty Years War was over at last. The Peace of Westphalia was signed in 1648, and a shattered Germany was redesigned. As regards the Wittelsbach territories, the Upper Palatinate was allotted to the man in possession, Maximilian of Bavaria, together with the title of First Elector of the Empire; but the Lower Palatinate was restored to its historic allegiance, and an eighth electorate, ranking last instead of first, was created. It was better than nothing, and Charles Louis, after all his years of struggle and intrigue, entered Heidelberg for the first time since his infancy to take up his inheritance.

The restoration brought out the best in the eldest of the surviving Palatines. No longer impelled to plot and trim to gain his ends, he proved an excellent ruler, moderate and benevolent, striving with all his not inconsiderable talents to restore his truncated and devastated domain to prosperity. His qualities of cool-headedness and astute judgement now found their proper sphere of action. He was still parsimonious, however, and indeed he had no money to spare. The Winter Queen, in the first flush of enthusiasm, thought her troubles were at an end; but she was speedily disillusioned. With her eldest and favourite son installed in the family domain she wrote confidently to him asking for financial support. She got nothing. Charles Louis insisted that the state of his treasury made it impossible to pay her the jointure to which she was entitled by her marriage to his father, or to recover for her the dower residence of Frankenthal assigned to her as Electress Palatine. Her position as titular Queen of Bohemia seems to have been advanced as an excuse for this latter refusal. 'The title of majesty,' wrote an informant at The Hague to John Thurloe, head of Cromwell's intelligence service, 'doth hinder her from going to dwell at Frankenthal, although the son also do take from her her dowry.'[5] Elizabeth felt his heartlessness bitterly. Henceforth in her tribulations she would turn more and more to Rupert in preference to her beloved but calculating eldest son.

One thing Charles Louis did do was to invite his sisters to Heidelberg, and the eldest and the youngest accepted. Elizabeth, 'La Grecque', aged thirty-three at the time of her sister Henrietta's death, had become known as one of the most learned women of her time. For years she had corresponded on philosophical subjects with Descartes, who treated her as an intellectual equal and dedicated to her his *Principia Philosophiae*. The friendship continued till Descartes died in Sweden in 1650, driven to his death by Queen Christina, who expected him to instruct her in philosophy at five o'clock in the morning in a semi-arctic winter. Sophia, the first to take up residence at Heidelberg, was a lively twenty-one-year-old who had already established herself as the devoted favourite of her eldest brother.

Edward, now living in Paris, also visited Heidelberg, four of the six Palatines being together there in the summer of 1652. Only Louise, the artist of the family, remained with her mother at The Hague.

Rupert was warmly greeted by his brother Edward, now back in Paris, but for the moment he took no steps to see the rest of his immediate family. Convalescent after his illness, he was content to relax in the society of his cousins Charles and James. A young Yorkshire squire, Sir John Reresby, passing through Paris in 1654, saw 'the King, the Duke of Yorke, and Prince Robert playing at billiards in the Palais Royal'.[6] The Prince also joined his cousins in swimming, and on one occasion came near to drowning. A letter from Paris quoted in the Evelyn correspondence thus describes the incident:

We have not much of newes here; but the river Seine had like to have made an end of your black Prince Rupert; for some nights since hee woulde needes coole himselfe in the river, where he was in danger of drowning, but by the help of one of his blackmores escaped. His Highnesse (it seems) has learnt some magic amongst the remote islands; since his coming hither he hath cured the Lord Jermin of a feaver, with a charme; but I am confident England is without the jurisdiction of his conjuring faculty.[7]

Another description of what was evidently the same incident was given in a quaintly spelt letter from Captain Edward Wogan to Major-General Massey:

The last night theare had licke to beane a most sad acksidinch: the King, ducke, and princh Rupertt beaing a swimming, princh Rupertt had licke to beane drountt, had it nott bene for on Hameltton, thatt saved him whin he was quitte gon under watter, took him up bey the hayre of the head, and swome asore with him. . . . Dear Sir, I am,

Your most affectinatt humbell sarvatt,
EDWARD WOGAN.

Valeroyal, the 19th of Jonge, 1653.[8]

Rupert had become a romantic figure, resplendent with the aura of distant climes and credited with magical powers born of the lore of strange and mysterious tribes. Quite possibly he had indeed cured Jermyn of a fever. Always keenly interested in scientific experiment, he may well have picked up some of their traditional medical knowledge from the natives of Africa or the West Indies. His 'blackamores' added to the glamour of his reputation. He had brought back others besides the boy who had clung to him at Cape Blanc, and 'Hameltton' was presumably one of them. They were evidently faithful and attached to him, and the fashion of keeping Negro pages, though it certainly did not originate with Prince Rupert, owed a good deal of popularity to his example.

Not unnaturally the ladies of Paris were enamoured of this austere but glamorous Prince. In Bromley's *Royal Letters* are printed a series of epistles in French, archly and somewhat obscurely worded, which, though neither sender nor recipient is identified, have been assumed to have been sent to Prince Rupert. Two are signed 'La Bohémienne', and one 'Chalendade'; the rest bear no signature, but are subscribed 'Votre tres-humble & obéissante servante'. One implores 'votre Altesse' not to be angry at the supplicant for taking the liberty of writing, and concludes: 'Si vous allez Dimanche a la chasse, & que cela n'incommode point votre Altesse, je la prie de passer par ici.'[9] Another assures him that 'je trouve toute ma satisfaction à vous dire que je ferai toujours à vous, malgré tout le monde'.[10]

The letters have a familiar ring, reading like the perennial fan-mail addressed by infatuated young women to popular heroes. The writer (or writers) may never have actually met Prince Rupert; alternatively the letters may not have been addressed to him at all. In any case there is no evidence that he took the slightest notice of them. There is, however, a passage in a letter of intelligence to Thurloe, sent from Paris on 1 April 1654, which suggests that the Prince did indulge in at least one affair of gallantry at this time.

. . . Last Sunday prince Rupert, with an Irishman called Homes, a captain, were returning from hunting at Cour de la reyne behind the Louvre, where two gentlemen rid in all haste coming into Paris, to which prince Rupert gave way; and after they passed, they returned back again, and drew their pistols against prince Rupert, and both failed; which the prince seeing, drew one of his own, and killed one of them, and wounded mortally the other; which the count de Mongiron their master, married to mareschal de Plessy Prastin's daughter, riding after them, and seeing one of his gentlemen killed, began to revenge him. Prince Rupert was to do with him as he had done with his man, till he cried, and told he was such a man. The prince said he could not believe him for such; yet seeing he said it, he would not meddle with him. So the matter passed, and the gentleman slain, the worse for him.[11]

The affair was apparently hushed up, and no more is heard of Rupert and the Comtesse de Mongiron, whose father, Plessis-Praslin, was one of France's most distinguished soldiers. But it would appear, if the account is accurate, that the Prince did acknowledge his involvement in the matter, even to the extent of sparing the outraged husband's life.

But Rupert still had business to do, and gradually he became once more engaged in public affairs. Holmes was in charge at Nantes, and Rupert visited him there in May 1653. There was much to be done: transporting the cargoes, disposing of what was left of the *Swallow*, paying off the crew and settling debts. Holmes had his troubles. Rupert's old flag-captain, Fearnes, always a difficult character, would not provide proper accounts of the stores; and there were threats of mutiny from the sailors when their pay was delayed. Then Cromwell put in a claim to the French Government for the seizure of Rupert's cargoes on the ground that they were taken from English merchant ships. He got no satisfaction. Cardinal Mazarin supported Rupert. 'What should his excellency my lord general Cromwell expect from the Cardinal,' wrote Thurloe's Paris correspondent, 'but a parcel of fair promises in answer to his letter? I assure you, the king and cardinal are resolved not to deliver prince Rupert's merchandizes, what language soever or fair words they give you. . . . I protest, they laugh at you, and think your demands so insolent, as nothing more.'[12]

The Cardinal's friendship was not entirely disinterested. He was a cold, calculating statesman; and the presence of Charles II on French soil, though agreeable to King Louis XIV (now fifteen years old), hampered his diplomacy, in effect debarring him from courting Cromwell's England should he wish to do so. King Charles for his part would gladly leave a country where he was not wanted, had he only the wherewithal to take himself elsewhere. Anything that would augment the royal funds would be welcome to both English king and French minister. But the money available was negligible, and Rupert in consequence found himself once more pitchforked into court intrigue reminiscent of Civil War days, and eventually into a furious quarrel with his cousin the King.

That Rupert must have returned to France with the wealth of the Indies to lay at the feet of his King was an article of faith at the court of St Germain. Charles was itching to get his hands on the treasure, which he hoped would enable him to leave France in becoming state. At the end of 1653 he wrote an ominous letter to Rupert:

My Dearest Cousin, If I had not thought you would have bene heare before this time, I would have written oftener and fuller to you. The truth is I do only deferr the setting downe the time of my goeing from hence, and the resolving of which way to goe, till I speake with you, you know what I am promised to receave from the french Court for my iorny, in the meantime I am sure I am not only without mony, but have been compelled to borrow all that I have spent neere these 3 moneths, so that you will easily iudge how soone three thousand and six hundred pistols will be gone, and yett I must expect no more from hence, but depend upon what you shall bring me, for my shipps, gunnes, and my share of the prise; I longe to have you here, and am intierly,

Your most affectionat Cousin
(Seal) Charles R.[13]

For the moment the matter of prize money hung fire. But acrimony was building up within the Privy Council. Rupert had taken his place on this body, and the King had reappointed him to the post of Master of the Horse, which he had held under Charles I; it seems that he was also granted a similar title by the King of France. In the exiled court two rival parties emerged. One consisted of Rupert's friends, the most important of whom was Sir Edward Herbert, now Lord Keeper of the Great Seal. There were also Lord Gerard, Lord Jermyn and Sir Marmaduke Langdale. The opposing party was led by Sir Edward Hyde, the Chancellor of the Exchequer. He had the weighty though relatively impartial support of the Marquess of Ormonde, who had joined King Charles in Paris. Others of the party were Lord Percy and Wilmot, who had recently been created Earl of Rochester.

Rupert's friends were eager to find him employment, and Langdale proposed that he should lead a new expedition to Scotland. Under the influence of Jermyn, and perhaps also inspired by her dislike of Hyde, Queen Henrietta Maria came forward as a supporter of Rupert, and enthusiastically espoused the idea. It was suggested that the Duke of York should be in nominal command, and to this both Rupert and the Queen were agreeable. Hyde was bitterly opposed to the whole plan. He rightly doubted the chances of success, and further believed that any hope there was would be blighted by the presence of Rupert, who would never be accepted by the Scots Presbyterians. Here the Scottish leaders themselves gave him the lie, for in May 1653 they issued a declaration, addressed to the King, in which, while beseeching Charles that he would 'not endure about his person any that are not eminent for righteousness',[14] gave their approval by name to Rupert, Ormonde, Gerard, Nicholas and Craven; Jermyn and Culpeper were specifically excepted.

Nevertheless there was still some doubt on the matter, and about this time one of the Duke of York's secretaries, Henry Bennet (the future Lord Arlington), received a letter, said to have come from a Scotsman in Holland, saying that the Scots had an aversion for Rupert. The writer 'did desyre, if the king did not come himself, to send the duke of Yorke to command in Scotland, but by no meanes to suffer prince Rupert to be there'.[15] The letter was shown to Rupert, who demanded to know from whom it came. Bennet refused to divulge the authorship, but shortly afterwards the writer himself appeared in Paris, and, finding that the letter had raised a stir, promptly admitted his responsibility. He was Daniel O'Neill, who had been one of Rupert's senior officers at Edgehill but had later, for reasons unknown, fallen out with him. O'Neill, though an Irishman, had spent a good deal of his life in Scotland. He stood by what he said and insisted that 'most of the friends of Scots and English were of that opinion'.[16]

Faced with this uncertainty, the King hesitated; and in the event the idea of a Scottish expedition petered out, as so many Royalist projects did. But the affair brought increased ill-feeling between the Chancellor of the Exchequer and the 'Swordsmen', as those who were in favour of military activity had come to be known. Hyde wrote scornfully to Nicholas on 4 July: 'The Lord-Keeper and Lord Gerard have a thousand projects to make Prince Rupert General in England, Scotland, and Ireland, and Admiral of two or three fleets together.'[17]

At the end of the year the Chancellor's enemies struck back, but in a singularly inept manner. Robert Long, a mischievous character who was in charge of some financial aspects of the Privy Council's work, brought forward an allegation that Hyde had been involved in conspiracy with Cromwell; behind him in this were Herbert and Gerard. The charge was so fantastic that it could only backfire on those who made it; Hyde himself ridiculed it. 'I hope you thinke it strange to heare,' he wrote to Sir Richard Browne, 'that I have bene in Englande, and have had a private conference with Cromwell, and [that you] are not sorry that my enimyes can frame no wiser calumny against me.'[18]

Absurd as the allegation was, it was brought up before the King in the council in January 1654, and Sir Richard Grenville, not the most reliable of witnesses, was named as the source of the information. Having listened to the exposition of the case by Herbert, Gerard and others, King Charles declared 'that he never heard soe frivolous an accusation in his life and wondred that such trash should come from some of those persons'.[19] He expressed his contempt for Long, and his faith in Hyde, whereupon Herbert 'urged it was strange the King should make such a difference betwixt Mr. Chancelor and Mr. Long, whereas he held Mr. Long as good a gentleman as Mr. Chancelor'.[20]

This was too much for Rupert. Herbert was his friend and Hyde his enemy; but his integrity would not allow him to acquiesce in a patently false charge, and he rounded on the Lord Keeper. 'Prince Rupert standing by said the King made not the difference from their blood, but from the honesty of the Chancelor and the dishonesty of Long.'[21] His intervention disconcerted those who looked to him as their leader. 'The accusers were much deceaved in their expectation from Prince Rupert, for his Highness intirely agreed in opinion with his Majesty for the frivolousness of the Chancelors charge.'[22]

In May a plan to assassinate Cromwell misfired in London. The leading spirit was John Gerard, Lord Gerard's cousin; he and his companions were captured and executed. How far King Charles and Prince Rupert were involved in this venture is uncertain. The 'Sealed Knot' had now been formed in England, and this Royalist fifth column had the King's blessing. But this particular attempt seems to have been a private venture of John Gerard's, though his cousin almost certainly gave it his support. An emissary of the conspirators named Thomas Henshaw had been sent over to the continent, and according to a Commonwealth account Henshaw 'went to Paris on this design, and conferred with prince Rupert; but the prince told Charles Stuart, who approved, and would have spoken with Henshaw but from a rumour that Henshaw was sent hence to abuse them'.[23] There is no reason to suppose that Rupert would have abjured a design to murder Cromwell, whom he regarded as a regicide and an ally of Satan. But the evidence is inconclusive.

It was in the explosive atmosphere induced by these events that the dispute over the prize money came to a head. King Charles had been bitterly disappointed when he found that Rupert had not brought a fortune back with him to France, and he demanded that what there was from the sale of the cargoes should be handed over to him. Rupert refused to comply. The ultimate residue was undoubtedly the King's, but two things mattered to the Prince. The seamen must receive their arrears of pay, and the debts of the merchants who had equipped his ships at Toulon must be settled. Rupert's honour was at stake; he was completely scrupulous in the matter of financial obligation, and in such a case he was immovable. The King's conscience on the other hand was more flexible, and particularly over money matters. In his view his own needs must come first; he cared little for the rights of merchants.

When the debts had been settled there would be little or nothing left, as Rupert explained to the King. Most of the booty he had acquired had been lost in the wreck of the *Constant Reformation*, and much of what remained had vanished with Prince Maurice. Egged on by Hyde, the King demanded an account. Furious at what he regarded as a slight on his honour, Rupert refused to give it. For the second time the Prince whose creed was loyalty defied his sovereign.

It was a bitter squabble. 'The King of England and Prince Rupert have quarrelled,' wrote Prince Edward to his sister Sophie. 'To tell you whether they have done so rightly or wrongly would be a relatively difficult thing for me to judge. I find that they are both of them in the wrong, for each of them is led by his fool, who governs them: and these fools hate one another like the plague.'[24] The two fools were presumably Hyde and Herbert.

King Charles did eventually get some of what he regarded as his due. The *Swallow* was so weather-beaten as to be unsaleable, but she bore fifty brass guns of considerable value, and these Rupert could hardly deny to be the property of the King. In the hope of preventing further argument Mazarin stepped in, and bought the guns on behalf of the French Government, handing over the money to Charles. But Rupert had not yet shot his bolt; he demanded half the sum raised. And once again he brought up the matter of the debts at Toulon. King Charles refused the demand.

Prince Rupert was beside himself with rage. He resigned his office of Master of the Horse and announced that he was going to Germany to seek what was due to him on the settlement of the Palatinate: 'from the prosecution of which purpose his majesty did not dissuade him, and possibly heard it with more indifferency than the prince expected'.[25] So wrote Hyde, whose account of the whole affair is envenomed against Rupert. But there is evidence that before the cousins parted tempers had cooled. Writing to the Winter Queen at the end of May, King Charles spoke kindly of her son and said that he 'doubts not but that in this short absence he will so recollect himself that they shall meet again with the more kindness and better understanding; for the King cannot but love him very much, and always be confident of his friendship'.[26] And Thurloe's agent in Paris wrote on 6 June (NS) that 'Prince Rupert is at last parted for Germany, having reconciled himself to Charles Stuart for the ordnancy of the ship the Swallow'.[27]

Whatever his relations with the King, Prince Rupert was not disposed to change his plan. For the first time in his life he was about to visit the principality of his ancestors.

CHAPTER 6

FATHERLAND

RUPERT had been contemplating a journey to the Palatinate before the quarrel with King Charles developed. By the Peace of West-phalia compensation for the loss of the Upper Palatinate was granted to the Elector by the Emperor, while to each of the younger brothers was accorded the sum of 100,000 thalers 'pour ayder a leur fournir leurs droits at appanages'.[1] Rupert hoped for an apanage, which by the custom of the Holy Roman Empire a younger brother might expect; but in any case he was entitled to the money, and to settle the matter he would have to travel to Germany. On 27 February 1654 he wrote to Charles Louis from Paris a letter in English (the brothers usually corresponded in French), which gave no hint of their recent differences:

Sir and dear brother. After being long at sea and since detayned here some months about settling the buisines I have had concerning what I brought with mee from thence this is the first time I could have for im-ploying my thoughts in considering the little fortune that may belong to me. It can not fall into my thoughts that I can soe fittly in any way apply myselfe as your brotherly care and affection where in I rest assured to find alle the assistance I can need which I will labour to deserve by alle meanes imaginable having thus determined for the way I meane to hould, I make it my first desire to you (to whom I wish to owe most) that I may hav the knowledge of what provision or portion can be thought due or fitt for me as a brother of your family or from any accord or establishment made upon the peace of that country and in the next place to lett me have your advice for what you think I may best doe in reference to the setting and advancing of what I may be capable of. In the last place that I may have your assistance (which I must rely upon in all things conduciable to my fortune).

After alle this (to make me the fitter for it) you will doe mee right to beleeve that I think I have not done and am resolved not to doe anything unworthy of my birth or unpleasing to you. I have been forced to loose much time which was not in my power to prevent, it must be your kind-ness to keepe me from loosing any more and therefore I beseech you lett me leave presently. . . .[2]

It is strange to find Prince Rupert adopting the tone of a submissive younger brother to one whom for years he had regarded as an enemy and a traitor to his house. But not only was Charles Louis now his sovereign in so far as he had acknowledged himself a Palatine subject; it lay in the elder brother's power to set Rupert up as a landowner and, in a small way, a semi-independent princeling. Rupert had at least learned a little diplomacy.

Charles Louis, however, viewed the prospect of a visit from his brother with little enthusiasm. It is difficult not to sympathize with him. He was striving against formidable odds to rehabilitate his truncated domain, and to parcel out further portions of it would make his task impossible; nor had he any money to spare. The advent of an importunate claimant, and that claimant the ferocious younger brother who, however humble he might appear for the moment, might quickly become 'Robert le Diable' once more if crossed, would be anything but welcome.

He put the bravest face he could on the matter. He answered Rupert's letter on 4 March, congratulating him on his safe return from sea but warning him at the same time of the distressed condition of the Palatinate, the small revenue derived from it, and his own grave problems of restoration. He suggested that French or English service would be more rewarding than anything he could do, and on the same day he wrote to Colonel Pawel, his agent in Paris, instructing him to endorse his own account of his difficulties and to tell Rupert that there was no possibility of providing an apanage. Pawel was to show Rupert the contract that the Elector had made the year before with his brother Edward, and try to persuade him to accept a similar settlement.

Rupert in his then mood of sweet reasonableness allowed himself to be persuaded. On the Elector's instructions Pawel drew up an agreement whereby Rupert was to receive an income of 2,500 thalers for the next five years, thereafter increasing to 4,000. He accepted this, and at the same time managed to raise ready money through the help of Edward's wife, who had influence at the French court and secured for him the arrears of pay that had been due to him since his French service in 1647.

He was not to be deterred, however, from his intention of visiting the Palatinate; and his rift with his royal cousin provided the occasion. He set out from Paris on 11 June 1654, 'with a very great train and brave'.[3] He travelled by easy stages, and his great train included the little African boy. 'Sunday last prince Rupert came on here from Paris,' wrote Thurloe's Strasbourg agent on 8 July, 'with 26 persons, among whom are three Black-moors, and an African lad of five years old, which is part of the prey which he brought over-seas from those parts'.[4] Rupert had evidently become much attached to this child, even though in the manner of the time he probably regarded him as a chattel; Hauck says that he 'treated him with an almost fatherly tenderness'.[5]

From Strasbourg it was only a short step to Heidelberg, and Rupert received a cordial welcome to his brother's capital city. Charles Louis received him at the city gates, and the two brothers rode together at the head of the procession, showing all the signs of genuine friendship. The people of the Palatinate greeted the famous warrior coming home for the first time with the warmest enthusiasm, and the throng was so great that there was hardly room for the exotic train to pass through the streets. The 'black-moors' aroused the liveliest curiosity.

Charles Louis and Rupert were now on better terms than, probably, they ever were before or after. Eight years had passed since their last meeting at Guildford. Much had happened since then, and they vied with each other in mourning the murder of an uncle and the loss of a brother. Old animosities were laid aside – at least for a time. And there were further reunions, for waiting at the castle were Rupert's sisters Elizabeth and Sophia, for both of whom he had a warm affection. 'I have had the joy of seeing a long-lost brother',[6] wrote Elizabeth, who had not seen him since he left the family home for England before the Civil War.

Rupert did not stay very long in Heidelberg, however. Financial arrangements had been settled with his brother. Further negotiations must be with the Emperor, and before the end of July Rupert was on his way to Vienna, a journey to stir up memories of the days after his release from his captivity at Linz. Charles Louis lent him a coach to take him as far as Donauworth, and in returning it he sent his brother a letter (in French) whose light tone emphasizes once more the pleasant and easy relations which had sprung up between them.

> I could not return your equipage, with which it pleased you to honour me, without informing you that they conducted me very well as far as this town without accident. On the road the Counts of Holck met me and accompanied us for some time, as today did another *with a hard name* [written in English] – at least my memory will not let me give you his name, nor have I time to discover it. I ducked the invitations both offered (and with great civility) the former to see their mother and the latter to see [omission in text] and postponed until another occasion giving myself this honour and pleasure. As for our conversation, it was naturally most reasonable in each case, but very hard to relate, which is why I shall do no more than make my excuses in this present letter.[7]

In Vienna he received another heart-warming welcome. He had made himself popular there in 1641, and he was not forgotten. Between him and the Emperor Ferdinand III there had been a strong mutual regard, and they were delighted to see one another again. At the same time Rupert received a further mark of favour from his brother in the shape of the insignia of the Palatine Order of St George. 'I send you herewith the St George,' wrote Charles Louis, 'which I could not manage sooner: the goldsmith has made it clumsily enough; but he is a drunkard from whom one cannot have what one wants.'[8] In writing to thank him Rupert offered his services in what looked like developing into a war between the Elector and the Bishop of Speyer. 'I would abandon all to serve you in it,' he wrote on 6 August, 'all the more because the interest of our house would impel me to do so.'[9] But Charles Louis assured him that it was a petty dispute not worth his attention.

In Vienna Rupert ran into difficulties. The imperial treasury – not for the first or last time – was in an exhausted state, and the Emperor's councillors proceeded to haggle over the money due to the Prince; it was quite impossible, they maintained, to pay over the full sum of 100,000 thalers, and an agreement on instalments must be made. Moreover Rupert must first sign an undertaking to renounce all claim to the Upper Palatinate for himself and his descendants. Rupert strongly objected to jeopardizing the future of his house, and deadlock appeared to be reached. But tempers cooled, and Rupert rather unexpectedly found a good friend in the Spanish Ambassador, the Marqués de Fuentes, who lent his good offices and advised him on ways of dealing with the imperial court. 'You will be glad to learn,' wrote the Prince to his brother on 2 September, 'that the Spanish Ambassador has worked extremely hard in my interests. . . . I beg you also to thank the said Ambassador for the care he has of me in everything, having not only lent me his carriage but even offered me one of his houses and, in fine, acted as if for himself.'[10]

Probably on the advice of this helpful envoy, Rupert appealed over the heads of the councillors to the Emperor himself. Ferdinand was as amicable as ever, and the two friends went over the whole question in a personal interview. The Emperor told his guest frankly of his financial problems and of the many claims made on him by the various princes of the Empire. In face of this friendly attitude, Rupert agreed to modify his demands, and an agreement was reached whereby he would receive 15,000 thalers in each of the next two years, and thereafter 10,000 thalers a year, with interest on the unpaid balance. He also asked for 10,000 thalers as past interest, and for the sum due to his dead brother Philip, which now devolved on the surviving Palatines. By the end of October all was concluded with an immediate payment of 18,000 thalers. No more seems to have been said about the renunciation of the Upper Palatinate.

Rupert was in a happy mood. Charles Louis, Elizabeth and Sophia sent him a joint letter in verse asking him how he was enjoying himself, and he replied in some French rhyming couplets with irregular scansion. 'My dear brother and sisters,' he wrote, 'I take delight in reading your verses, in which I recognised the writing of three hands, expressing in good sense that you desired to know how I pass the time.'[11] He had, he went on, so many fruitful vices ('fautes fecondes') that 'I prize first one, then another, and often desire to possess what a moment later I forget to dream of'.

Rupert's personal business in Vienna was satisfactorily concluded. He had also, however, been negotiating on behalf of his royal cousin: evidence that happy relations between them had now been fully restored. King Charles had managed to move his little court from France to Germany, and in the autumn of 1654 was at Cologne with his sister, Mary Princess of Orange. He apparently had hopes of hospitality at the imperial court, and Rupert on his behalf sounded out his friend the Emperor. Here he met with a rebuff. Ferdinand appears to have doled out some funds; '. . . the said P.C. [King Charles] writt a letter to the emperor concerning monie promised to him,' wrote one of Thurloe's spies, 'partes of which monies are paid'.[12] But it was made clear that Charles II would not be made welcome in Vienna. It seems that Charles Louis was in some way involved in the negotiations, for he wrote to Rupert: 'I have taken the liberty of despatching M. Bunckley to the King of Great Britain to warn him that he is not wanted at Vienna; doubtless you will be able to confirm this.'[13] King Charles thereupon blandly asserted that he had never intended to go there.

On 26 November Rupert left Vienna to return to Heidelberg. He travelled by way of the Upper Palatinate, and when he stopped at the small town of Neumarkt and was received with honour by the local dignitaries, of whom he made inquiries about the state of the country, some stir was caused at the Bavarian court. But Rupert had no ulterior motive, and after a brief stay he proceeded on his way. Bad roads delayed his journey, and it was not till 11 December that he reached Nuremberg. A few days later he was in Heidelberg.

After Vienna he found his brother's capital dull. His life for the moment was aimless; he wanted employment, but Charles Louis was reluctant to grant him any office at his court. A mood of restlessness seized him, and in the early months of 1655 he wandered here and there. His movements are not easy to trace, but in January he was with King Charles in Cologne. He did not stay there long; Hyde's influence was in the ascendant, and Rupert found the atmosphere of the court little to his liking. It would appear that about this time he also visited his mother at The Hague.

In the spring appeared the prospect of an escape from idleness.

Warfare between the petty princes of Italy was more or less continuous, and Duke Francis I of Modena, a pocket state to the east of Milan, wanted support. His pretext was that he needed troops for defence against the Papal States, but he really wanted to use them against the Spanish rule in Milan. He approached Rupert as a renowned soldier now out of employment, and invited him to enlist troops for Modena and himself assume the high command over them.

It was a small enterprise for a general of Rupert's fame, but it offered him something to do and he decided to accept. In the event it turned out an abortive affair which did nothing but harm to his reputation. At first he received cordial support. Charles Louis was delighted that his brother should find employment which he did not have to provide himself, and gladly offered quarters in the Palatinate for the troops raised for Modena. Mazarin, who favoured Duke Francis, allowed Rupert to recruit in France and helped him financially. On 17 April a contract was concluded in Heidelberg between Prince Rupert and the Modenese Ambassador, Colonel Pardi, by which Rupert undertook to raise one regiment of cavalry and two of infantry, recruitment for which was to be completed in ten weeks. Duke Francis himself offered an additional 2,000 men to be raised in France, with 1,000 Swiss and three other regiments; all to be under Rupert's command.

Throughout May Prince Rupert busied himself with raising his troops, offering commands to Craven, Gerard and Massey. Then troubles began to multiply. Mazarin refused to allow the French auxiliaries to come under Rupert's command, on the ground that it was not the custom for the King of France's soldiers to be commanded by a foreign general. Presumably this did not apply to the prince for whom they were raised, for Duke Francis now offered to take the supreme command himself; but Rupert rejected this as wounding to his own prestige. At the same time the Prince was finding it harder than he expected to raise troops in the German states, hard hit as they were in manpower by the campaigns of the Thirty Years War.

Wrangles dragged on through the summer, but Rupert was determined to take on no subordinate command. On top of all this King Charles begged him to give his services to nobody but himself. On 28 July Thurloe's agent in Cologne reported that the King had requested 'that he [Rupert] would quit all employments to serve him, and he would endeavour to defer his journey this summer, if a handsom conjunction might be procured with all parties, he would serve him with all his interest, either in men, money, arms, and friends'.[14]

Rupert's first loyalty was always to his English connection, and King Charles's intervention probably decided him. The breach of agreement over the command, and the discovery of the deception over Duke

Francis's objective for the troops, gave him the pretext for washing his hands of the whole business. He was able to withdraw without loss of honour. 'I cannot see how he can loose anie reputation by it,' wrote the Winter Queen to Charles Louis, 'since thay did not performe their promiss to him.'[15]

Nevertheless Rupert did lose some reputation. Mazarin considered, however unjustly, that he had been let down, and Rupert enjoyed his favour no longer. And Charles Louis, to his own great annoyance, was called to account by the Emperor for giving quarters and maintenance in the Palatinate to troops raised to fight against Spanish rule in Italy. He objected very reasonably that he had thought the troops were to be used against papal encroachments. But not unnaturally he harboured some resentment against Rupert, who perhaps might have inquired more deeply into the Modenese designs. It was the first step in the development of a new estrangement between the brothers.

King Charles's anxiety that his cousin should keep himself free for his own service was caused by the fact that hopes were rising of a Stewart restoration. Cromwell's difficulties were multiplying. There was widespread discontent with his arbitrary military government; Royalist conspirators were active in England, and there was talk of a new enterprise against the Protector based in Scotland. Lord Balcarres, one of the Scottish Presbyterian leaders, was at Cologne, and there Rupert joined the discussions in July 1655. 'Prince Rupert came on Sunday,' wrote Henry Manning, Thurloe's spy at King Charles's court, on 20 July. 'The swordsmen endeavour to gain the Presbyterians, the Prince declaring himself a Calvinist, as are the rest of his family. The Prince, Wilmot, Gerrard, and Balcarres, have had a private meeting with Lord Craven, who appears not in public here.'[16]

Nothing came of the proposed expedition, and Rupert next proceeded to Hesse-Cassel, whose ruler, the Landgrave William VI, was a distant cousin and Charles Louis's brother-in-law. It was now that Rupert formed one of the warmest friendships of his life. The Landgrave shared many of his interests, and for many years he continued to correspond with him on a wide variety of subjects.

Rupert next visited The Hague, and in October was with the King again. Charles had travelled to Frankfurt for a meeting with Queen Christina of Sweden, the eccentric daughter of Gustavus Adolphus, who had renounced her throne and was on her way to Rome, being received into the Catholic Church on the way. With his cousin, his sister Mary, and his youngest brother Henry Duke of Gloucester, King Charles met the fascinating lady at Königstein, and it was probably on this occasion that Rupert drew his caricature of Christina which is now in the British Museum.

At this time also Charles Louis visited Frankfurt, and Rupert did his best to effect a reconciliation between his brother and his cousin. But the two did not meet. Although they had apparently been in indirect contact over Charles's overture to Vienna, the King could not forget the part the Elector had played in the Civil War, and when Rupert hinted that his brother would like to invite the royal family to Heidelberg he met with no response.

From Frankfurt the Prince went once more to Vienna, apparently still hoping to enlist imperial support for his cousin. 'Prince Rupert has gone to negotiate with the Emperor on Charles Stuart's behalf,'[17] reported Manning in November. Nothing tangible transpired, but Rupert as usual had a cordial reception from Ferdinand, and did not return to Heidelberg till the following February.

He was still looking for occupation, and during these months he amused himself as best he could. His letters to the Landgrave of Hesse-Cassel were largely about hunting. 'As I hold myself to be one of St. Hubert's craft permit me to tell you the pleasure it has given me to hear what good hunting you have had,' he wrote from Heidelberg on 28 August 1655. 'I assure you it takes away my own displeasure at seeing our huntsmen returning from the woods every day singing the same song: "They have all fled again".'[18] 'This time we have been out catching larks,' he told the Landgrave two months later, 'but although there are many of them about here we cannot catch more than twenty at a time. . . . Let St. Hubert change our ideas or we shall catch nothing.'[19]

He was also pursuing his scientific and mechanical interests. In the letter last quoted he expressed the hope that he would soon be able to visit Hesse-Cassel again, and 'bring the turner's tool'. And on 31 May 1656 he wrote: '. . . with this I am sending you our local invention of a powder flask; I hope you will find it convenient enough and will not disdain so small a gift. Mr. Turrenberg [an official of the state of Hesse-Cassel] will also doubtless tell you of a tube I am having made here. If it succeeds I believe it will please you and I will bring one with me as an example when I come.'[20]

Relations with Charles Louis were deteriorating. Rupert had again taken up the question of an apanage, being to some extent influenced in this by his mother, who, despairing of direct help from her eldest son, wanted to spend her declining years with the younger. Both mother and son longed for a small independent court where they could live in dignity and state befitting their rank. The Elector was unwilling to oblige, but did not want to return a point-blank refusal, and fruitless argument continued throughout the summer of 1656. At one point there was talk of granting an estate at Huizburg on the border of the Upper Palatinate, which was jointly administered by Charles Louis and his kinsman Christian August, Duke of Huizburg. But the Duke turned Catholic, and the Elector withdrew the offer on the pretext that Rupert might be persuaded to do likewise.

Then came an episode in which neither brother shone with any distinction, and which contained all the elements of French farce.

Charles Louis had in 1650 married Charlotte of Hesse-Cassel, sister of Rupert's friend the Landgrave. She was a less amiable character than her brother, being haughty, bad-tempered and furiously jealous; and by 1656 husband and wife were bickering freely. Charles Louis for his part had fallen in love with one of Charlotte's maids of honour, Louise von Degenfeld, a pretty young woman who was accomplished enough to write her love letters in Latin.

Charles Louis was not Louise's only conquest. Rupert, not as a rule highly susceptible (or if he was, he had a soldier's skill in covering his tracks), was also attracted, to such an extent that when she rebuffed him he rashly bombarded her with letters upbraiding her for her coldness. One of these fell into the hands of the Electress, and as it bore no name she imagined that it was intended for herself. She was both pleased and flattered; she was apparently more ready to receive the non-existent overtures of the gallant Prince Rupert than was Louise to respond to his genuine advances. Next time she saw Rupert she greeted him archly with the words: 'I don't know why you should complain of me, or what reason I have ever given you to doubt my affection.'[21]

Rupert was not at his best in this sort of situation. He stammered and blushed and the Electress divined her error. She then took it out on Louise, who tried to convince her that she was quite indifferent to Rupert's attentions.

Nothing but humiliation came to Rupert in this affair. It was otherwise with his brother, who at least attained his end; the Electress Charlotte, her suspicions thoroughly aroused about her maid of honour, a few nights later found Charles Louis and Louise in bed together. There was a tremendous row, and the Elector managed to rescue his mistress only after his maddened wife had almost bitten the girl's little finger off. Thereupon Charlotte broke open Louise's desk, and found all her husband's love letters. There is no mention of any from Rupert. Probably Louise had destroyed these as being of no interest to her.

The sequel was final estrangement between Charles Louis and Charlotte. In the following year the Elector had his marriage declared null and void, and in 1658 he morganatically married Louise von Degenfeld. The Electress refused to recognize the nullity decree, and continued to live in Heidelberg.

The result of all this for Rupert was that the full story of his unrequited passion and his ludicrous conduct quickly became known to his brother, and relations between them declined still further. With the Landgrave William, on the other hand, Rupert remained on the best of terms. William VI had no illusions about his sister, and doubtless took a detached view of the affair.

There was little hope of an apanage now, and after further bickering Rupert left the Palatinate, to spend some months in Mainz as the guest of the Elector John Philip. 'The elector of Heidelberg is highly offended at his brother prince Rupert,' ran the inevitable report to Thurloe on 5 November, 'who parted from him in a rage, taking all his moveables with him, and is gone to live with the elector of Mantz: whether he will declare himself for the Roman Catholic religion, time will shortly discover.'[22]

Here we have another reference to the possibility of Rupert changing his faith, which was evidently taken seriously at this period. There is no evidence, however, that at any time after his adolescent flirtation with Rome in the 1630s he wavered in his loyalty to the Calvinist creed in which he was brought up. Probably the speculations rested on nothing more than his friendship with eminent Catholics such as the Emperor and the Archbishop-Elector of Mainz. There was no fanaticism in Rupert's religious outlook; he took men as he found them, and never bothered himself about whether or not their views were the same as his own.

From Mainz he reiterated his demands to his brother. Charles Louis was not unresponsive. He offered Rupert a further 1,000 thalers annually, and a residence either at Emstadt, a property in an area whose boundaries were continually in dispute between the Palatinate and Hesse-Darmstadt, or at Laubach; but he added a proviso which infuriated his brother. Rupert was not to set foot in Heidelberg without the express permission of the Elector.

Rupert was in one of his blackest moods. 'It seems that it will not please the Elector for me to be given any more than a thousand rix-dollars in addition to what he is otherwise already giving me, to be advanced annually,' he complained to William of Hesse-Cassel, 'and no other dwelling apart from Urmstadt or Laubach. With regard to the first, you know well what kind of state it is in. The other is a damnably watery place: no man can live there in good health. So I shall be obliged to adopt a different approach to my cause, and because the Elector would not have it otherwise, I must find a judge who will award and ascribe to me what is my due from God and nature.'[23]

He appealed to the Emperor to compel his brother to give him what he considered his due. But on 2 April 1657 Ferdinand III died, and in the interregnum before his son Leopold was formally elected his successor nothing could be done in that quarter. Then Lord Craven, that ever-ready friend in time of trouble, visited Heidelberg to try to induce Charles Louis to improve his offer; but he found the Elector adamant.

The quarrel rumbled on through the year 1657; but the climax was at hand. Queen Elizabeth was the next to try to effect a reconciliation. Rupert was now closest to her heart. 'I love you ever, my dear Rupert,'[24] she wrote to him, and 'I pray God to bless you, whatever you resolve to do.'[25] And she in a personal interview besought him to try once more to make peace with his brother.

Rupert yielded, and notified the Elector that he was returning to Heidelberg. Charles Louis, however, had other ideas. He himself retired to his country home at Alzei, which was, he said, unsuitable for receiving Rupert's train; and he instructed his brother to await further communication from him at Neustadt. At the same time he forbade the Governor of Heidelberg, Colonel John Jacob Frays, to admit anyone to the castle during his absence.

Frays was dismayed. He was well aware of Rupert's intention, and of his determined character. He asked for special instructions in case of the Prince's arrival, and Charles Louis shrugged him off by saying that Rupert would not come as he would know that in the Elector's absence the kitchens and cellars would be shut up. Frays then wrote to a member of Rupert's entourage imploring him to persuade his master to stay away, since he dared not disobey the Elector's orders and would be compelled to refuse him admittance.

The effect of this communication on Prince Rupert was predictable. His blood was up, and he would have it out with his brother once and for all. He rode to Heidelberg, presented himself at the castle gate, and demanded admittance. Frays reluctantly told him that his brother's orders were that he should not be admitted. Rupert demanded to see them in writing, and was shown them in Charles Louis's own hand. It was the end. He, a prince of the Palatine House, had been refused entrance by his own brother to the citadel of his ancestors. He paused for a moment in thought; then he wrenched his hat from his head and swore a solemn oath that he would never again set foot in the Palatinate.

Rupert returned to Mainz to lay his complaints before the Elector as State Chancellor of the Empire. He also approached the young Archduke Leopold who was on his way to Frankfurt for the imperial election. Charles Louis had also arrived there for the election, and Leopold was ready to do what he could with him in the way of friendly argument; but neither he nor John Philip of Mainz was prepared to antagonize one of the imperial electors on the eve of the election and so jeopardize the prospect of a unanimous choice.

Rupert himself repaired to Frankfurt, of course avoiding all contact with his brother. And it was there, at the end of 1657, that his attention was diverted from his own troubles by a new family crisis.

At seven o'clock on 19 December Princess Louise left the house of her mother Queen Elizabeth at The Hague, secretly and alone. A search was made, and a letter addressed to her mother was found in which she confessed that she had been received into the Catholic Church and was leaving for a secret destination to avoid having to take the sacrament on Christmas Day, against her conscience, according to a Protestant rite.

The Winter Queen was distracted. All her life she had regarded the Church of Rome with horror. Once she had feared for Rupert's conversion. He had remained faithful to Calvinism, but first Edward and now Louise had succumbed. Remembering the former, Elizabeth at once suspected that a lover was involved; but in this case there is no question that Louise's motive was simply and totally religious. Edward certainly had some influence over her; and a Catholic friend of his, the Princess of Hohenzollern, was at The Hague at this time and was admittedly privy to Louise's design, receiving Queen Elizabeth's venom in consequence. But Louise made up her own mind. 'At length it has pleased God to discover to me the surest way of salvation,' she wrote to her mother ,'and to give me to know that the Catholic religion is that only way out of which there can be no other. . . . I have no other aim than that of securing a tranquil retreat, where I may have full leisure for the service of God.'[26]

Louise made for the sea-coast, and sailed from Delftshaven to Bergen-op-Zoom and thence to Antwerp. Edward met her at Rouen and took her to Paris, and for a time she stayed at the convent of Chaillot as the guest of Queen Henrietta Maria. Shortly afterwards she was received as a nun into the convent of Maubuisson.

Elizabeth wrote bitterly to Rupert, complaining particularly of the conduct of the Princess of Hohenzollern. Rupert was himself angry: more, one may surmise, from sympathy with his mother, now left in dreary loneliness at The Hague, than in violent disapproval of Louise's change of faith. Characteristically he laid the blame on Charles Louis, who some years before had dissuaded Louise from entering the Lutheran convent of Herford in Westphalia, where her sister Elizabeth was to end her days as Abbess. On 28 December he wrote to William of Hesse-Cassel: 'The accursed tidings of my Sister Louise's desperate resolve have disturbed my mind and are the cause of my lapse [in not writing sooner]. The newspapers have written fully about her aforementioned folly, so I will trouble you no further with it. If the Elector had not prevented her entering the cloister at Herfurden she would not have thought of Chaillot.'[27]

When she had learned all the facts Queen Elizabeth seems to have taken a calmer and more resigned view of the affair, though she was still resentful against the Princess of Hohenzollern. On 29 April 1658 she wrote again to her second son:

> . . . Your sister Louys is arriving at Chaillot: her brother went and fetched her from Rouen: the Queen went to see her the next day: the King of France went the week aftor. They are very civil to her. The Queen wrote to me, that she will have a care of her as of her own daughter, and begs her pardon: but I have received it as handsomely as I could, and entreated her not to take it ill, but only to think what she would do if she had had the same misfortune. Ned doth not acknowledge his error in having so good an opinion of the P. of H. She is detested by Protestant and Papist. The next week I hope to have Louyse's justification against all her calumnies. . . . I have such a cold that I can say no more.

> Farewell, dear Rupert.[28]

Louise was to pursue her religious vocation long and happily at Maubuisson, where for many years she reigned as Abbess. Hers was the longest and serenest life of all the Palatines.

During the long-drawn-out process of the imperial election Prince Rupert stayed mainly at Frankfurt, playing little part in public affairs. For the first time since his captivity in Austria before the English Civil War he had leisure to devote to his artistic and scientific interests. His letters at this time to the Landgrave of Hesse-Cassel are fuller than ever of allusions to his inventions and experiments, and he frequently enclosed plans and drawings made by himself. On 31 August 1657 he wrote: 'With regard to the enclosure – the invention of the water machine – I have made a sketch on the other side but I do not know whether you will be able to understand it.'[29] On 10 November: 'With this I am sending you a sample of the varnish I have made myself. The ingredients can be seen from the enclosed paper.'[30] On 21 December: 'I am deeply sorry that my technique did not work, but I assure you that it only succeeds when the spirit is well prepared with which to ensure that the substances are pushed through impalpably.'[31]

Some of these references in the letters are clearly to the process of mezzotint engraving, which Rupert may or may not have invented.

He had disposed of the African boy. For some reason unknown he had handed him over to his cousin Frederick William of Brandenburg, who had him baptized and carefully educated. But the boy languished and died in the cold northern climate. The adult Negroes remained with Rupert, but they sometimes caused trouble by fighting among themselves. 'Brother Rupert's moors have wounded one another to death,'[32] wrote Charles Louis on 8 July 1658, perhaps not without a certain malicious relish.

At about this time Rupert seems to have set in motion the writing of his biography. Warburton prints a memorandum headed 'Suggestion for writing Prince Rupert's biography',[33] which makes it clear that part of the purpose was to vindicate the Prince's conduct in the more controversial episodes of the Civil War. The author of the memorandum, to whom Rupert had presumably applied for advice, wrote:

> In that business of Newark I would (with submission) pass also, with admittance of [some fault] as his Highness hath in some degree done already, and in that of Bristol (with favour) I conceive it will be the frankest way to write so much of it as was then made public, and after the Prince's just declaration and his acquittal, to insert the King's kindness and esteem in his own words with the Prince's reverence and generosity towards his uncle and an unfortunate prince, in continuing his loyalty and affection to him in all extremities, after this misunderstanding. . . .[34]

The result of this venture was in all probability the fragment known as the *Rupert Diary*, later to be developed into the still incomplete *Life* which was used by Warburton but has since been lost.

But Rupert was still brooding over the misdeeds of his brother, and in the early months of 1658 his anger led him into making overtures to the rival branch of the Wittelsbachs, with whom his family had been at daggers drawn during the whole of his life. The details are obscure, but Charles Louis and the Duke of Bavaria were in dispute over a matter of ecclesiastical patronage, complicated by the diverse laws of the Holy Roman Empire. The quarrel seemed likely to develop into war, and Rupert let it be known, through Dr Oxl the Bavarian Envoy at Main, that his support against his brother would be available in return for the promise of a grant of land for which he yearned so desperately. Whatever Charles Louis might have done, so gross a breach of loyalty to the head of the family could hardly be justified; and Rupert when his anger had cooled may well have been glad that the project came to nothing.

That it did so was owing to the good sense of the Elector of Bavaria. Maximilian had died in 1651, but his son Ferdinand Maria was a level-headed young man who knew better than to gain a temporary advantage at the cost of becoming involved in a domestic squabble between the Palatine brothers. He instructed Oxl to tell Rupert that he could promise no land, that even the imperial house had avoided taking up any decided position regarding the Palatine dispute, and that he had no intention of exacerbating the conflict; the Prince was to be dissuaded from visiting Munich as he was proposing to do. Thus was Rupert saved from perpetrating one of the worst errors of his life; one that would certainly have estranged him from the rest of his family for ever.

It was not till 16 July 1658 that Leopold King of Hungary, son of Ferdinand III, was elected Emperor at Frankfurt. There had never been any possibility of a different choice, but prolonged ceremonies and formalities had to be gone through, under the procedure laid down in the Golden Bull of 1356, before the appointment was valid. Rupert at once laid his grievances against Charles Louis before the eighteen-year-old Emperor. In the previous year he had drawn up a memorandum, presumably intended for presentation to Ferdinand, in which he argued his case with considerable cogency; and Leopold was now urged to take action as Charles Louis's overlord. Leopold, however, like Ferdinand Maria of Bavaria, was unwilling to be involved in the family dispute, and though he agreed to write to the Elector Palatine putting Rupert's case he would not exert his imperial authority. Charles Louis for his part refused to accede to the Emperor's representations, unsupported as they were by any threat of coercive action.

At the same time the Emperor Leopold I showed himself as friendly to Rupert as his father had been. He assured him of a cordial welcome in Vienna should he choose to go there, and of employment in the imperial service if he wanted it. Rupert accepted. In his quarrel with his brother he had renounced all financial aid from the Palatinate, and he was now finding it difficult to make ends meet. Leopold, who was crowned at Frankfurt on 11 August, therefore summoned him at once to Vienna. Rupert had been planning a visit to Hesse-Cassel, and he wrote rather sadly to the Landgrave two days after the coronation, at which he was present. 'I greatly regret,' he said, 'that I cannot conceal from you the fact that His Imperial Majesty's command to proceed at once to Vienna and there to await his orders robs me on this occasion of the good fortune of waiting on you. But I hope that this bad fortune will not persecute me for ever. Meanwhile I must patiently await a better time, hoping that you will not forget your poor cousin, who remains eternally devoted to you.'[35]

Having got to Vienna, Rupert awaited the Emperor's orders for a considerable time, for there was at the moment nothing for him to do. He therefore obtained leave of absence and visited his mother at The Hague. Whether he also paid his deferred visit to his cousin William at this time is uncertain, but it was not till the end of the following year that he took up a military command under Leopold. Meanwhile there was much to excite his interest in another quarter; for on 3 September 1658 Cromwell died at Whitehall. With the removal of the dictator's iron hand it seemed probable that in the inevitable struggle for power, and the disorder thereby engendered, thinking men would turn their eyes towards the King over the water. For the first time the hope appeared of a royal restoration other than by the way of armed invasion.

So it turned out. Richard Cromwell, successor to his father as Lord Protector, proved a broken reed, and resigned after a few months. The leading figures of the Commonwealth – Vane, Hazelrig, Desborough, Fleetwood, Lambert – were soon at each other's throats, and throughout the year 1659 England was in a state of rapidly growing chaos. General George Monk, the military commander in Scotland, alone preserved stability; and on 1 January 1660 he began his famous march to London which was to lead within a few months to the restoration of King Charles II to his father's realm.

Rupert, like his cousins, watched the events in England closely, and he was always ready to return to his first loyalty if he could do so with honour; but for the moment there was nothing he could do in that direction, and he was still the Emperor's servant. In November 1659 he took up the post of Lieutenant-Field-Marshal in the imperial army, and on 2 December left Vienna for the Baltic to take part in the Emperor's campaign against the Swedes. In April 1660 he gained a victory at Wismar in Mecklenburg, and Queen Elizabeth wrote to Charles Louis: 'I ame sorie my cosen Duke Christian of Mecklebourghs countrie is so ill used. It seldome falls out otherwise in a warr; I am confident Rupert will have hurt him as little as he can, he has had good luck of late in taking of a fort and beating of some troopes of the Swedes in Wismar.'[36]

Otherwise there was little of interest in the campaign, which was concluded soon afterwards by the Treaty of Oliva. The English Restoration was now imminent. King Charles, who in February 1658 had set up his court in Brussels, had moved to Breda in the Dutch Netherlands, and from there on 4 April he issued his declaration to his people promising to reign according to the laws of England. He then moved to The Hague, and soon everything was ready.

The King sent a message to his cousin assuring him that he would be very welcome to join him. But Rupert could not leave his command at once. When he had obtained leave, and set out for The Hague, he found himself too late to join in the festivities of the royal departure. He reached the Dutch capital on 29 May, the very day that King Charles entered London in triumph. It was the King's thirtieth birthday, and he was welcomed with all the pent-up enthusiasm of a people wearied with nearly twenty years of war and republicanism.

So Rupert, after a brief stay with his mother, returned to his command in Mecklenburg, where he fell ill with the malady, thought to have been malaria, which had troubled him intermittently since his return from sea. He remained at Rostock till August; then he asked the Emperor to release him to join the King of England, and his request was readily granted. Back he went to The Hague, and on his way was able to see two of his sisters, Both Elizabeth and Sophia had left Heidelberg. The former had taken the part of the Electress Palatine in the Degenfeld affair, and consequently found herself *persona non grata* with Charles Louis. Since 1658 she had been moving between Brandenburg and Hesse-Cassel, at both of which courts she was made welcome by her cousins. It was at Hesse-Cassel, where Rupert dropped in for a final visit to the Landgrave, that she and her brother met.

From Hesse-Cassel Rupert proceeded to Osnabrück, where Sophia was living. She had been married in 1658 to Ernest Augustus, younger brother of the Duke of Hanover, and Osnabrück was her home. Duke George William himself was there at the same time, and Sophia wrote cheerfully to Charles Louis: 'My brother Rupert made a great friendship with my Dukes, they agree so well in their amusements.'[37]

At The Hague Queen Elizabeth made one last effort to settle the difference between her two eldest sons, proposing that Rupert should be granted the family estate of Rhenen. Charles Louis was not unwilling, and some correspondence ensued, with the Queen as mediator; but the scheme was held up by disagreement over details, and it was some years yet before Rhenen came into Rupert's possession.

There was nothing now to impede the wanderer's return to the scene of his most famous exploits. Rumours of the impending event had been spreading in England, where it was reported that he was coming with a great train as the Ambassador of the Emperor Leopold. Nothing could have been further from the truth. At the end of September 1660, avoiding all ceremony, Prince Rupert of the Rhine slipped almost unnoticed into London.

BOOK FOUR

THE KING'S COUSIN
1690–1682

RESTORATION ENGLAND

IT was fourteen years since Rupert had left England after the defeat of the Royalist armies; it was twenty-three years since, wishing he could break his neck and so leave his bones in his mother's country, he had last seen Whitehall, where he was now given lodgings by the King: the same lodgings, ironically enough, that had been occupied by his brother Charles Louis under the rebel régime. He was forty now, but to the new generation coming to the front he seemed older, a semi-legendary, awe-inspiring figure, a picturesque survival from an earlier age. At the court of King Charles II, so different from that of the last monarch, he was regarded with respect tinged with an element of irreverence, as one who had done great deeds which were no longer in season. He was a resplendent figure. The portrait attributed to Lely, painted a few years later and now at Euston Hall, Suffolk, shows him in his Garter robes, stately and magnificent, strikingly handsome and superbly dignified, yet with an expression of kindliness and a suggestion of tolerant humour that seem a little at variance with his reputation.

Rupert was welcomed by King Charles as an honoured guest. 'Prince Rupert (as I am informed),' wrote the news-letter writer Stephen Charlton, 'is the only favourite of the King's, insomuch that he has given him 30 or 40,000*l*. per annum out of his own revenues for his present maintenance.'[1] The sum mentioned was something of an exaggeration; Charles II was in no financial position to distribute bounty on such a scale, and the actual allowance allotted to Rupert was £4,000 a year. This, however, was enough to enable him to support a household becoming to his rank.

King Charles II at thirty, tall, dark and active, was a mature, worldly-wise sovereign; shrewd, witty and humorous; one who had learned through years of hardship and misfortune to look with cynical, good-natured eyes on the doings and plottings of his fellow-men. He was also a man of iron nerve. He had none of the lofty idealism or the almost mystical conception of the kingly office that had characterized his father; but he had a far keener brain. He was not bookish, though he is said to have been 'well versed in ancient and modern history'.[2]

Nor had he the enthusiasm for art, or the knowledge thereof, that Charles I had had. His interests ran rather to scientific matters, and he had a real understanding of shipping and navigation. His conversation was brilliant, and his witticisms were treasured and repeated by his courtiers. He had no illusions, and like Cassius he could see 'quite through the deeds of men'. There could be no greater contrast than with Charles I, with his vacillations and his dependence on the last person he had spoken to. Charles II trusted few men, and placed little reliance on any opinions but his own. When he gave way to others (and he often found himself compelled to do so), it was from deliberate policy and political tactics.

His morals were lax. Objective truth meant little to him, and he would lie brazenly when it suited his purpose to do so. He was physically brave, but his moral courage was more questionable. He was apt to take the line of least resistance, and at certain times of crisis showed himself ready to sacrifice the lives of others for his own safety and convenience. As to his amours, they have become such a byword in history that it is hardly necessary to allude to them. It is sufficient to quote Dr Ashley: '. . . nobody has ever been able to make a complete count of his mistresses. He is said to have had seventeen during his exile alone; and he acknowledged fourteen illegitimate children'.[3] He was more like his maternal grandfather, Henry IV of France, than his father.

Yet with all his cynicism and his lack of scruple Charles II remains, probably, the most attractive character who has ever worn the English crown. He was easy of access, genial and friendly, the soul of good nature, totally free from pride or arrogance; he was able to maintain a kingly dignity without ever finding it necessary to assert his superiority; his easy, natural, witty talk enchanted those who came in contact with him and put them at their ease. Above all he was kindly and tolerant. He had no wish to persecute those who differed from him, and on his return to England did what he could to mitigate the severity of the treatment meted out to the erstwhile opponents of the throne; only those who had been directly concerned in his father's murder could expect no mercy from him. In religion he stood firmly for toleration. His own beliefs had been formed by circumstances. He was not deeply religious, but during the dark days after Worcester he had been helped by humble Catholics at the risk of their lives and ever afterwards he looked with kindly eyes on the Catholic faith, to which at the last he was reconciled. Conversely he had suffered misery and humiliation from the dour Scottish Presbyterians, and for Presbyterianism he retained a profound distaste. But for Catholics, Anglicans and dissenters alike he wanted freedom to worship God in their own way; again and again throughout his reign he fought for the unfashionable doctrine of tolera-

Margaret Hughes

Prince Rupert's daughter, Mrs Ruperta Howe

tion, though the persecuting zeal of his subjects proved too much for him.

The King's relations with Rupert were consistently cordial. They had had their differences in the past, but Charles had never completely out-grown the hero-worship he had felt for his martial cousin in early years, and though he smiled a little at Rupert's rigid scrupulosity and old-fashioned ways he rejoiced in his company. He was delighted that the gallant Prince had decided to take up residence in England, and the two were constantly seen in each other's company.

At the King's side was James Duke of York, his only remaining brother since Henry Duke of Gloucester had died of smallpox a fort-night before Rupert's arrival in England. James was the antithesis of Charles. Not overburdened with intelligence, he was highly capable in practical matters, earnest and painstaking, and a trained soldier. He was rigid where King Charles was flexible, single-minded where he was subtle, seeing things in black and white and pursuing what seemed to him the right path regardless of expediency. Perhaps in two things only did the brothers resemble each other: their love of feminine company and their belief in religious toleration.

With the Duke of York Prince Rupert's relations were probably closer than with the King. These two were more temperamentally attuned than were the King and the Prince, and in spite of the differ-ence in their religious views (for James was already inclined towards Catholicism) they saw eye to eye on most subjects, principally their interest in naval and military matters.

Nor was Prince Rupert at odds with the King's advisers. The effective head of government was Edward Hyde, now Lord Chancellor and soon to be created Earl of Clarendon. Here there might have been friction; but there was not. Both had mellowed with the years; Rupert for the moment held no public office, and there was no war in which Hyde could interfere in military strategy and Rupert could resent his inter-ference.

Others in high office were Ormonde as Lord Steward of the House-hold and Nicholas as Secretary of State: both tried friends of Rupert. The second Secretary of State was William Morrice, a cousin and protégé of General Monk (now Duke of Albemarle), an upright and retiring man with no taste for intrigue. The Lord Treasurer was the Earl of Southampton, who had remained in England under the Com-monwealth but had taken no part in public affairs. The Duke of Albemarle held the post of Captain-General of the Army, which was now being rapidly disbanded; his prestige as the architect of the Restoration was immense, but he never aspired to play any considerable part in political affairs.

The Government contained one sinister character – Anthony Ashley Cooper, who had taken over from Hyde as Chancellor of the Exchequer. Ashley Cooper, who had twice changed sides during and after the Civil War, was an able politician with a turbulent career of treachery and subversion ahead of him; he owed his present advancement to a family connection with the Earl of Southampton. Strangely enough, an incongruous friendship was to develop between Ashley Cooper and Prince Rupert which may possibly have had its beginnings at this time.

Others who might have caused trouble were no longer in a position to do so. Wilmot had died as Earl of Rochester in 1658; Culpeper almost immediately after the Restoration. Digby, now Earl of Bristol in succession to his father, had in 1657 become a Catholic convert and had been deprived of his Secretaryship of State, to which he had recently been appointed. He still had some backstairs influence with the King, but seems to have shown none of his old antagonism to Rupert.

All this suggests that Rupert's return to England was popular with all and sundry, and it is hard to understand what lay behind Samuel Pepys's acid comment on 29 September 1660: 'This day or yesterday Prince Robt. is come to Court; but welcome to nobody.'[4] Pepys was at this time an obscure clerk in the office of Sir George Downing at the Exchequer, and it is unlikely that he had ever seen Prince Rupert in the flesh; certainly he can have had no dealings with him. Yet the remark looks like pique. Later he was to develop an extreme dislike for the Prince, and it is possible that some episode which has escaped record had already prejudiced him against him.

For the time being Rupert held no official post. True, he had been appointed Lord High Admiral by Charles II in 1649, but this was at the King's pleasure and it had always been understood that he would relinquish the title when the Duke of York should take it up. When Algernon Earl of Northumberland had been made Lord High Admiral in 1638 the appointment was at the King's pleasure with a dormant patent to Prince James, who was then five years of age. Any other such appointment thereafter was to be of a temporary nature, and at the Restoration King Charles called on his brother to assume his post.

It does not appear, however, that Rupert was in any great hurry for employment. After all the storms and stresses of the past twenty years he may well have been glad to sit back and bask in the carefree atmosphere of Restoration England. The restless wanderings were over; now was the time to reap the reward in tranquillity. Moreover he was still the servant of the Emperor; and though his leave could certainly have been transformed into a termination of contract without excessive formality, Rupert, punctilious as always, had decided to visit Vienna once more and settle his affairs with Leopold in person.

He was by no means inactive. The sparse entries in the *Journals of the House of Lords* show that he was a regular attendant in that House, where he sat as Duke of Cumberland. The 'Convention Parliament', called to settle the restored constitution, first sat on 25 April and was dissolved on 29 December. When Rupert arrived in England the Houses were in recess, but they met again on 6 November, and from then on until the dissolution he was present nearly every day that Parliament sat. Nor was he simply a passive listener. There is no record of his having spoken in debate, but on 10 November his name was added to those composing the committee for the Bill to restore the Earl of Arundel to the Dukedom of Norfolk (Thomas Earl of Arundel, grandson of Rupert's old friend the art collector, was stated at this time to be 'a perfect Lunatic')[5] and on the same day it was ordered 'That the Duke of *Cumberland* be added to all Standing *Committees*'.[6] On 27 December, when a committee sat to consider a bill 'for the better ordering and selling of wines by retail, etc.' it was arranged for 'their lordships, or any Five; to meet tomorrow Morning, in the Prince's lodgings, at Nine a Clock'.[7]

On 30 October Queen Henrietta Maria arrived in England with her youngest daughter Henrietta Anne. The Duke of York, as Lord High Admiral, conducted them from Calais with a naval escort, and Prince Rupert, with the King and the Princess Royal, met them at Dover. No sign of the old enmity between the Prince and Queen was apparent, although a difference on a matter of policy soon followed. The primary cause of Henrietta Maria's return at this moment was the secret marriage between the Duke of York and Anne Hyde, daughter of the Lord Chancellor and a former maid of honour to the Princess Royal. The discovery of the *mésalliance* had set the court by the ears, and on hearing it Queen Henrietta had announced her intention of proceeding at once to England and breaking the match. On meeting her erring son at Calais she loaded him with reproaches, but her hostility had no support from the King and eventually she was persuaded to recognize Anne as Duchess of York.

There was, however, another reason for her journey. Henrietta Anne, Charles II's beloved 'Minette', was betrothed to Philip Duke of Anjou, younger brother of Louis XIV, and mother and daughter had come to England to complete the contract. Here Rupert intervened. He was well acquainted with Philip, and was revolted at the thought of his charming young cousin being handed over to a transvestite pervert. And he could, he insisted, arrange a happier and more illustrious match. This was with no less a person than his good friend the Emperor Leopold I, whom, it would appear, he had already sounded out on the matter, and who had expressed himself willing. Before the arrival of the Queen and Princess the Venetian Resident in London, Francesco Giavarina, had reported that Rupert 'may also negotiate the marriage between Princess Henrietta and the emperor, as that with the duke of Anjou seems colder than ever'.[8] Rupert's experiences in France had not attracted him towards a pro-French policy, whereas his ties with the court of Vienna were of the closest.

He was overruled, however. King Charles shared his cousin's view of Philip's character, but considerations of policy were paramount; a French alliance was dear to his heart. His mother doubtless urged the advantages of the match, and though Charles II was never influenced by her as his father had been her opinion probably carried some weight. In any case the betrothal was already in being, and no strong political reason existed for breaking it.

The marriage, predictably, proved extremely unhappy. But Minette at this time seems to have expressed no aversion for her future husband. She was, after all, French by upbringing, and was doubtless glad to be able to remain in Paris. Throughout her short life she was an ornament of the court of Louis XIV, at which she proved also a valuable agent for her brother Charles II.

In January 1661 came the episode of Thomas Venner's conspiracy, when a band of 'Fifth Monarchy' fanatics rose in London to dethrone King Charles and set up 'King Jesus'. They caused a surprising amount of bloodshed before being suppressed by the King's Guards, and in the scare that followed there was talk of raising a new standing army.

Rupert's name was mentioned as a possible commander, though the Duke of Albemarle was thought more likely. The scare died down, and nothing more was heard of the suggestion. But at the height of the trouble an incident occurred which bade fair to cause a rift between Rupert and Albemarle. One of the Prince's attendants, either overzealous or inspired for some reason by malice, gave information on the strength of which the Lord Chamberlain, Edward Montagu Earl of Manchester, the former Roundhead general, without further inquiry searched Albemarle's cellar at the Cockpit for gunpowder. Such impetuosity shows the extent of the fright that Venner's rising had aroused: to act on mere suspicion against the man who had restored King Charles to his throne was the wildest indiscretion. Albemarle was naturally furious, and when he learned the facts he 'cudgelled the informer with his own hand till he almost maimed him'.[9] Fortunately Rupert, who in earlier years might have reacted as precipitately as had Manchester where an attack on one of his own men was concerned, lent no countenance to his attendant's behaviour. According to Sir John Finch, on whom the authority for the story rests, 'the Prince not only put away his servant, but offered to fight any one who set the design on foot'.[10] Manchester acknowledged that he had acted over-hastily, and the affair was smoothed over.

As spring approached, Rupert prepared for his final visit to Vienna. He willingly agreed to act as an unofficial envoy for King Charles, and to keep him informed of what was happening at the imperial court; and for his agent in London he chose his old friend Will Legge. Legge, after all his vicissitudes, in which he had shown such a remarkable propensity towards being captured by his enemies – he was a prisoner in the Tower of London as late as 1659 – was now basking in royal favour as Groom of the Bedchamber, Master of the Armouries and Lieutenant-General of the Ordnance. Charles II had offered him an earldom, 'which he modestly declined, having a numerous family, with a small fortune: but told the King, he hoped his sons might live to deserve his Majesty's favour'.[11] His eldest son was created Baron Dartmouth by King Charles in 1682, and the Earldom of Dartmouth, created in 1711, remains in his family to this day.

Rupert sailed on 12 April (OS) 1661, and his progress can be traced in his letters to Legge. The passage was stormy, and it was three days before he landed in Holland. He proceeded to The Hague to visit his mother. The Winter Queen was old, sad and disillusioned. She had hoped once again, after Charles Louis's return to the Palatinate, that her troubles were at last at an end, and that she would be able to spend her old age happily in England as the guest of her nephew the King. But to her bitter disappointment Charles showed no disposition to accommodate her, and no hints from Prince Rupert could move him. 'I found the poore woman very much dejected that I could not tell her the time she might expect to be sent for,' wrote Rupert to Will Legge; 'pray acquaint the Chancelor with this, and the King with the news I tould you.'[12]

Charles II has been much blamed for indifference to Queen Elizabeth's misfortunes. But in truth he was in just the same position as that in which Charles Louis had found himself. As soon as he returned to his kingdom a swarm of petitioners for place and money flocked round him. All had suffered for the Cavalier cause, and all expected to be relieved and rewarded by a restored monarch whose purse they assumed to be bottomless. Charles's treasury simply could not cope with the demand, and the King was at his wit's end to provide for his importunate subjects. He shuddered at the thought of supporting, in a state appropriate to her rank, a penurious aunt loaded with debts who was notorious for her extravagance.

In May Rupert was at Cleves, where the ten-year-old Prince William

III of Orange was staying. War clouds were gathering. The Turks were advancing into Europe and threatening the Empire, and the Swedes were also arming. Rupert wrote giving full information for transmission to the King and the Chancellor. There were signs of coming trouble between England and the Netherlands over the herring fisheries. Rupert shrugged off Dutch bellicosity with contempt: 'I must add that the Hollanders boast much, avowing openly that if the King doth trouble the Hering fishing they will maintaine it with the sword. I tould some that butter and cheese would doe better.'[13] At Cleves he also met a man who aroused his old interest in military engineering:

> . . . I mett heere with on De Rues an Ingenir, the ablest man in his profession that ever I saw, of whoem I had alreddy spoken to the King. If the fortifications of Portchmouth goe on I wish his advice might be taken, for noen fortifys soe well and soe cheap and fast as he. . . . He makes any earth serve for his casemats and uses noe stones to them, he uses no sodds, he mingles his earth sometims with sands, some time with other earth or gravell as he finds occasion, and with beating makes it soe hard that the shaking of the guns can no waies desorder his batteries. . . Pray neglect not this man. . . .[14]

Two old friends came next on Rupert's list; on his way southward he visited the Landgrave of Hesse-Cassel and the Elector of Mainz. And at Mainz the news reached him that his mother had left The Hague for England. 'I heere for sertaine that the Queen of Bohemia is gone for England but on what terms I knowe not,' he wrote. 'Pray doe me the favor to lett me understand the truth of it, for when I left the Hage there was noe such thing in hand.'[15]

Still no invitation had come from King Charles, who had just been crowned in Westminster Abbey. But Elizabeth at this juncture was befriended by that old admirer who had never failed her. Lord Craven had returned to England at the Restoration, and he too had tried to persuade King Charles to bring his aunt home. Meeting with no response, he decided to take matters into his own hands and invited the Queen to come over without waiting for royal authority, and to take up residence in his own house in Drury Lane.

And so at last the Winter Queen returned to the country she had left after her marriage nearly fifty years before. She landed at Gravesend on 16 May (OS), proceeded by water to London, and settled down in comfort at Drury House. Her nephew the King, now that he was relieved of having to support her (though he did now grant her a pension), received her with affection.

Rupert arrived in Vienna in June and stayed for several months. His reception was not as cordial as might have been expected. The

Emperor was personally as friendly as ever, but his councillors were cold. The reason, as the Marqués de Fuentes (no longer Spanish Ambassador but still living in the imperial capital) explained, was the report that King Charles was contemplating marriage with the Portuguese Princess Catherine; this was held to be antagonistic to the Spanish-Austrian interest. Charles Louis, moreover, was suspected of intriguing against Rupert, to the extent of insinuating to the Viennese court that his brother was negotiating with the Turks. 'Deare Will,' wrote Rupert in a fury on 4 September (NS),

> I am not able to write to you of any subject but of one, which I confesse doth troble me in the highest degree, and doth concerne our Master as well as my selfe. The stori is this, the Elector Pallatin hath been pleased to write to a Prive Conseller of this court in these terms – what King of England's ambassador doth negotiate with the Porte, Elector Palatin knowes not nor what is intended by him against the hows of Austria, Prince Rupert whoe is intimate with King of England and his Privi counsellor can tell (if he please). All this is a brotherly trick you'l say, but I thank Good they heere doe little beleeve what he saies. . . . By heven I am in such a humor that I dare not write to any, therefore pray excuse me to alle for not writing this post.[16]

In spite of such difficulties Rupert was able to get on with his business, and gradually found the atmosphere more friendly, His name was suggested for the Generalship of the Imperial Horse; but his Protestantism was an obstacle, and in any case he was not minded to remain in Germany indefinitely. He saw little preparation for war; otherwise he might have thought differently. It was a good vintage year in Hungary, and he busied himself with arranging for a quantity of Hungarian wine to be shipped to England – '4 tonnes or 8 pipes which I hope will serve our Court this winter'.[17]

He had transported his hounds across Europe, and put them at the disposal of his host. 'The Emperor is gone to Ebersdorf 2 leages of,' he wrote on 9 September, 'where he expects my greihounds to course a stagge.'[18] And his enduring love of animals, particularly dogs, comes out in the sad ending to the next letter: 'If my Lord Lindsay be att court the same to him with the dolefull news that poore Royall att this instant is dying, after having been the cause of death of many a stagge. By heaven I would rather lose the best horse in my stable.'[19]

At length all was concluded. Rupert was given his discharge, took his leave of Leopold, and at the end of October started for England. He travelled by way of Frankfurt and Hesse-Cassel, where he found his sister Elizabeth and stayed some weeks. Early in the new year he was reunited with his mother.

It was a very brief reunion. Elizabeth had found tranquillity at last; but she was sixty-five now, a tired old lady who had endured many sorrows. She had been greatly distressed by the death at twenty-nine of her niece the Princess Royal on the previous Christmas Eve. She was still an indefatigable and sprightly correspondent. 'I could not give you thankes for your letter last week,' she wrote in her last letter to Charles Louis, 'because I was forced or persuaded by my two doctors Pridiau and Fraiser to take phisick, to be quite ridd of my colde, which I believe you dout not but I did very unwillingly, and it made me as sick as a dogg, but I think it did me good, yet my own phisick did me most good, which was letting of blood, for now I am very well, it is so hott weather heere as I have felt it colder in May. . . . Rupert is now heere and extreamly kindlie used by the king.'[20]

On 29 January 1662 she moved to Leicester House, on the site of the present Leicester Square, as tenant of the Earl of Leicester; and there, a fortnight later, she was taken ill with a haemorrhage from the lungs. King Charles now pressed her to take up residence in Whitehall Palace, but it was too late; she was too ill to be moved. On 13 February she died at Leicester House. King Charles and Prince Rupert were with her at the end.

Four days later she was buried in Westminster Abbey. Prince Rupert was chief mourner, supported by Lord Craven. Craven was deeply grieved. For thirty years he had served his royal mistress with unswerving devotion, always at her side in the stresses and misfortunes of her life. Rumour was later to declare that he was secretly married to her; but rumour almost certainly lied.

Queen Elizabeth had made her will at The Hague before sailing to England. In it she named Charles Louis as her principal heir, and then saw to it that he received no benefit; he was left all her possessions 'except what we give to our sons and daughters the Princes Edward, Rupert, and the Princess Elizabeth, and the Duchess of Brunswick (Sophia)'.[21] (Nothing, it may be noted, went to the errant Louise and, though as a nun she might be considered to have no use for worldly goods, this was presumably not the reason.) Certain jewels were bequeathed to Elizabeth and Sophia, and 'one of our large cut diamonds' (possibly the one left to the Queen by her brother Charles I) to Edward; the rest of her valuables and chattels, her plate and furniture, her papers, and 'all that is owing to us in money, and what we have in hand', went to Rupert, who was made executor of her estate.

The exceptions from the general bequest to Charles Louis in fact amounted to virtually everything his mother possessed. Such was the Winter Queen's way of showing her opinion of the way her erstwhile favourite had behaved to her in recent years. Naturally the Elector

Palatine was furious, and the result was a new fraternal quarrel which raged, albeit at a distance, for many years.[22] Charles Louis, without going quite so far as to accuse his brother of forging the will, protested that it had been opened without a plenipotentiary of the Palatinate being present, and that Rupert had had a completely free hand when he searched through the Queen's rooms, which were full of curiosities and books of all kinds, and opened and arranged her papers with the help only of a chambermaid.

The Elector fulminated in vain. Rupert was the man in possession, and he had the fullest support from King Charles. Certainly he took a gloating pleasure in this revenge for all the humiliations he had received at his brother's hands. To the scarcely veiled suggestion of forgery he replied by sending a certified copy of the will to Heidelberg, and refused to consider any further inquiry into the circumstances.

Charles Louis was not alone in his anger. His sisters, while sympathizing with their eldest brother, were averse from taking sides in a family quarrel; but acrimony arose between Rupert and Edward, who took the Elector's part with his customary warmth. Edward had recently come to England for the first time, and on 27 December 1662 he wrote from London to Charles Louis:

As soon as I arrived I did not wish to omit to inform you of how I found the matters in England that concern you. In a word, no formalities whatever have been observed with the Queen's will. To begin with, Prince Rupert, having seized all her [omission in text] and also the Queen's papers, where there must, no doubt, have been some instructions, both for creditors and the rest, I asked him for the letters I had written to my mother, and which I remembered having written about family matters – which I should be most annoyed for anyone to see. He refused to give me them, saying, 'I will burn those.' You can very well guess whom that concerns after I had been sent a receipt to sign for the diamond, which I have not seen and do not know if it is diamond or crystal. I replied to his man that I did not recognise the will at all and that even if I did recognise it I should have no need to give a receipt – by whatever gate we were to take it, but that I had already affirmed to my brother that I wanted none of it. He replied that he believed the two of us had reached agreement about it. I sent him away, just like that, after explaining to him what injustice had been committed; for none of the forms of justice had been preserved. . . .[23]

Rupert's inconsiderate behaviour to a brother with whom he had always been on good terms, and who indeed had cause to consider himself badly treated, can be explained only by the blind anger with which he looked on anyone who joined Charles Louis in disputing the validity of the will. Whether or not Edward got his diamond is uncertain; for he did not long survive his mother. He died in Paris on 10 March 1663 at the early age of thirty-eight.

With regard to Charles Louis, Rupert proceeded to counter-attack. Since the quarrel of 1657 he had asked for no financial help from his brother but he now demanded the arrears of his allowance and also the income promised, but not paid, to the Winter Queen in her last years, which he claimed was now due to him under the terms of her will. Charles Louis of course refused to hand over a penny, and when King Charles II called on him to fulfil his obligations to his dead mother he replied that the matter was no concern of England.

The squabble now had its repercussions in the Empire. Rupert appealed to the Elector Frederick William of Brandenburg, who rather reluctantly wrote to Charles Louis asking him to pay his brother's dues. Charles Louis's not unreasonable retort was that Frederick William should not take one party's side in a dispute before hearing what the other had to say. Next Charles Louis applied for an imperial edict calling for peace between the brothers. Rupert's friends William of Hesse-Cassel and John Philip of Mainz expressed themselves ready to help in the terms of such an edict; but nothing further happened in this direction, and Charles Louis complained to the imperial court that Rupert's word had been believed without inquiry and that he (Charles Louis) was being expected to give his hostile brother financial means which he would only use against himself. It was apparently seriously thought that Rupert might take up arms against his brother.

Rather unexpectedly, saner counsels prevailed. Probably the brothers came to the conclusion that the dispute was being blown up out of all proportion, and that they were both making themselves ridiculous. Charles II and his Chancellor, now the Earl of Clarendon, appealed for new negotiations, and on 21 July 1664 Rupert wrote a conciliatory letter to his brother suggesting an amicable settlement. Charles Louis reciprocated by intimating his willingness to pay the arrears of allowances if Rupert would acknowledge the agreement between them of 1654 as being still binding, and in addition hand over Elizabeth's papers, plate and furniture and provide a precise inventory of the estate.

This condition Rupert was not prepared to grant, and the haggling continued; now, however, in a much more friendly spirit. Mutual anger was appeased, and both brothers were ready for compromise. King Charles acted as mediator, and in February 1666 Charles Louis offered to pay all the money due to Rupert under the 1654 agreement, with the proviso that if Rupert valued his mother's silver plate he should pay for it by a modest deduction from the sum paid to him. Honour was satisfied, but it was not till 22 September 1670 that a new agreement was concluded.

As Prince Rupert resumed his peaceful existence in England, he gradually took a bigger part in public life. The 'Cavalier Parliament' had started on its lengthy career, second in duration only to that of the Long Parliament, and the Duke of Cumberland again sat regularly in the Upper House. On 4 November 1661 he was admitted as a member of the Inner Temple, and in April 1662 he was sworn a member of the Privy Council. In the following month he went to Portsmouth with the King to receive Charles's bride, Catherine of Braganza; she was the daughter of Rupert's old friend John IV of Portugal, who had died in 1656, and sister of King Alphonso VI. As her dowry Catherine had brought Bombay and Tangier to the English Crown, and in October 1662 Rupert was appointed to the committee formed to administer Tangier, together with the Dukes of York and Albemarle, Edward Montagu Earl of Sandwich, William Coventry and Samuel Pepys. Pepys, Clerk of the Acts of the Navy, thus now came into direct contact with Rupert, probably for the first time, and had little good to say of him. 'Prince Rupert doth nothing but swear and laugh a little,' he wrote of a meeting of the Tangier committee at a slightly later date, 'with an oath or two, and that's all he doth.' It is not a convincing portrait of the earnest warrior-prince.

Rupert took part in the social life of the court with zest. He was frequently to be seen with the King, walking in the Mall or riding on Epsom Downs. Often they played tennis together. For the rest, the Prince had leisure once more to pursue his artistic interests and to work on his scientific experiments.

But the prospect of war loomed ahead. Maritime and commercial rivalry between the English and Dutch was increasing ominously. When in the summer of 1664 it was reported that the formidable Dutch Admiral de Ruyter was on his way to the Guinea coast under the pretext of an expedition to punish the Barbary corsairs, it was proposed that Rupert should take a fleet to intercept him.

Rupert had visited West Africa in his wanderings in 1652. He was now a member of the company formed for the exploitation of the area, in which the Duke of York held substantial shares; and a fleet of twelve ships was fitted out for him to command. 'The equipage for Guinea is hastening,' ran a Dutch report to the States General on 23 September, 'and men are pressed in the North of England, as well as in London, and come in fast; 500 seamen are ordered from Scotland, and it is thought no more will be needed. The drums still beat for men to go to Guinea with Prince Rupert, and many come in, besides a number of reformadoes of good quality. The King has been to Woolwich, to view and hasten the ships; 30,000*l*. was brought in to the Royal Company, sums due by members, but not paid in before.'[24]

Pepys had a characteristic comment. 'Prince Robt. I hear this day is to go to command this fleet going to Guinny against the Dutch,' he wrote on 31 August. 'I doubt few will be pleased with his going, being accounted an unhappy [unlucky] man.'[25] A few days later, on 5 September, he recorded a meeting with the Prince himself at Whitehall, when Rupert commented: 'God damn me, I can answer but for one ship, and in that I will do my part; for it is not in that as in [an] army, where a man can command everything.'[26]

Seen off by the King and the Duke of York, Rupert sailed from Greenwich in the *Henrietta* on 4 October 1664, and assembled his ships at Portsmouth. But this fleet was not destined to put to sea. There was delay at Portsmouth while the ships, which were badly provisioned, were made ready for the voyage. The weather was rough, and for some days the fleet was wind-bound at Portsmouth. And now Rupert was in poor health. His old head-wound was troubling him, and he was in no condition to sail. He grew irritable, and complained bitterly of his chaplain, whom he accused of mutinous behaviour. He got rid of the cleric, but still complained of the condition of the fleet.

It was Will Legge who warned the Duke of York, as Lord High Admiral, of the state of Rupert's health. The Duke promptly sent his own surgeon, Anthony Choqueux, to Portsmouth, and himself wrote in great concern to his cousin:

Whitehall, 27th October.

As soon as Will Legg showed me your letter of the accident in your head, I immediately sent Choqueux to you in so much haste as I had not time to write by him; but now I conjure you, if you have any kindness for me, have a care of your health, and do not neglect yourself, for which I am so much concerned. . . . I write to you without ceremony, and pray do the like to me, for we are too good friends to use any. I must again beg you to have a care of your health; and assure you that I am yours.[27]

Pepys reported with relish a different diagnosis of Rupert's malady. '. . . my Lord Fitzharding come hither,' he reported a few months later, 'and fell to discourse of Prince Rupert, and made nothing to say that his disease was the pox and that he must be fluxed, telling the horrible degree of the disease upon him with its breaking out on his head.'[28]

The gossip of Pepys and his friends can be discounted. Choqueux performed an operation, and forbade Rupert to move; the Prince was agitating to get back to the fleet, but a dangerous illness followed. On 10 December a correspondent of the Hatton family wrote from Southampton: 'Prince Rupert by a chance has bruised his head and cannot gett cured. He is gone up to London, to endeavour it there; and, if effected, they say he comes downe this winter to Tichfield, my Lord Treasurer's house, and will live there. He is mightily worne away, and, in theyr opinions that are much about him, is not long-lived.'[29]

Rupert's constitution pulled him through, and in a few months he had recovered. But by then the Guinea expedition had been abandoned. The Anglo-Dutch situation had reached a climax nearer home.

CHAPTER 2

WAR AT SEA

CAUSES of hostilities between England and the United Provinces of the Netherlands in the seventeenth century were primarily commercial; there was constant friction over the herring fisheries in the North Sea, and over the wool trade. The two strongest maritime powers of Western Europe clashed at a multitude of points. The Navigation Act passed by the Long Parliament in 1651, requiring goods imported into England to be carried in English ships, infuriated the Dutch, and this measure was confirmed and extended by Charles II's Convention Parliament. But there were more fundamental rivalries. King Charles I had asserted British sovereignty over the Narrow Seas round the south and east coasts of England, and the claim was repeated and expanded by later governments. It was vigorously challenged by the Netherlands. Then there were the quarrels that were continually being waged by English and Dutch adventurers overseas; in Africa, in the East Indies, and in the Americas, where newly acquired rights and possessions were ill-defined and open to dispute. Spanish and Portuguese power in the new territories was waning. The English and the Dutch were staking their claims, and there was deadly rivalry between them. The three wars that took place were almost entirely naval. There was little scope for land operations, and little part for armies to play.

The First Dutch War broke out in 1652, in the days of the Commonwealth, and was concluded by the Treaty of Westminster in 1654. The English had the best of it, chiefly through the seamanship of Robert Blake, who handled Charles I's ship-money fleet, augmented by Cromwell, with the highest tactical skill. The Dutch conceded the honouring of the English flag in British seas, and agreed to pay an indemnity for English merchant losses in the East. But the seed of future conflict was sown.

From the Restoration onwards the outbreak of new hostilities became more and more certain; and well before any official declaration there was undeclared war in more than one part of the globe. Most of the aggression came from the English side, and Robert Holmes, Prince Rupert's old friend and faithful follower, played a prominent part. In

1663, under the auspices of the Duke of York and on behalf of the newly formed Royal Africa Company, he sailed for the coast of Guinea, where both English and Portuguese merchants were complaining of Dutch encroachments. Holmes's orders were to avoid hostilities if possible, but the Dutch fired on his ships and in retaliation he seized the fort at Cape Verde and the Castle of Cormantin. It was this episode that led to de Ruyter's expedition of 1664 and to the fitting out of a fleet under Prince Rupert to intercept him. In the meantime, on the other side of the Atlantic, Colonel Richard Nicholls captured the Dutch settlement of New Amsterdam, which was renamed New York in honour of the heir to the throne.

De Ruyter recaptured some of the strongholds taken by Holmes, who had returned to England, and then sailed for the West Indies. Rupert's fleet was immobilized by his illness. But war could not be long delayed. That it did not break out immediately was owing to the reluctance of the governments of both powers. The States-General of the Netherlands, preoccupied with their position in Europe, had no desire for a full-scale war at sea. In England neither King Charles nor Clarendon was anxious for drastic action. The country's need was peace to consolidate the Restoration settlement. Moreover the keystone of Charles's policy was alliance with France, and France and the Netherlands had, in 1662, signed a defensive alliance. In his effort to stave off hostilities the King even committed Holmes to the Tower of London pending an inquiry into his conduct off the Guinea coast. Holmes, however, was soon released.

But national sentiment, bellicose in the sanguine atmosphere induced by the Restoration, was strongly in favour of war; and there was a powerful war party. Its leader was the Duke of York, who had given his full support to Holmes and Nicholls in their martial exploits. The Duke was the moving spirit of the Royal Africa Company, the chief object of which was to wrest trade from the Dutch. Another strong influence was that of Henry Bennet Lord Arlington, a former Cavalier soldier and a close personal friend of the King and the Duke of York, who in 1662 had become Secretary of State on the retirement of Sir Edward Nicholas. Arlington, an ambitious politician, had been Charles II's representative in Spain and was accepted as an expert on foreign affairs, though his judgement was, to say the least, dubious. In his advocacy of war with the Dutch he was probably inspired more by opposition to Clarendon, whose place he coveted, than by the dictates of higher policy. The Duke of Albemarle was also regarded as being of the war party.

The final spark was ignited in December 1664 when Admiral Thomas Allin, commanding in the Mediterranean, attacked the Dutch merchant fleet homeward bound from Smyrna in the Straits of Gibraltar, sinking two ships and capturing two others. The attack was believed to have been instigated by Arlington, but whoever was responsible it was the signal for war. A formal declaration was made by the Dutch on 14 January 1665, though it was not till 4 March that King Charles followed suit. The House of Commons, in which the war party was predominant, voted £2½ million, an unprecedented sum, for the prosecution of the war.

Prince Rupert, though not fully restored to health, was eager for action, and was immediately given high command in the fleet now fitted out under the Duke of York. This fleet consisted of about a hundred[1] men-of-war, divided in accordance with the custom of the Restoration navy into three squadrons: the White Squadron to lead, the Red for the centre and the Blue for the rear. Each squadron was divided into three divisions having the same formation. The Duke himself, as was customary, took command of the Red or centre squadron as Lord High Admiral, and Rupert took the van as Admiral of the White. The Admiral of the Blue was Edward Montagu Earl of Sandwich, an experienced sailor who had seen much service under the Commonwealth before transferring his allegiance and personally conducting King Charles to England in May 1660.

The Netherlands fleet, now assembling in the harbours of the Texel in North Holland, consisted, says Laird Clowes, quoting an official Dutch source, of '103 men-of-war, seven yachts and dispatch vessels, eleven fireships and twelve galliots [small, swift galleys], mounting in all 4,869 guns, and having on board 21,556 officers and men'.[2] The two fleets were almost exactly equal in strength, but the Dutch divided theirs into seven squadrons, each made up of three divisions.

The English fleet assembled off Harwich, and there Rupert joined it on 23 March. His flagship was the *Royal James*, and as Admiral of the White he had thirty-five ships under his command. The next few weeks were occupied in fitting out and victualling the fleet, and in discussions among the senior officers on the strategy and tactics to be pursued. The Duke of York's aim was to cut off the homeward-bound Dutch East India merchantmen believed to be approaching, and to fight the Dutch fleet when it sallied out of harbour in their defence. All were agreed in principle on this design, but the vital question was: would the English fleet be able to compel the Dutch to give battle? Here Rupert differed from the rest. 'All, except Prince Rupert,' wrote the Duke to his brother on 5 April, 'think they will immediately come out and fight.'[3] Rupert's argument, based on more exacting seafaring experience than most of the others could boast, was that the English fleet could not be well enough provisioned to keep the seas until the Dutch were compelled to come out.

The position of the East Indiamen was not known, and the Dutch commander, Jacob van Wassenaer Lord of Opdam, would in these circumstances be in no hurry to risk a battle, particularly as de Ruyter was thought to be on his way back from the Americas.

Rupert was overruled, but his judgement proved correct. On 21 April the fleet sailed for the Texel, but once there it could do nothing but blockade the Zuyder Zee and capture a few stray merchantmen. At the end of a fortnight food was running short, and bad weather made it additionally advisable for the English to return to refit. On 8 May the Duke of York weighed anchor and took his ships home to Harwich. While they were there Opdam took his fleet serenely out of harbour and sailed into the North Sea, capturing a convoy of English merchantmen on the way.

The first trick had gone to the Netherlands, and there was a great outcry in London. Revenge for the humiliation became the prime consideration of the Lord High Admiral, and refitting was carried out with all possible speed. The initiative had passed to the Dutch, who were cruising off the east coast of England. But on 29 May the English fleet was ready for battle and sailed north from the Gunfleet, at the mouth of the Thames south of Harwich. That night it anchored off Aldeburgh, and the next day proceeded to Southwold Bay, some ten miles south of Lowestoft. There on 1 June news was received that the Dutch were about six miles to the east-south-east, and the Duke of York promptly put to sea. Opdam kept away to seaward, but was sighted the following morning. Both fleets, manoeuvring for the wind, sailed northwards and early on the morning of 3 June faced each other east of Lowestoft, ready for the first great sea battle of the reign of Charles II.

Principles of naval tactics in the Second Dutch War were laid down in detail in the 'Fighting Instructions' issued by the Duke of York in April 1665. These in turn were based on instructions drawn up by Blake, Deane and Monk, Generals-at-Sea in the First Dutch War, in 1653 and reissued in the following year. The primary object of a fleet was to sink or capture the enemy by gunfire or the use of fireships, or by boarding or forcing him on to a shoal. The first thing was to obtain the weather gage of the enemy, to get to windward of him and retain this tactical advantage throughout. The fleet having the weather gage had the initiative, since it could come down on the wind and attack, while fireships could drift down the wind towards the enemy.

Tactical formation had been evolved during the past century as the gun had come to dominate naval warfare. Warships of the early Tudor period had one gun-deck running the length of the ship; by the time of Charles II the first-rates of the fleet had three such decks, and their power lay in the ability to rake an enemy fleet with gunfire broadside on. Thus the system of advance in line abreast, generally employed in the sixteenth and early seventeenth centuries, had given way to that of line ahead, in which each ship, sailing parallel with the enemy, could employ its full fire-power in gun-broadside. The Duke of York's 'additional instructions' laid down that 'in all cases of fight with the enemy commanders of his majesty's ships are to endeavour to keep the fleet in one line, and as much as may be to preserve the order of battle which shall have been directed before the time of fight'.[4]

Within this general principle two rival schools of thought had emerged – known to naval historians as the 'Formal' and the 'Mêlée'.[5] The Formalists believed in observing strict rules of manoeuvre, both in approaching the enemy and in the actual fight. The commander-in-chief should keep a close grip on his fleet not only in the initial attack but throughout the action. Thus would an attacking fleet be able to bring the greatest possible controlled fire to bear, while in defence the danger of ships being isolated would be minimal and it would be possible for the commander to extricate his fleet if necessary.

Advocates of the 'Mêlée' believed in individual initiative. They accepted the principle of formal approach in line ahead under close and orderly control. Once battle was joined, however, they maintained victory would depend on the actions of subordinate commanders, each of whom would take advantage of any change in the situation as he saw it, without waiting for orders from a commander who might be well away from the action. He might be able to outflank the enemy at a particular point, to bring a superior force to bear on a weak part of the enemy line, or to break through and then wheel round to attack in the opposite direction. Thus, 'though great stress must still be laid upon the mutual confidence and co-operation among the units of the fleet, the general control of the action would gradually slip from the fingers of the commander-in-chief, and the outcome would largely depend upon the individual initiative and fighting qualities of subordinate leaders'.[6]

Adherence to each of these two schools of thought depended largely, and predominantly, on temperament. The leader of the Formalists was the Duke of York, whose rigid military mind ran to order and control in all things. He was supported by Sandwich, his Admiral of the Blue, and by his flag-captain Sir William Penn, who had chased Prince Rupert in the Mediterranean in 1651 and had subsequently fought in the First Dutch War.

Rupert himself was regarded as the chief advocate of the 'Mêlée'. Like the Duke of York he had been trained as a soldier before he had ever taken to the sea; but he had seen far more action than the Duke, and in the Civil War he had fought in many battles where control from the top had given place to the initiative shown by junior officers, whose dash and spirit had made the difference between victory and defeat. His own cavalry charges were a case in point, and his whole temperament called for attack uncontrolled by policy dictated from above. It was this doubtless that was in his mind when he said in Pepys's hearing that in a sea battle he would answer for only one ship. His principal supporter in this attitude was that other great soldier turned sailor George Monk, Duke of Albemarle; but Albemarle, one of Cromwell's commanders against the Dutch, was not now at sea. He was at home in charge of the Board of Admiralty.

James Duke of York, however, was in command off Lowestoft; so it could be assumed that formal tactics would be the order of the day. James performed the first duty of a commander by gaining the weather gage: when the first action began at about 3.30 a.m. on 3 June the wind was blowing from the south-west and the Dutch fleet was to the east of the English.

The two fleets passed each other on opposite tacks, the English northwest and the Dutch south-east, firing their broadsides as they went. This was the orthodox line-ahead manoeuvre; but neither fleet was in perfect formation, ragged encounters taking place at various points along the line. Rupert's squadron led the line, with Christopher Myngs, his Vice-Admiral of the White, in the van, and the Prince 'received the charge of their fleet, not discharging again till close to, and then firing through and through the enemy with great success'.[7] This was at about 6 a.m., and the shooting lasted about an hour as the fleet passed. At eight o'clock both tacked about for the second encounter. Each English ship turned simultaneously, so that now Sandwich was in the van and Rupert in the rear. The Dutch were striving to gain the weather gage, but English tactical skill kept the Duke's fleet in its advantageous position.

Soon, however, the conventional formation was broken. The Duke of York, to prevent the Dutch weathering Rupert's squadron, gave orders to tack into the enemy fleet, and Sandwich in the van broke through the centre of the Dutch line. Now there was a general mêlée, which went on for several hours; central control on both sides was lost, but the Dutch, with their line cut in half, were the more disorganized of the two fleets.

In the ship-to-ship encounters that now made up the battle the most notable was that between the two commanders-in-chief. The Duke of York in the *Royal Charles*, with her 78 guns, found himself during the afternoon in direct conflict with Opdam in the 76-gun *Eendracht*, and the two flagships became hotly engaged. There were continuous broadsides, and the Duke at one point was in danger of his ship being boarded. At another he very nearly lost his life. A single shot from the *Eendracht* carried off three of his officers – the Earl of Falmouth, Lord Muskerry and a Mr Boyle, son of the Earl of Burlington – and the Duke himself 'was so near the noble persons killed by that fatal shot that his clothes were besmeared with their blood'.[8]

But it was not the Duke but his rival commander who perished. Nobody knew how it happened, but at the height of the struggle the *Eendracht* blew up; probably an English shot had set the powder-room ablaze. Only five men survived out of a ship's complement of 400.

The catastrophe completed the disorganization of the Dutch. The command was assumed by the next senior admiral, Jan Evertsen, but so chaotic was the condition of the fleet that Cornelis van Tromp, son of the great Admiral Marten van Tromp who had died in the First Dutch War, took command of as much of the fleet as he could rally, not knowing that Evertsen had not been killed as well as Opdam, and thinking himself the senior commander left. Two days after the battle he was writing to the Dutch Government that 'perhaps also the L. [Lieutenant] Admiral Jan Evertsen, the L. Admiral Cortenaer, and Stellingwerf are dead'.[9] By seven o'clock in the evening the fighting was over and the Dutch were in flight. Evertsen made for the mouth of the Maas, van Tromp, with his section of the fleet, for the Texel, farther north. It was a splendid English victory. At least twelve Dutch ships had been sunk or burned, and half that number taken prisoner.

On the English side it is believed that not more than 250 men died, and about 350 were wounded. One ship, the *Charity*, was taken, and the Dutch claimed the capture of two more. But among the casualties were a number of senior officers. Vice-Admiral Sir John Lawson, who had been a distinguished sailor under the Commonwealth, died of his wounds, and Rupert lost one of his rear-admirals, Robert Sansum.

Such a victory might have put an end to the war. But, through dereliction of duty almost amounting to treachery on the part of one man, it was not followed up. The story is well known, and can be pieced together from the accounts by Clarendon, Burnet and others. When the Dutch were in flight the Duke, having been on deck for some eighteen hours, gave orders for pursuit and then retired to his cabin, and so did his flag-captain, Penn, leaving Captain John Harman in charge of the ship. During the night Henry Brouncker, brother of Lord Brouncker and a groom of the Duke's bedchamber, went on deck and told Harman that the Duke had ordered sail to be slackened as the chase was to be abandoned. Harman was surprised, but in view of Brouncker's position assumed that the order was authentic and obeyed it. As the *Royal Charles* was now leading this meant that the whole fleet fell back. In the morning, when the Duke emerged, the enemy were out of sight; he was naturally furious, and flatly denied having given any order for the chase to be given up. The chance of annihilating the Dutch fleet, or at any rate part of it (it was not certain which section was being pursued), had been lost.

Attempts were later made, when the Duke of York had lost popularity, to put the blame on him, with the implication that he was concerned with his personal safety. The charge hardly needs refuting; he had been in the thick of the fighting throughout the entire day, facing the immediate threat of death with serene composure, and he was not likely to show cowardice when the enemy were in retreat. There is no reason to doubt that Brouncker acted on his own responsibility, but his motives can only be guessed at. Possibly he was himself frightened, and took this nefarious means to ensure that there should be no more action; possibly he was genuinely concerned for his master's safety. But his conduct is difficult to explain; his duplicity was certain to be discovered as soon as the Duke came on deck. James dismissed him from his service, but although the matter was taken up in Parliament he was surprisingly not brought to trial.

Credit for victory must go in the first place to the Duke of York, though how far he acted under the advice of the more experienced Penn cannot be determined. But both Prince Rupert and Sandwich had distinguished themselves. Clarendon declared that Rupert 'did Wonders that Day'[10] and James Hickes, a civil servant, felt that justice had not been done to the Prince in the official reports. 'All are dissatisfied with last Friday's relation of the success of the fleet,' he wrote to Arlington's secretary, Joseph Williamson, on 10 June. 'There is no account of the Duke of York's singular encounter with Opdam, whose ship was sunk, though two other Dutch flag ships, and several others, tried to sink the Duke's ship and to kill him. Nor is a word said of Prince Rupert, though the seamen said none excelled him in valour and success.'[11] Sandwich also recorded his admiration of the Prince's gallantry.

Rupert himself was cheerful enough. On 13 June he wrote from Dunwich to Arlington:

My greatest joy is to have ben so happie as to have bin a small instrument in this last encounter, to chastise so high an insolency as that of the Dutch. I hope, with his Majesty's good liking, to continue so, till they be brought to their duty; which work will be very easy if we linger not out the time, for which this place is not unfitt and will give a thousand excuses for delays. What this day will be resolved on in the Council I know not, being laid by the leg, by a small mistake of the Surgeon, of which I shall not trouble you. This is writ abed, as you may see by the ill caracter, which I desire you not to take ill.[12]

It would appear from this letter that Rupert had been wounded, unless the leg trouble was a legacy of his recent illness. Sir John Denham, celebrating the victory over the Dutch, wrote with poetic exaggeration:

> *Rupert* that knew no fear, but Health did want,
> Kept State suspended in a Chair volant;
> All save his Head shut in that wooden Case,
> He shew'd but like a broken weather glass;
> But arm'd with the whole Lyon Cap-a-Chin,
> Did represent the Hercules within.[13]

Clearly Rupert was not so ill as Denham implied. But whether or not he had been wounded in the battle he was not in the best of health; it was probably just as well from his own point of view that his hope of continuing to fight against the Dutch was not for the moment fulfilled. He and the Duke of York were summoned to London soon after the return of the fleet, Sandwich being left in command. King Charles, whose marriage to Catherine of Braganza had not been blessed with issue, had decided that his brother should not be allowed to risk his life at sea again; he had come a little too close to being deprived of his heir.

It was now proposed that the fleet should be jointly commanded by Rupert and Sandwich. Both were in high repute after the Battle of Lowestoft, and Peter Lely was commissioned by the Duke of York this summer to paint their portraits as well as those of other senior commanders who had fought at Lowestoft. There was some doubt as to whether the two would work amicably in harness, and according to Sandwich Rupert objected and suggested 'that himself should command one squadron distinct and I another'.[14] This was clearly an impracticable plan; the arrangement was cancelled, and Rupert was told that Sandwich was to be in sole command. This was a snub to Rupert, but he remained in favour with the King and the Duke of York. A possible further factor was the likelihood that Rupert's health would not bear the strain of a new sea venture at this juncture. The King may have been glad of the opportunity to deprive him of his command

So Rupert joined the court; but he did not stay long at Whitehall. London this summer was ravaged by the worst pestilence it had known since the Black Death in the mid-fourteenth century. The Great Plague of 1665 was the last of its kind that the capital was to know; but it was far more severe than its many predecessors. The late Walter G. Bell estimated that at least 100,000 deaths were caused by the epidemic, though the official Bill of Mortaility showed only 68,000.[15]

It was a miserable time, with the poor of the city dying in their thousands. Those who could afford to do so fled to the country, in many cases taking the plague with them. The King himself showed no undue haste in making his escape; 'many blamed him for not leaving the peril behind earlier'.[16] But on 9 July the court moved up-river to Hampton Court, and later in the month to Salisbury.

Rupert went with the court. He was not the man to bolt from danger, but apart from the fact that the King had expressly demanded his company it would have been madness to stay in London in his current state of health. Two men of wealth and influence, both friends of the Prince, did risk their lives by voluntarily remaining in the capital. One was the Duke of Albemarle, who remained at the Cockpit in St James's and exercised control as the one senior representative of the Government. He maintained order by the force of his personality, ruling through such magistrates and minor officials as remained, at a time when the rule of law might easily have been overturned. With him was the Earl of Craven, whose qualities were never more in evidence. Regardless of personal danger he succoured the sick and welcomed the distressed at his house in Drury Lane, also distributing money to help them in their need. Both he and Albemarle, remarkably, escaped infection.

Rupert need hardly have worried himself at not having command of the fleet after Lowestoft. There were no further major engagements in 1665, and such actions as Sandwich undertook met with little success. He tried to intercept de Ruyter on his return from western seas, and also the Dutch East India fleet. This fleet made for Bergen in Norway, and while Sandwich and his second-in-command, Sir Thomas Tedde-man, were attacking it de Ruyter slipped by and got home to Holland. Sandwich captured a few merchantmen, but returned home with nothing to show for his efforts.

The prizes were valuable, but Sandwich was suspected of embezzling the proceeds; he was also attacked for allowing thirty Dutch ships to escape when they seemed to be within his grasp. A storm arose in the country on his return, and there were threats of impeachment. The King accepted the Admiral's explanations, but the popular outcry made it advisable to make another change in the naval command. Pepys, the protégé of Sandwich, bore witness to the state of public feeling when he recorded, on 6 November, that 'it was purposed by some hot-heads in the House of Commons to have, at the same time when they voted a present to the Duke of York, to have voted 10000*l* to the Prince and half a Crowne to my Lord of Sandwich'.[17]

It was generally felt that it was time Prince Rupert made a comeback. Sandwich's face was saved by his appointment as ambassador extraordinary to Spain, and he left England on 3 March 1666. The new arrangement for the fleet was once more a joint command this time by Prince Rupert and the Duke of Albemarle. There was little fear of friction between these two, and Albemarle declared that 'If the King pleased He would most readily serve under the Command of Prince *Rupert*'.[18] The Prince would doubtless have preferred to be in sole command, but he made no difficulties.

On 13 February 1666 'several sea commanders who had served under Prince Rupert invited him to dinner, and spoke cheerfully of going again together against the Dutch'.[19] And on 23 April the Prince and the Duke, together in the *Royal Charles*, took command of the fleet at the Nore.

CHAPTER 3

DOUBLE HARNESS

O N 16 January 1666 King Louis XIV, in pursuance of his defence treaty with the Netherlands, declared war on King Charles. Denmark also associated herself with the Dutch, but this alliance had little effect on the course of hostilities. France as a maritime state could not be compared with England or Holland, and King Louis's fleet was small; he probably intended no more than a token naval demonstration, designed to help his Dutch allies to challenge British supremacy at sea. Nevertheless the alliance had a nuisance value, for the main French fleet was concentrated at Toulon, with detachments at Brest and La Rochelle, and would therefore, if it moved to the attack, approach the English coast northwards from the direction of the Mediterranean. The danger was that the English, facing the Dutch enemy to the north-east, would be taken in the rear by the French.

Rupert and Albemarle commanded a fleet of eighty ships. Their condition appears to have been better than was usually the case in the seventeenth century. The Plague had taken its toll, and crews were by no means complete; while beer was in short supply. The general victualling situation, however, had improved. Samuel Pepys, Clerk of the Acts of the Navy, had in the previous October been appointed Surveyor-General of the victualling office, and here the ambitious young civil servant revealed his immense industry and his capacity for mastering detail. He produced an admirable report, and devised a system of local supervision at the ports which did much to bring order out of chaos.

The health situation gave cause for anxiety; the danger that the Plague, which in general was now under control, might spread through the fleet was not lessened by the presence on board in large numbers of the nautical equivalent of camp followers. 'The sickness increases,' wrote Sir John Mennes, the Controller of the Navy, to Pepys on 19 April, 'and they [the ships] are pestered with women; there are as many petticoats as breeches on board some of them, and that for weeks together.'[1] This was one of the first matters taken up by the Prince and the Duke. An order to Sir Thomas Allin, serving as Admiral of the White,

331

dated the day after they had taken up their joint command, instructed him to 'turn all the women to shore and suffer none to come aboard'.[2]

A month later, when these difficulties had been ironed out as well as they could be, Rupert and Albemarle, together in the *Royal Charles*, set sail from the Nore with their fleet to watch for the Dutch. Immediately, however, a new situation arose which brought about one of the most controversial decisions in the history of seventeenth-century naval warfare. No French warships, it had been believed, were any nearer English waters than the Mediterranean; but on 22 May a Captain Talbot, commanding the *Elizabeth*, sailed into Falmouth harbour with the startling news that a French fleet of thirty-six sail under the Duc de Beaufort was approaching the English Channel. He had seen it, he said, sailing northwards from Lisbon, and had made with all possible speed for home to give the news.

The news was false. What Talbot had seen was a detachment of the Spanish fleet cruising off the Portuguese coast; but this was not discovered until some weeks later, and at this sudden revelation there was intense excitement in London. Plans had been laid for such a contingency, and they were hurriedly put into operation. Orders were sent by the King to Prince Rupert to prevent the junction of the French and the Dutch. If, as now seemed likely, the French arrived first, they could be smashed before a battle with the Dutch took place.

The division of the fleet was subsequently condemned as strategically indefensible, and this contemporary verdict has been echoed by a number of naval historians. That the decision to divide the fleet turned out to be wrong is undeniable; but that decision was taken in the light of the information available, and the information on which the King and his ministers acted was that Beaufort and the French were at the mouth of the Channel, while the Dutch were not ready to come out of harbour. Actually the reverse was true. Beaufort was still south of Lisbon, and in the event did not sail further till the fight was over; while the Dutch fleet, under the formidable de Ruyter, was prepared for immediate battle.

There was without question a serious deficiency in intelligence, for which Lord Arlington, as Secretary of State with chief responsibility for foreign affairs, must bear most of the blame, though the commanders of the fleet were not guiltless. But the strategic error of the decision is less certain. To the school of thought that holds that the division of a fleet is in no circumstances defensible there is no problem; but not all naval authorities have held to this view. The English in May 1666 were faced with two possible threats, coming from opposite directions. Were they to wait to be attacked by one or the other or both? To concentrate the whole of their force against either the French or the Dutch and leave the country open to invasion from one direction? Or to endeavour to cope with both foes by division? 'When the order was given,' says one historian who defends the decision, 'the Dutch were believed to be in harbour and likely enough to remain there while the English united and prepared: consequently if Albemarle had gone with his whole fleet to meet the French he would have left the Thames open to de Ruyter, and, conversely, with all the fleet concentrated against the Dutch, Portsmouth and the Isle of Wight would have been exposed to Beaufort.'[3] With their knowledge of the quality of the French fleet the Government judged that Rupert's twenty-four ships, reinforced as they could expect to be by ten more from Plymouth, would be sufficient for the task; while Albemarle had a fleet of nearly sixty vessels to face the Dutch in the event of an attack. The decision was not an ideal one; but it is arguable that it was the only practicable one in the circumstances.

So much for the actual decision to divide the fleet, for which the Privy Council was responsible. But whether or not this was a strategical blunder, there was certainly a tactical error after the decision had been made. For when more accurate information came of the state of readiness of the Dutch fleet it was not too late to remedy the situation.

The sequence of events must be briefly reconstructed.[4] The first suggestion for diverting part of the fleet appears to have come from Prince Rupert, who on 10 May wrote to the Duke of York from the *Royal Charles*, referring to the report that Beaufort was on his way from Toulon and saying that, if the Dutch were not as yet likely to leave harbour, it would be a good opportunity to intercept him. According to what he said later he had already mentioned the possibility to the King, who had promised him the command if such an expedition should be undertaken. On the following day the two admirals wrote to Arlington to the same effect, saying that news had been received through Sir Edward Spragge, Rupert's Rear-Admiral of the Blue, that Beaufort was making for Belle Ile, off the coast of Brittany, where he would be joined by ships from Brest. Spragge himself then went to London as emissary of the admirals, and a meeting of the Privy Council was summoned on 13 May. As a result of this meeting two members of the council, Sir William Coventry and Sir George Carteret, Treasurer of the Navy, were sent next day to the fleet, now cruising off the Nore, to confer with Rupert and Albemarle. Rupert was on shore shooting when they arrived, but he joined the discussion later. Both he and Albemarle later wrote reports on the division of the fleet, and Albemarle recorded that Coventry and Carteret 'said the Dutch Fleet wd not be out in 6 weeks'.[5] It was then agreed that twenty ships and some fireships should be sent off in the direction of Belle Ile, and it was now that Rupert asserted that he had been promised the command. When Albemarle was asked if ho could spare the ships, he answered confidently: 'Leave us 60 sail, and we shall do well enough.'[6] He did, however, ask to be reinforced by any other ships that were available in the Thames.

Coventry and Carteret then returned to London to report to the King and the Duke of York, with a list of the ships to be detached, taken from all three squadrons. On 22 May the resolution was approved, and Rupert informed that he was to command the detachment. Meanwhile the admirals reported that they intended to sail from the Nore to the Downs, whence Prince Rupert would start on his southerly expedition.

Now, however, came fresh information, to the effect that the Dutch fleet was preparing to put to sea. Arlington notified Albemarle, but for some unexplained reason the message took three days to reach him. 'On 27th May at Night,' recorded Albemarle, 'I received a letter from my Lord Arlington dated 24th importing that he heard the Dutch fleet would be out suddenly, but mentioned no certain time of their coming out.'[7]

Rupert had not yet left the fleet, and it was open to the admirals to hold up his departure till the situation could be reviewed in the light of this new development. They did not do so. Their motives have been variously interpreted. It has been suggested that each of them wanted an independent command, and each was glad to be rid of the other. Such an insinuation is hardly consistent with the characters of the two men. They were fully in accord, and neither was the man to endanger the fleet over a matter of personal caprice. It would appear that Albemarle overrated his own strength and was confident that he could beat the Dutch with what remained of his force. As for Rupert, according to his later statement he 'concluded there could be no probable danger from the enemy in case they should come out, because the same wind which would bring them into the Channel would also serve to bring down our fleet to a conjunction with the squadron under my command'.[8] Moreover he had his orders; unless they were countermanded he would carry them out. At the same time, with his joy in battle and his delight in command, it can scarcely be doubted that he welcomed the opportunity.

So on 29 May Rupert, with his carefully selected ships, sailed southward in the *Royal James*. Albemarle was left in the Downs with fifty-four vessels (a few had been found unseaworthy), and now for the first time he appeared uncertain of his strength. He asked for instructions on whether or not he should risk battle with less than seventy sail. The Duke of York replied, not very helpfully, that the matter was best left to his own prudence, but that it would be better for him to shift his station to the anchorage on the Essex coast called the Gunfleet. There it would be easier for the Thames ships to join him, and there he would be able to fight or not as he judged expedient.

On the very day that Rupert sailed de Ruyter put to sea with about ninety ships. Albemarle received the news as he was starting on his journey towards the Gunfleet, and on the evening of 30 May the news reached Whitehall. The King promptly summoned the Privy Council, and it was decided that Rupert must be recalled. The Prince had not gone far on his voyage at this stage, but now there occurred one of those administrative lapses that have from time to time marked moments of crisis in national affairs, and not only in the seventeenth century. The Duke of York signed the orders for Rupert's return to the main fleet late that night, and Coventry was directed to tell Arlington to arrange for their despatch to the various Channel ports where Rupert might be expected to call. But Arlington had gone to bed, and when the messenger arrived at his house his staff were afraid to wake him. Thus many valuable hours were lost, and it was not till 5 p.m. on 31 May that the order reached Portsmouth, and a ketch was sent out to find Rupert.

But Rupert had not waited for orders. Cruising off Portsmouth, he heard the sound of guns, and his fighting spirit and speed of decision took little account of what Whitehall might be planning. When the ketch with its message reached him, he was starting out, on his own responsibility, to return to the Downs.

The battle, in fact, had begun. At eight o'clock on the morning of Friday, 1 June, Albemarle sighted the Dutch lying at anchor off the North Foreland. He called a council of his flag officers and captains, and discussed with them the question whether it was possible for his fleet to to get past the Dutch into the river without fighting. Opinion was unanimous: '. . . seeing most of our fleet were heavy ships we cd not avoid fighting, & thereupon the resolution was to fall upon them as they lay at anchor'.[9]

So the Duke of Albemarle, heavily outnumbered, moved gallantly in to the attack, hoping that shock tactics against a fleet at anchor would compensate for the discrepancy in strength. At eleven o'clock he gave the signal to draw into line of battle, and the fleet advanced in the conventional line-ahead formation: Sir George Ayscue leading the way as Admiral of the White, the Duke himself in the centre with the Red Squadron, and Sir Thomas Teddeman bringing up the rear with the Blue. They sailed eastwards towards the Dutch, with the wind blowing from the south-south-west. The English thus had the weather gage.

The Dutch immediately cut loose, but they were in some measure of disarray. De Ruyter was in the centre, with Cornelis Evertsen in the van to the north-west; but Cornelis Tromp in the rear was well to the south-east of the rest of the fleet. Albemarle sailed south-eastwards down the length of the Dutch line, but mostly out of gunshot. His windward position had the disadvantage that, in a fresh gale and choppy sea, it was impossible to use the lower tier of guns. It was not till the English reached Tromp's squadron that any close engagement was effected. Here Albemarle might have disabled Tromp, isolated as the Dutch admiral was from the main fleet; but his line of advance had become too much stretched out and he was unable to bring the full weight of his strength to bear. Meanwhile de Ruyter and Evertsen tacked to the south-west and, gaining the weather gage, bore down on the English.

The ensuing mêlée lasted some three hours. Sir William Berkeley in the *Swiftsure* was killed, and his ship taken by the Dutch; Albemarle's flagship the *Royal Charles* was considerably damaged. Then Albemarle tacked back to the north-west, and engagement became general all along the line. De Ruyter handled his ship with great tactical skill, and Albemarle found himself between two fires: de Ruyter and Evertsen to the north, Tromp to the south. Fierce fighting continued for the rest of the day, in the course of which the Dutch Admiral Evertsen was killed by a broadside from the *Henry*. At about 10 p.m. the Dutch tacked to southward, and the fleets separated for the night, the Dutch to the east and the English to the west.

The English had held their own against odds, but Albemarle's attempt to gain victory by surprise had failed. There was no great discrepancy in casualties: three English ships had been taken and two had had to run for port, while two Dutch vessels had been burnt and at least two had had to make for harbour. But the losses bore more heavily on the weaker fleet.

The night was spent in repairing the damaged ships, and early in the morning Albemarle prepared to renew the fight. The fleets engaged once more between seven and eight o'clock; Albemarle obtained the weather gage and the fleets passed on opposite tacks, west-north-west and east-south-east. The English fleet was now reduced to forty-four ships, while the Dutch had still about eighty. But the English were in better order; the Dutch were crowded together, and in some cases were masking each other's fire. This fact seems to have influenced Tromp in the rear when, on his own responsibility, he lay off from the Dutch line and tacked to try to gain the wind of the English van as it came up. He was followed by ten ships, but he failed to gain his advantage and found himself cut off from his comrades by the English. At the same time some ships in the Dutch van, in an act of rank insubordination, disengaged from the English line and stood off to the north.

De Ruyter was threatened with the disintegration of his whole line; but he was equal to the occasion. 'About 12 a clock,' writes the author of one of the anonymous English accounts of the battle, 'we thought we had routed the enemy: but de Ruyter, with great courage and skill, got them together again in good order.'[10] Ignoring the trouble in his van, he came down on the starboard tack to the rescue of Tromp, and succeeded in extricating him. Tromp had lost two ships sunk and three disabled, but Albemarle was compelled to stand away for fear of losing the weather gage. De Ruyter reformed his line on a southerly course and passed to leeward of the English.

Desultory fighting continued for some hours, but Albemarle had suffered considerable casualties and was unable to follow up such advantage as he had gained. His strength was now reduced to thirty-four ships, and when he tacked to the westward the captains of some damaged vessels 'stood for England without acquainting the General, who seeing that thought good likewise to hold our wind and make the best of our way home, having no more than 28 sail of fighting ships left'.[11] At 3 p.m. a council of flag-officers was held aboard the *Royal Charles*, after which what was left of the English fleet made for the mouth of the Thames. It was a fighting retreat. Albemarle put sixteen of his best ships in line abreast to hold off the enemy, with the weak and disabled vessels in front of them. The Dutch pursued in a straggling line, but they too had suffered heavily and de Ruyter's flagship, the *Seven Provinces*, severely damaged, lagged behind. Little attempt was made to molest the English, and at nightfall the Dutch fleet stood off.

Two days' hard fighting had left Albemarle's force badly crippled; but the battle was not over yet. On 3 June, Whit Sunday, the English drew near to the Thames, and as they did so suffered another severe loss. As the Dutch approached, Ayscue's flagship the ninety-gun *Royal Prince* – 'the best ship ever built', said Sir Thomas Clifford, 'and like a castle in the sea'[12] – ran ashore on the Galloper sands and fell into the hands of the Dutch who failed to get her off and so set her on fire, taking Ayscue prisoner. The rest of the ships continued on their way and the Duke of York sent Penn down to the river mouth to arrange for reinforcements and supplies.

At two o'clock in the afternoon a fleet of about twenty sail was seen approaching from the south. At first it was thought they were Dutch; then they were recognized. Rupert had arrived, full of fight and vigour, to aid the stricken fleet. The ships 'were received with great shouts',[13] and their arrival put new heart into the sailors. The Prince had made the best time he could. He had reached Dover on the previous afternoon, but then the wind had dropped and he was unable to make further headway. Now as he approached the main fleet the Dutch sent out a squadron of equal strength to his own as if to intercept him. He was quite ready for a skirmish, but Albemarle got a message through to him warning him of the danger of the Galloper sands, saying that 'he supposed that squadron was sent out as a decoy to draw his Highness and his first squadron upon the Banke'.[14] So Rupert eluded the enemy and linked up with his fellow-admiral. A council of flag-officers was held aboard the *Royal James*, and it was decided to return to the attack on the following morning. Rupert with his fresh crews and undamaged ships was to take the van.

> Thus re-inforc'd, against the adverse Fleet
> Still doubling ours, brave *Rupert* leads the way.
> With the first blushes of the Morn they meet,
> And bring night back upon the new-born day.[15]

So sang John Dryden, who a few years later was to become Poet Laureate, in his noble poem celebrating the events of the year 1666. Patriotic poets acclaiming warlike deeds are entitled to a little licence, and the Dutch fleet was now far from double the size of the English. Rupert and Albemarle had about sixty ships, the enemy sixty-four.[16] At daylight on Monday, 4 June, the Dutch were about twelve miles to the south, and Rupert led his squadron in their direction. Myngs was in the van leading his division in the *Victory*; with him in the *Defiance* was Prince Rupert's trusted friend Sir Robert Holmes, recently knighted. Rupert himself was in the centre in the *Royal James*, while Spragge brought up the rear in the *Dreadnought*.

The firing began around 8 a.m. Rupert attacked vigorously, and for about two hours the fight raged furiously: the wind was blowing from the south-west, and both fleets were sailing on the starboard tack. Albemarle with the main body of the fleet was following close up, and gradually the English forced their way into the Dutch line. A vivid description of Rupert's conduct at this point is given by an anonymous narrator:

> And here we cannot omit making reflection upon the Prince, who in this Pass was envision'd with as many dangers as the Enemy could apply unto him, they raked him Fore and Aft, plyed him on both sides, and to all that, were just clapping two Fireships upon him, but two of our Fireships that attended the Prince, got betwixt that danger and him, and bravely burnt the bold Assaylants; and though His Highness received very considerable prejudice in that different passage, in his Masts and Rigging, yet he answered the shot they poured on him, with as many close returns, which the Enemy felt and carried away with them; and in that whole day, to say no more, the Prince did manifest a Courage and Conduct Answerable to the other great Actions, which belong to the story of his Life, whereby he gave spirit to his friends and terror to the Enemy.[17]

Soon the fight developed into a general mêlée. Myngs headed the Dutch van, which in turn pursued him, while Tromp with the Dutch rear overhauled the van and on his own initiative brought the ships back to the main fleet. Five times Prince Rupert broke through the Dutch line, but the main body under de Ruyter kept its position. At some time in this confused action Myngs was shot through the throat. He refused to leave his post but remained standing on deck, pressing his finger on his neck to check the flow of blood, till another shot struck him down. He died a few days after the battle.

The mêlée continued till well on in the day, with no conspicuous advantage to either side. At length ammunition began to fall short, and with heavy casualties the fleets suffered from damage and exhaustion. The *Royal James*'s rigging was badly shattered, and for a time Rupert had to lay by to repair it.

> The warlike Prince had sever'd from the rest
> Two giant ships, the pride of all the Main;
> Which, with his one, so vigorously he press'd,
> And flew so home they could not rise again . . .
> When one dire shot, the last they could supply,
> Close by the board the Prince's Main-mast bore:
> All three now, helpless, by each other lie,
> And this offends not, and those fear no more.[18]

The fleets were now inextricably entangled, but de Ruyter with his usual admirable seamanship managed to exercise control over the bulk of his main body. He was to the south and to windward of Albemarle, but deciding that the moment had come to break away he gave the signal for his squadron to keep off before the wind, and broke directly through the English centre. At this time, which would appear to have been between 7 and 8 p.m., a heavy fog came up ('manifestly the work of Almighty God,'[19] said de Ruyter), though it did not last long, and the Dutch Admiral 'on a sudden fired a Gun, to call in the stragling Remains of his tatter'd Fleet . . . and bore away before the wind towards Flushing'.[20]

> This lucky hour the wise *Batavian* takes,
> And warns his batter'd Fleet to follow home:
> Proud to have so got off with equal stakes,
> Where 'twas a triumph not to be o'r-come.[21]

But the stakes were not equal. True, de Ruyter had been the first to break off the fight; to that extent Rupert and Albemarle might claim to have won. But though the battle was drawn, it was the English who had suffered most. They had lost ten ships, the Dutch only four. Killed and wounded on the English side are estimated at 5,000, with 3,000 taken prisoner; the Dutch lost some 2,000 killed and wounded.

Nevertheless the English sailors had not been dishonoured in the Four Days' Fight. They had fought against odds, and but for the division of the fleet victory might well have been theirs. Their discipline and morale were admitted to be superior to those of the Dutch, and there had been splendid examples of gallantry. Once again the verdict of the future Poet Laureate may be quoted:

> Thousands were there in darker fame that dwell,
> Whose deeds some nobler Poem shall adorn:
> And, though to me unknown, they, sure, fought well,
> Whom *Rupert* led, and who were British born.[22]

Yet when the news filtered through to London that the action had been less successful than was at first reported the recriminations began. According to Pepys the scapegoat was the Duke of Albemarle. 'All the commanders, officers, and even the common seamen,' wrote the diarist on 10 June, 'do condemn every part of the late conduct of the Duke of Albemarle. Both in his fighting at all – in his manner of fighting, running among them – in his retreat, and running the ship on ground – so as nothing can be worse spoken of.'[23] Rupert, on the other hand, escaped censure. Even Pepys, who disliked both admirals, recorded no criticism of the Prince.

Arguments were inevitable in the aftermath of a major engagement the results of which were a matter of controversy. The urgent need of the moment was to refit the fleet for further service, taking heed in the process of what lessons could be learned from the conduct of the battle. The English fleet anchored off Harwich on the evening of 5 June, and next day Penn went over the ships with authority from the Lord High Admiral to put matters in hand. The fleet began to reassemble at the Buoy of the Nore on 27 June, and early in July was ready to move down the river.

Prince Rupert personally issued three new fighting instructions, based on his experiences and designed to ensure closer cohesion in the fleet. The first laid down that 'in case of an engagement the commander of every ship is to have a special regard to the common good, and if any flagship shall, by any accident whatsoever, stay behind or [be] likely to lose company, or be out of his place, then all and every ship or ships belonging to such flag is to make all the way possible to keep up with the admiral of the fleet and to endeavour the utmost that may be the destruction of the enemy, which is always to be made the chiefest care'.[24] The second ordered that 'when the admiral of the fleet makes a weft [flag signal] with his flag, the rest of the flag officers are to do the like, and then all the best sailing ships are to make what way they can to engage the enemy'.[25] And the third: 'If any flagship shall be so disabled as not to be fit for service, the flag officer or commander of such ship shall remove himself into any other ship of his division, and shall there command and wear the flag as he did in his own.'[26]

The Duke of Albemarle as joint fleet commander must presumably have concurred in these instructions; but they were issued as from Rupert alone, and may be taken as having been devised by him. Another interesting order, which is to be found in a manuscript preserved at Greenwich, illustrates the two admirals' recognition of the dangers of service in fireships. Rupert and Albemarle promised on the King's behalf:

1. That if any of the King's fireships performs service expected from them in such a manner that any of the enemy's men of war of 40 guns or more shall be burnt by them every person remaining on the fireship till the service be performed shall receive on board the Admiral immediately after the service done ten pounds as a reward for the service over and above his pay due to him, and in case any of them should be killed in the service it shall be his executors or next relations over the ordinary provision to be made, for the relations of such as are in H.M.'s service. And the captain of such fireship shall receive a medal of Gold to remain as a mark of honour to him and his posterity. And shall receive such other encouragement by preferment and command as shall befit both to reward him and induce others to perform the like service. The inferior officers shall receive each ten pounds in money and shall be taken care of and placed in other ships before any other person whatsoever.
2. That in case any of the enemy's be fired the recompense shall be doubled to each man performing it. And the medal to the commander shall be such as shall particularly express the eminence of the service and his and other officers' preferment shall be suitable to it. . . .[27]

Entries in the *Rupert and Monck Letter Book* later in the year show that a number of these awards were made.

On 19 June the English fleet sailed from the Thames towards the Gunfleet. Rupert and Albemarle were again together in the *Royal Charles*, with Sir Joseph Jordan in the *Royal Oak* as Vice-Admiral of the Red and Sir Robert Holmes in the *Henry* as Rear-Admiral. The White Squadron was now commanded by Sir Thomas Allin in the *Royal James*; his principal officers were Sir Thomas Teddeman in the *Royal Katharine* and Richard Utber in the *Rupert*. The Blue was under Sir Jeremy Smith in the *Loyal London*, with Sir Edward Spragge and John Kempthorne as Vice-Admiral and Rear-Admiral.

The Dutch were already at sea. They had been quicker in their refitting than the English, and had left harbour on 28 June. De Ruyter was in command, with Lieutenant-Admiral Jan Evertsen, brother of the dead Cornelis, in the van and Cornelis van Tromp in the rear.

On Sunday, 22 July, the English discovered the Dutch under sail north-east of the Gunfleet. They were about six leagues off, and that evening the Prince and the Duke anchored in the Gunfleet.[28] 'The Generals were all day on deck,' recorded Sir Thomas Clifford, 'and sometimes a little rough with the pilots.'[29] Early next morning they weighed anchor and sailed northwards, the wind being south-south-east. The Dutch, being to the eastward, had the weather gage; the English were hoping to gain it from them, but conditions were against them, and at about 8 p.m., having temporarily lost sight of the enemy, they anchored off Orfordness.

Two ships were sent off to look for the Dutch, and on Tuesday they returned to report that the enemy were some five leagues to the south-east at the foot of the Galloper. The night before had been stormy, and the *Jersey*, her main topmast broken, had to return to Sheerness. The rest of the fleet bore down on the Dutch, but were driven into considerable disorder by the gale: 'they still kept the wind of us and if they had not been afraid to engage so near our sands they might have taken great advantage upon us for we were not only disordered and out of our line but very much separated and scattered from one another'.[30] At 8 p.m. both fleets anchored, the English thirty-three miles east of Orfordness and the Dutch twelve miles south-east of them.

Next day, the Feast of St James the Apostle, the two fleets converged. They were evenly matched, both having between eighty-five and ninety ships. The English weighed anchor at 2 a.m., and from then until 10 a.m. the fleets slowly approached one another. Neither was in perfect formation, but the English line, stretching for some five miles, was the straighter of the two. The Dutch were more in the form of a crescent, and there was a considerable gap between their centre and rear. When the rival forces met they were sailing parallel to each other almost due east, the English to the north of the Dutch.

The two vans were the first to engage, and the Dutch the first to fire. The signal to bear in was given from the *Royal Charles*, in accordance with the new fighting instructions, and soon the two centres were furiously engaged. In the rear, however, van Tromp, always inclined to pursue an independent line, instead of following the line put before the wind to weather the English Blue Squadron. It was a bold manoeuvre, and came near to succeeding; but it was no part of de Ruyter's plan and the Admiral was furious. The rear squadrons dropped away on the starboard tack, separated from the rest of the battle. The *Resolution* was disabled and burned, but Sir Jeremy Smith held his own in the confused struggle with Tromp.

In the rest of the action the fighting was fierce. Allin in the van asserted his superiority over the enemy. By one o'clock the Dutch van were in retreat to the eastward; Evertsen had been killed – the second of his family to die in this naval campaign – and two other flag-officers had fallen as well.

Action in the centre was the hottest of all. Rupert and Albemarle were in their element. The two foremost advocates of the 'Mêlée', they led their ships in a furious attack, grappling with the enemy and firing broadside after broadside. De Ruyter fought stubbornly. With Evertsen dead and his squadron beaten, and with Tromp out of sight to the westward, he had only his own centre squadron; but he was still full of fight. The two flagships fought each other at close quarters, and both suffered damage. 'The *Royal Charles* was much disabled by de Ruyter in yards masts and sails so that we were forced to give out to repair which held us almost an hour'.[31] As for de Ruyter, his *Seven Provinces* was completely dismasted, and he had to stand away.

The air was black with smoke, and the roaring of the guns drowned all other noises. The scene at the height of the fighting is vividly described by Prince Rupert's early biographer:

There you might see the Heads of some, the Arms, Legs, or Thighs of others, shot off, and others who were cut off by the middle with a Chain-Shott, breathing out their last in anguish and pain; some burning in ships fired, and others exposed to the mercy of the liquid Element, some of them sinking, whilst others who have learned the Art of Swimming, lift up their heads above water, and implore pity from their very Enemies, intreating them to save their lives, although with the loss of their Liberties: and yet in the midst of all these deplorable calamities, those that survive fight with as much resolution and fury as ever, their Courage and Valour being rather heightened than daunted or diminished thereby.[32]

By four o'clock the Dutch had had enough. De Ruyter with his usual skill gathered the remnants of his battered fleet together and began an ordered retreat, yet 'with great gallantry would make several tacks to fetch off his maimed ships and once endangered himself very much for his rescue of his second'.[33] Allin led the pursuit, but there was not enough wind for overtaking. During the night and next morning the chase continued, and Rupert sent in his little sloop the *Fan Fan* to harry de Ruyter's flagship. 'The little Fan Fan,' records Clifford,

. . . made up with her oars to de Ruyter and brought her two little guns on one side, and for near an hour continued plying broadside and broadside which was so pleasant a sight when no ship of either side could come near. There was so little wind that all ours fell into a laughter, and I believe the Dutch into indignation to see their Admiral so chased for he still shot his stern guns to the poor *Fan Fan* who came off with 2 or 3 shots between wind and water and had had one of her men killed by de Ruyter before as she lay behind the *Royal Charles* which put her upon the extraordinary chase to be revenged.[34]

By ten o'clock on the morning of 26 July the Dutch had gained the shallows off their own coast, and could be followed no farther. That evening they were joined by van Tromp, who had somehow learned of the defeat of the rest of the fleet and himself made for home, pursued by Smith. Tromp was promptly dismissed from his command for his insubordination.

The Four Days' Fight had been one of the longest sea battles in history, and the result had been inconclusive. On St James's Day the issue was decided in six hours, but it was quite as momentous a contest. It was a splendid English victory. Losses in ships were small on both sides, and de Ruyter had with his consummate seamanship been able to extricate the bulk of his fleet. But the ships were badly battered and damaged, and Dutch casualties were about 7,000, while the English were placed as low as 300.[35] The great Netherlands navy had been decisively beaten, and for the moment at least the English had command of the seas. It was a great triumph for Prince Rupert and the Duke of Albemarle. They had shown the dash and determination expected of them; they had kept admirable control of their ships (except for Smith's, which had been detached through the action of Tromp and which had played their part by preventing de Ruyter from being reinforced), and had shown in keeping to the new fighting instructions that they had learned the lessons of past reverses. The principle of concentrating the strongest possible force in breaking the enemy's line, put into practice on St James's Day, anticipated the tactics of Nelson.

The English admirals were quick to follow up their advantages. In the last days of July they appeared off Scheveningen, causing panic at The Hague. They then sailed triumphantly up the Dutch coast, arriving in sight of the Texel on 6 August. There news reached them that a large fleet of Indiamen was lying between the island of Vlieland and the mainland, and plans were laid to destroy it. Sir Robert Holmes was chosen for the command, and was given nine ships and a dozen fireships. He was to effect a landing and burn all stores as well as the ships in harbour; but it was made clear to him that there was to be no massacre. 'You are to issue your orders,' he was enjoined, 'that no violence be done to women or children, nor the inferior sort of people, unless in case of resistance, but you are to seize and secure the better sort of inhabitants and bring them aboard, to be disposed as we shall think fit. You are to take care there be some men allotted to the Dutch Capt. to preserve him from violence.'[36]

The expedition was a complete success. About 150 ships were destroyed, and all the storehouses on shore; while the orders to respect the lives of the inhabitants were strictly obeyed. The pecuniary loss to the Dutch was enormous, and 'Holmes's Bonfire' added immensely to the reputation of Prince Rupert's favourite captain.

This, however, was the last great English success of the war. Victuals were running short, and Rupert and Albemarle were forced to return to harbour. They continued to harry Dutch shipping on their way southwards, and captured a number of vessels laden with stores. On 15 August the fleet was back on the English coast, anchoring in Southwold Bay.

Meanwhile de Ruyter was making frantic efforts to prepare his fleet for renewed action. On 26 August he put to sea, making for the Channel where he hoped to link up with the Duc de Beaufort and the French fleet. Two days later the English, having revictualled and refitted, came out to prevent the junction. On 31 August the English and Dutch fleets were in sight of each other, but no engagement took place. The English became entangled in the Galloper shoals, the *Royal Charles* and other ships going aground. They soon broke free, but the fleet had to tack southward to get clear, and lost touch with the enemy. On the following day the Dutch were again sighted, and the English pursued them towards Calais. But a furious gale blew up and both fleets were compelled to make for harbour. The Dutch put in at Dunkirk, while the English fought their way westward to the Isle of Wight and anchored off St Helen's.

This was virtually the end of the naval campaign of 1666. The English held the straits, and from 6 September Rupert was in sole command. The reason for this lay in the vast calamity that had befallen England's capital city. On 2 September the Fire of London broke out, and for four days the town was a raging inferno. Almost the whole of what was then known as London (east of Temple Bar and excluding the city of Westminster) was reduced to a heap of smoking ruins. The King and the Duke of York made heroic personal efforts to restrict the damage, but with the narrow streets and wooden houses of seventeenth-century London the blaze defied the primitive fire-fighting apparatus of those days.

As the flames died down the King bethought himself of the great services rendered by the Duke of Albemarle during the Great Plague of the year before. Albemarle's brother-in-law Sir Thomas Clarges was sent with a message to the fleet, and the Duke left for London to take his part in the colossal task of rehabilitation.

345

There was little more. In mid-September Beaufort's fleet appeared briefly in the Channel, and Rupert made towards it. But King Louis had heard that Rupert's fleet stood between the French and Dutch and sent orders to Beaufort to return to Brest. He received them at the critical moment, and made for home. One ship became a casualty, and Clarendon tells a story characteristic of Rupert's behaviour in war:

> . . . But his (Beaufort's) Vice-Admiral, being the biggest and the best Ship but one in the Fleet, and carrying seventy Pieces of Cannon, pursuing the Course He was directed, in the Dark of the Night fell amongst the *English*, as the rest had done if it had not been for that Advertisement (of Beaufort's change of course); and after a little defending himself, which He saw was to no Purpose, was taken Prisoner, and desired to be brought to Prince *Rupert*, who knew him well and treated him as a gallant Person ought to be and caused many things which belonged to his own Person to be restored to him; and when he was brought into *England*, He found another Kind of Reception (though He was a Prisoner in the *Tower*) than any of the *English*, though of the same Quality, met with abroad. . . .[37]

On 25 September Rupert was at sea again, having heard that forty Dutch ships were off Dover. But once again the weather intervened, and both fleets put back. Thereafter English and Dutch broke off operations for the winter. The English anchored at the Buoy of the Nore on 3 October, and two days later Rupert presented himself at Whitehall.

He was given a warm welcome. There were murmurings and recriminations in plenty at shortcomings in the conduct of the war, but it was recognized that Rupert had proved himself a fine fighting leader and he was as popular with the generality of the English people as he had ever been. He took up residence at his lodgings in the Stone Gallery of Whitehall Palace amid general acclamation.

Nevertheless the Second Dutch War was not destined to end on the note of triumph resulting from the victory of St James's Day. Before a year had passed national rejoicing was to give place to shame and disaster.

First came accusations against the Commissioners of the Navy. Rupert himself had plenty of grievances against them, and no sooner had he returned to London than he launched out into denunciation. The fleet had been ill-supplied; food and beer were of inferior quality. Accounts had been falsified, and peculation, bribery and corruption were rife. An immediate inquiry was held by the King in person, and Pepys as Clerk of the Acts found himself called upon to put up a defence of the Commissioners. On 7 October he described what happened:

> . . . I with Sir J. Mennes to White-hall, where met by W. Batten and Lord Brouncker, to attend the King and Duke of York at the Cabinet; . . . And

anon were called in to the green-room, where the King, Duke of York, Prince Rupert, Lord Chancellor, Lord Treasurer, Duke of Albemarle, G. Carteret, W. Coventry, Morrice. Nobody beginning, I did, and made a current and, I thought, a good speech, laying open the ill state of the Navy – by the greatness of the debt – greatness of work to do against next year – the time and materials it would take – and our incapacity, through a total want of money. I had no sooner done, but Prince Rupert rose up and told the King in a heat that whatever the gentleman had said, he had brought home his fleet in as good a condition as ever any fleet was brought home – that twenty boats would be as many as the fleet would want – and all the anchors and cables left in the storm might be taken up again. This arose from my saying, among other things we had to do, that the fleet was come in, the greatest fleet that ever his Majesty had yet together, and that in as bad condition as the enemy or weather could put it. . . . I therefore did only answer that I was sorry for his Highness's offence, but that what I said was but the report we received from those entrusted in the fleet to inform us. He muttered, and repeated what he had said, and so after a long silence on all hands, nobody, not so much as the Duke of Albemarle, seconding the Prince, nor taking notice of what he said, we withdrew. I was not a little troubled at this passage; and the more, when speaking with Jack Fenn about it, he told me that the Prince will now be asking who this Pepys is, and find him to be a creature of my Lord Sandwiches, and therefore this were done only to disparage him. . . .[38]

Sir William Batten was sent to report on the condition of the fleet, but no further action was taken. The King had complete confidence in his commanders-in-chief; but he doubtless recognized that Pepys was right in that 'a total want of money' was at the root of all trouble. It was this lack of money that led directly to the humiliation of the following year.

Before this happened Rupert was taken seriously ill. His old head-wound was causing him great pain, and it appeared that a particle of his skull had been driven in upon the brain. In January 1667 he was so ill that it was reported on the Exchange that he was dead. Pepys reported with malicious glee that 'it seems, as Dr. Clerke also tells me, it is a clap of the pox which he got about twelve years ago, and hath eaten to his head and come up through his scull'.[39]

His life in danger, Prince Rupert was twice subjected to the fearsome operation known as trepanning. A hole was bored in his head, and the offending piece of bone extracted. When one considers the state of surgery at that time, the primitive instruments and the absence of anaesthetic, one can but wonder that he survived. But his robust constitution once more pulled him through, and when he began to recover he even used his scientific and mechanical ingenuity to assist his surgeons. 'Prince Rupert has again been trepanned,' wrote the news-letter writer Henry Muddiman on 21 February, 'the former not having gone down deep enough; this gave him present ease, by letting out a great quantity of corrupt matter, since which he has slept better, and is amending; he often diverts himself in his work house, where, among other curiosities, he had made instruments which the surgeons use in dressing him, which do it with more ease than any formerly used.'[40] On 13 February Pepys wrote that 'the Prince, I hear, is every day better and better'.[41]

Rupert was still a sick man, however, and for some weeks remained secluded. As late as 3 April Pepys, who was constantly in the vicinity of Whitehall, wrote: 'This day I saw Prince Rupert abroad in the Vane-room, pretty well as he used to be, and looks as well, only something appears to be under his periwigg on the crown of his head.'[42] Presumably he was wearing some sort of dressing or plate over the wound.

In the meantime the momentous decision had been taken not to fit out a fleet for the coming summer. The Treasury was on the verge of bankruptcy. The war, the Plague and the Fire of London had all played their part in depleting the nation's finances; while King Charles was having difficulties with the House of Commons. The first enthusiasm of the Cavalier Parliament was waning; the Commons disliked the King's policy of religious toleration, and for the rest of his reign became reluctant to supply funds unless he conformed with their views. At the same time peace negotiations with the Dutch had opened at Breda, and it was hoped that there would be no more hostilities. So in March the King and council decided to lay up the great ships in the Medway, at Harwich and at Portsmouth; to fortify these places as far as possible, and to keep only two small squadrons at sea for minor tasks.

In the circumstances it seemed a not unreasonable decision; yet it proved calamitous. Albemarle protested, and Rupert repeatedly warned the Government of the danger. But Rupert was in no condition to exert the force of his personality, and the peace party had their way.

Retribution came in June. On the 7th of that month the horrifying news reached London that de Ruyter with a fleet of seventy ships was off the Gunfleet; and there was no fleet to stop him. Unopposed, the Dutch sailed up the Medway. On 10 June they stormed Sheerness. Two days later they entered Chatham dockyard, burned five ships, and captured the *Royal Charles*.

In London crisis measures were put in hand; but it was too late to do much. Albemarle was sent to Chatham to take command; Rupert, in his still weakened state of health, to Woolwich. There the Prince, with a hurriedly raised regiment of foot, organized makeshift defences, pressing local carts and horses into service. But the Dutch did not get as far as Woolwich.

Albemarle was working against great odds. The dockyard officials had deserted their posts and fled; so had the population, and it was hard to find workmen. But the Duke had some land forces, and firing from the shore they succeeded in sinking two Dutch vessels below Gillingham. He then laid a strong iron chain, prepared beforehand as part of the defence measures, across the river, protected by a small shore battery at either end. His efforts were not in vain. There was a fierce bombardment, but the Dutch progressed no farther than Upnor Castle. They had expended nearly all their fireships, and could achieve no more. On 14 June they withdrew, towing the *Royal Charles* with them as a prize.

After the withdrawal de Ruyter continued to hang about the southeast coast of England, blockading the ports and making occasional attacks on English shipping. For more than a month the Dutch dominated the Channel, and the court at Whitehall was in constant fear of renewed invasion. Then, on 31 July, a treaty of peace was signed at Breda.

The Medway episode was a tremendous blow to English prestige, and its financial repercussions were considerable. It had, however, little effect on the Breda negotiations. The treaty indicated victory to neither side. Captures of territory during the war were recognized: England retained New York, and the Netherlands Surinam. All the ferocious fighting had resulted in stalemate, and it was highly probable that after a breathing space the struggle would be renewed.

CHAPTER 4

LAST COMMAND

THE most momentous result of the humiliation of the Medway was the fall of the Earl of Clarendon. Parliament and public opinion demanded a scapegoat, and the obvious one was the Chancellor, the King's principal adviser. King Charles, who had tired of him long since, made no attempt to save him, allowing himself to be carried with the tide. Parliament was prorogued in July 1667, and it seemed certain that when it met again a motion for the impeachment of the Chancellor would be passed. The King therefore suggested, through Clarendon's son-in-law the Duke of York, that his chief minister should resign before this happened. Clarendon was obstinate, saying that he would not deliver up the Great Seal unless he was deprived of it; the King thereupon dismissed him. The anger of Parliament was not appeased, and before the end of the year Clarendon had fled abroad to escape impeachment.

Charles II has been much blamed for his treatment of the minister who had been his right-hand man since the Restoration as well as through most of the years of exile. But in truth the Chancellor had done much to bring about his own downfall. Always pompous and self-important, he had in his years of power become progressively more autocratic. He would brook no opposition and he antagonized his master by bullying him about his private life and by opposing his plans for religious toleration, a matter in which the King felt deeply.

As for the failure of the Second Dutch War, Clarendon may not have been the most guilty party; but as the King's chief minister he could fairly be blamed. He had exerted little authority over the sequence of events, and did not disguise his ignorance of the sea. 'He confessed that he did not even know where Sheerness was and that when he was on the river Thames his sole thought was how to get on shore again as soon as possible.'[1]

It is at least arguable that the King's action saved his Chancellor from the worst consequences of his own behaviour. Parliament and people were howling for Clarendon's blood, much as they had howled for the blood of Strafford twenty-six years before. And King Charles had no need to be reminded of what had happened on that occasion. He was far from all-powerful, and could not have saved his faithful servant had Lord and Commons concurred in destroying him. Yet he was unquestionably glad to be rid of him. 'The truth is,' the King wrote to Ormonde, 'his behaviour and humour was grown so insupportable to myself, and to all the world also, that I could not longer endure it, and it was impossible for me to live with it and do those things with the Parliament that must be done or the government will be lost.'[2]

Clarendon had no successor as Chancellor. Sir Orlando Bridgeman received the Seal, but with the inferior title of Lord Keeper and with little or no political authority. Arlington was now the most influential minister, with responsibility for foreign affairs as Secretary of State. He was the King's close personal friend and always ready to defer to his master. During the next few years others came to share his power. Southampton, the Lord Treasurer, died in 1667, and the Treasury was entrusted to a commission, the most important member of which was Sir Thomas Clifford, an able administrator, a man of principle and integrity, and a gallant sailor who had served with Prince Rupert in the late war. Of a very different nature was the Duke of Buckingham, brilliant and unstable, who held no official high office but exercised influence through his membership of the Privy Council, his wealth and the greatness of his name. Others were the slippery Lord Ashley (Anthony Ashley Cooper), Chancellor of the Exchequer, and James Maitland, Earl of Lauderdale, a blunt and extremely intelligent Caledonian who was responsible for Scottish affairs. These five, through the coincidence of their initials, became known as the Cabal. They did not constitute a cabinet. The King would consult now with one, now with another; state secrets which he shared with some were withheld from others.

What Rupert thought of these changes can only be conjectured. The old enmity between him and Clarendon had been replaced by a degree of mutual respect; but he was on no very cordial terms with either Clarendon or Arlington. On at least one occasion the Prince's dislike for Arlington flared into open hostility. According to a news-letter on 2 September 1667 the two had 'High words in Council',[3] and it was even reported, though not on very reliable authority, that 'Prince Rupert had struck Lord Arlington a box on the ear, and knocked off his hat and periwig'.[4]

With the other members of the Cabal, however, relations were better. Rupert thought highly of Clifford, and during the Second Dutch War had recommended him to the King for promotion in the navy. With Buckingham, the brother of his great friend the Duchess of Richmond, he had in the past been on cordial terms, though there was friction at times. Lauderdale was an old comrade in Royalist politics during the interregnum, and Ashley was a surprisingly consistent friend.

Nevertheless, in the years of peace that followed the Second Dutch War, Prince Rupert took no prominent part in public affairs. He did, however, continue to concern himself with naval matters. He fought for the rights of his officers whose pay was in arrears, demanding that the matter should 'come before the King and Council, and so the poor men have that which is due to them'.[5] According to Pepys, his championship of his officers led him into a dispute with the Duke of York, who protested at the supersession of a certain Captain Batts by an officer named Greene who had previously been dismissed for drunkenness. Rupert hotly defended Greene, and an argument took place. When it was over, Rupert commented to Pepys: 'God damn me, if they will turn out every man that will be drunk, they must turn out all the commanders in the fleete. What is the matter if he be drunk, so when he comes to fight he do his work?'[6]

When in the autumn of 1667 Rupert and Albemarle were invited to write their reports on the management of the Second Dutch War, Rupert's narrative contained furious allegations of neglect by those responsible for supplies during the 1666 campaign. Casks were delivered staved in, provisions were seriously defective, beer barrels were twenty gallons short in quantity. 'This want of provisions,' concluded the Prince, 'did manifestly tend to the extraordinary prejudice of his Majesty's service in that whole summer.'[7]

Rupert's criticism aroused considerable controversy, and Parliament appointed a committee to investigate his charges of neglect. But in the way of parliamentary committees it came to no firm conclusions, and little was done to improve naval administration. Rupert and Albemarle were formally thanked in the Lords for their services in the late war.

For the rest, Prince Rupert in these years devoted himself largely to social life, to his artistic and scientific interests, and to sport. He played tennis regularly at Whitehall; probably also at Hampton Court, where the tennis-court, still in use today, had been built by King Henry VIII in 1530. Pepys on 2 September 1667 'went to see a great match at tennis, between Prince Rupert and one Captain Cooke, against Bab. May and the elder Chichly; where the King was, and Court; and it seems are the best players at tennis in the nation'.[8]

Rupert was constantly with the King and the Duke of York in their leisure hours. In the same month of September 1667 the three went together to Bagshot for two days' hunting, and in the following March Rupert was with his cousins at Newmarket, already renowned as the centre of English racing. In May 1670 he accompanied them to Dover to meet Charles II's beloved sister 'Minette', now Duchesse d'Orléans, on her second and last visit to the land of her birth. At some time during this period also Rupert joined the court at Tunbridge Wells where he formed that association with the actress Margaret Hughes which was to prove the most durable of his life.

His popularity with the people at large had grown with the years. The country was in a disturbed state. Fire, plague and war had bred unrest and discontent, and neither court nor government could boast of much support among the populace. But nobody blamed the Prince for the nation's troubles. His stern integrity and his freedom from the shackles of clique and faction had caught the public imagination; courtiers might laugh at him behind his back, but the people loved him, and acclaimed him when he appeared in public.

One lifelong passion that had not faded with the years is illustrated in the files of the *London Gazette*. He still surrounded himself with animals, particularly dogs. But dog thieves seem to have been exceptionally active at the court of Charles II. The King more than once had to complain of his famous spaniels being stolen, and his cousin was similarly the victim of robbers. At the end of October 1667 the *Gazette* reported: 'Lost in Deans-yard . . . a young white spaniel about six months old, black head, red eyebrows, & a black spot on his back. Lost also about the same time near Camberwell, a York: buck-hound, having black spots upon his back, red ears & wall-eye & P.R. upon his near shoulder; both belong to H.H. Pr. Ru.' A few months later the loss was reported of 'a light fallow coloured greyhound bitch, with a sore under her jaw & a scar on her side'. And in March 1668 'was lost out of Whitehall a small blue Bitch greyhound, with a white neck and breast of H.H. Pr. Ru.'. Anybody finding her would be 'well rewarded for his pains'. How many thieves 'found' the dogs and were rewarded for their pains there is no means of knowing. Obviously the canine friends of so celebrated a popular hero had their market value as well as being prized as souvenirs.

In September 1668 Rupert was appointed Governor and Captain of Windsor Castle – 'fee 10s. a day; the first payment to commence from Michaelmas 1668'.[9] Hardly a princely salary, even by seventeenth-century values; but the post was congenial.

The early days of 1670 saw the death of George Monk Duke of Albemarle; a comrade in arms, on and off, since the 1630s, and a man for whom Rupert had a deep liking and respect. Many of the Prince's old friends were now departed. William of Hesse-Cassel had died shortly after the Restoration. Lord Craven still survived, and so did Will Legge, but the latter's death was only two years off. Rupert must have felt the loneliness of advancing years; but he had Margaret Hughes now. And he still corresponded occasionally with his sisters. Louise was remote in her convent at Maubuisson, but Elizabeth and Sophia wrote sometimes to him, more often to Craven, with whom he was always in close touch. Elizabeth, writing from Herford to the old family friend on 23 October 1668, thanked him for a portrait of himself which had found a place in her bedroom beside one of Rupert. On 24 July 1671 she wrote saying how glad she was that Rupert had had his home (Windsor Castle?) fitted up so well, but thought he must put away his dogs if he wanted to have good furniture. A fortnight later she had changed her mind. Writing again to Craven, she asked him to tell Rupert that 'she esteems his content more than a clean house and therefore does not wish him to put away his dogs'.[10]

Sophia, now Duchess of Brunswick, received a portrait of Rupert from Craven, but when it reached her in November 1669 she found that 'it does not do justice to his martial appearance'.[11] But she expressed the warmest affection for her brother, whom she described to Craven as 'le meillure Prince du monde'.[12]

All in all, Rupert in those early days at Windsor was probably as contented as he had ever been. But the clouds of war were again gathering.

The causes of the Third Dutch War were basically the same as those of the previous conflict, augmented by the desire for revenge for the humiliation of the Medway. But the war was preceded by several years of tortuous diplomacy with which Prince Rupert was not concerned.

There was one important difference between the two wars. Throughout the first ten years after the Restoration King Charles had kept his eyes fixed on his diplomatic goal, an alliance with Louis XIV's France; a goal which was opposed by many of his ministers and by the bulk of the House of Commons. In 1670 he had achieved his aim in the Secret Treaty of Dover, by which the two monarchs agreed to join forces against the Dutch Republic. So when hostilities opened on 17 March 1672 France, which had been in alliance with the Netherlands in the earlier conflict, was England's ally.

The means by which hostilities were brought about were flagrantly cynical, Sir Robert Holmes being ordered to get himself embroiled with the naval escort to a Dutch merchant convoy. The English were palpably the aggressors, but King Charles promptly declared war. The French King followed suit in accordance with the terms of the Treaty of Dover.

The war that now began was waged by land and sea, for France had the most powerful army in Europe and the arrangement was that this army should invade the Netherlands overland, assisted by a small English contingent. It was obvious, however, that the main campaign would be by sea; the Dutch could not be overcome without the defeat of their formidable navy. France was to supply a fleet of thirty-six vessels, but by the Treaty of Dover the supreme naval command was to go to an English admiral.

For this combined command it was essential that an officer of the highest prestige should be appointed, and though the Duke of York was still the heir to the throne, for Catherine of Braganza had failed to produce a child, it was decided that the Lord High Admiral should be allowed once more to risk his life at sea. Rupert would have fulfilled the conditions almost as well, and the fact that he was not appointed has led a number of his biographers to conclude that he was opposed to the war. Eva Scott categorically states, though without producing any evidence, that 'Rupert and Ormonde vigorously opposed the declaration of war',[13] and suggests that the Prince remained at home for this reason.

This alleged dislike of the war has been attributed to Rupert's reluctance to fight in alliance with Frenchmen against a country with which he had been closely associated for a great part of his life. It is doubtful if such sentiments influenced him. His sympathies were with the House of Orange, which had befriended his family so warmly in days gone by. But no Prince of Orange now ruled the Netherlands as Stadtholder. Since the death of William II, Charles II's brother-in-law, the Netherlands had been a republic in fact as well as in name; power was mainly in the hands of John de Witt, Grand Pensionary of Holland. The young Stadtholder William III, posthumous son of William II, was about to come into his own and was now appointed Captain-General of the Dutch land forces; but as yet he was rigidly excluded from political power.

In fact, from the opening of the war, Rupert played a vital part. Like Albemarle when the Duke of York took command of the fleet at the beginning of the Second Dutch War, he was chosen to look after naval affairs ashore as the Lord High Admiral's deputy. The appointment was announced in a letter to the Prince from his cousin James, dated 2 May 1672:

> His Majesty requiring my attendance with H.M. fleet now bound forth to sea, it will be necessary that some person be authorised in my absence to take care of the affairs of H.M. Navy at London. And the great zeal and affection which you have always had for the service, and your large experience and ability in these affairs, having fully assured me that I could not make a choice more advantageous for H.M. Service, I do therefore desire you will take upon you the charge, care and management of

355

the business of the Navy at London in my absence. . . . And I do hereby require the several officers of H.M. Navy, yards and ships, carefully to obey and observe such commands and orders as they shall from time to time receive from you.[14]

The appointment, though in effect it made Rupert Vice-Admiral and Lieutenant of the Admiralty, was an informal one; and so had Albemarle's been. The reason in both cases was that there already was a Vice-Admiral of England in the person of the Earl of Sandwich, who had been appointed to the office shortly after the Restoration. In 1665 Sandwich was at sea with the Duke of York, and so he now was again. The cloud of scandal which had driven him to Spain after the Bergen affair had dispersed, and he was chosen as Admiral of the Blue and the Duke's right-hand man.

Whatever the reason for his not being sent to sea, Rupert gave no sign of dissatisfaction; he threw himself into the task which he had been given with his customary vigour. He had been a bitter critic of the administration of the previous war; he would see that there was no cause for complaint now. The Lord High Admiral's letter was followed on 3 May by the issue of a warrant to the Prince 'to take charge of the business of the Navy at London during the Duke of York's absence',[15] and the next day he called a meeting of the Navy Commissioners. Samuel Pepys, now coming into his own as an efficient and painstaking civil servant, found himself as Clerk of the Acts of the Navy Board subjected to the full force of the Prince's administrative zeal. On the same day, 4 May, he received a peremptory demand from Sir Joseph Williamson, Clerk of the Privy Council:

Prince Rupert desires that you and the rest of the Board attend him and some other of the Lords at his lodgings at Whitehall, at nine on Monday morning, and be prepared as thoroughly as you can to give account of these particulars:– An exact list of the fleet and all other the King's ships, their stations and condition. The want of small stores in the ship, if there be any. The condition of victuals – and that particular, not general only. The stores of cordage hemp, pitch, tar, etc. Fireships, in what condition they are, and where? What bulks there are, and where? And in the meantime look out for ten of the stoutest merchant ships in the river, to know their force, conditions, etc.[16]

As Rupert began, so he went on. He kept in close touch with the Duke of York at sea, maintained a constant correspondence with Navy Board officials, issued orders to local authorities on victualling and maintenance of the fleet, went down to Sheerness to inspect the regiments stationed there, and personally superintended the fortification of the coast. As a result there were no grumbles this time at inefficient management on shore.

The years of peace that followed the Third Dutch War were to see the development of the Royal Navy into a highly organized and efficiently administered force, with a cohesion that had been lacking in the haphazard, *ad hoc* arrangements hitherto in evidence when war brought the fleet into action. The major portion of the credit for this revolution has been rightly given to Pepys; but Prince Rupert's energy in the summer of 1672, and his influence thereafter, played a vital part. The administrative capacity of the bustling civil servant, his hard work and devotion to detail, worked wonders. But the driving force was Rupert's.

While a stream of orders, covering every aspect of naval administration, poured forth from the Prince's office, the Duke of York put to sea. Early in May the French contingent arrived at Portsmouth, and the junction of the allied fleets was effected. The French formed the White Squadron, designed to fight in the van. Its commander was the Comte d'Estrées, Vice-Admiral of France, whose career up to this time had been almost entirely on land; his second-in-command, Abraham Duquesne, was an experienced seaman, but was on consistently bad terms with his superior.

The Duke of York had a total of ninety-eight ships: a formidable battle array to confront the seventy-five which were all the Dutch could muster. The Dutch, however, were a homogeneous force, free from the danger of national rivalries; they had, moreover, the inestimable advantage of being commanded once more by the illustrious de Ruyter, the greatest sailor of his time.

In the event there was only one naval battle in 1672, and that, like so many of the engagements in the Anglo-Dutch wars, was indecisive. It took place on 28 May off Southwold Bay (or Sole Bay as it was more commonly called).

The allies, whose intelligence was faulty, were caught on a lee shore, with little room for manoeuvre, when de Ruyter attacked from the north-east. D'Estrées either misunderstood his orders or failed to carry them out; a gap opened between the White and the other two squadrons. The Duke in the *Prince* and Sandwich in the *Royal James* fought furiously for several hours, and Admiral van Ghent, de Ruyter's second-in-command and leader of the Dutch van, was killed, but the English had a comparable loss when Sandwich, transferring to another vessel when the *Royal James* was set ablaze, was drowned.

The Duke of York, who had been compelled during the battle to shift his flag from the *Prince* to the *St Michael*, had behaved with the greatest gallantry, but he had been outmanoeuvred by de Ruyter. Sole

Bay was a drawn battle, but English losses were heavier than the Dutch, and de Ruyter with an inferior force had so crippled the English fleet that it could attempt no further action that year.

The 1672 campaign was followed by important changes in both countries. King Louis's troops had overrun large areas of the Netherlands and a surge of popular discontent led to the overthrow and murder of John de Witt. The young Prince of Orange, who had put up a brave resistance, was restored to all the offices held by his father, and henceforth as Captain-General and as Stadtholder of Holland was to guide the fortunes of the Dutch Republic.

In England the changes were less spectacular but equally far-reaching. The death of Sandwich enabled Rupert's appointment to be placed on a regular footing, and on 15 August 1672 an order was made for the 'grant for life to Prince Rupert . . . of the office of Vice-Admiral of England, and Lieutenant of the Navy'.[17]

More important were the developments that led to the gradual break-up of the Cabal and the defeat of King Charles's policy of religious toleration. Largely through the financial acumen of Clifford, the King had been able to carry on the war without the help of the House of Commons, which had become increasingly suspicious of his religious designs; two days before the outbreak of hostilities he issued his second Declaration of Independence. But his failure to win the war in one campaign meant that he would have to recall Parliament, which had been prorogued in April 1671.

In March 1672 King Charles rewarded the Cabal with a hand-out of titles: Clifford became Lord Clifford of Chudleigh, Ashley Earl of Shaftesbury, Arlington an earl and Lauderdale a duke. But now new rifts appeared. Lauderdale and Buckingham became opposed to Clifford and Arlington, while a new figure came to prominence in the person of Sir Thomas Osborne, another financial expert. In November the King, preparing to face a parliamentary storm, reshuffled his ministry. Shaftesbury was made Lord Chancellor and Clifford Lord Treasurer, an appointment which led to a breach between Clifford and Arlington who had hoped for the post. Osborne was made a privy councillor, and Henry Coventry, elder brother of Sir William, a Secretary of State.

Parliament met in February 1673, and quickly showed its temper. A wave of 'no popery' agitation was sweeping the country. Details of the Secret Treaty of Dover, under which King Charles had announced his intention of becoming a Catholic at an unspecified date, had leaked out, and suspicions increased that both the King and the Duke of York were Catholic converts. In the case of the Duke they were true. When his wife, Clarendon's daughter, died in 1671, it was revealed that she had been a Catholic for the last year of her life; and he himself, though this was not yet known, had been received into the Church of Rome on a visit to Ghent in 1669.[18]

King Charles faced his Parliament with his usual equanimity, and demanded supplies to carry on the war. But the Commons were adamant. Penal statutes in matters of religion, they maintained, could not be suspended except by Act of Parliament; therefore King Charles's Declaration of Indulgence was unconstitutional. The King manoeuvred to defeat the opposition; then he gave in. No monarch ever knew better when to yield than Charles II; in this he was the antithesis of his father. He would fight and run away, so long as he lived to fight another day. The King got his money, and the Declaration of Indulgence was withdrawn.

Parliament proceeded to consolidate its victory. On 29 March 1673 was passed the Test Act, 'for preventing changes which may happen from popish recusants and quieting the minds of His Majesty's good subjects',[19] under which any person holding public office in the Government or in the Royal Navy, or in the service of the King or the Duke of York, was required to take the oaths of supremacy and allegiance, to receive the sacrament according to the Church of England in public on or before the first of August following, and to abjure the doctrine of transubstantiation. Any such person who failed to comply was to be held incapable of public office.

Two men in the highest counsels of the King were affected by the Act. Lord Clifford appears to have become a Catholic at some recent date, though the fact has never been established; at any rate he refused to take the sacrament in an Anglican church, and on 19 June he resigned the office of Lord Treasurer. He was succeeded by Sir Thomas Osborne.

The Test Act was aimed first and foremost at the Duke of York, who had become anathema to the House of Commons. He too refused to take the sacrament, and on 15 June he laid down all his official appointments, including that of Lord High Admiral. As to the command of the fleet at sea, it appears that the Duke, whether because he foresaw what was to come or because it was once more considered inadvisable for him to risk his life in battle, had resigned this post even before the Test Act became law. There was only one possible successor. Prince Rupert alone possessed both the naval experience necessary for the appointment and the position and prestige required for the commander of a joint Anglo-French fleet. Presumably, in spite of his Calvinism, he made no scruple about taking the Anglican sacraments. He was not, however, reappointed to his old post of Lord High Admiral; the Admiralty went into commission.

Exactly when the Prince took over his first sole command of the

English fleet, except for a brief period in the latter part of 1666, is uncertain, but it would seem to have been before the end of March. On 6 April the King, writing to him to give him authority to receive a commission from the King of France, mentioned 'having given you supreme command of the fleet for this year's campaign';[20] and Rupert had apparently asked for this authority some days earlier.

Having taken up his command, the Prince almost immediately met with a major frustration. He wanted to have with him his faithful follower and friend Sir Robert Holmes, and he applied to the King for Holmes's appointment to one of the senior posts in the fleet. 'I therefore once more desire you,' he wrote to Arlington on 10 May, 'to try to get Sir R. Holmes into play. . . . Pray propose this way to his Majesty, which is to make him a Lieut-General, or send him aboard, and I will give him the command, when there's occasion and without any disturbance to the officers of the fleet; in the meantime he shall go in my ship.'[21]

To this and later representations he met with a polite but definite refusal. King Charles, it appeared, had no intention of sending Holmes to the fleet. Why this should have been so is a puzzle. The solution has been widely advanced that the thwarting of Rupert's wishes was the result of intrigues by adherents to the Duke of York who wanted the Duke's successor to fail. This view stems mainly from the eighteenth-century naval historian John Campbell, who wrote that Rupert was at odds with the Cabal, whose members plotted to introduce officers into the fleet who would make the commander's task impossible. Campbell continued:

All the captains in the fleet were the creatures of the duke of York, and were told, though perhaps without truth, that glancing at the prince's character would oblige his royal highness. There needed no more to set these folk to work. They began to find fault with every order he gave, and to misrepresent every measure he took, but the prince quickly convinced them, that, instead of hurting his character, they would, by such conduct totally destroy their own.[22]

Campbell seems to have based his allegations on the pamphlet *An Exact Relation of the several Engagements and Actions of His Majesty's Fleet under the command of His Highness Prince Rupert*, whose author, 'a person in command in the fleet',[23] threw out rather vague remarks about some unspecified 'persons of high trust under His Majesty', who 'had such an influence upon affairs, that when they could no longer hinder the issuing forth of His Highness's Commission, they took care so to qualify and curtail it, that they left him not power to make so much as one

Officer in the whole fleet, unless he could upon request obtain the favour so to do'.[24] The theory that the Cabal and the Duke's naval followers were the villains of the piece has been followed by biographers of Rupert. But Campbell wrote in the Whig tradition of his time, according to which all papists and James Duke of York in particular, were agents of the devil. That there were intrigues going on at court may be accepted; in the seventeenth century (as in every other period) there always were. But the Duke's supersession by Rupert was not caused by any personal difference. The Cabal, moreover, so far as it had any real entity at all, was in process of dissolution. Buckingham was out of favour; Clifford was on the point of resignation, and in any case was a friend and admirer of Rupert. With Shaftesbury the Prince was on excellent terms, and Lauderdale, who was now appointed to the Admiralty Commission, had hitherto taken little part in English affairs and belonged to no particular faction. Only Arlington can be classed as an enemy. As for the fleet, the senior officers were those who had served in the Dutch wars under both Rupert and James, and were attached at least as much to the one as to the other.

A more probable explanation of the rejection of Holmes is that of a clash of personalities. After the death of Sandwich Sir Edward Spragge had been appointed Admiral of the Blue. He and Holmes, both forceful characters, were well known to be on terms of rivalry if not enmity, and it may well have been considered that to give senior posts in the fleet to both of them would be asking for trouble. The author of the *Exact Relation* states indeed that this was the official pretext given, but hints that it was merely a cloak for some deeper design. Holmes's biographer, however, is inclined to accept it as genuine.[25] Nevertheless the continued refusal of the Government to accede to the wishes of the commander-in-chief is not easy to explain.

Spragge had always been a follower of Rupert, being the brother-in-law of Will Legge, who had died in 1672. But his appointment to the highest subordinate post in the fleet was to have unfortunate consequences.

Meanwhile Rupert had taken up his post. According to the agreement signed with the French the two allied fleets were to assemble off Portsmouth on 5 April 1673; but neither was ready by this date, and the plan was altered by events. Most of the English ships had wintered in the Thames, where the Prince embarked in the *St Michael* early in April. Some light vessels were in the Downs, and there were other ships at Portsmouth; these included the new *Royal Charles* under Captain Richard Haddock, built to replace the proud vessel captured by the Dutch in the Medway and intended as Prince Rupert's flagship. The French were assembling in Camaret Bay near Brest, but it was May before d'Estrées put to sea. On the same day Rupert set sail for the Downs. His orders were to make for the Dutch coast, attack the enemy fleet in harbour, and land troops on the Netherlands coast in support of the French army. Five thousand soldiers were to be embarked in the ship, while a further 6,000 men were assembling at Yarmouth. The strategic aim was to destroy the Dutch fleet so that the coast could be blockaded and the campaign ashore maintained.

It was, however, the Dutch who moved first. De Ruyter had assembled his fleet off Flushing, and on 2 May he emerged with some forty ships and made for the Thames estuary. His plan was to block the entrance to the river by sinking ships in the narrow channel along the Essex coast, and then, having imprisoned the main body of the English fleet, to confront the rest with a numerical advantage. It was a daring man-oeuvre, and England was faced with a repetition of the Medway disaster. But Rupert was equal to the occasion. He quickly summed up the situation, and dispatched sufficient ships to the danger-point to prevent the sinking of ships. The Dutch were held up for a day by fog, and when they reached the narrows they found the English massing in some force. De Ruyter turned tail and made for home. Meanwhile Rupert sent ketches to mark the sands, and 'turned through with the whole fleet, though this was never done before on an ebbing tide and is expressly forbidden in the rules of Trinity House'.[26] The move, he reported, was effected with great facility.

The initiative now passed to the English. On 13 May Rupert shifted his flag to the *Royal Charles* in Rye Bay, and three days later d'Estrées arrived with the French contingent. On the same day King Charles came to Rye with the Duke of York, still his chief naval adviser though in an unofficial capacity, and at a council of war held on 17 May it was decided to sail immediately to the attack, making for the Schooneveld, a funnel-shaped channel off Flushing, where de Ruyter's fleet was known to be assembling. In the belief that the outnumbered Dutch might withdraw within the sands, a pursuit force of thirty-five light vessels and ten fireships was to be sent ahead to make chase. This force was in three divisions and no single commander was appointed; the senior captain of each division was to act on his own initiative.

Rupert sailed with his fleet on 20 May, and two days later reached the Dutch coast, where he saw that the Dutch were anchored in the Schooneveld. The weather was stormy and continued so till the morning of the 27th, making any offensive action impracticable. That day the wind dropped, and at a council of war north of Ostend, where the English had anchored, it was decided to attack next day.

The English superiority in ships and fire-power was pronounced. Rupert had a fleet of seventy-six vessels carrying a total of 4,812 guns;

de Ruyter fifty-two ships and 3,171 guns.[27] Against this the Dutch were ensconced in a strong defensive position within their own waters.

Rupert led the fleet in the *Royal Charles*. With him as Vice-Admiral in his Red Squadron was Sir John Harman who was unfortunately afflicted at this time with gout; according to the *Exact Relation* he was unable to move from his cabin. The Rear-Admiral of the Red was Sir John Chicheley.

Second-in-command of the fleet was Sir Edward Spragge as Admiral of the Blue in the *Prince*; his Vice-Admiral was Sir John Kempthorne. As Rear-Admiral he should have had Sir John Narbrough, but Narbrough had been sent on a convoy to the Mediterranean. In his place was appointed the Earl of Ossory, son and heir of the Duke (as he had now become) of Ormonde; deficient in naval experience, but in courage and character a worthy son of a worthy father.

As in the year before, the French formed the White Squadron. D'Estrées was still in command, flying his flag in the *Reine*, but Duquesne had fallen out with him and had been sent home. D'Estrées's senior commanders were Rear-Admiral the Marquis de Grancey and Rear-Admiral Hector des Ardents. There was a significant change in the formation of the fleet. The White Squadron, instead of leading the way as was customary, was placed in the centre, while Rupert himself took the van as Admiral of the Red. Doubtless he distrusted the French after what had happened at Sole Bay, and preferred to keep d'Estrées between himself and Spragge.

De Ruyter's flagship was the *Seven Provinces*, and his squadron was in the centre. Tromp had emerged from the cloud under which he had been living since his insubordinate conduct at the St James's Day battle, and now commanded the van. Commander of the rear was Adriaen Bankert, Lieutenant-Admiral of Zeeland.

On the morning of 28 May the wind was from west-south-west, veering to west-north-west. At nine o'clock Rupert gave the signal by the firing of a gun, and the allies steered towards the enemy, the advance detachment leading. It was fully expected that the Dutch would retreat within the shoals, but de Ruyter had other ideas. He promptly ordered a counter-attack and stood to the northward, Tromp's squadron leading, hugging the wind. The light advance force was soon thrown into confusion; some ships withdrew to the main line of battle, while others went into action against Tromp but to little effect.

Seeing that the pursuit-force plan had failed, Rupert led his whole fleet to the attack. At noon he steered his Red Squadron east by north towards the north end of the enemy fleet, fearing that Tromp would get to windward. 'We were forced to engage sooner than I intended,' he reported later to Arlington, 'to prevent the enemy getting the wind.'[28] The Prince attacked at long range at about 1 p.m.; then he sailed in to the attack. Soon Tromp's flagship was disabled, and he was forced to shift his flag. About the same time his Vice-Admiral, Volkhart Schram, was killed.

The action became general about two o'clock. To the Dutch it seemed that the allies were approaching in crescent formation, owing to the fact that Rupert and Spragge in the van and rear moved more quickly than d'Estrées in the centre. Then, while d'Estrées was moving forward against de Ruyter, his rear commander de Grancey, instead of attacking the aftermost ships of the Dutch centre, closed with Bankert's leading vessels at the southward end of the line. This should have been Spragge's province as Admiral of the Blue. Spragge for his part waited for de Grancey to come up, and then their combined force of some twenty-five ships engaged with the less than twenty commanded by Bankert.

This was de Ruyter's chance. D'Estrées had been slow in moving in, and the nine French ships that had formed part of the advance force had joined Rupert's Red Squadron. With the defection of de Grancey d'Estrées's White Squadron was reduced to a strength of about a dozen ships to face the eighteen under de Ruyter's immediate command. The great Dutch Admiral was not the man to let such an opportunity slip. Tacking to the south-west and leaving Tromp to fight it out with Rupert, he burst through the French line to cut the allies in half.

He was only partially successful. A few French ships, including d'Estrées's *Reine*, remained to windward, while de Grancey and Spragge staved off danger by skilful tacking off to westward. But the allied line was in confusion, Bankert was relieved from pressure, and there could be no attack by the White Squadron on the Dutch centre. De Ruyter was unable to drive home his advantage, but his centre and rear were intact and the tactical advantage was his. He could turn back north-eastwards to help Tromp.

Rupert meanwhile had been forcing Tromp back in a north-easterly direction. But he was hampered by shallow water, and to his fury his new flagship the *Royal Charles* 'proved so crank-sided, and fetched so much water in at the ports, that her lower tier of guns could not be made use of'.[29] At length, finding themselves dangerously near the shore, the attackers were compelled to stand off to the westward. 'Had it not been for fear of the shoals,' commented the author of the *Exact Relation*, 'we had driven them to their harbour'.[30] The fight was continued at long range until, towards eight o'clock in the evening, de Ruyter and Bankert arrived to rescue Tromp. The rival forces sailed southward on parallel lines, the English to the windward. Rupert was able to reassemble his scattered fleet, but de Ruyter had no intention of risking any further engagement or of being lured into the open sea. At about 10 p.m., when darkness came on, the Dutch returned to their anchorage in the Schooneveld. The allies stood out to sea, and anchored early next morning some twelve miles to westward.

It was another indecisive encounter, but the honours rested with de Ruyter who with an inferior force had staved off a formidable attack. The allies had hoped either to destroy the Dutch fleet or to drive it into the inner waters and, anchoring in its place, effect the landing of troops. This they had signally failed to do, and Rupert's semi-apologetic dispatch to the Secretary of State showed his disappointment. 'I hope His Majesty will be satisfied,' he wrote, 'that considering the place we engaged in, and the sands, there was as much done as could be expected.'[31] He was generous to his subordinates. D'Estrées and the French, he wrote in the same dispatch, had behaved themselves very bravely, and Sir Edward Spragge had maintained the fight with courage and resolution.

King Charles hastened to assure his cousin that he was perfectly satisfied with his conduct. 'You have done all that was possible,' he wrote on 1 June, 'with those circumstances the enemy afforded you. . . . In a word, I am very well pleased with your success.'[32]

Casualties in the First Battle of the Schooneveld were not heavy. Losses of ships were insignificant on both sides, and the total of killed did not exceed a few hundred. These, however, included a considerable proportion of senior officers.

De Ruyter nevertheless had regained the initiative. Being within his own waters, he could refit with ease, and choose his own moment for renewing the fight.

Rupert was under no illusions as to the danger of the situation. He put all his energy into effecting what repairs were possible in the open sea, but they were sadly inadequate. He complained bitterly to Arlington. 'It is now four days since I sent to you concerning our wants,' he wrote on 3 June. 'I hoped to have supplies ere this in sight, but nothing comes, and the wind being easterly little is hoped for. . . . If this be neglected, and the Dutch recruit, as doubtless they may, being so near their magazines, I know not what game they have to play better than to fall on us in the condition we now are in, being in so great want of men that captains of the best ships come with tears in their eyes to tell me the few seamen they have on board.'[33]

On 31 May he shifted his flag, transferring from the unsatisfactory *Royal Charles* to the *Royal Sovereign*. 'I am now changing my ship,' he wrote, 'which proves a mere table, ships water with the least breath of wind, and in great gales her topsails may overset her.'[34]

There was a gale blowing for most of the week following the First Battle of the Schooneveld, and this at least staved off the expected Dutch attack. When the weather became calmer, on the evening of 3 June, de Ruyter planned his assault. Rupert was expecting it, and according to the *Exact Relation* even thought it might come at night, an unusual manoeuvre in seventeenth-century naval warfare; 'imagining the enemy might attack us that night, he went not to bed, but waited till morning'.[35]

The allies were anchored in a series of lines running north-west and south-east: the Blue Squadron was to the north, the White in the centre and the Red to the south. Distances between squadrons were so great that Spragge reported that his flagship was ten miles from Rupert's. Relative strengths were much as before; the Dutch had fifty-one ships, the allies seventy-four.[36]

The Dutch left their anchorage soon after eleven o'clock on the morning of 4 June, a fresh breeze from the north-east giving them the weather gage. They were assisted by the singular conduct of Sir Edward Spragge. The Admiral of the Blue must presumably have been as conscious as Prince Rupert that a Dutch attack was to be expected this day; yet he chose this moment to leave his post to seek a conference with the commander-in-chief. He left his flagship, the *Prince*, at 10 a.m., and when he reached the *Royal Sovereign* at noon the enemy were in sight and the Red Squadron ready to sail. Not surprisingly, Spragge was curtly told to return to his ship and make sail. It was two o'clock before he was back in the *Prince*, and the Blue Squadron, which had been ordered to stand away to the northward, had not moved in the absence of its commander. Nor had the French of the White Squadron, which should have followed the Blue. Seeing the van immobile while waiting for Spragge, d'Estrées 'took occasion to lay by and delay time'.[37]

This muddle dictated the course of the Second Battle of the Schooneveld. Rupert's plan had been to draw the Dutch away from their own coast and rely on the allies' superior strength in the open sea. But now the Dutch were upon them, well within reach of their own harbours. They could conduct the fight as they chose, and break off easily if it should go against them.

Rupert lost patience, and decided to take the lead himself. Cutting his cable, he led his squadron through the French ships with the intention of putting it at the head of the line. It was a rash move. He had not made his design clear to d'Estrées, and the Red and White Squadrons were thrown into confusion. Sir John Chicheley, Rear-Admiral of the Red, found himself fighting next to the French second-in-command des Ardent. Meanwhile Spragge had got his squadron moving and was sailing northwards.

The Dutch, however, launched no very vigorous attack. De Ruyter, in view no doubt of his inferiority in numbers, seems to have been content to inflict damage with the aim of driving the allies away from the Dutch coast. D'Estrées summed up the battle accurately enough: 'It was a grand skirmish rather than a straight fight, which consumed a lot of powder, which makes me think they did not intend a decisive battle, but just to gain time and waste our powder.'[38] The two fleets sailed side by side on the starboard tack with the Dutch to the windward, firing at long range. It was the classic line-ahead formation, but the Dutch were sailing in good order and control, while the allies were in confusion.

The firing started about four o'clock in the afternoon, and went on till nightfall. Tromp with the Dutch van caught up with Spragge, whose flagship was badly damaged. Rupert, now in the centre, engaged de Ruyter, who made a show of accepting the challenge and then suddenly withdrew.

It was about 10.30 when de Ruyter broke off, signalling his fleet to return to the Schooneveld. The allies followed half-heartedly, but seeing that they could not catch the enemy before they reached the sands Rupert discontinued the pursuit at 2 a.m. Four hours later his fleet tacked and made for the English coast.

There was no loss of ships on either side, and casualties were not heavy. But de Ruyter had gained his objective. Damage to vessels and expenditure of ammunition were sufficient to prevent the allied fleet from embarking on another bout before returning to England to refit. The result of the battle reflected little credit on Rupert, or on anybody else on the allied side.

Rupert was deeply disappointed at the negative outcome of the two battles, and came home in a thoroughly disgruntled frame of mind. He felt that he had been let down by the administration at home, and he reacted with characteristic fury. He had himself, in the previous summer's campaign, seen to it that the Duke of York was adequately supplied; at least when he was in command at sea the Government might have given him similar support. In this mood he lashed out at all and sundry. Contemporary reports are full of his outbursts of rage. A letter dated 26 June to Sir Joseph Williamson, Under-Secretary of State, then on a mission to Cologne, said a story was going round London 'that the Prince at his first comeing to towne, when the Commissioners of the Navy came to waite upon him, fell into such a passion against them, that he had like to have made use of his cane upon some of them, and it is reported he did; certaine it is he was very angry with them for not haveing taken better care to supply the fleet with necessaries'.[39]

The Prince's anger was vented in higher quarters than the Navy Commission. When the fleet had anchored at the Nore the King and the Duke of York went down on a visit of inspection, and in their presence, reported another correspondent, Rupert 'stormes extreamely att the want of provision that they had, and declares he shall never thrive att sea till some are hanged att land'.[40] The easy-going Charles accepted the rebuke in typical fashion: '. . . the King sayd merrily, the day before he went to see him, that he must expect a chideing but had sweetend by letter all he could'. Whether the more serious-minded Duke took so tolerant a view of the accusations is not recorded; but it may be that some temporary bad blood arose between the cousins. In the following month Sir George Fletcher wrote to Daniel Fleming: 'There is a report that the Duke and Prince had some words before the King which made them draw, the Duke calling the Prince coward, which compliment the Prince returned with calling him traitour.'[41] The correspondent added, however: 'What truth in this I know not.' Almost certainly the report was false. If Prince Rupert had drawn his sword against the King's brother in the presence of the monarch himself, much more would have been heard of it.

At any rate Rupert got some satisfaction from the King. He demanded more power for himself, with freedom from administrative control. And his wishes were respected. On 16 June he was granted a fresh appointment as 'admiral and commander-in-chief of the fleet for the present expedition',[42] and a week later a new commission was chosen 'for executing the office of Lord High Admiral, vacant by the surrender of the Duke of York'.[43] The first name in the list of commissioners was that of Prince Rupert. The Prince then became in effect First Lord of the Admiralty, and the prime voice in deciding naval policy was his.

Meanwhile both sides were preparing for a renewal of the conflict. Rupert's rages had galvanized the sluggish administration into action, and the refitting of the fleet was proceeding apace. But it was the Dutch who were ready first. On 25 June de Ruyter appeared with a total of a hundred sail off the mouth of the Thames, and Rupert prepared to meet him with what ships he could muster. But de Ruyter got no further. His fleet was riddled with sickness, and he was forced to return to Holland.

On 6 July Rupert reported that he would be ready to put to sea in two days. Councils of war were held at which the King and Duke of York were present, and it was decided that the Prince should sail towards the Schooneveld but 'not for any consideration whatsoever adventure upon attacking the enemy'[44] there without the authority of the King. The stratagem was to sail northwards towards the Texel, where the homeward-bound East India fleet was expected. The threat to this convoy would draw the Dutch fleet out, and the next battle could be fought in the open sea. Then, with victory achieved, a landing could be effected on the Dutch coast.

On 17 July Rupert sailed from the Nore with ninety ships of the line and a total of 'near 200 sail, and in men 28,000'.[45] He had with him some 8,000 soldiers in hired ships, and in connection with this there occurred next day a somewhat absurd but most unfortunate incident.

The troops were placed under the command of Count Frederick Schomberg, a German who, born in the Palatinate, had had a distinguished and highly varied military career in the continental wars. He had become acquainted with Charles II in the King's years of exile, and when he appeared in England in July 1673 he was promptly welcomed as an experienced soldier such as was needed for the command of a continental expedition. He was given the rank of lieutenant-general on 4 July, and promoted to that of captain-general a week later.

The day after Rupert set sail, Friday 18 July, Schomberg took his troops to join the fleet, himself sailing in the frigate *Greyhound*. With him was the Earl of Mulgrave, whom Schomberg consulted on the advisability of flying some sort of signal by which the subordinate military commanders could recognize the vessel in which their commander travelled. One of the colours of Mulgrave's regiment happened to be lying on the deck, and with the concurrence of Captain Clements of the *Greyhound* this was run up at the masthead.

The next thing that happened was that Schomberg and Mulgrave 'heard a bullet whizzing over our heads, and another in the same manner presently after; at which we began to think cannon-bullets that came so near a little worth the minding, but were extremely surprized to perceive they came from the Admiral'.[46] Rupert had seen the signal, and, aghast at the presumption of a subordinate captain flying an unauthorized flag in his fleet, ordered shots to be fired across the *Greyhound*'s bows. He then sent a lieutenant to order the flag to be lowered immediately, but in the meantime Captain Clements himself had set out in a boat to explain the reason for the signal. When Clements reached the *Royal Sovereign* he found the commander-in-chief in one of his towering rages. Rupert had noted that the lieutenant's boat was returning without the flag having been struck, and promptly clapped the frigate's captain in irons. He then commanded his gunner to sink the *Greyhound* if the flag was not immediately taken down.

At this some of Rupert's senior officers, in particular the Earl of Carlisle, intervened, venturing to suggest that the Admiral was letting his feelings run away with him. Rupert's anger cooled, he released Clements, and allowed Carlisle and others to go to the *Greyhound* and explain the situation to Schomberg. The flag was promptly lowered, but Schomberg, not unnaturally, was deeply affronted by what had happened. His mortification was increased when he received an order to take his transports to Yarmouth and await orders there. This he attributed to pique on Rupert's part. More probably the Prince had decided that the presence of all these vessels would merely hamper the movement of the fleet; the troops could always be sent for when the moment arrived. In the event they were never needed, and remained idle throughout the rest of the campaign.

Schomberg was undoubtedly at fault in running up the colour; none but the King of England's flags were entitled to fly in the royal fleet. But the Count and Mulgrave were landsmen, with little knowledge of naval etiquette; though it is surprising that Clements did not put them right on this point. Rupert's behaviour is hard to excuse. He regarded the flying of the flag as an insult both to his King and to him as commander-in-chief. But in acting in so overbearing a manner without so much as inquiring into the circumstances he exaggerated the incident in a ridiculous manner. One wonders whether there was some bad blood between Rupert and Schomberg. The episode was not closed. From Yarmouth Schomberg, smouldering with resentment, complained to the King through Arlington of the insult he had received. Rupert, evidently conscious that he had gone too far, wrote in conciliatory terms to Arlington on 3 August:

> . . . I am very sorry that Mons. de Schomberg had any mortification by what was done in that business of the flag. I intended him none, and shall always show him the contrary, yet, he being an old commander, I cannot but wonder he should give way for a foot colour to be stripped off from the staff, putting ribands to it, and so making it fit to hoist and lower. But I shall say no more, leaving all to his Majesty's consideration.[47]

Schomberg was not mollified, and after the campaign he sent Mulgrave with a challenge to the Prince. The King, however, forbade any duel to take place.

The Schomberg episode was an irritation, but it did not affect the progress of the campaign. Rupert proceeded to carry out his orders, sailing towards the Schooneveld where he saw the Dutch at anchor. On 21 July he anchored some twelve miles to the west-north-west.

Next day the two fleets were soon in contact. De Ruyter began to put in an attack, but the wind changed and the rival forces were driven apart. After some manoeuvring the Dutch returned to their anchorage.

After this the allied tactics developed according to plan. The fleet sailed slowly up the Dutch coast, and on 25 July anchored off the Texel. So far de Ruyter had made no move, but on the 28th he was ordered

Prince Rupert's demands relating to his naval appointment

That I may have my commission as soon as may be
That His Majesty & his Royal Highness be pleased to name the
ships designed for this fleet, and that none be diverted
for convoys, guard of coast etc.
That I may have power to command all the yards, victuals,
stores and what shall be necessary to set out this fleet.
That I may have power from His Majesty to punish all misdemeanours according
to the custom of war and the Seas.
& a power to sink, burn, destroy or take any ships,
men, or country in possession of the Dutch.

Instructions given to Prince Rupert by King Charles II at the Nore, 26 July 1673, in the handwriting of Pepys by the Prince of Orange to keep in touch with the enemy and seek battle when opportunity offered. He put to sea at once, but paused off Scheveningen to ask for further orders.

Rupert had also been consulting his sovereign. On 27 July he wrote to Arlington asking for guidance on three points. Was he to send for the land forces? Was he to attend the Dutch East India fleet if he got intelligence of it, and in what ports might he attack it? And was he to attack the Dutch in the Schooneveld if they did not come out? He also took the occasion to ask once more for his most trusted officer: 'If his Matie will have either of them well done, he must send me Sir Robert Holmes. If there were not a necessity of this I would not, after so many denials, press it. I do it only to save the King's honour, which if we do nothing more this year will suffer.'[48]

The answer did not come till 9 August, well after intelligence had been received of the approach of the Dutch fleet and when action was imminent. The Prince, ordered the King, was not to send for the troops before a sea battle had been won; he was not to attack in the Schooneveld, and he was not to go in search of the East India fleet. The request for Holmes's services was ignored. The situation now in being rendered the instructions academic.

De Ruyter, in accordance with new orders from the Prince of Orange, resumed his northward voyage on 3 August, and that evening anchored fifteen miles south of the Texel. Rupert was at this time twenty miles north-west of the Texel. His aim was to get southward of the Dutch and so prevent them returning to the Schooneveld; but for several days rough weather kept both fleets at anchor. It was not till the morning of 10 August that any movement was possible. The allies then steered southward, the Dutch northward; and about 10 a.m. they came in sight of one another. The Dutch tacked and sailed in the same direction as the allies, and a day of manoeuvring found them five miles apart, nine miles west of the Texel on the morning of the 11th. Both fleets were now steering east-north-east; there was a light wind from the south-east, and the Dutch were directly to windward.

There was little change in relative strengths. De Ruyter had sixty ships of more than forty guns as against the allies' eighty-six – fifty-six English and thirty French. In guns the figures were 5,386 for the allies and 3,667 for the Dutch. There were few changes in the higher command on either side, but the Marquis de Martel had succeeded de Grancey as second-in-command to d'Estrées. Narbrough had returned from the Mediterranean and was serving as Ossory's flag-captain in the Blue Squadron.

Both fleets tacked and headed south. The White Squadron of French ships was now the van; Rupert was in the centre with the Red, and the

Blue under Spragge in the rear. Rupert's plan was for the van to run ahead to tack and attempt to weather and gain the wind of the evening while the other two squadrons sustained the shock of the expected attack. It was essential that the Red and Blue Squadrons should be in close touch, and Spragge had express orders to keep well up with Rupert. At a council of war he gave a solemn assurance that he would not be far from his side.

De Ruyter was as usual in the centre of his line; his own van was commanded by Bankert and his rear by Tromp. His plan was to hold the French in check with the van of Bankert's squadron, which would enable him to engage the rest of the allied fleet on something approaching equal terms.

The battle began at about 8 a.m. De Ruyter attacked Rupert's Red Squadron with his own centre and two divisions of his van while Bankert's leading division, under Cornelis Evertsen, faced the French ships. Meanwhile the Marquis de Martel, with the van of the White Squadron, sailed south in accordance with his orders to weather the Dutch. Whether or not he succeeded is open to doubt. D'Estrées and Martel were at loggerheads after the battle, and their accounts of what happened conflicted. D'Estrées criticized his subordinate for tacking too soon and failing to carry out his orders, but Martel insisted that he 'was ordered to get the wind and got it'.[49] It seems probable that he did get to windward of the Dutch, though possibly with only a few of his ships and by breaking through the line rather than weathering it.

D'Estrées for his part was slower off the mark, and a gap opened between his main force and Martel's van. Evertsen attacked with gunfire and fireships and burst through the French line, and simultaneously d'Estrées, followed by his rear commander des Ardents, broke through the Dutch. The French White Squadron and the leading Dutch division thus exchanged places, with the French to windward, but unfortunately d'Estrées, in the words of Mr R. C. Anderson, 'appears to have looked on getting to windward of the enemy as an object in itself rather than a step towards attacking on his own terms'.[50] Instead of returning to the attack he stood off to the south-east and virtually dropped out of the battle, while Evertsen was left in a position to reinforce the main body of the Dutch fleet.

Meanwhile Rupert with his Red Squadron was bearing the full weight of de Ruyter's attack. That he had to do so was the fault of his second-in-command. For here came the great defection. Ever since the St James's Day fight in 1666 Sir Edward Spragge had apparently looked on Cornelis van Tromp as a hated personal rival, and it was said that he had made a pledge that he would bring him in dead or alive. Now was his chance, for he knew that Tromp was in command of the Dutch rear and would come up against him. His task was clear; he was to keep close up behind his commander's squadron, and this was to be his first priority. But nothing seemed to matter to him but his personal feud with Tromp. In flat contradiction of his orders he slackened sail and lay by waiting for his enemy.

In the encounter that followed Spragge showed the greatest gallantry. Tromp too recognized the rivalry, and for three hours a furious battle raged. The two flagships, Spragge's *Royal Prince* and Tromp's *Gouden Leeuw*, hotly engaged each other, and both admirals had to shift their flags. Spragge transferred to the *St George*, after the *Royal Prince* had suffered heavy damage, and then when this vessel was disabled in its turn he decided to move on to the *Royal Charles*. Now retribution overtook him. On his way from ship to ship a chance cannon-ball sank his boat and he was drowned.

Ossory took over command and the fighting went on. The Blue Squadron held its own, but the Dutch gunnery was superior. Gradually Tromp began to wear his enemy down.

Abandoned by both his van and his rear squadrons, Rupert faced de Ruyter's onslaught. He had some thirty ships as against the more than forty that the Dutch admiral now brought to bear upon him. His tactics were, while engaging his enemy at long range, to bear to westward to draw the Dutch further away from their own shore. But de Ruyter managed to push in between the Prince and his rear division under Sir John Chicheley. Chicheley was isolated, and Rupert, his force cut in two, found his strength reduced to twenty ships. De Ruyter outnumbered him by two to one.

Rupert's fighting spirit came to his aid. He found himself attacked on both sides, but he would not give way. He rallied his ships, sent fireships among the Dutch, and inflicted heavy damage on the stronger fleet. Between 9 and 10 a.m. a heavy shower of rain fell, and thereafter the wind veered to south-west, giving the English the weather gage. Rupert, ably assisted by George Legge, the twenty-five-year-old son of his old friend, in the *Royal Katharine*, broke through to the north-west and reunited his ships with Chicheley's division.

De Ruyter was still attacking, but about noon Rupert caught sight of his Blue Squadron some nine miles to leeward, and bore away to the north-east to help his rear forces and to reunite his fleet. De Ruyter followed, and the two fleets ran down side by side within cannon-shot of each other without firing.

Closing with the Blue Squadron, Rupert found many ships, including the *Royal Prince*, disabled; but Ossory was defending gallantly against the onslaught of Tromp. With Rupert joined with Ossory and de Ruyter with Tromp, the main body of each fleet was now engaged. De Ruyter

373

was striving to get in among the disabled English ships and destroy them, but Rupert and Ossory held him off, steering in between the Dutch and the lame vessels.

The French, it appears, had at last moved back towards the scene of battle. All this time they should have been attacking de Ruyter in the rear, but d'Estrées had remained idle, to the fury of Martel who was anxious to give all the support he could to Prince Rupert. Now, at about four o'clock in the afternoon, the White Squadron hove in sight. The allies had the weather gage, and if a united attack was made victory could be achieved.

It was not to be. Rupert put out 'the usual signal to bring all ships into the general's wake or grain, which is the blue flag upon the mizen peak, and sent ketches, sloops and boats to the ships to windward to command them in'.[51] The response was inadequate. Many of the English ships were too badly damaged, and the French squadron, fresh and intact, held off, d'Estrées pretending he did not understand the signal and 'thinking he ought to keep the advantage of the wind, to renew the fight next day'.[52] Standing by the Prince in the *Royal Sovereign*, his flag-captain Howard said to him: 'Does your Highness see the French yonder?' 'Yes, God zounds, doe I,' was Rupert's terse reply.[53] Later, in his report on the battle, he commented that this was 'the greatest and plainest opportunity ever lost at sea'.[54]

At five o'clock de Ruyter closed, and there was a sharp mêlée; but both fleets were now weary and neither could gain advantage over the other. Rupert was anxious to take off his damaged ships, and de Ruyter to seek the sanctuary of his own harbours. At sunset the action was broken off, and Rupert confessed that he was glad of it.

When it was all over, so Rupert reported, 'a message came from Comte d'Estrées to receive orders to know the meaning of the blue flag being on the mizen peak, which I wonder at, seeing there was no instruction plainer to be understood, or more necessary among the general instructions for fighting, which he had laid before him, and besides it wanted neither signal nor instructions to tell him what he should have done, the case was so plain to every man's sight in the whole fleet'.[55]

So yet another battle ended in stalemate; once again no major ship had been lost in either side. But it had been a fiercer fight than those at the Schooneveld, and its effect was to put an end to the allies' attempt to destroy the Dutch fleet. This was not immediately apparent, and there was talk of fitting out another expedition. But damage and casualties were heavy, the English treasury was in a precarious state, King Charles was having trouble with his Parliament, and other political preoccupations took precedence of naval affairs. There were no more major engagements in the Third Dutch War. The Dutch successfully resisted the French invasion, and de Ruyter had saved his country.

Rupert anchored north-west of the Texel, and for some days hung about in the expectation of further action. But bad weather supervened, and towards the end of August the fleet returned to the Nore. Rupert struck his flag on 27 August, and proceeded to London. He had left the shores of England for the last time.

There were the usual recriminations. At first the tendency was to blame the Prince for the lack of success. It was hard for him to put up a strong defence. He had been badly let down; but Spragge was dead and could not be court-martialled, while his complaints against the French had to be tempered by diplomatic considerations. Here, however, he had the warm if surprising support of the Marquis de Martel, who published a statement condemning his commander:

> Prince Rupert, seeing us coming with that fair wind, gave us the signal to bear into his wake. Monsr. Martell laid his sails to the west and expected Monsr. d'Estrées would advance with his whole squadron, and fall altogether with his fair wind on the body of the enemy and send his fireships among them, but instead he kept the wind, and contented himself with letting his ship fire at more than a cannon and a half distance from the enemy. Monsr. Martell saw very well how shameful this was, but having express order to attempt nothing without the order of Monsr. d'Estrées and besides having been so ill-attended that morning by the captain of his own division that he could have no assurance they would follow him, he shrugged up his shoulders, and forbade any firing from his ship.'[56]

The honest Martel's reward, perhaps not surprisingly, was a spell in the Bastille.

In the event Rupert was fully vindicated and 'was received with the greatest dearness possible as well from the King as people'.[57] His popularity was undimmed.

There was no further co-operation between French and English in arms. D'Estrées sailed home in September 1673, and Schomberg's military contingent was disbanded. On 9 February 1674 the Treaty of Westminster was signed, which put an end to the war. The terms were advantageous to England. The Dutch acknowledged the right of English men-of-war to a salute, places taken by either side were restored, and the Netherlands agreed to pay a substantial indemnity.

With the Battle of the Texel Prince Rupert's martial career came to an end. As First Lord of the Admiralty he continued to preside over the affairs of the navy, but he 'never heard guns again'. It is therefore time to attempt a brief assessment of his capacity as a commander at sea.

Clearly Rupert was no great naval tactician. He was outmanoeuvred by de Ruyter in the Third Dutch War as he had been by Blake in his wandering days in the Mediterranean. But in both cases he was up against quite exceptionally able men. De Ruyter was the greatest sailor of his age, with the possible exception of his compatriot the elder van Tromp; Blake the greatest English seaman. Naval tactics were at this time hardly out of their infancy. Fleets of up to a hundred small vessels, tossed to and fro at the mercy of wind and weather, were almost impossible to control; a few brilliant commanders such as de Ruyter and Blake were alone beginning to master the problem. Only the simplest rules of tactical procedure could be laid down with any success, and when battle was joined even these usually went by the board. The result was the 'Mêlée', and Rupert being an advocate of that mode of battle was probably on the right tack. He knew he could not exercise close control of the ships under his command. His famous remark to Pepys – 'I can answer but for one ship, for it is not as in an army where a man can command everything' – is revealing.

Yet if his methods at sea were rough and ready he was a superb fighting sailor. The dash and vigour that he had shown as a cavalry commander he brought to his new element. He was always in the thick of the fight, leading his ships, showing the aggressive spirit at all times and in all situations, encouraging his men by his own example. He was a popular commander who could always be sure of the loyalty of his seamen – at least those of his own ships who were in immediate contact with him. Owing to imponderables such as weather, and the occasional insubordination of his senior subordinates, his plans were apt to go awry, but in his personal encounters he was uniformly successful. He was always quick in initiative, as when he so promptly turned back to the assistance of Albemarle when he heard the guns of the Four Days Battle. With Albemarle he showed himself at his best, and on St James's Day 1666 the two admirals achieved their greatest success.

Rupert's strategy was generally laid down for him, and it can hardly be said that he had any far-reaching insight into wider aspects of sea warfare. His design in the Third Dutch War of drawing the Dutch away from their shores and keeping them in the open sea was sound but obvious.

He was an admirable administrator. No detail was too small for him, and he worked with all his dynamic energy to see that his men and ships were ready for war. His work at the Admiralty in the summer of 1672 paved the way for more systematic management of the navy. The time was not far off when-well-set up fleets, of fewer but larger ships, would make Britain the undisputed mistress of the seas. Rupert was not the least of those who played their part in bringing this about.

He was present in all but one of the major engagements of the Second and Third Dutch Wars; more than could be said of any other English admiral. And in every one he was in the forefront of the fighting. Judged on the results of battles, the sea career of Prince Rupert of the Rhine was not marked by conspicuous success. But in almost every way he can be regarded as the outstanding sailor of Restoration England.

CHAPTER 5

SEEDS OF EMPIRE

RUPERT was condemned to be a wanderer from his birth. Born in the capital of Bohemia, he had been taken as a fugitive through Germany before he was a year old. Growing up in the Netherlands, he had seen military service in northern Europe in early youth; at sixteen he first visited England, and was within measurable distance of leading an expedition to Madagascar. Before he was out of his teens he was a prisoner in Austria, and after his release he saw Vienna and Prague (his birth-place) before his four years' fighting in England, during which he became acquainted with almost the whole of his mother's native country. His rovings at sea thereafter took him to Ireland, to Portugal, to the Spanish coast and the eastern Mediterranean, to the Azores and the Cape Verde Islands, to West Africa, to the West Indies and finally to France. In subsequent years he visited his Palatinate fatherland and roamed once more over much of Germany, with a brief excursion to the Baltic. His last twenty years saw him settled in the land of his choice, established as very much an Englishman; but until the Restoration he had never in his life lived more than a few years continuously in any one country.

He had become acquainted with all sorts and conditions of men, from sophisticated officials of the imperial court to primitive natives of Africa and the western isles; everywhere he went he interested himself in local customs and life in little-known parts. He was renowned as a linguist; he certainly spoke fluent English, French, German and Dutch, with probably a smattering of Spanish, Italian and Portuguese. It is worth noting that during the Civil War his Puritan enemies, who constantly attacked him as a German interloper, never in their pamphlets made fun of his manner of speech. Had he spoken broken English, they would surely have made it a subject of ridicule.

It would have been strange indeed if so cosmopolitan a character, once he had made England his permanent home, had not extended his vision over wider fields. And Rupert with his keen brain and his questing mind in fact took the closest interest, from the Restoration onwards, in the development of Britain's overseas possessions.

The British Empire grew up almost by accident, and the driving force was commercial expansion. England in the seventeenth century had no policy of deliberate territorial acquisition; nor, as was the case with Spanish and Portuguese colonialism, was missionary fervour in evidence. What happened was that, in the wake of the sixteenth-century corsairs, groups of pioneers set up trading posts, known as 'factories', in undeveloped parts to exploit the local resources and drive bargains with the natives. From the first these traders sought the support and protection of their home government, which they obtained in greater or lesser degree. Many influential persons, from monarchs downward, interested themselves financially in a private capacity in the trading ventures, which as time went on, and as local difficulties and rivalries grew, became increasingly involved with the central administration and national foreign policy. In the eighteenth and nineteenth centuries this involvement would lead to annexation and an extension of British rule never envisaged by the Stewart sovereigns.

Exceptions to the general rule were Bombay and Tangier, outright possessions which came to England as part of the dowry of the Portuguese Princess Catherine of Braganza on her marriage to King Charles II in 1662. Bombay was remote from England and was placed at once under the powerful East India Company, which had been in existence since 1600 and was very much in control of its own affairs. At the time of acquisition Tangier seemed the more important possession. This vital port, on the extreme north-west coast of Africa, was in a position to command the Straits of Gibraltar and the sea route between Europe and Africa. Since 1471 it had been subject to the crown of Portugal, but the Portuguese had found it by no means easy to control. Constant harassment by the warlike Berber tribes of what is now Morocco had forced them to expand their dominion by conquest, but owing to various vicissitudes these extra possessions had largely been whittled away. The union of the Spanish and Portuguese crowns between 1580 and 1640 further complicated the situation, for after the re-establishment of Portuguese independence Spain, which retained other possessions in North Africa, was added to the list of local enemies. To seaward, moreover, the depredations of the Barbary pirates of the Mediterranean, which reached their zenith in the mid-seventeenth century, were a further vexation.

The delivery of Tangier to Britain was, then, by no means an unmixed blessing; the port was isolated and beset by dangerous foes. It was, however, accepted with enthusiasm; and indeed, had it been imaginatively handled, and had there been sufficient resources available in men and money to maintain it adequately, it might have proved as strategically valuable as superficially it appeared to be. At first all went

well. A board of privy councillors was appointed to administer the
territory, two new regiments were raised for its defence, and work was
begun on the construction of a harbour mole 1,425 feet long with an
average width of 100 feet.

Prince Rupert was a member of the board, but if we are to believe
Pepys he took little part in its proceedings. Pepys, however, seldom
mentioned Rupert without malice, and his comment need not be taken
too seriously; nor need his later remark when, writing on the subject of
Tangier, he stated that the King looked on the Prince as 'a madman'.[1]
The fact remains that Rupert does not seem to have taken any profound
interest in Tangier. In papers concerned with its administration his
name seldom occurs. In view of his lifelong concern with military and
naval strategy, and his enthusiasm for British development, this is
strange. Possibly he saw that England had in this case taken on something beyond her capacity to handle, and decided to have as little to
do with it as he reasonably could. If this was so, his foresight was
justified. Tangier proved a white elephant. The drain on the Treasury
was incessant; the attacks of the Berbers and the presence of the pirates
negatived the city's strategic value; a succession of weak and tactless
governors antagonized the Portuguese population and made efficient
administration impossible. In 1683, the year after Rupert's death, the
decision was taken to destroy the fortifications, including the mole, and
abandon Tangier to the Berbers.

Curiously enough, Rupert showed a much more active interest in
those ventures whose primary concern was trade than in the one whose
value was strategic. Immediately on his return to England in 1660 he
set himself to promote developments in that part of the west coast of
Africa where he had had such stirring adventures during his sea
wanderings eight years before.

In 1652, when he sailed into the Gambia River, the Prince had
listened to stories told by natives of rich gold-mines in the region. He
saw no reason why these stories should not be true, and presumably
interested his royal cousins in the possibilities even before the Restoration; for within a month of his return, in October 1660, plans were
being made in London under his auspices for an expedition whose
purpose was to dig for gold in Guinea and the Gambia. His protégé
Robert Holmes was chosen to lead the expedition, which set out at the
beginning of 1661. The commander's orders were to send barges up the
Gambia; which barges, it was optimistically enjoined, were to be
brought back 'full of Gold or the richest sands'.[2]

Holmes found no gold; but his expedition was not unsuccessful. He
encountered opposition from the Dutch, who were the strongest
European settlers in the area, and held his own in a number of skirmishes.

He established English factories in Guinea and Sierra Leone, and he brought back a cargo of ivory, wax and hides.

Simultaneously with the dispatch of Holmes to the Gambia, moves were set on foot to establish a company to take charge of trade with the region. It was not the first to be formed. European settlements in West Africa had been in existence for two centuries; the vast and under-developed area could provide gold, ivory and many other products, and trade was there for the taking. As in many other places, the Portuguese were the first in the field. They were followed by the Dutch, and later came the French and the English. On a smaller scale the kingdoms of Sweden and Denmark, the Duchy of Courland and the Electorate of Brandenburg, took their pickings.

In England the 'Company of Adventurers of London trading to Gynney and Bynney [Guinea and Benin]' was incorporated in 1618, and the 'Company of Merchants trading to Guinea' in 1630. The new organization formed at the Restoration, on the initiative of Prince Rupert, was the 'Company of the Royal Adventurers of England trading into Africa'. By its charter, granted by King Charles on 10 January 1662, it was given 'the privilege of exclusive trade from Sallee to the Cape of Good Hope'.[3] W. R. Scott, historian of early joint-stock companies, states, though without giving his authority, that the first governor of the company was Prince Rupert. If so, the Prince must have soon handed over to the Duke of York, who appears as holding that office in July 1664.[4] Rupert, however, continued to take the keenest interest in the proceedings of the company, and regularly attended meetings of the court of assistance.

The company, however, was not successful. Its finances were haphazard; 'the whole venture,' says the chronicler of its successor, 'was more reminiscent of an aristocratic treasure-hunt than of an organised business'.[5] After some years it was heavily in debt, and the trading returns were inadequate. Rupert did what he could. In August 1664 he offered to lead a new expedition to Guinea, with the express purpose of countering Dutch movements under de Ruyter. Bad weather and his own state of health frustrated him, and eventually Holmes went once more in his place. The voyage was eventful, but the whole issue had now become bound up with preparations for the Second Dutch War. Holmes consolidated the British presence on the West Africa coast, but his exploits belong more to military history than to the expansion of British trade overseas.

Meanwhile a new development was linking the work of the Africa company with another region in which Prince Rupert also took a keen interest. The slave-trade had flourished for centuries in West Africa, but it does not seem to have figured conspicuously in the first plans of the Company of Royal Adventurers. In the West Indies, however, the cultivation of sugar had been introduced, and soon became a major industry. For success it required an abundance of cheap labour, and the demand for slaves from Africa brought a new importance to trade with that part of the world.

What Prince Rupert thought personally about the slave-trade is impossible to determine. Probably he took it for granted as an economic fact of life, as did most of his contemporaries. He had in his time had many dealings with Negroes, and so far as the evidence goes one can say that he had always treated them with consideration; he had been genuinely fond of the 'little nigger' whom he had adopted during his African adventure. But the traffic in slaves was everywhere an accepted fact until towards the end of the eighteenth century. The people concerned were slaves in their own regions before ever they passed into European possession. Some were born in servitude; some were debt slaves or convicted criminals; most were prisoners of war captured in the internecine conflicts of Africa. All were victims in the first place of their fellow-Africans.

This commerce in human bodies soon became the most lucrative and flourishing part of the trade with West Africa, and Rupert certainly encouraged it. But it did not solve the problems of the Royal Adventurers; nor did the formation in 1669 of a daughter company called the Gambia Adventurers, to which was leased the trade of north-west Africa at a rent of £1,000 a year. In 1670 it was decided to wind up the whole concern, and to form a new company on a sounder financial basis.

The intention was to raise at least £100,000 by public subscription and to take over the assets and debts of the Royal Adventurers. In the event some 200 individuals underwrote stock to the value of £111,600; Rupert was among the number, and so was Craven. The new venture was able to start with adequate capital and clearly defined aims.

The Royal African Company received its charter from King Charles II on 27 September 1672. The company was granted the monopoly of trade in the regions 'lying and being within the limits and bounds hereafter mentioned, that is to say, beginning at the port of Sallee in South Barbary inclusive and extending from thence to the Cape of Good Hope inclusive, with all the islands near adjoining to those coasts and comprehended within the limits aforesaid . . . unto the full end and term of one thousand years, yielding and rendering therefor unto us, our heirs and successors, two elephants whensoever we, our heirs and successors or any of them, shall arrive, land or come into the dominions.'[6] No subject of the Crown was to visit West Africa without the permission of the company, which was empowered to seize ships and goods belonging to those who infringed its monopoly. Gold, silver and Negroes were mentioned as the principal objects of trade; the company was authorized to set up forts and factories, to make war and peace with local chieftains, to raise troops and declare martial law. The charter came nearer than any of its predecessors to advocating the annexation of territory.

Charles II never set foot in Africa; so he never got his elephants.

The list of persons to whom these privileges were granted consisted of twenty-four names; the first three were those of 'our said dearest brother James, duke of York, his highness Prince Rupert, Anthony, earl of Shaftesbury'.[7] The stockholders were to elect annually a governor, a sub-governor, a deputy governor and twenty-four assistants.

Rupert had been the inspiration of the whole movement, but once the Royal African Company was established and set on its course it does not appear that he took a leading part in its administration. The Duke of York, as the company's royal patron, was elected Governor, and the first Sub-Governor was Shaftesbury. Rupert continued to take an interest in West Africa, and was a regular attendant at meetings of the company; but he was content to leave the direction of its affairs to others.

This was one of the ventures in which Rupert found himself a business partner of Anthony Ashley Cooper, Earl of Shaftesbury. A warm friendship developed between the two men. A correspondent of Sir Joseph Williamson wrote in 1673: 'Prince Rupert and he [Shaftesbury] are observed to converse very much together and are very great, and indeed I see his Highnesses coach often at his doore. They are lookt upon to be the great Parliament men, and for the interest of Old England.'[8] Later, when Shaftesbury was ill and in trouble, Rupert was again a frequent and sympathetic visitor at his house.[9]

This prolonged friendship has led some historians to associate Prince Rupert with the political activities for which the Earl is most famous. In the 1670s and early 1680s Shaftesbury, Dryden's 'false Achitophel', devoted himself with an almost fanatical single-mindedness to stirring up every kind of trouble for his King, and still more for the Duke of York, that his ingenious mind could concoct. In the discreditable episode of the Popish Plot, and in what is known as the Exclusion Crisis, he led the opposition to the Crown in a manner that prompted the probably correct belief that his ultimate design was to overthrow the restored monarchy and bring back the 'Commonwealth' régime. There is no evidence that Rupert had any sympathy with this policy, and Professor K. H. D. Haley, author of the latest, very complete, biography of Shaftesbury, considers there is no ground for the suggestion. Shaftesbury was a man of considerable charm, and the Prince doubtless admired his keen brain, his business acumen, and his devotion to the same interests as his own. But his relations with him were on a personal and business footing. It would have been contrary to the whole tenor of his life for Prince Rupert to have dabbled in any form of anti-Royalist politics.

During the ten years that Rupert was concerned with the Royal African Company its trading was highly successful. In the three years 1676–8 50 guineas per cent was paid, or nearly 55 per cent.[10] It was not till after the Prince's death that the company began to run into trouble, chiefly owing to difficulty in maintaining its monopoly.

The overseas project, however, with which Prince Rupert's name is most closely associated, developed in a different part of the world. Since the discoveries of Columbus at the end of the fifteenth century the American territories had, like Africa, attracted the attention of European explorers and traders. The usual powers – England, France, the Netherlands, Spain and Portugal – were all involved; but in the latter part of the seventeenth century the vast territory now known as Canada was largely in the hands of the French. 'New France', however, did not extend to the area around the great gulf or inland sea called Hudson Bay (after the English navigator Henry Hudson), in the north-east. This region was largely unexplored.

The dream of discovering a north-west passage to the China Seas had haunted the imagination of navigators for centuries. Hudson's own expedition in 1610 had been in search of the north-west passage, and a number of explorers had sailed through the Hudson Strait into the bay. But the land remained undeveloped. However, in the late 1650s two French fur-traders, Médart Chouart des Groseilliers and Pierre Radisson, pushed into the region of Lake Superior. Disappointed at the lack of support accorded to them by the French authorities in Quebec, these two began in the years that followed to look about for help from other nations. At the beginning of 1668 they arrived in England and made contact with Prince Rupert, the Duke of Albemarle and Lord Craven. They reported not only 'that in that part of America there is great hope of finding some passage through those lakes into the South Sea',[11] but that a monopoly of fur-trading was to be had for the taking.

It was the very thing to appeal to Prince Rupert. He went straight to the King, and Charles ordered the Duke of York to hand over the *Eaglet* ketch to Rupert and Albemarle for an expedition to Hudson Bay. Meanwhile an Englishman, Zachariah Gillam, had also reached Hudson Bay in the *Nonsuch* ketch, building there a fort which he named after the King. Gillam returned to England about this time, and in the summer of 1668 the two ketches set out on the officially sponsored expedition. Radisson sailed in the *Eaglet*, and Groseilliers – or 'Mr.

Gooseberry'[12] as he rather delightfully appears in the instructions for the voyage – with Gillam in the *Nonsuch*.

The *Eaglet* failed to reach the bay, but Radisson set out again in May 1699 on board the *Wivenhoe* pink. The *Nonsuch* achieved her objective and returned on 9 October 1669 with a rich cargo of furs and skins; Gillam and Groseilliers, it was announced, 'report the natives to bee civill and say Beaver is very plenty'.[13]

The outlook was promising, and preparations were being made for the establishment of a joint-stock company. Rupert put up £270 towards the costs, and Craven as always was a generous supporter. In the winter of 1669–70 the adventurers put in hand a ship of their own, a full-rigged three-masted frigate to be called the *Prince Rupert*. She was ready by the summer of 1670 and sailed from Gravesend in June, together with the *Wivenhoe*, which had apparently returned from the 1669 expedition though whether or not she had reached the bay is uncertain.

When the charter of the Hudson's Bay Company was granted on 2 May 1670, Rupert was nominated as the first Governor, to hold office 'untill the tenth of November then next following if hee the said Prince Rupert shall soe long live and soe untill a new Governor bee chosen by the said Company in forme herafter expressed'.[14] In fact Rupert remained Governor until his death. His Deputy-Governor was Sir John Robinson, Lieutenant of the Tower of London, and among the eighteen original members of the company to whom the charter was issued were Christopher second Duke of Albemarle (whose father had died in the previous January), Craven, Arlington, Ashley (not yet Earl of Shaftesbury) and the wealthy banker Sir Robert Vyner, whose financial support was invaluable. These eighteen were described as having 'at their owne great cost and charge undertaken an *Expedicion* for Hudsons Bay in the Northwest part of America for the discovery of a new Passage into the South Sea and for the finding some Trade for Furrs Mineralls and other considerable Commodityes'.[15]

In the years that followed, expedition after expedition was fitted out, the region was developed, and the fur-trade increased. The company had its ups and downs. It took time to make it profitable; no dividend was declared in Rupert's lifetime. But the Prince and his associates never lost faith. At last, in 1681, a cargo of furs sold in London brought in the remarkable sum of £15,721 4s 9d. It was the turn of the tide.

Minutes of the Hudson's Bay Company show that Prince Rupert was far more than a titular governor. He was regularly present at the general courts of the company, which as a rule were held at his house in Spring Garden. He was the link between the company and the King, and more than once he interceded with his cousin on the company's behalf, on one occasion procuring for it the privilege which the Royal African

Company enjoyed of sending out provisions to the factories without paying customs duty. For day-to-day administration he worked through James Hayes, who had been his secretary since 1666 and was knighted in 1670. Hayes was a live-wire, who quickly became the moving spirit of the Hudson's Bay Company. By 1679 he had become Deputy Governor, and after Rupert's death he continued in that office under the new Governor, the Duke of York. To Sir James Hayes above anybody else the eventual success of the company was due. But Hayes was Rupert's man, and the two can share the credit.

The formation of the Hudson's Bay Company sowed the seeds of the British Dominion of Canada. The initiative came from Prince Rupert, and he watched over the fortunes of the company throughout the last twelve years of his life. 'The old hero of so many fights on land and sea, with his high station, his many interests, and his chequered, adventurous memories, had stood up for the Company well', was Sir George Clark's verdict.[16] The territory developed under his inspiration was named after the Prince, and for long was known as Rupert's Land. It has ceased to exist as such, but the Prince's name lives on in the Rupert River.

CHAPTER 6

SCIENCE AND ART

THE seventeenth century was a time of intense scientific curiosity and activity. The areas of knowledge were being continually enlarged, and scholars in every land, with the generous support of princes and prelates, devoted themselves to experiment and discovery. England, rent though she was by civil war in the middle of the century, was by no means backward in the quest for scientific advancement. The names of Bacon at the beginning of the period and Newton towards its end, with many others of comparable distinction in between, are sufficient witness to English achievement in the natural sciences.

Prince Rupert with his questing mind and restless intellectual energy took the keenest interest in the new ideas that found vent during his lifetime, and in his later years himself made no inconsiderable contribution. In early days his interests were artistic rather than scientific. He was a competent draughtsman, and at Leyden, in company with his sister Louise, had the benefit of the tuition of the Dutch painter Gerard van Honthorst. Yet this very preoccupation with the pictorial arts led him in the direction of science. His facility in drawing brought appreciation of the art of design, and this in turn led him to the development of mechanical invention which proved so fertile in the years after the Restoration. The fusion of artistic and scientific skill was to find its fulfilment in the process of mezzotint.

Art, then, played an important part in bringing Rupert to scientific experiment. A second influence, and perhaps a more potent one, was war. The Prince made a close study of weapons and equipment. Gunnery, cartography and engineering were techniques that lay close to his heart, and it is possible that, had circumstances not dictated otherwise, he might have chosen to be an artillery rather than a cavalry officer. In the English Civil War he kept a constant eye on the engineering side of the conflict, bringing his own experts Bernard de Comme and Bartholomew La Roche from the continent to take charge of it; and at the siege of Lichfield he was responsible for laying the first mine ever to be sprung in England.

In the wandering years at sea he showed the same interests. His resources were too limited to allow of any spectacular development, but his concern with naval gunnery dates from that time; and at Lisbon he came near to blowing up one of the enemy English ships with one of his own inventions.

It was after his return to Europe in 1653, and particularly after he left France for Germany in the following year, that Rupert began to concern himself with the wider issues of science, and from the mechanics of war advanced to chemical and physical experiment and invention. In the intervals between his bickerings with his brother Charles Louis he had abundant opportunity for study, and in his letters to his friend William VI of Hesse-Cassel one can see the lines along which his mind was developing. On 31 May 1656, when in Heidelberg, he sent William a powder-flask invented by himself. On 31 August 1657, writing from Frankfurt, he enclosed details of his invention of a water machine: 'I have made a sketch on the other side,' he wrote, 'but I do not know whether you will be able to understand it.'[1] Later references in the letters mainly concern the perfecting of mezzotint engraving, but are interspersed with allusions to other inventions which are difficult to identify without external evidence.

After the Restoration he was able further to develop his ideas. In the years of peace before the outbreak of the Second Dutch War he again had time on his hands, and conducted experiments at his lodgings in Whitehall. And with the Restoration came the official foundation of the Royal Society.

The Royal Society of London for Improving Natural Knowledge was not a new institution when King Charles II gave it is first charter in 1662. It evolved from meetings of intellectuals held from at least the beginning of the Civil War period, and its origins have always been a matter of controversy. Recently a contemporary historian, in a distinguished work of scholarship,[2] has found the genesis of the society in Oxford rather than London and shown that its spiritual progenitor was Francis Bacon. Be that as it may, the Royal Society quickly became one of the most influential and respected scientific bodies in Europe. It held weekly meetings at Gresham College in the City of London, and among its early fellows were Robert Boyle, Christopher Wren, John Evelyn, John Dryden, Edmund Waller, John Locke, Samuel Pepys and Isaac Newton.

Rupert was elected a fellow in March 1665, but even before that his experiments had been brought to the notice of the society. In 1661, the year before the granting of the first charter, the curious invention known as 'Prince Rupert's Drops' was demonstrated. These drops, popular until quite recently as toys, are formed by allowing droplets of molten glass to fall into a vessel of warm water. They then set rigidly into the shape of a tadpole, tapered into a tail at one end. The glass body can be struck violently and will resist all attempts to break it, but if the tail is pressed with the hand near its end the whole piece crumbles into powdered glass. The device seems a curiously frivolous invention on the part of the severely practical Prince Rupert, who probably stumbled on it by chance.

Once elected a fellow, Rupert does not seem to have been a regular attendant at the Royal Society's meetings, if indeed he attended at all. But he continued to send in his inventions, and his name constantly crops up in the society's records.[3] The source of communication was usually Sir Robert Moray, the society's first president, an old Royalist soldier and a personal friend of the Prince.

Many of these inventions were concerned with the military art. One was a tiny automatic pistol which shot needles through a piece of oak three inches thick. Another was a noiseless musket. Moray also told the society of the Prince's method of blowing up rocks – an echo of the Lichfield mine. A chemical invention was a form of gunpowder ten times the strength of that normally used. This aroused great interest, and Rupert issued a warning to users that the charges must be less 'in all small guns, and especially in pistols, for else they will break'.[4]

But Rupert was long past the days when his mechanical experiments were all designed to improve the quality of a fighting force; he had extended his range to embrace the arts of peace. Inventions included a water-raising engine, a quadrant for measuring altitudes at sea, a method of making black lead run like a metal in a mould so that it could be used again, and a method of painting colours on marble which when polished would be permanent. In 1677 an experiment in wound-healing was described – a piece of pig's gut which had been incised when the animal was alive, and treated by Rupert's method, being shown perfectly healed. 'This gut being sent by his highness prince Rupert, who had himself caused the said incision to be made, it was ordered, that the humble thanks of the Society should be returned to him, and that it be intimated, that it would be worth while to try, whether such an incision would not heal of itself without the application of any thing.'[5]

Medical experiments were an important part of Rupert's scientific studies. He had taken the keenest interest in his own treatment for his old head-wound, and at an earlier date his remedies for his friends' maladies had caused him to be suspected of witchcraft. Membership of the Royal Society brought him a new circle of intellectual friends: John Evelyn the diarist, a rather pedantic scholar but a man of wide knowledge and culture; Christopher Wren the pre-eminent architect, astronomer and mathematician; John Locke, rising to fame as one of the greatest philosophers of the age. To these three Rupert showed the results of his experiments, and it was Locke who recorded in his note-book the Prince's remedy for burns:

> ... Sweet cream 3 gallons in May, Boyle it till it come to a Curd (continually stirring it to avoid burning) then hang it up in a long woollen bag that the Oyle may drop clear from it. Then take Moonwort, Mousear, plantin, Sanicle, Adders tongue and the roots of Solomons Seale an $\frac{1}{2}$ lb. Cut and beat them in a stone mortar, then Boyle them in the Oyle till crisp always stirring it, then strain it out and twice a day anoint the part with a feather.
>
> This is Prince Ruperts oyntment for a Burne or Scald, wherewith the Lady Chichley cured her son Mr. Norton when his face was exceedingly burnt with Gunpowder.[6]

Rupert also invented some form of drops which he recommended to his sisters; but Elizabeth's physician Helmont failed to follow the pre-scription. 'I should gladly send you the formula,' wrote Rupert to Sophia in 1679, 'if it could profit you to have it. But as it is impossible to make them without knowing all the tricks of the trade this would be useless to you. That is why even Helmont failed to make them at Herford.'[7] Apparently Rupert changed his mind, for on 26 December he wrote to Sophia: 'I am sending you, dear sister, the formula for my drops, from which you will see how Helmont went wrong when he tried to make them. . . . My sister, E[lizabeth] writes to me that the doctors will have it that the drops cause vomiting. This cannot be the case, for on the contrary, they cure it if one takes them again as soon as one has vomited; that is, unless one has taken some poison; in that case they *do* make one vomit. . . . When you have tried them you will be astonished at their efficacy.'[8]

Metals were a particular interest of Prince Rupert's, and in company with Locke and others he advocated a reform of the coinage. These were days when, for lack of an adequate monetary supply, innkeepers and tradesmen issued their own token coins, greatly adding to fiscal confusion. In March 1668 the Prince and Henry Howard, son of the late Earl of Arundel, proposed to the King the making of farthings (virtually a new coin, though a few had been minted in the reign of James I): '. . . showing their necessity, the loss and inconvenience by private tokens in case of removals, etc., as appeared in the late fire of London; also arguments for the model proposed by the Prince, as made of metals of the kingdom and difficult to cultivate, rather than for farthings of copper, which would be very bulky, and being of intrinsic value, would yield no benefit to the King'.[9] In November 1669 it was reported that Rupert 'is desiring leave of the King to make halfpence, to go throughout the kingdom, at which all rejoice, for now every pitiful shopkeeper coins farthings and halfpence at his pleasure'.[10] Rupert's designs were not adopted, at any rate as regards farthings; for though the general minting of halfpennies and farthings dates from the reign of Charles II, they were made, from the first, of copper.

The Prince also busied himself with the making of steel. On 17 November 1671 a warrant was issued 'for a licence to Prince Rupert, at the yearly rent of 20s., of the sole exercise for fourteen years from 6 May last of his inventions of converting edged tools and other forged instruments and iron wire into steel; also of softening cast or melted iron so as to be wrought like forged iron, and also of tincturing copper upon iron; with commission to him to take oaths from all the workmen employed in the said arts not to divulge them'.[11] In this venture, as in so many others, Rupert was associated with Shaftesbury. A document bearing both their signatures, recording an agreement for the forging of iron into steel, is in the Public Record Office.

In his last years at Windsor Rupert was able to indulge his scientific tastes to the full. He set up a laboratory, forge, workshop, studio and library, and conducted his experiments free from the cares of state. In the words of his contemporary biographer, he

> ... found himself at leisure to prosecute his Chymical & Philosophical Studies; wherein he had made some progress before, but now applied himself to it with more seriousness & attention than ever, & took so much delight therein, that it rendered the hardest and most unpleasing part of it sweet and pleasant to him, actually performing the most difficult and laborious Operations himself; not disdaining the most sooty and unpleasant labour of the meanest Mechanick; witness his Forge and his Furnesses, from which he hath by his industry furnished us with many curious Arts and useful Inventions, whilst others are forced to content themselves with empty speculation, because they onely study the Theory, and instruct others to perform the practick part from them.[12]

True, this peaceful existence was sometimes rudely disturbed. In January 1677 he was the victim of riotous behaviour by some of King Charles's more unruly followers. The episode is thus described by the writer of a news-letter:

> ... His Majesty, whom God preserve, went on Munday last to Windsor to see his workemen, and with a design to stay all the weeke there, but on Wednesday night some of his courtiers fell to their cups and drunke away all reason, at last they began to despise art to, and brake into Prince Rupert's Laboratory and dashed his stills and other chymicall instruments in pieces. His Majesty went to bed about 12 aclock, but about 2 or 3 aclock one of Henry Killigrew's men was stabbed in the company in the

next chamber to the King. They say he murdered himselfe amongst them because of some distast betwixt his master and him: how it was God knowes: but the Duke ran speedily to His Majesty's bed and drew the curtaine, and said 'Sir, will you lye in bed till you have your throat cut?' where upon His Majesty got up at 3 aclock in the night and came away immediately to Whitehall.[13]

It may be that King Charles's precipitate departure was caused by fear at least as much of his cousin's wrath as of the rioters; in such a matter Rupert was not the man to mince words, even to his sovereign. But history is silent on any repercussions there may have been.

In general, however, Rupert was left undisturbed; and at Windsor he pursued his vocation to the end of his life. He kept in touch with fellow-scholars on the continent. The German scientists Johann Glauber and Johann Becher were his friends, and in 1679 he invited Becher to England so that that eminent mineralogist could study tin-mining in Cornwall.

Rupert's scientific inventions, though not on a large scale, were substantial and of an astonishing variety. But his greatest claim to the gratitude of posterity lies in a development belonging more to the realm of art than to that of science.

From an early age the Prince was attracted to the visual arts. At the request of Queen Elizabeth, Honthorst gave lessons in drawing and painting to all the young Palatines at Leyden, but only Rupert and Louise appear to have benefited from them. Rupert had not the talent of Louise, some of whose pictures have been confused with Honthorst's own; but he developed a high competence. A number of his drawings and prints survive, mostly in the British Museum, and some of them are probably from this early period.

A further stage in his artistic education came with his first visit to England in 1636. At the court of Charles I he had access to the superb collection of pictures acquired by that cultured monarch, which included masterpieces by Raphael, Titian, Rubens, Correggio, Mantegna and Caravaggio. And he was able to meet the artists whom the King had attracted to his court: Van Dyck, Dobson, Inigo Jones. King Charles himself was his guide and tutor, and Rupert almost certainly made the acquaintance at this time of that other great English collector the Earl of Arundel.

That Rupert made a serious study of art and artists is certain, and he seems to have shown a particular interest in Albrecht Dürer, the German Renaissance painter and engraver who had died nearly a hundred years before his birth. His studies bore fruit after his return to the continent. In the enforced idleness of his three-year captivity in Austria he spent much of his time drawing and engraving. An etching which he made of a galloping horse bears an inscription showing that the print was made at this time.[14] At the same time he was already interesting himself in the technical aspects of drawing, as a passage in the *Rupert Diary* reveals. While in captivity, we are told, he 'perfected the Instrument to draw all things into perspective' which Dürer had conceived but never developed. The *Diary* adds that 'it was not made practicable to put it into a way of exercise; and the instrument is after presented to the Royall Society'.

During the Civil War Rupert had little time for the arts; yet it was either during this period or, more probably, in the subsequent years of exile that he first gave thought to a new method of engraving, the development of which constitutes his greatest claim to artistic fame and the one which has aroused the greatest controversy.

The process known as mezzotint, as now practised, is quite different from any other method of printing. The procedure is to roughen a polished copper-plate with a special tool called a 'rocker', not unlike the blade of a chisel but ground with a curved edge. The face of the tool is incised with vertical lines, thus giving a series of teeth when sharpened. The blade is pressed into the surface of the plate, making innumerable punctures and a corresponding 'burr'. The whole plate is traversed by the rocker, which gives it the appearance of a copper 'velvet'. A reversed picture on thin paper is then traced on to the prepared plate, and the engraving begins. The light areas are gradually scraped down with a 'scraper', a piece of steel not unlike a pen-knife blade; the highlights are scraped down to the bare metal, and the untouched parts print an intense black.[15]

The main difference, therefore, between mezzotint and all other forms of engraving is that the process works from dark to light, not from light to dark.

This process, and the tools it required, were brought to perfection in the eighteenth century. But the art of mezzotint had reached an advanced state, and needed little further development, when Prince Rupert introduced it to England immediately after the Restoration. That he did so introduce it is not in dispute. The question at issue is whether or not he invented it.

Mezzotint and its tools crop up in a series of letters which Rupert wrote to William of Hesse-Cassel in 1657 and 1658, shortly after he had visited his cousin at Cassel. On 28 December 1657 Rupert wrote:

These enclosures are based on a better original but the copyist is the same as before, so I am sending it. You will be so good as to overlook the mistakes that you find and to look only at the manner, with which one can achieve as much as with the paintbrush. You can rest assured that bone-black is best of all for the varnish [ink], but it must first of all be well rubbed and crushed with something and it will then mix very well. . . .[16]

On 2 January 1658:

. . . Meanwhile, in accordance with your command, please find herewith, fixed on paper, what you requested. I believe you will understand it. The weight does not matter and the shape matters little. What is important is the teeth – these must be even – for which I have invented an instrument which is now in hand being made; other wise I think it would be difficult to get good instruments. But I have several on the way from Vienna, which will be at your service.[17]

On 5 February:

. . . So that you should not have to wait any longer for the health of our file cutter, I am sending with this several instruments that have already been completed. You should simply whet them on an oilstone until they draw evenly upon the copper. The proofs which you promise will be a heartfelt delight to me. I have another [instrument] here which is made in quantity from steel.[18]

Finally, on 26 March:

. . . I must inform you that I have invented an instrument that works over the whole of the copper with little effort and time. I also have other things in hand which will soon be completed.[19]

These observations present a far from complete picture, but no scholar has doubted that they refer to mezzotint, on which Rupert was now busily working; the last extract is a clear allusion to the rocker in its first, rudimentary form. By the time he returned to England in 1660 he had finished the job, and the first person to whom he communicated the results was John Evelyn. Evelyn lost no time in proclaiming the invention in print, which he did in the book, published in 1662, the full title of which is *Sculptura: or the History, and Art of Calcography and Engraving in Copper. With an ample enumeration of the most renowned Masters, and their Works. To which is annexed A new manner of Engraving, or Mezzo Tinto, communicated by his Highness* Prince Rupert *to the Authour of this Treatise.* Chapter VI, in which this new method is dealt with, is headed 'Of the new way of Engraving, or *Mezzo Tinto*, Invented, and communicated by his Highness Prince Rupert, *Count Palatyne of Rhyne*, etc'.[20]

Here we have, in the first book to mention mezzotint, a categorical statement that the process was invented by Prince Rupert. Earlier, on 24 February 1661, Evelyn had written in his diary: '*Prince Rupert* first shewed me how to Grave in M[e]zzo Tinto.'[21] Again, in an entry dated

13 March of the same year but obviously not written till later, he wrote: 'This after noone his hig[h]nesse *Prince Rupert* shewed me with his owne hands the new way of Graving call'd *Mezzo Tinto*, which afterwards I by his permission publish'd in my Historie of *Calcographie*, which set so many artists on Worke, that they soone arrived to the perfection it is since come, emulating the tenderest miniature.'[22]

Nobody at that time suggested any other name than Prince Rupert's in connection with the invention of mezzotint. And in the next century George Vertue, eminent alike as engraver and antiquary, who was born twenty-two years before Evelyn died and derived much of his information from him, had no doubts on the question. 'Varner Vaillant,' he wrote in his notebook, 'drew in Black & White from the Life very well . . . he assisted P. Rupert in his invention & performance of Metzotint grounds.'[23] And again: 'Mr. Evelyn gave the name Metzotint to the new art of Graving found out by Prince Rupert.'[24]

Vertue also recorded the story, which had reached him at second hand from Evelyn, of how Rupert had got the idea that led to his invention. The incident, he implied, had occurred when the Prince was fighting in the Low Countries after the Civil War:

. . . the Prince going out one morning privately, observ'd the Citinel [sentinel] that was that one night upon Duty remov'd from his post at some distance. & was busily employ'd in doing something to his peice. which the Prince observing steppt up to him & asked what he was about. his answer was that night the Dew had fell & had rusted & cancer'd his fusee. & he was a Scraping & clearing of it which the prince looking at, perceived some kind of odd figure accidentally eat into the barrel of the gun, with innumerable small holes clos'd together like friz'd work in Gold & Silver, which the fellows accidental scraping with his knife had taken partly away, & left it clear again.

this immediately struck into the Princes mind that some contrivance might be made to cover a brass plate with such a grain'd ground of fine pressed holes it would undoubtedly make an Empression all Black & then by Scraping as he had remark'd the figure or form of any thing might be made. this conception of his was not lost, for communicating his thoughts on that head to Warner Vaillant an Enginious limner whom he employ'd in his house & who drew neatly in Black and white they made experiments of several kinds. & found that invention of a steel roler cutt with tools to make teeth unto a file or rasp, with points projecting, did effectually make the black grounds on the Copper plates ready to Scrape, by rolling too & froo over & over again. from this improv'd experiment the Prince made his prints known by his particular *mark* to be done by him. . . . .[25]

Here we have an exceptionally clear description of the mezzotint process in its early years, with a plausible description of how it came about; all on the authority of John Evelyn. Yet this same Evelyn had in his old age (he lived to be eighty-five) made a written observation which appears to contradict his previous confident statements that Prince Rupert had invented mezzotint engraving. In 1697, thirty-five years after the publication of *Sculptura*, Evelyn produced *Numismata, a Discourse of Medals, Antient & Modern*. And in this work, recording the names of 'eminent chalcographers', he mentioned 'the late *Melanochalcographer N. de Seigen*; who in the Year 1648, first produced the *Mezzo-Tinto* Graving'.[26]

This rather casual reference appears to be the first suggestion of any claim to the invention of mezzotint by Lieutenant-Colonel Louis von Siegen, a German officer who was for many years a groom of the bedchamber to none other than the Landgrave William VI of Hesse-Cassel. Von Siegen, who was born in 1609 and died about 1680, made no such claim himself, though he did claim to have invented some form of engraving. Vertue, if he knew of Evelyn's 1697 reference (and as a scholar and student of engraving and art in general he must surely have read *Numismata*), brushed it aside as of no importance. He certainly knew of von Siegen's work, since he described one of the earliest of that officer's engravings as '*something like* mezzotint'.[27] The qualification is important.

It was not till nearly three-quarters of a century after the publication of *Numismata* that any serious attempt was made to establish the Siegen claim. In 1771, in a work published at Leipzig, Baron Heineken put forward the thesis that Rupert learned the art from von Siegen, who in 1643 produced, in his portrait of the Landgravine Amalia of Hesse, the first known specimen of mezzotint. This was the engraving which Vertue said was '*something like* mezzotint'.

From then on the case in favour of von Siegen was developed, and it has been widely accepted by art historians and by biographers of Rupert (not by Warburton, who, however, expressed himself 'little qualified to act as an advocate').[28] It was discovered that two plates bearing Siegen's signature existed, dated 1642 and 1643, and two more dated 1654; and that in an extant letter to William of Hesse-Cassel, accompanying the earliest plate, he wrote of a print from copper as the fruit of 'a new and singular invention of a kind never hitherto beheld'.[29]

The earliest signed mezzotint by Rupert is dated 1657, and it was now held that Rupert must have learned the new art from von Siegen at some time during the 1650s. This theory, which held the field for so long, was challenged in 1936 by Mr George Edinger, who argued the case for Prince Rupert more lucidly and effectively than had been done since the days of Evelyn and Vertue.[30] His argument may be briefly summarized.

Two places and dates have been put forward for the meeting between Rupert and Siegen: Brussels in 1654 and Vienna in 1658. There is no reason to suppose that either man was in Brussels in 1654, and the latter date is of no significance since Rupert's first plate is dated 1657. Rupert undoubtedly claimed the invention as his own, 'and the word of Prince Rupert is not to be lightly dismissed'.[31] The Prince, according to Vertue, gave Evelyn his story of how the invention came about, and said that it happened when he was serving in the Low Countries. This was in 1647, so unless either Rupert, Evelyn or Vertue was lying the Prince could not have learned the secret from Siegen in 1654.

Siegen produced two engravings in 1642–3, and claimed a new invention. But he did not say what this invention was, and Vertue, a considerable authority, described his work only as *something like mezzotint*. Then, when these engravings had been produced, nothing more appeared, nor was the invention referred to again, for twelve years. Yet Rupert, while a prisoner in Austria in 1637, produced a signed etching which, as Warburton says, 'probably bears as much resemblance to mezzotinto as the head of the Princess Amelia does'.[32]

Siegen was in the service of William of Hesse-Cassel, to whom he communicated the fact of his new invention. Yet Rupert in 1657–8 was expounding to this same ruler his own inventions as something quite new. Considering his intimacy with the Landgrave, he would surely have known if William was familiar with the mezzotint process already.

Mr Edinger argues from this that it is far more probable that Siegen learned the secret from Rupert than Rupert from Siegen. The two may well have met in or about 1654, not at Brussels but at Cassel, and Rupert, knowing of Siegen's work and his studies in engraving, may then have told him about the process which he had been developing since 1647.

Nobody to my knowledge has made any serious attempt to challenge Mr Edinger's reasoning, though the claim for von Siegen continues to be made. But in recent years a manuscript has been discovered which has been held to throw fresh light on the question. The document, found by Mr W. G. Hiscock, sub-librarian of Christ Church, Oxford, among the Evelyn papers deposited at that college, is a fuller account of mezzotint than appears in *Sculptura*, and is apparently the draft for a lecture which Evelyn intended to read to the Royal Society. It gives a rather different version of the incident of the musket. In this paper, which is of unknown date but certainly much later than 1661, Evelyn gives a full description of the process, referring to the 'hatcher' which was the earlier version of the rocker. Then comes the relevant passage:

This invention, or new manner of *Chalcography* His Highness Prince Rupert was pleas'd to show me with his owne hands in the year 1661, He told me it was the devise of a common souldier in *Germany*, by observing something which had scraz'd his Musquett, upon which (being an ingenious fellow) he refind, 'till he had brought it to that perfection on Copper, as to exceede all the sorts of Graving, especially for heads and figures, that are hitherto extant, for it appeares more like miniature than graving and resembles the best designes of the old Masters for its manner and delicacy; I have the honour to be the first of the *English* to whom it has be[e]n communicated and, by a special Indulgence, to Instruct in it whom I thinke fitt, and which was first by presenting it to our *Royal Society*. There is another way of Engraving, by Rowelling a plate with an Instrument, made like that which Scrivenors use to direct their rulers on parchment; only the poynts are thicker set; and when the plate is sufficiently freckl'd with it, abated and wrought on as we shewd above; of this kind I have seen an head of the *Queene* of Sweden, made as bigg as the life; it was pretty, but not comparable to the Mezzo-Tinto of P. *Rupert* describd above.[33]

The contents of this paper were revealed to the Walpole Society in 1960 by the late Orovida Pissarro, artist and historian. She argued that the 'common souldier' referred to was clearly von Siegen, 'whose rank Evelyn misunderstood'.[34] From this she reasoned that Siegen was indeed the inventor of the mezzotint, but that Rupert was not dishonest in his claim, since to him the technical development of the discovery was due.

This may be so if we accept Miss Pissarro's contention that von Siegen and the hero of the musket story were one and the same person. I must confess, however, that I find this quite unconvincing. Evelyn might have confused a common soldier with a colonel, but what was von Siegen, a senior officer and a court official, doing with a common soldier's weapon? And if for some reason he possessed one, he surely would not have cleaned it himself. Had he no batman? Moreover, would Rupert have referred patronizingly to such a man as 'an ingenious fellow'? And if they were not the same man, are we to believe that the real inventor of mezzotint was an unnamed private soldier, who brought a new system of engraving to perfection and then disappeared into oblivion, leaving a prince to claim the credit which truly belonged to him? This seems to be straining credulity too far.

All that this new discovery seems to reveal is that Evelyn became confused as to what precisely Rupert had told him. At the time of *Sculptura*, when it was all fresh in his mind, he had no doubt that Rupert was the inventor of mezzotint. *Sculptura* does not contain the story of the soldier and his musket, and when Evelyn set it down later, at an unknown date, the details had become vague to him. The later document is after all a rough draft, and he may have meant to check the details (it does not appear that the paper was ever presented to the Royal

Society). Later still, when the name of von Siegen had become known to him (probably through Rupert), he mentioned him as the inventor of mezzotint, without any suggestion of what had caused him to change his mind. Evelyn was then seventy-seven. Old men forget.

The Evelyn paper, and Miss Pissarro's comments, do not seem to refute in any way Mr Edinger's version of the facts. There remains the evidence of the pictures themselves. In this one must bow to the views of experts, but the portrait of the Landgravine Amalia for instance does not give the impression of being worked from dark to light, the essential distinguishing mark of mezzotint. 'The Great Executioner' (the executioner of St John the Baptist), Rupert's best-known engraving, on the other hand, seems indistinguishable in style and method from the more matured mezzotints of the eighteenth century. Siegen would appear to have used the 'rowelling' method which Evelyn categorized as 'another way of Engraving' with the 'roulette', an instrument for mechanically scoring a plate with dotted lines. The 'hatcher' or 'rocker' was invented by Rupert. In the words of a recent writer, 'Rupert was concerned more with tones, working from black to white, von Siegen more with line, since the degree of tone achieved by Rupert simply was not possible with the roulette.'[35]

About a score of Prince Rupert's mezzotints survive, together with a handful of etchings and drawings. The most striking of the etchings is his portrait of Queen Christina, half caricature, which gives a vivid impression of the idiosyncrasy of that highly individual sovereign. Of the rest, none is without merit and all are pleasing to the eye. To quote again Mr P. H. Hulton of the British Museum, 'they are enough to show that Rupert was an amateur of talent and the best of his mezzotints are among the finest ever produced'.[36]

CHAPTER 7

FEMININE COMPANY

P RINCE RUPERT, officially at any rate, was never married; and he
never paraded his love-affairs. This alone made him something of
an alien at the court of Charles II, where such discretion was unfashionable; and the unravelling of his sex-life is not easy.

One possibility must be mentioned, if only to be discarded. In an age
whose intelligentsia have decided that every historical character, from
Adam onwards, was homosexual in greater or lesser degree, it is unlikely
that Rupert would escape. Yet only one of the Prince's biographers has
even hinted at such a thing, and that most tentatively. 'There is, perhaps,' wrote James Cleugh, 'a streak of homosexuality in every exceptionally virile man whose inclination to women is something less than
normal. Such a streak the Princes [Rupert and Maurice] probably
had.'[1] Cleugh produced no evidence – not surprisingly, since there is
none. Rupert's worst enemies during the Civil War never accused him
of sexual deviation. Nothing in his career gives the slightest suggestion
that he was not a man of perfectly normal passions, however much he
may have preferred to keep the details of his love-life to himself.

The truth seems to be that in the constant activity of his early life he
allowed himself little time for dalliance. His stern temperament would
not let him put pleasure before business, and there was abundant business to keep him occupied until he was well into his thirties. But more
than one love-affair dates from the easier days after the Restoration.

Undoubtedly he was gauche in the company of women. At the time
of his first visit to England his mother had compared him unfavourably
with his elder brother; had described him as an 'ill courtier', and
expressed misgivings on how he would get on with the ladies. Much
later, in the 1650s, he had made an egregious ass of himself in the affair
of Louise von Degenfeld and the Electress Charlotte. And his association
with Margaret Hughes excited the ribaldry of courtiers who thought
the austere old soldier incapable of conducting an affair of gallantry.

Yet even in his younger days his name was linked with those of
various ladies. He showed no enthusiasm for the proposed match
with Marguerite de Rohan, and evidently had no intention of getting

married at that time; but during the captivity at Linz came the idyllic
romance with Susanne von Kuffstein. It was a boy-and-girl affair of no
great depth, and probably it left no lasting impression on either of them;
but there is no reason to doubt that Rupert and Susanne were in love.

During the Civil War itself, when his days were packed with military
activities, he does not appear to have dedicated himself to total celibacy.
If we are to believe the assertions of some of the Parliamentary pamphleteers, he was even something of a lady-killer; but such sources cannot
of course be taken too seriously.

It was at this time that he became associated with the Duchess of
Richmond, and their friendship was eagerly seized on by the pamphleteers. Mary Villiers was the daughter of the first Duke of Buckingham
and elder sister of the second; she was born in 1623, and was thus three
years younger than Rupert. In her infancy she had been proposed as a
bride for Frederick Henry, eldest of the Palatines; but Frederick was
drowned when she was six years old, and in her eleventh year she was
married to Charles Lord Herbert, son and heir of the Earl of Pembroke.
Within a year she was a widow, and was taken into the household of
King Charles I, who had been so devoted to her father. In 1637 she was
married for the second time to the King's cousin James Stewart, Duke
of Lennox and later to be created Duke of Richmond. Richmond died in
1655, and Mary's third husband was Thomas Howard, brother of the
Earl of Carlisle.

During the Civil War the name of Mary Duchess of Richmond
constantly crops up in letters, memoirs and pamphlets; often in connection with Prince Rupert. Yet authentic details of her life are hard to
come by. Most of what has been written of her is based on the memoirs
of Marie de la Mothe, Comtesse d'Aulnoy, whose name was frequently
written as 'Dunois'. The Countess was a gossip-writer of by no means
negligible talent, with a gift of merry narrative and a fine disregard for
historical truth. Being involved with intrigues at the court of Louis XIV,
she fled to England in 1654, and she claimed that while there she became
an intimate friend of the Duchess.

Whether this was really true or not, 'Madame Dunois', while the
facts she recorded are not to be taken too literally, built up a recogniz-
able portrait of the Duchess which accords with what details are known
from more reliable sources. She paints her as 'extremely Beautiful, and
of a Mien and Presence very Noble and Majestic';[2] gay, spirited and
unconventional; courageous and quick-witted, and in youth something
of a tomboy. Her best-known story is of an incident said to have occurred
just after the death of her first husband, when the eleven-year-old Lady
Herbert was still in widow's weeds. She climbed a tree in the King's
garden (presumably at Whitehall) to pick some fruit, her black garb

and veil, spread over the tree, looked in the distance like wings, and the King, spotting her from a window, thought some large strange bird had got into the garden. He called a Mr Porter (presumably not Endymion), a young courtier who was a good marksman, and told him to go into the garden and shoot the bird; and Porter promised the King that 'he would take his Fusee, and in a moment bring him the Butterfly'.[3] But when he got into the garden he found that the strange bird was the young widow, who promptly pelted him with the fruit she had gathered. And when she heard he had come to shoot her, she entered into the spirit of the joke and sent for a large hamper and got into it. Porter and an attendant took the hamper into the palace, and Madame Dunois's story goes on:

> ... Mr *Porter* presenting it to the King told him, he had had the good fortune to take the Butterfly alive; which was so beautiful, that had he killed it, he should never have outlived it himself. His Majesty, eager to see it, opens the Hamper, and the young Countess clasping her Arms about his Neck, furnish'd matter for a most agreeable suprize. 'Tis not to be admired [wondered at], that she embraced the King in so familiar a way, everybody knows they were bred up together, and he look's upon her no otherwise than his own Sister. Ever since that time, she has been known by the name of Butterfly, and in several Courts of *Europe*, that name is oftener given her, than her own Title.[4]

It would be churlish to disbelieve so pleasant a little tale, which may possibly have some foundation in fact. But it serves as an example of the Countess's historical method. Charles I was the King of England at this time, but the king with whom Mary Herbert had been brought up was the future Charles II, who was at this time not more than five years old. Which of them gave the order for the shooting of the 'Butterfly'? Incidentally, Mary was not a countess.

The main purpose of the story seems to have been to lead up to Madame Dunois's relation of the lifelong and unrequited passion of 'Mr Porter' for the Duchess, which takes up a substantial portion of her book. The details, mainly connected with rivalry in love at the time of Mary's marriage to Thomas Howard, are too theatrical to be regarded as other than the purest fiction.

The Duke and Duchess of Richmond were among the closest friends and supporters of Prince Rupert throughout the Civil War. Through all the intrigues of the court they never wavered in their loyalty. The Duchess was always sending messages to the Prince, regardless of any effect they might have on her own reputation. 'I had an express command to present the Duchess of Richmond's service to you,'[5] wrote Lord Percy, no friend to Rupert, in 1643. And Will Legge in the dark

Remains of Prince Rupert's house in Cripplegate in 1791

Old Guard Chamber, Round Tower, Windsor Castle, arranged by Prince Rupert

AN
ELEGY
ON
That Illustrious and High-Born
PRINCE RUPERT,
Who Dyed on *Wednesday November* the 29th.
1. *Dec.* 1682.

Farewell, thou Bravest of the Great, Farewell,
When Fame shall thy Unbiast Virtues tell;
Thy Match no History shall ever find,
Thou Universal Favourite of Mankind;
Whilst Factions Boyl, whilst Bandying Parties clash,
And meeting Tydes their angry Billows dash,
Whilst Heat meets Heat, and thwarting Ferments Reign,
Rupert alone, firm to Truths Golden mean
Held his, even Souls miraculous Ballance right,
The Countries Darling, yet the Courts delight;
Honour in Thee, united all Her Charms,
In glories Race, in Battle and in Arms;
No fiercer Fires e're fill'd a *Heroes* Breast,
In Peace thy mind a perfect *Halcyon* Nest,
Where Manly Virtue kept Her Princely Throne,
Yet so retir'd as if Her State were gone:
A mind so firm, all irregular Heat,
The restless Burning Feavour of the Great;
A mind where all Perfections mixt so well,
The equal Glory of a Camp or Cell.
When future Ages shall with Honour tell
Things Dismall, that black Master-peice of *Hell*,
The Royal Martyrs Wound, a Blow so great,
Posterity shall start but to repeat:
In the sad Tale, Great *Ruperts* Deeds shall come,
And blossom on his Sacred Masters Tomb.

No hand more Active, and no sharper Sword,
The Throats of *Englands* Rebel *Hydra* gor'd;
And if in that lost day, when Fates dire Blow,
Had destin'd Truth and Loyalties overthrow;
Inth' Universal wrack, Great *Rupert* sunk,
Whilst starting Fortune from his Bannors shrunk;
His Courage only swel'd his Sails too High,
Till his great Soul onset his Victory:
Our *English* Hannibal, like him, alone
By his unmannaged Conquests overthrown.
Whilst that mad Chandteer, with fury hurl'd,
Ambition drives the *Jehues* of the World;
Whilst Ensignes fly, Drums beat, and Trumpets sound,
Or Conquering *Heroes* are with *Lawrels* Crown'd,
Fames deathless Book shall keep in Leaves of Brass,
Proud *Ruperts* Name enrou|'d till Times last Glass:
Nor is thy Memory here only Crown'd,
But lives in Arts, as well as Arms renown'd;
Thou Prideless Thunderer, that stoop'd so low,
To force the very Bolts thy Arme should throw,
Whilst the same Eyes Great *Rupert* did admire
Shining in Fields, and sooty at the Fire:
Perceiving thee advanced in Fields and Arms so far
At once the *Mars* and *Vulcan* of the VVar,
Till Dancing *Cyclops* shall thy praise repeat,
And on their Anvils thy tun'd Glorys Beat.
Written by a Person of Quallity.

LONDON, Printed for Langly Curtis, 1682.

An Elegy on Prince Rupert, anon.

days after the surrender of Bristol in 1645, writing to the Prince from Oxford after his release from arrest, added a postscript: 'You must thank Duchess of Richmond for she furnished a present to procure this messenger, I not being so happy as to have [any money] myself.'[6]

The Puritan propagandists of course made the most of what scandal was going. A pamphlet called *The Ladies Parliament*, published in 1647, but probably written earlier, opens with the words: 'The rattle-headed being assembled at Kate's in Covent Garden [probably a brothel, but possibly the house of Kate, Lady d'Aubigny, a lively lady of the court], and having spent some time in chusing their speaker, (it having been objected against the Lady Duchess, that she had used beating up of quarters, and other sports, too frequently with Prince Rupert,) they at last resolved upon the Lady Isabella Thynne, hoping thereby that the acts might have the great influence upon the King's majesty.'[7]

The ladies voted to raise a troop, 'consisting of one hundred tryed and able men, which should be always ready (both in peace and warre) to obey their commands'; and debated on the appointment of a commander-in-chief. Digby was proposed, and Goring, and Mrs Kirke (reputed to be Prince Maurice's mistress) urged the merits of her lover; 'but then the Duchess of Richmond assured them, that none was to be compared to Prince Rupert, against whom nothing could be urged, but that his labour was not alwaies crowned with the desired and wish't for success; but being cleared of the imputation by Mrs Legge (who assured the house that that did not depend upon him but his companions in armes) he was generally thought the fittest man for the employment; and it was ordered that the Lady Aubigny, attended by the Lord Hawlye, should be sent into France to receive the command'.

There is more than one version of this pamphlet, and one copy ends with a piece of doggerel which reads in part:

> Richmond she is brisk & jolly,
> wch makes Rupert malencoly
> but both he now & his brother
> may go to visit their Mother. . . .
> Andover did much desire,
> that Rupert should her admire;
> her Lord gave her good advice,
> yet some say she was too nice. . . . [8]

Another pamphlet, called *Newes from the New Exchange, or the Commonwealth of Ladies* and published in 1650, pursued the same subject. In this the Ladies Parliament received intelligence of the birth of the future second Duke of Richmond: 'Newes, newes. The Duchess hath a son and heir, in the absence of Prince *Rupert*.'[9]

The question then that arises is whether or not Mary Duchess of Richmond was Prince Rupert's mistress. The Roundheads of course took it for granted that she was, but there were clearly suspicions in Cavalier circles as well. Daniel O'Neill, a volatile Irishman but a consistent Royalist and an old friend of the Palatine family, lost the Prince's favour in 1645 after speaking carelesly in Ireland of 'the amours off Prince Rupert and the duches of Richmond'.[10] When the Duke of Richmond died in 1655 it was widely believed that Rupert and Mary would be married. The Duke's death was reported in Paris before it actually happened, and a correspondent wrote to Lord Hatton: 'I hope the news of yesternight is false that the Duke of Richmond should be dead. If soe, there is a widdow; whose she shall [be], I know not but *Pr. Ruperts*.'[11] Nine years later, when tentative suggestions were being made for a marriage between Rupert and some member of the French royal family, a lady who was watching his interests in France wrote to him that she was doing what she could, 'quoiqu'on ait appris que vous êtes fort engagé auprès d'une Duchesse il y a long-tems'.[12]

A final indication that such a marriage had been expected to take place comes from Rupert's sister Louise, Abbess of Maubuisson, who in 1667 met the Duchess and her third husband, Thomas Howard. 'I have recently seen the Duchess of Richmont,' she wrote to her brother Charles Louis, 'with her young husband. She is in the best humour in the world and says everything that comes into her head . . . she boasts much of the contentment she feels at being remarried, although it is said that she is greatly disturbed when her husband speaks to young beauties, or when she does not see him always beside her. She would have been unfortunate indeed if she had had Prince Rupert, who would not have kept her company so faithfully.'[13]

These allusions certainly suggest that Rupert was in love with the Duchess, and probably she with him; but about any sexual relationship between them nothing can be proved one way or the other. Some sort of conclusion can be drawn, however, from the characters of the three persons concerned. Mary Richmond was of an open nature, frequently indiscreet and defiant of convention; clandestine intrigue does not accord with what we know of her. Rupert was the soul of honour; and so was James Duke of Richmond. Clarendon describes the Duke as 'of a great and haughty spirit, and so punctual in point of honour that he never swerved a tittle'.[14] It seems inconceivable that such a man could have continued to serve Rupert, as he did, with unfaltering loyalty to the end of his life if his wife had all the while been carrying on a liaison with Prince Rupert, of which he could hardly have failed to be aware. It is equally unlikely that two such people as Rupert and the Duchess would have conducted a secret love-affair behind the back of one who was so firm a friend.

Little is known of the later years of the Duchess, who kept her title after her third marriage. She is said to have supported Nell Gwynn in her rivalry with Charles II's French mistress, Louise de Kéroualle Duchess of Portsmouth; while according to some lines attributed to that most scandalous of court poets the second Earl of Rochester (Henry Wilmot's son), she took to the bottle in her old age. The lines, quoted by the eighteenth-century social historian J. H. Jesse, were said to be addressed to the King:

> Old Richmond, making thee a glorious punk,
> shall twice a day with brandy now be drunk:
> Her brother Buckingham shall be restor'd,
> Nelly a countess, L— be a Lord.[15]

Jesse, who used sources now lost and is usually found to be accurate when he can be checked, suggests that L— was probably Sir John Lawson, father of a girl whom, he claims, the Duchess brought to court as an additional rival to the Duchess of Portsmouth.

The Duchess of Richmond died in 1685, three years after Prince Rupert.

In what other directions Rupert's sexual passions had outlet during the Civil War period is hidden in obscurity, but occasional glimpses can be caught in the Roundhead satires of the time. Two of the more scurrilous of these merit quotation. Clearly from the same pen, they refer, ostensibly, to a pet monkey belonging to Prince Rupert. The first pamphlet, published in 1642, is entitled *An exact description of Prince Rupert's Malignant She-Monkey, a great Delinquent: Having approved herselfe a better servant, then his white Dog called BOY. Laid open in these particulars: 1. What she is in her owne shape. 2. What she does figuratively signifie. 3. Her malignant tricks and qualities.* It is thought, the pamphlet opens, that the she-monkey 'was formerly some proud dame, that pulling up her cloathes, and setting her looking-glasse a good distance from her, would needs view her white belly in that immitating mirrour; where-upon the gods being angry at her obscene wantonnesse, did convert her into the shape of a lascivious she-monkey'. A later passage runs:

A monkey for her petulant and wanton tricks may resemble a wanton creature, I will not say a whore (for that name will make the Devill blush) but a necessary instrument of recreation, into which pretty peeces of delight it is no doubt but Prince *Robert* doth stand well affected, and though a souldier, he doth love the soft embraces of a faire laidy, since Mars himself did not scorne to dally with *Venus*, *Eneas* had a *Dido*, and it is like that Prince *Rupert* is not only a souldier but a courtier, it being naturall to the most witty and valiant to love a woman. But let that passe, certain it is that the Prince doth love this Monkey exceedingly; and the Monkey doth by all her gestures, and actions tempt the prince to lascivious desires. . . .

After describing some of the animal's endearing ways, the pamphleteer concludes that

. . . this monkey is a kind of movable body that can cringe and complement like a Ventian curtisan, though her face be not so handsome; yet all her gestures and postures are wanton and full of provocation, she being nothing els (as many others are) but a skin full of lust; her eyes are full of lascivious glances, and generally all her actions do administer some temptation or other; so that she cannot chuse but work upon Prince *Ruperts* affections; and if he were any thing effeminate as it is not to be doubted but he is foreward enough in expressions of love as wel as valour; for as the Spanish painter wrote in a Church window *sunt* with a *C.* which was an abomination, so her name is an embleme of wantones, *sunt* written in that manner being often called a Mon*k*ey, which is a *k*ind of prophanation, and thus you see what Prince *Ruperts* Mon*k*ey both nominally and figuratively signifye, she being in all her postures the picture of a loose wanton, who is often figuratively called a Mon*k*ey.

The second pamphlet, published in London a year later, is equally uninhibited. The full title is *The Humerous Tricks and Conceits of Prince* Roberts *Malignant She-Monkey, discovered to the world before her marriage. Also the manner of her marriage to a Cavalier and how within three dayes space, she called him Cuckold to his face.* The monkey, says this effusion, for some time despaired of getting a husband,

. . . she having no portion to guild over these faults or tricks following: First, she was always unconstant changing her affection, oftner than her smock, and it is supposed that she learnt her giddy actions either from Brownists, or her halfe cosins, which are Baboones: And when as maids should simper and dissemble there desires, this Monkey had a licorish tongue and a licorish taile, she would eat no oatmeal nor lome of walls to cure her green infirmitie, but the longest whitest sugar plums she could put in her mouth were most delightful to her taste, and had such a ravinous appetite to fruit that she would swallow all but the stones, and having gotten a delectable bit in her mouth (according to the manner of monkeys) she would only suck the juice out of it and then spit out the rest. . . .

There is more in the same vein. Matrimony still eluded the she-monkey, the chief trouble being that 'she could never keep her legs together, but would throw them abroad in such an obscene manner, that any of the Cavaleers with a carbine charged with two bullets might easily enter her maiden Fort, rifle all the treasures of her virginity, and come off safe and sound with a poxe to them, and so she would be revenged of her ennemies. . . .'

The rest follows a predictable course. The monkey finally entrapped a Cavalier into matrimony; but the marriage did him no good, and he 'took many restoratives to fortifie his back again, intending to keep a good while out of his Monkeys mouth, having been so shrewdly bitten on his wedding night'. And while he so absented himself 'a Scholar of *Oxford* had a great desire to leave off poring on his book, and instead of plodding on the deep liberall Sciences, he had a minde to peep into the Monkeys black Art or Arse, and so according to former appointment the Scholar thought to have about with the Monkeys *Numquam Satis*, and thereupon slipt off his breeches and slipped into bed, and so the Scholar perfectly performed his Acts, and came off with grace'.

Prince Rupert, with his love of animal pets, may well have kept a she-monkey, perhaps one from his mother's menagerie. But it does not need much perspicacity to deduce that these scurrilities were aimed at a human target. Who then was the lady? It cannot have been the Duchess of Richmond. She was a *grande dame* who, whatever her eccentricities, would hardly have behaved like a whore. Such a satire on her conduct would have been so wide of the mark as to have no point. It may well be that no particular individual was being pilloried; the author may simply have tried to achieve an exaggerated picture of what he imagined life at the Oxford court to be like. If any special woman was intended, a possible candidate is Lady Catherine Scott.

Lady Catherine, daughter of the Earl of Norwich and sister of George Goring, was one of the more colourful ornaments of Charles I's court at Oxford. A lady of great charm and no morals, she was the female counterpart of her brother. She was credited with a host of lovers, and lived apart from her husband, Edward Scott, the son and heir of Sir Edward Scott of Scott's Hall and of Nettlestead in Kent. He, a quiet, studious scholar, inclined to the support of Parliament, but he wanted only to be left in peace and spent the war years in retirement at Nettlestead. His wife was an ardent Royalist, and did all she could to enhance the morale of the Oxford garrison in her own charming way.

The evidence for Prince Rupert's association with Lady Catherine is tenuous in the extreme, consisting as it does of a single entry in the diary of John Evelyn. Catherine had a son Thomas, knighted in 1663; and on 6 July of that year Evelyn, who in a previous entry had described Lady Catherine as 'that pleasant Lady',[16] recorded: 'This evening came Mrs *Bennet* (sister to the Secretary) to visit us: we all sup'd at Sir Geo: Carterets Treasurer of the Navy, who had now married his daughter *Caroline* to Sir *Tho* · *Scot* of Scots hall: This gent: thought to be begotten by *Prince Rupert*.'[17]

It is little enough to go on; but Evelyn knew Rupert well, and may have known what he was talking about. The entry at least indicates that Rupert's name was coupled with that of Lady Catherine Scott.

Catherine's exploits did not end with the Civil War. In 1646 she startled Kentish society by taking forcible possession of Nettlestead House and defying her husband to dislodge her. He, however, succeeded in starving her out, and when the siege was raised she escaped by a window. Two years later, during the Second Civil War, she made her way through the Roundhead lines to visit her father, Lord Norwich, then besieged in Colchester. Fairfax with his usual courtesy allowed her through, and she entered the town, where she and her companions 'were entertained with a collation of horseflesh stewed in claret, and a bottle or two of wine, the best we could treat them with'.[18]

But Lady Catherine's greatest notoriety came at the end of 1656, when Edward Scott petitioned for a divorce (attainable at that time only by Act of Parliament). Reporting of parliamentary proceedings was forbidden, but Thomas Burton, MP, jotted down the details in notebooks in tiny and barely legible script. Burton's diary was edited by John Towill Rutt and published in 1828. Rutt performed a notable feat in deciphering the diary but left out most of the evidence in the Scott case as being unsuitable for publication.

Scott's petition alleged that Lady Catherine had 'eloped from him, and at Oxford, and other places, had children by other men'.[19] There was plenty of evidence to support his contention, and a whole procession of servants testified to having seen Catherine with her lovers. Thus a German who had served with the Roundhead forces gave evidence that 'about 9 years since he was desired to waite upon this lady to putney to the head quarters for a protection (it seems it was in time of warr) where she meeting with one of the king's chaplaines took an occasion to be a little with him. She had lockt her door to her & the german peeping in at the key hole saw her clothes upp and the Chaplain upon her thrashing in his longe cloak'. The German hastened to add that 'he saw noe nakedness'.[20]

A woman servant testified that a number of men whom she named had been 'familiar' with Lady Catherine: in particular Colonel Howard, brother of the Earl of Suffolk: 'One night he had left his waxe Poll [?] burning on the table, wch sett all on fire. I rose to put out the fire & saw them both in naked bed together. . . . I could not endure it. I would lay noe longer in her chamber. Soe another maid there till she and I fell out. When I told her what I heard of abroad of her, my lady would answ: She cared not what they said of her.'[21]

Much of the evidence suggests kinship with Prince Rupert's she-monkey. The biographical details, however, do not tally. The date of

Catherine's marriage is not known, but it must have been before the start of the Civil War. And Edward Scott could hardly be described as a Cavalier.

Rather surprisingly, Scott finally withdrew his petition and recognized Sir Thomas as his heir. Catherine lived till 1686. Her relations with Rupert remain enigmatic.

Of love-affairs during the interregnum no details are available. It is scarcely likely that Rupert led a celibate existence throughout his continental wanderings, but as usual he kept what happened to himself. The letters from admiring females during his Paris days are unimportant. Only the story of the affair with the Comtesse de Mongiron, Marshal de Plessy Praslin's daughter, appears to have had some basis.

Both before and after the Restoration suggestions were made for Rupert's marriage to one or another foreign princess. One of these was his cousin Mary, eldest daughter of Charles I and widow of William II of Orange. But none came to anything. Rupert was not a matrimonial catch – a landless prince with a comparatively small and uncertain income, dependent for his living on an unfriendly brother and an ever-impecunious cousin. There is little doubt that he would have liked to found a family. But marriage with anybody but a lady of royal or near-royal blood would have been unthinkable, and such brides required more than Prince Rupert had to give. This at least in part accounts for his passionate yearning for an apanage in the Palatinate, and his fury when the Elector refused to grant him one.

However, nothing materialized; and soon after the Restoration Rupert probably gave up all thought of a dynastic marriage. But it was in these years, when he was well on into middle age, that the two most important love-affairs of his life developed. Neither is at all well documented, and a particular mystery attaches to the Prince's association with Francesca (or Frances) Bard. She was the daughter of Henry Bard, Viscount Bellomont,[22] a gallant Cavalier officer who lost an arm in the Civil War. Bellomont was a scholar and traveller as well as a soldier, and before the war had made an excursion on foot through France, Italy, Turkey, Palestine and Egypt. In 1660 Charles II appointed him envoy to the Shah of Persia, a country which he had previously visited in 1654, and to the Great Mogul. He reached Persia but perished in a sandstorm on his way to India.

Rupert was undoubtedly personally acquainted with Bellomont, for it was he (then Sir Henry Bard) who appealed to the Prince to save the life of Francis Windebank after the surrender of Bletchingdon House in 1645. His son, moreover, who became the second viscount, was named Charles Rupert, and we may infer that Rupert was his father's hero. Bellomont left his wife and children in straitened circumstances, and in

September 1660 his widow petitioned for a pension, saying that she was 'so reduced by the loss of her husband and property that she must else go to gaol, and her children, one of them His Majesty's godson, be left "to the cold charity of others" '.[23] A month later she renewed her petition, asking for 'some relief of her great distress, having four children with titles of honour upon them, and little or nothing to maintain them'.[24]

Rupert may well have felt impelled to come to the help of the family and it at least seems likely that it was this that brought Francesca Bard to his notice. How old she was at this time is uncertain. A Latin epitaph written after her death in 1708 described her as dying 'aetatis suae 52'.[25] This would place her date of birth at 1656, which cannot possibly be right, since it would have made her a mother at ten years old. Probably '52' was a mistake for '62'. She was the eldest of three sisters, and if she was born in 1646 she was the eldest of the family, as her brother was born in 1648.

Francesca then was about fourteen when Rupert either made or renewed her acquaintance; within a few years they had become lovers, but the details are unknown. The only thing that can be said with certainty about their association, which seems to have lasted for only a few years, is that about 1666 a son was born who was christened Dudley. Rupert acknowledged paternity, and sent the boy to Eton, where his grandfather had been educated and where he was registered as Dudley Bard.

After leaving Eton Dudley was placed under the care of Sir Jonas Moore, a distinguished mathematician and military engineer, at the Tower of London; his father having decided to train him for a military career. After the Prince's death, when he would have been about sixteen, he visited the Palatinate to take possession of the house at Rhenen which had been left to him by Rupert. There were difficulties about the entail, and in 1685 Dudley was back in England, where he fought for King James II against Monmouth. The following year he returned to Germany to take part with other English volunteers in the Emperor's war against the Turks. In August 1686 he was killed in a gallant attempt to storm the walls of Buda. He was nineteen or twenty years old.

Dudley Bard was a worthy son of Prince Rupert, and the manner of his death would have filled his father with pride. At Eton he was described as being of gentle temper and amiable behaviour: qualities not altogether characteristic of his sire. He seems to have been universally popular. A career of bright promise was cut short in 1686.

The romance between Dudley's parents seems to have faded out within a year of his birth. Up to that time Francesca remains a shadowy figure; but later she was a well-known character. She took up residence at the court of Rupert's youngest sister, Sophia Electress of Hanover, who was enchanted with her. 'She is an upright, good and virtuous woman,' wrote Sophia in 1697; 'there are few like her; we all love her!'[26] In 1704 she wrote of her as one 'who makes us all laugh'.[27] Many years earlier, however, and long before she met her, Sophia had written to Rupert of Francesca: 'She cannot be very good-natured if she has offended you'[28] – the only evidence that Rupert and his mistress had parted with ill-feeling.

Francesca was evidently a lively character, who developed a strain of lovable eccentricity. She was an ardent Catholic, and after the 1688 Revolution became an equally ardent Jacobite. She even tried to enlist Sophia's sympathy for the Jacobite cause, regardless of the fact that that lady had been declared the eventual heiress to the English throne when the line of James II was excluded. Sophia took it in good part, and Francesca continued to enjoy her friendship.

The Bellomont peerage died out with the death of the second viscount, Charles Rupert Bard, in 1667. Thereafter Francesca took to calling herself 'Lady Bellamont'. She appears in correspondence sometimes with that title, sometimes as 'Madame Bellamont'.

In her later years Francesca consistently maintained that she had been lawfully married to the Prince. Sophia regarded the claim with scepticism; but there were plenty of people who believed it. Dudley was widely known as 'Dudley Rupert', and it was as 'Captain Rupert, the Prince's son', that he appeared at the Battle of Norton St Philip in 1685. A letter in the Verney correspondence records that 'some say Prince Rupert in his last sickness owned his marriage'. A contemporary note by Edmund Verney on the same page adds: '. . . if so, his son is next heir after him to the Palegrave, for he has no child nor is like to have any by his wife.'[29]

There is no further corroboration of any acknowledgement of a marriage by Prince Rupert. But in 1899, just after the publication of Eva Scott's biography of the Prince, Mrs Deedes of Saltwood Castle, Kent, revealed to Mrs Scott, a descendant of Francesca's youngest sister Persiana, the existence of an alleged marriage certificate.[30] This document, a small strip of paper now among the Surrey County Archives, is inscribed in a seventeenth-century hand:

July the 30th 1664

These are to certifie whom it may concerne that Prince Rupert and the Lady ffrances Bard weare Lawfully married at petersham in Surry by me

Henry Bignell
minister

411

There are obvious difficulties in the way of accepting this document as genuine. In the first place no official certificate would have alluded to the bridegroom simply as 'Prince Rupert'. It would have been 'His Highness Prince Rupert, Count Palatine of the Rhine, Duke of Cumberland, Duke of Bavaria', etc. etc. Secondly, it seems certain that Henry Bignell was not the incumbent of Petersham in 1664. He had been there from 1656 till about the time of the Restoration, when he was succeeded by John Crane. Presumably he was expelled as a Cromwellian, but he evidently made his peace with the authorities as he returned to Petersham for a second spell in 1666. At the same time, a circumstance of which much has been made tends to suggest that something may have happened at Petersham. Two pages of the parish church register, which included the year 1664, appear to have been deliberately cut out. Examination of the register, however, reveals many other such gaps, which lessens the importance of this negative evidence. The register seems to have been very carelessly kept.

There is little other evidence. The Latin epitaph previously mentioned refers to Francesca as 'Serenissimo Principi Roberto Palatine quondam matrimonio juncta'. Rupert's niece, Elizabeth Charlotte Duchesse d'Orléans, daughter of Charles Louis, asserted much later that Rupert had deceived Francesca with a false marriage: an act incredible to anybody with any knowledge of Rupert's character. 'Liselotte', however, added statements that reveal how unreliable her evidence is, saying that at the time of the 'marriage' Rupert was lodging with Francesca's father, who had then been dead four years. In truth Liselotte knew little of the affairs of her uncle, whom she had never met.

More pertinent are the comments of one who did know the Prince intimately – his sister Louise, Abbess of Maubuisson. A letter to her brother in which Louise mentions a meeting with his alleged wife is dated only 'the 27th April', but it must of course date from the time of Francesca's continental wanderings, while the second half of it indicates a date when both Rupert and his sister were growing conscious of advancing years: It reads:

> It is true, dearest brother, that I had heard that Mistress Bard had spoken at Pontoise as if she had some sort of promise of marriage, but I can assure you that she said nothing of that sort to me. I saw her only once, because she did not take a carriage, and she could not come here often on foot from Pontoise in the bad weather we have had. She made it clear to me that she has always held you in all the respect and esteem that she ought to do, but one may forgive her if she wished to make others think her situation more unfortunate than guilty. One is always inclined to excuse such faults, and, even if she had told me anything like that I should not have

believed her, for I know that these ladies are quicker to tell lies than you would be to engage yourself to marry.

However that may be, this matter has given me the honour to realise by your letter your continued affection. Although I cannot do you even the most humble service, I always pray God that he may keep you, and that I may not have the grief of seeing you depart before I do, being, with all the affection and respect which I owe to my dearest brother, your very humble and very obedient servant.

Sister Louise P[rincess] Abbess.[31]

This letter provides no hard evidence one way or the other. But it does give some indication of what members of the Palatine family (other than Liselotte) thought of the marriage claim. And the fact that Francesca, who talked so freely to others, did not venture to mention that claim to the formidable Abbess of Maubuisson, a sister much closer in age to Rupert than Sophia, the baby of the family, is surely significant.

Not much importance need be attached to the so-called marriage certificate, which was probably a forgery devised by some member of the Bard family to bolster Francesca's claim. Such devices were common at the time. Charles II was reputed to be married to Lucy Walter, Queen Henrietta Maria to Jermyn; even Elizabeth of Bohemia to Lord Craven. And in more than one such case a certificate was produced or alleged to exist. It is at least possible, however, that there was some form of morganatic marriage, recognized by the parties concerned but not by official authority, such as was common among princely houses on the continent. If there was, unless we accept the dubious evidence of the Verney letter, Rupert never acknowledged it, even in his will. And he was a truthful man.

By the late 1660s Rupert had apparently broken with Francesca Bard. Whether or not the parting of the ways was connected with the Prince's acquisition of a new mistress can only be a matter of conjecture; but it seems likely. For it was at this time that Rupert embarked on the love-affair which was to prove the most enduring and satisfying of his life. It was to lead him into the world of the theatre, a *milieu* far removed from any in which he had hitherto moved.

The romance with Margaret Hughes had its origin at Tunbridge Wells, and for the sole account of its beginnings we are indebted to Anthony Hamilton, author of the so-called 'Gramont Memoirs'. The healing spring which brought fame to the Kentish spa was discovered by Lord North in 1606, and since then Tunbridge Wells had become a popular resort. The court of Charles II moved to the town a number of times; there the gay and gallant courtiers and their ladies diverted

413

themselves much as the court of Louis XVI and Marie Antoinette did at Trianon in the later years of Versailles. They would take the waters in the morning, then stroll along the delightful shady avenue now known as the Pantiles, doing their own shopping in the market, flirting with the country maidens and behaving with a freedom from etiquette impossible in Whitehall. The evenings were devoted to dancing and to love.

Hamilton gives no dates, but it was almost certainly in the summer of 1668 that the company were diverted by the spectacle of the austere and ageing Prince Rupert falling head over heels in love with an actress from Drury Lane. Queen Catherine had sent for the players of the King's Company to entertain the court. Hamilton suggests that she had an underlying motive, for among the actresses was Nell Gwynn. King Charles was in the throes of his infatuation for Frances Stewart, one of the few court beauties who resisted his advances and whom he pursued with indefatigable but futile ardour. The Queen, according to Hamilton, brought down the fascinating Nelly as a counterblast to 'la belle Stewart'. It seems an unlikely stratagem for the demure and unworldly Catherine of Braganza.

Hamilton's account throws light on how Prince Rupert appeared to the more frivolous element of Restoration society:

. . . He was brave to the point of rashness, but eccentric and incredibly obstinate about his eccentricities. His mind delighted in mathematics, and he had some talent for chemistry. He was excessively polite when the occasion did not demand it, and haughty almost to the point of brutality when he should have been civilised. He was a large man with a rather clumsy air; his face was plain and severe, even when he was trying to display tenderness, and when he was in a rage his expression was positively criminal.

The Queen had arranged for the actors to accompany the Court, so that nothing should be lacking for their pleasure, or perhaps so that she might repay Miss Stewart for some of the anxiety she had caused her by ensuring that Miss Gwynn was present. Prince Rupert was greatly attracted to another little actress, whose name was Hughes; the result of this attraction was to put a stop to all his normal seriousness. Farewell to alembics, crucibles, furnaces and the black tools of alchemy; farewell to mathematical instruments and speculations! Powder and perfume now filled his whole mind. The wicked creature insisted on being besieged in the most formal manner. By proudly resisting bribes in order to sell her favours more dearly later on she made such an odd character of this poor prince that he seemed too extraordinary to be in real life at all. The King was delighted by all this; and there was general rejoicing at Tunbridge. However, no one was bold enough to joke about it, although all the other visitors had suffered severely.[32]

It is interesting to note that, while Prince Rupert was a figure of fun to the courtiers, nobody dared to laugh at him publicly. Hamilton's sneers at the actress's designing tactics can be discounted. Disinterested love was foreign to the notions of the Restoration court, and the gay and cynical author of the memoirs was not in the habit of attributing any but the basest motives to anybody.

As with other women in Rupert's life, there is tantalizingly little detail on which to build up a picture of Peg Hughes's personality. The Restoration brought women players to the English stage, to replace the boys who had played female parts in Elizabethan and Jacobean days, and Margaret Hughes has sometimes been acclaimed as the first English actress. This she was not. Mrs Charles Coleman had appeared in an entertainment, for which her husband had composed music, at Rutland House as far back as 1656; and in public theatres the name of Ann Marshall appears at an earlier date than that of Peg Hughes. High-born ladies also acted regularly in the court masques of the reigns of James I and Charles I. Peg, however, was certainly one of the first. She played Desdemona at Drury Lane in 1663, and her name appears on and off from then until 1669. She was the original Theodosia in Dryden's *Evening Love* in 1668, and in the following year played Panura in Fletcher's *Island Prince*. She does not seem to have acted at all regularly, which may possibly indicate that she had another lover (or lovers) before Rupert, but when she did appear she was consistently seen in leading parts. It can be assumed that she was at least a competent actress.

If Prince Rupert ever knew domestic peace it was with Peg Hughes. He took her from the stage and installed her in a splendid house at Hammersmith. It had formerly belonged to Sir Nicholas Crisp, a very wealthy man and an old Royalist officer, who before his death in 1666 had taken a prominent part in the development of African trade and had doubtless been associated with Rupert in that sphere. This mansion subsequently became known as Brandenburg House, and was for a time the residence of George IV's estranged wife Caroline.

Here Rupert spent as much time as he could with his mistress, and she was also frequently with him at Windsor. Sophia, in a letter to Charles Louis, referred to her being there in July 1674; she described her as clever, and suspected her of having got possession of the Queen of Bohemia's jewels.[33] And at Windsor in June 1670 she was apparently the innocent cause of a violent episode which again reminds us that all was not peace and quiet at the castle. 'One of the K[ing's] servants,' wrote Lady Chaworth to her brother Lord Roos, 'hath killed Mr Hues, Peg Hues' brother, servant to P[rince] Robert upon a dispute whether Mis Nelly [Gwynn] or she was the handsomer now at Windsor.'[34]

In 1673 Peg Hughes gave birth to a daughter, named Ruperta after her father. A passage in a letter of 9 June of that year to Arlington from the Buoy of Nore – 'I must beg leave to steal to London the first westerly wind. It shall be very private, and shall in no way hinder any business'[35] – may refer to Ruperta's birth. Rupert doted on her, and from then on till his death spent more and more time at Hammersmith.

In 1676 Peg returned to the theatre, playing Cordelia in D'Urfey's *Fond Husband* at Dorset Garden, the new house built for the Duke's company in Salisbury Court. Subsequently she appeared in plays by Sir Charles Sedley, whose mistress she is said to have been in pre-Rupert days, and Aphra Behn. Since there is no indication of even a temporary rift in her relations with Rupert, this can only mean that she had a genuine love of the stage. Rupert perhaps encouraged her. At any rate he was frequently seen at the theatre during the last few years of his life.

Scanty as are the contemporary references to Margaret Hughes, one gets the impression of a woman of warmth and good sense, who took her awesome lover in hand and did all she could to soften the hardness of his nature. She was an acknowledged beauty, but no scandal was attached to her name after she had settled down with Rupert. Sophia, whose earlier references to Peg indicated disapproval, described her in 1679 as 'très modeste'. She added: 'I was going to say the most modest of the court, which would have been no great thing.'[36] And in some of the last letters she sent to her brother she spoke warmly of his mistress. In July 1681 she said that she wished 'Mistress Hus' had borne him a son; and in September 1682, two months before Rupert's death, she wrote: 'I am much indebted to Mistress Hews for the care she takes of you and I should like to embrace pretty Ruperta and to be of assistance to her in some way.'[37]

Peg Hughes was perhaps fond of gambling, as were most people in Restoration society. Genest, the historian of the English stage, quotes a fictional correspondence taken from Thomas Brown's *Letters from the Dead to the Living*, published in 1702, in which Nell Gwynn is made to reproach her fellow-actress with gambling away her lover's money. 'Sister Peg,' runs Nell's letter, 'Of all the concubines in christendom, that ever were happy in so kind a keeper, none sure ever squandered away the fruits of her labour so indiscreetly as yourself; whoring and gaming I acknowledge are two very serviceable vices in a common-wealth, because they make money circulate; but for a woman who has enriched herself by the one, to impoverish herself by the other, is so great a fault, that a harlot deserves correction for it.'[38]

Peg's answer is a dignified admission of the charge of gambling; but her justification of her actions contains a passage which, while having no foundation in fact whatever, is perhaps a fair reflection of her attitude to Rupert:

> . . . Beauty's the reward of great actions, and I generously bestowed mine upon a prince that deserv'd it, abstractly from the thoughts of interest, but rather to shew my gratitude, in return of his noble passion for me; and since he had made me the object of his affections, I resolved thro' the true principle of love to surrender the ultimate of my charms to make him happy: my embraces were all he wanted, and the utmost I could give, and if a prince would submit to take up with a player, I think on my side there was honour enough, without interest, to induce me to a compliance.[39]

Margaret Hughes lived till 1719, dying at Lee in Kent. Ruperta married Emanuel Scrope Howe, who in 1705 was appointed Envoy Extraordinary to the court of Hanover by Queen Anne. He and Ruperta were at Hanover at the time when Francesca Bard was conducting her Jacobite campaign there. Ruperta's granddaughter married into the Bromley family, who have carried on Prince Rupert's line till the present day. Sir Rupert Bromley, the tenth baronet, is a direct descendant.

From what is known of the ladies whose names were linked with Prince Rupert's, it seems clear that he was not one of those men of action who are attracted by insipid women. Mary Richmond was a dashing extrovert, Catherine Scott a joyous strumpet, Francesca Bard an amusing eccentric. Peg Hughes is harder to place; but all indications are that she was a woman of character. She was the consolation of his mature years. Whether or not she was deeply in love with him, at all events she gave him enduring affection. It was due above all to her that in his last days he found, probably, greater happiness than he had ever known before.

CHAPTER 8

WINDSOR CASTLE

PRINCE RUPERT was appointed Governor and Constable of Windsor Castle, 'and keeper of the forest, parks and chases thereof',[1] on 29 September 1668, and from then on the castle became his principal residence. As he gradually withdrew (though never completely) from participation in public affairs, he devoted more of his time to the Berkshire countryside. Soon after his appointment he became High Steward of the Borough of Windsor, and in 1670 Lord-Lieutenant of Berkshire. He was also in command of the small military garrison maintained at the castle.

From the first he took the keenest interest in the welfare of his new home. Windsor Castle, though never besieged, had been severely damaged in the Civil War, and not till Rupert's appointment were any serious repairs taken in hand. Now, with his cousin in charge, King Charles authorized a lavish programme. The King was fond of Windsor, and in spite of his perennial impecuniosity was prepared to spend more money on embellishments than any sovereign for centuries. There was extensive rebuilding under Hugh May, Controller of the Works; the Italian artist Antonio Verrio was brought in to adorn walls and ceilings with his paintings, and the rooms and staircases were decorated with the exquisite wood carvings of Grinling Gibbons.

All this work was supervised by Rupert. He himself took up residence in the Round Tower, where bonfires and feasting celebrated his arrival, and in his own quarters he made extensive alterations. His paramount interests – the military, the scientific and the artistic – found full play in this work; he set up his laboratory, and his bedroom was hung with pictures. The hundred steps leading up to his private rooms were adorned with arms and armour, and so was the great hall known as the Old Guard Chamber, now called the Armoury. There, on 28 August 1670, John Evelyn visited him, and thus recorded his impressions:

> . . . *Prince Rupert Constable* had begun to trim up the *Keepe* or high round tower, and handsomely adorn'd his hall, with a furniture of Armes, which was very singular; by so disposing the Pikes, Muskets, Pistols, Bandilers,

418

holsters, Drumms, Back, brest & head pieces as was very extraordinary: & thus those huge steepe stayres ascending to it, had the Walls invested with this martial furniture, all new & bright, & set with such study, as to represent, Pillasters, Cornishes, Architraves, Freezes, by so disposing the bandalliers, holsters, & *Drums*, so as to represent festoons, & that with out any Confusion, Trophy like: from the Hall, we went into his Bedchamber & ample roomes which were hung with tapissrie, curious & effeminate Pictures, so extreeamely different from the other, which presented nothing but Warr & horror, as was very surprizing & Divertissant.[2]

There is little to be seen of these rooms as they were in Prince Rupert's time. When Sir Jeffry Wyatville, architect to George IV, increased the height of the Round Tower, he doubled the thickness of the walls to support the extra weight, and this completely altered the appearance of the rooms, which were moreover remodelled to form a suite of guest chambers. Since then the quarters have again been altered to accommodate the Royal Archives, and they now bear virtually no resemblance to those occupied by Rupert.

Prince Rupert was happy at Windsor. 'He took extraordinary delight in the Castle,' says his early biographer, '. . . bestowing no small part of his time and Art in Beautifying and adorning it, being now one of the finest Ornaments the Kingdom has, and is preferred by his Majesty above any of his Palaces'.[3] Nor was he concerned only with the castle. He hunted regularly in the country around, often accompanied by the King and the Duke of York, and as Lord-Lieutenant of Berkshire presided at local functions and made himself known to the people of the countryside.

Windsor, however, was never his only home. Official duties continued to take him frequently to the capital, and in 1668 he had a house built in Spring Garden, close to the Palace of Whitehall. In addition he had a house in the City of London, Drury House in Beech Lane, Barbican, which stood until the early nineteenth century. There was also the great mansion at Hammersmith in which he had installed Peg Hughes.

These establishments must have absorbed a good deal of money. Details of how he managed to make ends meet are meagre. He was certainly never a rich man, but he seems to have kept out of debt. Until 1672 he had an account with the goldsmith Edward Backwell, but the Backwell ledgers, which still exist in the files of Child's Bank, are not revealing. They record various payments and receipts, but cannot represent the whole of Rupert's wordly wealth. He had his pension of £4,000 a year from the King, and a varying income from his shares in colonial ventures. He had certain perquisites as Constable of Windsor, and an allowance for food and entertainment when in London.

He was still Vice-Admiral of England and First Lord of the Admiralty. He regularly attended meetings of the Admiralty Commission and on at least two occasions matters arose regarding his pay. On 9 March 1674 it was agreed that 'the arrears of pay due to his Highness Prince Rupert as Vice-Admiral of England, be paid out of the first money applicable thereto'.[4] A fortnight later Pepys, as Secretary to the Navy, was instructed to prepare a warrant for £4 a day while Prince Rupert had been at sea.

Two years later, in May 1675, some discussion took place on an alleged overpayment to the Prince of £1,104. It was decided to resolve the dispute by allowing the bill for the sum to 'run in the style of his Majesty's free gift and bounty', but Rupert objected to this formula and it was then agreed, 'for the satisfaction of His Highness, that the said words should be left out, and the Officers of the Navy were directed at the same time to cause the bill to be drawn accordingly'.[5]

Throughout the 1670s Rupert continued to watch carefully over the affairs of the navy; but he did not always get his way. In 1677 Pepys, zealous and far-sighted Admiralty official that he was, introduced a scheme for ensuring a more highly professional officer corps. There were too many high-born commanders who knew little of their craft; under Pepys's new establishment for lieutenants every candidate for that rank would have to have served three years at sea and at least one as a midshipman. It was a practical proposition, but Rupert, together with Craven and Ossory, objected that service as a midshipman was 'beneath the quality of a gentleman'.[6] It is surprising to find Prince Rupert, with his long experience of the hard school of war by land and sea, opposing the subjection of officers to a routine that must give them invaluable experience: a sign perhaps that with increasing age he was becoming somewhat hidebound in conservative instincts. In this case he was overruled, and Pepys, rightly, had his way.

Rupert's last years were tranquil, spent 'in a sweet and sedate repose, free from the confused noise and clamours of War, wherewith he had in his younger years been strangely tost like a ship upon the boisterous Waves of fickle and unconstant Fortune'.[7] His name now occurs more often in connection with ceremonial affairs than with matters of state. Distinguished visitors to England paid their respects to him, pleased and somewhat awed to meet the almost legencary hero of battles long ago. One such was Cosimo III, Grand Duke of Tuscany, who wrote an account of his visit in 1669 and related how he dined with the King and the Duke of York and the Prince at Newmarket, after which they 'went on horseback to a place a little distance from Newmarket, and amused themselves with the game of tennis'.[8] It was the Grand Duke who recorded that 'Prince Robert adheres to Calvinism at its rigidest and purest form, as it is professed at Heidelberg by the family of the Counts Palatine of the Rhine'.[9]

In 1677 came the young William III of Orange. England and the Netherlands were at last at peace, and William, in full control of his country's fortunes, had come to establish a dynastic link by marrying the Duke of York's elder daughter Mary. Rupert, with his happy memories of friendship with the House of Orange in earlier days, received his kinsman in state at Windsor Castle and gave him a salute of guns.

Three years later two other young princes, both nephews of Rupert, paid visits to England. One was George Louis, eldest son of Sophia, and himself, like William of Orange, a future King of England. He too was seeking a bride. Sophia's husband, Ernest Duke of Brunswick, in 1679 became, by the death of his brother John Frederick, Duke and Elector of Hanover, and the Elector and Electress planned a marriage between their son and heir and Anne, the younger daughter of the Duke of York. So George, a youth of twenty, rough and uncouth but a good soldier, was sent to England in 1680 to press his suit.

He arrived at Greenwich in December, to find that no arrangements had been made to receive him; either because his visit really was unexpected or through an administrative lapse not uncharacteristic of the somewhat casual court of Charles II. But George knew to whom he could best apply. A message to his uncle quickly set matters to rights, and George reported to his mother:

> . . . I arrived here on December 6, having remained one day at anchor at Greenwich till M. Beck went on shore to take a house for me. He looked up Uncle Rupert and let him know of my arrival, and he, on his part, informed King Charles at once. His Majesty immediately allotted me an apartment at Whitehall. M. Beck requested Uncle Rupert to excuse me; but King Charles insisted that I should be treated like a cousin, and after that no more could be said. . . .[10]

George Louis, with Rupert watching over him, was treated with all due courtesy. But he was no courtier. Neither King Charles nor the Duke of York was favourably impressed; nor was Princess Anne. The marriage proposal came to nothing.

The other nephew of Rupert to come to England in this year was none other than Prince Charles, only son of Charles Louis and soon to be the last Palatine ruler of the senior Wittelsbach branch. Charles Louis, who had brought peace and prosperity to what remained of his ancestral domain, in his last years found himself a pawn in the continental game of power politics. Louis XIV was at war with the Empire, and in accordance with his marriage alliance (Charles Louis's daughter 'Liselotte' was now the second wife of Philippe Duc d'Orléans) demanded the use of the Palatinate as a base for his troops. The Elector refused, and his territory was overrun.

In the troubles of these years Charles Louis turned his eyes towards his one surviving brother. The young Prince Charles was a delicate youth, unlikely to live long or beget children; the only hope for the future of the Palatine family lay in Rupert. In 1674, before the French threat had been fulfilled, Charles Louis asked his brother to return. If Rupert would come back to Heidelberg, marry and found a family, he could make his own terms.

Rupert, advanced in years though he was and happily settled at Windsor, must have been tempted to accept the offer. He had always cherished his links with his fatherland. The thought of an apanage there never quite left him, while in recent years he had renewed his memories by importing his country's famous wine in bulk. Both brothers had mellowed, but Rupert was a man of his word and this exchange revealed him at his most rigid. 'Your belovedness,' he wrote to the Elector, 'has caused me to take a solemn oath to God that I will never more set foot in the Palatinate; and my sworn, if regrettable, oath I will keep.'[11] Yet it was not only a matter of his oath; his innermost inclinations were against uprooting himself at this stage of his life. When his sister Elizabeth, appealed to by Charles Louis, added her entreaty, his reply to her was that he was quite comfortable at Windsor, and had no intention of moving.

With his brother's heir, however, Rupert had no quarrel. A temporary peace with King Louis was concluded in 1679, but the Palatinate had been devastated by the French troops and it was highly probable that the same thing would happen again. Early in 1680 Charles Louis sent his son to England to see what help and sympathy he could enlist. Rupert received him warmly, and entertained him nobly. He was pleased with the young man. 'I am full of admiration for our nephew, the Elector,' he wrote to Sophia a little later. 'His piety is very great.'[12] Young Charles's mission, however, was predictably unrewarding. Rupert gave him advice and sympathy; he had nothing else to offer. Friendship, however, was established; during the remaining two years of Rupert's life uncle and nephew corresponded regularly.

For the other members of the Palatine family Rupert's affection was undimmed. He never lost touch with his sisters, though Elizabeth and Sophia wrote more often to him than he to them. But on 12 February 1680 Elizabeth died at Herford. She had been in great pain for many months, suffering from what is now believed to have been cancer; and Rupert's drops, distrusted by her own doctors, had done her no good. In her last years she had been befriended by her cousin the Elector of Brandenburg, who had helped her with money when the Abbey of

Herford was in financial difficulties. So when she came to make her will she made him her principal heir, explaining why she had done so. And she added:

> To Prince Rupert, who has always been a dear and faithful brother to me, I intended to leave all I have; but for the above-mentioned reasons I must change my purpose and trust that he will not take it amiss. I leave to him all my claims in England, and will ever pray for his temporal and eternal welfare.[13]

On 28 August the same year Charles Louis died, broken by the disasters of his last years. He was greatly mourned among his own people, and very deeply indeed by his youngest sister the Electress of Hanover, to whom he had been almost a father. 'My grief passes the power of words to express,' wrote Sophia in the concluding passage of her memoirs. 'He had always loved me as a daughter, and put such confidence in me that he wrote by every mail, and in a style of such fire and charm that the correspondence formed one of my chief pleasures. This loss has so increased my malady of the spleen that it constantly reminds me that I am now fifty years old, and must soon follow my sister and brother.'[14] There she was wrong. She lived for another thirty-four years, dying at the age of eighty-four.

Young Charles, 'Karellie' as he was called, succeeded his father and ruled for five troubled years. On his death in 1685 the Palatinate passed to a distant cousin. In 1689 it was again devastated by the French.

And now, with the death of Charles Louis, out of the thirteen children born to the Winter King and Queen of Bohemia only three were left – Rupert, the eldest survivor, and his sisters Louise and Sophia. Louise was ideally happy in her convent at Maubuisson. As Abbess she practised all the austerities of the religious life: she ate no meat, slept on a hard bed, sat only on a straw stool, and rose at midnight every night for her devotions. But her asceticism did not affect the gaiety and vitality that had always characterized her. She went on painting almost to the end of her life; she was always the best of company, and her relations loved to visit her. When she was eighty her niece the Duchesse d'Orléans, who was particularly fond of her, wrote: 'She is better tempered, more lively, sees, hears and walks better than I do. She is still able to read the smallest print without spectacles, has all her teeth complete, and is quite full of fun, like my father when he was in a good humour.'[15] She lived to be eighty-eight.

Sophia too was happy at the Hanoverian court. She had her family troubles, but her innate good sense and strength of character enabled her to overcome them. After the death of Elizabeth and Charles Louis she became even more attached to Rupert, taking a close interest in all his affairs, though it was twenty years since they had met.

As Prince Rupert's life became more settled at Windsor, the turmoil of politics and public affairs passed him by. In 1678 came the extraordinary episode of the 'Popish Plot', when the disreputable Titus Oates spread the story of a Catholic conspiracy to assassinate the King and bring in a Jesuit reign of terror. England was gripped by a 'no-popery' hysteria, and this was followed by what is known as the Exclusion Crisis. The Earl of Shaftesbury, using the 'Plot' for his own ends, launched a campaign to exclude the Duke of York from the succession as a papist and set up Charles's bastard son James Duke of Monmouth as a candidate for the throne. For a time King Charles's crown was in danger, but he handled the crisis with his usual sang-froid and shrewdness and in the end it was the contumacious Shaftesbury who fell from power and influence to ignominy and shame.

Throughout this prolonged crisis, which shook the nation to its depths, Rupert, like his King, preserved his unruffled calm. Shaftesbury was his friend, and he showed that his personal feelings were unchanged by visiting him when the Earl fell ill in September 1680. But he gave not the slightest sign of either approving or disapproving the course on which his friend had embarked. His own loyalty to his King was unassailable, and there was no need to assert it.

He became a familiar figure in the Berkshire countryside; sometimes riding, sometimes walking in the company of a large black dog whose name has not come down to us. The old warrior was still a formidable figure, but the peace and domesticity he had found at last had softened the fierceness of his nature and he won the love of the people among whom he moved. 'In respect of his private life,' wrote John Campbell, who was born in 1708 and spent his childhood at Windsor, 'he was so just, so beneficent, so courteous that his memory remained dear to all who knew him. This I say of my own knowledge, having often heard old people in Berkshire speak in raptures of Prince Rupert'.[16]

At the end of the decade Rupert's health began to deteriorate. His old head-wound was troubling him again, and he suffered from an open sore on his leg. At times he was immobile. 'I went to see Uncle Rupert, who received me in bed,' wrote George Louis of Hanover to his mother during his visit to England in 1680, 'for his ailment in his leg often keeps him to his bed. He has to take care of himself.'[17]

For a time he made use of an invalid chair, possibly some sort of wheelchair. In August 1682 he wrote from Windsor to Sophia: 'As for my chair, I will send you one when it is made to send to the Elector, By God's mercy I do not have much use for it now. I walk pretty well once again but they won't allow me to be cured altogether.'[18] His letter went on to refer to his sister's kind remarks about his mistress and their daughter, giving a pleasant glimpse of the family life they were now enjoying. 'What you have been told about Mme Hews is very true,' he wrote. 'She took great care of me during my illness and I am obliged to her for many things. I assure you that, as for the little one, she cannot resemble me, she is turning into the prettiest creature. She already rules the whole house and sometimes argues with her mother, which makes us all laugh.' Ruperta was now nine years old.

Sophia replied with cheerful encouragement: 'I am very pleased indeed that you no longer need your chair, and that they are of the opinion that your leg should be left open, for there is nothing more dangerous than to allow it to close. On the contrary, it is better than a cauterization because it collects all the bad humours. A gentleman in this district lived in that way for nearly a hundred years, and would perhaps be still alive had he not allowed his leg to close up. He ate and drank enough for four.'[19]

There were still occasional excursions into public affairs when the Prince felt fit enough to get to London. On 5 October 1681 Lord Fauconberg protested in the Privy Council at the intended sale of 'the great guns of Prince Rupert's invention' to the King of France. 'The Prince was present and spoke of the value of the invention on the experiments made abroad, but it was undervalued here. Therefore he was not to blame, while the Act is in force, which will expire next November, to seek his market.'[20] In the following January it was recorded that the Ordnance Commissioners had agreed to buy the guns.

This is the last recorded instance of Prince Rupert's having any part in national affairs. As he approached his sixty-third birthday his health troubles increased once more. But the end when it came was quick, and he was active almost to the last.

In the final week of November 1682 he was in London. On the 25th a General Court of the Hudson's Bay Company was held in his house in Spring Garden, at which the principal business was the re-election of the Prince as Governor. It may have been for this that he had come to town; but in the event he was not present at the court, though he was in the house. On the previous day he had been at a theatre, but in the morning he fell ill. For some days he lingered on, in considerable pain, suffering from 'an intermitting feavor'[21] and pleurisy. He still had a will of his own. In the seventeenth century bleeding was the accepted panacea for every kind of malady, but Rupert flatly refused to be bled; with his interest in medical science he evidently had little faith in the universal remedy. On Wednesday, 29 November, between five and six in the morning, he died.

The head-wound, the sore in the leg, the pleurisy, all played their part. But there were other complications, and it may be surmised that only the Prince's splendid natural constitution had kept him alive so long. A news-letter dated 2 December 1682 recorded:

Last Thursday Prince Rupert's body being opened, three strange things were found in him. The first was a stone in his kidneys bigger than a great nut which lay so that it would have stopped the passage of his urine, but, what is strange, there was a hole in it, through which the water passed so freely that he in his whole life was never troubled with any pain of the stone. Another was that in the skin that covers the brain there grew a bone and in his heart another. His body is embalmed and will lie some time in state, an express being sent to Germany to acquaint the Prince Elector with his death. . . .[22]

Two days before the end, when he felt the hand of death upon him, Prince Rupert made his will, naming Lord Craven as his executor. To his son Dudley Bard he left, in addition to his house at Rhenen the legacy of his mother, all money owed to him by the Emperor, the Elector Palatine, 'or by any other person or persons whatsoever not naturall borne subject of the King of England'.[23] To the servants in his employ at the time of his death he left all money owed to him by the King, to be distributed among them at the discretion of Craven and Margaret Hughes. The document proceeded:

. . . All the rest of my goods, chattells, jewells, plate, furniture, household stuffe, pictures, armes, coaches, horses, stock in companies interested, or shares in patents to myselfe or in copartnershipp with others, and all other my estate, rights, properties, and interest whatsoever not hereby before bequeathed, (my just debts being paid and satisfyed,) I do hereby give and bequeath unto William Earl of Craven, in trust neverthelesse to and for the use and behoofe of the said Margaret Hewes and of Ruperta my naturall daughter begotten on the bodie of the said Margaret Hewes, in equall moyeties as aforesaid; and I doe hereby desire, charge, and command my said daughter upon my blessing to be dutiful and obedient to her mother, and not to dispose of herselfe in marriage without her consent and the advice of the said Earle of Craven, if they or either of them shall be then living. . . .[24]

A name conspicuously absent from the will is that of Francesca Bard. The details of how Craven fulfilled his trust are contained in a document printed by Warburton.[25] 'Found in the Prince's iron chest' was the sum of 1,694 guineas, and 'found there also in silver' £1,000. Plate sold realized £2,070. Some of the jewellery was also sold, the largest sum received being £4,520 for 'the great pearl necklace', bought by Nell Gwynn. Among payments to servants the biggest share, £800, went to Thomas Benett, who was Rupert's secretary at the time of his death. A curiosity among sums received for goods sold was £1 for 'an old blind mare'.

The funeral took place on Wednesday, 6 December. According to custom the King and Duke of York did not attend, but the court went into mourning, the King being 'three weeks in purple and plain linen and three weeks in black cloth'.[26] Also according to custom, the ceremony took place at night. The procession from the Painted Chamber to the South Door of Westminster Abbey was an impressive spectacle.[27] First marched two companies of Foot Guards, followed by the Prince's watermen, footmen, postilions and grooms; gentlemen servants of knights of privy councillors, of nobles, of the Duke and Duchess of York and of the King and Queen; the Prince's pages, physicians, surgeons, lawyers and chaplains. Then came his secretary, the Master of the Jewel House, younger sons of peers, pursuivants and heralds, the Vice-Chamberlain of the Household, the Principal Secretary of State; next the members of the House of Lords – barons, bishops, earls and the Dukes of Hamilton, Beaufort, Monmouth, Albemarle and Somerset. Windsor and York Heralds followed; then the Duke of Ormonde, Lord Steward of the Household, and the Marquess of Halifax, Lord Privy Seal.

Norroy King of Arms carried the Prince's coronet in front of the coffin, which was borne by Yeomen of the Guard from Windsor Castle. Six of Rupert's gentlemen servants held the canopy above the bier, and behind them came Clarenceux King of Arms with the Garter. Finally, with the Duke of Grafton, the Earl of Feversham and six other peers in attendance, and Yeomen of the Guard bringing up the rear, came the chief mourner.

This chief mourner was none other than William Earl of Craven, seventy-six years old now and destined to live another fifteen years: Craven the loyal and devoted family friend, the last link, apart from Louise in her convent far away, with Rupert's earliest days. Craven had consecrated his life to the service of Elizabeth Queen of Bohemia and her family. Now he was paying his final tribute to the last of the Winter Queen's sons.

Rupert was laid to rest in Henry VII's Chapel. But there have been changes in the Abbey since that day, and no monument survives to mark his tomb. He who searches for his resting-place today will find, with great difficulty, an obscure plaque on which the name of Prince Rupert is inscribed among those of many others of his contemporaries. It is a poor memorial to one who in his day served his sovereigns and his adopted country well.

NOTES AND SOURCES

BOOK ONE

Chapter 1: The Winter Prince

1 *Elizabeth of Bohemia*, pp. 22–3.
2 Mary Anne Everett Green, *Elizabeth, Electress Palatine and Queen of Bohemia*, p. 29.
3 Elizabeth Godfrey, *Heidelberg: Its Princes and Palaces*, p. 226.
4 S. R. Gardiner, *History of England*, Vol. II, p. 158; *Letters of John Chamberlain*, Vol. I, p. 390.
5 Oman, op. cit., p. 76.
6 Sir George Bromley, *A Collection of Original Royal Letters*, p. 2.
7 *Vide* Oman, op. cit., pp. 172–3, and S. C. Lomas, Introduction to Green, *Elizabeth, Electress Palatine*, pp. xiv–xviii.
8 L. M. Baker, *Letters of Elizabeth, Queen of Bohemia*, p. 49.
9 *Calendar of State Papers of Venice*, Vol. XVI, p. 135.
10 op. cit., pp. 224–5.

Chapter 2: First ventures in arms

1 Green, *Elizabeth, Electress Palatine*, p. 250; C. V. Wedgwood, *The Thirty Years War*, p. 149.
2 Baker, *Letters of Elizabeth, Queen of Bohemia*, p. 73.
3 Ibid., p. 81.
4 HMC (Historical Manuscripts Commission), *Rev. Francis Hopkinson*, p. 265.
5 *Memoirs of Sophia, Electress of Hanover, 1630–1680*, pp. 3–7.
6 Bromley, *Royal Letters*, p. 21.
7 *The History of Prince Rupert (Lansdown MSS)*. This anonymous biography, which records Rupert's career up to the opening of the Civil War, appears to have been written soon after the Restoration.
8 *The Life of Prince Rupert*, MS transcribed by Eliot Warburton, *Memoirs of Prince Rupert and the Cavaliers*, Vol. I, p. 449. Warburton dates this *Life* at *c.* 1678 and thinks it was probably compiled by Colonel Benett, Prince Rupert's secretary. Hereafter in these notes where the volume number is given, the main title will be excluded.
9 Eva Scott, *Rupert, Prince Palatine*, p. 13. (*Vide* note 14 below)
10 In this interpretation of events, and the career of Gustavus Adolphus, I

have followed Wedgwood, op. cit., G. Pagès, *The Thirty Years War, 1618–1648* and Michael Roberts, *Gustavus Adolphus and the Rise of Sweden.*

11 Eva Scott, *Prince Rupert* (unpublished – *vide* note 14 below); Green, op. cit., p. 303.

12 Green, op. cit., p. 303.

13 *Pyne MS*, quoted by Warburton, Vol. I, p. 49. Pyne says the incident occurred during Rupert's captivity at Linz, but it would appear that Rupert had no English attendant there.

14 My authority is Eva Scott, whose *Rupert, Prince Palatine* was published in 1899. However, many years later she wrote a revised biography, entitled *Prince Rupert*, which has never been published. It is here that the episode of Johann of Zweibrucken is recorded. The typescript came into the possession of Dame Veronica Wedgwood, to whom I am deeply indebted for the loan thereof. I have not had personal access to the letters in question, but I accept these and other quotations given by Miss Scott, who was a most conscientious historian.

15 Scott, *Prince Rupert.*

16 Warburton, Vol. I, p. 449.

17 Ibid.

18 Green, op. cit., p. 312.

19 Scott, *Prince Rupert.*

20 *History of Prince Rupert.*

21 Warburton, Vol. I, p. 449.

22 Ibid., p. 450.

23 *History of Prince Rupert.*

Chapter 3: Motherland

1 *The Great Rebellion: The King's Peace, 1637–1641*, pp. 152–3.

2 *The Earl of Strafforde's Letters and Despatches*, Vol. I, p. 489; Scott, *Rupert, Prince Palatine*, p. 22.

3 *Earl of Strafforde's Letters and Despatches*, Vol. I, p. 490.

4 *Cal. SP, Venice*, Vol. XXIII, p. 518.

5 *Calendar of State Papers, Domestic Series*, Charles I, 1635–6, pp. 206–7; Green, *Elizabeth, Electress Palatine*, pp. 323–4.

6 *Cal. SP, Dom.*, 1636–7, p. 69.

7 Scott, *Prince Rupert.*

8 Green, op. cit., p. 325.

9 Scott, *Prince Rupert.*

10 Bromley, *Royal Letters*, p. 86.

11 *Cal. SP, Dom.*, Charles I, 1635–6, p. 351.

12 Ibid., p. 402; Scott, *Rupert, Prince Palatine*, pp. 24–5.

13 Scott, *Prince Rupert.*

14 Bromley, *Royal Letters*, pp. 56–7. Bromley gives the letter as sent from Oatlands on 16 September 1632, but this is obviously an error; 1636 is the only year in which it could have been written.

15 *Cal. SP, Venice*, 1636–9, p. 106.

16 *The Sydney Papers: Letters and Memorials of State*, Vol. II, p. 545.
17 *Autobiography of Phineas Pett*, pp. 162–3.
18 James Howell, *Epistolae Ho-Eliamanae: Familiar Letters, Domestic and Foreign*, p. 257.
19 Warburton, Vol. I, p. 59. I have tried to trace this pamphlet, which Warburton says is in the British Museum. It is not to be found under the reference he gives.
20 *The Works of Sr William D'avenant Kt.*, p. 205.
21 Ibid., p. 211.
22 *Cal. SP, Dom.*, 1636–7, p. 91.
23 Ibid., p. 92.
24 Anthony à Wood, *History and Antiquities of the University of Oxford*, Vol. II, p. 408.
25 William Laud, *Works*, Vol. V, p. 149.
26 *Cal. SP, Dom.*, 1636–7, p. 113.
27 Ibid., p. 559.
28 Ibid., 421.
29 Ibid.
30 Ibid., 1637, p. 82.
31 *Earl of Strafforde's Letters and Despatches*, Vol. II, p. 85.

Chapter 4: Imperial captive

1 Warburton, Vol. I, p. 450. The perdu was the van or 'forlorn hope', the term in general use at this time. Fortescue describes this phrase as a corruption of the German *Verlorner Hauf*, *Hauf* being the word used for any mass of soldiers. (*History of the British Army*, Vol. I, pp. 83–4.)
2 Warburton, Vol. I, p. 451.
3 *Rupert's correspondence and his log-book*. This bound MS, now among the Wiltshire County Archives at Trowbridge, consists of miscellaneous letters and notes, apparently materials for a biography of Rupert. The passage here quoted and some others occur in all the same words, but slightly expanded, in the *Life of Prince Rupert* reproduced at length by Warburton; showing that this work, the present whereabouts of which are unknown, is in fact the biography based on the Log-Book and manuscript which Warburton calls the *Rupert Diary*, which is in the same collection and is also in narrative form.
4 A 'field-marshal' in continental warfare at this time was an officer charged with the control of the encampment and sustenance of the army. (*Oxford English Dictionary*.)
5 Warburton, Vol. I, pp. 452–3.
6 Ibid., p. 453.
7 Ibid., p. 454.
8 Ibid.
9 Ibid.
10 Ibid.
11 *History of Prince Rupert.*

12 Warburton, Vol. I, p. 455.
13 Ibid.
14 Ibid., p. 456.
15 *Cal. SP, Dom.*, 1638–9, p. 103.
16 Baker, *Letters of Elizabeth, Queen of Bohemia*, p. 110.
17 Ibid., p. 111.
18 Warburton, Vol. I, p. 457.
19 The *Rupert Diary*. I have retained Warburton's name for this document, which was formerly in the Benett collection and is now among the Wiltshire County Archives at Trowbridge. It is, however, in no sense a diary; nor is it written by Rupert. It appears to be a rough draft for the *Life of Prince Rupert*, but contains some material not in the parts of that document reproduced by Warburton.
20 *Rupert Diary.*
21 *History of Prince Rupert.*
22 Baker, *Letters of Elizabeth*, p. 131.
23 Warburton, Vol. I, p. 457.
24 *History of Prince Rupert.*
25 Ibid.
26 Ibid.
27 Ibid.
28 *Rupert Diary.*
29 *History of Prince Rupert.*
30 *Cal. SP, Dom.*, 1641–3, p. 83.
31 Ibid., p. 124; Scott, *Prince Rupert.*
32 Warburton, Vol. I, pp. 458–9.
33 *Cal. SP, Dom.*, 1641–3, p. 131.
34 Warburton, Vol. I, p. 459.
35 *Cal, SP, Dom.*, 1641–3; Scott, *Prince Rupert.*

BOOK TWO

Chapter 1: Raising an army

1 Letter from J. du Perron to the Marquis de Fonteney: HMC, *Duke of Portland*, Vol. I, p. 12.
2 *Cal. SP, Dom.*, 1641–3, p. 198.
3 *Rupert Log-book.*
4 Wedgwood, *The Great Rebellion: The King's Peace*, p. 21
5 Sir John Southcote: John Morris, *The Troubles of Our Catholic Forefathers*, p. 392.
6 *History of Prince Rupert.*
7 *Rupert Diary.*
8 *Cal. SP, Dom.*, 1641–3, p. 302.
9 Edward, Earl of Clarendon, *History of the Rebellion and Civil Wars in England*, Vol. II, p. 214.
10 *Rupert Diary.*
11 Thomas May, *History of the Parliament of England.* p. 160.

12 Warburton, Vol. I, p. 461.
13 *History of Prince Rupert.*
14 Warburton, Vol, I, pp. 461–2.
15 Ibid., p. 462.
16 Ibid.
17 *Rupert Log-book.*
18 In the survey that follows I have relied mainly on the following works: S. R. Gardiner, *History of the Great Civil War*; J. W. Fortescue, *History of the British Army*; C. V. Wedgwood, *The Great Rebellion: The King's Peace* and *The King's War*; A. H. Burne and Brig. Peter Young, *The Great Civil War*; and Brig. Peter Young, *The British Army* and *Edgehill, 1642: The Campaign and the Battle.*
19 Burne and Young, *The Great Civil War*, p. 5.
20 *Vide* Young, *Edgehill*, p. 68.
21 Gardiner, *History of the Great Civil War*, Vol. I, p. 465.
22 *Edgehill*, p. 19.
23 op. cit., p. 293.
24 Roberts, *Gustavus Adolphus*, Vol. II, p. 261.
25 Ibid., p. 256.
26 Warburton, Vol. I, pp. 393–4.
27 Ibid., pp. 395–6.
28 Sir Philip Warwick, *Memoires of the reigne of King Charles I*, p. 227.

Chapter 2: Edgehill

1 John Vicars, *God in the Mount*, pp. 155–7.
2 *History of the Parliament of England*, p. 160.
3 *Natural History of Stafford-shire*, p. 336.
4 Wedgwood, *The King's War*, pp. 122–3.
5 Warburton, Vol. I, pp. 400–1.
6 Green, *Elizabeth, Electress Palatine*, p. 357.
7 *Cal. SP, Dom.*, 1641–3, p. 398.
8 *Somers Tracts*, Vol. IV, p. 498.
9 *Rupert Diary.*
10 Warburton, Vol. II, p. 12.
11 Burne and Young, *The Great Civil War*, p. 23.
12 King James's account: Young, *Edgehill*, p. 257. In this book Brig. Young has assembled all the essential contemporary authorities, and I have therefore used it as my main source-book for the battle. The future King James II was nine years old when he was present at Edgehill with his elder brother Charles. His clear and soldierly story of the battle was of course written many years afterwards. For the 'Swedish Brigade' see de Gomme's plan: Young, op. cit., pp. 64–5, 83.
13 It is sometimes maintained that the future King Charles II was never Prince of Wales. The truth seems to be that he was 'declared' Prince of Wales when he became a Knight of the Garter in 1638; but owing to the troubles in England his formal installation was postponed, and in

the event never took place. In the later stages of the Civil War he was generally alluded to as Prince of Wales. *Vide The Complete Peerage*, Vol. III, p. 176.

14 Sir Richard Bulstrode's account: Young, op. cit., pp. 269–70.
15 *Rupert Diary*.
16 James Heath, *Chronicle of the Late Intestine War*, p. 40.
17 Sir Philip Warwick's account: Young, *Edgehill*, p. 282.
18 *History of the Rebellion*, Vol. II, p. 353.
19 King James's account: Young, op. cit., p. 278.
20 Sir John Hinton's account: Young, op. cit., p. 301.
21 Edward Walsingham's account: Young, op. cit., p. 298.
22 *Vide Edgehill*, p. 138.

Chapter 3: Friends and enemies

1 F. J. Varley, *The Siege of Oxford*, p. 37.
2 C. H. Firth (ed.), *Journal of Prince Rupert's Marches: EHR*, Vol. XIII, p. 731.
3 Ibid., p. 732.
4 *Rupert Correspondence*: Scott, *Prince Rupert*.
5 Ibid.
6 *Rupert Correspondence* (British Museum).
7 Morris, *Troubles of Our Catholic Forefathers*, p. 392.
8 The houses of these two ladies at Colchester were sacked in August 1642. Lady Rivers, as a Catholic, was particularly obnoxious to the Puritan mob. *Vide* Gardiner, *The Great Civil War*, Vol. 1, p. 14.
9 Lord Northampton's house at Compton Wynyates was occupied by the Parliamentary forces in 1643 and much damaged. *Vide Victoria History of the County of Warwick*, Vol. V, p. 60.
10 I am unable to identify this place-name.
11 *Memoires of the reigne of King Charles I*, pp. 227–8.
12 Clarendon, *History of the Rebellion*, Vol. II, p. 351.
13 Ibid., p. 354.
14 Ibid., Vol. III, p. 67.
15 HMC, *Verney Papers*, Vol. II, p. 160.
16 So on the title-page. The signature at the end is 'T.P.'.
17 *Observations upon Prince Rupert's White Dogge, called Boye.*
18 *Prince Rupert's Burning Love to England.*
19 *Observations upon Prince Rupert's White Dogge.*

Chapter 4: Cavalier ascendancy

1 *EHR*, Vol. XIII, p. 732.
2 *Historical Memoires of the Life and Death of That Wise and Valiant Prince Rupert*, p. 7.
3 *Bibliotheca Gloucestrensis*, p. 183.
4 Ibid.
5 Gardiner, *History of the Great Civil War*, Vol. I, p. 94.

6   Clarendon, *History of the Rebellion*, Vol. III, pp. 18–19.
7   Warburton, Vol. II, p. 144.
8   Warburton, Vol. III, p. 19.
9   *Four Tracts relative to the Battle of Birmingham*, pp. 31–3.
10 Ibid., pp. 22–3.
11 *History of the Rebellion*, Vol. III, p. 21.
12 Ibid., p. 22. The 'graff' was the moat.
13 Letter sent from a captain in Lichfield to his wife in London; Warburton, Vol. II, p. 166.
14 Ibid., p. 168.
15 *Rupert Diary*; Firth, *Journal of Prince Rupert's Marches: EHR*, Vol. XIII, p. 733.
16 *Rupert Correspondence* (British Museum).
17 Ibid.
18 *EHR*, Vol. XIII, p. 733.
19 *Rupert Correspondence*: Warburton, Vol. II, pp. 189–90.
20 Essex wrote that not more than 300 of his horse were present at Chalgrove, but Brig. Young estimates the strength as between 600 and 800.
21 *His Highness Prince Rupert's late beating up the Rebels' quarters at Postcomb and Chinnor* (Bodleian Library), p. 7.
22 Ibid.
23 Ibid., p. 8.
24 *History of the Rebellion*, Vol. III, p. 62.
25 *Rupert Diary*.
26 *Journal of the Siege of Bristol*: Warburton, Vol. II, p. 237. This account, reproduced by Warburton, is believed to have been written by Sir Bernard de Gomme, Rupert's chief engineer.
27 Ibid., p. 238.
28 *Pythouse Papers*, p. 54.
29 *Rupert Diary*.
30 Warburton, Vol. II, p. 240.
31 Ibid., p. 247.
32 Ibid.
33 Ibid.
34 Richard Atkyns: Brig. Peter Young, *Military Memoirs: The Civil War*, p. 28.
35 Warburton, Vol. II, p. 250.
36 Ibid., p. 254.
37 Ibid., p. 255.
38 Ibid.
39 Ibid., p. 261.
40 Ibid.
41 Ibid., p. 262.
42 *A Relation made to the House of Commons by Colonel Nat. Fiennes*: Warburton, Vol. II, p. 267.
43 *Bellum Civile: Hopton's Narrative of the Campaign in the West*, p. 59.
44 *History of the Rebellion*, Vol. III, p. 124.

45 *Bellum Civile*, p. 59.
46 op. cit., pp. 122–3.
47 May, *History of the Parliament of England*, p. 217.
48 *Rupert Diary*.
49 Ibid.
50 Ibid.
51 Byron's account: Walter Money, *The First and Second Battles of Newbury and the Siege of Donnington Castle*, p. 44.
52 *History of the Rebellion*, Vol. III, p. 189.
53 Ibid., p. 190.
54 Whitelocke, *Memorials of the English Affairs*: Scott, *Rupert, Prince Palatine*, pp. 121–2.

Chapter 5: Defeat in the north

1 *Pythouse Papers*, p. 54.
2 Ibid., p. 55.
3 Ibid., p. 56.
4 Ibid., p. 57.
5 Thomas Carte, *Life of James Duke of Ormonde*, Vol. V, pp. 520–1; Scott, *Prince Rupert*.
6 C. V. Wedgwood, *Thomas Wentworth, First Earl of Strafford*, p. 159.
7 Carte, op. cit., Vol. VI, p. 41.
8 *EHR*, Vol. XIII, p. 735.
9 *Rupert Diary*. This episode is usually assigned to a later date. The *Diary* makes it clear that it occurred at this time.
10 *Rupert Correspondence* (BM).
11 *Historical Memoires of Prince Rupert*, p. 10.
12 *Pythouse Papers*, p. 4.
13 Sir Richard Baker, *Chronicles of the Kings of England*, p. 486.
14 Ibid.
15 Warburton, Vol. II, p. 392.
16 Baker, op. cit., p. 487.
17 *The Letter Bookes of Sir Samuel Luke, 1644–45*, p. 334.
18 *Historical Memoires of Prince Rupert*, p. 12.
19 Lucy Hutchinson, *Memoirs of the Life of Colonel Hutchinson*, Vol. I, p. 323.
20 *Historical Memoires of Prince Rupert*, pp. 13–14.
21 John Rushworth, *Historical Collections*, Pt III, Vol. II, p. 307.
22 Baker, op. cit., p. 48.
23 *Historical Memoires of Prince Rupert*, Vol. II, p. 304.
24 Rushworth, op. cit., p. 308.
25 op. cit., p. 325.
26 op. cit., p. 308.
27 *Vide Newark on Trent: The Civil War Siegeworks*, p. 19.
28 *Rupert Correspondence* (BM).
29 Wedgwood, *The King's War*, pp. 109–10.
30 Thomas Carlyle, *The Letters and Speeches of Oliver Cromwell*, Vol. III, p. 65.

31 Warburton, Vol. II, p. 397.

32 *Vide* Margaret Toynbee and Brig. Peter Young, *Cropredy Bridge, 1644: The Campaign and the Battle*, p. 40.

33 Brig. Peter Young, *Marston Moore, 1644: The Campaign and the Battle*, pp. 63–9; also Peter Wenham, *The Great and Close Siege of York, 1644, passim.*

34 *Carte MSS* (Bodleian Library).

35 *Rupert Diary.*

36 Warburton, Vol. II, p. 429.

37 *Rupert Diary.*

38 *Letter Bookes of Sir Samuel Luke*, p. 660.

39 *Rupert Diary.*

40 Warburton, Vol. II, p. 429.

41 The original of this letter is in the Victoria and Albert Museum.

42 This is stated by Warburton (Vol. II, p. 438), quoting a note in the diary of Dr Watts, Prince Rupert's chaplain. Dame Veronica Wedgwood has pointed out (*The King's War*, pp. 327–8) that the story 'sounds like a subsequent elaboration; there was no reason to suppose, when the letter was written, that if Rupert fought the results must necessarily be disastrous'.

43 So Warburton (Vol. II, p. 437), quoting from memory the copy of Heath's *Chronicle* in the London Library, with its annotations in a seventeenth-century hand, which has already been mentioned. This edition is dated 1676, six years before Rupert's death. The note in the margin is not easy to decipher, but appears to read: 'Prince R. had recd these commands from the K to fight which he has about him to this day.'

44 *Memoires of the reigne of King Charles I*, p. 274.

45 Carte, *James Duke of Ormonde*, Vol. VI, p. 151.

46 *EHR*, Vol. XIII, p. 736.

47 *The Fairfax Correspondence*, Vol. I, p. 1.

48 *Pythouse Papers*, p. 19.

49 Young, *Marston Moor*. As in the case of Edgehill, I have used Brig. Young's work as my main source-book for the Battle of Marston Moor. It contains reproductions of most of the essential documents.

50 C. H. Firth, *Two Accounts of the Battle of Marston Moor: EHR*, Col. V, p. 347.

51 The *Diary* habitually refers to the Marquis of Newcastle as 'the Earle'.

52 So says Cholmley. This timing is accepted by Brig. Young (*Marston Moore*, p. 111) and by Dame Veronica Wedgwood (*The King's War*, p. 337). The *Rupert Diary* says 11 o'clock.

53 Cholmley's narrative: *EHR*, Vol. V, p. 348.

54 Ibid.

55 Young, *Marston Moor*, p. 113.

56 In describing the ground and orders I have followed Brig. Young in *Marston Moor*, pp. 93–110.

57 *A Full Relation of the late Victory*, p. 4; Young, op. cit., p. 113.

58 This is Brig. Young's opinion, based largely on Lumsden's recently discovered plan. Previous estimates have been in the region of a total of 27,000 men.

59 *EHR*, Vol. V, p. 348.

60 Vol. III, p. 376.

61 The Duchess of Newcastle's account: Young, op. cit., pp. 219–20.

62 Scoutmaster-Gen. Watson's account: Young, op. cit., p. 230.

63 *EHR*, Vol. V, p. 348.

64 Sir Thomas Fairfax's account: Young, op. cit., p. 244.

65 Lt-Col. James Somerville's account: Young, op. cit., p. 262.

66 op. cit., p. 129.

67 Mr Ogden's account: Young, op. cit., p. 217.

Chapter 6: *Extinction of hope*

1 Sir Edward Walker, *Historical Discourses*, p. 37.

2 *History of the Rebellion*, Vol. III, p. 374.

3 *Rupert Correspondence* (BM).

4 Firth, *Journal of Prince Rupert's Marches: EHR*, Vol. XIII, p. 737.

5 Ibid.

6 Ibid.

7 Walker, op. cit., p. 53.

8 *History of the Rebellion*, Vol. III, p. 390.

9 Walker, op. cit., pp. 57–8.

10 *Rupert Diary*.

11 op. cit., p. 107.

12 *Rupert Diary*.

13 *History of the Rebellion*, Vol. III, p. 345.

14 *Rupert Diary*.

15 *Life of James Duke of Ormonde*, Vol. VI, p. 206.

16 Ibid., p. 205.

17 Ibid.

18 *Memorials of the English Affairs*, p. 114.

19 The word 'treaty' was used for negotiations with a view to a pact as well as for the pact itself.

20 *The King's War*, p. 390.

21 Warburton, Vol. III, p. 54.

22 Ibid., p. 52.

23 Warburton, Vol. III, pp. 68–9.

24 Ibid., pp. 69–70.

25 *The Great Rebellion*, Vol. IV, p. 38.

26 Ibid.

27 Ibid., p. 39.

28 *Letter Bookes of Sir Samuel Luke*, p. 298.

29 op. cit., p. 129.

30 *The Great Rebellion*, Vol. IV, p. 43.

31 I have founded these figures on those given by Brig. Peter Young and

John Adair in *Hastings to Culloden*, pp. 172–3. They are based partly on the contemporary battle plan in Joshua Sprigge's *Anglia Rediviva*. Sprigge was a chaplain in Fairfax's army, and his account is one of the main sources for the Battle of Naseby.

32   *Anglia Rediviva*, p. 34.
33   Ibid., p. 37.
34   op. cit., p. 130.
35   *Memorials of the English Affairs*, p. 151.
36   op. cit., p. 131.
37   *The Great Rebellion*, Vol. IV, p. 45. Clarendon's account is clearer and slightly more detailed than Walker's, but Walker wrote earlier and was himself at Naseby. Clarendon's account of the battle is obviously based on Walker's, though he probably had independent sources of information.
38   op. cit., p. 131.
39   Ibid.
40   *Vide* Austin Woolrych, *Battles of the English Civil War*, p. 136.

Chapter 7: Bristol and after

 1   *Rupert Diary*.
 2   Warburton, Vol. III, pp. 119–21.
 3   *Rupert Correspondence* (BM).
 4   Warburton, Vol. III, p. 129.
 5   Ibid., p. 131.
 6   Ibid., p. 148.
 7   Ibid., p. 149.
 8   *Rupert Correspondence*: Clarendon, *History of the Rebellion*, Vol. IV, pp. 74–5.
 9   Clarendon, op. cit., p. 91.
10   Sprigge, *Anglia Rediviva*, pp. 97–9.
11   *A Declaration of His Highness Prince Rupert*: Rushworth, *Historical Collections*, Pt IV, Vol. I, p. 71.
12   Ibid.
13   Ibid.
14   Sprigge, op. cit., p. 106.
15   Ibid.
16   Rushworth, op. cit., p. 82.
17   Ibid.
18   Ibid., p. 83.
19   Warburton, Vol. III, p. 181.
20   Ibid., p. 183.
21   *Nicholas Papers*, Vol. I, p. 65.
22   Clarendon, op. cit., p. 93.
23   *EHR*, Vol. XIII, p. 740.
24   William Bray (ed.), *Diary and Correspondence of John Evelyn*, Vol. IV, pp. 164–5.

25 *Cal. SP, Dom.*, 1645–7, p. 144.
26 Ibid., p. 143.
27 *Vide* Warburton, Vol. III, pp. 164–80.
28 Ibid., p. 180.
29 *Rupert Diary.*
30 Ibid.
31 Ibid.
32 *Cal. SP, Dom.*, 1645–7, p. 140.
33 Ibid., p. 141.
34 Walker, *Historical Discourses*, p. 145.
35 Ibid., p. 146.
36 Warburton, Vol. III, pp. 201–3.
37 *History of the Rebellion*, Vol. IV, p. 123.
38 Vol. III, p. 203.
39 Walker, op. cit., p. 147, Walker's is the best and most authoritative account of the episode, though it is not entirely clear; Clarendon's is based on it. The account in the diary of Richard Symonds, who had the story from Willis, is fragmentary and disjointed (*vide* note 41 below).
40 Walker, op. cit., p. 147.
41 Richard Symonds, *Diary of the Marches of the Royal Army*, p. 269.
42 Walker, op. cit., p. 147.
43 Ibid.
44 Ibid.
45 Ibid.
46 Joshua Moore, *A Brief Relation of the Life and Memoires of John Lord Belasyse*: HMC, *Marquess of Ormonde*, new series, Vol. II, pp. 389–90.
47 *Mercurius Britannicus*: quoted by Warburton, Vol. III, p. 206.
48 Warburton, Vol. III, pp. 211–12.
49 *Pythouse Papers*, pp. 27–8.
50 *William Salt Collection of Autograph Letters.*
51 *Rupert Diary.*
52 Ibid.
53 Ibid. In the margin of the *Diary* at this point are the cryptic words: 'D. Dutchesse of Richmond'.
54 Ibid.
55 Ibid.

BOOK THREE

Chapter 1: Soldiering in France

1 *EHR*, Vol. XIII, p. 741.
2 John Bruce (ed.), *Charles I in 1646: Letters of King Charles I to Queen Henrietta Maria*, p. 58.
3 *Rupert Log-book.*
4 Ibid.
5 *Memoirs of Mademoiselle de Montpensier*, p. 93.
6 Ibid., p. 95.
3 *Rupert Log-book.*

8 The *Rupert Log-book* is here at variance with the *Rupert Diary*, which says that this episode took place at La Bassée. I have followed the *Log-book* as the *Diary* account appears confused.

9 *Rupert Log-book.*

10 Ibid.

11 *Rupert Diary.*

12 *Rupert Log-book.* Holmes's biographer points out that this must be an exaggeration, in view of the victim's fitness in later years. *Vide*, Richard Ollard, *Man of War: Sir Robert Holmes and the Restoration Navy*, p. 21.

13 *Rupert Log-book.*

14 Ibid.

15 *Rupert Diary.*

16 Ibid. The *Diary* says that this incident, which is not mentioned in the *Log-book*, took place near Arras, which is between Landrécis and La Bassée.

17 *Vide* George Edinger, *Rupert of the Rhine: The Pirate Prince*, pp. 117–18.

18 Vol. III, pp. 243–4. Warburton's account of this campaign, 'given *verbatim* as I find it among Prince Rupert's papers', consists mainly of extracts from the *Diary* and the *Log-book*. The passage quoted is not in either. Warburton presumably had some other source as well.

19 In the *Rupert Log-book*. The account in the *Rupert Diary*, which ends with this episode, appears to have been rather hastily and carelessly compiled.

20 Warburton, Vol. III, p. 248.

21 The sequence of events is related by Daniel O'Neill in a long letter, dated 9 October 1647, to the Marquess of Ormonde. *Vide* Carte (ed.), *A Collection of Original Letters and Papers*, Vol. I, pp. 146–59.

22 Carte, op. cit., p. 152.

23 Ibid.

24 Ibid., p. 153.

25 Ibid., p. 154.

26 Ibid., p. 155.

27 Ibid.

28 Ibid., p. 158.

29 *Hamilton Papers*, p. 178.

30 Warburton, Vol. III, pp. 82–3.

31 Bromley, *Royal Letters*, p. 136.

32 *Vide* Oman, *Elizabeth of Bohemia*, pp. 365–8. I have followed Miss Oman's account, which seems to me the most coherent and authoritative that has been published.

33 Bromley, op. cit., pp. 133–4.

Chapter 2: For the King again

1 Rushworth, *Historical Collections*, Pt. 4, Vol. I, p. 141.

2 *Nicholas Papers*, Vol. I, p. 95.

3 *Calendar of Clarendon State Papers*, Vol. II, p. 115

4 *Memories of Sir John Hinton*, p. 23.
5 Ibid., p. 24.
6 *Memoirs of Ann Lady Fanshawe*, p. 48.
7 R. C. Latham and W. Matthews (eds), *Diary of Samuel Pepys: A New and Complete Transcription*, Vol. V, p. 169.
8 *Cal. Clarendon SP*, Vol. II, p. 415.
9 Ibid. The quotations are from 'A Relation concerning the Management of the Fleet under the Prince', written by Sir Edward Nicholas.
10 *Rupert Log-book*.
11 *Rupert Correspondence*: Scott, *Prince Rupert*.
12 Ibid.
13 *Rupert Log-book*.
14 *History of the Rebellion*, Vol. IV, p. 425.
15 *Rupert Log-book*.
16 Ibid.
17 Warburton, Vol. III, pp. 263–4. Warburton appears to be quoting the *Rupert Log-book*, but I cannot find this last passage therein.
18 *Nicholas Papers*, Vol. I, p. 96.
19 Ibid.
20 *Cal. Clarendon SP*, Vol. II, p. 407.
21 Ibid., p. 408.
22 Ibid.
23 Ibid., p. 409.
24 Ibid.
25 Mark Napier (ed.), *Memoirs of the Marquis of Montrose*, Vol. II, p. 677.
26 Ibid., p. 678.
27 Warburton, Vol. III, p. 266.
28 op. cit., p. 423.
29 Scott, *Prince Rupert*.
30 Ibid.
31 Carte, *Life of James Duke of Ormonde*, Vol. VI, p. 587.
32 *Cal. Clarendon SP*, Vol. II, p. 424.
33 Warburton, Vol. III, p. 272.
34 *William Salt Collection of Autograph Letters*.
35 *Vide* W. L. Clowes, *The Royal Navy*, Vol. II, p. 114.
36 Warburton, Vol. III, p. 283.
37 Ibid., p. 285.
38 *Declaration of His Highnesse Prince Rupert*, p. 2.
39 Ibid., p. 6.
40 *Cal. SP, Dom.*, 1649–50, p. 85.
41 Bromley, *Royal Letters*, p. 296.
42 For these operations I have followed R. C. Anderson, 'The Royalists at Sea in 1649', *Mariner's Mirror* (1928), by far the best and fullest account.
43 Ibid., p. 331.

Chapter 3: Confrontation with Blake

1   *Vide* Anderson, 'The Royalists at Sea in 1649', *Mariner's Mirror*, p. 336.
2   *Rupert Correspondence* (BM).
3   Ibid.
4   S. R. Gardiner, *Prince Rupert at Lisbon: Camden Miscellany*, Vol. X, p. 1.
5   Henry Cary, *Memorials of the Great Civil War*, Vol. II, p. 164.
6   *Prince Rupert at Lisbon*, pp. 1–2.
7   Ibid.
8   *Rupert Correspondence* (BM).
9   *Prince Rupert at Lisbon*, p. 12.
10   Ibid., p. 15.
11   Warburton, Vol. III, p. 303. Warburton is here quoting the *Rupert Sea Narrative*, the early part of which is not traceable.
12   Ibid.
13   *Cal. SP, Dom.*, 1649–50, p. 483.
14   From now on I have adopted New Style dating for the Lisbon and Mediterranean episodes.
15   J. R. Powell (ed.), *Letters of Robert Blake*, pp. 54–5.
16   *Rupert Sea Narrative*: Warburton, Vol. III, p. 304.
17   Ibid., p. 305.
18   *Prince Rupert's Declaration to the King of Portugal*, p. 1.
19   Ibid., p. 4.
20   *Prince Rupert at Lisbon*, p. 18.
21   *Cal. SP, Dom.*, 1650, p. 104.
22   Powell, op. cit., p. 60.
23   Ibid., p. 61.
24   Ibid.
25   *Vide* Ollard, *Man of War*, p. 36.
26   Warburton, Vol. III, p. 313.
27   HMC, *Duke of Portland*, Vol. I, p. 548.
28   Anderson, 'The Royalists at Sea in 1650', *Mariner's Mirror*, Vol. XVII, p. 162.
29   Warburton, Vol. III, p. 316. A fireship was an old vessel filled with combustible material, designed to be sailed close to an enemy ship and then set alight, the crew escaping by boat at the last minute.
30   HMC, *Portland*, Vol. I, p. 548.
31   Warburton, Vol. III, p. 316.
32   Ibid.
33   Ibid., p. 317.
34   Powell, op. cit., p. 66.
35   Rupert (1619–82) and Condé (1621–86) were almost exact contemporaries. Both were of royal blood. Both made their names as brilliant and dashing military commanders when in their early twenties. Both fought in civil wars. Both had periods of exile. And both ended their days as loyal and revered figures in their respective kingdoms, engaged in cultural pursuits.

36 Warburton, Vol. III, p. 320.
37 *Cal. Clarendon SP*, Vol. II, p. 93.
38 *History of the Rebellion*, Vol V, p. 100.
39 Warburton, Vol. III, p. 324.
40 Ibid., p. 322.
41 *Historical Memoires of Prince Rupert*, p. 33.
42 Warburton, Vol. III, pp. 324–5.
43 Ibid., p. 325.
44 *Historical Memoires of Prince Rupert*, p. 33.

Chapter 4: The western seas

1 Warburton, Vol. III, p. 325.
2 Ibid., p. 326.
3 For the western adventure, in which continental custom is not in the main relevant, I have reverted to Old Style dating.
4 Warburton, Vol. III, p. 327.
5 Ibid.
6 *Rupert Sea Narrative.* The portion of this document now among the Wiltshire County Archives begins with the arrival at the Azores, and henceforth I have used the original in preference to Warburton's transcript.
7 *Rupert Sea Narrative.*
8 *Vide* Anderson, 'The Royalists at Sea, 1651–1693', *Mariner's Mirror*, Vol. XXI, p. 72. I have adopted Mr Anderson's dates where they are not given in the *Rupert Sea Narrative*.
9 *Rupert Sea Narrative.*
10 Ibid. The term 'Admiral' at this time was used either of a commander or of his ship. A vessel is said to 'start' or 'spring' a butt when a plank is loosened at the ends (*Oxford English Dictionary*).
11 *Rupert Sea Narrative.*
12 Ibid.
13 Ibid.
14 Ibid.
15 *Vide* Anderson, op. cit., p. 73, and Ollard, *Man of War*, p. 39.
16 *Rupert Sea Narrative.*
17 Ibid.
18 Ibid.
19 Warburton, Vol. III, pp. 534–5.
20 *Rupert Sea Narrative.*
21 Ibid.
22 Ibid.
23 Ibid, which thus gives the sequence of events. Pitt's own account, as quoted by Warburton (Vol. III, p. 535), says that the canvassing of the officers' opinions took place on 13 September, before the loss of the *Constant Reformation*. This date does not seem compatible with Chester's decision to leave the fleet.

24 *Rupert Sea Narrative.*
25 Ibid.
26 Ibid.
27 Ibid.
28 Ibid.
29 Ibid.
30 Ibid.
31 Warburton read this name as 'Jacus', and in this has been followed by subsequent biographers of Rupert. The name when it first appears in the *Rupert Sea Narrative* certainly looks like 'Jacus', but in most subsequent references, both in the *Sea Narrative* and in the *Log-book*, it is clearly 'Jaques'.
32 *Rupert Sea Narrative.*
33 Ibid. The *Rupert Log-Book* says that the natives 'put all the men to the sword except one boy'.
34 *Rupert Sea Narrative.*
35 Ibid.
36 Ibid.
37 Ibid.
38 Ibid.
39 Ibid.
40 Ibid.
41 Ibid.
42 Ibid.
43 *Cal. SP, Dom.,* 1651–2, p. 309.
44 *Rupert Sea Narrative.*
45 Ibid.
46 Ibid.
47 Ibid.
48 Ibid.
49 Ibid.
50 Ibid.
51 Ibid.
52 Ibid.
53 Warburton, Vol. III, p. 544.
54 *Rupert Sea Narrative.*
55 Baker, *Letters of Elizabeth, Queen of Bohemia,* p. 209.
56 *Vide* HMC, *J. M. Heathcote.* pp. 134–9.
57 Ibid., p. 117.
58 Ollard, op. cit., p. 125.

Chapter 5: A court in exile

1 Warburton, Vol. III, pp. 418–19.
2 Ibid., p. 419.
3 Ibid., p. 420.
4 *Historical Memoirs of Prince Rupert,* p. 35.

5   *Thurloe State Papers*, Vol. II, p. 684.
6   *Memoires of Sir John Reresby, 1634–89*, p. 7.
7   Bray, *Diary and Correspondence of John Evelyn*, Vol. IV, p. 282.
8   *Thurloe SP*, Vol. I, p. 306.
9   Bromley, *Royal Letters*, p. 158.
10 Ibid., p. 163.
11 *Thurloe SP*, Vol. II, p. 186.
12 Ibid., Vol. I, pp. 344–5.
13 The original of this letter, which is reproduced in the *Pythouse Papers* (p. 34), is in the Trowbridge collection (Wiltshire County Archives). Pasted to it is a note in seventeenth-century writing: 'Paris Dec: 18 no further date I suppose 1650'. But it cannot be of any year but 1653. Rupert must have been at the time once more at Nantes, clearing up the accounts.
14 *Cal. Clarendon SP*, Vol. II, p. 211.
15 *Thurloe SP*, Vol. II, p. 141.
16 Ibid.
17 *Cal. Clarendon SP*, Vol. II, p. 222.
18 Bray, *Diary and Correspondence of John Evelyn*, Vol. IV, p. 298.
19 *Nicholas Papers*, Vol. II, p. 49.
20 Ibid., p. 50.
21 Ibid.
22 Ibid.
23 *Cal. SP, Dom.*, 1655, p. 407.
24 Karl Hauck, *Die Briefe der Kinder des Winterkoenigs*, p. 97.
25 Clarendon, *History of the Rebellion*, Vol. V, p. 338.
26 *Cal. Clarendon SP*, Vol. II, p. 358.
27 *Thurloe SP*, Vol. II, p. 327.

Chapter 6: Fatherland

1   Scott, *Prince Rupert*. The thaler, or Rix-dollar, was equal to about 3 shillings.
2   Hauck, *Briefe der Kinder des Winterkoenigs*, p. 94. This chapter is founded to a considerable extent on the researches of Hauck, who had access to documents not used by English biographers of Rupert. (The subsequent references to Hauck in this chapter indicate this work.) *Vide* also his *Rupprecht der Kavalier*.
3   *Thurloe SP*, Vol. II, p. 327.
4   Ibid., p. 405.
5   Hauck, op. cit., p. 100.
6   Scott, op. cit.
7   Hauck, op. cit., p. 98.
8   Bromley, *Royal Letters*, pp. 169–70.
9   Hauck, op. cit., p. 100.
10 Ibid., p. 102.

11   'Je me plais a la lecture
        de vos vers dont jay connu la lescriture
        de trois mains expriment en bon sens
        que desirais savoir come je passe le temps' (Ibid., p. 105).
12   *Thurloe SP*, Vol. II, p. 644.
13   Bromley, *Royal Letters*, p. 315.
14   *Thurloe SP*, Vol. III, p. 659.
15   Baker, *Letters of Elizabeth, Queen of Bohemia*, p. 254.
16   *Cal. SP, Dom.*, 1655, pp. 235–6.
17   *Cal. Clarendon SP*, Vol. III, p. 67.
18   Hauck, op. cit., p. 114.
19   Ibid., p. 116.
20   Ibid., p. 118.
21   *Memorien der Herzogin Sophie*, p. 57.
22   *Thurloe SP*, Vol. V, p. 541.
23   Hauck, op. cit., p. 128.
24   Bromley, *Royal Letters*, p. 189.
25   Ibid., p. 295.
26   Green, *Elizabeth, Electress Palatine*, p. 391.
27   Hauck, op. cit., p. 129.
28   Baker, *Letters of Elizabeth, Queen of Bohemia*, pp. 271–2.
29   Hauck, op. cit., p. 124.
30   Ibid., p. 128.
31   Ibid., p. 130.
32   Scott, op. cit.
33   Vol. III, p. 434.
34   Ibid., p. 435.
35   Hauck, op. cit., p. 138.
36   Baker, *Letters of Elizabeth, Queen of Bohemia*, p. 304.
37   Scott, op. cit.

BOOK FOUR

Chapter 1: Restoration England

1   HMC, *Appendix to Fifth Report (Duke of Sutherland)*, p. 170.
2   Maurice Ashley, *Charles II: The Man and the Statesman*, p. 104.
3   Ibid., p. 316.
4   Latham and Matthews, *Diary of Samuel Pepys*, Vol. II, p. 255.
5   *Old Parliamentary History*, Vol. XXIII, p. 31.
6   *Lords Journals*, Vol. XI, p. 183.
7   Ibid., p. 228.
8   *Cal. SP, Venice*, 1659–61, p. 205.
9   *Cal. SP, Dom.*, 1660–1, Vol. I, p. 471.
10   Ibid.
11   Arthur Collins, *The Peerage of England*, Vol. IV, p. 301.
12   HMC, *Earl of Dartmouth*, p. 4.

13 Ibid.
14 Ibid., pp. 4–5.
15 Ibid., p. 5.
16 Ibid., p. 7.
17 Ibid., p. 8.
18 Ibid.
19 Ibid.
20 Baker, *Letters of Elizabeth, Queen of Bohemia*, pp. 351–2.
21 John Gough Nicols and John Bruce (eds), *Wills from Doctor's Commons*, p. 109. The will is drawn up in French.
22 *Vide* Hauck, *Rupprecht der Kavalier*, pp. 83–9.
23 Hauck, *Briefe der Kinder des Winterkoenigs*, p. 193.
24 *Cal. SP, Dom.*, 1664–5, p. 16.
25 Latham and Matthews, *Diary of Samuel Pepys*, Vol. V, p. 258.
26 Ibid., p. 262.
27 Bromley, *Royal Letters*, pp. 283–4.
28 H. B. Wheatley (de.), *Diary of Samuel Pepys*, Vol. IV, p. 311.
29 E. M. Thompson, *Correspondence of the Family of Hatton, A.D. 1601–1704*, Vol. I, pp. 44–5.

Chapter 2: War at sea

1 Richard Ollard, the latest authority, says 98 (*vide Man of War*, p. 133). Previous estimates have been slightly higher. Laird Clowes put the strength of the fleet at 109 men-of-war, with 28 fireships and ketches, mounting in all 4,192 guns and with 21,006 men (*vide The Royal Navy*, Vol. II, p. 256).
2 Clowes, op. cit., pp. 257–8.
3 *Cal. SP, Dom.*, 1664–5, p. 294.
4 J. S. Corbett, *Fighting Instructions, 1530–1816*, p. 126.
5 *Vide* Michael Lewis, *The Navy of Britain*, pp. 455–8.
6 Ibid., p. 457.
7 *Cal. SP, Dom.*, 1664–5, p. 420.
8 Ibid., p. 408.
9 A. W. H. Pearsall, *The Second Dutch War, Described in Pictures and Manuscripts of the Time*, p. 12.
10 *Continuation of the Life of Edward Earl of Clarendon*, p. 508.
11 *Cal. SP, Dom.*, 1664–5, p. 420.
12 *Cal. SP, Dom.*: Scott, *Rupert, Prince Palatine*, pp. 309–10.
13 *Poems on Affairs of State*, p. 26.
14 *Journal of Edward Mountagu, First Earl of Sandwich, 1659–1665*, p. 236.
15 *Vide The Great Plague of London in 1665*, p. 325.
16 Ibid., p. 66.
17 Wheatley, *Diary of Samuel Pepys*, Vol. VI, p. 291.
18 Clarendon, op. cit., p. 591.
19 *Cal. SP, Dom.*, 1665–6, p. 252.

Chapter 3: Double harness

1   *Cal. SP, Dom.*, 1665–6, p. 357; A. W. Tedder, *The Navy of the Restoration*, p. 151.
2   J. R. Powell and E. K. Timings, *The Rupert and Monck Letter Book, 1666*, p. 13.
3   Tedder, op. cit., p. 152.
4   *Vide* R. J. A. Shelley, 'The Division of the English Fleet in 1666', *Mariner's Mirror*, Vol. XXV, pp. 178–96.
5   *Duke of Albemarle's narrative of the miscarriages in the Dutch War (Coventry MSS).*
6   Shelley, op. cit., p. 182.
7   *Albemarle's narrative.*
8   Warburton, Vol. III, pp. 481–2.
9   *Albemarle's narrative.*
10 Powell and Timings, op. cit., pp. 238–9.
11 Ibid., p. 245.
12 *Cal. SP, Dom.*, 1665–6, p. 431.
13 Ibid.
14 Rupert's account of the Four Days' Battle: Powell and Timings, op. cit., p. 242.
15 *Annus Mirabilis*, stanza 119: James Kinsley (ed.), *The Poems of John Dryden*, Vol. I, p. 73.
16 In this and other details of the final stages of the Four Days' Battle I have followed Rear-Adm. A. H. Taylor, 'The Four Days Fight and St. James's Day Fight', *Naval Review*, Vol. XLI, and Tedder, op. cit.
17 *A True Narrative of the Engagement between His Majesties Fleet and that of Holland*: Pearsall, *The Second Dutch War*, p. 22.
18 Kinsley, *Poems of John Dryden*, Vol. I, p. 73.
19 De Ruyter's Journal: Pearsall, op. cit., p. 24.
20 *A True Narrative* . . . : Pearsall, op. cit., p. 22.
21 Kinsley, *Poems of John Dryden*, Vol. I, p. 76.
22 Ibid., p. 83.
23 Wheatley, *Diary of Samuel Pepys*, Vol. VII, p. 158.
24 Corbett, *Fighting Instructions*, pp. 129–30.
25 Ibid., p. 130.
26 Ibid.
27 *Wyn Papers* (National Maritime Museum).
28 *Vide* R. C. Anderson, 'Naval Operations in the Latter Part of the Year 1666', *Naval Miscellany*, Naval Record Society, Vol. III, pp. 1–27. The document reproduced gives the full account of the St James's Day Battle.
29 Powell and Timings, op. cit., p. 266.
30 Sir Thomas Clifford's account: Powell and Timings, op. cit., p. 276.
31 Ibid.
32 *Historical Memoires of Prince Rupert*, pp. 44–5.
33 Powell and Timings, op. cit., p. 277.

34 Ibid.
35 These are Adm. Taylor's figures. *Vide* Taylor, op. cit., p. 302.
36 Powell and Timings, op. cit., p. 123.
37 *Continuation of Life*, pp. 244–5.
38 Wheatley, *Diary of Samuel Pepys*, Vol. VII, pp. 311–12.
39 Ibid., Vol. VI, p. 151.
40 *Cal. SP, Dom.*, 1665–6, p. 523.
41 Wheatley, *Diary of Samuel Pepys*, Vol. VI, p. 174.
42 Ibid., p. 253.

Chapter 4: Last command
 1 Ashley, *Charles II*, p. 138.
 2 Arthur Bryant, *The Letters of King Charles II*, p. 204.
 3 *Cal. SP, Dom.*, 1667, p. 437.
 4 Ibid., p. 439.
 5 Ibid., 1667–8, p. 505.
 6 Wheatley, *Diary of Samuel Pepys*, Vol. VII, p. 264.
 7 Warburton, Vol. III, p. 483.
 8 Wheatley, *Diary of Samuel Pepys*, Vol. VII, p. 96.
 9 *Cal. SP, Dom.*, 1667–8, p. 608.
10 HMC, *Craven Papers* (National Register of Archives), p. 61.
11 Ibid., p. 65.
12 Ibid., p. 66.
13 *Rupert, Prince Palatine*, p. 322.
14 L. G. Carr Laughton, 'The Vice-Admiral of England', *Mariner's Mirror*, Vol. XIV, pp. 176–7.
15 *Cal. SP, Dom.*, 1671–2, p. 457.
16 Ibid., pp. 465–6.
17 Ibid, 1672, p. 491.
18 The date and place have only recently been established. *Vide* Sir Hughe Knatchbull-Huggeseon, *Kentish Family*, p. 50.
19 *English Historical Documents, 1660–1714*, Vol. VIII, p. 389.
20 *Cal. SP, Dom.*, 1673, p. 123.
21 Ibid., p. 232.
22 *The Naval History of Great Britain*, Vol. II, p. 306.
23 R. C. Anderson, *Journals and Narratives of the Third Dutch War*, p. 371.
24 Ibid., p. 374.
25 *Vide* Ollard, *Man of War*, pp. 182–3.
26 *Cal. SP, Dom.*, 1673, p. 222.
27 These are Mr Anderson's figures. *Vide Journals and Narratives of the Third Dutch War*, p. 29.
28 *Cal. SP, Dom.*, 1673, p. 309.
29 *An Exact Relation*: Anderson, op. cit., p. 377.
30 Ibid.
31 Anderson, op. cit., p. 388.
32 Bryant, op. cit., p. 266.

33 *Cal. SP, Dom.*, 1673, p. 333.
34 Ibid.
35 Anderson, op. cit., p. 378.
36 Mr Anderson's figures. *Vide Journals and Narratives of the Third Dutch War*, p. 37.
37 *An Exact Relation*: Anderson, op. cit., p. 378.
38 Rear-Adm. A. H. Taylor, 'Prince Rupert and de Ruyter, 1673', *Naval Review*, Vol. XLII, p. 295.
39 W. D. Christie (ed.), *Letters Addressed from London to Sir Joseph Williamson while Plenipotentiary at the Congress of Cologne in the Years 1673 and 1674*, Vol. I, p. 48.
40 Ibid., p. 39.
41 HMC, *S. H. Le Fleming*, p. 102.
42 *Cal. SP, Dom.*, 1673, p. 377.
43 Ibid., p. 385.
44 Taylor, op. cit., p. 295.
45 *Journal of John Narbrough*: Anderson, op. cit., p. 342.
46 John Sheffield, Earl of Mulgrave and Duke of Buckingham, *Works*, Vol. II, p. 18.
47 *Cal. SP, Dom.*, 1673, p. 476.
48 Ollard, op. cit., p. 184.
49 Anderson, op. cit., pp. 48–9.
50 Ibid., p. 48.
51 *Cal. SP, Dom,.* 1673, p. 521.
52 Taylor, op. cit., p. 297.
53 Christie, *Letters to Sir Joseph Williamson*, Vol. I, p. 174.
54 *Cal. SP, Dom.*, 1673, p. 521.
55 Ibid., pp. 521–2.
56 Ibid., p. 530.
57 Thompson, *Hatton Correspondence*, Vol. I, p. 114.

Chapter 5: Seeds of empire

1   *Tangier Papers of Samuel Pepys*, p. 219.
2   Ollard, *Man of War*, p. 64.
3   W. R. Scott, *Constitution and Finance of English, Scottish and Irish Joint-Stock Companies to 1730*, p. 17.
4   *Vide* Hilary Jenkinson, *Records of the English African Companies*: Royal Historical Society transactions, 3rd series, Vol. VI, p. 199.
5   K. G. Davies, *The Royal African Company*, p. 41.
6   *English Historical Documents*, Vol. VIII, p. 571.
7   Ibid., p. 372.
8   Christie, *Letters to Sir Joseph Williamson*, Vol. II, pp. 21–2.
9   *Vide* K. H. D. Haley, *The First Earl of Shaftesbury*, pp. 343, 587.
10 Scott, op. cit., p. 21.
11 *Cal. SP, Dom.*, 1667–8, p. 220.
12 Sir John Clapham, *Minutes of the Hudson's Bay Company 1671–1674*,

p. xxv. In this sketch of the Hudson Bay venture I have in the main followed the admirable introductions, by Sir John Clapham and Sir George Clark, to the volumes of minutes. But I think the minutes themselves indicate a closer personal interest on the part of Prince Rupert in the company affairs than Clapham is inclined to credit him with.

13 Ibid.
14 Ibid., p. 133.
15 Ibid., p. 131.
16 Clapham, op. cit., *1679–1684*, p. xxiii.

Chapter 6: Science and art

 1 Hauck, *Briefe der Kinder des Winterkoenigs*, p. 124.
 2 Margery Purver, *The Royal Society: Concept and Creation*.
 3 *Vide* Kenneth Dewhurst, 'Prince Rupert as a Scientist', *British Journal for the History of Science*, Vol. I, pp. 365–73. Mr Dewhurst has surveyed all the evidence for Rupert's scientific activities, and this section is based largely on his paper.
 4 Thomas Birch, *History of the Royal Society of London*, Vol. I, p. 285.
 5 Ibid., Vol. III, p. 337.
 6 Dewhurst, op. cit., p. 372.
 7 Hauck, op. cit., p. 279. This letter is undated and Hauck places it after that of 26 December. But it should clearly come before.
 8 Ibid., p. 278.
 9 *Cal. SP, Dom.*, 1667–8, p. 178.
10 Ibid., 1668–9, p. 575.
11 Ibid., 1671, p. 572.
12 *Historical Memoires of Prince Rupert*, pp. 73–4.
13 HMC, *Duke of Rutland*, Vol. II, pp. 37–8.
14 *Vide* P. H. Hulton, 'Prince Rupert, Artist and Patron of the Arts', *The Beaver* (Winter 1960), p. 5.
15 *Vide* Lawrence Josset, 'The Careful Art of the Mezzotint', *Art and Antiques Weekly* (7 December 1968). Mr Josset, believed to be the only contemporary British artist working in mezzotint, has kindly explained the process to me.
16 Hauck, op. cit., p. 129.
17 Ibid., p. 132.
18 Ibid., p. 133.
19 Ibid., p. 137.
20 *Sculptura*, p. 145.
21 E. S. de Beer (ed.), *Diary of John Evelyn*, Vol. III, p. 271.
22 Ibid., p. 274.
23 *Vertue Note Books* I: Walpole Society, Vol. XVIII, p. 33.
24 Ibid., p. 40.
25 *Vertue Note Books* II: Walpole Society, Vol. XX, pp. 18–19.
26 *Numismata*, p. 283.

27 Hugh W. Diamond, 'Earliest Specimens of Mezzotinto Engraving', *Archaeologia*, Vol. XXVII, p. 405.
28 Warburton, Vol. III, p. 439.
29 Edinger, *Rupert of the Rhine*, p. 214.
30 *Vide* Edinger, op. cit., pp. 213–17.
31 Ibid., p. 215.
32 Warburton, Vol. III, p. 438.
33 Orovida C. Pissarro, *Prince Rupert and the Invention of Mezzotint*, p. 5.
34 Ibid., p. 6.
35 Hulton, op. cit., p. 9.
36 Ibid.

Chapter 7: Feminine company

1 *Prince Rupert: A Biography*, p. 212.
2 Countess of Dunois, *Memoirs of the Court of England*, p. 1.
3 Ibid., p. 398.
4 Ibid., pp. 399–400.
5 *Pythouse Papers*, p. 57.
6 Warburton, Vol. III, p. 212.
7 *Somers Tracts*, Vol. V, p. 473.
8 *The Ladies Parliament: Thomason Tracts*, E. 1143.
9 p. 13.
10 Carte, *Life of James Duke of Ormonde*, Vol. VI, p. 277.
11 *Nicholas Papers*, Vol. II, p. 158.
12 Bromley, *Royal Letters*, p. 252.
13 Hauck, *Briefe der Kinder des Winterkoenigs*, pp. 209–10.
14 *History of the Rebellion*, Vol. II, p. 528.
15 John Heneage Jesse, *Memoires of the Court of England*, Vol. IV, p. 80.
16 Beer, *Diary of John Evelyn*, Vol. II, p. 560.
17 Ibid., Vol. III, p. 358.
18 James Renat Scott, *Memorials of the Family of Scott*, p. 234.
19 J. T. Rutt (ed.), *Diary of Thomas Burton, Esq.*, Vol. I, p. 205.
20 *Burton's Diary MS* (British Museum).
21 Ibid.
22 I have used the spelling given in the *Complete Peerage*, Vol. II, p. 105. The name was later spelt Bellamont, and this has usually been adopted.
23 *Cal. SP, Dom.*, 1660–1, p. 300.
24 Ibid., p. 331.
25 Eva Scott, *The Marriage of Prince Rupert: EHR*, Vol. XV, p. 761.
26 Scott, *Rupert, Prince Palatine*, p. 361.
27 Ibid.
28 Original letter in the colletion of the late Donald Nicholas.
29 HMC, *Seventh Report* (*Verney*), p. 479. The letter is dated 2 May 1681, which must be wrong since Rupert did not die till the end of the following year. The Palsgrave was the Elector Charles, son of Charles Louis.
30 *Vide* Scott, *The Marriage of Prince Rupert: EHR*, Vol. XV, pp. 760–1.

Mrs Scott investigated the marriage question exhaustively, and nothing has since transpired to throw new light on the matter.

31 MS in the collection of the late Donald Nicholas.
32 Anthony Hamilton, *Count Gramont at the Court of Charles II*, pp. 154–5.
33 *Correspondance de la Duchesse Sophie de Hanovre*, p. 194.
34 HMC, *Rutland*, Vol. II, p. 17.
35 *Cal. SP, Dom.*, 1673, p. 357.
36 *Correspondance de la Duchesse Sophie*, p. 368.
37 MS in the collection of the late Donald Nicholas.
38 John Genest, *Some Account of the English Stage*, Vol. I, pp. 385–6.
39 Ibid., pp. 386–7.

Chapter 8: Windsor Castle

1 *Cal. SP, Dom.*, 1667–8, p. 608.
2 Beer, *Diary of John Evelyn*, Vol. III, p. 560.
3 *Historical Memoires of Prince Rupert*, p. 75.
4 J. R. Tanner, *Naval Manuscripts in the Pepysian Library*, Vol. IV, p. 20.
5 Ibid., p. 205.
6 Arthur Bryant, *Samuel Pepys: The Years of Peril*, p. 187.
7 *Historical Memoires of Prince Rupert*, p. 75.
8 *Travels through England of Cosimo the Third, Grand Duke of Tuscany*, p. 208.
9 Ibid., 457.
10 Ruth Jordan, *Sophie Dorothea*, p. 46.
11 Scott, *Rupert, Prince Palatine*, p. 290.
12 Hauck, *Briefe der Kinder des Winterkoenigs*, p. 302.
13 Elizabeth Godfrey, *A Sister of Prince Rupert*, p. 350.
14 *Memoirs of Sophia, Electress of Hanover*, p. 261.
15 Scott, op. cit., p. 347.
16 *Naval History of Great Britain*, pp. 310–11.
17 Jordan, op. cit., p. 46.
18 Hauck, op. cit., p. 303.
19 Original letter in the collection of the late Donald Nicholas.
20 *Cal. SP, Dom.*, 1680–1, p. 493.
21 Thompson, *Hatton Correspondence*, Vol. II, p. 20.
22 *Cal. SP, Dom.*, 1682, p. 560.
23 Nichols and Bruce, *Wills from Doctors' Commons*, p. 163.
24 Ibid., pp. 143–4.
25 *Vide* Warburton, Vol. III, pp. 558–60.
26 *Cal. SP, Dom.*, 1682, p. 556.
27 The details are preserved in the College of Arms.

BIBLIOGRAPHY

This bibliography is probably not complete. In the robbery mentioned in my preface I lost all the bibliographical notes which I had been making as I wrote, and I have had to reconstruct the details as best I can.

THE TROWBRIDGE DOCUMENTS

After Rupert's death the bulk of his papers went into the possession of Colonel Thomas Benett of Norton Bavant, Wiltshire, secretary to the Prince and subsequently MP for Shaftesbury. They were handed down through his descendants and collateral descendants the Benetts and Benett-Stanfords of Pythouse in Wiltshire, and formed the main source used by Eliot Warburton in his monumental *Memoirs of Prince Rupert and the Cavaliers*. Later this collection, consisting of more than a thousand documents, was dispersed. Some papers appear to have been destroyed; some found their way to the British Museum, others to the Bodleian Library in Oxford. The most important manuscripts, however, alluded to by Warburton, somewhat indiscriminately, as the *Rupert Diary*, disappeared (so far as historians were concerned) until 1959, when Brigadier Peter Young discovered by chance that they were among the Wiltshire County Archives at Trowbridge. Curiously enough, a detailed examination of them was made in 1914 by H. J. Bell of the British Museum, whose report is also at Trowbridge.

The main documents are in three bound volumes. The first contains miscellaneous notes relating to Rupert's career; I have called this the *Rupert Log-book*. The second is a more or less chronological account of the Prince's career up to his campaign in France after the First Civil War, evidently a rough draft for a biography; for this I have retained Warburton's title the *Rupert Diary*. Finally there is an incomplete narrative of the wanderings at sea after Charles I's death, which I have called the *Rupert Sea Narrative*. The whole collection was evidently designed as a basis for the *Life* which was partly written (possibly by Colonel Benett) and was liberally used by Warburton, but is now lost.

Brigadier Young has used these documents in his recent books on the Civil Wars. Their existence, however, was unknown to biographers of Rupert subsequent to Warburton except through the latter's very inaccurate transcripts.

455

BIOGRAPHIES

The History of Prince Rupert, taking the story of his life up to the beginning of the Civil War, is in the *Lansdown* MSS in the British Museum. The following ten biographies have been published:

Historical Memoires of the Life and Death of That Wise and Valiant Prince Rupert (1683). This work, according to Warburton, 'would scarcely amount to a modern obituary notice'. But obituary notices were long in Warburton's day; it in fact runs to some 10,000 words and contains valuable material.

Memoirs of Prince Rupert and the Cavaliers, by Eliot Warburton (1849). This huge three-volume work is less a biography than a repository of documents, many of them now lost; with all its faults it is the basis of all modern studies of Rupert.

Rupert of the Rhine: The History of a Brave Prince, by Mary C. Bushe (1869).

Rupert of the Rhine: A Biographical Sketch, by Lord Ronald Gower (1890).

Rupert, Prince Palatine, by Eva Scott (1899). The last fully documented biography. Before her death some fifty years later Mr Scott wrote a revised and expanded version, *Prince Rupert*, which was never published. The typescript came into the possession of Dame Veronica Wedgwood, who very kindly lent it to me. It was stolen from me in 1972, and so far as I know there is now no copy in existence.

A Royal Cavalier: The Romance of Rupert Prince Palatine, by Mrs Stewart Erskine (1910).

Prince Rupert: A Biography, by James Cleugh (1934).

Prince Rupert the Cavalier, by Clennel Wilkinson (1934).

Rupert of the Rhine: The Pirate Prince, by George Edinger (1936). The only biography to deal adequately with Rupert's career after the Restoration.

Rupert of the Rhine, by Bernard Fergusson (1952).

There are also three lives in German:

Leben des Prinzen Ruprecht von der Pfalz, by A. von Treskow (1854).

Pfalsgraf Rupert der Cavalier, by Karl von Spruner (1854).

Rupprecht der Kavalier, by Karl Hauck (1906).

The first two of these are little more than *précis* of Warburton for German readers. Hauck, however, used documents not available to English writers.

MANUSCRIPT SOURCES

Backwll Ledger (Glyn, Mills & Co.)
Carte MSS (Bodleian Library)
Colonial Papers (Public Record Office)
Coventry MSS (Longleat)

Danny Papers (Sussex Record Office)
Diary of Thomas Burton (British Museum)
Firth Transcripts (Bodleian Library). These transcripts are not by Sir Charles Firth, but were bought by him about 1889. He believed them to be transcripts used by Warburton. They appear to be of widely varied date.
Funerals of Kings, Princes, etc. (College of Arms)
Lansdown MSS (British Museum)
Letters to Rupert from His Sisters Louise and Sophia (Collection of the late Donald Nicholas)
Pepys MSS (Magdalene College, Cambridge)
Rupert Correspondence (British Museum)
Westminster Abbey Register
William Salt Collection of Autograph Letters (William Salt Library, Stafford)
Wyn Papers (National Maritime Museum)

Historical Manuscripts Commission:

> *Earl Cowper*
> *Craven Papers* (National Register of Archives)
> *Earl of Dartmouth*
> *Earl of Denbigh*
> *Family of Gawdy*
> *Mrs Harford*
> *J. M. Heathcote*
> *Rev. Francis Hopkinson*
> *S. H. Le Fleming*
> *Lord Montagu of Beaulieu*
> *Newark on Trent: The Civil War Siegeworks*
> *Duke of Northumberland*
> *Marquess of Ormonde*
> *Duke of Portland*
> *Duke of Rutland*
> *Somerville College, Oxford*
> *Duke of Sutherland*
> *Verney Papers*

PRINTED WORKS

Dates are those of editions I have used – not necessarily the first, or even early editions.

AFRICA COMPANIES, *The Company of Royal Adventurers Trading into Africa, 1662–72* (1919).
ALLIN, SIR THOMAS, *Journals of, 1660–1678*, ed. R. C. Anderson (Navy Records Society, 1939).
ANDERSON, R. C., "The Royalists at Sea, 1648–1653", *Mariner's Mirror* (1923–35).

ANDERSON, R. C., *Journals and Narratives of the Third Dutch War* (Navy Records Society, 1946).

ASHLEY, MAURICE, *Oliver Cromwell: The Conservative Dictator* (1937).

——, *Charles II: The Man and the Statesman* (1971).

ASHTON, ROBERT, *James I by His Contemporaries* (1969).

ATKYNS, RICHARD, *Memoirs of*, ed. Brig. Peter Young and pub. in *Military Memoirs: The Civil War* (1967).

BAKER, SIR RICHARD, *Chronicle of the Kings of England* (1679).

BARTON, MARGARET, *Tunbridge Wells* (1937).

BELL, WALTER GEORGE, *The Great Plague of London in 1665* (1924).

BENGE, THOMAS, *The History of Tunbridge Wells* (1766).

Bibliotheca Gloucestrensis: A Collection of Scarce and Curious Tracts, Relating to the County and City of Gloucester (1825).

BIRCH, THOMAS, *The History of the Royal Society of London* (1754).

BLAKE, ROBERT, *Letters of*, ed. the Rev. J. R. Powell (Navy Records Society, 1937).

BLOK, P., *The Life of Admiral de Ruyter*, trans. G. J. Renier (1933).

BOURNE, DOROTHEA ST HILL, 'Daughter to Prince Rupert', *The Beaver* (1962).

——, 'They Buried him among the Kings', *Royal Martyr's Annual* (1969).

BRANDT, GEERAERT, *La Vie de Michel de Ruiter*, trans N. Aubin (1698).

BROMLEY, SIR GEORGE, *A Collection of Original Royal Letters* (1787).

BRYANT, ARTHUR, *Samuel Pepys: The Years of Peril* (1935).

BURNE, LT-COL. A. H., and YOUNG, P., *The Great Civil War, 1642–1646* (1959).

Calendar of Clarendon State Papers (1869–76).

Calendar of State Papers, Domestic Series, 1636–82.

Calendar of State Papers and Manuscripts in the Archives and Collections of Venice, 1619–82.

CAMPBELL, DR JOHN, *The Naval History of Great Britain* (1818).

CARLYLE, THOMAS, *Letters and Speeches of Oliver Cromwell* (1897).

CARTE, THOMAS, *Life of James Duke of Ormonde* (1735–6).

——(ed.), *A Collection of Original Letters and Papers* (1739).

CARTWRIGHT, JULIA, *Madame: A Life of Henrietta, Daughter of Charles I and Duchess of Orleans* (1894).

CARY, HENRY, *Memorials of the Great Civil War* (1842).

CHAMBERLAIN, JOHN, *Letters of*, ed. Norman Egbert McClure (1939).

CHAPMAN, HESTER W., *The Tragedy of Charles II* (1964).

——, *Privileged Persons: Four Seventeenth-Century Studies* (1966).

CHARLES I, KING, *Charles I in 1646: Letters of King Charles I to Queen Henrietta Maria*, ed. John Bruce (1856).

——, *Letters, Speeches and Proclamations*, ed. Sir Charles Petrie (1935).

CHARLES II, KING, *Letters, Speeches and Proclamations*, ed. Arthur Bryant (1935).

CHRISTIE, W. D. (ed.), *Letters Addressed from London to Sir Joseph Williamson while Plenipotentiary at the Congress of Cologne in the Years 1673 and 1674* (1874).

CLARENDON, EDWARD, EARL OF, *The Continuation of the Life of Edward Earl of Clarendon* (1759).

——, *The History of the Rebellion and Civil Wars in England*; re-ed. W. Duncan Macray (1888).

CLARK, SIR GEORGE, *The Later Stuarts, 1660–1714* (1955).

CLOWES, WILLIAM LAIRD, *The Royal Navy* (1897–1903).

COLLINS, ARTHUR, *The Peerage of England* (1779).

CORBETT, JULIAN S. *Fighting Instructions, 1530–1816* (Navy Records Society, 1905).

COSIMO THE THIRD, GRAND DUKE OF TUSCANY, *Travels through England of*, trans. from the Italian (1821).

CROMWELL, OLIVER, *Letters and Speeches of*, ed. T. Carlyle (1845).

DAVENANT, SIR WILLIAM, *The Works of Sr William D'avenant Kt.* (1673).

DAVIES, GODFREY, *The Early Stuarts* (1959).

DAVIES, K. G., *The Royal African Company* (1957).

DAY, MAJOR FRANCIS J., *Professional Papers of the Corps of Royal Engineers* (Royal Engineers Institute, 1888).

DEWHURST, KENNETH, 'Prince Rupert as a Scientist', *British Journal for the History of Science* (1963).

DIAMOND, HUGH W., 'Earliest Specimens of Mezzotint Engraving', *Archaeologia* (1838).

DOWNES, JOHN, *Roscius Anglicanus, or, an Historical Review of the Stage* (1789).

DRYDEN, JOHN, *Poems of*, ed. James Kinsley (1958).

DUNOIS, COUNTESS OF, *Memoirs of the Court of England* (1707).

EDGAR, F. T. R., *Sir Ralph Hopton: The King's Man in the West* (1968).

Elizabeth Charlotte, Princess Palatine and Duchess of Orleans: Letters from Liselotte, trans. and ed. Maria Kroll (1970).

ELIZABETH, QUEEN OF BOHEMIA, *Letters of*, compiled by L. M. Baker (1953).

English Historical Documents, 1660–1714, ed. Andrew Browning (1953).

Eton College Register.

EVELYN, JOHN, *Sculptura: or the History and Art of Chalcography and Engraving in Copper* (1662).

——, *Numismata: A Discourse of Medals, Antient & Modern* (1697).

——, *Diary and Correspondence*, ed. William Bray (1879).

——, *Diary*, ed. E. S. de Beer (1955).

Fairfax Correspondence, The, ed. G. W. Johnson (1848).

FANSHAWE, ANN LADY, *Memoirs of* (1907).

FIRTH, C. H., (ed.), *Two Accounts of the Battle of Marston Moor* (*EHR*, 1890).

——, *The Journal of Prince Rupert's Marches* (*ERH*. 1898).

FLATMAN, THOMAS, *On the Death of the Illustrious Prince Rupert; A Pindarique Ode* (1683).

FORSTER, JOHN, *The Statesmen of the Commonwealth of England* (1840).

FORTESCUE, J. E., *History of the British Army* (1899–1912).

GARDINER, SAMUEL RAWSON, *History of England* (1863–82).

——, *History of the Great Civil War* (1886–91),

——, 'Prince Rupert at Lisbon', *Camden Miscellany* (1902).

GENEST, REV. JOHN, *Some Account of the English Stage* (1832).

GODFREY, ELIZABETH, *Heidelberg: Its Princes and Palaces* (1906).

——, *A Sister of Prince Rupert* (1909)

GREEN, MARY ANNE EVERETT, *Lives of the Princesses of England* (1849–55).

——, *Elizabeth, Electress Palatine and Queen of Bohemia* (1909).

GWYN, JOHN, *Memoirs of*, ed. Norman Tucker and pub. in *Military Memoirs: The Civil War* (1967).

HALEY, K. H. D., *The First Earl of Shaftesbury* (1968).

HAMILTON, ANTHONY, *Count Gramont at the Court of Charles II*, ed. and trans Nicholas Deakin (1965). The most recent translation.

HAMILTON PAPERS, ed. S. R. Gardiner (1880).

HAUCK, KARL, *Die Briefe der Kinder des Winterkoenigs* (1908).

HEATH, JAMES, *Chronicle of the Late Intestine War* (1676).

HINTON, SIR JOHN, *Memoirs of*, (1679).

HOPTON, SIR RALPH, *Bellum Civile: Hopton's Narrative of the Campaign in the West*, ed. C. E. H. Chadwyck Healey (1902).

HOWELL, JAMES, *Epistolae Ho-Eliamanae: Familiar Letters, Domestic and Foreign* (1795).

Hudson's Bay Company, Copy-Book of Letters Outward of the, ed. E. E. Rich (Champlain Society, 1942).

Hudson's Bay Minutes, ed. E. E. Rich (Champlain Society, 1942–6).

HULTON, P. H., 'Prince Rupert, Artist and Patron of the Arts', *The Beaver* (1960).

HUTCHINSON, LUCY, *Memoirs of the Life of Colonel Hutchinson* (1810).

JENKINSON, HILARY, *The Records of the English African Companies* (Royal Historical Society, 1912).

JESSE, JOHN HENEAGE, *Memoirs of the Court of England* (1840).

JORDAN, RUTH, *Sophie Dorothea* (1971).

JOSSET, LAWRENCE, 'The Careful Art of the Mezzotint', *Art & Antiques Weekly* (1968).

KETTON-KREMER, R. W., *Norfolk in the Civil War* (1969).

Kingdomes Weekly Intelligence, The (1643).

KNATCHBULL-HUGESSEN, SIR HUGHE, *Kentish Family* (1960).

LAUD, WILLIAM, *Works* (1847–60).

LAUGHTON, L. G. CARR, 'The Vice-Admiral of England', *Mariner's Mirror* (1928).

LEWIS, MICHAEL, *The Navy of Britain* (1948).

London Gazette, The.

Lords Journals.

LUKE, SIR SAMUEL, *The Letter Bookes of Sir Samuel Luke, 1644–45*, ed. H. G. Tibbutt (Bedfordshire Historical Record Society, 1963).

MAHAN, CAPT. A. T., *The Influence of Sea Power upon History, 1660–1783*. (1890).

MARCUS, G. J., *The Formative Centuries*, Vol. I of *A Naval History of England* (1961).

MARSHALL, JULIAN, *The Annals of Tennis* (1878).

MATHEW, DAVID, *James I* (1967).

MAY, THOMAS, *The History of the Parliament of England* (1812).

MONEY, WALTER, *The First and Second Battles of Newbury and the Siege of Donnington Castle* (1884).

MONTPENSIER, ANNE DUCHESSE DE, *Memoirs of Mademosielle Montpensier*, trans. G. H. Seely (1928).

MORRIS, JOHN, *The Troubles of Our Catholic Forefathers* (1872).

MULGRAVE, JOHN EARL OF, *Works* (1753).

NAPIER, MARK, *Memoirs of the Marquis of Montrose* (1856).

Naval Operations in the Latter Part of the Year 1666, ed. R. C. Anderson (Navy Records Society, 1928).

NEWCASTLE, MARGARET DUCHESS OF, *The Life of the [1st] Duke of Newcastle* (1915).

Nicholas Papers, ed. G. F. Warner (Camden Society, 1886–97).

NICHOLS, JOHN GOUGH, and BRUCE, JOHN, *Wills from Doctors' Commons* (Camden Society, 1863).

OLLARD, RICHARD, *Man of War: Sir Robert Holmes and the Restoration Navy* (1969).

OMAN, CAROLA. *Henrietta Maria* (1936).

——, *Elizabeth of Bohemia* (1938).

PAGÈS, G. *The Thirty Years War, 1618–1648*, trans. David Maland (1970).

PAMPHLETS

Prince Rupert his Declaration (1642).

The Parliaments Vindication, in Answer to Prince Rupert's Declaration (1642).

An exact description of Prince Rupert's Malignant She-Monkey (1642).

Observations upon Prince Rupert's White Dogge, called Boye (1642).

Prince Rupert his reply to a Pamphlet, Entitled, The Parliaments Vindication (1642).

Prince Roberts Disguises (1642).

The Humerous Tricks and Conceipts of Prince Roberts Malignant She-Monkey (1643).

An Answer to Prince Rupert's Declaration (1643).

A briefe Relation of a most Hellish, Cruell, and Bloudy Plot against the City of Bristol (1643).

The Best Newes That ever was Printed (1643).

Prince Rupert's Burning Love to England (1643).

His Highness Prince Rupert's late beating up the Rebels' quarters at Chinnor (1643).

A Dogs Elegy, or Rupert's Tears (1644).

A Declaration of Prince Rupert concerning Bristol (1647).

The Ladies Parliament (1647, Thomason Tracts, E. 1143).

The Declaration of His Highnesse Prince Rupert (1649).

Newes from the New Exchange (1650, Thomason Tracts, E. 590).

Prince Rupert's Declaration to the King of Portugal (1650).

Four Tracts relative to the Battle of Birmingham (Central School of Arts and Crafts, 1931).

Parliamentary or Constitutional History of England (1762–3), Usually known as 'The Old Parliamentary History'.

Parliamentary History of England, The (1806 10).

PARTINGTON, J. R., *A History of Chemistry* (1961).

PEARSALL, A. W. H., *The Second Dutch War, Described in Pictures and Manuscripts of the time* (1967).

PEPYS, SAMUEL, *Tangier Papers*, ed. Edwin Chappell (Navy Records Society, 1935).

——, *Diary*, ed. Henry B. Wheatley (1946).

——, *The Diary of Samuel Pepys: A New and Complete Transcription*, ed. Robert Latham and William Matthews (1970–; in process of publication). I have used this edition up to 1666, the last volume to appear before my book was completed.

PERRIN, W. G., 'The Lord High Admiral and the Board of Admiralty', *Mariner's Mirror* (1926).

PETT, PHINEAS, *Autobiography of*, ed. W. G. Perrin (Navy Records Society 1918).

PISSARRO, OROVIDA C., *Rupert and the Invention of Mezzotint* (Walpole Society, 1960).

PLOT, ROBERT, *Natural History of Stafford-shire* (1686).

Poems on Affairs of State (1703).

POWELL, REV. J. R., *Robert Blake: General-at-Sea* (1972).

——, 'Sir George Ayscue's Capture of Barbados in 1651', *Mariner's Mirror* (1973).

POWELL, REV. J. R., and TIMINGS, E.K., *The Rupert and Monck Letter Book, 1666* (1969).

PURVER, MARGERY, *The Royal Society: Concept and Creation* (1967).

PYNE, W. H., *The History of the Royal Residences* (1819).

Pythouse, Papers, The, ed. William Ansell Day (1879).

RERESBY, SIR JOHN, *Memoirs of, 1634–89*, ed. J. J. Cartwright (1875).

RICH, E. E., *The History of the Hudson's Bay Company 1670–1870* (1958).

RICHMOND, ADM. SIR HERBERT, *Statesmen and Sea Power* (1946).

ROBERTS, MICHAEL, *Gustavus Adolphus and the Rise of Sweden* (1973).

ROGERS, COL. H. C. B., *Battles and Generals of the Civil Wars, 1642–1651* (1968).

ROGERS, P. G., *The Dutch in the Medway* (1970).

ROOTS, IVAN, *The Great Rebellion, 1642–1660* (1966).

ROUTH, E. M. G., *Tangier: England's Lost Atlantic Outpost, 1661–1684* (1912).

ROY, IAN, *The Royalist Ordnance Papers, 1642–1646* (1964).

ROYAL SOCIETY, THE, *The Record of the Royal Society of London* (1901).

RUSHWORTH, JOHN, *Historical Collections* (1659–1701).

RUSSELL, CHARLES E. 'Some Problems of the Early History of Mezzotinting', *Print Collector's Quarterly* (1929).

Sandwich, Journal of Edward Mountagu, First Earl of, 1659–1665, ed. R. C. Anderson (Navy Records Society, 1929).

SCOTT, EVA, *The Marriage of Prince Rupert* (EHR, 1900).

SCOTT, JAMES RENAT, *Memorials of the Family of Scott* (1876).

SCOTT, WILLIAM ROBERT, *The Constitution and Finance of English, Scottish and Irish Joint-Stock Companies to 1720* (1910).

SHELLEY, ROLAND J. A., 'The Division of the English Fleet in 1666', *Mariner's Mirror* (1939).

Somers Tracts (1809–15).

SOPHIA, ELECTRESS OF HANOVER, *Memorien der Herzogin Sophie* (1879).

——, *Correspondance de la Duchesse Sophie de Hanovre* (1886).

——, *Memoirs of, 1630–1680*, trans H. Forester (1888).

SPRAT, THOMAS, *History of the Royal Society of London* (1667).

SPRIGGE, JOSHUA, *Anglia Rediviva: England's recovery, being the history of the Army under Sir Th. Fairfax* (1647).

STEINBERG, J. H., *The 'Thirty Years War' and the Conflict for European Hegemony, 1600–1660* (1966).

STRAFFORD, THOMAS, EARL OF, *The Earl of Strafforde's Letters and Despatches*, ed William Knowles (1739).

STUART, GRAHAM H., *The International City of Tangier* (1931).

Sydney Papers, The: Letters and Memorials of State, transcribed by A. Collins (1746).

SYMONDS, RICHARD, *Diary of the Marches by the Royal Army* (Camden Soc., 1859).

TANNER, J. R., *Naval Manuscripts in the Pepysian Library* (Navy Records Society, 1904).

TAYLOR, REAR-ADM. A. H., 'The Four Days Fight and St James's Day Fights', *Naval Review* (1952).

——, 'Prince Rupert and de Ruyter, 1673', *Naval Review* (1952).

TEDDER, ARTHUR W., *The Navy of the Restoration* (1919).

THOMPSON, EDWARD MAUNDE (ed.), *Correspondence of the Family of Hatton, A.D. 1601–1704* (Camden Society, 1878).

THORNBURY, WALTER, *Old and New London: A Narrative of Its History, Its people, and Its Places* (1881).

Thurloe State Papers (1742).

TOYNBEE, DR MARGARET, *King Charles I* (1968).

TOYNBEE, DR MARGARET, and YOUNG, BRIG. PETER, *Cropredy Bridge, 1644: The Campaign and the Battle* (1970).

TUCKER, JOHN, and WINSTOCK, LEWIS S., *The English Civil War: A Military Handbook* (1972).

TUCKER, NORMAN (ed.), *Rupert's Letters to Anglesey and Other Civil War Correspondence* (Anglesey Antiquarian Society & Field Club, 1958).

TURNER, E. J., *Gallant Gentleman: A Portrait of the British Officer, 1600–1956* (1956).

TURNER, SIR JAMES, *Memoirs of His Own Life and Times* (Bannatyne Club, 1829).

UNDERDOWN, DAVID, *Royalist Conspiracy in England, 1649–1660* (1960).

VARLEY, FREDERICK JOHN, *The Siege of Oxford* (1932).

VERTUE, GEORGE, *Vertue Note Books* (Walpole Society, 1929–30).

VICARS, JOHN, *God in the Mount* (1643).

WALKER, SIR EDWARD, *Historical Discourses* (1705).

WARNER, REBECCA, *Epistolary Curiosities* (1818).

WARWICK, SIR PHILIP, *Memoires of the Reigne of King Charles I* (1701).

WAYLEN, JAMES, *A History, Military and Municipal, of the Town of Marlborough* (1854).

WEDGWOOD, (DAME) C. V., *The Thirty Years War* (1944).

WEDGWOOD, (DAME) C. V., *The Great Rebellion: The King's Peace 1637–1641* (1953).

——, *The Great Rebellion: The King's War, 1641–1647* (1958).

——, *Thomas Wentworth, First Earl of Stafford* (1961).

WELD, CHARLES RICHARD, *A History of the Royal Society* (1848).

WENHAM, PETER, *The Great and Close Siege of York, 1644* (1970).

WHITELOCKE, BULSTRODE, *Memorials of the English Affairs* (1732).

WINGFIELD-STRATFORD, ESME, *King Charles and King Pym* (1949).

——, *King Charles the Martyr* (1950).

WOOD, ANTHONY A., *History and Antiquities of the University of Oxford* (1792–6).

WOOLRYCH, AUSTIN, *Battles of the English Civil War* (1961).

YOUNG, BRIG. PETER, *The British Army* (1967).

——, *Edgehill, 1642: The Campaign and the Battle* (1967).

——, *Marston Moor, 1644: The Campaign and the Battle* (1970).

YOUNG, BRIG. PETER, and ADAIR JOHN, *Hastings to Culloden* (1964).

YOUNG, BRIG. PETER, and HOLMES, RICHARD, *The English Civil War: A Military History of the Three Civil Wars, 1642–1651* (1974).

ZOOK, GEORGE FREDERICK, *The Company of Royal Adventurers Trading into Africa* (1919).

INDEX

INDEX